Nurturing Faith Commentary, Year A, Volume 1
Lectionary Resources for Preaching and Teaching: Advent, Christmas, Epiphany

Nurturing Faith Commentary, Year A, Volume 2
Lectionary Resources for Preaching and Teaching: Lent, Easter, Pentecost

Nurturing Faith Commentary, Year A, Volume 3
Lectionary Resources for Preaching and Teaching: Season after Pentecost, Proper 1–14

Nurturing Faith Commentary, Year A, Volume 4
Lectionary Resources for Preaching and Teaching: Season after Pentecost, Proper 15–29

*

Nurturing Faith Commentary, Year B, Volume 1
Lectionary Resources for Preaching and Teaching: Advent, Christmas, Epiphany

Nurturing Faith Commentary, Year B, Volume 2
Lectionary Resources for Preaching and Teaching: Lent, Easter, Pentecost

Nurturing Faith Commentary, Year B, Volume 3
Lectionary Resources for Preaching and Teaching: Season after Pentecost, Proper 1–14

Nurturing Faith Commentary, Year B, Volume 4
Lectionary Resources for Preaching and Teaching: Season after Pentecost, Proper 15–29

*

Nurturing Faith Commentary, Year C, Volume 1
Lectionary Resources for Preaching and Teaching: Advent, Christmas, Epiphany

Nurturing Faith Commentary, Year C, Volume 2
Lectionary Resources for Preaching and Teaching: Lent, Easter, Pentecost

Nurturing Faith Commentary, Year C, Volume 3
Lectionary Resources for Preaching and Teaching: Season after Pentecost, Proper 1–14

Nurturing Faith Commentary, Year C, Volume 4
Lectionary Resources for Preaching and Teaching: Season after Pentecost, Proper 15–29

Nurturing Faith Commentary

Year A, Volume 3

Lectionary Resources for Preaching and Teaching:
Season after Pentecost, Proper 1–14

TONY W. CARTLEDGE

Nurturing Faith Commentary is sponsored
by a generous gift from Bob and Pat Barker.

© 2023

Published in the United States by Nurturing Faith, Macon, GA.

Nurturing Faith is a book imprint of Good Faith Media (goodfaithmedia.org).

Library of Congress Cataloging-in-Publication Data is available.

ISBN: 978-1-63528-216-0

Unless otherwise indicated, all scripture citations come from the New Revised Standard Version (NRSV).

Contents

Publisher's Preface

More than a decade in the making, *Nurturing Faith Commentary* is unique in its intent and content. Anyone seeking to teach, preach, and/or learn from a broad swath of carefully explored biblical texts will find this to be a reliable, helpful, and treasured resource.

Tony Cartledge brings the mind of a scholar, the heart of a pastor, and the writing skills of an experienced author to this extensive yet accessible multi-volume resource. Rooted in a trusted weekly Bible study, lessons are provided for every possible Sunday of the Christian Year.

Following scripture texts as found in the three-year cycle designated by the Revised Common Lectionary, these lessons are both scholarly and applicable.

The purpose of these Bible studies goes beyond gaining knowledge — although the insights are plentiful — to discovering the inspiration and fresh possibilities for living out biblical truth in one's daily experiences and spheres of influence.

The many years of excellent work in which Tony poured himself into writing thoughtful, weekly Bible studies now form the basis of these volumes. These lessons reflect his wisdom, interpretive skills, diligence, and humility that never prescribe how others are to think and believe.

"Nurturing Faith" is more than just the overall title of this multivolume resource. Learning is seen as the road to redemption and transformation by an individual encountering not just facts, but a living God.

Each week, Tony's lessons have impacted individuals and classes of all shapes and sizes in seeking to learn and apply biblical truths. Having these volumes easily at hand will provide access to a multitude of ideas, insights, and illustrations for those heeding the call to equip disciples to more faithfully follow in the ways of Jesus.

A unique mark of these lessons is the way readers and listeners are treated respectfully and intelligently regardless of their backgrounds. The lessons are never dumbed down to the point of ignoring known scholarly findings.

Yet the purpose is not to impress, but to communicate. Though a Bible scholar and teacher of note, Tony seeks to convey biblical insights effectively rather than using language exclusive to the scholarly community.

When it comes to sharing helpful insights from biblical scholarship with his readers, Tony — intentionally using double negatives for effect — has often said: "I'll never not tell you something I know if it's relevant."

This honest and appreciated approach contrasts with a long history of Bible study curriculum providers that "hand-cuff" writers and therefore "mind-cuff" learners with narrow doctrinal and marketing parameters.

In contrast, *Nurturing Faith Commentary* has no such restrictions — allowing for the freedom of both writer and readers to question, pray, seek, disagree, or apply whatever arises from the exploration of these ancient texts.

The Nurturing Faith approach to Bible study does have a lens, however. It is based on the belief that Jesus is God's fullest revelation, the Living Word through whom all else is filtered in a search for truth.

These insightful and inspiring lessons are a gift — coming from the sharp mind and generous spirit of a minister-scholar who helps us dig more deeply into the rich soil of truth formed by the many layers of experiences, reflections, and stories compiled in what we know and value as the Bible. Dig in!

John D. Pierce
Executive Editor/Publisher
Good Faith Media

Introduction

The 12 volumes of *Nurturing Faith Commentary* are the product of a committed desire to provide quality Bible study for Christians who come to the scripture with open minds and a desire to go beneath a surface reading. Our goal has been to provide pastors, teachers, and other Bible students with both academic and pastoral insights in approachable language.

The project began in early 2011, when John Pierce, editor of what is now *Nurturing Faith Journal*, envisioned the idea of including a weekly Bible study in the print version of the journal, along with additional resources provided online. The studies were to be based on texts from the Revised Common Lectionary and use the New Revised Standard Version as the primary text. Use of the lectionary had become increasingly common in worship among progressive Baptists, who had been our primary audience, but resources for Bible study were lacking.

With many years of experience as a pastor, academician, professor, writer, and editor, I was asked to take on the challenge of writing these studies. With some trepidation, I accepted, and the first studies appeared in the July 2011 issue of *Baptists Today*. The studies have continued now for more than a decade, even as the newspaper-style *Baptists Today* morphed into the magazine format of *Nurturing Faith Journal and Bible Studies*.

For those who subscribe to the journal, additional resources are available online, including detailed insights through "Digging Deeper," helps for troublesome issues through "The Hardest Question," a weekly video in which I offer a summary of the lesson, plus additional teaching resources for youth and adults prepared by other writers. In this resource, Digging Deeper and The Hardest Question are incorporated into print.*

As years of publication and lectionary cycles piled up, we thought it fruitful to update and compile these lessons in a convenient format for teachers, preachers, or others who rely on helpful Bible studies, especially when lectionary based. That, plus the addition of many new commentaries for texts not previously covered, is now coming to fruition in a 12-volume set of Bible studies, with four volumes for each of the three lectionary years.

The project is a massive undertaking, and we are grateful to all who have contributed time, energy, and finances to the project.

---

*All photos used in Digging Deeper and The Hardest Question, unless otherwise indicated, are by Tony Cartledge.

Using This Resource

The Revised Common Lectionary (RCL), devised by a consortium of Protestant and Catholic representatives on the Consultation of Common Texts, was published in 1992. Since then, it has become a standard resource for both Roman Catholics and mainline Protestants.

The lectionary contains hundreds of texts chosen to reflect a progressive study of primary texts in the Bible, along with texts representative of the church year. It follows a three-year cycle known as "Year A," "Year B," and "Year C," then repeats the cycle, using the same texts. Year A relies mainly on Matthew for the gospel readings, while Year B focuses on Mark, and Year C draws mainly from Luke. Selections from the gospel of John are scattered through the three years.

Most days on the lectionary calendar include four readings. These typically follow a pattern of one reading from the Old Testament narratives, prophets, or wisdom; one text from Psalms; one text from the New Testament gospels; and one text from the epistles. Exceptions are many, especially during the Season after Pentecost, when most Sundays include two additional readings as options.

The RCL includes texts for both Sunday worship and other special days. *Nurturing Faith Commentary* focuses on texts for Sundays rather than every "feast day" on the church calendar, many of which are not observed through active services, especially in Protestant churches. We do include texts chosen for New Year's Day, Epiphany, and All Saints' Day, however, because sometimes they fall on Sunday.

A small handful of optional texts from the Apocrypha or "Deuterocanonicals," which are regarded as scripture by Roman Catholics, appear in the lectionary. Given that I write as a Protestant and our audience is mainly Protestant, apocryphal texts are not included in this resource.

The studies in these volumes are not dated, because we want them to be useful in any calendar year, and no year contains all the potential Sundays. Persons who use the text for preaching and teaching may easily consult online and print resources for the specific dates associated with each lectionary Sunday. (Vanderbilt University's library provides an ideal resource at https://lectionary.library.vanderbilt.edu.)

The RCL sometimes uses the same texts on multiple Sundays. When those occur, the study for that text will be printed only once per volume, with appropriate notes to indicate where it may be found if it is indicated on multiple Sundays.

Lectionary texts follow the church year rather than the calendar year, beginning with Advent, the four Sundays prior to Christmas day. Three optional sets of texts are provided for use on Christmas Eve or Christmas Day. These are sometimes referred to as "Christmas 1, 2, and 3," or as "Proper 1, 2, and 3" for Christmas. The first three potential Sundays after Trinity Sunday are also called "Proper 1, 2, and 3," so in this resource we will use the terms "Christmas 1, 2, and 3."

For the sake of completeness, we include studies for all three Christmas options in Volume 1. Many churches hold Christmas Eve services, and Christmas Day sometimes falls on Sunday.

One or two Sundays may follow Christmas, depending on the number of Sundays between Christmas Day and Epiphany. Texts for the second Sunday after Christmas are rarely used and always the same. Studies on those texts are also provided in Volume 1. The texts are sometimes similar to texts for New Year's Day.

Epiphany is celebrated with special texts on January 6, which commonly occurs during the week, but studies on these texts are also included in this resource because Epiphany sometimes occurs on a Sunday. Ministers also sometimes choose to use texts for Epiphany on the Sunday nearest January 6.

The season of Epiphany may include from four to nine Sundays before concluding with Transfiguration Sunday. The number of weeks depends on the date of Easter, which moves about on the calendar, likewise affecting the dates of Ash Wednesday and the beginning of Lent. The last few weeks of Epiphany aren't used in each cycle, but they are included for the sake of those years that do have them. Their location is in Volume 3 of each year, as will be explained below.

Lent always includes six Sundays, concluding with Palm Sunday, which can be celebrated with texts focusing on Jesus' entry to Jerusalem, or on the following passion. Both are provided.

The Season of Easter has seven Sundays leading up to the day of Pentecost, 50 days after Easter.

The first Sunday after Pentecost is always Trinity Sunday. Depending on the calendar, from 23 to 29 Sundays follow Pentecost, ending on the last Sunday before Advent. These are called "Proper" Sundays. The RCL handles the dilemma of differing calendars by starting at the end with Proper 29 as the Sunday before Advent, then working backward. In this system, the texts for Proper 7 through Proper 29 appear in each year's cycle. Texts for Proper Sundays 1–6 are not always used, but are provided for those calendar years in which they appear.

Since Epiphany 6–9 and Proper 1–4 are the least likely to occur, they share the same texts: Epiphany 6 = Proper 1, Epiphany 7 = Proper 2, Epiphany 8 = Proper 3, and Epiphany 9 = Proper 4. Studies for these Sundays are included in Volume 3 for each year, which begins the Season after Pentecost, with their location noted in Volume 1, which contains lessons for the Season of Epiphany.

The number of "Sundays after Pentecost" for a given "Proper" Sunday is different from year to year, so in this resource they will be designated by the "Proper" number, which can be coordinated with each year's number of "Sundays after Pentecost," which will vary.

Texts, especially from the psalms, are often short and designed more for liturgical reading than for individual study. Even so, all texts receive full treatment in Bible study form.

Readers familiar with the RCL know that texts are often chopped and spliced for liturgical reading, which isn't always ideal for a connected Bible study. In many of those cases, the Bible study in these volumes will expand the RCL selection to provide greater context and continuity. Texts listed in the Table of Contents, with each lesson/commentary, and in the index, are based on the actual text examined, which may be longer than the RCL text, but not shorter.

The basic outline of the series is as follows, for each of the three cycles:

Volume 1 – Advent through Epiphany
Volume 2 – Lent through Pentecost
Volume 3 – Season after Pentecost (Propers 1–14)
Volume 4 – Season after Pentecost (Propers 15–29)

Abbreviations

BCE	Before the Common Era
cf.	confer
ch., chs.	chapter, chapters
cp.	compare
CE	Common Era
CEB	Common English Bible
CSB	Christian Standard Bible
e.g.	for example
et. al.	and others
etc.	and others
f., ff.	the following verse, verses
HCSB	Holman Christian Standard Bible
KJV	King James Version of the Bible
LXX	Septuagint
MT	Masoretic Text
NASB95	New American Standard Bible, 1995 edition
NASB20	New American Standard Bible, 2020 edition
NET	New English Translation of the Bible
NET2	New English Translation, 2nd edition
NIV11	New International Version, 2011 edition
NJPS	New Jewish Publication Society
NRSV	New Revised Standard Version of the Bible
RCL	Revised Common Lectionary
v., vv.	verse, verses

Trinity Sunday /
First Sunday after Pentecost*

First Reading
Genesis 1:1–2:4a**

Beginning to Begin

God saw everything that he had made, and indeed, it was very good. (Gen. 1:31a)

Every culture, both ancient and modern, has a creation story. Whether it is the Cherokee account of a water beetle bringing up mud to build earth in the primeval ocean, or a scientific portrait of the big bang or evolution, humans have sought to explain our beginnings.

The Egyptians had at least two creation stories, quite different, one crediting the god Ptah with creating the earth by the spoken word, and another attributing creation to Amun, who used more hands-on methods. [**Creating with words**]

The Hebrews had several creation stories, but just one of them constitutes our text for today. Others are found in Gen. 2:4b-25, Prov. 8:23-31, Ps. 33:6-7, Psalm 104, Jer. 10:12-13, Isa. 40:21-26, and Job 38–39. All these stories describe creation in different ways, and *all* of them rely on the language of metaphor.

The Bible as we have it – written, compiled, and edited over hundreds of years – begins with two contrasting accounts of how God created the heavens, the earth, and all that is in them. Genesis is often called one of the "books of Moses," but the careful reader can find many internal literary and theological clues to suggest that the book is a composite of several hands.

The first story of creation (Gen. 1:1–2:4a) was probably composed later than the second (Gen. 2:4b-25), and

> **Creating with words:** The ancient Egyptians had multiple accounts of creation, generally attributed to different gods. The "Hymn to Ptah," a god favored by the priests of Memphis, claimed that Ptah created all things by the spoken word alone, while Atum, the patron god of Heliopolis, could only create by masturbating things into existence. In doing so, the priests of Ptah declared Ptah's supremacy over Atum.
>
> The Hymn to Ptah is similar to Gen. 1:1–2:4a in that Ptah spoke the earth into existence, albeit by creating lesser gods to do the dirty work of further creation. And, like the God of Gen. 1:1–2:4a, "When all these things were done, Ptah rested" (translation from Victor H. Matthews and Don C. Benjamin's *Old Testament Parallels: Laws and Stories from the Ancient Near East*, 4th ed. [Paulist Press, 2016], 8-9).

was added as a hymnic introduction to the larger work. The polished poetry and stately theology of Gen. 1:1–2:4a have led scholars to propose that it came from one or more priestly writers who may have begun their work before the exile, and continued it in the postexilic period. The second story's earthy language, anthropomorphic images of God, and use of "Yahweh" as a name for God are characteristic of an early writer commonly known as "the Yahwist."

The first story portrays creation as taking place over a seven-day period. In the first three days, God creates a

---

The first Sunday after Pentecost is always Trinity Sunday. From 23 to 29 Sundays will follow between Pentecost and Advent, depending on the Easter date. These are called "Proper" weeks: the dates and number of weeks after Pentecost will vary from year to year. Proper 1–6 may not be used in all years.

**Genesis 1:1-5 is also read for the first Sunday of Epiphany in Year B.*

substrate or framework for animal life, similar to an artist who sketches an outline as the foundation for a painting. During the next three days, God fills in the canvas with colorful creations of light and life. On the seventh day, God rests. [Orders of creation]

Orders of creation: The stories found in Gen. 1:1–2:4a and 2:4b-25 derive from different sources and tell the story in different ways, but they convey the same essential message: God created all things, made them good, and invited humankind to live in relationship with God while sharing in the work of caring for the world.

Some Bible teachers argue that the second creation story is merely a more detailed account of the first, but the differences are so stark that the claim doesn't hold up. The biblical writers and editors knew that the stories were different, but they preserved both because the stories complement each other, offering richer material for those who try to imagine how God brought all things into being.

The two stories describe the order and manner of creation in quite different ways, as seen in the comparison below:

Gen. 1:1–2:4a
Order of creation: Seven-day format
1. Light (1:3-5)
2. The firmament (1:6-8)
3. Dry Land and land-based vegetation (1:9-13)
4. Heavenly bodies: sun, moon, stars (1:14-19)
5. Creatures of sea and sky (1:20-23)
6. Creatures of the earth, animals, reptiles (1:24-25), and humans (1:26-31)
7. Rest (2:1-3)
Conclusion: 2:4a

Gen. 2:4b-25
Order of creation: "the day," perhaps meaning "when" (2:4b)
1. Earth and heavens (2:4b-6)
2. A man (2:7)
3. A garden, trees (2:8-17)
4. Beasts of the field and birds of the air (2:18-20)
5. A woman (2:21-25)

Creation: round one
(1:1-13)

In the first creation story, the author portrays God as being high and remote, creating all things by the spoken word alone. All that exists of the world is a watery chaos called *tōhû wabōhû*, a "formless void" (NRSV) or "welter and waste" (Robert Alter's translation, from *The Five Books of Moses: A Translation with Commentary* [W.W. Norton, 2004], 17).

Many ancient peoples, including both Hebrews and Mesopotamians, imagined creation emerging from a dark and watery tumult. The writer envisioned God's Spirit as somehow moving or brooding over the waters of chaos prior to the act of creation.

The first thing needed was order, and order needs light. Thus, the Bible's first record of God speaking is this: "Let there be light."

And there was light, the writer says. Light was created before the sun and moon, because the purpose was to show that God created the whole notion of light, not just sources of light. It is God's light that overcomes darkness.

As we will see below, it was also important for the writer – who probably wrote during or after the exile – to distinguish Israel's creation account from familiar stories told by the Babylonians and other ancient peoples who considered the sun, moon, and stars to be gods.

With light bringing some order to the universe, God spoke again, and day two was marked by the creation of a solid "firmament" to separate and to protect a safe place within the waters of chaos, like a giant bubble in the waters where life-giving air could exist.

The Hebrews lived long before the invention of the telescope, and could only interpret the world as they saw it. The writer of Genesis 1, like others of his day, envisioned a three-story universe in which the earth existed within a primordial sea as a disk-like land mass with supporting pillars below and a solid, dome-like firmament above. The sun, moon, and stars ran on fixed courses across the firmament, moving beneath the earth at night and re-emerging during the day.

Having created a space for life to exist, God spoke again on day three, and dry land drew apart from the oceans, providing a substrate for earth-bound life. With another divine word, land-based plants emerged, even before the sun and moon were set into the sky.

The emergence of plants offers a clear reminder that the order of events was designed for theological and rhetorical purposes, not as science or history. By introducing green plants before warmth or light provided by the sun, the author attributes life's existence to God alone and moves the celestial bodies further down the list as a subtle way of pointing out that in Israel's belief system, they were not gods.

Creation: round two
(1:14-27, 31)

Having established sky, sea, and dry land with vegetation in place, God was ready to fill in the lines with life. The ancients knew that the sun's warmth and light were essential for continuing life, but the author wanted to affirm that the sun was merely one part of God's creation.

Thus, when God spoke and the heavenly bodies appeared, the author carefully avoided naming them. He described the sun and moon as "the greater light" and "the lesser light" rather than using the Hebrew words for them. The Babylonian sun god was named "Shamash," an obvious cognate to the Hebrew word for "sun" (*shemesh*), and the writer wanted no confusion: he added "and the stars also" as if their creation was an afterthought. The intent was to leave no doubt that the sun, moon, and stars were objects created for God's purpose, not deities.

On the fifth day, animal life came to the fore: God spoke, and creatures of the sea and sky appeared to bring life to the oceans and the air, joining plant life on the dry land.

This is a good place to notice that the author has arranged creation in two corresponding, ordered sequences. Light on day one is followed by creation of the heavenly bodies on day four. Creation of the sea and sky on day two corresponds to the birds and fish that occupy them on day five. We can expect, then, that the creation of the dry land and plants on day three will be matched by the emergence of animal life to inhabit the land on day six.

So, when God speaks again, creatures of *terra firma* emerge in every corner of the earth. Insects and worms that creep and crawl join larger animals that feed on the pre-existing vegetation. Although humans do not yet exist, the

---

"Let us make … what?" The familiar phrase from v. 26 is "let us make man," because that is how the KJV translated it. Some modern versions hold to the traditional translation (HCSB, NASB, NIV), usually with a footnote. Others avoid gender-specific language with "let us make humankind" (NRSV, NET). The Hebrew word is 'ādām, which can serve as a proper name, or it can mean "a man," or it can mean "humankind" in the collective sense.

In v. 26, the context makes it clear that the latter option provides the best translation, for "in the image of God he created them" (v. 27b). This text (unlike the story in Gen. 2:4b-25) does not say that God created a male first, and then a female, but that men and women were brought into existence together. The creation of humans is described in the same manner as the creation of fish, fowl, and beasts of the earth, in that the image depicts creation en masse, rather than assuming that God made one pair of each species, from whom all other examples descended.

---

writer distinguishes between wild animals and those that would be domesticated.

With all else in place, God spoke into being the human race, male and female together, as the crowning glory of all creation. With the creation of humankind, a literary shift describes God as being more personally involved. The word *bara'*, a specific term that refers to God's creative action, is found in v. 1, but does not appear again until v. 27, where it occurs three times. The author thus emphasizes God's personal role in human creation.

According to the story, God said "Let us make humankind in our image, according to our likeness … (v. 26a, NRSV).

This comes as a surprise. Who is this "us," and what does it mean for humans to be made in God's image? [**"Let us make … what?"**]

Some readers have imagined a reference to the Trinity here: that God the Father/Creator was speaking to the preexistent Son and the Holy Spirit. This notion would have been completely alien to the writer.

People throughout the ancient Near East imagined that the earth was ruled by a heavenly council of divine beings. In Canaanite belief, the chief god El held council on Mount Zaphon with lesser gods such as Baal, Dagon, Mot, Yam, and Asherah. In Babylonian thought, Marduk presided over a council of lesser gods that met each year to determine the fates of humankind.

Hebrew religion had no place for multiple gods, but imagined that God also ruled over a heavenly court of supernatural beings called "sons of God" (see Job 1–2) who served God in various ways. Hebrew tradition thought of them as angels: other religions might call them lesser gods.

The writer was too theologically precise to suggest that humans could be created in God's exact image, but believed that we share something of God's image, perhaps a step down from the heavenly court. (See "The Hardest Question" below.)

Creation: round 3
(1:28-29, 2:1-4a)

God's creation of humankind did not come without instructions. As the highest order of creation, humans have a responsibility to care for the earth, sea, and sky – and for the creatures that inhabit them.

God instructed humans to "have dominion" over creation (v. 28). The word does not imply exploitation, but proper stewardship or management. Humans are put in charge of the earth, but not just for their own benefit.

Some readers may be surprised to learn that vv. 29-30 call for both humans and animals to eat only plants. It was only after the flood, according to the primeval stories, that people were authorized to eat meat, and then only with respect and care (Gen. 9:1-4).

Having created the earth and given it over to humans to enjoy and to manage, God rested on the seventh day: "So God blessed the seventh day and hallowed it …" (2:3a). The text does not instruct humans to follow the same pattern, but the author of Genesis 1 clearly considered it as a model for humans to follow in observing the Sabbath. In a brief commentary on the commandment to "Remember the Sabbath day and keep it holy," Exod. 20:11 specifically recalls how God rested on the seventh day after creating the heaven, earth, and sea, adding "therefore the LORD blessed the Sabbath day and consecrated it."

The emphasis on the Sabbath day, an element that is not present in any of the other creation stories, is a clear indication that the first creation story derives from a priestly writer. As we contemplate his imaginative account, we can recognize that it is clearly metaphorical rather than a literal account of creation. More than anything, it is designed to make the theological claim that God created all things, that

God created them good, that humans are called to join God in the ongoing work of caring for creation, and that humans are to regard the seventh day as holy.

As we go about our daily lives, most of us are in far closer contact with the earth and the concerns of physical life than we are with God. The majestic story of creation we find in Gen. 1:1–2:4a reminds us that we can't fully separate the two: our text declares that the earth upon which we stand, the air we breathe, the vistas we enjoy, the water we drink, the food we eat, and even the rest we take are all gifts of a loving God.

And the responsibility of caring for this magical creation is the first biblical word of God to humankind. That's something worth thinking about.

The Hardest Question
What does it mean to be made in God's image?

There is no easy answer to this question, and no one can claim to have fully plumbed its depths or to speak with full authority. Yet, there are many potential ways to approach the issue of what it means to be made in God's image.

God's physical image?

God said "Let us make humankind in our image, according to our likeness." The word "image" comes from *tselem*, which carries the physical connotation of "image," "copy," or "statue." The word "likeness" derives from *dᵉmût*, which has a less specific meaning. The second word qualifies the first and shows that while we are made in God's image, we are not an exact copy.

Does the text suggest that our physical appearance looks like God? Some Old Testament writers could refer to God as Spirit, while others used anthropomorphic (human-like) terminology to imaginatively describe God's appearance. God was said to have delivered Israel with a "mighty hand and an outstretched arm" (Deut. 4:34). God would not allow Moses to see God's face, but only his backside (Exod. 33:23).

Hebrew thought was more holistic than ours: to be in God's image was not just to have a spirit, but to be like God in some greater sense. Note the text of v. 27: "So God created humankind in his image, in the image of God he created them; male and female he created them."

This verse suggests that to be in God's image is not to be either male or female (despite Paul's rabbinic comment in 1 Cor. 11:7). The fullest expression of God's image is found in the complementary relationship between the two.

One implication of this truth is that gender, race, cultural background, and social status are all meaningless in God's eyes. We all share equally in the divine image, and all are worthy of respect and honor and equal treatment. Paul affirmed this same truth for the Christian church: "There is neither Jew nor Greek, slave nor free, male nor female, for you are all one in Christ Jesus" (Gal. 3:28, NIV).

A second implication has to do with the decisions we make concerning our physical bodies. How well do we take care of them? What kinds of harmful or addictive substances do we put in them? Do we bring glory to God with our bodies, or shame? When Paul emphasized the proper use of our bodies as the "temple of the Holy Spirit" (1 Cor. 6:12-20), he was reflecting the belief that we are made in God's image.

God's spiritual image?

Is it natural to assume that the image of God is more spiritual? We must be aware that the separation of the spirit from the body is more of a Greek idea than a Hebrew one. The Hebrew word often translated as "soul" or "spirit" is *nefesh*. In Old Testament thought, one's *nefesh* is not a soul that is separate from the body, but refers to one's life in all its aspects, including the physical. Animals also have a *nefesh*, but only humans have the spark of divinity that makes them capable of relating to God and being renewed by God's gift of grace.

Our humanity involves more than just bodies, and our needs go far beyond the physical and material things to which we devote so much of our time. We are made from a different mold than other earthly creatures. If we were only animals, guided by instinct, we would have a good excuse for living by physical desires alone, but we are not ordinary animals. We are made in the image of God, and our lives should reflect the presence of God in us.

God's relational image?

Another way to understand God's image is relationally. Humans have the ability to speak and relate to others on a much deeper and meaningful level than any other creature. Only humans (so far as we know) consciously seek communion with God through prayer and praise, or look to God for direction in how we should live and relate to one another.

This implies that we are most like God when we intentionally relate to God and to others in the way Jesus taught us – through love. We can use our relational ability to build good, healthy relationships, to seek peace and goodwill, and to help others come into a personal relationship with God.

Those who are most successful in building good human relationships are those who first pay heed to their own relationship with God. As we come to experience divine love and grace more fully, we can share it more freely.

God's rational image?

Another potential aspect of God's image is our capacity for rational thought. Only humans can think and plan on a significant level. Only humans can use their minds to better the world. Only humans have the intellect necessary to have dominion over the earth (v. 28).

This suggests that God has given us a mind, and God expects us to use it. We are to learn whatever can be learned and to continually send our minds into new frontiers. Intellectual growth is a part of good stewardship of life.

This is true even of our faith. Many Christian leaders would have us to believe that God doesn't want us to think, but to blindly obey. We are indeed called to obedience, but not to blind obedience: we must understand that the voice of God and the voice of an authoritarian minister with an inerrantist view of scripture are not one and the same. Christians have not only the right, but also the responsibility to constantly work toward a fuller understanding of the scriptures and how they relate to our own daily life in this present world.

God's responsible image?

Along with our ability to think, God has given to humans the ability to choose. We can use our remarkable intellectual capacity to scheme a murder, or to plan a disaster relief effort. We can design a bomb, or plan for peace. We can think evil thoughts (Matt. 9:4), or use our minds for good (Phil. 4:8). The "dominion over the earth" God has granted humanity (v. 28) implies a high level of responsibility.

Only humans are truly responsible creatures, guided by choice and not instinct or conditioning. We alone are truly free to choose how we will live and how we will behave. Every choice we make bears consequences for good or evil, and we are responsible for those choices.

God could have created us in such a way that we could only do good, but then we would have been like many robots. We would be less than human. Our freedom to choose reflects the image of God in us, and the possibility of evil is the price we pay for humanity.

To be made in God's image is to be physical, spiritual, and relational. It is to be rational in our thinking, and responsible in our decision-making. To maximize God's image is to use all these capabilities for good, reflecting that image most clearly.

Second Reading
Psalm 8*

Not Quite Angels

O LORD, our Sovereign, how majestic is your name in all the earth! (Ps. 8:1)

One of the great challenges we all face is finding our place in the world. For some people, it's less difficult because choices are more limited: local culture or parents tell children what their place is, opportunities are few, and people may assume from childhood that they will live in the same village and watch cattle or plant rice until they grow old, with their own children following them. Other children may grow up obeying their parents' instructions to do well in school and become a doctor or an engineer; even to marry a person of their parents' choosing.

Those who live in freer circumstances have more opportunities and options, but sometimes feel overwhelmed and at a loss to find and establish their identity. In America, young adults are waiting longer and longer to get married, have children, or settle into a career. Many feel lost even into their 30s or 40s, unsure of who they want to be, what they want to do, or where they belong.

Psalm 8 cannot point us to a career or a mate, but it does help us to understand where we fit in the larger scheme of things – indeed, in the *largest* scheme of things – in relation to God and the world. [**What's a *gittith*?**]

A majestic God
(vv. 1-2, 9)

Have you ever stood beneath a clear night sky studded with stars, feeling overcome by how big the universe is and how

> **What's a *gittith*?** The superscription to Psalm 8, like others in the psalms, is an ancient notation added by a scribal copyist at an early date, but is not original to the psalm. Many superscriptions suggest a setting for the psalm, or associate it with an author or collection. Some, such as this one, include musical instructions.
>
> In Psalm 8, the note is directed "To the director: according to (or "upon") the *gittît*." The Hebrew word is not translated because we don't know what it means. Some believe the *gittît* was a type of stringed instrument such as the lyre, and would translate "upon the *gittît*." Optionally, the word could indicate the name of a tune, and would translate "according to 'the *gittît*.'" The word is similar to the plural form of *gat*, which means "wine-presses" (*gittôt*), so some commentators think the tune may have been sung at harvest time, perhaps during the Feast of Booths.
>
> The superscription identifies the psalm as a "psalm of/ by/to David." Whether the annotator believed David wrote the psalm or simply associated it with a collection dedicated to David is unclear.

puny we are? As impressive as it is just to look at the stars – which the ancients believed were inside a dome over the earth – those who understand even a hint of our current knowledge of the universe must feel even smaller. We live in a small solar system near the edge of a massive galaxy containing more than 100 billion stars, and it's just one of an estimated 100 billion galaxies or more. The expanse of the universe boggles the mind.

---

*Psalm 8 is also read on Trinity Sunday in Year C and for Proper 22 in Year B.

The psalmist had no way of understanding that the earth is a planet rather than the center of the universe, or that there are untold billions of star systems surrounded by other worlds. Still, he didn't need to know, any more than we do. A starlit sky is all we need to realize how small we are.

If we consider the size of the universe, and we also believe that God created all things, how could we think of God as anything other than possessing magnificence beyond our comprehension? Thus, the psalmist writes "O LORD, our Sovereign, how majestic is your name in all the earth! You have set your glory above the heavens" (v. 1).

Those who recall the familiar KJV may remember the opening words as "O LORD, our Lord." The initial "O" is not in the text, but added for English style. Literally, the text has "Yahweh, our Lord." Yahweh is a personal, covenant name that God revealed to Israel (Exod. 3:15), always rendered in English by LORD, or occasionally GOD, in all upper-case letters. The word translated as Sovereign ("Lord") comes from the word 'ădôn, which means "lord," or "master" (it is often spelled in English letters as 'adonai, an optional spelling of "my lord"). In different contexts, it could be used of human persons in positions of authority, but here it clearly refers to God.

English translations don't convey it, but the word translated as "our Lord/Sovereign" ('adōnēnû) is a plural form of the word. Grammarians refer to this as a "plural of majesty," a way of making God's lordship even more emphatic, as in the name 'elōhîm, a plural form of 'ēl that is commonly translated as "God." When used for God, 'ădôn usually appears in the singular form, but here the psalmist is particularly interested in emphasizing God's greatness, so he uses the plural.

Having addressed God by the covenant name "Yahweh," the psalmist connects divine splendor to the divine name: "How majestic is your name in all the earth!" [The origin of "Jehovah"]

The closing words of v. 1 offer an interesting translational conundrum. The word translated "You have set" in the NRSV, or "You have revealed" in NET, is actually an imperative form of the word meaning "to give." Translators generally regard the text as corrupt and read it as another form of the word, nuanced as "set" or "reveal." The unusual word is preceded by another word that normally means "which" or "that," but seems a bit out of place here.

The origin of "Jehovah": At some point, the Hebrews came to regard God's revealed name as so sacred that humans should no longer pronounce it, so when readers came to the name *yhwh* (Hebrew was written without vowels), they would pronounce it as "Adonai," a more generic name meaning "Lord." The Jews' reticence to speak the name Yahweh (our best guess as to how the name was pronounced) is responsible for its familiar rendering as "Jehovah." When Jewish scribes, called Masoretes, added vowel points to the text, they left the consonants for *yhwh*, but pointed them with the vowels for *'adônî* as a reminder that readers should pronounce it that way. In the German language, the consonants *yhwh* would be transliterated as *jhvh*. Reading the consonants for *jhvh* with vowels for *'adônî*, early German scholars translating the Bible into their language rendered the name as "Jehovah," and this was picked up in later translations, including the KJV.

Some translators now prefer an option, first suggested by Mitchell Dahood, in which the two three-letter words are put together, forming a longer word that means "to minister" or "to serve." This leads to the potential translation, "I will worship your majesty above the heavens" (Peter C. Craigie, *Psalms 1–50*, vol. 19 of Word Biblical Commentary [Zondervan, 1983], 104.) As high as the heavens might be, said the psalmist, God's glory is elevated even higher.

With v. 2, we come to the most puzzling part of the text, an apparent declaration that God can use even the praise of infants to silence all foes. The verse is clearly designed to expand upon the theme of God's magnificence, but its imagery interrupts the main flow of the psalm, so we'll leave a further discussion of that thorny verse for "The Hardest Question," below.

A privileged people
(vv. 3-5)

When most of us read Psalm 8, we tend to skip over the puzzling reference to babies and enemies, because it is the following question that grabs our attention: "When I look at your heavens, the work of your fingers, the moon and the stars that you have established; what are human beings that you are mindful of them, mortals that you care for them?" (vv. 3-4).

The psalmist struggled with the staggering notion that God could create something as massive as the heavens and earth and still care for human beings. We can't know if the psalmist conceived of God in anthropomorphic terms, or just happily used the metaphor, but he used the idea that God created the universe using only fingers as a way of emphasizing Yahweh's limitless power. If such a God could be bothered to care about puny, squabbling humans, how amazing is that?

But God does care, he concluded, because Yahweh not only created human beings, but also "made them a little lower than God, and crowned them with glory and honor" (v. 5). Again, those who grew up reading the KJV will remember a different translation: "For thou hast made him a little lower than the angels ..."

Which is it? Are we to think of ourselves as a little lower than God, or than angels? As usual, the answer is a matter of interpretation. The word is 'elōhîm, the plural form of a word meaning "god" that could be translated as "gods" in a generic sense, as in Exod. 18:11, "Now I know that the LORD is greater than all gods." Most of the time, however, it was used as an alternate term for the God of Israel, with the plural form being a "plural of majesty" designed to indicate that no singular term for God would be adequate.

The Old Testament also speaks of supernatural beings, created by God, who served on a divine council and did God's bidding, often as intermediaries between heaven and earth. Hebrew commonly refers to these beings as "sons of God" (benê 'elōhîm), as in Job 1:6, where the NRSV uses the term "heavenly beings." We typically think of such beings as "angels," and the Septuagint translators read 'elōhîm in that sense, using the Greek term 'aggelous (the double gamma [gg] was pronounced as "ng"), the root of the English word "angel."

How do we decide? The psalmist may have had Gen. 1:26-27 in mind, where God spoke to the divine council and said "Let *us* make humankind in *our* image" before creating humans, both male and female. Thus, the idea is that humans were created not only in the image of God, but also in the image of the angelic assembly. [**To whom was God speaking?**] Thus, some interpreters prefer to translate 'elōhîm as "angels," while others prefer the more common meaning of "God." It could also be translated as "a little lower than gods," which calls to mind Ps. 82:6.

At the end of the day, the meaning is little different. Humans are not only made by God, but also share

To whom was God speaking? Some readers mistakenly assume that when God said "let us make mankind in our image" (Gen. 1:26), it was an early reference to the Trinity, in which God the Father was speaking to God the Son and God the Holy Spirit. The author of Genesis (like the psalmist) had no such concept, but shared the ancient Near Eastern belief, common in many religions, that the high god often met in council with lower-level supernatural beings. Israel adapted the concept to the extent that Yahweh's divine council consisted of heavenly beings who were clearly suprahuman, but not considered gods. They, too, were part of God's created order.

something about God's image, and in making them this way God has "crowned them with glory and honor."

A responsible dominion
(vv. 6-8)

The poet's recollection of the creation story continues in vv. 6-8, which recalls God's instructions that humankind should "Be fruitful and multiply, and fill the earth and subdue it; and have dominion over the fish of the sea and over the birds of the air and over every living thing that moves upon the earth" (Gen. 1:28).

The psalmist had seen such dominion in action, and praised God for having given humans charge "over the works of your hands," putting "all things under their feet" (v. 6). Sheep and oxen, the beasts of the field, the birds of the air, fish and everything living in the sea had come under human control (vv. 7-8). [**Not just sheep**] The psalmist's point is that all life, from land to sea and sky, was subject to humankind: the work of God's hands was put into human hands, both to use and to preserve.

For the psalmist, the notion that God had not only taken notice of humans, but also given them control of life on earth, was such an astonishing notion that he could not resist bursting into praise once again, closing the psalm by

Not just sheep: Translators typically render v. 7 as "all sheep and oxen, and also the beasts of the field," mainly for lyrical purposes: it sounds better. The word translated as "sheep," however, is tsōneh, which refers to a mixed flock of sheep and goats. Such mixed flocks were typical: sheep were raised mainly for their wool, while goats provided meat and milk.

repeating his initial thought: "O LORD, our Sovereign, how majestic is your name in all the earth!" (v. 9).

How do you think the psalmist might have responded if he could see just how greatly humans have multiplied, and to what extent they have exercised dominion? We must remember that God's granting control over the earth to humans in Gen. 1:28-30 includes accountability along with authority. God did not put the earth into our hands so that we might exhaust its resources, pollute its water, and overheat its atmosphere.

The psalmist lived in a time when the earth's population was small, air pollution was limited to cooking fires, and animals were not being forced into extinction on a regular basis. If the ancient poet could catch a glimpse of what humans have done – and are doing – to the planet, he might not have thought it was such a good idea for God to put them in charge.

The poet has testified that God's greatness is beyond comprehension, and yet God cares enough for humankind to grant them stewardship of the earth, and to desire a relationship with them. When we contemplate the beautiful poetry of Psalm 8, and the staggering majesty of creation, what challenges us the most?

The Hardest Question
What do babies have to do with it?

Verse 2 is the most difficult part of the psalm to interpret: The NRSV has, "Out of the mouths of babes and infants you have *founded a bulwark* because of your foes, to silence the enemy and the avenger." The NET renders it differently: "From the mouths of children and nursing babies you have *ordained praise* on account of your adversaries, so that you might put an end to the vindictive enemy" (emphasis added).

What could baby noises have to do with establishing strength (the literal meaning of "bulwark"), or with silencing enemies and avengers? The verse has perplexed interpreters from at least the third century BCE, when early Greek translations were being done.

How should we interpret this puzzling text? Some writers suggest this approach: As a baby's cry leads to a response from the parent to deal with the problem, so Israel could cry to God, who would deliver them from their foes.

Another approach looks back to the previous emphasis on God's name and glory to propose that God's name is so powerful that even babies could pronounce the divine name and God would silence Israel's enemies.

One may also think of the baby's cry as a metaphor for weakness, and as a reminder that God often used weak or unassuming people to accomplish great things: the Old Testament contains many examples of "little come big," when unexpected heroes such as Ehud (Jdg. 3:12-30), Deborah (Judges 4–5), or Gideon (Judges 6–8) arose to lead Israel to victory over their foes.

Yet another approach notes that the Septuagint, an early Greek translation, used the word "praise" instead of "strength," suggesting that the translators' copy of the text had a different word. This leads to the idea that God displayed divine greatness by drawing praise even from infants (see the NET translation above).

Whatever nuance we put on the psalmist's precise meaning, his purpose was clearly to magnify the glory and power of God over all creation, from infants to enemies.

Third Reading
2 Corinthians 13:11-13

As Close as It Gets

The grace of the Lord Jesus Christ, the love of God,
and the communion of the Holy Spirit be with all of you. (2 Cor. 13:13)

Among the four lectionary readings, this brief text offers the most obvious reminder that the first Sunday after Pentecost is always "Trinity Sunday." Paul's benedictory words in v. 13 are as close to a Trinitarian statement as anything we have in the New Testament.

Before we get to the benediction, however, we find a fervent, last-ditch appeal to a troubled church. Paul's letters to the church in Corinth are a clear indicator that church conflict has been around from the emerging movement's earliest days. That can be cold comfort for a pastor who is currently trying to guide a conflicted church, however, and

Paul's authoritarian approach would not work well in most contemporary settings.

In 2 Corinthians 10–13, Paul adopts such a strident tone that some commentators have suggested it may represent a portion of the severe letter Paul described in 2 Cor. 2:4 as being written "out of much distress and anguish of heart and with many tears," one that he acknowledged could be painful to read.

Paul had spent at least two years with the young congregation, kept up a lively correspondence with them, and returned for visits at least twice. As the founder of the

---

A little background: It may be helpful to remember some highlights (and lowlights) in Paul's ongoing relationship with the people of Corinth:

Paul first visited Corinth and founded the church during his second missionary journey (Acts 18:1-18, c. 50–51 CE). The letter we know as 1 Corinthians was written from Ephesus during Paul's third journey, but it presupposes an earlier letter dealing with immorality in the church (1 Cor. 5:9). Some scholars think a fragment of this earlier letter has been preserved as 2 Cor. 6:14–7:1, which deals with immorality and doesn't really fit into its present context.

After sending the first letter, Paul heard from a group in the church he identifies as "Chloe's people" (1:11), and he also received a letter from Corinth (7:1). He responded with the letter we call 1 Corinthians, apparently dealing with the issues raised by Chloe's people in chs. 1–6, and with matters from the letter in chs. 7–16 (cf. 7:1, 7:25, 8:1, 12:1).

The Corinthians responded to Paul's letter with some hostility, requiring him to make a "painful visit" from Ephesus to the church (2 Cor. 2:1). After returning to Ephesus, he wrote a strongly worded letter and sent it by Titus (2 Cor. 2:3-9, 7:12). Parts of this "severe letter" may be preserved in 2 Corinthians 10–13, which is harsher than the conciliatory tone of the surrounding text.

Paul was still burdened for the Corinthians when he left Ephesus. He hoped to meet Titus in Troas and learn how the letter was received, but he did not find Titus there, and restlessly moved on to Macedonia (2 Cor. 2:12). There he met Titus, who reported that the Corinthians had accepted the letter with grace and had been reconciled to Paul (2 Cor. 7:5-16). Paul then wrote 2 Corinthians to express his joy and to encourage the church at Corinth to raise a worthy offering for the poor in Jerusalem (2 Corinthians 9). He later wintered in Greece, probably at Corinth (Acts 20:1-3) before proceeding to Jerusalem with the offering.

church, he considered himself to be like a parent who had authority over his "children" in the faith. In his absence, however, certain traveling preachers that Paul sarcastically calls "super-apostles" (11:4, 12:11) had gained influence over the church and challenged Paul's authority while teaching aberrant doctrine. **[A little background]**

Paul offered a spirited defense of both his teaching and his authority in chs. 10–13, concluding with the hope that his letter would have the desired effect so that "I may not have to be severe in using the authority that the Lord has given me for building up and not tearing down" (13:10). Rather than continuing his critique upon arrival, he wanted to devote his in-person efforts to more constructive work.

With the last few verses, Paul's heated rhetoric gives way to a sweeter, if still imperative, appeal.

A closing appeal
(vv. 11-12)

Verse 11 marks a transition to Paul's closing thoughts with the word "Finally" (*loipon*) before he launches into five summary directives, all in the form of second-person plural imperative verbs, though only four are apparent from the NRSV's translation.

Following the KJV, the NRSV translates *chairete* as "farewell," even though it is clearly the imperative form of the verb *chairō*, "to rejoice." Forms of the word could be used as a salutation in the sense of "be happy" or "be well," and perhaps the translators adopted that, thinking that "rejoice" might be a strange command to people who had just been taken to the woodshed.

Since it introduces a string of five imperatives, though, it is best to go with the basic translation "rejoice," possibly in the sense of a comforting "Cheer up!" – Paul wanted to close on a positive note.

"Put things in order" renders *katartizesthe* in a direct sense, though in the middle form it can also be translated reflexively as something akin to "get it together." If considered together, the first two directives could bear the friendly sense of "Come on now, cheer up and put things right." In giving the instructions, Paul is showing confidence that the Corinthians are capable of positive change.

The third imperative (*parakaleisthe*) can also have a reflexive sense, and adds to the theme of encouragement or consolation. The NRSV's "listen to me" is a possible render-

ing, but "be consoled" or "encourage one another" seems to better fit Paul's calming close after his earlier tirade against those who had fallen in with the "super apostles."

The fourth and fifth imperatives counsel an end to the conflict and a return to unity in the church as Paul urges his readers to "agree with one another" (literally, "think the same") and to "live in peace." The apostle knew better than to expect a complete uniformity of opinion, but he urged them to have the same goal, to agree that the unity and mission of the church were more important than doctrinal quibbles or personality cults.

If the people were willing to do their part to overcome division and work together, Paul believed, they would experience a renewed sense of God's presence in the congregation: "and the God of love and peace will be with you."

Though I have read this in a conditional sense, it is also possible that Paul was offering a promise that God would be at work to promote love and peace as the people sought to pull themselves back together and right their foundering congregational ship.

Only with repairs to broken relationships would the people be able to obey Paul's last command to "Greet one another with a holy kiss" as they remembered others who were sending best wishes to them.

Few people in the English-speaking world have a tradition of greeting each other with a peck on the cheek – or both cheeks – but it was apparently customary in Roman society, and it remains popular in some cultures today.

Paul counseled a "holy kiss" rather than an amorous one, but even a perfunctory buss requires people to get close enough for a rather intimate touch. Paul's directive may remind us more of a teacher who breaks up a fight and tells the participants to apologize and shake hands. Or, we may think of friends who have had a spat but manage to get past it enough to "kiss and make up" or to "hug it out."

Touch can be a very powerful thing. It's hard to remain overly critical of someone while shaking their hand or exchanging a hug. Paul understood that.

An intriguing benediction
(v. 13)

Having concluded his counsel, Paul closed with a memorable benediction, often repeated by worship leaders even today: "The grace of the Lord Jesus Christ, the love of God, and the communion of the Holy Spirit be with all of you."

Paul's intent was not to teach a doctrinal lesson on the Trinity, but to wish for the people he loved to have the fullest experience possible of God's presence among them. One way to speak of the Trinity is to describe the concept in social terms. The whole notion of "one God in three persons" demands significant elasticity of the brain to try and comprehend, but one way is to think of Father, Son, and Holy Spirit as being eternally coexistent in a mutual, social relationship.

Another way is to think of God as one being with three aspects who over time has related to humans primarily as Creator, Redeemer, or Sustainer, while never losing any of the other aspects. [**Common, but inadequate**]

God's existence as Father, Son, and Holy Spirit, however difficult it is to comprehend, is true in relation to all people and at all times. We might have a tendency to think that God the Father/Creator came first, the uniquely begotten Son came later, and the Holy Spirit emerged after Christ's ascension, but that is not the biblical picture.

John's gospel declares that the Son (as the "Word") was coexistent with the Father from the beginning (John 1:1), and the Spirit of God is active in the Old Testament, empowering judges from Othniel (Judg. 3:10) to Gideon (Judg. 6:34) to Jephthah (Judg. 11:29) and Samson (Judg. 13:25, 14:6, 19; 15:14). The Spirit of the Lord came upon King Saul but later departed (1 Sam. 10:6, 16:14), but when David was anointed, "the Spirit of the LORD came mightily upon David from that day forward" (1 Sam. 16:13).

Though Paul was not elaborating on the Trinity, his benedictory words in v. 13 may help us to think of the Trinity in a functional sense: he wished for his friends to

know "the *grace* of the Lord Jesus Christ, the *love* of God, and the *communion* (or fellowship) of the Holy Spirit."

The Old Testament's core understanding of God's character was grounded in steadfast love and mercy (Exod. 34:6; Ps. 86:5, 15; 103:8; 145:8; 2 Chron. 30:8-9; Neh. 9:17; Jon. 4:2). New Testament writers believed that God's grace had been revealed preeminently through the incarnation and work of the Son, a free gift of grace to humankind (Rom. 5:15). Jesus promised to send the Holy Spirit as an advocate, comforter, or "paraclete" to testify of God's continuing presence that would both empower the church and bind it together in fellowship (John 14:26, 15:26).

It may be worth noting that Paul's closing benediction to 1 Corinthians mentions only "the grace of the Lord Jesus" (1 Cor. 15:23), Galatians closes with "the grace of the Lord Jesus Christ" (Gal. 6:18), as does Philippians (Phil. 4:23). Ephesians closes with a wish for peace and love "from God the Father and the Lord Jesus Christ" (Eph. 6:24).

Only here, following his sharp critique of the Corinthian church, does Paul appear to reach deeper or pull out all the stops in his appeal for his children in the faith to stop squabbling and renew their fellowship. Every way of thinking about God – as Father, Son, or Holy Spirit – should challenge them to remember their former state and trust the fullness of God to restore their unity and witness.

When we consider the state of our own congregations today, many of them fractured and declining, perhaps Paul's comprehensive appeal could speak to us, too.

The Hardest Question
How can thoughts of the Trinity inform our own relationships?

Many creeds, essays, treatises, and books have been written attempting to explain the concept of the Trinity, and none can claim to have done so completely. Some things are simply beyond our full comprehension.

Here I simply offer David Gushee's description of the Trinity in social terms, with special attention to how Paul's benediction applied to the people of Corinth, who were lacking in the area of their own social relationships:

> To say that God is triune is to mean that God is
> social in nature. It is also to say that those made in

Common, but inadequate: A pastor once tried explaining the Trinity to my young ears by pointing out that he was simultaneously a son, a father, and a husband. The thought was helpful at the time, but the analogy doesn't carry when we consider that those varying identities are in relation only to certain people, not to all. He could have added that he was also a pastor, a Little League coach, and a Democrat. Human analogies fall short when considering the nature of divine being.

the image of God are likewise intrinsically social. There is one God, and the unity of this one God is absolute; yet this God is described in Scripture as three persons: Father, Son, and Holy Spirit. Scripture speaks primarily of the roles that each person plays in relation to human salvation: the Father sends the Son to redeem the God-created world, the Son lives and dies for the world, the Spirit draws people to salvation and into community. (*Feasting on the Word,* Year A, vol. 3 of Accordance electronic ed. [Westminster John Knox Press, 2011], para. 13239.)

Trinity Sunday / First Sunday after Pentecost

Third Reading
Matthew 28:16-20

The World Needs the Gospel

Go therefore and make disciples of all nations, baptizing them in the name of the Father and of the Son and of the Holy Spirit, and teaching them to obey everything that I have commanded you. And remember, I am with you always, to the end of the age. (Matt. 28:19-20)

The closing challenge of Matthew's gospel is so familiar that many readers might wonder why we bother to study it anew. As children, many of us were encouraged to memorize Matt. 28:19-20. Long-time church attenders have no doubt heard any number of sermons based on the text, especially during those seasons when donations for missions were being collected.

Our terminology and methodology of mission work have changed considerably through the years, but not our love for what came to be known as "the Great Commission." On close study, we may find more than one reason to call this commission "great." It's not about evangelizing alone.

On the liturgical calendar, this week celebrates Trinity Sunday, which is why the gospel reading skips to the end of Matthew, where we find what appears to be a Trinitarian formula.

Meeting Jesus
(v. 16)

The closing verses of Matthew must be read and understood within the context of the entire 28th chapter, a narrative that begins with Mary Magdalene and "the other Mary" standing wide-eyed and open-mouthed before an empty tomb. The careful reader may notice that *twice* in this short account of Easter morning (vv. 7 and 10), Jesus sent word to his disciples that he had gone ahead of them to Galilee,

and that they should follow him there if they wanted to see him.

Why was this so important that Matthew spelled it out twice to be sure we don't miss it? If Jesus wanted to see the disciples again, why didn't he just drop in on their sullen hideout in Jerusalem, which is precisely what Luke and John describe him as doing (Luke 24:36-49, John 20:19-29)? Why was it important for Matthew to insist that Jesus would go straightway into *Galilee*, and first meet the disciples there? [**Why so different?**]

In the first century CE, the region of Galilee was fairly well defined by the Jordan valley to the east and the Phoenician border to the west, extending as far north as Lake Huleh (a small lake about six miles north of the Sea of Galilee), and as far south as the plain that begins at Megiddo and reaches southeast through the Valley of Jezreel, which joins the Jordan rift valley some 15–20 miles south of the Sea of Galilee.

At least two things about this location may be significant. First, Galilee was Jesus' earthly home. Though born in Bethlehem, he was raised in Nazareth, a small town in southern Galilee. Though he traveled south for his baptism and may have visited Jerusalem for religious festivals, he spent the bulk of his ministry in the green hills and lakeside towns of Galilee. [**Jesus in Jerusalem**]

During the short years of his active ministry, the closest thing Jesus had to a home was the town of Capernaum,

Why so different? The post-resurrection accounts of Mark, Luke, and John are quite different from that in Matthew. Mark's gospel ended so abruptly, with the women running from the tomb in fear, that ancient scribes added two alternate endings following the dramatic stopping place in Mark 16:8.

Luke describes post-resurrection appearances of Jesus in Jerusalem rather than in Galilee, including the familiar stories of Jesus walking and dining with followers in Emmaus (Luke 24:13-35); Jesus' sudden appearance among the gathered disciples to confirm his resurrection and instruct them to remain in Jerusalem until he sent the Spirit upon them (Luke 24:36-49); and Jesus leading the disciples to the nearby village of Bethany, where he blessed them and ascended into heaven (Luke 24:50-53).

John's gospel says that Jesus appeared on Easter evening to the disciples (minus Thomas) who were gathered behind locked doors in Jerusalem (John 20:19-25); appeared again a week later when Thomas was present (John 20:26-29); and "did many other signs in the presence of his disciples" (John 20:30-31) before appearing again to the disciples on the shores of "the Sea of Tiberias" (an alternate name for the Sea of Galilee, and obviously in Galilee), where he confronted Peter and told him to "feed my sheep/lambs" (John 21:1-23).

We should not be surprised that the shock of Jesus' resurrection inspired many different stories, and it is not possible to reconcile them all. It is likely that none of the gospels are eyewitness accounts: Mark and Luke came along later, and though the other two gospels bear the names of Matthew and John, they were written many years after Jesus died, though in the name of the disciples.

The authors of the gospels, probably 30–70 years removed from Jesus' death and resurrection, had no videotape or newspaper accounts of what had happened so long before. Instead, they had access to traditions that had been developed from the early stories, some of them written and some of them not. In seeking to tell their version of the story of Jesus, each author chose those stories that matched their special interests. We can be sure that Matthew and Luke drew much from Mark's earlier gospel, but both also borrowed material from another unknown source that scholars call "Q" (from the German *quelle*, meaning "source"). Matthew, Luke, and John also had access to traditions that the other gospel writers may or may not have known about, but did not include in their accounts.

While the obviously different accounts might trouble someone whose faith depends on the existence of an "inerrant" Bible that has no internal contradictions, it should not trouble us. We cannot measure the historical accuracy of the various accounts, but we can still learn from what the author intended to get across, and that is the task at hand.

Jesus in Jerusalem: The Fourth Gospel indicates that Jesus visited Jerusalem three times during his active ministry, each time for a religious festival. John places the "scourging of the temple" early in Jesus' ministry (John 2:1-17), while Luke locates it in the context of the passion week (Luke 19:45-46). The Fourth Gospel also has Jesus going to Jerusalem for an unnamed "feast of the Jews" (John 5:2), and another time for Hanukkah (John 10:22-30), before his final visit, beginning with the Palm Sunday account in John 12 and extending through the remainder of the gospel. Thus, John records four visits to Jerusalem, along with an additional visit to Bethany, on the outskirts of Jerusalem, when he raised Lazarus from the dead (John 11).

In contrast, the synoptic gospels record only one visit to Jerusalem during Jesus' ministry, that being the final week before the crucifixion (Mark 11:1, Matt. 21:1, Luke 19:28). Luke frames much of his gospel around Jesus' final journey to Jerusalem, from when he "set his face toward Jerusalem" in 9:21 to his final ascent toward Bethany and the Palm Sunday road in 19:28.

This need not bother us greatly. Each gospel writer chose to include material that was particularly important to him, and we cannot expect any of them to be comprehensive. Writing 30–70 years after Jesus' ministry, we cannot expect any of them to have an accurate chronology of events: they were all working from sketches of memory and tradition that had been handed down for a generation or more.

where Simon Peter lived, hard by the north shore of the sea of Galilee. According to Matthew, as Jesus began his active ministry, "He left Nazareth and made his home in Capernaum by the sea, in the territory of Zebulun and Naphtali" (4:13).

More importantly, Matthew may have seen important symbolism in Jesus' return to Galilee. First-century Galilee was a very cosmopolitan community. There were Jewish towns and villages such as Nazareth and Capernaum and Cana, but Jews were likely a minority in the area. The cities of Tiberius on the Sea of Galilee and Sepphoris in the hill country just north of Nazareth were both Hellenistic centers with few, if any, Jews. Many villages were populated then, as now, by people of other ethnic backgrounds. Galilee was a melting pot of the ancient world.

Jesus' ministry stretched far beyond the narrow confines of Judaism. Matthew often cited Old Testament texts that he believed Jesus came to fulfill, so it's often thought that his gospel was directed primarily toward Jews. The author, however, clearly understood Jesus' concern for all people. So, it was important for him to highlight a tradition that Jesus did not stay in Jerusalem but went into Galilee, perhaps because it symbolized the larger world he had come to save.

Jesus was not content to return to Galilee alone, for he had business yet to accomplish with his disciples. Thus, he instructed the women: "Do not be afraid; go and tell my brothers to go to Galilee; there they will see me" (v 10). Jesus in his resurrection was not limited by geography, and neither was the mission he was leaving the disciples.

For Jesus' work to continue, his disciples would need to be willing to follow him into the world. And, it was only when his 11 remaining disciples had gone by faith into Galilee, Matthew says, that Jesus met them on a mountain and declared to them the church's ongoing commission.

Worship, and wonder
(v. 17)

When the disciples found Jesus, Matthew tells us, "they worshiped him." The last time they had seen Jesus, he was suffering under the humiliation of Roman cruelty and the cross. Now, however, they saw him resurrected and glorified. Perhaps we are to imagine they had discussed his prior predictions of death and resurrection while on the way to Galilee. No one could do what he had done apart from God. No one could do what he had done unless, in some mysterious way, he was in some way related to God.

Worship was appropriate then, as it is appropriate now: worship that confesses the Lordship – the *Godship* – of Jesus, the Christ, the dead and risen and lifted up; worship that declares our human unworthiness to stand in the presence of the creating and redeeming God. It is no wonder that the disciples were moved to worship.

"They worshiped him," Matthew says, "but some doubted." What? Here they are on the ground before the risen Christ, but *some doubted*? The Greek text allows considerable ambiguity in translation. Was there doubt among the 11 disciples Matthew identifies as being present? Or, does the text suggest there were others gathered around who doubted that the man before them was truly the risen Christ?

While some worshiped, others doubted. Has anything really changed from that spring day until now? Some

> **An exercise:** Consider closing your eyes and taking some time to imagine yourself standing (or kneeling) among the disciples in a Galilean mountain meadow. If you could see Jesus with your eyes and fall to your face before him, what would you say? How would you worship him? How does that compare with what you normally do in church, where we still claim to be in the presence of Christ?

worship, but others doubt. And is it not true that sometimes we who worship may also doubt? Thinking Christians may have honest questions about their faith – even as they worship, and to their potential profit.

We can be grateful that Matthew's gospel offers space for the doubters among us. It is possible both to adore and to doubt, and Jesus honors our questions along with our worship. In that sense, this text is a real gift to those who travel with Thomas, who was portrayed by the Fourth Gospel as harboring doubts before he saw Jesus for himself (John 20:20-25). Jesus appeared undisturbed by the mixed minds of those who worshiped him. He understood their uncertainty and extended the same challenge to them all. **[An exercise]**

Witness
(vv. 18-20)

Jesus declared to his confused-but-still-worshiping disciples that he had been granted "all authority in heaven and on earth" (v. 18). Matthew's gospel begins with the claim that Jesus was the promised scion of David, the true messianic king (1:1), but for most of his ministry, Jesus avoided such language. Now, despite the lack of regal trappings or evidence in that isolated mountain setting, Jesus affirmed his role as king, not only of Israel, but of all things. "All authority in heaven and on earth has been given to me," he said. Think about that claim: *All authority in heaven and on earth.* The resurrection marked a new phase of Christ's eternal reign.

Jesus' authority implies the power to command, the power that lies behind the "therefore" of v. 19: "Go therefore and make disciples of all nations ..." Jesus' followers – doubting or not – were called to obey Christ, the last word in authority. When Jesus calls us to "go," we are expected to go.

But where do we go, and what do we do? We go to every place and to every people who need the love of Christ.

Indeed, we are always "going" here and there, and the responsibility of making new disciples rests with all believers, not just with those who feel called to "go to the mission field." In this age of post-Christendom, America is as greatly in need of the gospel as any other place – and more than some.

Interpreters often point out that the word for "go" is a participle in Greek, and only the word meaning "make disciples" is in the imperative form. Thus, it is possible to translate the command in this way: "As you are going, make disciples …" No believer is exempt from the responsibility of living in a way that inspires others to discipleship, and we are to do that as a matter of course in our daily lives – as we are going.

The text appears to reflect an early baptism formula used by the church, but it does not reflect a full-blown understanding of the Trinity, something that developed over many years.

Baptism is important, for it marks the first step on the road of discipleship. But, for too many of us, our spiritual growth stalls along the way. If we take seriously Jesus' command to care about others' spiritual formation, however, if we are doing our best to "make disciples," it's much more likely that we'll look to our own spiritual development also.

Jesus did not promise that the task would be easy. Living with a Jesus-centered worldview calls us away from easy selfishness and toward a life of loving sacrifice. How can we succeed in such an enterprise? We can do it because we have the full support of God working in us and through us – God known to us as the One who creates all things, the Redeemer who brings salvation, and the Spirit who empowers us for confident action in following Christ's command.

In this we receive an amazing blessing, but also a major challenge. How are we responding?

The Hardest Question
Does Matt. 28:19-20 teach the Trinity?

Matthew 28:19-20 includes a formula that was no doubt used in the early church, probably as a baptism formula. Matthew presented them as the words of Jesus. Does this mean that the author of Matthew believed in the Trinity?

The answer must be both yes and no. It is "yes" in the sense that Matthew speaks of God in three ways: as Father, Son, and Holy Spirit – and he apparently believed this did not contradict the Hebrew teaching that there is only one God (Deut. 6:4). A few other texts, such as the apostolic benediction in 2 Cor. 13:13, also used trinitarian language: "The grace of the Lord Jesus Christ, the love of God, and the communion of the Holy Spirit be with all of you." Similar references to Father, Son, and Holy Spirit are found in 1 Cor. 12:4-5, Eph. 4:4-6, 1 Pet. 1:2, and Rev. 1:4-5.

It is "no" in the sense that a word for "Trinity" does not appear in the New Testament, and its writers could not have been familiar with the long-running and highly contentious theological debates about the nature of God that led to the doctrine of the Trinity through a series of councils at which church leaders gathered to debate doctrine and draw conclusions.

Church history is complicated by the existence of multiple traditions, but church councils held in Nicea in 325 CE and Constantinople in 381 CE ultimately settled on an accepted formula. Known both as the Niceno-Constantinopolitan Creed and in shorthand as the Nicene Creed, the resulting text depicted God as triune in nature.

The creed was written in Greek, and is used in various English translations. The following translation is derived from earlychurchtexts.com:

We believe in one God, the Father almighty, maker of heaven and earth, of all things visible and invisible; And in one Lord, Jesus Christ, the only begotten Son of God, begotten from the Father before all ages, light from light, true God from true God, begotten not made, of one substance with the Father, through Whom all things came into existence, Who because of us men and because of our salvation came down from the heavens, and was incarnate from the Holy Spirit and the Virgin Mary and became man, and was crucified for us under Pontius Pilate, and suffered and was buried, and rose again on the third day according to the Scriptures and ascended to heaven, and sits on the right hand of the Father, and will come again with glory to judge living and dead, of Whose kingdom there will be no end; And in the Holy Spirit, the Lord and life-giver, Who proceeds from the Father, Who with the Father and the Son is together worshipped and together glorified, Who spoke through the prophets; in one holy Catholic and apostolic Church. We confess one baptism to the remission of sins; we look forward to the resurrection of the dead and the life of the world to come. Amen

The biblical texts were just one step on a long road that led to the doctrine of the Trinity.

First Reading
Deuteronomy 30:15-20*

Choose Rightly!

Choose life so that you and your descendants may live, loving the LORD your God,
obeying him, and holding fast to him … (Deut. 30:19b-20a)

If you've ever seen the musical *Fiddler on the Roof,* you will no doubt remember Tevye, the father, singing and dancing to celebrate his daughter's engagement. Again and again he sang "To life, to life, *l'chayim, l'chayim, l'chayim,* to life …"

Chayim, beginning with a rough "h" sound, is the Hebrew word for life, and it plays a starring role in today's text, which portrays Moses as challenging Israel to choose life by choosing faithfulness to God, known to the Israelites as Yahweh.

A bit of background

Deuteronomy is the last book of the Pentateuch, or the Torah. "Pentateuch" comes from Greek and means "Five books," namely the first five in the Hebrew Bible. "Torah," which is often translated as "law," refers more broadly to instruction or guidance.

The book is written in the form of speeches or sermons proclaimed by the law-giver Moses as the Israelites came to the end of their journey from Egypt and camped just across the Jordan from the Promised Land. Deuteronomy may preserve Mosaic traditions, but it was written many years later, just before or during the exile, when Israel had both occupied the land of promise and later lost it.

As written, the stern warnings given by Moses to the nascent Israelites provided a theological explanation for the Hebrews' loss of their land to the Assyrians and Babylonians, but also offered hope that God would redeem them from exile and return them to the land if they could prove more faithful than their ancestors.

The book is set on the verge of Israel's initial entry to Canaan, a time of sharp transition. The people were about to end their wandering ways and enter the Promised Land – if they could be faithful enough to have God's aid in subduing it. Just as importantly, however, they were about to lose Moses as the only spiritual leader they had ever known. God had told him he could not enter the land: they would have to learn to live without him.

On more than one occasion, the people had proven faithless even when traveling together and with Moses' stern leadership. Now they would be scattered throughout the land in their tribal allotments. Being obedient and faithful to God would prove even more difficult when the people were dispersed, with no central authority to keep them accountable – something the author (or authors) of Deuteronomy had seen firsthand.

Canaan was already populated by many people who worshiped other gods, and the Israelites would be tempted to follow their example. Even a cursory reading of 2 Kings

---

Deuteronomy: The Deuteronomic writers built their work on the theme of blessing and cursing, the premise being that God would bless the righteous and curse the wicked. Later writers in Judah used this same theology as the basis for the books of Joshua–2 Kings (with the exception of Ruth), commonly known as the "Deuteronomistic History." Their purpose was to explain the exile by showing that Yahweh had not been defeated or deserted his people. Rather, the exile was a natural result of Israel's sinful ways that had been practiced over many years. Even Josiah's revival, they concluded, was too little and too late to stop the impending invasion of the Babylonians, which was nothing more than God's punishment for Israel's errant ways.

Here's one way to outline the book of Deuteronomy.

Introduction and Moses' First Sermon (1:1–4:43)
Historical review of the wilderness journey (1:6–3:29)
Exhortations to give heed (4:1-43)

Moses' Second Sermon (4:44–26:19)
The giving of the law at Sinai (5:1–11:32)
Additional statutes and ordinances (12:1–25:19)
Rituals, and an interlude (26:1-1)

Covenant Making at Ebal and Gerizim (26:20–28:68)
A charge to accept the covenant stipulations (26:20–27:10)
Twelve curses proclaimed and acknowledged (27:11-26)
Moses' summary of blessings and cursings (28:1-68)

Moses' Third Sermon (29:1–30:20)

Moses' Last Days (31:1–34:12)
A final charge and the writing of the law (31:1-13)
The commissioning of Joshua as Moses' successor (31:14-23)
The Song of Moses (31:30–32:47)
The blessing of Moses (33:1-29)
The death of Moses (34:1-12)

and the prophets reveals that many Israelites adopted other gods in addition to Yahweh from the point of their entry into Canaan right up to the time of the exile – a primary reason why the phrase "until this day" appears so frequently in Deuteronomy. [**Deuteronomy**]

Options and consequences
(vv. 15-18)

Calling for Israel to stay on the straight and narrow, the author has Moses call the people to pledge their loyalty to God – or else. His lengthy speech occupies two chapters, beginning at 29:1 with the marker "These are the words of the covenant that the LORD commanded Moses to make with the Israelites in the land of Moab." This was not to be just a renewal ceremony, but a second covenant "in addition to the covenant that he had made with them at Horeb."

Horeb is an alternate term for "Sinai." While the Yahwistic and Priestly writers called the mountain of law-giving "Sinai," the Elohistic and Deuteronomistic writers called it "Horeb."

The speech begins with a reminder of how God had delivered the Israelites from Egypt, brought them through the wilderness, and helped them defeat King Sihon of Heshbon and King Og of Bashan, taking their land for themselves (29:2-9). [**Heshbon and Bashan**]

Covenants typically name the parties involved, and Moses made it clear that all the Israelite people were included, from the elders to the children, men, women, and even the servants who chopped their wood and fetched their water – characteristics that portray a settled life long after Moses (29:10-15). The phrase "this day" occurs twice as a call for an immediate decision.

The anticipated problem is spelled out in 29:16-19. Some of the people might have been attracted to other gods by the idols they had seen among other peoples, and may have anticipated serving other gods when they came into the land. That would bring disaster, Moses declared, inciting the devastating curses that are spelled out in 29:20-29, the same sort of disasters that had taken place prior to the exile.

The speech then called later readers to remember, when they went into captivity, that Moses had warned them and called them to return to God and to "obey him with all your heart and with all your soul, just as I am commanding you today" (30:1-2).

Heshbon and Bashan: Little else is known about these two reported kings. The land of Bashan was a hilly but fertile area east of the Sea of Galilee, known for its rich pasturage. Amos would later excoriate the luxurious lifestyle of the rich by describing them as "fat cows of Bashan" (Amos 4:1). Bashan extended southward to meet Heshbon, which was later controlled by the Ammonites. The northern part of this territory was then assigned to half of the tribe of Manasseh, and the southern part to the tribes of Reuben and Gad.

Repentance would elicit divine compassion and God would "restore your fortunes … gathering you again from all the peoples among whom the LORD your God has scattered you." Even "to the ends of the world" God would return them to "the land that your ancestors possessed" (30:3-5).

There God would "circumcise your heart and the heart of your descendants, so that you will love the LORD your God with all your heart and with all your soul, in order that you may live" (30:6-10).

The narrator has Moses insist that the commandment "is not too hard for you, nor is it too far away." Understanding it did not require an ascent to heaven or a voyage across the sea: "the word is very near to you; it is in your mouth and in your heart for you to observe" (30:11-14).

Finally, we come to the climax of the story, the moment of decision. As the people entered the promised land, they would have to make a choice about their allegiance to Yahweh.

"See, I have set before you today life and prosperity, death and adversity" (v. 15), Moses declared. [**Adding color**] Observing the commandment by "loving the LORD your God, walking in his ways, and observing his commandments, decrees, and ordinances" would lead to life and prosperity in the land, while those who turned to other gods would perish (vv. 16-18).

For the Deuteronomist, theology was a simple transaction.

A challenge to choose
(vv. 19-20)

"Choose," Moses insisted. "I call heaven and earth to witness against you today that I have set before you life and death, blessings and curses. Choose life so that you and your descendants may live, loving the LORD your God, obeying him, and holding fast to him; for that means life to you and length of days, so that you may live in the land that the LORD swore to give to your ancestors, to Abraham, to Isaac, and to Jacob" (vv. 19-20).

Ancient covenants typically called on the gods of both parties as witnesses, but Israel had just one god, so "heaven and earth" served as metaphorical stand-ins.

Note how repetitive the challenges are. Love God. Obey God. Hold fast to God. Avoid other gods. Do that

Adding color: The NRSV translates v. 15 as "See, I have set before you today life and prosperity, death and adversity." That gives a rather floral cast to the Hebrew's straightforward "life and good or death and evil." Prosperity is not quite the same thing as good, and adversity is not the same thing as evil. Good can lead to prosperity (though not always), and evil can lead to adversity (but good people may also face adversity).

The black-and-white portrayal of obedience = blessing and disobedience = cursing fits the rhetoric of the Deuteronomistic covenant, but does not reflect the realities of life.

and live long and happy lives. Turn away from God and meet the bad end of a short life.

Choose.

What does this text mean when we read it today? As an interpretive principle, it is essential to remember that this was remembered as a covenant for Israel, not for the church.

Christians who read this text as a promise that God will grant long life and prosperity to the obedient but stir up trouble for the disobedient are not only misreading the text, but also failing to take notice of the world around them.

It is a world in which people who are faithful to God may suffer poverty and hardship, or die young of cruel diseases. It is a world in which liars and cheaters and self-worshipers can make out like bandits or achieve high office with no punishment in sight.

Proclaimers of the misguided "prosperity gospel" pick and choose verses such as these to make false promises, urging followers to believe that God wants them to be rich, and to prove their faithfulness, in part, by donating money to the shysters who pass as preachers.

Christians may read the text in all sincerity but without attention to context, and mistakenly take it as a promise to modern believers. Jesus never promised financial success or good health or long life to his followers. He promised *abundant* life, life in the kingdom of God, life that has meaning and purpose beyond selfish goals. He also told his followers to expect hardship in life.

Christian preachers sometimes update the challenge to choose by tying it to Jesus and making it a call for conversion, a choice between eternal life in heaven or eternal death in hell, but it is never as simple as that. Some evangelists sell the gospel as if it were fire insurance, but the question we should really ask is this: Do we serve God only for what we think we can get out of it, or because we believe that being faithful to God makes us better people, doing our part to build up the kingdom, reflecting God's love in the world?

In other words, if there were no clear tangible rewards for serving God – even if we were to one day discover that life after death isn't what we think it is – would we still want to follow Jesus?

Choosing to serve God is always better than serving self, or power, or money. We also have choices to make, but the option of gaining rich rewards through serving God is not one of them.

The Hardest Question
Did Moses really preach this sermon?

The book of Deuteronomy is shaped in the form of one or possibly three connected sermons that Moses reportedly delivered as Israel stood on the verge of entering the land of promise. As presented, it amounts to a lengthy challenge and farewell address from Moses before his death. The book includes a restating of the Ten Commandments, along with supplemental commentary and additional laws. This gave rise to its English name: "Deuteronomy" means "second law" (from Greek *deuteros* [second] *nomos* [law], used as a title in the Greek translation known as the LXX). The Hebrew name of the book is *ha-d'bārîm*, meaning "The Words," because that is the first word in the book.

Deuteronomy is written as if these are the very words of Moses, who supposedly wrote them down. But did he?

During Moses' lifetime, so far as we know, Hebrew had not yet become a written language. The earliest – and rather primitive – proto-Hebrew inscriptions we know are 200 years later than the time attributed to Moses. Traditions and stories associated with Moses, like the rest of the Pentateuch, were passed down in oral tradition for hundreds of years.

While the speeches in Deuteronomy may have roots in ongoing Mosaic traditions, it's likely that they are the work of someone who lived long after Moses, constructing speeches designed to support the theological agenda of the priests in the late seventh and early sixth centuries BCE. Purporting that Moses was responsible for the law would give the writing an added sense of authority.

The final edition of Deuteronomy was probably compiled during the exile, but an earlier version was known as early as 621 BCE, when it was "found" during renovations in the temple ordered by King Josiah and presented to the king as a book of law that had fallen from use and been lost. Josiah apparently used the teachings of the book as the basis for promoting a revival of Yahwism and various religious reforms in Judah (2 Kings 22–23).

Thus, while Deuteronomy purports to be an address to Israelites who had not yet entered the land, it was mainly a message to people who had lived in the land for many years but were in danger of losing it – or had lost it already.

We do not live under the same covenant as Israel, but we can learn from Israel's experience and profit from the challenge to serve God faithfully – not just to gain rewards, but because it is the right way of life.

Second Reading
Psalm 119:1-8*

Law Lovers

Happy are those whose way is blameless, who walk in the law of the LORD. (Ps. 119:1)

Did you have an "ABC book" as a child, or buy one for your own children? Such books help young readers learn the alphabet by associating each letter with words beginning with that letter: "A is for apple," "B is for ball," and so forth.

The ancient Hebrews had a related but more advanced practice of making religious poetry easier to memorize by beginning each line, couplet, or stanza with sequential letters of the alphabet.

The book of Lamentations uses this pattern, as do some of the psalms. The longest and most complex of these is Psalm 119. Its 176 verses encompass 22 stanzas of eight couplets each, one for each letter in the Hebrew alphabet – or *alefbet*. [**Alefbet**]

Each couplet of each stanza begins with the same letter: each of the first eight verses begin with the letter *alef*, the next eight with *bet*, the next eight with *gimel*, and so on to the final eight verses, which begin with *tav*.

As the poet built his prolonged prayer on the scaffold of the Hebrew *alefbet*, he utilized as building material the theme of God's Torah, or teaching. Eight different synonyms for the concept appear repeatedly: some stanzas contain all eight terms, and all stanzas include at least six.

The poet believed that rules are important. The thought of life without restrictions may be appealing, but the lack of guidelines could lead to personal or societal chaos. The psalmist recognized the value of holding to certain standards

> **Alefbet:** The English word "alphabet" is derived from the first two letters of the Greek alphabet: *alpha* and *beta*. The Hebrew collection of letters begins with *alef* and *bet*, so we call it the "*alefbet*." Although Hebrew and Greek are very different languages, many of their letters descend from the same roots. Both Hebrew and Greek begin with corresponding letters that make the sounds for a, b, g, and d before the order diverges (*alef, bet, gimel, dalet* in Hebrew; *alpha, beta, gamma, delta* in Greek). This is helpful to know when we consider the acrostic form of Psalm 119. This also explains the strange headers many Bibles have above each section: "*alef, bet, gimel,*" etc. The headers are the names of the Hebrew letters that begin each verse in that section.

of behavior in individual or corporate life. He encouraged readers to take comfort in knowing basic and acceptable guidelines for living, and to follow them.

In the psalm, he speaks lovingly of God's *torah*, God's word, and God's way, in addition to God's laws, statues, decrees, commands, precepts, and ordinances. He firmly believes in the value of studying and following the written law.

We should note that this indicates a shift from a religion based largely on temple sacrifices to one based on obedience to the written law. In this sense Psalm 119 has much in common with the book of Deuteronomy, and likely reflects a post-exilic setting, when the Pentateuch was completed.

---

*Psalm 119:1-8 is also read on Proper 26 in Year B.

Psalm 119 has many characteristics of wisdom psalms such as Psalm 1 and Psalm 19, which have similar themes. It also contains elements of personal lament, however, and these give the psalm an added sense of passion. The psalmist repeatedly professes a love for God's law, which should be read more appropriately as God's "teaching." He earnestly desires to follow God's way, and he hopes that his obedience will motivate God to save him from distress and preserve him from his enemies.

In some ways the psalm is like a long-play rap song, filled with wordplay and repetition, a paean of praise for God's teaching and a plea that God will recognize the psalmist's devotion. Commentator Leslie C. Allen waxed poetic himself in describing Psalm 119: "This elaborate acrostic is a literary festival of prayer and praise held in honor of Yahweh's self-revelation to Israel" (*Psalms 101–150*, Word Biblical Commentary, vol. 21 [Thomas Nelson, 1983], 184).

A happy claim
(vv. 1-3)

Tackling all 176 verses of Psalm 119 would be quite a chore, and with its repetitive themes, unnecessary. This week's lesson considers the first eight verses, in which the poet sets forth the subject he will then explore at great length.

Those who look to the psalm as a guide to specific behavior may be disappointed, for the poet consistently speaks of God's teaching in an abstract fashion. He doesn't cite specific laws or commandments, such as "don't steal," or "show kindness to strangers." He assumes that readers are familiar with the content of God's instructions, and focuses on his commitment to them.

Needing words that begin with *alef* to use as the first word in the eight verses of this section, the poet chose *'ashrê*, meaning "happy" or "blessed," for the first two. Many years later, Jesus would begin each of the Beatitudes (Matt. 5:3-11) with a similar word, translated into Greek as *makarios*.

"Happy are those whose way is blameless," he wrote, "who walk in the law of the LORD" (v. 1). The psalmist does not anticipate that he or anyone else can live a perfect life, but he knows that those who pattern their lives after God's teachings – who "walk in Yahweh's *torah*" – will have little cause for censure.

Success requires a full measure of commitment: "Happy are those who keep his decrees, who seek him with their whole heart, who also do no wrong, but walk in his ways" (vv. 2-3).

"Decrees," like "law," serves as one of the eight synonyms for God's teaching, and "ways" serves the same purpose. "Decrees" could be translated as "rules" or "guidelines." The word for "keep" could also mean "watch" or "observe." To be faithful is to follow the rules wholeheartedly.

The psalmist understood that life without rules is not freedom, but a path to misery. Think of a 5th grade classroom: Without some guidelines for respecting both the teacher and fellow students, chaos would reign, and no learning would take place.

Or consider traffic regulations. We may occasionally resent them, but we wouldn't want a system in which everyone drove in whatever lane they chose, at whatever speed, with no stop signs or traffic signals. Appropriate rules are essential for a pleasant and safe driving experience.

The psalmist understood that following God's way by honoring God's rules was the pathway to happiness.

A divine command
(vv. 4-6)

The next few verses set forth the psalmist's basic understanding of one's relationship with God. It begins with a belief that God makes the rules: "You have commanded your precepts (yet a third synonym for God's teaching) to be kept diligently" (v. 4). The word for "commanded" is the verbal form of the noun "commandments."

God's rules are not suggestions, but directives to those who would experience the fullness of life in harmony with God. The poet desires this above everything: "O that my ways may be steadfast in keeping your statutes!" (a fourth synonym, v. 4). "Then I shall not be put to shame, having my eyes fixed on all your commandments" (synonym number five, v. 5).

Note the idiom of "fixed eyes." I remember the first time my father allowed me to climb on our old John Deere tractor to turn over a field with a disk harrow. After explaining how to raise and lower the harrow, he got me positioned correctly on one edge of the field and told me to focus on a tree at the other end.

> **A broader view:** Regarding the illustration about plowing a straight furrow, I confess that I successfully harrowed only half the field. I concentrated so hard on keeping the front wheel aligned with the furrow that I failed to notice a guy wire supporting a telephone pole in the middle of the field. When I ran the front axle up the guy wire, I was quickly replaced, thus ending my plowing career and reminding me that it is possible to be *too* focused on one thing.

By driving straight toward the tree, I could plow a straight furrow. That furrow would then serve as a guide: by keeping a front wheel just inside it, the next furrow would also be straight, and I could successfully harrow the field and not be embarrassed by a string of crooked rows. **[A broader view]**

How could the psalmist live without shame? By "having my eyes fixed on all your commandments." He had not one tree to aim toward, but the sum of God's teaching as it was depicted in the written law.

Many of us have memorized a similar thought from v. 11 of this same psalm, probably from the KJV: "Thy word have I hid in mine heart, that I might not sin against thee."

A promise and a plea
(vv. 7-8)

The section closes with a pledge and a prayer. "I will praise you with an upright heart, when I learn your righteous ordinances," he promised, with "ordinances" being yet a sixth synonym for God's law, or teaching (v. 7).

The word is *mishpat*, often used to mean "judgment," in this case God's "righteous judgment." The poet promises to praise God even as he continues to learn more of God's way, and he pledges to put his lessons into practice: "I will observe your statutes" (v. 8a).

He is not motivated by love for the law alone, however. As he devotes himself to God, he expects God to look out for him. He pleads, "do not utterly forsake me" (v. 8b).

Was the poet in some danger or facing difficult times? He did not want to feel alone, but wanted God to remain present and active in his life.

Most of us know what it is like to feel alone in the face of hard days, longing to know the presence and care of God. We know what it is like to pray for divine comfort or rescue from testing situations.

We may also have combined our plea for help with a promise to do better. It's unlikely that we couched our prayers in the same terms as the psalmist, praising God's guidance with a barrage of synonyms for "law" and promising to obey them.

But many people have prayed along the order of "O Lord, if you will please (insert request), I promise that I will not (insert wrongdoing) again," or "I will (insert faithful behavior) from now on."

We may have sought help with family troubles, or financial trials, or in dealing with an illness. We may have promised to stop drinking or some other harmful habit, or we may have pledged a renewed commitment to church attendance or tithing.

In either case, we have tended to understand faith as a transactional affair in which we do something for God, and God does something for us. Texts such as today's reading can encourage such thinking, but is that how it should be?

If God's teaching and God's ways are good and praiseworthy, should we not seek to follow them because it is the right thing to do, and not just because we expect rewards or special treatment from God?

True wisdom acknowledges that all are better served when we follow God's ways rather than our own.

The Hardest Question
What are the synonyms used for "law" in Psalm 119?

As noted in the lesson, the psalmist developed Psalm 119 on an acrostic pattern in 22 sections, utilizing eight thematic terms to refer to God's teaching. He repeats these key words again and again, with each of the 22 sections including at least six of the eight terms, and some using all eight, or using some of the same terms more than once in a section.

But what were these terms? Are they fully synonymous, or do they have variations in meaning? The central and most frequent term is *tôrâ*, used 25 times, which is typically translated as "law," but should be understood with reference to the whole of what was believed to be God's revealed teaching as found in the first five books of the Hebrew Bible. Christians often refer to them as the "Pentateuch" (meaning "Five Books"), but Jews refer to them as the "Torah."

The books depict the various laws and commandments as having been dictated by God to Moses, though much of the material developed over time and dates to a much later period as part of the scribal tradition that appears to have been completed in Babylon during and after the exile (c. 587–538 BCE). Ezra, known as a scribe and expert in the law, reportedly returned with a later group of exiles and brought with him the completed "book of the law." A large assembly was held in Jerusalem so that he could read it to the people (in Hebrew), while certain Levites among the people translated to Aramaic so they would understand (Ezra 8). This would have taken place in the mid-fifth century. Psalm 119, with its focus on allegiance to the written law, probably dates to the same general period.

As noted, the poet used eight or more close synonyms to indicate divine directives, and it was common to combine them to indicate completeness, especially the combination "statutes and ordinances" (Lev. 26:46; Deut. 4:1, 5, 8, 14, 45; 5:1; 11:32; 12:1; 26:16; Josh. 24:25; Ezra 7:10).

"Decrees" is sometimes added. Deut. 4:45 claims to present "the decrees and the statutes and the ordinances that Moses spoke to the Israelites when they had come out of Egypt." The *sh'm'a* instructs parents to teach the law to their children, especially when they ask "What is the meaning of the decrees and the statutes and the ordinances that the LORD our God has commanded you?" (Deut. 6:20).

The word "decrees" comes from *'edût*. It appears 23 times in Psalm 119, and often has the sense of "covenant terms." Deuteronomy portrays God as entering a covenant with Israel in which the Hebrews were required to "obey the LORD your God, by diligently observing all his commandments that I am commanding you today" (Deut. 28:1), with the promise that God would bless them in return.

The term often rendered as "statutes" (*chōq*) appears 22 times in the psalm. It refers to something that has been prescribed as a task or something that is due. In the psalm, it carries the sense of a divine order to prescribe proper behavior.

"Ordinances" (from *mishpat*) also occurs 22 times in Psalm 119. It is often used in the sense of "judgments," especially divine determinations for acceptable human actions.

The word translated as "commandments" or "commands" (*mitswâ*) is found 21 times in the psalm. It is the term used in Exodus 20 with reference to the Ten Commandments, and describes a direct order.

The emphasis on the written law is evident in the use of "word" (*dābar*), always in the sense of God's word revealed in the law, which appears 24 times in the psalm. It speaks of directions presumed to have been spoken by God and written down for the people's instruction.

The term translated as "precepts" or "charges" (*piqûd*) is used 20 times in Psalm 119. It can refer to accounts of expenses and by extension, to the accountability of humans to God, what humans owe to God.

The last of the eight primary synonyms is *'imrâ*, translated "promise" or "saying." It is used 20 times in the psalm, where it refers to things God was thought to have said in directing human behavior.

These are not the only synonyms used, however. Occasionally the psalmist uses terms such as God's "paths" or "ways" to get across the same ideas. The first section, our text for today, includes six of the eight terms plus the near synonym "ways," and "statutes" appears twice.

James Luther Mays described the effect of the acrostic structure and repetitive lexicon of stock words in this way: "The resulting poem of 167 lines has an impressive literary structure that combines a sharp simplicity with constant variation. Within the control of the formal structure, the same thing is said in 167 different ways, in a progression that moves through the alphabet without ever moving from its single subject" (*Psalms*, Interpretation: A Bible Commentary for Teaching and Preaching [Westminster John Knox Press, 2011), 382]).

Third Reading
1 Corinthians 3:1-9

Growing Children

For as long as there is jealousy and quarreling among you, are you not of the flesh,
and behaving according to human inclinations? (1 Cor. 3:3)

Don't you love babies? Many adults love to smile at them and rub their sweet little heads, but have no desire to raise them. It takes an amazing level of love and commitment to care for children and help them grow from being totally helpless to becoming mature and functioning human beings. Parents who do a faithful job of that are worthy of great admiration.

Infants can bring both transcendent joy and persistent trials to life. They cry in the wee hours and require sleep-deprived parents to feed and change and comfort them. Babies soil their diapers at the most inopportune times, spill things with great frequency, and often totter on the edge of danger, leaving their caretakers emotionally ragged.

As children grow older and approach adulthood, some accept increasing responsibility for themselves, while others seem to avoid maturity at all costs. Parenting is a challenge.

Paul, the parent

Today's text is about infants of the spiritual kind. The Apostle Paul approached his work of growing churches as a parent with his children, and often used that terminology (1 Cor. 4:14-16). He knew the prodigious joy of seeing people forsake their sins and come to Christ, but he also knew the predictable frustrations of nurturing those same persons to maturity.

The letter of 1 Corinthians suggests that believers in Corinth were slow to mature, causing Paul considerable aggravation and sleepless nights as he tried to clean up some of the messes they made. His letters mention issues such as open immorality, elitism, and infighting between various factions within the church. Some church members considered themselves to be more spiritual than fellow Christians, or privy to secret knowledge that others had not attained.

Paul dealt with some of these matters in the previous chapter in an ironic, almost sarcastic manner, and then focused on factionalism as a particular issue in 3:1-9. Instead of taking sides with those who considered themselves to be more spiritual or wise than the others, Paul accused them of acting like babies.

Spiritual infants
(vv. 1-4)

Some Corinthians had complained that Paul was not introducing them to the deep mysteries of the faith, but his reply was straightforward: spiritual things can only be revealed to spiritual people, and "I could not speak to you as spiritual people, but rather as people of the flesh, as infants in Christ" (v. 1).

Thus, Paul kept the Corinthians on a steady diet of the most basic truths. Until they proved themselves mature enough to digest spiritual milk, he knew they would not be ready for more solid food (v. 2; cf. 1 Pet. 2:2, Heb. 5:12-14). Even then, Paul insisted that all they really needed to know was what he had already taught: God was at work through

> **Fleshly people:** Paul's reference to the Corinthians as being "fleshly" derives from adjectives built off the word *sarx*, which refers to the bodily aspect of human life (the English "sarcoma" describes a cancer that affects soft tissues or bones). The words are not limited in meaning to one's literal flesh, but to one's human nature as a mortal being as opposed to one who is guided by the Spirit of Christ.

Christ to bring about a new age of salvation. To be faithful was to focus on Jesus and follow his teachings.

What evidence of immaturity did Paul see? "You are still of the flesh," he said in v. 1. "For as long as there is jealousy and quarreling among you, are you not of the flesh, and behaving according to human inclinations?" (v. 3). Words such as "fleshly," or "merely human" are awkward translations for the words *sarkinos* (v. 1) and *sarkikos* (v. 3), which carry the sense of being earthly-minded rather than spiritually directed. **[Fleshly people]**

Paul charged that his readers were self-centered, "behaving according to human inclinations" (v. 3b), directed by their own interests rather than God's. They were more concerned with supremacy than service, more devoted to factionalism than to friendship (v. 4).

Paul was not implying that the Corinthians had no experience with the Spirit: there had been any number of spiritual manifestations among them, from speaking in tongues to healing and other demonstrations of power.

They wanted to have the Spirit, but had not let the Spirit possess them. God's Spirit was alive within them just as surely as human life is present in the tiniest baby, but they had given the Spirit scant room for promoting growth.

As long as human persons remain self-serving in their behavior and relationships with others, they cannot experience the spiritual growth that comes through humility and service. Division, strife, and jealousy are not the product of the Spirit's work, but of human nature – of the "flesh" (see Gal. 5:16-21). As Richard Hays summarized Paul's point in 3:1-4, "The real measure of spiritual maturity is unity and peace in the community" (*1 Corinthians*, Interpretation [John Knox Press, 1997], 49).

That is why Paul insisted that he had fed the Corinthians only with milk, and that they were still too immature for spiritual pabulum, much less anything more substantial (v. 2).

In the opening section of his letter, Paul said he had learned that some church members claimed to follow Paul, others Apollos, and others Cephas (Peter), while another group apparently claimed to follow Christ alone (1:12). Paul returned to this problem of factionalism in 3:4 to illustrate his contention that they were still thinking and acting on a human level rather than a spiritual one.

When one claimed to be of Paul's party while another pledged allegiance to Apollos, Paul wrote, "are you not merely human?"

Faithful Christian leaders are not focused on taking selfies with crowds of followers, but on selfless service to God and "the least of these" whom God loves (Matt. 25:40).

This text challenges us to think about our own lives and the relationships we see within our church. What signs do we see of spiritual maturity, or the lack of it? When we think of how our church relates to other congregations, do we cooperate in service to others, or compete for more members to serve our cause?

If Paul were to visit our homes, where would he direct the conversation? If he were to speak in our church, what might be on his preaching menu? What worldview would he be promoting?

Spiritual growth
(vv. 5-9)

Having introduced the subject in vv. 1-4, Paul spoke directly to the folly of factionalism in vv. 5-9. Why should the Corinthians align themselves with one leader or the other when all the leaders were working for the same goal (v. 5)?

When Paul spoke of himself and Apollos in v. 5, he used the neuter form of the interrogative pronoun *ti* rather than the personal form, *tis*. As such, he did not ask "Who is Paul?" and "Who is Apollos?" Instead, he inquired "*What* is Paul? *What* is Apollos?"

By speaking in this way, Paul put himself and Apollos in the category of things, of instruments used by God for a common purpose. Paul would still have regarded this as honorable and praiseworthy work, but he sought by every means to downplay the personality cults that had arisen in Corinth.

> **Metaphors:** While modern teachers of English composition might cringe at the mixed metaphors, in ch. 3 Paul moves smoothly between three figurative symbols as he describes the church as God's field (vv. 5-9a), God's building (vv. 9b-15), and God's temple (vv. 16-17).
>
> In every case, it is imperative to remember that Paul is not talking about a literal building or even the church as an institution, but the gathered community of believers in a given place.

Were Paul and Apollos guided by ego or the desire for fame, determined to build up a personal following and start rival television networks?

No, Paul insisted. They were both servants of the same God "through whom you came to believe." They were simply people who were doing what God had led them to do, proclaiming the gospel and the teachings of Jesus (v. 5).

The word we translate as "servants" in v. 5 is *diakonoi*, the same root from which we get the word "deacon." Paul uses it as a simple metaphor, however. He and Apollos were not deacons in the modern sense of the word, but servants of God seeking to do God's work.

Paul described himself and Apollos as field hands who had worked among the Corinthians at different times, but for the same purpose: "I planted, Apollos watered, but God gave the growth" (v. 6). We learn elsewhere that Paul had begun the work (Acts 18:1-8), and Apollos came after to build it up (Acts 18:24–19:1). **[Metaphors]**

Take note of the emphasis Paul gives to the work of God in calling forth believers, redeeming them, and establishing the church. Paul and Apollos were instruments through whom God worked, even as the Corinthian believers were called to serve while acknowledging that it is God who gives the growth. Our calling is no different.

It was only natural that church members would feel closer to one leader than the other, even as any of us can name our favorite pastors or teachers. Paul, the straight-talking rabbi from Tarsus, would have been popular with many people, especially those from a Jewish background. The eloquent Apollos, from the city of Alexandria, would have resonated better with others, particularly Greeks who were enamored with oratory.

It is unlikely that doctrinal issues were involved in the factionalism involving Paul and Apollos. According to

Acts 18:24-28, Apollos knew the scriptures, taught them accurately, and had been tutored by Paul's friends Priscilla and Aquilla in understanding the way of God (probably a reference to Christ's work) more accurately.

Paul wanted the Corinthians to get past their human favoritism and realize that both he and Apollos were nothing in comparison to Christ. They both played a role in planting and watering the Corinthian fields, but it is "only God who gives the growth" (v. 7). Human leaders cannot take credit for God's work of grace, nor should they claim the personal loyalty of persons saved by Christ. God's servants will receive appropriate rewards in due time (v. 8, cf. 3:3, 4:5): it is not for them to organize fan clubs to sustain their egos.

Paul pointed to himself and Apollos as examples of the kind of unity the Corinthians should be pursuing. They saw themselves as God's fellow servants, working together in God's field or cooperating to construct God's great building project of the church (v. 9).

Just as Paul and Apollos were different persons but united in ministry, so Paul called the Corinthians to a new solidarity in faith. Unity in the congregation would have to come from surrender to the Spirit of God and devotion to following Jesus.

Only a fortunate few among today's Christians have escaped some aspect of church conflict, from temperamental tiffs over minor issues to heated disagreements that lead to division and an exodus of church members, even a church or denominational split.

While we sometimes make wry jokes about churches "multiplying by division," Christ is not honored by infighting among those who are called to be peacemakers. Working for unity among believers is serious business, and it is the work of the spiritually mature. It is the way of Jesus, the way those who follow a "Jesus worldview" should adopt.

What kind of work are we doing?

The Hardest Question
Were Paul and Apollos competitors?

As Paul condemns the factionalism present in the Corinthian church, he speaks of those who follow him and those who follow Apollos as examples – which likely suggests that those were the two largest factions fracturing the fellowship.

Although Paul appears to insist that neither he nor Apollos should receive any glory, since both were merely servants of God, he does subtly remind the Corinthians that he preceded Apollos in planting the church, while Apollos came along later to water it, though both would acknowledge that God gave the growth.

By reminding them that he was there first, Paul seems to assume a place of superiority above Apollos, at least regarding leadership or influence over the church. In the next few verses, Paul goes on to insist that *he*, "like a skilled master builder," laid the foundation of the Corinthian church, and that others were building upon it (3:10). Others could build well, or poorly, he pointed out, and would be judged accordingly.

In the conclusion to the major section of the letter (3:5–4:21) in which this discussion occurs, Paul insisted that the Corinthians should regard him as their spiritual father and look to him for guidance: "I am not writing this to make you ashamed, but to admonish you as my beloved children. For though you might have ten thousand guardians in Christ, you do not have many fathers. Indeed, in Christ Jesus I became your father through the gospel. I appeal to you, then, be imitators of me" (1 Cor. 4:14-16).

This directive suggests that Paul wanted the Corinthians to think of him as father, and Apollos or other leaders as guardians. We have no way of knowing what Apollos thought of all this, as we have no letters from Apollos to the church. Commentators are divided in their view of whether there was tension between Paul and Apollos.

It is clear from Paul's comments that there were factions in the church, and that some favored the eloquent Apollos while others favored plain-spoken Paul. The outward show of favoritism was not a good thing, and so Paul played it down by insisting there was no competition between the two traveling evangelists – but he never backed down from insisting that he had primary responsibility for the church, and that the Corinthians should look to him for leadership.

Sixth Sunday after Epiphany / Season after Pentecost: Proper 1

Fourth Reading
Matthew 5:21-37

Then, and Now

So when you are offering your gift at the altar, if you remember that your brother or sister has something against you, leave your gift there before the altar and go; first be reconciled to your brother or sister, and then come and offer your gift. (Matt. 5:23-24)

What do you do when touchy subjects come up in conversation? Some people speak boldly and don't seem to care if they cause offense. Others prefer to leave delicate issues alone. While Jesus was known for his compassion and care, Matthew's gospel suggests that he sometimes took on topics that he knew might cause consternation, but he did so to speak to the high ideals of the kingdom.

The collection of teachings Matthew has set into Jesus' famed "Sermon on the Mount" (Matthew 5–7) begins with the encouraging "Beatitudes" (5:1-12) before moving to a charge for believers to be salt and light in the world (5:13-16). Jesus then prepared to launch into a series of challenges to current understandings of the law by insisting that his teaching did not violate or abolish the law, but established its true intent (5:17-20). As Matthew relates it, Jesus then addressed several sensitive subjects: anger (5:21-26), lust (5:27-30), divorce (5:31-32), oaths (5:33-37), revenge (5:38-42), and love (5:43-48). **[A matter of the heart]**

Today we consider what Jesus had to say about anger, lust, divorce, and oaths.

Buckle your seatbelts.

Murder and anger
(vv. 21-26)

Everyone understood that murder was against the law (v. 21, Exod. 20:3), but Jesus explained that it was not enough to simply refrain from killing people. Holding

> **A matter of the heart:** Ben Witherington III introduces Jesus' antithetical teachings about the law in this way: "One of the things that characterizes this teaching is that Jesus is literally trying to get to the heart of the matter. The root of the problem lies in the human heart, which prompts various kinds of misbehavior. Thus he will deal not only with actions like oaths or adultery and divorcing, but with things like anger, lust, revenge, and love. Jesus also intends to return to first principles, as we shall see" (*Matthew*, Smyth & Helwys Bible Commentary [Smyth & Helwys, 2006], 229).

on to anger or rage toward others was also sinful, Jesus said. There is a righteous kind of anger that Jesus would endorse, but this kind of interpersonal anger is not it. Jesus was not suggesting that believers should never get angry: he displayed anger in his own life (Mark 1:41, 3:45; Matt. 21:12-17), mainly when he saw others being mistreated or oppressed. What he had in mind is selfish and sinful anger that leads to harmful actions. Bearing grudges against others may not end in murder, but it results in harmful, poisonous feelings. If we don't control our anger, it will control us.

Words were thought to have power in the ancient world, and the act of name-calling was a more serious matter than today. There is nothing magic about using the word "fool" that will make one liable to judgment: the Aramaic word *raqa'* meant something akin to "idiot," in a particularly derogatory sense. Using it was wrong (v. 22), just as objectifying others with any derogatory term is wrong.

> **The hell of fire:** The New Testament term translated "hell" is "Gehenna," a Greek version of the Aramaic *gē hinnâm*, a valley southwest of Jerusalem where residents dumped all manner of garbage and refuse, including their chamber pots. In ancient times, a fire pit used for human sacrifice to the god Molech was said to be located there (2 Kgs. 23:10, Jer. 7:31). With its constant stench of rotting and wormy garbage, along with a smoking pile of rubbish and the unsavory memory of people being burned there, the site came to symbolize a horrid place of divine punishment, a concept unknown in the Old Testament and intended as an unsavory metaphor for judgment, not a literal description of it.

Note that Jesus was speaking mainly of behavior within the community, toward Christian brothers and sisters. Not being able to see beyond our own anger can escalate into insults and degrading words, and words are weapons. They can kill both reputations and relationships. If believers cannot act with love toward each other, how can they be a witness to the world?

In first-century Judaism, character defamation could make one subject to discipline from the local council or even the Great Sanhedrin in Jerusalem. Ultimately, Jesus said, hateful attitudes could lead to "the hell of fire." In this he was using hyperbole as a rhetorical device, not condemning angry people to everlasting torment. [**The hell of fire**]

Jesus understood that those who bear hatred or unresolved grievances toward others cannot truly worship God in good conscience. As Jesus would teach in "the Lord's prayer," we cannot expect God to forgive us if we do not forgive others. Coming to church and bringing our tithes is important, but resolving grudges or differences with others is even more important.

Jesus' teaching that starts with murder and extends to unhealthy expressions of anger that interfere with worship may reflect the story of Cain (Genesis 4), who grew angry at his brother Abel over an issue related to offerings, and then killed him.

Note that Jesus extends this responsibility to those who share reciprocal anger or are objects of others' wrath: we should take the initiative to be reconciled. In vv. 25-26, Jesus moves to an example in which the accuser appears to have some standing to take the believer to court. This suggests a relationship that goes beyond the church community. Again, Jesus challenges those who have been accused by others to initiate reconciliation. Otherwise, even the innocent might end up being jailed until they paid whatever the judge declared. As in other cases, Jesus calls upon believers to go above and beyond in reaching out to others.

Adultery and lust
(vv. 27-32)

Moving from murder to adultery, Jesus again showed that the core problem is one of the heart and mind, not just of actions. The prohibition of adultery was well known (Exod. 20:4, Deut. 5:17), and it could bring severe penalties for perpetrators, including death. Jesus insisted that believers are accountable for lustful thoughts as well as adulterous behavior (vv. 27-28).

For ancient Hebrews, adultery referred primarily to a man having sex with another man's wife, rather than being a blanket term for extramarital sex. The sin, in Judaism, was against the husband or father of the woman, as it damaged someone who, though not exactly his property, was under his control and of considerable economic value. [**Responsibility**]

The directives to gouge out one's right eye or chop off one's right hand rather than face eternal destruction are intended as hyperbole (vv. 29-30). Though such punishments were known in Jewish law, Jesus knew that lust is conceived in the heart and mind: one-handed or one-eyed people are at no handicap when it comes to lechery. The point is that we should take whatever actions are necessary to get lascivious thoughts under control.

Some commentators consider the saying on divorce in vv. 31-32 as a separate antithesis, while others interpret it as a natural extension of the teaching on adultery (a similar

> **Responsibility:** Early Jewish literature often portrayed women as temptresses, but Ben Witherington III has pointed out that the phrase "everyone who looks at a woman with lust has already committed adultery with her in his heart" could also be translated as "anyone who so looks on a woman that she becomes desirous has already led her astray into adultery in his heart" (*Matthew*, Smyth & Helwys Commentary [Smyth & Helwys, 2006], 132). In either case, Jesus put greater moral responsibility on the males, who generally had the upper hand in power relationships.

teaching is found in Matt. 19:3-9). In Jesus' day, Jewish women could leave their husbands or pressure them for a divorce, but only husbands had the legal standing to authorize a "bill of divorcement." This is referenced in Deut. 24:1, which allows a husband to divorce his wife if "she does not please him because he finds something objectionable about her." The rabbis interpreted this differently: the school of Shammai argued that the only sufficiently objectionable quality was sexual sin on the part of the wife. Hillel and his followers, in contrast, argued that a man could count it as "something objectionable" if his wife burned the dinner or failed to be as attractive as some other woman.

As Matthew relates it, Jesus taught that God intended for marriage to be permanent and that divorce should be allowed only "on the ground of unchastity." This translates the word *porneia*, which described a broader field of sexual misbehavior than the typical word for adultery. While Matthew has Jesus allow for an exception in the case of a partner's unchastity, both here and in 19:9, a similar teaching in Mark does not include it (Mark 10:2-11).

From the perspective of Jesus' teaching, men should not divorce their wives for selfish reasons, thus violating the law and putting their wives – and any future husbands – in the position of becoming adulterers in the eyes of the law.

Again, the problem is in the heart. For either the husband or the wife, thinking so highly of one's selfish desires that he or she would dismiss the person who should be closest to them in favor of another is a sinful and harmful act that falls far short of God's ideal.

Oaths
(vv. 33-37)

Jesus next turned to the subject of oaths and keeping one's word. There was no Old Testament command that one should make oaths, though they were allowed, and the breaking of oaths was roundly condemned (Exod. 20:7, Lev. 19:12, Zech. 8:17). Unfortunately, many translations and commentaries fail to distinguish between oaths and vows, using the terms interchangeably when they were in fact two different things.

In the Old Testament world, continuing into the first century, vows were conditional promises made directly to God: one would ask God for a particular benison, and promise to give God something in return if the prayer was

---

Oaths in the ancient world: Oaths functioned orally to reinforce the veracity of a promise by invoking punishment from a higher power if one's word proved false. Oaths were typically located in informal but intense settings of social interaction, as when Abraham swore he would not take anything from Sodom's king because "I have raised my hand to Yahweh, to the Most High, creator of heaven and earth" (Gen 14:23); or when Joseph swore (by Pharaoh) that his brothers could not return without Benjamin (Gen 42:15).

Despite the self-imprecations, oath-takers could also be oath-breakers, a theme that helped drive written narratives, especially in conflict situations that reflect negatively on the oath-taker. Saul (1 Sam. 14:44), David (1 Sam. 25:22), Jezebel (1 Kgs. 19:2), Ben-hadad (1 Kgs. 20:10), and Jehoram (2 Kgs. 6:31) all made oaths that they failed to keep.

More positively, oaths could be used to pledge loyalty. Ruth swore that she would never leave her mother-in-law Naomi (Ruth 1:17), even as Jonathan and David swore fealty to each other (1 Sam. 20:13-17). (From my article on "Oaths" in *The Dictionary of the Bible and Ancient Media* [T&T Clark, 2016].)

---

answered. Hannah, for example, asked God for a son, and promised to return the boy to God if the prayer was granted (1 Samuel 1).

An oath, on the other hand, consisted of a promise to do something, accompanied by a self-imprecation that invited God to bring punishment if the person did not fulfill the promise. King Jehoram, for example, pledged to assassinate Elisha, saying "So may God do to me, and more, if the head of Elisha son of Shaphat stays on his shoulders today" (2 Kgs 6:31, NRSV). In most cases, the full form was abbreviated, and over time people came to swear, not only by God, but by Jerusalem, by the temple, the gold in the temple, the temple's altar, or the gift on the altar. [**Oaths in the ancient world**]

This led to a practice of equivocating, as the rabbis distinguished between which oaths were binding, and which were not. Jesus took such interpretations to task, insisting that believers should not break any oaths, but live up to their word (v. 33). To those who sought to make impressive but non-binding oaths, Jesus reminded them that anything they swore by – whether the earth, Jerusalem, or even one's head – belonged to God, so that every oath appealed to God and was therefore binding (vv. 34-36).

It's better yet, Jesus said, to avoid swearing at all. Believers should live with such integrity that they need no oaths to reinforce the truthfulness of their word or the faithfulness of their promise. "Let your word be 'Yes, yes' or 'No, no,'" Jesus said. This did not suggest a new form of swearing by repeating the word "yes" or "no," but was simply a method of emphasis indicating the sincerity of one's word. Feeling the need to swear by our mother's grave or anything else automatically implies that we are untrustworthy and subject to the temptation to break our promise.

Unlike some religious sects, we should not take this as a programmatic ban on submitting to an oath when testifying in court or being "sworn in" to public office. Jesus' challenge is that we should be people of our word who have no need to initiate an oath: his concern was not to create a new law prohibiting believers from participating in legal requirements of society.

Whether the subject is spiteful anger, endangering lust, or breaking one's word, Jesus' teaching goes deeper than the law. The heart of the matter is a matter of the heart – and a willingness to follow the one who rules our heart.

The Hardest Question
Is there grace for divorce?

Jesus' teaching in vv. 31-32 appears unduly hard if it is interpreted to rule out the possibility of divorce for people who find themselves in abusive, unhealthy, or even extremely unhappy marriages.

Should we interpret the text in such a legalistic sense? One can argue that emotional or physical abuse within a marriage can be just as damaging as sexual infidelity. Coldness and an apparently irredeemable lack of love could be seen in the same way. Some people would contend that an unloving and disconnected spouse has become metaphorically "dead" to his or her partner.

Jesus' intent was to uphold the ideal sanctity of marriage as a lifetime commitment, not to condemn poorly matched or mistreated persons to a lifetime of misery because they made a poor decision to marry in the first place.

Reading Jesus' teaching as a determinative rule about marriage and divorce would be tantamount to setting up a new series of laws, when Jesus' clear desire was for believers to base their living on an ethic of love rather than law. Divorce is always painful. Bad choices may fall into the category of sin and cause harm to self and others. But they are not unforgiveable sins, and do not preclude the possibility of honoring God in the context of another marriage, and hopefully making better choices.

Seventh Sunday after Epiphany / Season after Pentecost: Proper 2

First Reading
Leviticus 19:1-18 (RCL 19:1-2, 9-18)*

Being Holy

You shall not take vengeance or bear a grudge against any of your people, but you shall love your neighbor as yourself: I am the LORD. (Lev. 19:18)

How often do you think about holiness? It comes up at church when we sing "Holy, Holy, Holy," or "Take Time To Be Holy," or "We Are Standing on Holy Ground." It may show up in a sermon from time to time, or in one's daily Bible reading – but I suspect few of us begin each day with the thought "I'm going to be holy today."

That may be in part because many people assign a negative connotation to the idea of people seeking to be holy, possibly because we've known someone who carried around a "holier than thou" attitude. [**Holy Joe**]

For those who read the book of Leviticus, the theme of holiness is pervasive: an entire block of the text, Leviticus 17–26, is commonly known as "The Holiness Code." Today's text is drawn from that section. Readings from the book of Leviticus occur only twice in the three-year Revised Common Lectionary cycle, and it is basically the same text, used twice. Given the paucity of readings from this important book of the Old Testament, the least we can do is include all of vv. 1-18 in our study. [**Leviticus**]

Holy being
(vv. 1-4)

The Holiness Code is marked by a repeated refrain: "You shall be holy, for I am holy," as in Lev. 19:2. The Hebrew concept of holiness was not just about purity, piety, or the

> **Holy Joe:** In my den is a rocking chair with a well-crafted wooden frame, deep burgundy upholstery, and extra wide arms. It was custom made more than 100 years ago for Josiah Bailey, the son of a Baptist pastor who served both as editor of the North Carolina Baptist *Biblical Recorder* and as president of the state's "Anti-Saloon League" before leaving both in 1907 to enter a career in law and politics. Bailey, whose political views mixed both progressive and conservative ideas, was elected as a United States senator representing North Carolina in 1931, serving until his death in 1946.
>
> Bailey's personal piety stood out so strongly in Washington that he reportedly acquired the nickname "Holy Joe." A traditional claim that Josiah was the original "Holy Joe" may be apocryphal, but I like to believe it is true.

absence of sin: to be holy was to be set apart as a distinct people. Thus, rules about circumcision, letting sideburns grow, eating scaly fish but not catfish, or not weaving two kinds of thread together may have no practical purpose other than as marks of religious or ethnic identity: "This is how we do it."

In that sense, the Holiness Code spells out what "being holy" meant for the Hebrews in daily life – how it set them apart from the Canaanites, Philistines, Romans, or whoever else was living around them.

The code includes rules about what foods are kosher, when nakedness is allowed, how sacrifices should be made,

Leviticus: From a geographical standpoint, the entire book of Leviticus, along with Exodus 19–40 and Numbers 1:1–10:10, is set at Sinai. This long section portrays the Israelites as remaining at the mountain for an extended time while receiving several sets of additional laws and ritual requirements following the Ten Commandments, constructing the Tabernacle and its accoutrements (including the Ark of the Covenant), ordaining the priests and instituting worship according to the rules given, and so forth.

Though it has a narrative framework, most of Leviticus consists of legal materials. Here's a general outline:

Instructions for Sacrifice (chs. 1–7)
Burnt offerings (1:1-17)
Cereal offerings (2:1-16)
Sin offerings (3:1–6:30)
Guilt offerings (7:1-27)
"Peace" (*shelamim*) offerings (7:28-38)
This section bears the marks of an extended insertion into the narrative.

The Beginnings of Worship in Israel (chs. 8–10)
The consecration of Aaron as high priest reportedly sets in motion a new cultic system based on the rules for worship previously given. This appears to take up the narrative from Exod. 29:35.

Regulations on Cultic Purity (chs. 11–15)
Laws about individual purity, cleanliness/uncleanliness
Laws about identifying clean food and clean water (ch. 11)
Rules for women regarding childbirth and bleeding (ch. 12)
Rules about skin diseases (chs. 13–14)
Rules for men regarding "discharges" and "emissions" (15:1-18)
More rules for women regarding menstruation (15:19-33)

The Day of Atonement (ch.16)
This is likely a late insertion: it is rarely mentioned elsewhere.
Rules for annual sacrifices and a "scapegoat" ceremony

The Holiness Code (chs. 17–26)
This is thought to be the oldest part of the book, designed to spell out what "being holy" means in practical terms.

Dedicatory Gifts (ch. 27)
The closing chapter adds equivalent values for people or things promised to God through conditional vows, as well as monetary substitutions for agricultural tithes.

and how people should relate to one another. Further rules govern the breeding of animals (no hybrids allowed), avoiding witchcraft, respecting elders, sexual partners permitted or forbidden, qualifications for priests, rules for the observance of religious festivals including the Sabbath, and further directives about debts, slavery, and the Jubilee year. The Holiness Code closes with a section (26:3-46) that sounds as if it came straight from Deuteronomy, promising blessings on those who obey and curses upon those who do not.

Chapter 19 begins with rules that recall several of the Ten Commandments, instructing the Hebrews to honor their parents, keep the Sabbath, and eschew the making of idolatrous images (vv. 2-4). They are to do this because Yahweh said so: "I am the LORD your God" or "I am the LORD" is repeated in vv. 3, 4, 10, 12, 14, 16, and 18, reinforcing the belief that these behaviors identified Israel as God's special people, called to be holy.

Leviticus 19, though part of the larger Holiness Code (Leviticus 17–26), bears marks of having existed earlier as a standalone collection of separate sayings. Though the larger code began with "The LORD said to Moses …," ch. 19 begins with another introduction: "The LORD spoke to Moses, saying …"

The text is a collection of individual commands, most of which are injunctions written as second-person directives, though vv. 20-22 are written in the third person. It is not obvious in most modern translations, but some of the sayings are written in the plural (vv. 11-12, 27-28, 30, 31, 35-36), while others address individuals (vv. 9-10, 15-16, 17-18, 29, 32). In modern English, "you" can be singular or plural. In the KJV, "you" indicated singular, and "ye" was used for plural.

Chapter 19 follows a general progression of thought, with vv. 1-8 mainly concerned with obligations to God, vv. 9-18 addressing responsibilities to others, and vv. 19-36 focusing on forbidden practices that were apparently common among Israel's Canaanite neighbors.

Holy worship
(vv. 5-8)

Although the first seven chapters of Leviticus set out details for various sacrifices, vv. 5-8 repeat previous instructions from 7:16-18 insisting that meat offered as a sacrifice must be eaten within two days. [**An altar, not a grill**]

An altar, not a grill: Few animal sacrifices were burned whole on the altar, and those were not eaten by humans, but "sent up in smoke" to God in a primitive attempt to offer something tangible to the deity.

In Israel's life, most animal sacrifices were ritually slaughtered with the blood being poured out before God or sprinkled on the altar, for it was believed the life was in the blood and therefore belonged to God. After the animal was skinned and butchered, only the visceral fat and the fat tail of the sheep went into the sacrificial fire. The rest of the animal was divided between the priest and the worshiper, to be cooked elsewhere, with strict provisions that it be eaten on that day or the next: anything left until the third day was not to be eaten.

Regulations for cooking varied at different times in Israel's history. At Shiloh (1 Samuel 1) the meat was to be boiled, but at other times it was roasted over an open fire.

The sacrificial rules of Leviticus describe a time before worship had become centralized at the temple in Jerusalem, and the annual festivals became times of feasting. During earlier periods, sacrifices could be made at other sanctuaries or altar sites, but the book of Deuteronomy – probably finalized during the time of Josiah – called for them to be offered in Jerusalem only.

Such a rule makes perfect sense, for without refrigeration, even cooked meat is subject to spoilage by the third day. For the Hebrews, however, the issue was not that the food had "gone bad," but that it was considered "an abomination."

Rules about animal sacrifice are of little concern to Christians, who believe that Christ's sacrifice is all sufficient, and no further sacrifices are necessary. Most Jews also believe the age of sacrifice is past. Only the most orthodox show any interest in returning to a sacrificial system, but there is no longer a temple in Jerusalem where sacrifices could be legitimately offered. This is one of the reasons other distinctive Jewish practices, such as kosher eating and highly ritualized Sabbath keeping, came to be more prevalent.

Holy behavior
(vv. 9-18)

Beginning with v. 9, the regulations shift from the sacramental to the personal, offering guidelines for how humans in community can thrive by practicing social justice. The first requirement may surprise us, for the rules do not begin with family members or neighbors, but with poor strangers. When harvest time came, the Hebrews were to intentionally leave some of their grain in the field and grapes in the vineyard, allowing "the poor and the alien" free access to come and glean from what was left (vv. 9-10).

Few of us depend on grain fields or grape vines for sustenance – but "the poor and the alien" are still among us. What might the principle behind this commandment suggest about our responsibility to the poor and homeless people we often seek to avoid, or to the immigrants who find a wall instead of a welcome? What might it say about industry leaders who seek to accumulate every possible penny of profit with little concern for those who do the actual work?

The text returns to themes from the Ten Commandments in v. 11, which insists that God's holy people are not to steal from others or to deceive others by swearing falsely or lying to each other. While speaking of oaths, the text enjoins the Hebrews to remember that oaths sworn in God's name are sacred, so God's name should not be used in vain (v. 12).

In the ancient Near East, persons wanting to reinforce promises with an oath commonly swore in the name of their patron god. The Hebrews followed the same practice, using a typical formula that began "May God do so and so to me if I do not do …" One should do that only with the greatest respect, not to hide deceit behind a religious façade.

The following verses address other aspects of life together. "You shall not defraud your neighbor" (v. 13) includes a rather weak translation of a word that commonly means "to oppress" someone, treating them badly or taking advantage of them. The act is paired with "you shall not steal," using a more forceful verb for theft or robbery than in v. 11. **[Stealing and robbing]**

Refusing to pay a laborer at the end of the day was considered as offensive as outright theft, for it oppressed and shamed those who lived hand-to-mouth as poor day laborers and needed to be paid every evening so they could buy food for that day (v. 13b).

A concern for the powerless continues in v. 14, which demands that the Hebrews show respect to deaf or blind people, whether by shortchanging persons who can't see or saying cruel things to those who can't hear. We demonstrate respect for God in the way we treat others.

> **Stealing and robbing:** Careful readers will note that both v. 11 and v. 13 contain the injunction "you shall not steal." Though translated the same way in the NRSV (unfortunately), they reflect different verbs. The word in v. 11 comes from *gānav*, which suggests a secret theft of something when the owner is away. The word in v. 13 is derived from *gazal*, which was used to describe robberies in which one person forcefully took something away from another, either through violence or through some other wrongful exercise of power.
>
> The difference calls to mind a line from The Beatles' 1969 *Abbey Road* album. The song "She Came in Through the Bathroom Window" includes the comment "She could steal, but she could not rob."

The heart of this section is a concern for justice, and v. 15 exemplifies that with a call for right judgment that is not partial to the poor or the wealthy. Likewise, holy people do not slander others, put them down, or profit from their misfortune (v. 16).

The clause translated as "you shall not profit by the blood of your neighbor" uses common words but in an uncommon way, rendering its meaning uncertain. A literal translation would be "you must not stand on the blood of your neighbor," which must have been an idiomatic expression. NRSV takes it to mean "profiting by the blood of your neighbor," but it may also suggest potential violence toward one's neighbor, as in v. 13. Thus, NIV11 has "Do not do anything that endangers your neighbor's life."

The approach taken by NET is appealing: assuming that "standing on the blood" of one's neighbor might imply standing by while a neighbor is in danger of poverty or harm, the NET has "You must not stand idly by when your neighbor's life is at stake."

Justice was a special concern of prophets such as Isaiah, who saw wealthy Hebrews finagle and scheme to get their neighbors indebted to them, and then foreclose on their property to expand their own estates. Addressing those who were called to do justice but who oppressed their neighbors instead, Isaiah pronounced woes on those "who join house to house, who add field to field, until there is room for no one but you" (Isa. 5:8).

Do these commands have something to say to an increasingly stratified society in which the rich get richer and the poor get poorer, or to government leaders who want to further increase the wealth disparity by cutting taxes for the wealthy while reducing needed services for those who face old age, disabilities, illness, or poverty?

Verse 17 is a direct challenge to those who exhibit animosity toward certain races or groups as well as for those who deny their disregard but act with opprobrium toward disfavored people: "You shall not hate in your heart anyone of your kin" (NRSV), or "You shall not hate your brother in your heart" (NET). The reference to kinship does not limit the command to blood relatives. All Hebrews considered themselves to be related. Sharing a common humanity, we all owe respect and care to one another. There is no place for hatred among God's people.

Caring for our neighbors includes holding them accountable for their own role in the community. Those who fail to reprove their neighbors when needed are also guilty of falling short in their responsibilities (v. 17b).

The opposite of hatred or uncaring attitudes is love, and our text concludes with the familiar challenge to "love your neighbor as yourself" (v. 18b). Though we often cite this verse, and remember that Jesus endorsed the call to love others as second only to loving God, many are unaware that the challenge is the second part of a verse that begins "Do not take vengeance or bear a grudge against any of your people" (v. 18a). One cannot hold vindictive feelings or bear a grudge against someone and truly love them at the same time. The word "forgive" is not used, but that is what the verse is about. To love someone in the present, we must first be willing to forgive them of wrongs from the past.

In this context, the word "love" does not suggest the presence of sentimental feelings, but a genuine and loyal commitment to the well-being of others, whether they belong to our family, live in our community, or have come from a far country. This is what sets God's people apart – what makes them "holy."

Perhaps we should think about holiness more often.

The Hardest Question
What is the purpose of Leviticus?

Most modern scholars believe the Pentateuch was composed by several different writers and editors, despite a tradition that refers to them as "the Books of Moses." Critical scholars regard the claim of Mosaic authorship as an attempt by later priestly writers to insert customs that developed over a long period of time into a single protracted law-giving event attributed to Moses, which would make the laws seem more foundational and authoritative.

Many of the rules clearly relate to settled agrarian or urban life, not to the nomadic existence the Israelites would have experienced during their time at Sinai, where the material is set. And, while the book may contain earlier material, it appears to reflect the ritual practices of the second temple period (post 515 BCE). Thus, the final edition of this work should probably be dated to 500 BCE or later.

The final form of the legal sections in the Torah appears to reflect a response to the destruction of the northern kingdom (Israel) in 721 BCE, the southern kingdom (Judah) in 586 BCE, the exile that followed, and the desire for ethnic distinctiveness following the exile. The ritual texts – stressing ways in which the Hebrews were to be different from their neighbors – became more and more dominant following the exile, when the Persians defeated the Babylonians and allowed the Hebrews to return to re-establish their temple and cultic system in Jerusalem.

The priestly leaders of postexilic Israel appear to have believed that the nation's fall was due to a failure to faithfully support the temple and observe cultic rituals, some of which had likely developed over time. As constructed, the book of Leviticus seems designed to inspire future faithfulness by doing several things, including these:

- Preserving foundational laws, in danger of being forgotten, but attributing them all to Moses at Mount Sinai.
- Explaining the various defeats Israel and Judah had suffered as punishment for failing to keep the ritual laws.
- Encouraging present and future adherence to laws of holiness (set-apartness) that would cultivate a sense of ethnic and religious identity among the Hebrews.
- Redefining some sacrifices as a means of atonement.

By characterizing these very specific rules as laws handed down by Moses, the priestly writers hoped they would be regarded as more authoritative and therefore more likely to be observed. As time went by, rabbinic Judaism developed more and more specific rules designed to "build a hedge about the law" by instituting so many minor regulations that those who tried to keep them would not come close to breaking the more serious commandments.

While modern Christians may find this approach tedious and ill-founded, the growing stress on preserving the Hebrews' ethnic identity through practices such as Sabbath observance and kosher eating played a major role in the Jews' ability to persevere through centuries of persecution and multiple attempts to exterminate them as a people.

Second Reading
Psalm 119:33-40*

Teach Me, Lord

Give me understanding, that I may keep your law and observe it with my whole heart. (Ps. 119:33)

I once knew a minister who was famed for his long prayers. L-o-n-g prayers … prayers that could start in the a's and b's but leave me cutting z's. At first, I cringed when he got up to pray, but after a while I welcomed the naps.

That says nothing good about my personal spirituality, but it does suggest something about the wisdom of stretching public prayer to the limit.

The Old Testament's longest prayer is found in Psalm 119, a full 176 verses that would literally go from a to z except the Hebrew alphabet ends in a different letter, so it goes from *alef* to *tav*.

The psalm contains some elements of lament, but it's mainly a wisdom psalm, designed to display an absolute love for God's *torah* – not so much God's law, as often translated, but the sum of God's teaching.

The psalm is long, repetitive, and filled with wordplay, all devoted to the veneration of God's teaching and a plea that divine instruction might be embedded in the psalmist's heart.

The psalmist built his prolonged prayer on the framework of the Hebrew "*alefbet*," which contains 22 letters, beginning with *alef* and *bet*. The psalmist composed 22 stanzas to correspond to the 22 letters, with each stanza consisting of eight verses. Adding to the psalm's over-the-top complexity, all eight verses in each stanza begin with the same letter. That is, the first eight verses each begin with

---

Law language: The psalmist populated Psalm 119 with eight thematic terms describing God's teaching, repeating them again and again: most of them appear in each of the 22 sections. The eight terms are generally translated as:

1. "law" (*tôrâ*, used 25 times)
2. "decrees/covenant terms" (*'edût*, 23 times)
3. "statutes/laws" (*chōq*, 22 times)
4. "commandments/commands" (*mitswâ* 21 times)
5. "ordinances" (*mishpat*, 22 times)
6. "word" (*dābar*, 24 times)
7. "precepts/charges" (*piqûd*, 20 times)
8. "promise/saying" (*'imrah*, 20 times)

Occasionally the psalmist uses terms such as God's "paths" or "ways" to get across the same ideas.

James Luther Mays described the effect of the acrostic structure and repetitive lexicon of stock words in this way: "So he used the alphabet to signal completeness and the whole vocabulary to represent comprehensiveness…. Within the control of the formal structure, the same thing is said in 167 different ways, in a progression that moves through the alphabet without ever moving from its single subject" (*Psalms*, Interpretation: A Bible Commentary for Teaching and Preaching [Westminster John Knox Press, 2011], 381-382).

---

alef, the next eight with *bet*, the next eight with *gimel*, and so on to the final eight verses, each of which begin with *tav*.

The psalmist furthermore interweaves eight thematic allusions to God's commandments or teachings into the

---

psalm so that all of the 22 sections include at least six of the eight terms, along with a few others. [**Law language**]

This week's reading, the fifth of the 22 stanzas (vv. 33-40), provides an excellent summary of the psalmist's concern.

The eight verses of this section begin with the letter *hē* (pronounced "hay"). This made alliteration easy, because the causative (*hifil*) stem of the Hebrew verb system adds the letter *hē* to the beginning of the word. Verses 33-39 all begin with verbs in that form, and v. 40 begins with the interjection *hinēh*, which means "look," "behold," or "see."

A whole heart
(vv. 33-35)

The verbs that begin vv. 33-35 also have first-person pronoun suffixes attached: "teach me," "give me," "lead me." This gives the verses a very personal appeal: the psalmist recognizes his lack and asks God to guide him in a closer walk.

The poet wants to follow God's way, but he knows that staying on the path is not easy. "Teach me, O LORD, the way of your statutes, and I will observe it to the end" (v. 33). He appeals to Yahweh as the ultimate guide, and pledges to remain faithfully on the road of obedience.

Memorizing precepts and understanding them are two different things, so the psalmist asks to go deeper. He doesn't want to know just the content of the divine *tôrâ*; he wants to truly grasp its meaning and make it a part of his life: "Give me understanding, that I may keep your law and observe it with my whole heart" (v. 34).

For the Hebrews, the heart was the seat of one's thoughts and decision-making. To observe the law with one's whole heart was to do so with all of one's being. No doubt the psalmist was familiar with the command of Deut. 6:4 to "love the LORD your God with all your heart, and with all your soul, and with all your might."

Verse 35 appeals again for divine assistance in remaining true: "Lead me in the path of your commandments, for I delight in it." Note the psalmist's thematic words "statutes," "law," and "commandments." He does not define the terms or draw any fine distinctions between them. His concern is that God's teachings, in whatever form, help him to walk in the way that pleases God, "for I delight in it."

The skilled sage recognized that God's teachings are far more than rules people could recite and think they have arrived. Rather, life with God is a journey in which we are to be constantly engaged with learning about and living out God's way.

Do the psalmist's words resonate with us? How often do we give even the least thought to seeking God's way as we go through the day? Consider how it would profit our spiritual lives if we began each morning with a prayer that God would teach us, touch our hearts, and guide us through the hours. These verses would be a good place to begin.

A divided heart
(vv. 36-37)

The psalmist's desire to live faithfully was genuine, but he recognized his human weakness and the allure of going off track. Thus, he prayed that when tempted to stray, God would direct him back to the right way.

Would any of us deny that we live in a materialistic, self-driven culture – and that it affects us? Our natural tendency is to be more concerned with financial prosperity than with spiritual growth. Perhaps we need to pray with the psalmist "Turn my heart to your decrees, and not to selfish gain. Turn my eyes from looking at vanities; give me life in your ways" (vv. 36-37).

Notice the difference: the psalmist asked God to turn his heart *toward* a life in keeping with God's teaching, and to turn his eyes *away from* "selfish gain" and "vanities." The word translated as "vanities" refers to things that are worthless or empty. We can't model divine lovingkindness if our lives are ruled by selfishness.

In our quest for success, do we pursue things that are truly worthwhile, or things that have little value in the ultimate scheme of things? What the psalmist wanted was not the comforts of life, but life in its deepest meaning: "give me life in your ways."

What are some ways in which a life focused on God-inspired justice and kindness might be different from the self-directed and materialistic life patterned after our culture?

A devoted life
(vv. 38-40)

In the final section, the poet pleads that God will be true: "Confirm to your servant your promise, which is for those who fear you" (v. 38). Hebrew has no word that specifically means "promise." The assumption was that one's words constituted a promise. Often, however, the term *'imrâ*, which can mean "word" or "saying," carried the sense of "promise," especially if the words came from God.

But what promise did the psalmist have in mind? The writer was clearly familiar with the book of Deuteronomy, which taught that God and Israel lived in a covenantal relationship. As long as the people were faithful, God promised blessings, but if they turned after other gods (including self), God would punish them. Deuteronomy 28 is a prime example of the teaching: the first 14 verses promise prosperity to those who obey the commandments, while vv. 15-58 take three times the space in threatening punishment to those who disobey.

Thus, it is likely that the psalmist believed God would recognize his desire to follow God's teachings by granting security, prosperity, and long life, and he asked God to confirm the covenant promise.

Here we should point out that the covenant in question was taught as binding upon the ancient Israelites, but it is not the covenant under which Christians live. Even for the Hebrews, it did not always play out as expected: the books of Job and Ecclesiastes were both written in large part to deal with the question of why the righteous often suffered while the wicked prospered.

God has not promised that health and wealth will follow faithful Christians wherever they go. Indeed, the New Testament contains many passages encouraging believers to be strong in the face of suffering.

That does not mean, however, that there are no promises. Through Christ we have the promise of the Spirit's presence with us in all the trials and the joys of life. Through Christ we have a mission to love others in a way that brings true purpose to life. And, through Christ we have the hope of being in God's presence even beyond the grave.

Through Christ we also have the promise of forgiveness for our shortcomings. The psalmist knew something of this, too. "Turn away the disgrace that I dread" could be a roundabout way of asking for forgiveness (v. 39). The word translated "turn away" could more literally be read as "cause to pass by." The psalmist hoped for God to bless his obedience and forgive or pass over the dreaded reality of his failures.

> **Give me life:** The closing line of v. 40, translated "in your righteousness give me life" in the NRSV, is subject to varying translations. In Hebrew it consists of two words that require multiple words to express in English: "in your righteousness" (*bezîdqāteka*) and "give me life" (*chayēnî*). The basic stem of the verb used means "to live" or "to have life." Here it appears in the emphatic *pi'el* form, so that it means "let live," "give life," "revive," or "refresh." With the first-person ending, it is "give life to me."
>
> Thus, NIV 11 has "preserve my life," while NASB 95 and NET have "revive me." Though the nuances may differ, the central thought is the same: the psalmist wants to experience the best life possible, which he believes is found in following God's way.

Verse 40 closes the section with a declaration of the psalmist's deep desire to be so devoted to God's way that he could experience the fullness of God's life: "See, I have longed for your precepts; in your righteousness give me life." **[Give me life]**

The psalmist knows that God is the author of life, and he wants to know life to the fullest. That is the kind of life the prophet Micah described much more succinctly: one that finds its meaning in the deep joy of faithfully pursuing justice, displaying kindness, and walking humbly with God. That, Micah said, is what God wants from us (Mic. 6:8).

What kind of life do *we* want?

The Hardest Question
How does the alliteration work in vv. 33-40?

For readers who might be interested in more insight to the poet's craft, here are the verbs that introduce vv. 33-39. We note that they are all in what is called the *hifil* form, which gives them a causative sense. This allowed the poet a great deal of freedom: he could use almost any verb he wanted, because the causative form would add a *hē* prefix.

Verse 33 begins with *hôrēnî*, from the verb *yārâ*. The suffix *-nî* is the first-person pronoun, "me." The meaning of the verbal root is "to cast" or "to shoot." In the causative form it was used to mean "to teach" or "to show." Indeed, it is the same verb that gave rise to the noun form *torah*, which is often translated as "law" but really refers to the wide range of divine teachings. Here *hôrēnî* means "teach me" or "instruct me."

Verse 34 begins with *hᵉbinēnî*, the causative form of *bîn*, "to understand" with the first-person suffix: "cause me to understand" or "give me understanding."

Verse 35 begins with *hᵉdrîkēnî*, from *dārak*, which means "to walk." The causative form with the first-person suffix means "cause me to walk," or more elegantly, "lead me."

Verse 36 begins with *hat-libî*. The verb is *hat* (sometimes transliterated as *hath* to distinguish the letter *tet* from *tav*, which has a sharper sound). It comes from the root *nātāh*, which means "to incline" or "to bend." In the *hifil* form the initial *nun* and the final *hē* both disappear, leaving the imperative *hat*, which can mean "stretch out," "turn," or "incline" when used with an object. In this case, the object is *lebî*, "my heart." The psalmist wants God to incline or turn his heart toward God's teachings.

Verse 37 begins with *haᵃvēr*, the *hifil* form of *ʿāvar*, which means "to pass over" or "pass by." In the causative form it can mean "cause to pass over" or "cause to pass by." In this case, the psalmist wants God to cause his eyes to pass over or turn away "from looking at vanities."

Verse 38 begins with *hāqēm*, from the verb *qûm*, which means "to arise" or "to stand." The *hifil* form means, as we might expect, "to cause to stand," or "to raise." The idea of "causing to stand" can carry the idea of "establish" or "confirm," and that is the sense here, where the psalmist prays for God to confirm or establish God's words/sayings, translated by the NRSV as "promise."

Verse 39 begins with the same verb as v. 37: *haᵃvēr*. Here, instead of praying for God to turn the psalmist's eyes away from vanities, it has the sense of asking God to "cause to pass by" or "turn away" any disgrace or reproach from the psalmist.

Verse 40 concludes the section, though with a different beginning. Here the first word is *hinēh*, an interjection that means something akin to "behold" or "see."

Third Reading
1 Corinthians 3:10-23 (RCL 3:10-11, 16-23)

Quality Construction

For you belong to Christ, and Christ belongs to God. (1 Cor. 3:23)

Have you ever built a house – even a playhouse, a doghouse, or a toy house constructed from wooden logs or plastic bricks? Building something new can bring both satisfaction and challenges. Houses are hard to hide: the use of poor construction techniques or inferior building materials will be obvious to everyone. If you dare to build a house, you had best do it carefully.

Today's text continues the theme that Paul has been hammering from the opening verses of 1 Corinthians: Christians are called to live in unity within cooperative communities of faith that are focused on Jesus. Paul had heard of sharp divisions in the church at Corinth, factions based on things such as social status, spiritual elitism, and personality preferences.

Paul labeled their ongoing conflict as a sign of immaturity. Noting a division that existed between those who favored Paul and those who preferred Apollos, Paul insisted that both he and Apollos were servants of Christ – and that the Corinthians should focus on serving Christ, too.

The church's one foundation
(vv. 10-15)

After describing the church as God's field (3:5-9a), Paul added metaphors of the church as God's building (3:9b-15) and God's temple (3:16-17). When reading, we must remember that Paul was not talking about the church as a literal building or even as an institution. His subject was the gathered community of believers.

Western culture is so individualistic that we often misread this text as a treatise on personal behavior and the final judgment, but Paul's concern was with those who serve the church.

Any building needs a well-designed foundation, and Paul described himself as a "skilled (or wise) master builder" who laid a firm foundation for the church in Corinth (v. 10a). Paul's apparent lack of humility was not braggadocio, but a realistic appraisal of his work. He was a proficient and practiced church planter, a pioneer who blazed new trails and who trained others to follow in his steps.

When Paul described himself as a "skilled master builder," he used the word *sophos*, which can mean "wisdom" when applied to knowledge, or skill, when applied to a trade. He did not claim that his expertise was innate, but "according to the grace of God given to me" (v. 10).

"I laid a foundation," Paul said, and now "someone else is building on it." That did not trouble Paul. Like a modern building contractor, he laid a firm foundation and entrusted subcontractors to build upon it while maintaining oversight of the project.

"Each builder must choose with care how to build on it," Paul said (v. 10b). Paul had earlier taken issue with those who sought or claimed to have esoteric knowledge about the faith. Paul insisted that Christ was the only foundation needed (v. 11). Without Christ as its basis, there is no church, no matter who its leader might be.

The cornerstone: Paul's insistence on Christ as the only foundation may have been drawn in part from Isaiah's prophecy about God's anointed, who would be rejected by many but become the cornerstone of faith: "Therefore thus says the Lord GOD, See, I am laying in Zion a foundation stone, a tested stone, a precious cornerstone, a sure foundation: "One who trusts will not panic" (Isa. 28:16).

Early Christians believed the prophecy was fulfilled in Christ. It is quoted specifically (though loosely) in Gal. 1:6-7 and 1 Pet. 2:6.

The church at Corinth could not be built on Paul, on Apollos, or on Peter – only Christ. Paul's point is echoed in the words of a favorite hymn: "The church's one foundation is Jesus Christ, the Lord," by Samuel John Stone. The hymn's words grew out of a painful schism in the Church of South Africa in the 1860s.

Was Paul's choice of metaphors coincidental, or is it possible that the "Peter party" in Corinth had championed Jesus' promise to Peter: "… upon this rock I will build my church" (Matt. 16:18)? Paul insisted that the foundation of the church was not Peter, Paul, or Apollos, but Christ. [**The cornerstone**]

The type of division experienced in Corinth remains a constant threat to the body of Christ. Many of us have observed churches that grow as a pastor's personality cult, or churches that split when members declare allegiance to different leaders within the church.

Churches and their leaders may build upon the foundation of Christ in different ways. They may focus on a hard

Reward and loss: With regard to Paul's comments about church builders being rewarded or suffering loss in the judgment, Scott Nash has written: "The metaphor stresses that one who builds well gets paid while one who does not pays a penalty, in accordance with the building contract. Applied to the church, the metaphor suggests that preachers who actually do harm to the church (God's building) are liable for the damages, though they themselves may be spared bankruptcy" (1 Corinthians, Smyth & Helwys Bible Commentary [Smyth & Helwys, 2009], 114).

Richard Hays puts it this way: "Paul's point is that some leaders are building with valuable fireproof material (the gospel of Christ crucified) while others are building with ephemeral fluff (the fads of human wisdom) that will be consumed by flames in God's coming building inspection" (1 Corinthians, Interpretation [John Knox Press, 1997], 55).

line of doctrine (orthodox or otherwise), on political activism, on catering to members' needs, on missional outreach to the community, or on other things – some more appropriate than others. The results of those efforts will become obvious in time, for good or ill.

Expanding his analogy, Paul spoke of teachers who might build upon the foundation with the metaphorical equivalent of gold, silver, or precious stones, while incompetent or self-focused teachers would add to it wood, hay, or straw (v. 12).

Every ancient city contained fine dwellings made of brick and stone, in addition to rustic buildings of mudbrick and thatch. On those occasions when floods, earthquakes, or fires struck the town, it became obvious which buildings were most substantial.

Paul's challenge to churches then and now is to remember that one day all will know what kind of materials and workmanship have gone into building the community of faith (v. 13). Those who have built well will have the reward of seeing their efforts stand firm (v. 14). Those who added shoddy construction will see their misguided efforts come to naught.

No church built on the foundation of Christ will be lost altogether, but for some builders, Paul said, it will be as if they escaped from a burning house with nothing to show for their efforts (v. 15). [**Reward and loss**]

The church as God's temple
(vv. 16-17)

In v. 16, Paul shifted from the general idea of a building to the specific image of a temple: "Do you not know that you are God's temple and that God's Spirit dwells in you?" English translations don't distinguish between the singular and plural sense of the pronoun "you," but the Greek does – and Paul routinely used the plural form in this section.

Elsewhere Paul spoke of individual Christians as the temple of the Holy Spirit (1 Cor. 6:19, 2 Cor. 6:16), but here (as in Eph. 2:21) his subject remained the believing community. The Spirit dwells in the hearts of individual believers, but is best experienced and communicated to others through the gathered body of the church. [**A new temple**]

It is hard to experience the Spirit in a fractured church. Internal strife can destroy the witness of God's people, who

> **A new temple:** In speaking of the church as God's temple, Paul could be reflecting the Jewish belief that God would erect a new and glorious temple in the last days (Isa. 28:16, Jubilees 1:17, Enoch 91:13; cp. Mark 14:58). Like Peter (1 Pet. 2:5), Paul saw the church as the fulfillment of Jewish hopes; a new community in which one could approach and worship the Spirit of God.
>
> We should recognize that this was a rather audacious idea, for the Jerusalem temple was still standing when Paul wrote, and Jews believed the Spirit of God was particularly present in the inner sanctuary. Paul's assertion was that the Spirit was fully present in the gathered community of faith.
>
> As Richard Hays describes it: "... when Paul now transfers this claim to the community of Gentile Christians in Corinth, he is making a world-shattering hermeneutical move, de-centering the sacred space of Judaism (cf. John 4:21-24).... He believes that the Spirit of God is present in the community and that the community is now the place where praise and worship are rightly offered up to God" (1 Corinthians, Interpretation [Westminster John Knox, 2011], 57).

are called to stand like an impressive sanctuary, revealing God's glory to others. Paul underscored the seriousness of the matter with v. 17: "If anyone destroys God's temple, God will destroy that person. For God's temple is holy, and you are that temple."

This troublesome verse seems to predict divinely directed capital punishment for those who cause dissension. Yet, in v. 15, Paul had argued that even those who built with "wood, hay, and straw" would be saved despite the loss of their labors.

The church belongs to Christ
(vv. 18-23)

Paul concluded his discussion about true wisdom and the dangers of factionalism with a sharp warning against boasting that reprises earlier themes. Those who claim to be wise in this age are lost in their own self-conceit, Paul said. Rather, "you should become fools so that you may become wise" (v. 18).

In other words, "You must become fools (as far as the world is concerned) by accepting the wisdom of God displayed in the crucified Christ – only then can you become truly wise."

Returning to the refrain he began in 1:18–2:5, Paul labeled worldly wisdom as foolishness to God (v. 19), even

as the world might think of a crucified "savior" as a crazy way to start a religion. The wisdom of the world is folly because it assumes people can save themselves by their own efforts, while true wisdom does not come by human effort, but through what God reveals in the cross of Christ.

[Quotations]

Wise and mature believers do not divide the church with pride-inspired divisions, but build it up as a community focused on Jesus.

Through God's work in Christ, all things "belong to" the church, Paul said. Whether it is the teaching of any leader or anything related to "the world or life or death or the present or the future," all is done for the sake of the church (v. 22).

Philosophers of Paul's day, both Stoics and Cynics, taught that the wise learned to become master of all things, and thus, to possess them. Paul argued that all things belong to the church – including its leaders – because all things belong to Christ, in whom believers live. Believers must remember, however, that they also belong to Christ. All that they have and all that they are is a gift – including their relationship with God through Christ (v. 23).

God graces individuals with the gifts of teaching and leadership, but gives no one the right to fracture the fellowship through seeking personal power or acclaim. The church's leaders belong to the faith community in the same

> **Quotations:** Paul's scripture quotations in vv. 19 and 20 are variations on Job 5:13a and Ps. 94:11a.
>
> The text from Job ("He takes the wise in their own craftiness") comes from the first speech of Eliphaz, which consists of traditional wisdom that Job refutes as too simplistic, but it reinforces the point Paul wants to make.
>
> Paul stretches the latter quotation ("The Lord knows our thoughts, that they are but an empty breath") by adding the word "wise," quoting it as "The Lord knows the thoughts of the wise, knowing that they are futile." The term for "wise" does not appear in either the Hebrew or the LXX (the Greek translation of the Old Testament), but Paul apparently felt justified in adding the word because of the verse's larger context, which does discuss wisdom.
>
> Paul cited the two verses to support the point that humans may think they are wise, but those who rely on their personal cleverness will be caught in their own traps and amount to nothing.

way that all other things belong to the church: to be used in service for the greater glory of God.

Paul concluded the section with a powerful rhetorical chain: all things belong to the church, the church belongs to Christ, and Christ belongs to God. Thus, just as Christ can be described as subordinate to God (in Paul's thinking, cf. 15:28), the church is subordinate to Christ, and individual leaders must recognize their place as servants of the church.

When things are set in proper order, the church's witness will be more impressive than the most majestic cathedral, declaring the love of Christ to all.

This passage challenges church leaders and members alike to take a close look in the mirror. Do we utilize the church as if it belongs to us? It's easy to speak of "my church," but we must remember that means "the church to which I belong," not "the church that belongs to me." The church, Paul has reminded us, belongs to Christ, and Christ belongs to God.

The Hardest Question
What did Paul mean by "If anyone destroys God's temple, God will destroy that person"?

This can be a troublesome verse, as it seems to predict a death sentence for those whose divisive spirit fractures the church and destroys its witness.

It may be helpful to note that Paul was not talking about one's eternal destiny, but pointing out that the judgment would reveal the quality of their work, and whether anything would be left of it.

Paul did not explain what he meant by "God will destroy that person." The same word was used for the one who "destroys" the temple and the prediction that God will "destroy" him. The Greek word (*phtheirō*) usually means to ruin or corrupt in a financial or moral sense, rather than utter annihilation, and that seems to be the best sense here.

Perhaps it would be helpful to remember Jesus' stern warning that those who become a stumbling block to "little ones" (either children or new believers, perhaps) would be better off being cast into the sea with a heavy millstone around the neck. Both are apparent examples of hyperbole, or exaggeration for effect. They are not to be taken literally, but still seriously.

And this is serious business. As Hans Conzelmann has noted (*1 Corinthians*, Hermeniea [Fortress Press, 1975], 78), whether one violates a temple or a virgin, something is lost that cannot be regained. One cannot engineer a breach of fellowship within the church without also experiencing a loss of relationship with others and with God's Spirit. Something has been destroyed.

Fourth Reading
Matthew 5:38-48

Seriously?

Be perfect, therefore, as your heavenly Father is perfect. (Matt. 5:48)

"Seriously?" Perhaps you've said that when someone made a request or demand that you thought was ridiculous, stretching it, over the top.

We might have responded in the same way if we had been there when Jesus spoke the words in today's text. We might do the same when we read them today. "Really?" "You've got to be kidding!"

Give to anyone who asks? Love my enemies? *Be perfect? Seriously?*

Let's find out.

Don't retaliate?
(vv. 38-39)

Today's text continues a series of antithetical teachings in which Jesus offered a new take on the Jewish law, going beyond legalistic traditions to get at the underlying principles of behavior that God desires. Jesus insisted that he had not come to abolish the law and the prophets, but to fulfill their true intent for human behavior and divine relationship (v. 17).

Accepted norms in our culture expect everyone to look out for himself or herself. We live in a world of retaliation and retribution, a world of tit-for-tat relationships where good begets good and evil begets evil – and sometimes, even good is met with evil. At an early age, children learn to excuse their misbehavior by saying "He hit me first!"

We know the rules of this world, and we are pretty good at playing by them. We know how to win by these rules, but Jesus' teaching messes with our understanding of how the game is played. His ideas sound very much like a recipe for being a loser, and we don't want to be losers.

The truth is, when Jesus proclaimed what it is like to be children of God and citizens of the kingdom of heaven, he was describing the rules for a different game altogether. It's not a game in which the winners gain the most money and bankrupt everyone else, as in Monopoly. It's not a game in which we root for others' misfortune because it's good for our business or stock positions. It's not a game in which the winners physically outplay their opponents and run up more points, as in basketball or soccer or wrestling.

The winners in this game are those who love other people so much that they are willing to put the interests

---

Extreme measures: It's likely that Jesus employed hyperbole when talking about the measures one should employ to avoid certain sins. For example, in vv. 29-30 Matthew reports that Jesus said "If your right eye causes you to sin, tear it out and throw it away; it is better for you to lose one of your members than for your whole body to be thrown into hell. And if your right hand causes you to sin, cut it off and throw it away; it is better for you to lose one of your members than for your whole body to go into hell."

Jesus knew that chopping off a hand might deter a thief, but wouldn't change his spirit – and one-eyed people are perfectly capable of lust. Though employing physical symbols, Jesus was more concerned with inner motivations than outward behavior. His kingdom ethic called for radical surgery to the mind and heart that rules our hands and eyes.

of others first, even when the others don't deserve it, even when the others are ungrateful and wicked.

And Jesus expects us to play by these rules?

Seriously?

In Matt. 5:21-37, Jesus radically reinterpreted traditional laws concerning murder, adultery, divorce, and oaths. Consistently, his teaching went beyond the letter of the law to focus on the purpose behind it. Murder is the unhealthy outgrowth of spiteful anger, and adultery is the product of sinful lust. Both need to be controlled, by whatever measures necessary. Believers should live with such faithful integrity that neither divorce nor oath taking should be necessary. [**Extreme measures**]

Still, in every case, Jesus challenged believers to move past the law and focus on a new kingdom ethic. In today's text, we find him continuing that pattern with further teachings about a proper response to people who mean us harm: "You have heard that it was said, 'An eye for an eye and a tooth for a tooth.' But I say to you, 'Do not resist an evildoer. But if anyone strikes you on the right cheek, turn the other also'" (vv. 38-39).

Hammurabi's law code: The famed stele of Hammurabi is housed at the Louvre in Paris. Used by permission of Wikipedia Creative Commons.

Can't you imagine his disciples looking at each other with raised eyebrows that asked the unspoken question: *"Really?"*

The law of "an eye for an eye," commonly known as *lex talionis*, is attested as far back as the 18th century BCE, where it appears in the famous law code of Hammurabi, the sixth king of the first Babylonian dynasty. References to the law appear three times in the Old Testament, where damaged eyes and teeth are not the only things subject to reciprocal penalties: hands, feet, fractures, and even lives are cited as examples (Exod. 21:24, Lev. 24:20, Deut. 19:21). [**Hammurabi's law code**]

The purpose of *lex talionis*, or "lawful retaliation," was to limit vengeance and keep conflict from escalating. The principle was stated in terms suggesting that victims of injury could retaliate with equivalent injuries to the one who harmed them. But by the time of Jesus, things were usually settled with monetary payments rather than eyes and teeth. The law was also designed to curb immediate vengeance that could get out of hand: cases were taken to court and the penalty had to be authorized by a judge.

The custom was so old and well known that it was probably never questioned until Jesus came along and demanded, not equal retaliation, but *no* retaliation. In the first-century world, a backhanded slap to the right cheek was particularly demeaning, bringing insult with injury. Jesus taught that the victim of such opprobrium should not slap back, but stand his ground and turn the other cheek, inviting a second blow.

Can you imagine? Jesus must have shocked his listeners by replacing permission to retaliate with a call to repay evil with good, but he wasn't done.

Give freely?
(vv. 40-42)

Responding to a physical insult with grace was just one example of how one could subvert the evil in another's hurtful behavior. Jesus cited an instance in which someone sued another person, asking for his tunic (a better translation than the NRSV's "coat"). The tunic was a person's main article of clothing: like a shirt, but knee length or longer. Jesus did not address whether the lawsuit was legitimate, any more than whether the blow to the right cheek was deserved. He simply said something like "If they

---

A frivolous lawsuit? Why would someone sue another person for his or her tunic? The situation would probably reflect a small-time lender who had loaned someone money, with his or her outer tunic as collateral. Old Testament law spoke to similar loans, insisting that someone who took a poor person's outer cloak as collateral should return it each night, lest the person have nothing to guard against the evening chill.

"If you take your neighbor's cloak in pawn, you shall restore it before the sun goes down; for it may be your neighbor's only clothing to use as cover; in what else shall that person sleep? And if your neighbor cries out to me, I will listen, for I am compassionate" (Exod. 22:26-27).

---

demand your clothes, give them your outer cloak, too" (v. 40). [A frivolous lawsuit?]

It's unlikely that Jesus was encouraging his followers to leave the courtroom and walk around naked: his shocking demand was designed to support the principle of loving grace over prideful reprisals.

The same principle would apply if a Roman soldier should conscript a citizen to carry his gear for a mile – a custom that applied in Jesus' time (v. 41). The Roman measure of a mile was just under 5,000 feet, a bit shorter than the 5,280 feet that currently defines a mile.

Jesus suggested that one who was ordered to carry a soldier's gear for one mile should volunteer to double the distance, showing grace by going beyond what was required.

Jesus' further commands that his followers give to beggars and make loans without question (v. 42) follow the same theme. Jesus wanted his disciples to model a profoundly different approach to relationships: one that elevated grace over law, service over recompense, love over power, and generosity over greed. In every case, these examples took the Old Testament law into entirely new territory.

Love enemies?
(vv. 43-48)

Jesus' shocking new demands culminated in his commands to love one's enemies and pray even for abusive people (vv. 43-44). In this way, Jesus' followers could get a taste of what it meant to be "children of your Father in heaven" – who set the example of loving generosity by providing life-giving sunshine and rain to all people, whether righteous or not (v. 45).

Jesus expanded the traditional interpretation of the law that limited one's responsibility of care to fellow Jews or family members. Showing love only to those who love in return is inherently selfish; learning to love the unloving is a lesson in selflessness (vv. 46-47). In Jesus' teaching, foreigners, strangers, and the despised Samaritans alike were neighbors in need of love and compassion. Even enemies – people who intentionally intended harm – fell into the category of people in need of our love and prayers.

Old Testament writers knew that God's self-declared character was "merciful and gracious, slow to anger, and abounding in steadfast love and faithfulness" (Exod. 34:6, cited or reflected in Num. 14:18; Ps. 86:15, 103:8, 145:8; Joel 2:13; Jonah 4:2; Nah. 1:3). In a sense, Jesus was challenging his followers to look past the law to the lawgiver, and to act in the same merciful, gracious, patient, loving, and faithful way that God related to the world. For disciples to follow God's example, they must go beyond reciprocal expressions of love to people who love them back, and show grace even to those who are hateful.

Jesus concluded with a call to "be perfect," even as God is perfect (v. 48). Once again, we ask, "Seriously?"

It may help a bit to know that the Greek word Matthew used (*teleios*) does not mean absolute perfection as we might think of it. Rather, it means "complete," "whole," "mature," or "having attained the end." It is the Greek equivalent to the Hebrew *tamîm*, used to speak of persons who were ethically upright (Noah in Gen. 6:9, Job in Job 1:1). It is comparable to God's challenge in the Torah to "Be holy, for I am holy" (Lev. 19:2). In Luke's version of this same teaching, he has Jesus conclude with "Be merciful, just as your Father is merciful" (Luke 6:36).

Context is our best guide to meaning. Here, to be perfect or spiritually mature is to live as Jesus lived, to follow his teachings by demonstrating unselfish grace and love to others. When responding to others' actions, whether loving or indifferent or hateful, we typically base our behavior on who they are or what they have done. Jesus challenges us to respond on the basis of who we know ourselves to be as God's children, and to act out of the Spirit-empowered love that dwells within us.

Is that radical? Absolutely. Was Jesus being serious? Yes. Can we do it? That remains to be seen.

The Hardest Question
How literally should we take these teachings?

Jesus' teachings may not seem very practical. It's obvious that Jesus was upholding an ideal that is the opposite of selfishness, but was he speaking in hyperbole? Was he intentionally exaggerating to make a point? That's possible. I doubt Jesus expects his followers to walk around shirtless or with two black eyes. I don't think he expects us to empty our bank accounts when a homeless person on the corner holds up a cardboard sign. There's a difference between having a loving, generous spirit and being a total patsy. Jesus didn't heal or feed every needy person he saw.

But let's not get too comfortable. Jesus clearly expected his followers to do more than they were accustomed to doing, and he expects more of us, too. Most of us don't get punched in the face very often. We rarely have someone ask for the shirt off our backs.

Jesus was more concerned about relationships than finances. In every situation, Jesus expects us to think of what the other person needs, not just what we need, and to do what we can to help that other person. He calls us to be so generous of spirit that we show grace to every person we meet.

Often what others need most is not material goods or a chance to hit us again: what they need most is forgiveness, or understanding, or acceptance. Few things in this world are harder than to love someone who hates us, or to forgive someone who has hurt us. It just doesn't seem natural. But what Jesus teaches here is that what seems natural is not necessarily what is best. For Christian people, *our* actions and attitudes are not to be determined by the actions and attitudes of someone else.

We should not let someone else's negative behavior make us negative. We should not let others' hostility make us hostile. We should not let someone else's insensitivity make us insensitive, or let their meanness make us mean. Even though we may be victims of others' actions, we are not required to live as victims, or to continue being victimized by living with a cancerous grudge.

What an incredible thought! God is kind to the ungrateful and the wicked – and God calls us to act in the same way. That may not seem fair to us, and we may think it is not fair of God to expect us to act the same way. But if God were not kind to the ungrateful and the wicked, if God were not merciful, then where would we be?

But God *is* kind to the ungrateful and the wicked. Because of that, Jesus came into the world and allowed ungrateful and wicked people to treat him terribly and then hang him on a cross, and just before he breathed his last, he had the love and the courage to forgive them.

It may seem to us that forgiving someone who has hurt us or being kind to someone who hates us is impossible, but Jesus insisted that nothing is impossible with God. We can be merciful, even as our Father in heaven is merciful.

We may not always feel like being merciful, but it's important to remember that love and forgiveness are *actions*, not just *feelings*. We can *act* in a merciful and loving way, even when we don't *feel* very kind toward the one who has hurt us.

It sounds radical, but Jesus insisted that we should not base our love and generosity on whether others are loving and generous. Rather, we love others – even when it seems crazy – because that is what Jesus does, and what he has called us to do. That is who God is and who God calls his children to be: loving, forgiving – even to those who don't deserve it. Really.

First Reading
Isaiah 49:8-16a

Show Yourselves!

Sing for joy, O heavens, and exult, O earth; break forth, O mountains, into singing!
For the LORD has comforted his people, and will have compassion on his suffering ones. (Isa. 49:13)

Most of us can recall times in our lives in which we felt stuck and wondered if we would ever be free. The time might be as petty as an 11-year-old who thinks the day's end bell will never release him from school. It may be the memory of long nights of studying, with graduation fading seeming far off. We may recall the sense of being stuck in dead-end jobs that seemed to suck the life out of us, leaving us longing for a change.

Today's text addresses a group of Hebrew exiles who had been in Babylon for 40 years or more. Some of them had been born in exile, but had grown up hearing stories about Jerusalem and the beloved temple upon Mt. Zion.

As the older generation died out and younger Hebrews wondered if they would ever see the land of their ancestors, a prophet inspired by Isaiah of Jerusalem arose to comfort and challenge his fellow captives. [**Second Isaiah**]

Beginning with the thematic words "Comfort, O comfort my people, says your God" (40:1), Second Isaiah promised the coming of a new day – and of new responsibilities for those who considered themselves to be God's people.

Comfort and challenge
(vv. 8-12)

Today's lectionary reading follows the second of four "Servant Songs" (vv. 1-6), which speaks of a God-empowered chosen one who would restore the people of Israel and

> **Second Isaiah:** As often noted, the book of Isaiah addresses at least three historical periods and is thought to have at least two, if not three authors.
>
> The first Isaiah, the son of Amoz, prophesied in Jerusalem for much of the latter half of the eighth century BCE. His prophecies typically decreed coming judgments upon Israel, Judah, and other nations. With the probable exception of the "Little Apocalypse" in chs. 26–29 and a historical section in chs. 36–39, the original Isaiah's work is found in Isaiah 1–39.
>
> Isaiah 40–55 takes us from Jerusalem to Babylon more than 150 years later. Around 540 BCE, as Cyrus the Persian began to threaten the weakening Babylonians, a student of Isaiah's work felt called to comfort the people who were experiencing the judgment predicted by the first Isaiah: we typically call him "Second Isaiah" or "Deutero-Isaiah." His words are primarily messages of comfort and challenge, predictions that the exiles would return.
>
> Isaiah 56–66 reflects a setting in and about Jerusalem after Cyrus had allowed willing exiles to return in 538 BCE. Those who returned found life among the ruins of Jerusalem's former glory to be disappointing and hard. Second Isaiah may have returned with them and continued to speak, but it is more likely that yet another arose in the spirit of Isaiah to offer comfort and challenge. We call him "Third Isaiah," or "Trito-Isaiah."

become a "light to the nations, that my salvation may reach to the end of the earth" (v. 6). The verse echoes a similar sentiment in an earlier oracle, which speaks of one called to be a light to the nations who frees the imprisoned (42:6-7).

Verse 7 is a transitional verse that moves from the servant to Israel as God's chosen one, and introduces an oracle predicting deliverance for those who lived as captives in a foreign land.

We should note that the Hebrew exiles, for the most part, did not live as prisoners. They were assigned land and allowed to live as farmers, to operate businesses, and to marry as they wished. They were integrated into Babylon's economy and, to the extent they wished, into its society.

Though free to go about their business, they were not free to return to Jerusalem. In a sense, they must have felt like today's residents of Bethlehem, a Palestinian city that is surrounded by fences and walls controlled by the Israeli government. Residents of Bethlehem can go about their business inside the city, but they cannot leave without a permit allowing them to pass through a checkpoint manned by Israeli soldiers. They long for the freedom to go and come as they choose, to visit relatives in nearby Jerusalem, to explore greater economic opportunities, or even to shop for goods that are hard to find in Bethlehem.

God was aware of the exiles' longing and was about to act on their behalf, the prophet said. Speaking in the oracular style of one who had been given a message by God, he declared "Thus says the LORD: In a time of favor I have answered you, on a day of salvation I have helped you" (v. 8a, NRSV).

Or is that what Isaiah intended? The verbs are in the perfect tense, which would normally be translated in the past, as in NRSV. This is sometimes referred to as the "prophetic perfect," in which someone speaks of something yet to come, but in the perfect tense, as if it has already happened.

The KJV and NASB20 also translate the verbs as past tense, but the NIV11 and NET see it as a future (but sure) promise: "In the time of my favor I will answer you, and in the day of salvation I will help you" (NIV11).

The verbs shift to imperfects in the next line, more commonly translated as present or future, but the NRSV renders them as a present perfect: "I have kept you and given you as a covenant to the people." NET has "I will protect you and make you a covenant mediator for people."

We note that the promise of God's delivering act is combined with a description of a call to vocation: the "chosen one" is to mediate the covenant in ways that benefit others, "to establish the land, to apportion the desolate heritages; saying to the prisoners 'Come out,' to those who are in darkness, 'Show yourselves'" (vv. 8b-9a).

Most interpreters read this promise and command as being addressed to Israel. The second-person pronouns associated with God's answer, protection, help, and commission are all in the singular, but one could understand the singular as referring to corporate Israel.

Some interpreters, however, such as John D. Watts in the *Word Bible Commentary*, believe the oracle is addressed to the Persian king Cyrus, who freed Israel, or Darius, who supported later returns. If that is the case, the singular pronoun would be appropriate.

Whether it is a Persian king, the prophet, or the people, what is the commission about? The charge is for prisoners to come out of their bondage, and for those in darkness to come into the light. Whether "those in darkness" refers to prisoners or to people in hiding is unclear, but the point is the same: the people of Israel will be set free to enter a new time of life "as a covenant to the people, a light to the nations, to open the eyes that are blind, to bring out the prisoners from the dungeon, from the prison those who sit in darkness" (42:6-7).

In both cases, there is an apparent shift from a single mediator to Israel as the responsible party in living as a faithful, covenant community.

Using the thinly veiled metaphor of the people as sheep led by a shepherd, the oracle declared "They shall feed along the ways, on all the bare heights shall be their pasture; they shall not hunger or thirst, neither scorching wind nor sun shall strike them down, for he who has pity on them will lead them, and by springs of water will guide them" (vv. 9-10).

The promise recalls the image of a new Exodus in which God's people will be redeemed from captivity and led through the wilderness. Rather than experiencing hardship along the way, as tales of the initial wilderness wandering recount, the people would find adequate food and water along the way, for they would be led by "he who has pity," or better, "the compassionate one."

God would not only provide for the people, but also metaphorically ease their way by turning mountains into roads and valleys into highways (v. 11), an image that reflects the earlier promise that "Every valley shall be lifted

> **A blessed hope:** Isaiah 2:2-4, a hopeful prediction from Isaiah of Jerusalem, would have been known to Second Isaiah, so it comes as no surprise that we find similar vocabulary:
>
> "In days to come the mountain of the LORD'S house shall be established as the highest of the mountains, and shall be raised above the hills; all the nations shall stream to it. Many peoples shall come and say, 'Come, let us go up to the mountain of the LORD, to the house of the God of Jacob; that he may teach us his ways and that we may walk in his paths.' For out of Zion shall go forth instruction, and the word of the LORD from Jerusalem. He shall judge between the nations, and shall arbitrate for many peoples; they shall beat their swords into plowshares, and their spears into pruning hooks; nation shall not lift up sword against nation, neither shall they learn war any more."

up, and every mountain and hill be made low; the uneven ground shall become level, and the rough places a plain" (Isa. 40:4).

The travel language of v. 11 leads to a reminder that the captives in Babylon were not the only Hebrews to have been scattered from their home. The Assyrian defeat of Israel in 722 BCE had led to massive relocations of its citizenry, and following Babylon's defeat of Judah, many had fled to Egypt. Trade ventures or other migratory forces had brought Israelites into many parts of the world.

Thus, when God called the people home, the Babylonian exiles would come from the east, but they would not be alone. Others would come "from the north and from and from the west, and these from the land of Syene" (v. 12). The Hebrew text has "Sinim," but an Isaiah text among the Dead Sea Scrolls has "Syene," a region of Egypt, indicating that others would come from the south.

On the one hand, the vision appears to speak of Israelites returning to Jerusalem, but it may also look to the time when people from across the world would seek God in Jerusalem, being drawn by the "light to the nations" (see also the hope expressed in Isa. 2:2-4). **[A blessed hope]**

Doubt and assurance
(vv. 13-16a)

The prophet makes a surprising shift in v. 13, calling the heavens, the earth, and the mountains to sing praise to Yahweh, who "has comforted his people, and will have compassion on his suffering ones."

The note of praise, however, is dampened by a complaint attributed to a personified Zion, who cries "The LORD (*yahweh*) has forsaken me, my Lord ('*adonāy*) has forgotten me" (v. 14, parentheses added).

Isn't that the way it often is? God makes promises, but we can't see past our isolation to believe it, even when the distance between God and us is our own doing.

The hill of Zion and the people who longed for it may have felt abandoned by God, but the prophet declared otherwise. "Can a woman forget her nursing child, or show no compassion for the child of her womb?" (v. 15a).

He speaks as in disbelief: *"Can a mother forget the child at her breast?"*

Sadly, we know that on rare occasions some human mothers have abandoned their children for various reasons. In times of exigency, a human mother might leave her child behind, but Yahweh would never abandon Israel: "Even these may forget, yet I will not forget you" (v. 15b).

Readers may recall the plaintive speech of Hosea, who spoke of how Yahweh grieved over Israel like a parent grieving over a recalcitrant child, but persisted in love: "How can I give you up, Ephraim? How can I hand you over, O Israel?" (Hos. 11:8a).

The oracle's closing line was unfortunately numbered as the first half of a verse that also appears to begin a new charge. In it, the prophet expressed the depth and permanence of Yahweh's love: "See, I have inscribed you on the palms of my hands" (v. 16a).

A literal translation would be "Look: on the palms I have engraved you." The anthropomorphic image of God in human form, God as a loving mother, is intensified with the picture of a knife cutting Israel's name into the divine palms. Such an act would be accompanied by pain, intended as a permanent sign of devotion.

Like a tattoo that cannot be removed or a scar that no plastic surgeon can cover, Israel's name would be ever before God. Yahweh would never forget.

Though we often speak of such psalms as having messianic characteristics and Isaiah certainly did not have it in mind, modern Christians might meditate on Isaiah's imagery and recall that Christ's hands were pierced for our sakes – wounds that John claimed were still evident when shown to Thomas (John 20:24-29).

Such thoughts may lead us to ponder times – even now – when we may have doubted God's love or felt abandoned by the divine presence.

Isaiah's word to Israel may also speak to all who find themselves in the dark. He calls us to show ourselves, believe the promises, and get on the road.

The Hardest Question
What do we mean by "Servant Songs"?

Second Isaiah's "Servant Songs" are often identified as Isa. 42:1-4, 49:1-6, 50:1-11, and 52:13–53:12, but scholars disagree on their precise limits. Some, for example, consider the first song to be comprised of Isa. 42:1-4 only, while others see it as 42:1-7 and others stretch it to 42:1-9. The second song is often delimited as 49:1-6, but some scholars see it continuing through v. 13. Some identify the third song as 50:1-11, but others include only 50:4-11. There is little question about the limits of the fourth song, marked as 52:13–53:12. Some scholars interpret Isaiah 55 as a fifth servant song.

Who is the servant? At times, the "servant" clearly appears to be Israel in a corporate sense, but in other instances, as here, the servant is depicted as an individual. In some instances, Isaiah may have thought of an individual like Cyrus the Persian, who allowed the exiles' return, as the servant.

More commonly, the servant is pictured as one who suffers, not for his own sin or shortcomings, but for the sake of others (compare the charges against Israel in Isa. 40:1-2, 42:22-25, 43:22-28, 47:6, 50:1 with descriptions of the servant in Isa. 50:5-6; 53:4-6, 9, 11-12).

Early Christian believers took Isaiah's description of the "suffering servant" as prophecies of Christ as the anointed one who suffered for others without complaint.

Second Reading
Psalm 131

Humility and Hope

O Israel, hope in the LORD from this time on and forevermore. (Ps. 131:3)

Psalm 131 is short and easily overlooked, but it shouldn't be relegated to the liturgist as a cursory reading. The psalm is not only profound in its meaning, but also intriguing in its nature. Perhaps most interesting, it may have been written by a woman. It's worthy of some prime-time homiletical exploration.

A humble approach
(v. 1)

The psalm bears a superscription identifying it as a "Song of Ascent." [**An ascending psalm**]. Like many others, the psalm is also associated with David, though "*l'dawîd*" is more likely to mean "to" or "for" David than "by" him.

David, indeed, seems an unlikely candidate as the author. David was capable of humility, but more commonly

---

An ascending psalm: Psalm 131, like all of the psalms between Psalm 120 and 134, has a superscription identifying it as a "Psalm of Ascent." The meaning of this is obscure: there are 15 Songs of Ascent, and some interpreters have suggested that these psalms were sung by priests ascending the 15 steps into the women's court of the temple.

It's more likely that the Songs of Ascent are associated with pilgrims coming into Jerusalem for the annual festivals. Jerusalem is surrounded by valleys, so any approach to the city involved climbing uphill. Jerusalem also bore a symbolic role as the center of worship. Whether people departed from a higher or lower elevation, in biblical language they always "went up" to Jerusalem.

---

appears as an aggressive personality, a mover and shaker who believed he belonged on top.

In contrast, Psalm 131 begins with what sounds like an apology, as if the postulant feels out of place or unworthy of speaking up. "O LORD, my heart is not lifted up, my eyes are not raised too high" (v. 1a).

A quick reading might lead one to think the person is sad or depressed, like the wag who claimed he was so low that he had to pull down his socks to see.

That's not what the statement is about, though: the unlifted heart and downcast eyes do not indicate sorrow, but humility.

The words could have been spoken by a man who did not want to give the impression of questioning or challenging God, but they sound more like the voice of a woman who dares to tread on male-dominated religious territory and offer a public prayer, even though that was not normally a woman's "place" in ancient Israel.

The author of Psalm 131 could have been a highly respected woman, but still hesitant to appear "above her station" in offering her brief but insightful prayer.

"I do not occupy myself with things too great and too marvelous for me," the psalmist said. Whether male or female, the poet acknowledged that there are things we can know, and things we can never understand. Some humans may claim to know what God thinks or wants – prophets among them – but this person was content with not knowing.

She or he did not complain that God had forgotten them, or express dissatisfaction with their situation in life. They did not ask why faithful people suffer, as Job did. They did not fret over the uncertainty of life and the surety of death, as the author of Ecclesiastes did.

They were happy to let God be God and tackle the life that was before them.

A place of trust
(v. 2)

Others might stress, "But," the poet says, "I have calmed and quieted my soul, like a weaned child with its mother; my soul is like the weaned child that is with me" (v. 2). If this was not written by a woman, it was penned by a very observant man.

The translation of the last phrase could literally be "like the weaned one upon me, my soul." A woman would be more likely to speak of a weaned child being "upon me," or "with me." Some have suggested that the implication is one of a child still being weaned, and thus sticking especially close to its mother.

Children were often breastfed for three years or more in the ancient world, building close bonds with their mother. Even after weaning, small children found – and continue to find – great comfort in being near her.

We have all experienced or observed a young child who clings to her mother, occasionally venturing out to explore a new environment, but always returning to climb in her lap or seek reassurance. Except in rare circumstances, small children feel safe in their mother's arms, confident of her care and protection.

We cannot overlook the feminine imagery of God that is pictured here. The psalmist does not find solace in God as a father, but as a mother. Her confidence in God is comparable to the trust that a small child puts in the mother who has nursed it and cared for it from birth.

While other motherly images of God are found in scripture, Christians may immediately recall Jesus' plaintive prayer over the people of Jerusalem: "How often have I desired to gather your children together as a hen gathers her brood under her wings, and you were not willing!" (Matt. 23:37, Luke 13:34).

What the later children of Jerusalem were unwilling to do, the author of Psalm 131 was delighted to do, finding perfect comfort in the maternal arms of God.

A word of advice
(v. 3)

Having testified of her own confident relationship with God, the psalmist addresses others who might read or hear her composition: "O Israel, hope in the LORD from this time on and forevermore" (v. 3).

The placement of this psalm may be due to the closing verses of the previous psalm, which concludes "O Israel, hope in the LORD! For with the LORD there is steadfast love, and with him is great power to redeem. It is he who will redeem Israel from all its iniquities" (Ps. 130:7-8).

While Psalm 130 uses masculine pronouns for God, it offers the balance of a maternal image of the divine as the source of hope "from this time on and forevermore."

People who have experienced great trials know the power of hope. When all else fails, there is hope. No matter how dark things look, as long as we're praying or even complaining, we are holding on to hope that things might get better.

It is when we lose hope that we open the door to even more difficult days by failing to try or even adopting destructive behaviors that bring death closer.

We don't know anything about what was happening in the life of the perceptive poet behind Psalm 131. She or he may have been living an ordinary life, or could have been facing trauma they could not understand.

In either case, they chose trust in God over fearful stress or angry questioning, and because of that, they could remain calm through the day and sleep like a baby.

Today's stressed-out society could benefit from reflecting on this psalm that is brief, but deep.

The Hardest Question
Are there other texts where God is described as a mother?

While masculine imagery for God is predominant in scripture, and the New Testament especially speaks of God as "Father," the Bible contains many instances of motherly metaphors for the divine.

Psalm 131's reference to the weaned child calls to mind Moses' complaint against God in Numbers 11. When he had grown tired of hearing the people's complaints, Moses cried out to God, "Why have you treated your servant so badly? Why have I not found favor in your sight, that you lay the burden of all this people on me? Did I conceive all this people? Did I give birth to them, that you should say to me, 'Carry them in your bosom, as a nurse carries a sucking child,' to the land that you promised on oath to their ancestors?" (Num. 11:11-12).

The implication is that bearing and nursing young children was God's job.

Imagery of God as a mother eagle that saves her faltering young in flight by catching and carrying them on her back is found in Deut. 1:30-31 and 32:10-18. The latter of those verses speaks of God setting Israel down in a fertile land, then *nursing* the people "with honey from the crags, with oil from flinty rock; curds from the heard and milk from the flock ..." (Deut. 32:13-14a).

Hosea 11:1-4 speaks of God's love for Israel in maternal terms: though the people rebelled against God's way, God could not forget. "Yet it was I who taught Ephraim to walk, I took them up in my arms; but they did not know that I healed them. I led them with cords of human kindness, with bands of love. I was to them like those who lift infants to their cheeks. I bent down to them and fed them" (Hos. 11:3-4).

Isaiah 49:15 combines images of longing and nursing. When Zion complained of being forgotten, Isaiah declared Yahweh's response: "Can a woman forget her nursing child, or show no compassion for the child of her womb? Even these may forget, yet I will not forget you."

Birth imagery is also attributed to God, even with regard to creation. In a series of blustery questions for Job, God asks "Or who shut in the sea with doors when it burst out from the womb? – when I made the clouds its garment, and thick darkness its swaddling band, and prescribed bounds for it, and set bars and doors, and said, 'Thus far shall you come, and no farther, and here shall your proud waves be stopped?'" (Job 38:8-11).

Isaiah 46:3-4 uses masculine pronouns for God, but speaks of God bearing Israel from his womb: "Listen to me, O house of Jacob, all the remnant of the house of Israel, who have been borne by me from your birth, carried from the womb; even to your old age I am he, even when you turn gray I will carry you. I have made, and I will bear; I will carry and will save."

Elsewhere, Isaiah relates God's grief over Israel to the pangs of birth: "For a long time I have held my peace, I have kept still and restrained myself; now I will cry out like a woman in labor, I will gasp and pant" (Isa. 42:14).

The latter Isaiah used maternal imagery in describing God's care for Israel: "For thus says the LORD: I will extend prosperity to her like a river, and the wealth of the nations like an overflowing stream; and you shall nurse and be carried on her arm, and dandled on her knees. As a mother comforts her child, so I will comfort you; you shall be comforted in Jerusalem" (Isa. 66:12-13).

It's no wonder that Jesus illustrated the proper attitude of welcome to his disciples by placing a little child on his knee and insisting "Whoever becomes humble like this child is the greatest in the kingdom of heaven. Whoever welcomes one such child in my name welcomes me." (Matt. 18:4-5; see also Mark 9:33-37 and Luke 9:46-48).

Though we know that God's true nature is far beyond human gender, our vocabulary and point of view are limited. While attempts to describe God lean toward the masculine, God has a strong feminine side, too.

Third Reading
1 Corinthians 4:1-5

A Very Small Thing

Therefore do not pronounce judgment before the time, before the Lord comes, who will bring to light the things now hidden in darkness and will disclose the purposes of the heart. Then each one will receive commendation from God. (1 Cor. 4:5)

The task of leadership is plagued with potential pitfalls. The Apostle Paul knew this well, having fallen into several of them that were not of his own making. Trying to exercise some modicum of leadership over the church he founded in Corinth was particularly frustrating, because substantial portions of the congregation didn't necessarily want or respect his leadership efforts.

Paul had spent at least two years getting the young congregation off the ground, and had kept up a lively correspondence with them. He sent Titus as a mediator once, and returned for visits at least twice. As the founder of the church, he considered himself to be like a parent who had authority over his "children" in the faith.

Early on, some Corinthians bickered over whether Paul, Apollos, or Peter should get star billing. Later, certain traveling preachers that Paul sarcastically called "super apostles" (2 Cor. 11:4, 12:11) gained influence over the church and challenged Paul's authority while teaching aberrant doctrine.

The Corinthian culture was one of seeking honor or prestige by associating in some way with high profile people. Why be loyal to hardscrabble Paul with his bad eyes and scratchy speech when a handsome celebrity preacher with a golden voice brought his eloquent rhetoric to town?

Some former pastors might have written it off and just moved on, but Paul felt an ongoing responsibility to the church, so he sought ways to walk the tense line between expressing humility and exerting authority.

Trustworthy stewards
(vv. 1-2)

At this point, Paul seems mainly concerned with the favoritism that some Christians had shown toward Apollos, while others remained faithful to him. In this, he is revisiting his earlier argument from 3:5-9 in which he described both himself and Apollos as fellow servants of God who had labored in their behalf: he had planted and Apollos watered, but God had given the growth.

Again, he says, "Think of us this way, as servants of Christ and stewards of God's mysteries" (v. 1). Several things stand out in this short sentence.

The word translated "servants" is not the more common *diakonos*, which came to be used for deacons, but *hyperétas*, literally "under-rower." The term was used in a variety of circumstances, typically of someone serving under an official, including guards or attendants who worked for government or religious leaders (Matt. 5:25, 26:58; John 18:18). Luke uses it in the expression "eyewitnesses and

---

The faithful servant: In a parable concerning faithful or unfaithful servants, Jesus used the example of a slave who also served as master of the house: "And the Lord said, 'Who then is the faithful and prudent manager (*oikonomos*) whom his master will put in charge of his slaves, to give them their allowance of food at the proper time? Blessed is that slave whom his master will find at work when he arrives'" (Luke 12:42-43).

servants of the word" (Luke 1:2), and Paul used the verbal form in describing Christ's command in his vision on the road to Damascus: "But get up and stand on your feet; for I have appeared to you for this purpose, to appoint you to *serve* and testify to the things in which you have seen me and to those in which I will appear to you" (Acts 26:16).

Paul employed the term, then, to speak of himself and Apollos as servants who acted directly under Christ. The second significant term, "steward," conveys a similar sense. "Steward" translates "*oikonomos*," or "master of the house." An *oikonomos* was basically a business manager placed in charge of a wealthy family's estate, looking after daily financial and organizational affairs. That person could be a free person or a slave, but one who was trusted and put in charge of the other servants. **[The faithful servant]**

Both terms portray Paul and Apollos as servants of Christ who had been given responsibility over others – namely members of the Corinthian congregation or other churches they had established or nurtured. All are servants of Christ, but some have leadership responsibilities over others. Despite the "servant" terminology, it was a claim of authority over the church but under the lordship of Christ.

But what did Paul mean by saying they were "stewards of God's mysteries"? He had earlier spoken of "God's wisdom, secret and hidden," which had been revealed to him and presumably, to Apollos (2:7). It is unlikely that Paul had in mind esoteric knowledge known only to a select few. For Paul, the gospel message of Christ's advent and redeeming work was the essence of the mystery, a part of God's plan from the beginning, but unknown prior to its revelation in Jesus. **[God's mysteries]**

Paul and Apollos, then, were stewards of the gospel, appointed by Christ not only to proclaim the message, but also given responsibility to oversee how the gospel was received and acted upon in the lives of those who received it.

The primary characteristic needed in a steward is integrity: "Moreover," Paul said, "it is required of stewards that they be found trustworthy" (v. 2). The manager of an affluent estate could be tempted to misuse the position to either enrich himself or to abuse those who served beneath him. In addition to a requisite amount of business acumen, only the most reliable, principled, and incorruptible servant could be trusted with the task. That point was indisputable. The question at hand was whether Paul was qualified for the job: some in the congregation had apparently raised the issue.

One trustworthy judge
(vv. 3-5)

With v. 3 Paul shifts from the plural (referencing both himself and Apollos) to the singular, clearly defending himself against those in the congregation who preferred another leader. He does so, curiously, by insisting that he is *not* defending himself and doesn't really care what they think: "But with me it is a very small thing that I should be judged by you or by any human court. I do not even judge myself" (v. 3).

It clearly matters a lot to Paul what the congregation thinks of him, but he insists that it is not their opinion that matters, but God's. The expression "that I should be judged by you or by any human court" literally ends with "by any human day." Most translations render "human day" as "human court" on the basis that he was speaking of an appointed time for human judgment.

We will see, however, that Paul's main concern is the difference between divine judgment and human appraisal, even his own. Paul claimed that he did not judge himself and was unaware of any shortcomings on his part, though that did not mean he was innocent of wrongdoing or not guilty of potential missteps in leadership. "It is the Lord who judges me," he said (v. 4).

God's mysteries: Earlier in 1 Corinthians, Paul spoke of God's mysteries in this way:

"But we speak God's wisdom, secret and hidden, which God decreed before the ages for our glory. None of the rulers of this age understood this; for if they had, they would not have crucified the Lord of glory. But, as it is written, 'What no eye has seen, nor ear heard, nor the human heart conceived, what God has prepared for those who love him'–these things God has revealed to us through the Spirit; for the Spirit searches everything, even the depths of God" (1 Cor. 2:7-10).

Here, Paul draws a direct connection between a mystery hidden "for our glory" and the crucified Jesus, "the Lord of glory." The quotation comes from Isa. 64:4. People of former ages did not know the mystery of "what God has prepared for those who love him," but the Spirit had now revealed it.

We cannot know the fullness of what Paul had in mind, but the gospel message was at the heart of it.

An eschatological element enters the discussion with v. 5, as Paul looks toward the final judgment: "Therefore do not pronounce judgment before the time, before the Lord comes, who will bring to light the things now hidden in darkness and will disclose the purposes of the heart. Then each one will receive commendation from God."

Paul goes on to say that he had applied the argument to himself and Apollos "for your benefit … so that none of you will be puffed up in favor of one against another" (v. 6).

So, there we have it: the congregation has questioned Paul's leadership, and some clearly favor another leader. Paul's defense does not speak to his qualifications, his preaching skills, or his pastoral presence. In essence, he seems to be saying "God appointed me as steward over you, and God's judgment is the only one that matters – end of discussion."

That's well enough until someone who is less than trustworthy comes along and makes the same argument. Is there no room for human judgment in calling – or keeping – congregational leaders?

The truth is that human judgment is an essential element of all relationships, including relations between a congregation and its pastors or other staff members. The challenge is for all to work together in humility, carefully seeking to know what best serves God's will for all concerned.

We must certainly be careful when judgment is concerned, as it's easy to become overly critical toward others.

Jesus was the only person fully qualified to judge others, but he often refused to do so. That put him out of favor with those whose religion depended on categorizing who's in and who's out. "Judge not, that you be not judged," Jesus said (Matt. 7:1-5). Jesus refused to judge the woman caught in the act of adultery (John 8:1-11) and confounded the self-righteous by demanding that only the sinless cast the first stone. Then he forgave the woman. In John 9:1-41, Jesus taught that forgiveness and healing are more important than the attribution of sin. In the story of the "prodigal son" (Luke 15:11-32), Jesus emphasized not only the forgiveness of the father, but the judgmental attitude of the older brother, who would not forgive.

Jesus' teachings about judgment were in a different context than Paul's displeasure with the way he was being judged, but both situations remind us that human judgment should always be subject to God's desire that believers should love and support one another.

Too often, we make flippant judgments about others when we have no idea what they have been through, or what they are up against. Jesus demonstrated a generosity of spirit and grace that stood out against the harshly critical attitudes of others. Paul, on his better days, also demonstrated gracious efforts to include everyone in the church's common mission.

Our natural temptation is to judge, but we must remember that love, forgiveness, healing, and restoration keep us closer to God's desire for the church.

The Hardest Question
How does Paul's teaching speak to today's pastors and churches?

Paul's self-defense before the Corinthian church may give the impression that issues of church leadership are written in black and white, but we know that congregational relations are often experienced as gray. It's not for one person to determine God's will for a church.

Churches that operate independently, not relying on a bishop to appoint their leaders, seek pastors who are called by God, but also called by the congregation. While a potential leader might express a belief that God has called them to a particular church, the call must be confirmed by the congregation.

Persons who have served on pastoral search committees have had the experience of wading through stacks of resumés and cover letters from prospective ministers, and noting that multiple applicants profess a sense of calling to that particular church.

They can't all be right.

The first half of my working life was spent as pastor of five different congregations over 26 years. In each case, the churches felt led to call me. I felt led to accept, and we both did so in an attitude of prayer, believing that God was in it.

Even denominations that practice ministerial appointments don't do so without human judgment from the appointing bishop and some knowledge of prospective congregations.

But what about relationships after the initial call? If a pastor turns out to be less than competent, or seeks to lead the church in a new direction that doesn't jibe with the church's past sense of mission or tradition, what happens then?

We know what happens. Tension mounts. People take sides. Churches split. It can be an ugly business, especially when a dictatorial pastor insists that the church must follow him because God called him and that's that.

We also know what happens when an influential faction of a congregation turns against a pastor for some perceived fault. Perhaps the pastor is promoting a shift in worship styles, or is preaching ideas deemed too liberal or too conservative for some members' personal tastes.

Paul's method of admonishing the Corinthians for questioning his leadership may have been appropriate in the early days of the church when reputable leaders were few, but ineffective leaders should not take his teaching out of context and use it as a stick to browbeat their congregations into submission.

Pastor-church relations must be mutual if they are to be effective and congenial. Sometimes relationships break down. Sometimes pastors and congregations are mismatched. Sometimes people change, or their ideas change.

Times such as these call for careful evaluation and renegotiation from both parties – again in a prayerful spirit that seeks God's leadership for the church.

Fourth Reading
Matthew 6:24-34

What, Me Worry?

Therefore I tell you, do not worry about your life, what you will eat or what you will drink, or about your body,
what you will wear. Is not life more than food, and the body more than clothing? (Matt. 6:25)

When I was a boy, I enjoyed reading high quality materials, such as *Mad Magazine*. The *Mad* mascot, who's still around, is a character named Alfred E. Neuman, a round-headed guy with a freckled nose and prominent ears. Alfred's motto is "What, me worry?"

Most of us are more inclined to fretting. I enjoy the music of the late Doc Watson, who preserved much of the traditional mountain music of the Appalachians. One of his standards was called "I'm Worried Now." Are *you* worried now? Anxious? Stressed out? Frazzled?

The gospel reading for the day is found in the Sermon on the Mount, a sort of summary statement of Jesus' new kingdom ethic. In his teaching, Jesus spoke to the existential anxiety experienced by so many persons. His advice, simply stated, was this: "Don't worry!"

Think clearly
(v. 24)

It's easy to assume that Jesus' advice might apply to ancient peasants, but certainly not to our modern age. Didn't the poet W.H. Auden call our time the "age of anxiety"? Yet the farmers, merchants, homemakers, fishermen, homeless persons, and retirees who gathered around Jesus that day had the same concerns that we have. If we had to live under the primitive conditions they endured, we would probably be even more stressed.

John Savage, for many years a popular seminar leader on human understanding and relationship skills, used to distinguish between sources of anxiety and types of anxiety. He would point out the many sources of anxiety: concerns about our family, job, finances, health, and relationships. He categorized four types of anxiety: reality-based anxiety (real problems), moral anxiety (when our behavior doesn't match our value system), neurotic anxiety (groundless fears), and existential anxiety (the awareness of human finitude).

Jesus' comments appear to deal with the latter two types of anxiety. Some people worry needlessly about their finances, so intent on stockpiling funds for their own future use that they fail to appreciate the present or to see the needs of others. Others are so anxious about the possibility of death that they cannot enjoy life.

The first type comes to the fore with Jesus' memorable reminder that "No one can serve two masters." Translating Jesus' culture-related illustration of a slave to today's workplace, we understand how frustrating it would be for an employee to have two supervisors, both competing for the worker's best efforts. Jesus likened that to one's attempt

---

Mammon: The word "mammon" came into English via the KJV, which did not translate the word, but merely transliterated the original: "Ye cannot serve God and mammon." The word *mammon* is Aramaic, and simply means "wealth." Thus, the NRSV has "You cannot serve God and wealth," and the NET has "You cannot serve God and money."

to serve God while also being devoted to the pursuit of wealth (v. 24). No one can serve two bosses when both demand full allegiance. [**Mammon?**]

Jesus was not criticizing money as inherently evil, but he recognized that the desire for wealth can overpower our best nature and leave us greedy for accumulating personal wealth while ignoring the needs of others. Money itself is not evil, but as noted in 1 Tim. 6:6-10, it "is a root of all kinds of evil" that leads people away from God.

Trust God
(vv. 25-33)

Thoughts of wealth are tied up with further causes of anxiety, but Jesus said "do not worry about your life, what you will eat or what you will drink, or about your body, what you will wear. Is not life more than food, and the body more than clothing?" (v. 25).

There is more to life than eating fine foods, wearing fashionable clothes, and checking things off our bucket list. Many in Jesus' audience weren't concerned about gourmet meals or *haute couture*, however: they worried about going hungry and being cold for lack of a cloak.

Even then, Jesus counseled trust that God had created a world with sufficient resources to feed all its inhabitants, from birds to people. Worry alone won't provide needed sustenance, but we can trust God to help us find what we need (vv. 26-31).

Another anxiety producer is the fear of death. I once worked at an orphanage, and befriended a young man I'll call Billy. Several times I invited him for dinner or to participate in some enjoyable activity. He would come, but often sat alone with a dark look on his face. Engaging him in conversations often led to his expressing a fear of death. Billy was so afraid of dying that he often missed out on living.

Jesus knew people like that, so he asked: "Can any of you by worrying add a single hour to your span of life?" (v. 27). Some translations use the literal translation, "add a single cubit to his stature," but the Greek words were often used metaphorically. If anything, the extra worry may take years off our lives.

Billy Graham used to tell a story about a farmer driving a wagon who offered a ride to a weary traveler carrying a heavy bag. The sojourner accepted the ride, but refused

> **Three things:** Jesus' encouragement that we need not worry about what we will eat, drink, or wear is a symbolic way of referring to all our physical needs. As we trust God to provide for *our* needs, however, it is helpful to remember that Jesus said we will be judged by how we respond to the needs of others as a way of serving him.
>
> In the parable of the sheep and goats, Jesus congratulated those who had given him food when he was hungry, drink when he was thirsty, and clothes when he was naked – insisting that providing for "the least of these" was also a ministry to him (Matt. 25:31-46). When we care enough to provide food, drink, and clothing to those in need, we become God's means of providing for them, so they need not worry.

to put down his bag, even though the wagon was already carrying the weight of it.

If we can learn to trust in God's providence, we won't have a great problem with either reality-based anxiety or neurotic anxiety. "Gentiles" worry about such things, Jesus said, speaking of people who don't know God (v. 32). Jesus did not promise that we could sit back and all our needs would be met. Seeds and worms don't just jump into the mouths of hungry birds. As we do our part to meet daily needs, we can trust that God's resources are sufficient.

With v. 33 Jesus moved from advice to a promise that can be misunderstood: "But strive first for the kingdom of God and his righteousness, and all these things will be given to you as well." [**Three things**]

What does it mean to seek the kingdom of God, and the righteousness of God? It is more than setting out on a quest similar to Indiana Jones in search of ancient treasure: it is embracing the adventure of life in cooperation with God. The kingdom of God is not a place, but the reign and rule of God over all places. The righteousness of God is not just an unattainable state of perfection, but a pathway of life guided by the teaching of scripture and the prompting of the Holy Spirit.

If we can bring ourselves to trust God and follow the kingdom road, we won't have to worry about moral anxiety, because we will find ourselves obedient to God's way. Even when we fail, our anxiety is short-lived, because we also know the pathway to forgiveness. Nor will we need to worry about reality-based anxiety, for God's provision is adequate for our basic needs.

Worry can be a significant detriment to spiritual growth. In the familiar parable of the sower and the seed, Jesus pointed out that some seed failed to grow because, even though they sprouted well, the worries and cares of this world sprouted along with them and choked them out (Mark 4:19, Matt. 13:22, Luke 8:14).

Reinhold Neihbur described worry as a "precondition of sin" because it sets us up to either accept or reject God's care. To deal with this issue, he composed the little prayer that, slightly adapted, now adorns the walls and desks of countless people: "God grant me the serenity to accept the things I cannot change, the courage to change the things I can, and the wisdom to distinguish the one from the other."

That prayer works because it focuses on God, rather than on our problems. When we seek earnestly to know God's way and to live within God's will, we learn to be content with what God provides. Note again that Jesus did not promise financial prosperity commensurate with our faith. "All these things" refers back to concerns for food, drink, and clothing – not to BMWs, beach houses, and big bank accounts.

Live today
(v. 34)

Jesus concluded with a reminder that overcoming worry is a daily thing: "So do not worry about tomorrow, for tomorrow will bring worries of its own. Today's trouble is enough for today" (v. 34). Jesus was not saying we should not plan for tomorrow or have goals for the future, but that we should not worry about them. Jesus lived with a clear awareness of where his earthly road was leading, but he focused on each day as it came.

We all make mistakes, but continuously replaying mental tapes of our past failures will not improve anything. We live in today, and we live toward tomorrow. The future

Two days: In *How to Encourage Others* (Broadman Press, 1983), Bill Bruster and Bob Dale advised that we can be happier by giving God just two days of our lives. We give God yesterday, because it's gone and we don't need to worry about it anymore. We give God tomorrow, for it isn't yet ours. Today is what we have. We can use it, live it, and make of it all that we can. When we focus on seeking God's kingdom on the day that is before us, we'll find more joy and less sorrow.

may be laced with both blessings and disasters, but worrying about it will get us nowhere. We control what elements of life we can; we learn to make peace with the rest.

Breaking life into manageable pieces is an important secret. Some managers call it "chunking down," dividing a job into realistic parts. Members of 12-Step groups learn that life must be lived one day at a time. Recovery and spiritual health last only if we are committed to it each day. Every day has enough trouble of its own, but it also has enough blessing and joy, if we are open to it. **[Two days]**

By the time we reach the end of v. 34, we realize that we've circled back to the beginning of Jesus' talk about worries in v. 24. We are reminded that we cannot serve two masters. We must choose one, and when we choose Jesus, focusing on the kingdom path, daily worries no longer dominate our lives.

What — *me* worry? Not if Jesus has his way.

The Hardest Question
What *should* we worry about?

One of the Bible's most common injunctions is some variation of "fear not," or "don't worry." We may think of it as something less threatening, but worry is just another word for fear. We fear that we won't have enough money to retire. We fear that our children will make huge mistakes (and maybe that we'll have to pay for them). We fear that our health won't hold up.

We deal with such fears in various ways. Some people fight the fears by seeking financial security. Some try to mute their worries by self-medicating with alcohol or drugs. Some deal with anxiety by obsessively preparing for everything.

Jesus said we shouldn't worry about our lives, but that doesn't mean there's nothing to fear. What we should fear is Jesus.

That may sound surprising, but has a more fearsome person ever walked the earth than Jesus, God incarnate? Jesus shook up his world. People quailed before the power he demonstrated, even though he used it only for good. The religious officials were so afraid of his influence that they sought to eliminate him.

We ought to fear Jesus – because a healthy fear puts us on the right road.

Much of what Hebrew wisdom teachers taught was centered on a single mantra: "the fear of the LORD is the beginning of wisdom" (Prov. 1:7, 4:7, 9:10; Ps. 111:10). Abraham was said to have feared God (Gen. 22:12), as did Joseph (Gen. 42:18), the midwives in Egypt (Exod. 1:17), and Job (Job 1:1).

In this context, "fear" does not suggest that we cringe in fright before God, but that we stand in awe or reverence before God and trust that God's way is right.

The Pentateuch is replete with commands to fear God (Lev. 19:14, 32; 25:17, 36, 43; Deut. 6:13, 24; 8:6; 10:12, 20; 13:4; 14:23; 17:29; 31:12). In addition,

- Samuel counseled Saul to fear God (1 Sam. 12:14).
- King Uzziah set out to learn the fear of God (2 Chron. 26:5).
- Nehemiah challenged the former exiles to walk in the fear of God (Neh. 5:9).
- The psalmists criticized those who did not fear God (Ps. 36:1, 55:19) and celebrated those who did (Ps. 40:3, 61:5, 64:9, 66:16).
- The prophets called upon Israel to fear God (Isa. 50:10, Jer. 5:24).

Admittedly, the Hebrew Bible's counsel to fear God included an element of "fear God … or else," because most Old Testament theology was grounded in a belief that God and Israel lived in a covenant relationship that promised blessings for obedience and curses for disobedience – reason enough to fear.

But there was more to it. It was because people feared God that they had no need to fear either people or circumstances: "Do not fear, for I am with you, do not be afraid, for I am your God" (Isa. 41:10; see also 41:13, 44:8).

Jesus' counsel not to fear began and ended with a command to choose which lord we will follow, which master we will fear. There's more to it than the fear that if we don't follow Jesus, we'll miss out on eternal life. God's call is more than a transaction of this for that. It is a call to relationship and responsibility. When we "fear" Jesus by putting our trust in him and prioritizing his teaching for our lives, we're on the kingdom road, and need not fear what comes our way.

First Reading
Genesis 6:1–9:17 (RCL 6:9-22, 7:24, 8:14-19)

A Flood of Trouble

The LORD saw that the wickedness of humankind was great in the earth,
and that every inclination of the thoughts of their hearts was only evil continually. (Gen. 6:5)

Few Old Testament stories have as much impact as the story of the flood. Any child who has spent time in Sunday School will know the story of Noah's ark. Any number of children's books and nurseries have been festooned with cartoon images of elephants and tigers and sheep filing peacefully onto a big wooden boat.

Most people who think they know the story have not read it closely, however, or they would notice that the account is internally inconsistent and sometimes repeats things in different ways. The reason for this is that the Priestly editor, who put together the final version of Genesis, interwove his own account (P) with an earlier story from the Yahwistic tradition (J), with no real effort to reconcile them.

The Revised Common Lectionary picks and chooses a few verses comprising a very small fraction of the flood account. Here we will take a much broader view.

A grieving God
(6:1-13)

Reading the flood stories introduces us to a writer who believed that God could be disappointed, which suggests that he did not consider God to be omniscient, at least with regard to the future. He pictures a God who grieves for having created a people who turned out so badly.

The story is introduced twice, first by J's account (6:1-8), and then by P (6:9-13). Both observe that human-kind had become so corrupt that God decided to clean the slate and reset the table with Noah.

This brings to light the first glaring difference between the biblical account and the well-known Mesopotamian accounts, which attribute the deluge to a petty god who grew angry because he found humans to be noisy and irritating.

In contrast, the biblical story speaks of God as being deeply grieved over the failures of humankind and struggling with the necessity of judgment. Genesis 3–4 describes a trend in which Adam's descendants fall deeper into sin, then Genesis 6 claims that certain "sons of God" looked upon the "daughters of men" with desire and had sex with them (6:1-2). The interaction apparently gave rise to giant warriors known as the "Nephilim," which means "fallen ones." **[Bad and getting worse]**

God decided to address the issue, according to the narrator, though the meaning of 6:3 is unclear. Some interpreters take it to mean that God decided to cut down on sin by limiting the length of human life to a maximum of 120 years: "Then the LORD said, 'My spirit shall not abide in mortals forever, for they are flesh; their days shall be one hundred twenty years'" (NRSV).

Verse 3 can also be interpreted, however, to mean that God decreed a 120-year grace period between the announcement of judgment and the coming flood: the NET translation has "My Spirit will not remain in human-

Bad and getting worse: Genesis 6 is the capstone of a developing saga in which God's wonderful and sinless creation (Genesis 1–2) degenerated into a moral morass. Genesis 3 recounts how the first humans disobeyed God, and the next chapter portrays the crime of fratricide, as Cain murdered his own brother (4:8), and how a descendant of Cain named Lamech boasted of killing for no good reason (4:18-24).

The writer is building a case for how the sinfulness of humankind grew as quickly as the people who populated the earth. Even worse things were to come with the introduction of the misguided "sons of God," who cohabited with human women to produce descendants with superhuman qualities. The thought was not entirely new: the Gilgamesh epic identifies Gilgamesh as being born from the union of a human king named Lugalbanda and the goddess Ninsun, making him "two-thirds god and one-third human," so big and strong and prone to trouble-making that the gods created the wild man Enkidu to keep him occupied.

A strange boat: The P account in Gen. 6:13-21 describes the ark as a giant floating box 300 x 50 x 30 cubits in size. A cubit is about 18 inches, so the ark would have been about 450 feet long, 75 feet wide, and 45 feet tall, with three interior floors, a window on the top, and a door in the side. It had no prow, rudder, or sail, and would have looked nothing like a ship.

Noah's ancestor Enoch had also "walked with God," and was taken up by God without needing to die (Gen. 5:24).

As the last man of the old age and the first of the new, as the writers portray it, Noah is the last person in the Bible who is said to have walked with God, though the prophet Micah still upheld that ideal (Mic. 6:8).

The Priestly writer then supplements his earlier genealogy from 5:25-32 by introducing Noah's sons Shem, Ham, and Japheth (vv. 9-10). The writer explains again God's motives for sending the flood (vv. 11-13), and provides instructions for building the ark and filling it with two of each kind of animal, plus food (vv. 14-21).

Mesopotamian stories are written as if the high gods had sworn the lower gods to secrecy about the plan, but a lower god known as Enki or Ea cared for humans and provided an indirect warning to a certain man known variously as Ziusudra, Artahasis, or Utnapishtim by whispering to the wall outside of his home. In contrast, Gen. 6:13 insists that God spoke directly to the righteous Noah, explaining what was coming and giving explicit directions for a rectangular houseboat large enough for his family, representative animals of every type, and sufficient rations for all. **[A strange boat]**

A cleansing flood
(7:1–8:14)

The J account of the flood itself begins in 7:1-5 with a second set of instructions about what animals to bring into the ark. Instead of two from each species, as in P, the J account says Noah was to bring seven pairs of all "clean" (edible) animals, and one pair of all "unclean" animals.

The extra "clean" animals would be used for sacrifices and to provide breeding stock for human consumption. We might expect the Priestly account to have included animals for sacrifice, but P was careful not to speak of rules for sacrifices and kosher eating prior to the giving of the law following the Exodus.

kind indefinitely, since they are mortal. They will remain for 120 more years." Either translation is possible.

The Yahwist offers an editorial comment in 6:5-6, noting that humans were not just irksome, as the Mesopotamian tales held, but exceedingly wicked. Repetitive wordplay is evident in v. 5: "The Lord saw that the wickedness of man was great on the earth, and that *every* intent of the thoughts of his heart was *only* evil *continually*."

God's heart was not piqued, but mournful: "And the LORD was sorry that he had made man on the earth, and he was grieved in his heart. So the LORD said, 'I will blot out from the earth the human beings I have created— people together with animals and creeping things and birds of the air, for I am sorry that I have made them'" (6:6-7).

The decision to send a flood seems as much for humanity's own sake as for God's divine sense of ethics, as a world so depraved would not be a good place for people to live.

One human, however, stood out from the rest: "Noah found grace in the eyes of the Lord" (6:8). That observation, from the Yahwist, is followed by the Priestly writer's introduction to the flood story in 6:9-13. Noah was a *tsadîq*, the text says, a righteous man, "blameless (*tamîm*) in his generation." The word *tamîm* suggests a state of complete integrity. Moreover, Noah "walked with God." No greater praise could be offered. The Priestly writer claimed that

The story includes two accounts of boarding the ark (7:7, 10 [J] and 7:8-9, 11, 13-16a [P]), in addition to dual descriptions of the flood.

In J, the flood is a rain event lasting 40 days (7:4), while P describes it as a disturbance in the entire cosmic order. The word for "flood" is *mabbul*, which suggests the waters of chaos, not a simple flood. For P, "the fountains of the great deep burst forth, and the windows of the heavens were opened" (7:11). With water both spouting up and raining down, all of creation was threatened by a return to chaos.

The Yahwist's account seems to assume that the waters began to subside immediately after the rain ceased, so the total length of the flood event would be about 61 days (40 days of rain plus three weeks in which Noah experimented with releasing birds [8:6-12]).

The Priestly writer claimed that the waters "swelled on the earth" for 150 days (7:24) before God closed the windows of the heavenly firmament and blocked the subterranean waters, then sent a wind that caused the water to recede over several months before the ark grounded on Mount Ararat, with months to go before the land was dry enough for the ark's passengers to depart, a year and 10 days from the beginning of the flood (8:1-5, 13-14).

A gracious God
(8:15-22)

Noah had found grace before the flood (6:8), and later "God remembered Noah" and all that were with him in the ark (8:1).

The flood's aftermath is described in both the Priestly (8:15-19) and Yahwist (8:20-22) versions. Both people and animals were sent out to "be fruitful and multiply upon the earth" (8:17).

The Yahwist focuses on the theological impact of the flood, as he describes Noah's initial offering of sacrifices from every acceptable bird and animal (8:20). Yahweh took notice of the sacrifice and "smelled the pleasing odor" (8:21). Unlike the Babylonian flood story, in which Utnapishtim offered sacrifices and the "gods swarmed like flies" through the smoke due to hunger, Yahweh responded with pleasure by promising an ongoing relationship with humans, despite their sinful nature. For the Yahwist, God understood that destroying all but one family had not changed human nature: "for the inclination of the human heart is evil from youth" (8:21).

The reported commitment not to curse the earth again is not said aloud, even to Noah, but in God's heart. We note that J does not say that Yahweh promised not to curse humans, but only that God would not curse the ground. Israel's covenant theology assumed that humans were fully subject to divine blessing or cursing (Deuteronomy 28, for example).

Humans would remain responsible for the created order, but God promised to guarantee orderly seasons "as long as the earth endures" (Gen. 8:22).

A new start
(9:1-17)

A Priestly account of God's response follows, with the promise of a new day. The command to "be fruitful and multiply and fill the earth" is repeated (9:1, 7), but the Edenic peace between humans and animals came to an end. Animals would now fear humans, as humans were granted permission to eat their flesh but not their blood, which was to be reserved for God as the author of all life (9:2-4).

The *lex talionis* ("an eye for an eye") command of 8:5-6 demonstrates the value of human life by declaring a severe penalty for murder. This reflects an early belief that God sanctioned blood vengeance. The practice was also found in Mesopotamian law codes and reappears in the Hebrew Bible, though Jesus questioned it (Matt. 5:38-48), calling for forgiveness rather than vengeance.

A new "covenant," to use P's language, is described in 9:8-17, but it was more of a promise than a covenant, and it is not mentioned anywhere else in the Old Testament. No human responsibilities are described. Instead, it is a declaration of divine grace toward the earth, and a promise.

The Yahwist's version of a post-diluvian promise (8:21) was a pledge that God would not again curse the ground or destroy all living things. Here, P's version promises that God would never again destroy the earth with a flood.

As a sign of the "covenant," according to P, God put a "bow in the clouds" as a comforting reminder, so humans would not fear another flood. We understand this, naturally, as a rainbow, though Hebrew has no specific word for that spectral phenomenon. The word for "bow" commonly indicates a weapon, and the ancients often imagined weather gods shooting lightning bolts toward the earth, but the bow was now pointed away from the earth, as a sign of peace.

Significantly, the bow is portrayed as a reminder to God, not humans, of the divine commitment not to destroy again by means of a flood.

What can we learn from these odd and ancient stories? They declare, first, that God's rule over creation is adaptable and open to changing circumstances on the earth.

We are reminded of the perils of sin and the reality of judgment, but also find the ultimate triumph of grace and redemption for sinful humanity.

The story also suggests an attempt to understand competing values in the heart of God. God is portrayed as wiping out every person on earth save Noah and his family, but of being grieved by the action and determined to work redemptively for humans to survive despite their many failures.

The story also speaks to the importance of obedience, even under difficult circumstances. God's offer of grace calls for human cooperation. Noah's willingness to wait for God's direction before leaving the ark also says something about the importance of patience before God.

The story reminds readers that the future of the earth and all who live on it are interconnected. Humans are given responsibility for caring for the planet in all its aspects, from its animal life to the atmosphere.

Finally, the story speaks to the importance of hope amid our own troubles. We may at times feel overwhelmed or under water, but God's redemptive care persists despite our troubled circumstances.

The Hardest Question
Was the flood story borrowed from Mesopotamia?

While we cannot demonstrate priority, the biblical flood story undoubtedly shows points of contact with Mesopotamian traditions about a punitive flood sent by the gods, and they were far older – at least in written form – than the biblical flood narratives.

Ancient Israel shared much in terms of a common cultural background with their neighbors. Abraham reportedly came from "Ur of the Chaldees," which may refer to the ancient city of Ur in Sumeria (now near Basra, in southern Iraq), or from a northern site now called Urfa, in southeastern Turkey. Genesis 11 says that Abraham's family moved and spent many years in the northern Mesopotamian city of Haran.

Isaac's wife Rebekah came from Haran, and Jacob returned to spend decades in the same Mesopotamian city.

In addition to stories of Mesopotamian links with the ancestors, the people of Judah spent 50 years or more in Babylonian exile, scattered in settlements across the region. The Israelites would have had multiple exposures to Mesopotamian legends about the ancient past.

The oldest of the flood stories was written in Sumerian. Its fragmentary remains speak of how the gods grew angry at the humans they had created to build cities and maintain the canals for them, and decided to send a flood that would drown them. Enki, known as the god of fresh water and a patron of wisdom, felt compassion for the humans. To avoid offending the other gods, he approached the home of Ziusudra, a priest (or possibly the king) of the city of Shuruppak, and whispered the plan outside a thin wall so the pious priest would hear him. Ziusudra then heeded Enki's warning and built a large boat for himself, his family, and a number of representative animals.

The story holds that "all the windstorms, exceedingly powerful, attacked as one, at the same time, the flood swept over the cult centers" for seven days and nights (translation by Samuel Noah Kramer, *History Begins at Sumer* [Doubleday, 1959], 153). When the waters had receded, Ziusudra opened a window and saw the rays of Utu (the sun god) shining into the boat and drying the waters from the earth. In gratitude, Ziusudra killed an ox and worshiped Utu. He then bowed before the high gods Anu and Enlil, who gave him life "like that of a god" in an idyllic place known as the land of Dilmun.

The Babylonian version exists in multiple, but similar versions, with the hero's name varying from Atrahasis to Utnapishtim, who appears in the famed Gilgamesh epic. In that account, the high god Enlil was angry because humans were making too much noise and disturbing his sleep, so he decided to destroy them with a flood. He ordered the other gods to keep the plan secret, but Ea (an alternate name for Enki) went to Shuruppak and whispered the secret to the walls of Utnapishtim's reed hut. Utnapishtim heard the warning and followed Ea's advice to build a huge boat in the shape of a giant cube, an acre in size, with six decks, to which he brought "all the living creatures along with his wife, a pilot for the boat, and some workmen."

The flood lasted seven days and was so great that it frightened even the gods before the boat came to rest on a mountain called Nisir. Unable to see from the boat, Utnapishtim released a series of birds to determine the state of the earth:

The seventh day when it came,
I brought out a dove, I let it loose:
Off went the dove but then it returned,
there was no place to land, so back it came to me.
I brought out a swallow, I let it loose:
Off went the swallow but then it returned,
There was no place to land, so back it came to me.
I brought out a raven, I let it loose:
Off went the raven, it saw the waters receding,
finding food, bowing and bobbing, it did not come back to me.

(From Gilgamesh Tablet XI, Standard Babylonian, lines 147-156. Translation by Andrew George, *The Epic of Gilgamesh* [Penguin, 2003], cited by Christopher B Hays, *Hidden Riches: A Sourcebook for the Comparative Study of the Hebrew Bible and the Ancient Near East* [Westminster John Knox, 2014], 80).

As Utnapishtim offered sacrifices, the gods realized how hungry they were with no humans to feed them by offering sacrifices. They smelled the aroma and "gathered like flies around the man making sacrifices." Enlil's anger was unappeased, but Ea convinced him to be merciful, and he granted immortality to Utnapishtim and his wife.

The biblical flood story contains obvious similarities along with distinct differences as the Babylonians told the story from the perspective of their own deities. Given their shared background, it should come as no surprise that the Hebrews had their own version of a flood story. More precisely, they had two: as noted in the study above, differing stories preserved by the Yahwist and the Priestly writer were editorially intertwined in the biblical account.

Both the Sumerian flood story and some early versions of the Babylonian account date at least as far back as 2000 BCE, though they continued to evolve. The most complete version of the Gilgamesh account comes from an Assyrian composition recorded on 12 tablets from the seventh century BCE. Though oral traditions may be older, the actual writing of the sources behind the book of Genesis probably ranges from the ninth to the fifth centuries BCE.

Ninth Sunday after Epiphany / Season after Pentecost: Proper 4

Optional First Reading
Deuteronomy 11:18-28 (RCL 11:18-21, 26-28)

A Call to Remember

You shall put these words of mine in your heart and soul, and you shall bind them as a sign on your hand,
and fix them as an emblem on your forehead. (Deut. 11:18)

Why do observant Jews adorn every external door to their homes or businesses with a little rectangular box, perched at an angle? Why do Orthodox Jewish men sometimes wrap long leather strips containing black leather boxes around their heads while praying?

Today's text is one of several that explain these customs. For more, read on.

A sign of remembrance
(vv. 18-21)

The optional Old Testament reading for the day is part of a lengthy sermon that was probably written in the late seventh century, but was attributed to Moses. It derives from one of several sermons Moses is said to have preached to the Israelites as they camped east of the Jordan following 40 years of wandering in the wilderness after their escape from Egyptian slavery.

The sermon is based on a tradition that God and Israel entered a covenant agreement at Mount Sinai (often called Mount Horeb by the Elohist and in Deuteronomy). God had issued the Ten Commandments and promised that, if Israel proved to be obedient, God would cherish and bless them as a special people (Exodus 19–20).

The Deuteronomistic writers took this covenant idea to extreme lengths, promising rich blessings for obedience and threatening woeful curses for disobedience. Moses' purported sermons recite the Ten Commandments in

> **The Shema:** Deuteronomy 6:4-5, one of the most important texts in Jewish life, is known as the "*Shema*" (pronounced "*shmáh*) after the first word of the text, an imperative verb that means "listen" or "hear."
>
> "Hear, O Israel: The LORD is our God, the LORD alone. You shall love the LORD your God with all your heart, and with all your soul, and with all your might."

5:1-21 and recall them in 10:1-7, with various commentary providing much of the structure for the book.

The content of Deuteronomy is very repetitive, as if the author or authors were trying to hammer home their insistence on obedience by repeating promises, threats, and appeals again and again.

Deuteronomy 11 begins with a call to "love the LORD your God" and "keep his charge, his decrees, his ordinances, and his commandments always" (v. 1). Here and in similar texts, "love" is better understood as "loyalty." The overall pattern of Deuteronomy follows that of ancient suzerainty treaties made between a conquering king and vassal nations. They call for the new vassals to "love" the king, but they clearly do not expect a defeated people to have warm affection for their conquerors. They do, however, expect loyalty rather than rebellion.

Verses 2-7 recall the former captives' deliverance from Egypt, and vv. 8-12 insist that obedience will be required if the people are to occupy Canaan. Verses 13-17 contain the promise of rain and fertility for the land if the people obey, but threaten drought and disaster if the people turn after other gods.

This brings us to today's text, which repeats previous instructions from Deut. 6:8-9, where they follow the familiar command to "love the LORD your God with all your heart, and with all your soul, and with all your might" (6:5).

[The *Shema*]

Both texts suggest the use of mementos designed as aids to remembrance, here described as follows: "You shall put these words of mine in your heart and soul, and you shall bind them as a sign (*'ōt*) on your hand, and fix them as an emblem (*tôtafōt*) on your forehead. Teach them to your children, talking about them when you are at home and when you are away, when you lie down and when you rise. Write them on the doorposts of your house and on your gates, so that your days and the days of your children may be multiplied in the land that the LORD swore to your ancestors to give them, as long as the heavens are above the earth" (vv. 18-21).

Both texts reflect a tradition associated with the origin of the Passover, a story that appears in conjunction with the Israelites' departure from Egypt. Observance of the ritual was said to "serve for you as a sign (*'ōt*) on your hand and as a reminder (*zikrôn*) on your forehead, so that the teaching of the LORD may be on your lips; for with a strong hand the LORD brought you out of Egypt" (Exod. 13:9).

The theme is repeated with slight variations a few verses later: "It shall serve as a sign (*'ōt*) on your hand and as an emblem (*tôtafōt*) on your forehead that by strength of hand the LORD brought us out of Egypt" (Exod. 13:16).

Deuteronomy 6:8-9 calls for parents to teach the words of the *shema* to their children, and to "Bind them as a sign (*'ōt*) on your hand, fix them as an emblem (*tôtafōt*) on your forehead, and write them on the doorposts of your house and on your gates."

We have no way of knowing how these commands were understood or followed in ancient Israel, especially prior to the exile. As with the Passover, the "sign" and "emblem" appear to be metaphorical. Reciting and teaching the *sh'ma* served as a sign on the hand and a mark on one's home that the residents there were faithful to God.

In a similar way, the female lover in the Song of Songs asked her partner to "Set me as a seal upon your heart, as a seal upon your arm" (Song 8:6a), using the imagery of a cylinder seal to symbolize remembrance.

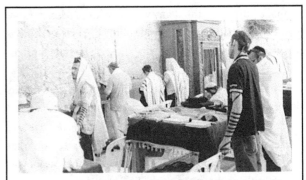

Tefillin: Orthodox Jews, especially the Ultra-Orthodox, continue the pattern of wearing *tefillin* during prayer times, along with special prayer shawls. Here, some are praying near the Western Wall in Jerusalem.

By the first century, however, the most orthodox of Jews had begun interpreting the commands quite literally. When praying, they bound leather boxes to their foreheads and upper arms using long leather strips. Inside the boxes were small rolls of parchment bearing the texts cited above from Exod. 13:1-16, Deut. 6:5-9, and Deut. 11:13-21. The implements were called phylacteries or *tefillin*, from the word for prayer, *tefillâ*.

Jesus noted that some people appeared to flaunt their faith in a pretentious way, wearing their religion on their sleeve, as it were, and criticized scribes and Pharisees who didn't follow their own teachings but "do all their deeds to be seen by others; for they make their phylacteries broad and their fringes long" (Matt. 23:5).

Orthodox Jews of today continue the practice, fashioning the *tefillin* of black leather with the straps following a prescribed pattern of wraps around the arm and fingers of the left hand. [*Tefillin*]

The instruction to "write them on the doorposts of your house and on your gates" would remind residents and their guests of the challenge to live in obedience to Yahweh. Though not explicitly stated, the practice could also recall the blood of the Passover lamb to be placed on the doorposts of Hebrew homes so their firstborn would not fall victim to the tenth plague striking the Egyptians (Exod. 12:21-27).

In contemporary life, many Jews also attach rectangular boxes of various shapes, often quite decorative, to the doorframes of all exterior doors, including interior doors to hotel rooms in Israel. Known as *mezuzahs*, these ideally would contain the same scriptures, though many serve the symbolic purpose without any writing within. *Mezuzahs* are typically attached to the right side of the door frame, always at a slight angle to indicate that no one is fully upright before God.

In addition to the physical reminders, the related texts also emphasize the importance of teaching the *sh'ma* and the commandments to the children "so that your days and the days of your children may be multiplied in the land that the LORD swore to your ancestors to give them, as long as the heavens are above the earth" (v. 21).

Note that the promise was conditional, as God had reportedly promised the land for all time, but possession of the land was contingent on obedience. Both training and allegiance would be necessary if the people were to prosper and to persist in the land.

The sermon from which this text is excerpted is credited to Moses before the people ever crossed into the land, but it was written after the northern kingdom of Israel had been conquered by the Assyrians and its population dispersed. A primary purpose of the sermon, when written, was to warn the people of Judah that a similar fate could befall them if they did not prove faithful.

Judah fell to the Babylonians about 125 years later, and the promised land was no longer their home.

A promise of land
(vv. 22-25)

Verses 22-25, not included in the lectionary reading, is yet another strong reminder that the promise of God's help in taking the land would be conditional. Note how many words of emphasis accompany the promise: "If you will *diligently* keep *this entire* commandment that I am commanding you, loving the LORD your God, walking in *all* his ways, and *holding fast* to him …" (v. 22, italics added). [A double positive]

Only with such obedience could they be assured that "then the LORD will drive out all these nations before you, and you will dispossess nations larger and mightier than yourselves" (v. 23).

There were no "nations," in the modern sense of the word, to drive out: a better translation would be "peoples." The Hebrew word *goyîm* could be translated as "nations" or "peoples." In this case, it refers to the various ethnic groups or small political entities that occupied the land, most of

> **A double positive:** Many languages, including Hebrew, allow double negatives for emphasis. Proper English grammar decries their use, but we often use double negatives for emphasis: "I can't get no satisfaction," sang the Rolling Stones. Or we may have heard someone say "There ain't no way …"
>
> Hebrew also used a type of "double positive" for strong emphasis, combining the infinitive absolute of a verb with its conjugated finite form. In v. 22, the Hebrew *'im-shâmar tishm'rûn* uses two forms of the verb "to guard" or "to keep." What looks like "if keeping, you will keep" has the sense of "if you will *diligently* observe" (NRSV) or "if you will *carefully* keep" (NIV11, NET).

them serving as vassal states beholden to Egypt, which exercised considerable control over the area.

During the Late Bronze Age, political structures in Canaan consisted of small city-states in which centers such as Hazor, Gezer, Lachish, and others existed as walled cities that controlled an area that could extend for 10–20 miles around it. The leader of the city was called a "king," and in the eyes of the Hebrews, each city-state constituted a nation.

If the Hebrews numbered even a tenth of the population attributed to the wilderness travels in Numbers, they could have overwhelmed any of those city-states. The statement that the various entities were "larger and mightier than yourselves" points to the situation that more likely reflected reality: the Hebrews were not really that numerous.

Nor were the Israelites as organized or well-equipped as the settled populations who inhabited the land and were practiced in war. Still, Moses promised that strict obedience would win them such divine favor that "Every place on which you set foot shall be yours," such that their territory would extend from the southern wilderness to Lebanon in the north, and from the River Euphrates in the east to the Mediterranean Sea in the west (v. 24).

Victory would not be due to the Israelites' military prowess, but to divine aid: "the LORD your God will put the fear and dread of you on all the land on which you set foot, as he promised you" (v. 25).

A blessing and a curse
(vv. 26-28)

The sermon continues with a section on blessing and cursing that serves as both a summary reminder and an introduction to the following section. The theme is unchanged: obedience leads to blessing, and rebellion brings a curse. The land and the promise await, but only if the people prove to be faithful—something they continually struggled to do.

Can Christian people find profit in this time-conditioned promise to a group of ancient Israelites when we are neither ancient nor Israelite? Many modern believers make the mistake of reading texts like this as if the promise of blessing and cursing applies to contemporary Christians. Prosperity preachers encourage such beliefs, emphasizing promises of blessings with little focus on the call for obedience or the flipside potential of cursing.

The conditional promises and threats were understood to be central aspects of a binding covenant between God and Israel. Christians are also challenged to live in relationship with God, but one that is based on grace rather than commandments, ordinances, decrees, statutes, or other synonyms for laws and rules to be obeyed. Believers are challenged to follow Christ's "new commandment" to love one another. We are assured of abundant and eternal life – but there are no promises of earthly prosperity or military victory.

Our best entry to the text may be to consider the directive for God-followers to institute daily reminders of their faith and their responsibilities. What are effective ways of doing that? Some may find that wearing a cross on a necklace or carrying one in their pocket could serve as a helpful memory jog. A candle in the window or a cross in the yard might label a house as a place where Christians dwell, but such practices can also become as rote and meaningless as wearing *tefillin* for show or mounting a *mezuzah* by the door only because it is culturally expected.

Physical symbols can be helpful, but daily habits are what make a real difference. Regular prayer, Bible study, and worship attendance are more likely to inspire faithful living. A conscious effort to live each day with a "Jesus worldview" will improve the chances of showing the kind of love Jesus calls for. What reminders work for you?

The Hardest Question
How does Deuteronomy reflect ancient treaty practices?

Elements of the book of Deuteronomy, and also a more compact covenant ceremony in Joshua 24, bear a strong similarity to ancient near eastern suzerainty treaties commonly struck between conquering kings and their new vassals. Examples commonly cited can be found in both Hittite and Assyrian documents.

In these treaties, the triumphant king (the "suzerain") sets the conditions for future peace between himself and his subjects. It is clear that the king makes the rules: the vassals choose to accept the conditions and live in peace, or to reject them and run the risk of further humiliation.

Such treaties had six typical elements:

1. The ruling king is identified by name.
2. The king's "gracious acts" to the conquered are named.
3. The vassals' covenant obligations, including "to love the king," are enumerated.
4. The document is to be placed in a public sanctuary and read periodically.
5. The gods of the parties involved are invoked as witnesses.
6. Blessings are promised for obedience to the treaty, and penalties are listed for those who rebel.

For Yahweh and Israel, since the covenant was entered voluntarily rather than through conquest, and since the covenant was between Israel and their one God, obvious adaptations had to be made, but the underlying structure is still apparent.

In Joshua 24, the Lord (Yahweh) is identified as the ruling power in v. 2, and God's great acts of redemption and grace are recited in vv. 2-13. God's kindness to the patriarchs (vv. 2-4), during the Exodus from Egypt (vv. 5-7), in the Transjordan area (vv. 8-10 and in the conquest of Canaan, vv. 11-13) are all remembered. Verses 14-15 issue a call for Israel to "revere the LORD and serve him in sincerity and in faithfulness," and vv. 16-18 constitute the people's promise to do so.

Since multiple gods could not be called to witness, the people served as witnesses against themselves (v. 22). Joshua reportedly "wrote these words in the book of the law of God; and he took a large stone, and set it up there under the oak in the sanctuary of the LORD" (v. 26), with the stone to serve as an ongoing witness of the covenant (v. 27).

The book of Deuteronomy is both longer and more repetitive, but it contains the same elements of covenant making.

Second Reading
Psalm 46*

When All Else Fails

Be still, and know that I am God! I am exalted among the nations, I am exalted in the earth. (Ps. 46:10)

Few psalms are more devoted to pure thanksgiving than Psalm 46. Reading it offers an appropriate reminder of how important it is to recognize how much we have to be thankful for, and how many blessings should inspire gratitude. Some of us have far more in the way of material goods or money in the bank than others, but we may have observed that some of the poorest people are the richest in thanks. Perhaps it is because, when one has so little, every blessing is appreciated more. Or, perhaps those who are not distracted by bank accounts, big houses, and expensive toys find it easier to stay in touch with the daily blessings of food, health, and life itself.

When you stop to think about thanksgiving, what comes first to your mind?

A refuge
(vv. 1-3)

The poet behind Psalm 46 thought first of security: those who are at home with God can face even cataclysmic events without fear. The psalm expresses profound confidence and inner security, something the wealthiest of people can lack. It's no wonder, then, that Psalm 46 has become a favorite "go to" text for those who face troubling days when life experience seems to be preaching a contrary message.

The superscription of the psalm is interesting but not overly helpful. It is one of 11 psalms attributed to the "Korahites" or "sons of Korah," who served various

> **Earthquakes:** Israel's prophets also called on the imagery of earthquakes to speak of the power of God. Isaiah of Jerusalem predicted a coming day of judgment: For the windows of heaven are opened, and the foundations of the earth tremble. "The earth is utterly broken, the earth is torn asunder, the earth is violently shaken. The earth staggers like a drunkard, it sways like a hut; its transgression lies heavy upon it, and it falls, and will not rise again" (Isa. 24:19-20; cp. Hag. 2:6).
>
> In contrast, Isaiah of the exile believed that God would show mercy to a faithful remnant. In words that could have inspired a poem such as Psalm 46, he promised: "For the mountains may depart and the hills be removed, but my steadfast love shall not depart from you, and my covenant of peace shall not be removed, says the LORD, who has compassion on you" (Isa. 54:10).

functions in the temple, from gate keeping to "the work of the service" (1 Chron. 9:17-19). Psalms 42, 44–49, 84–85, and 87–88 are all attributed to the "sons of Korah."

The superscription, an ancient notation not to be considered an original part of the psalm, includes instructions for the musical director, perhaps related to the tune or style of the music. Unfortunately, "according to Alamoth, a song," is too cryptic to be informative. The word *ʿălāmôth* means "young women," but whether that describes a tune, a style, or that young women are preferred singers is unclear.

What is clear is that the psalmist is supremely confident in God's care, no matter what comes: "God is our refuge and strength, a very present help in trouble" (v. 1).

---

*Psalm 46 is also read for Proper 29 in Year C.

That introduction is followed by a celebration of God as a refuge against natural disasters (vv. 2-3), a section that honors God's protection against other nations (vv. 4-7), and a closing meditation that brings the two together (vv. 8-11). The image of God as a refuge begins the first section and concludes the other two (vv. 1, 7, and 11). **[Earthquakes]**

The Jordan Rift Valley, between Israel and the Palestinian West Bank to the west and Jordan to the east, marks a fault line that runs from the Jordan River's origin north of the Hula Valley, through the Sea of Galilee, the Dead Sea, and on through the Arabah and the Gulf of Aqaba, then as far as Mozambique in southern Africa. It is a deep rift: land around the Dead Sea is the lowest point below sea level on earth (about 1,400 feet), and the deepest part of the Dead Sea is another 1,000 feet below. The fault remains seismically active, and earthquakes have been occurring since ancient times. Strong temblors in 1837 and 1927 reportedly killed about 4,000 and 300 people, respectively. Newspapers in Israel and Jordan regularly report minor quakes felt throughout the area.

The New Testament speaks of an earthquake powerful enough to split rocks and open tombs when Jesus was crucified (Matt. 27:50-53). Notably, the prophet Amos dated the beginning of his ministry to "two years before the earthquake," a memorable temblor that probably occurred around 760 BCE.

We cannot know if the psalmist had experienced this earthquake or another one, or if he knew of them only from stories passed down, but he felt no trepidation at the possibility of natural disaster. Trusting God as a refuge and help in times of trouble, he insisted: "Therefore we will not fear, though the earth should change, though the mountains shake in the heart of the sea; though its waters roar and foam, though the mountains tremble with its tumult" (vv. 2-3).

The psalmist draws a picture of a major quake that changes the landscape and sends mountainous landslides tumbling into the sea, resulting in massive tidal waves that crash back against the shore and threaten to wash away coastal residents who weren't already buried beneath the rubble. **[Mountains and seas]**

The poet's words should not be read as confidence that God would never allow the faithful to be harmed by temblors or tsunamis, but as an assertion that God has control over the forces of chaos, typically symbolized by the churning sea,

Mountains and seas: On December 26, 2004, in one of the worst natural disasters in recorded history, a powerful earthquake off the coast of Indonesia spawned a series of tsunamis that killed an estimated 230,000 people. Most of the deaths occurred in Indonesia, with Sri Lanka, India, and Thailand also suffering great loss of life.

Although Sri Lanka was nearly 1500 miles from the epicenter of the earthquake, the massive tsunami washed ashore with such force that it demolished buildings, tossed train cars from their tracks, and drowned thousands who lived in towns and villages along the shore.

The psalmist understood that the danger of earthquakes may arise from the sea as well as the earth.

which no human can conquer. As an obedient worshiper, the psalmist does not fear whatever God may choose to bring.

The psalmist's confidence in God grew in part from Hebrew beliefs about creation. Genesis 1 imagines a universe consisting of nothing but dark chaos waters before God began the creative work of bringing order to the primordial world: light from dark, land from sea, and earth from sky. The psalmist believed that God had conquered chaos – which periodically reared its head in the form of earthquakes or tidal waves.

A happy stream: Hezekiah's Tunnel, also known as the Siloam Tunnel, was dug during King Hezekiah's reign, according to 2 Kgs. 20:20.

Though the Gihon Spring was already protected by a strong tower and was inside the city's outer wall, channeling the water through the underground tunnel provided easier access for the city's inhabitants, and made it impossible for besieging forces to take advantage of the water. Advancing Assyrian forces that had already conquered strong cities – including Lachish, second only to Jerusalem in Judah – threatened to conquer Jerusalem, too. Hezekiah responded by blocking off the Gihon Spring and bringing it entirely into the city, according to 2 Chronicles 32. The date would have been in the mid-to-late 720s BCE.

In the photo, Professor Barry Jones of Campbell University Divinity School stands knee deep in water near the end of Hezekiah's Tunnel, where the tunnel widens and the water enters an outdoor channel on the way to the Pool of Siloam, a large and beautiful pool surrounded by wide steps.

The Hebrews were not the only ancient people who had creation stories in which chaos waters played a role. The Babylonian creation myth claimed that Marduk, one of many gods spawned by the mother god Tiamat and her partner Apsu, entered the chaotic sea controlled by Tiamat and slew her, using her body to create the earth and sky.

A river
(vv. 4-7)

The psalmist believed that God's power over the forces of nature also extends to dominion over human nations, and this is the subject of vv. 4-7. Having spoken of waters and mountains in the previous verses, the poet skillfully transitions to the next section by shifting to another mountain, a river, and "the city of God."

The imagery of the verse is captivating: "There is a river whose streams make glad the city of God, the holy habitation of the Most High" (v. 4). The meaning of the verse, however, is a bit confusing.

On the one hand, a reader may assume that the city is Jerusalem, where the Hebrews believed God's presence, in some fashion, dwelt above the cherubim in the Holy of Holies. There is, however, no river in Jerusalem, which sits atop a low mountain. It is possible that the psalmist is speaking metaphorically, for though Jerusalem is perched on a steep crest and has no river, at the base of the hill is the strong Gihon Spring, which gushes clear water from the earth and provides the city with adequate water. In Hezekiah's time, a deep tunnel was cut through bedrock, bringing the spring's water into the city, where it fed the pool of Siloam. That dependable stream surely brought gladness to the city. [**A happy stream**]

Imagery from both Canaanite mythology and early traditions about Melchizedek may also have influenced the picture. The Canaanites believed that the high god El sat enthroned at the head of two streams on lofty Mount Zaphon, a mythical mountain in the north, sometimes identified with Mount Hermon, whose snowy heights feed the Jordan River with meltwater.

The imagery of a stream emerging from God's throne also appears in Ezekiel's vision of heaven (Ezek. 47:1-12), later adapted by the author of Revelation: "Then the angel showed me the river of the water of life, bright as crystal, flowing from the throne of God and of the Lamb"

(Rev. 22:1). Zechariah also prophesied of a day when "living waters shall flow out from Jerusalem" to both east and west, continuing in both the rainy winter and the dry summer season (Zech. 14:8).

We note that in v. 4, "the city of God" uses the title *'Elohîm* for God, while "holy habitation of the Most High" refers to God by the title *'Elyôn* (suggesting a "high" god). The story of Abraham and Melchizedek (Genesis 14) describes "King Melchizedek of Salem" as the "priest of God Most High." The term "Salem" almost certainly refers to Jerusalem, and "God Most High" translates *El 'Elyôn*. The Hebrews came to believe that *'El 'Elyôn* of "Salem" and Yahweh of Hosts, the God of Jacob (v. 7), must be the same God.

As far as our text is concerned, the poet's point is that because God dwells in the city (probably Jerusalem), "it shall not be moved; God will help it when the morning dawns" (v. 5). Other psalms also speak of forlorn believers finding help in the morning: "Weeping may linger for a night, but joy comes in the morning" (30:5). "Satisfy us in the morning with your steadfast love, so that we may rejoice and be glad all our days" (90:14). "My soul waits for the Lord more than those who watch for the morning, those who watch for the morning" (130:6).

Israel's narratives also celebrated victories that took place at dawn. As the Hebrews departed from Egypt and crossed the sea with the Egyptians in pursuit, it was at dawn that Moses stretched out his hand and the sea returned to its place, destroying the Egyptian army (Exod. 14:7). A more likely referent is a story in Isaiah, related to the same siege for which Hezekiah reportedly prepared the tunnel described above. According to Isa. 37:36, the besieged Israelites awoke one morning to find 185,000 Assyrians dead in their camp, victims of "the angel of the LORD."

The temple was in Jerusalem, and it is most likely that the psalmist was, too. He did not fear attacks from other nations, because he did not believe God would allow the city to be conquered. The psalmist must have been confident that the people in his day were living up to their covenant obligations, because God's promises of victory were conditioned on Israel's obedience. **[Safe in Jerusalem?]**

The psalmist again flashes poetic skill by using some of the same words to describe the nations that he had previously used for the earthquake-stricken mountains and sea.

Safe in Jerusalem? The belief that God would always protect Jerusalem was popular, but not entirely correct. God's promise of protection was always conditioned on Israel's obedience. Jeremiah preached against those who thought they were safe from attack because they were close to the temple – even though they were guilty of oppressing their neighbors and failing to keep the law. Jeremiah told them:

"Thus says the LORD of hosts, the God of Israel: Amend your ways and your doings, and let me dwell with you in this place. Do not trust in these deceptive words: 'This is the temple of the LORD, the temple of the LORD, the temple of the LORD'" (Jer. 7:3-4).

In 587 BCE, both the temple and the city of Jerusalem were destroyed by the Babylonian army of King Nebuchadnezzar.

The city of God does not "totter" (better "slip" or "slide"), as the tottering mountains slid into the sea, but "the kingdoms totter" and fall. As the seas "roared," so "the nations are in an uproar" (using a different form of the same verb). When God "utters his voice" – a reference to the sound of thunder – "the earth melts," as do God's enemies.

The section concludes with a confession that "The LORD of hosts is with us; the God of Jacob is our refuge" (v. 7). The same confession, which echoes v. 1, will be repeated at the end of the psalm, in v. 11.

A reminder
(vv. 8-11)

The psalmist closes by bringing together God's rule over both the earth and its people. God has brought desolations on the earth (v. 8) while bringing wars to an end, presumably in Israel's favor. In language reminiscent of the "swords into plowshares" prophesies of Micah and Isaiah (Mic. 4:1-4, Isa. 2:2-4), the psalmist speaks of Yahweh breaking and burning the weapons of war to bring peace to the earth (v. 9).

This brings us to v. 10, a much-loved and often quoted but generally misunderstood verse. "Be still, and know that I am God! I am exalted in the earth." We usually read the verse as an invitation to pause in our busy days and meditate on the goodness of God, but in context – whether addressed to Israel or the defeated nations – it calls for humans to cease their striving ("Stop it!"), recognize that

God is king, and let God be about God's work of ruling the earth and bringing peace.

This does not diminish the importance of being still and pondering our place in God's world – its main purpose is to remind us of our place: God is king; we are not.

The Hardest Question
What does "Selah" mean?

Each of the three sections of Psalm 46 (vv. 3, 7, and 11) ends with the word *selâ*, a Hebrew term that is transliterated into English letters, but not translated into English words. The reason for this is straightforward: we don't know what it means.

The word – which was probably pronounced "*I-la*" – appears 71 times in Psalms (scattered among 39 different psalms) and another three times in Habakkuk 3, which is a psalm. It may appear at the end of a stanza or section (as in today's example or in Ps. 32:4, 5, and 7; at the end of a psalm; or even at the end of a quotation [Ps. 44:9]).

The term is scattered throughout the book of Psalms, suggesting that it was in use over a long period of time. Whether it was original to each psalm or added by a later hand is unclear.

Some commentators have suggested that the term means something similar to "Amen," another Hebrew word that we don't translate, though we know it's a sign of confirmation or agreement. But, there are many places where an "Amen" would be appropriate that it does not appear.

The most likely suggestion is that *selâ* has some musical significance. We must remember that the psalms were written as poetry, and many of them, if not most, would have been sung in worship at the temple. In some cases, superscriptions supply a title or even the name of a tune (none of which is known).

The term appears most commonly in psalms that have titles, and most of those connect the psalm with David or one of the known temple singers such as Asaph. Three quarters of the hymns with titles in which *selâ* appears have the indication "to the choirmaster."

But if the term has musical significance, what is it? Some think it might mark the spot for an instrumental interlude, a pause for reflection, or even a clash of cymbals.

A tradition reflected among early Palestinian Jews and some Christians was that it meant "forever," although the Hebrew Bible uses other terms when it clearly intends to suggest that concept.

At least one interpreter, Sigmund Mowinkel, proposed that it might indicate a place where worshipers were expected to lie prostrate before God.

One possible interpretation is that *selah* could be derived from the root *sll*, which means "to raise" or "lift up" – which could imply raising the voice, singing louder, or raising the volume of any instrumental accompaniment. This, however, is not certain.

We read from Psalms today and sometimes set them to modern music without any knowledge of the original tune, but still find them profitable. That the word "Selah" remains as mysterious as the tune named "The Deer of the Dawn" (Psalm 22) should not trouble us. It probably refers to an unknown musical instruction, and unless additional insight is forthcoming, we'll have to be satisfied with that.

(The above explanation leans heavily on Peter Craigie, *Psalms 1–50*, Word Biblical Commentary, vol. 15 [Word Books, 1983], 76–77, and on John Durham, "Psalms," in *The Broadman Bible Commentary*, vol. 4 [Broadman Press, 1971], 175.)

Though extensive treatments can be found in dictionaries or journal articles, all conclusions remain tentative, and most commentaries offer little attempt at explaining the term. Robert Alter's recent work states simply: "Though there is general agreement that this is a choral or musical notation, there is no way of determining the meaning or the etymology" (*The Book of Psalms: A Translation with Commentary* [W.W. Norton & Co., 2007], 8). Mitchell Dahood's massive contribution to the Anchor Bible likewise provides a single comment: "Selah. A liturgical direction; its meaning and etymology still elude scholars" (*Psalms 1–50*, [Doubleday, 1965], 21).

Ninth Sunday after Epiphany / Season after Pentecost: Proper 4

Optional Second Reading
Psalm 31 (RCL 31:1-5, 19-24)*

Refuge and Redemption

*Psalm 31:1-5, 5-15 is also read on the Fifth Sunday of Easter in Year A and for the Liturgy of the Palms on the Sixth Sunday of Lent in Years A, B, and C. Psalm 31:9-16 is read on that Sunday for the Liturgy of the Passion in Years A, B, and C. A commentary on Psalm 31 appears in Year A, Volume 2 of this resource, under the Sixth Sunday of Lent, Liturgy of the Passion.

Third Reading
Romans 1:16-17, 3:21b-31 (RCL 1:16-17, 3:22b-28 [29-31])

Hope for the Guilty

… all have sinned and fall short of the glory of God. (Rom. 3:23)

Most of us are well acquainted with guilt and shame. Some people may have a psychotic condition that leaves them unable to feel guilt, but even the holiest of us are unlikely to think we have met God's standard every day, in every way. We may have known people who suffered from excessive guilt, constantly feeling unworthy.

Today's text addresses the guilty, but also offers them hope. It begins with one of Paul's most familiar statements in 1:16-17, and then moves to an elaboration on the consequences of sin in 3:22b-28. Our study will continue through the end of the latter pericope in v. 31.

I am not ashamed
(1:16)

Paul understood shame, but there was one thing of which he was pointedly *not* ashamed: "For I am not ashamed of the gospel"; "it is the power of God for salvation to everyone who has faith, to the Jew first and also to the Greek.

By saying he is "not ashamed" of the gospel (good news), Paul is using a rhetorical figure of speech to emphasize his positive commitment to the gospel. We may also use negative words to stress a positive reality: if we want to stress how clean something is, we say it is "spotless." Likewise, a perfect diamond is "flawless." If a person is really nice, "there's not a mean bone in his body." For Paul to say "I am not ashamed of the gospel" is an emphatic way of saying "I'm more proud of the gospel than you can imagine."

Alexamenos and his god: This graffito, probably dating to about 200 CE, was scratched into a wall near Palatine Hill in Rome. Sadly, it is one of the earliest pictorial representations of Christ. Stone rubbing by Rodolfo Lanciani, 1898, Public Domain.

The Romans lived in a world that considered the gospel to be foolish. Some years ago, a bit of first-century graffiti was uncovered on an ancient stone wall. There was a crude drawing of a man kneeling before Christ on the cross, with the head of a donkey. An inscription said "Alexamenos worships (his) god." [**Alexamenos and his god**]

With this kind of ridicule, many early Christians were ashamed to profess their faith publicly, but not Paul. He was jeered for his faith, jailed for his faith, beaten for his faith, and run out of town for his faith, but through it all he continued to say "I am not ashamed of the gospel."

Paul's impetus for sharing the gospel was clear: "it is the power of God for salvation to everyone who has faith" (1:16b). Paul was like a research scientist who had just discovered a universal cure for cancer. He could not keep the good news to himself. He would burst if he did not share the gospel with every person in need of the saving knowledge it brought.

There is power in the gospel. The word Paul uses is *dynamis*, the root of our words "dynamic" and "dynamite." The gospel has power to shake us loose from sin-hardened ways and to bring us into relationship with the Lord of the universe that lasts through this life and beyond. We call that "salvation," and it is available to everyone who believes, and that is good news. It is not something to be ashamed of, but to be excited about.

The righteousness of God
(1:17)

Why was Paul not ashamed of the gospel? He explained: "For in it the righteousness of God is revealed through faith for faith; as it is written, 'The one who is righteous will live by faith'" (1:17). [**Martin Luther and faith**]

We know the words, but what did Paul mean by them? The salvation we experience is the result of the righteousness of God that is granted to us. In Hebrew thought, righteousness was not so much a moral quality as a legal standing. The Bible declares that God is righteous in every way. We know that none of us can attain moral perfection or righteous standing based on our own merits. Paul's great discovery was that God through Christ is willing to impute God's own righteous standing to those who believe (v. 17).

Some interpreters suggest that the phrase often translated as "from faith to faith" may mean something akin to "faith from first to last." One who comes into a relationship with God through faith can only continue that relationship in the same way – through faith.

The phrase can be translated differently, however, and its meaning is not necessarily self-evident, because the referents of "faith" are not clear. Charles Talbert has suggested that Paul intended to say salvation arises from/out of the faith/faithfulness of Christ and *for* the faith of humans. It is not a judicial decision, but a relational act (*Romans*, Smyth

---

Martin Luther and faith: The Reformer Martin Luther struggled with what Paul meant by "faith." In August of 1513, the University of Wittenburg professor offered a series of lectures on the book of Psalms. Despite being a professor of theology, he found his legalistic faith to be frustrating and empty. In his own words, he was engaged in an agonizing search "to find a gracious God."

Luther was enamored with a prayer from Ps. 31:1, "in thy righteousness deliver me," but he struggled to understand it. He had always thought of God's righteousness as his righteous judgment on sinners, so he thought of "condemnation" rather than "deliverance." Luther was so plagued by feelings of guilt that he would resort to fasting, hours of prayer, and even physical pain in seeking a sense of atonement. Some commentators claim that he went to confession so often that the monks on duty would hide when they saw him coming.

Ultimately, Luther began to study Paul's claim in Rom. 1:17 that "the righteousness of God is revealed through faith for faith; as it is written, 'The one who is righteous will live by faith.'" Later, Luther wrote:

> Night and day I pondered until ... I grasped the truth that the righteousness of God is that righteousness whereby, through grace and sheer mercy, he justifies us by faith. Thereupon I felt reborn and to have gone through open doors into paradise. The whole of scripture took on new meaning, and whereas before 'the righteousness of God' had filled me with hate, now it became to me inexpressibly sweet in greater love. This passage of Paul became to me a gateway into heaven.

(Drawn from F.F. Bruce, *Romans* [IVP Academic, 2008], 56-57 and James E. Hightower Jr., *Illustrating Paul's Letter to the Romans* [Baptist Sunday School Board, 1984], 13-15.)

& Helwys Bible Commentary [Smyth & Helwys, 2002], 41, 47). [**Righteousness**]

Paul's quotation of Hab. 2:4b has also been translated and interpreted in different ways. Does he mean "the one who is made righteous by faith will live (eternally)"? Or does he mean "The one who is already righteous will continue to live by faith"? Both statements are true. From the human standpoint, our experience of God's grace is a matter of faith from beginning to end.

Righteousness: Charles Talbert makes this observation about "righteousness" in Rom. 1:17: "In Paul, God who is righteous (= faithful) reveals His righteousness (= saving acts), resulting in justification (= salvation) of people. Of what does that salvation consist? In Romans, one sees it involves at least (1) acquittal/forgiveness of guilt, so that one is at peace with and able to stand before God at the Last Day; (2) freedom from sin's power and enablement to be faithful to God; (3) freedom from legalistic religion; (4) freedom from death's ultimacy; (5) participation in the people of God made up of Jew and Gentile who are justified through Christ; and (6) involvement in a distinctive lifestyle that reflects a transformed mind" (*Romans*, Smyth & Helwys Bible Commentary [Smyth & Helwys, 2002], 40).

The righteousness God grants
(3:21-31)

After considering the power of the gospel and the righteousness of God (1:1-17), Paul elaborated on the power of sin that affects every person and leaves us in such dire need of divine grace (1:18–3:20). Paul made it clear that all have sinned, even those who have the benefit of the law, but none are able to obey the law perfectly and thus find righteousness. This leads to the question: "Is there any hope?" Is there any way for sinful humans to experience the righteousness of God?

Paul answers that question, beginning with 3:21. The answer is a message of grace, a grace so unexpected and different from our everyday experience that it is difficult for us to comprehend.

Some years ago, when the investment firm of Smith-Barney needed a spokesperson for their television commercials, they chose John Huston. With his craggy looks, gray hair, and weathered voice, he convinced viewers that Smith-Barney earned money the old-fashioned way: "We *earn* it!" he said.

The theme reflected American values: we respect people who earn their wealth more than those who inherit it or have it given to them or win the lottery. Perhaps that is one reason why it is so hard for many persons to accept God's offer of *grace*. We want to be saved, but we want to *earn* it by our own works. To think it could be freely given seems like cheating, or too good to be true.

Paul declared the amazing truth that God has engineered the possibility of righteousness, despite human-

kind's penchant for sin. Both Jews and Gentiles are hopeless without God's grace, but God is gracious: Paul's use of "the righteousness of God" does not just describe divine holiness, but also the way in which God imputes righteousness to those who trust in Christ.

"But now, apart from law, the righteousness of God has been disclosed," Paul wrote, "and is attested by the law and the prophets, the righteousness of God through faith in Jesus Christ for all who believe" (3:21-22a).

None of us are righteous on our own: "all have sinned and fall short of the glory of God" (3:23), but those who believe "are now justified by his grace as a gift, through the redemption that is in Christ Jesus" (3:24).

The word "redemption" (*apolytrōseōs*) is a slave market term. Jesus paid a price to redeem us from slavery to sin. This text is often quoted in support of the "ransom theory" of the atonement. Similar ideas are found in 1 Cor. 6:20 ("buy"), Gal. 3:13 ("redeem"), and Acts 20:28 ("purchase").

There are other approaches to understanding the atonement, including the "moral influence" theory (Christ's self-sacrificial example calls us to righteousness) and the "Christus Victor" theory (Christ conquered Satan through his death and set sinners free). The ransom theory is similar to the view of Christ's work as a "penal substitutionary atonement," and in vv. 25-26 Paul turned to sacrificial imagery in a further attempt to explain the atonement.

There he speaks of Christ, "whom God put forward as a sacrifice of atonement by his blood, effective through faith. He did this to show his righteousness, because in his divine forbearance he had passed over the sins previously committed; it was to prove at the present time that he himself is righteous and that he justifies the one who has faith in Jesus" (3:25-26).

The word translated "atonement" is *hilastērion*. In the Septuagint (an early Greek translation of the Old Testament), it is the word used to describe the covering of the Ark of the Covenant (e.g., Exod. 25:17, 31:7), and often translated as "mercy seat." The only other appearance of the word in the New Testament is Heb. 9:5, which speaks of the "mercy seat" beneath the cherubim in the Old Testament tabernacle.

In the present verse, some interpreters translate the word as "propitiation" (KJV, NAS20). The CEB speaks of Jesus as "the place of sacrifice where mercy is found by means of his blood," and the NET says "God publicly displayed him at his death as the mercy seat accessible through faith." As the Israelites thought of themselves as meeting God and finding forgiveness on the Day of Atonement when the high priest went in before the mercy seat, so Paul sees God meeting us in Jesus' cross, to offer forgiveness of sin.

As a rather odd aside in vv. 25-26, Paul suggests that God had not fully judged those who lived before Christ in accordance with their sins, but had withheld punishment out of mercy so that Christ's sacrifice could also apply in retrospect to the faithful who had lived before him.

Lest his hearers think this statement nullified the Old Testament, Paul adds vv. 27-31, showing that redemption comes through God alone and in accordance with the law:

"Then what becomes of boasting? It is excluded. By what law? By that of works? No, but by the law of faith. For we hold that a person is justified by faith apart from works prescribed by the law. Or is God the God of Jews only? Is he not the God of Gentiles also? Yes, of Gentiles also, since God is one; and he will justify the circumcised on the ground of faith and the uncircumcised through that same faith. Do we then overthrow the law by this faith? By no means! On the contrary, we uphold the law."

For Paul, the Hebrews' failure to keep the law did not reflect the value of the law, but the fallen nature of humankind. God's offer of grace in Christ was not an indictment of the law, but a gift for those unable to live by the law.

We should be careful to note that Paul was not setting up "faith" as a human work that gains divine acceptance, as a new kind of law. Faith is the human response to divine grace, an option open to everyone.

That is a gospel of which no one should be ashamed.

The Hardest Question
What are some misperceptions about faith?

Charles Talbert's commentary on Romans examines Paul's discussion of faith, which is easily misunderstood. Talbert lists a series of helpful comments relative to common misperceptions about the meaning of faith (*Romans*, Smyth & Helwys Bible Commentary [Smyth & Helwys, 2002], 125-127). Briefly, they are:

• One is not saved by faith: God saves. Faith is the human reception of God's salvation.
• Faith is not a work, a necessary precondition we must initiate. Faith is our response to God's justifying work in Christ, our acceptance and experience of it.
• Faith is not believing doctrinal propositions: it is a relational term, not intellectual.
• The difference between works and faith is not that works are actions and faith is a feeling or attitude. Feelings, attitudes, and actions go together. The difference in faith and works lies in whether those feelings, attitudes, and actions are designed to gain God's favor, or come in response to God's favor.
• Faith is not a one-time event. It begins the Christian life (Rom. 10:9) and describes an orientation by which the Christian life continues (Gal. 2:20).
• Faith is not a partial response to God, but involves the whole person.
• Faith is not my decision to follow Jesus. It is God's gift that opens the door for my relationship with Jesus.

Fourth Reading
Matthew 7:21-29

Firm Foundations

Everyone then who hears these words of mine and acts on them will be like
a wise man who built his house on rock. (Matt. 7:24)

My daughter loved the songs she learned in Sunday School, and one of her favorites included hand motions to go with the lyrics: "The wise man built his house upon the rock, the wise man built his house upon the rock, the wise man built his house upon the rock and the rains came tumbling down…." You probably know how the rest of that little song goes. Children particularly enjoy the last line: "and the house on the sand went *smash!*" (If you're not familiar with the song, several versions can be found on YouTube.)

Young children don't contemplate the deeper meaning of the song, but it is one of the most important lessons any child or adult will ever learn.

Saying and meaning
(vv. 21-23)

Today's gospel reading concludes Jesus' Sermon on the Mount, a lengthy collection of sayings Matthew portrayed as Jesus' teaching from the side of a mountain. The symbolism is obvious: as Moses taught Israel the law at Mount Sinai, so Jesus – who was greater than Moses – spoke on a mountain as he reinterpreted the Old Testament law and taught how people could live in a sincere and meaningful relationship with God as children of God's household and participants in the kingdom of heaven.

The importance of sincerity was at the heart of Jesus' teaching here: he said what he meant and meant what he said, and he expected his followers to do the same. Jesus did not countenance lip service: "Not everyone who says to me, 'Lord, Lord,' will enter the kingdom of heaven," he said (v. 21).

Today we know many people who claim to be Christians and seem quite confident that heaven awaits them, but their manner of living bears little familiarity with Jesus' teaching.

The basic thrust of Jesus' statement seems clear: words without actions do not a Christian make. Verse 21 has an eschatological cast, as Jesus looked toward a day of judgment and discernment regarding who would "enter the kingdom of heaven" and who would not.

Verse 22 speaks of people who would approach Jesus at the judgment, call him "Lord, Lord," and claim to have prophesied, cast out demons, and done mighty works in his name, only to have Jesus respond "I never knew you; go away from me, you evildoers" (v. 23).

Some readers imagine that the people in question would have been making false claims, while others think of them as having done real works but for selfish reasons (see "The Hardest Question" below for more on this).

Regardless of how we read vv. 22-23, the centrality of sincerity is clear: those who enter the kingdom are those whose faith is true and whose motives are genuine.

Hearing and doing
(v. 24)

The theme of sincere belief and living with integrity continues in the final saying of Jesus' Sermon on the Mount, the familiar comparison of earnest faith and the firm foundation of a house built on a rock: "Everyone then who hears these words of mine and acts on them will be like a wise man who built his house on rock," Jesus said (v. 24).

"These words of mine" refers back to the lessons taught in the Sermon on the Mount. As Jesus looked into the eyes of those who were gathered around, we can imagine that he saw differing levels of response. Some were listening on a mental level, while others were listening with their hearts *and* their minds. We might think of the crowd that day as being like the audience at a rock concert. Some listen politely, and applaud when each song is done. Others let the music flow through them, and they dance.

There were some in the crowd, perhaps, who had listened to every word, and who might have said "Amen!" Maybe they smiled when Jesus finished speaking and shook his hand and said they enjoyed it, but nothing changed inside them. They were impressed, but not converted — still closed to the real presence of God, still devoted to the inner god of self.

But there were others who listened more deeply. Jesus' words had penetrated both their ears and their hearts. They took Jesus seriously, followed his lead to the narrow way, and ventured out in faith to a new kind of life. They not only *heard*, but they also *obeyed*. To obey is to hear with our hearts and respond with our lives. [**To hear and obey**]

To hear and obey: In the Hebrew Bible, the word for "to obey" is the same as the word for "to hear," though often expressed in a more intensive form. When I was a boy and my father would tell me to do something, I did not always respond immediately. If I delayed too long, he would say "Did you *hear* me?" The implication was, if I truly heard, I would obey. The biblical expectation is the same.

When we think about our devotional activities, Bible study experiences, and opportunities for worship, how often can it be said that we truly hear with our hearts as well as our minds? How can others tell?

Standing and falling
(vv. 25-29)

As Jesus had earlier used the metaphor of the wide and narrow roads to stress the importance of decisions (vv. 13-14), so now he turns to the analogy of two men who are building houses, places to dwell and find security. We know the importance of building on a firm foundation, and in a good location.

In the past few years, while severe drought has prevailed over the American West, unusual weather patterns related to climate change have brought heavy flooding to the Mississippi River, to the Ohio River Valley, to North Carolina's Neuse and Cape Fear rivers, and to many others. National and local news programs alike have beamed frightening pictures of the flooding to homes across the country. We have seen horrifying pictures of broken houses floating downstream, while other homes remain standing, but covered with water and filled with mud.

That graphic image was also known in Palestine, which remained dry most of the year, but was also subject to periodic flooding during the seasonal rains. Those who were wise learned to build their homes on firm, high ground. Those who built on the sandy soil of dry riverbeds were taking chances with future floods, and often paid the price.

Houses in Palestine were sometimes built mainly of stone, but often consisted of a stone foundation with walls made of mudbrick, sometimes plastered. A flat roof was made of thatch interwoven with poles laid across the walls, with mud plaster packed in as a sealer. [**Mud and stone**]

In a version of the parable recorded by Luke (6:47-49), Jesus spoke of two houses built side by side near a river. One had a deep foundation that reached to the underlying rock, while the other was built on a shallow foundation of sand.

Matthew's version suggests that the difference was not just one of *foundation*, but of *location*. The first man – the wise man who not only hears but also obeys – goes about building his house with special care. He searches out a location on high ground, even though it is harder to get to and may be unlevel. He digs until he reaches solid rock, and then lays a solid foundation for his house.

The second man – the one who hears but does not act – seems more nonchalant about his efforts. He chooses a broad and sandy valley that is easy to access. Since the

Mud and stone: A story told by the rabbi Elisha ben Abuyah (born sometime before 70 CE) also contrasted two men who built houses and the effects of a flood. In his story, the rabbi compared a man who sought to learn the law but did no good works, and another who not only studied the law, but also devoted himself to good works. In his parable, "bricks" refers to mudbricks that have not been fired or cured for hardness, so that they melt when they get wet.

"ELISHA ben Abuyah says: One in whom there are good works, who has studied much Torah, to what may he be likened? To a person who builds first with stones and afterward with bricks: even when much water comes and collects by their side, it does not dislodge them. But one in whom there are no good works, though he studied Torah, to what may he be likened? To a person who builds first with bricks and afterward with stones: even when a little water gathers, it overthrows them immediately" (From *The Fathers According to Rabbi Nathan*, translated by Judah Goldin [Yale University Press, 1955], 103).

surface is already level, he builds directly upon the firm ground.

Both houses seem equally sturdy until a storm comes raging across the land. Heavy rainstorms in Palestine do not occur often, but have devastating effects when they do. The house on the hill is built on a solid foundation, and it weathers the storm.

The house in the sandy valley is not so fortunate. Too late, the owner realizes that the valley is really a dry wadi, or riverbed. Soon the waters come rushing by, and what seemed to be hard ground quickly washes away, leaving the mud-brick house to collapse and dissolve in the storm.

One can see in this parable a suggestion that those who build their lives on following Christ are better prepared to persevere in faith and deal with the storms of life that all of us will face. Most scholars agree, however, that the main point of the parable concerns the final judgment.

The houses we build are the lives we live in this world. We may think that this world, this life, is all there is. One day, however, the final judgment will break upon us like a raging storm. If our lives are built upon the strong foundation of life-changing faith in Christ and obedience to his way, we will weather that storm and live on. If our lives are built on the shifting sands of self-directed thinking and behavior, the house will fall.

The wide road to destruction and the house on a sandy foundation both come to the same end: eternal death, but Jesus came and lived and died for the express purpose of saving us from that death. We can choose the narrow way and follow him. We can build our faith on the solid rock of his love for us. And when the storms come, we will endure. When the judgment comes, we will live on.

When Jesus finished teaching, Matthew says, the people were "astounded," because he taught as one who had "authority" (vv. 28-29). This final note reminds modern readers that Jesus did, in fact, teach with authority. He has the right to teach us how to live, and to expect our obedience. He has the authority to explain and to enforce future consequences based on our willingness – or lack of it – to follow the kingdom path.

The decisions we make in this life are important. It matters *whether* we believe, and it matters *what* we believe. It matters *how* we live and how we love. It matters now, and it matters in eternity.

Jesus has laid a heavy challenge *before* us, *on* us, and *in* us. It is a challenge to change our way of living, to turn from self, to trust in God. It is a challenge to walk the narrow path, to live in fellowship with God's Spirit, to reach *up* to God in trust for our needs, and to reach *out* in love to those persons God brings our way.

The Hardest Question
How should we interpret v. 22?

Jesus' main point about sincere belief and action seems clear, but we run into a wall of questions in reading v. 22: "On that day many will say to me, 'Lord, Lord, did we not prophesy in your name, and cast out demons in your name, and do many deeds of power in your name?'"

We may wonder how anyone could do such mighty works and still be so insincere that Jesus could say "I never knew you; go away from me, you evildoers" (v. 23).

One option for understanding this verse is to note that the prophecy, exorcism, and deeds of power in question may exist only in the words of those who claim to have done them. It is helpful to note that vv. 21-23 follow a warning against false prophets in vv. 15-20, and many interpreters consider vv. 15-23 to form a unit, with v. 24 beginning a new unit.

One may speak his or her own ideas and call them prophecy, even when the words did not originate with God. One may lay hands on an afflicted person and claim to have cast out a demon, but how is anyone to know for sure? One may claim to have done mighty works that may not have been done at all. In our own time, we are quite familiar with padded résumés and politicians who lay claim to accomplishments they never achieved.

So, it's possible that Jesus was being sarcastic, speaking sardonically of false prophets whose actions don't live up to their claims.

When we remember that Matthew was writing from the perspective of many years later, however, he would have known that "gifts of prophecy" were known in the early church (Acts 2:17-18, Rom. 12;6, 1 Cor. 12:10). Early believers were said to have cast out demons (Acts 5:16, 16:18, 19:12) and to have done mighty works (Acts 3:6,

5:15-16, 9:34, 14:10, 19:11-12). Paul spoke of people who had the gift of "miracles" (1 Cor. 12:10, Gal. 3:5).

So, some interpreters suggest that Jesus spoke of people who might legitimately preach, cast out demons, or do mighty works, but on the day of judgment it would be revealed that their motives were self-centered: they had sought personal attention or glory rather than focusing on serving Jesus.

One might even argue that Jesus portrayed persons thought to be in league with Satan and thus empowered to perform miracles even though they played for the other team, but such persons would be unlikely to call Jesus "Lord" and claim that they had done such things in his name.

Whether Jesus was thinking of outright charlatans or of believers who were in it for themselves, his claim is that they never truly knew him – and as a result, he did not know them.

Season after Pentecost: Proper 5

First Reading
Genesis 12:1-9*

A New Start

*Genesis 12:1-4a is also read on the Second Sunday of Lent in Year A. A commentary on Gen. 12:1-9 appears for that Sunday in Year A, Volume 2 of this commentary.

Optional First Reading
Psalm 33:1-12

An Attitude of Gratitude

Rejoice in the LORD, O you righteous. Praise befits the upright. (Ps. 33:1)

Have you noticed how vocabulary shifts, and how some perfectly good words can come to take on an entirely negative connotation? Take the word "attitude." There was a time when you needed an adjective to describe someone's attitude. You might describe someone as having a "positive attitude" or a "bad attitude."'

Used alone, however, "attitude" has taken on a decidedly unfavorable sense. I have taught on every level from elementary school to junior high to high school, college, and divinity school. On every level, "teacher's lounge" conversation often concerns certain students who "have an attitude."

But that works both ways. When my sons came home with poor grades on their report cards, they sometimes claimed it was because the teacher "had an attitude."
[Finding joy]

One of the most important values a church can uphold is a joyful attitude of worship and praise. We live in a world that seems more and more negative in its outlook, but gratitude can offer benefits for us as individuals, and as a church family.

Studies have shown that our mental attitudes have a strong influence on our health, whether we are recovering from surgery or dealing with diseases. People with positive attitudes tend to recover more quickly and have better functioning immune systems.

The same sort of system is at work in the church. When a positive attitude pervades the congregation, the church is more likely to be healthy and functioning well. But, when a church is overtaken by a spirit of negativism, love and

> **Finding joy:** Perhaps you have heard the old story of a man who went to church on a dark and gloomy day. It was pouring down rain and getting colder by the minute. The heat wasn't working in the sanctuary, and everyone appeared to be absolutely miserable. The grouchy parishioner knew that the pastor always opened the service with a prayer of thanksgiving, but he thought to himself: "He'll never find anything to be thankful for this morning!" When the pastor stood up to pray, he said: "We thank you, Lord, that it's not always like this."
>
> Even in wretched weather, he found his way to an attitude of gratitude—and that is at the heart of true worship.

forgiveness are in short supply. Stinginess and suspicion take over, and the church's health will suffer.

This is a primary reason for worship: it keeps us focused on who we are and why we are here. Corporate worship is a public manifestation of an attitude of gratitude to the Lord of all. Many of the psalms were written to assist God's people in the worship and praise of God. Psalm 33 is one of them. Let's take a closer look.

A call to worship
(vv. 1-3)

The righteous are called to "sing for joy," because "praise is becoming to the upright" (v. 1). If we find it hard to put our hearts into worshiping God, this verse may offer a clue to the problem: praise is characteristic of those who are "upright." The word comes from a root that means "to be straight," and it carries the sense of one who seeks to follow God's way.

If our lives follow a different path, it will be harder for us to praise God. We can't praise God for deliverance if we have not been delivered. We can't praise God's goodness if our lives are wicked. We can't praise God's grace when we haven't sought forgiveness.

This is why effective worship incorporates times of meditation and prayers of confession. We need that time to clean house. We need that time to renew our focus. We need that time to center our thoughts and find forgiveness, to put the past week behind us and open our hearts to the future God has for us.

Then, we can worship and sing the new song that v. 3 speaks about. The call to sing a new song may suggest that worship is not static. We don't worship in the same way the early church did. Most of us don't worship like the church of the Middle Ages. We don't worship just like the Reformers did. Many of us don't worship like our grandparents did. The forms, the hymns, and the expressions of worship can change with time and culture.

Indeed, one could argue that we are called to find new ways to express our praise and sing new songs that are relevant to contemporary culture. The psalmist instructed his hearers to give thanks with the lyre and a harp of 10 strings. Today, he might suggest electric guitars and a keyboard synthesizer. The important thing is not the instrument, but how it is played, and why.

Throughout the ages, the most important instrument is our voice. Whether we have a beautiful singing voice or not is immaterial. Some church choirs are backed by an orchestra and sing so beautifully that they could record albums. Others may be small and struggle to stay on key, but still praise God to the best of their abilities.

God appreciates the depth of spirit more than the heights of harmony.

We are called to praise! But the important question is: *Why?*

Reasons for worship
(vv. 4-12)

The psalmist speaks of three primary reasons for praising God. First, God is faithful: "For the word of the Lord is upright, and all his work is done in faithfulness" (v. 4).

All of us know unfaithful people. We have had our trust abused and our hearts broken by people who said one thing and did another. There may have been occasions when we were the ones who were unfaithful, who didn't come through or do what we had promised.

Our human fickleness makes it difficult to trust God's total faithfulness, but the scriptures attest to God's care through all the ages. God has not promised to protect us from trials and troubles, because we remain free people who can make mistakes and do foolish things.

Worship celebrates God's faithfulness, and it may inspire us to turn back in the right direction.

Second, God is loving: "He loves righteousness and justice; the earth is full of the lovingkindness of the Lord" (v. 5).

The Lord does not just love righteousness and justice out of a desire for control, but because that is what is best for God's people, and for all peoples. God knows that when we do what is right, the world is a better place. God knows that when we practice justice and care for all people, we will also experience greater peace and joy.

We often have a negative attitude about Old Testament law, but the heart of the law was a call to live peaceful and productive lives that honored both God and others with the same kind of steadfast love that God showed to the Hebrews.

We know our world harbors injustice, violence, abuse, pride, selfishness, and greed – everything that opposes what it means to be loving and kind. God would not be loving and kind if we were not allowed free will. The fact that we abuse our freedom does not negate the love God has shown us.

The gospels insist that God became incarnate in Jesus Christ for the express purpose of experiencing the violence and abuse that humankind can devise. Jesus died on a cross that humans made, and in doing so he demonstrated that despite our darkest sin, God's lovingkindness is still there, and it is ultimately victorious.

The largest part of this psalm is given over to a third cause for worship, a recognition of God's power. God is not only faithful and kind, but also capable of action.

Verses 6-9 speak of God's power as seen in creation. God spoke, and the universe was made. As a result, all people have reason to stand in awe. That is a part of worship – to stand in awe before the power of God. That is why cathedrals are built so huge and breathtaking: they are meant to inspire reverence and awe.

We may feel the same kind of awe when we stand on a mountaintop or on the edge of a gorge, or when we look out the window of an airplane or contemplate the beauty of a single tree or flower. We don't need a cathedral to stand in awe of God's work.

God's power is also seen among the nations (vv. 10-12). It is not only appropriate but also essential that Christians pray concerning world and national events, believing that God has power to influence entire nations and guide those who trust.

Verse 12 declares "Happy is the nation whose God is the Lord, the people whom he has chosen as his heritage."

We must remember that those words addressed ancient Israel, and not America. A common belief holds that America is the new promised land and that Americans are the new Israelites, but God has no more and no less love for the political entity we call America than for Germany or Brazil or Malaysia.

The people God has chosen as an inheritance are those who trust in God and follow God's way. In our world, it is not the responsibility of the government to sponsor religious instruction or prayer at public events. It is the responsibility of the church to teach, and to pray, and to uphold the values of justice and compassion. Blessed indeed is the nation that has a mature church that understands Jesus' compassion for its conscience.

The lectionary reading stops at v. 12, but the psalm does not. God's power is also expressed toward individuals (vv. 13-19). The Lord made our hearts, the psalmist said, and watches us (v. 15). God knows that we seek meaning and purpose on many dead-end roads. God knows our tendency to place all our hopes in our own strength. God allows us to go down blind alleys, and when we realize we are lost and call out for help, God is there to pick us up. "Truly the eye of the Lord is on those who fear him, on those who hope in his steadfast love" (v. 18).

That is more than enough reason for worship.

The Hardest Question
What comes next?

The lectionary reading from Psalm 33 stops at v. 12, but the psalm has 22 verses. We offered a brief description of vv. 13-19 above, but for someone who wants to teach or preach from the entire psalm, what comes next? Should we not honor all that the psalmist had in mind?

The conclusion of the psalm takes the truth that has already been expressed and makes it a corporate statement of faith and worship.

"Our soul waits for the Lord," the psalmist said, because "he is our help and our shield" (v. 20). This is a statement of trust, and that is a crucial aspect of worship.

The poet's declaration or explanation of worship continues: "Our heart is glad in him, because we trust in his holy name" (v. 21).

Do our hearts rejoice when we come to worship? The truth is, many of us have difficulty with that, especially many men or anyone who tends to keep their feelings close to the vest. We may be somewhat scared of feelings because we never learned to express them well, or even to recognize them. We may be like the guy in the country song who said "I wish you could have turned my head and left my heart alone." Even in worship, we would rather relate on a "head" level and not get the heart involved.

But we cannot have a true relationship without involving the heart. We cannot love another person without involving the heart. And we cannot have a relationship with God that does not involve the heart.

Worship involves our head, our heart, and our soul: Recall the memorable command of Deut. 6:5: "You shall love the LORD your God with all your heart, and with all your soul, and with all your might." Jesus endorsed that command, according to Matt. 22:37-40, Mark 12:28-31, and Luke 10:25-28.

True worship gets as deep as we can go.

Season after Pentecost: Proper 5

Second Reading
Hosea 5:8–6:6 (RCL 5:15–6:6)

Crocodile Tears

Come, let us return to the LORD; for it is he who has torn, and he will heal us;
he has struck down, and he will bind us up. (Hos. 6:1)

It is a hard thing to live with no sense of the presence of God, to live with the thought that we are alone in this world, to live with an almost tangible feeling of emptiness inside. This is especially hard if we can remember what it was like to know God's feeling before. If we have experienced the tender warmth of his love and the overwhelming joy of God's grace, then the feeling of God's absence can be devastating.

Can such a thing happen? Yes. And it may have happened to us. Our text today describes what it was like for Israel to hear a prophet proclaim that they were no longer God's people. The lectionary text begins at 5:15, but our study cries out for background. A quick review of what has preceded in 1:1–5:7 can be found in "The Hardest Question" below. Rather than beginning our study with the last verse of ch. 5, we will begin at v. 8.

When God disciplines
(5:8-15)

Hosea's oracular declaration continues a lengthy courtroom scene that began at 4:1, but marks a shift in the prophet's rhetoric. Here, Hosea not only predicts a coming time of trial, but also calls for it to begin: He could see no hope for Israel beyond a serious dose of discipline designed to shock the people into their senses and lead them to change their ways and return to worshiping Yahweh alone. The prophet saw war in Israel's future, and it would not be pleasant. "Blow the horn in Gibeah," he said, "the trumpet in Ramah" (5:8). Both "trumpet" and "horn" could refer

to the ram's horn *shôfār* commonly used to assemble the people with its high-pitched blare.

Hosea connects the symbols of war with the cities of Gibeah, Ramah, and Bethel (assigning Bethel the pejorative name "Beth-Aven," meaning "House of Sin"). The cities were all located in the southernmost part of the northern kingdom, near the border with Judah. Because of their location, some scholars think this may be a reference to the Syro-Ephraimitic war of 734–732 BCE, in which Israel and Syria joined in attacking Judah to force the southern kingdom into their military coalition. The location of the cities suggests a counterattack by Judah. Ultimately, Judah escaped defeat, but only by calling on Assyria for assistance.

In 5:9-14, Hosea continues his tirade against Israel (Ephraim) by predicting a gloomy future for the nation's inhabitants. Property in the ancient world was marked by boundary stones, which an unscrupulous person could easily move. Hosea puts Israel in the category of those who would blatantly infringe on others' rights by moving the boundary stones and claiming others' land. The people would feel God's wrath, Hosea said, but because they were so intent on pursuing success through idolatry, they would be trampled by judgment before they even heard it coming (5:10-11).

Judgment would come in ways both fast and slow. In 5:12, God is described as one who gradually eats away at the people like maggots or wood rot, but in 5:14, God is portrayed as a great lion that rips the people to shreds and carries them away before anyone can rescue them. Israel or

So many things: Hosea's prophecy criticized Israel and Judah for so many things, on so many fronts. Primarily, the people had turned away from worshipping Yahweh alone to serving other gods. Hosea's marriage to a prostitute who had taken another lover symbolized God's dilemma in loving someone who was also prone to stray.

Hosea's charges against Israel may speak loudly to modern believers who commonly chase after prosperity and pleasure with far more energy than they express in seeking God. How can idolatrous ideals make us blind to God's call?

Judah might call on Assyria or other nations to come to their aid, but they would be unable to interfere with God's judgment: their wound would be incurable (5:13).

The purpose of these chilling judgments comes to the fore in v. 15: "I will return again to my place until they acknowledge their guilt and seek my face. In their distress they will beg my favor."

Hosea pictures God as abandoning Israel altogether, using discipline as a means of snapping Israel from their trance-like devotion to foreign gods. With God's presence and blessings gone from the land, the people would come to recognize their plight and their need for God. Then they would be motivated to seek God's favor through repentance and renewed devotion. [**So many things**]

That was the plan. But would it work?

The result of discipline
(6:1-6)

How do we interpret the first few verses of ch. 6? Scholars are divided. Is this Hosea's appeal to the people to seek the Lord and live? Or is Hosea mocking the empty words of those who speak words of repentance, but do not follow them?

The first three verses attest belief in a simple formula: If Israel returns to Yahweh, Yahweh would return to them. "Come, let us return to the LORD; for it is he who has torn, and he will heal us; he has struck down, and he will bind us up" (6:1).

Whether the words are an appeal from Hosea or a depiction of the people, they offer the same awareness of sin and hope of forgiveness. The appeal acknowledges hard times as divine discipline, and it expresses confidence that a return to God will bring healing and a relationship of presence between God and the people (6:1).

Verse 2 offers the interesting prediction that "After two days he will revive us; on the third day he will raise us up, that we may live before him." The numerical movement from two days to three builds upon a typically Hebrew literary convention used to add suspense or emphasis. Many readers also see a remarkable (though unintentional) foreshadowing of Christ's resurrection on the third day, which also makes it possible for Christian believers to be "raised up" to experience life eternal and abundant (6:2).

Hosea puts special emphasis on the importance of *knowing God*, of experiencing God in fullness. "Let us know, let us press on to know the LORD…" (6:3a). The Hebrew word translated "to know" implies more than intellectual knowledge. To "know" in Hebrew means to know by experience. It can express intimate experience to the point of being used as a euphemism for sexual intercourse: "Now the man *knew* his wife Eve, and she conceived and bore Cain" (Gen. 4:1).

How does one "know" God? For Hosea, knowing God came through worship and prayer and faithfulness to the law. For modern believers, knowing God also comes through worship and prayer but is enhanced through Bible study, fellowship with other believers, and seeking to live as Jesus would have us to. All of these are simply aids or aspects of a relationship with God.

Hosea wanted his fellow Hebrews to recognize that it is not enough to know a lot of facts or theories *about* God: our great need is to know God *in* a personal relationship. When Jesus confronted Peter by the Sea of Galilee following his resurrection, he did not ask Peter "Do you understand all about me?" He asked "Do you *love* me?"

The appeal found in 6:1-3 suggests that God would not turn back toward Israel or restore divine blessings until the people repented, sought God's favor, and recognized the mutual responsibilities of a covenant relationship. Only then could Israel expect to experience the refreshing "showers" symbolic of God's return, "like the spring rains that water the earth."

Israel, however, was a hard case. Though 6:1-3 seems to suggest a movement toward repentance, God's response in 6:4-6 is less confident: "What shall I do with you, O Ephraim? What shall I do with you, O Judah?" God mourns

> **Ephraim:** Ephraim, like Manasseh, was a son of Joseph. Biblical narratives suggest that Ephraim and Manasseh became the largest tribes of the northern kingdom. Though Manasseh was larger, people from Ephraim were more influential. Prophets sometimes used "Ephraim" as a symbolic name for the entire northern kingdom, more formally known as Israel (Isa. 7:8-9, 17; 11:13; Jer. 31:18, 20; Zech. 9:13, 10:7). This is especially characteristic of Hosea, whose home was in Judah, but whose preaching often targeted the north (Hos. 5:3, 11-14; 6:4; 7:1, 8, 11; 8:11; 9:3, 8, 13, 16; 10:6, 11; 11:3, 8, 9, 11; 12:1, 8, 14; 13:1; 14:8).

for a people whose love is no more lasting than the morning mist, for people who might repent in their morning prayers, and then sin before the dew has evaporated from the grass (6:4). **[Ephraim]**

It was Israel's empty and hypocritical rituals of repentance that had sparked Yahweh's punishment as well as the fiery words of his prophets, who had pronounced God's judgment. Symbolically, Hosea speaks for God: "Therefore I have hewn them by the prophets, I have killed them by the words of my mouth, and my judgment goes forth as the light" (6:5).

With 6:6 we come to the heart of the matter: "For I desire steadfast love and not sacrifice, the knowledge of God rather than burnt offerings" (6:6). As Samuel had criticized Saul for offering sacrifices without obedience (1 Sam. 15:22), Hosea charged that Israel was long on ritual, but short on relationship. Contemporary prophets Amos and Micah also charged Israel with paying lip service to God through ritual sacrifices while living without regard to God or God's teaching (Amos 5:21-24, Mic. 6:6-8). They had taken God's love for granted.

In a similar way, modern believers might associate religion or faithfulness to God with actions such as going to church or taking the sacraments or even tithing. We also must know, however, that the rituals of religious life are meaningful only when they manifest a deeper relationship between God and the believer.

When Jesus confronted this same issue in dealing with the Pharisees, he quoted to them this very scripture from Hosea. The religious elite once criticized Jesus for spending so much time with unsavory types such as sinners and sick people. Jesus responded: "Those who are well have no need

of a physician, but those who are sick. Go and learn what this means, 'I desire mercy, not sacrifice.' For I have come to call not the righteous, but sinners" (Matt. 9:12-13).

On another occasion, the Pharisees condemned Jesus and the Twelve for violating the oral tradition by rubbing grain between their hands to prepare a snack on the Sabbath. Jesus' reply was quick and forceful: "If you had known what these words mean, 'I desire mercy, not sacrifice,' you would not have condemned the innocent" (Matt. 12:7). Satisfying the hunger of a real person is more important than satisfying an unnecessary regulation concerning the Sabbath.

It is not ritual alone that brings us into relationship with God, nor is it the legalistic following of rules and regulations. To know God's presence is to live in relationship, and that relationship derives from covenant love – loyal love – lasting love. "I desire love, not sacrifice."

Modern believers need not assume that every illness or financial setback is a divine punishment for spiritual failure, but that does not mean a worldly focus has no consequences. When we experience bleak periods in our spiritual life, it is worth asking if we have substituted Sunday ritual (or no ritual) for an ongoing, intimate relationship. Our relationship with God is akin to any other relationship in that it requires effort to maintain it. We would do well to ponder what we are doing to foster and enrich our own relationship with the God who does not wish to give us up.

The Hardest Question
What came before?

The book of Hosea stands out as unusual, even among Israel's prophets, who were often prone to bizarre behavior. The book begins with a family drama written by a third person narrator who claims that God instructed Hosea to marry "a wife out of whoredom and have children of whoredom" to symbolize Israel's abandonment of God: "for the land commits great whoredom by forsaking the LORD" (1:2).

Hosea then married Gomer, according to 1:3, and three children were born, though Hosea appears to question whether he was the father.

He named the first son "Jezreel" in memory of a bloody coup in that city when Jehu murdered both King Joram of Israel and Ahaziah of Judah before slaughtering many royal descendants and also worshipers of Baal (1:4, 2 Kings 9–10).

The second child was a daughter Hosea named "Lo-ru-hamah," meaning "Not Pitied," indicating that God would no longer forgive or save the recalcitrant people of Israel (1:6-7).

A third child was a boy whom Hosea named "Lo-ammi," or "Not my people," a sign that God had foresworn any further allegiance to the apostate people.

Chapter 2 is an extended oracle in which Hosea speaks for God, predicting judgment on Israel (2:1-13) but also offering "a door of hope" if the people should repent and return (2:14-23).

Chapter 3 opens with a command for Hosea to reclaim his wife, who had abandoned him and fallen into sexual slavery, bringing her back into his home but under strict conditions that symbolized Israel's need to return to God and change their behavior (3:1-5).

The marriage metaphor gives way to a courtroom scene throughout ch. 4, and it continues into ch. 5, where Hosea brings formal charges against Israel because of their sin. The charge is directed toward every level of society (5:1a), including the *priests*, the *people* (house of Israel), and the *princes* (house of the king).

Hosea charges that Israel's behavior has also endangered others: "you have been a snare at Mizpah, and a net spread upon Tabor, and a pit dug deep in Shittim" (5:1b-2a). Mizpah, Tabor, and Shittim were locations that had positive connotations from the time of Israel's entry into the promised land, but had since become known as hotbeds of corruption. The people may have thought they could act without consequences, but Hosea portrays God as observing: "I know Ephraim, and Israel is not hidden from me" (5:3a). The prophet accuses the entire nation of having adopted a wholesale "spirit of whoredom" that renders them so lost in sin that they neither know the Lord, nor have the ability to find him (5:3b-4).

Hosea's "snare" terminology seems to be inspired by the bad influence he believed the northern kingdom of Israel had exerted upon their kindred in Judah, leading the southern kingdom astray. The prophet observes that, while Israel had set traps for others, they had also stumbled into their own snare (5:5).

The observation in 5:4 that Israel was too sinful to return to God finds further elaboration in 5:6. Hosea declares that people may take their sacrificial animals to "seek the LORD" through sacrifice, but "they will not find him," because "he has withdrawn from them." In essence, Hosea claims that God no longer showed up for worship in Israel. The people's ritual actions, so entangled with cultic prostitution and other pagan practices (5:7) was such an abomination that God could no longer bear to be present, and intentionally withdrew his presence.

Modern believers would do well to consider Hosea's warning, and ask whether their own worship is attractive to God, or if their everyday behavior repels the divine presence.

Optional Second Reading
Psalm 50 (RCL 50:7-15)

What God Wants

Offer to God a sacrifice of thanksgiving, and pay your vows to the Most High. (Ps. 50:14)

Psalms come in many shapes, sizes, and even temperatures. This one comes in hot. Psalm 50 sounds as if it came straight from one of the prophetic books, and we can safely assume that its author thought of himself as a prophet. Like Psalms 73–83, the text bears a superscription that associates it with Asaph, who David reportedly installed to lead the music program in the temple.

Psalm 50 sounds more like preaching than singing, however. It is a foot-stomping, toe-bashing, finger-pointing sermon that could have set the congregation's ears ringing.

As a pastor, I learned that while most congregants squirmed at the thought of such sermons, there were always a few who found a pulpit-pounding, sin-condemning peroration to be cathartic and helpful in spurring personal repentance.

Convicting or not, our study of Psalm 50 should lead us to ponder whether we might find ourselves as targets of the psalmist's sharp tongue. The RCL reading comprises only vv. 7-15, but if we are to grasp the writer's meaning, we should consider the full text.

When God is scary
(vv. 1-6)

The psalm begins with a theophany. It is not the kind of majestic and inspiring appearance such as we find in Psalm 104, but a frightening show of power and storm. God is identified as "The mighty one, God the LORD," an unfortunate translation that masks the psalmist's sequence of three divine names: "*'El, 'Elohim, Yahweh*," perhaps a reflection of Josh. 22:22, which uses the same sequence twice. The

> **Another triplet:** For emphasis, perhaps, the NRSV translation of Josh. 22:22 inverts the three names and translates as "The LORD, God of gods! The LORD, God of gods! He knows; and let Israel itself know …" Like Ps. 50:1, the Hebrew text is "*'El, 'Elohim, Yahweh*." The NET translates it in order as "El, God, the LORD!"

Hebrew was not written with punctuation, so another translation could be "God of Gods, Yahweh." [**Another triplet**]

The multiplied title contributes to the powerful image of God who shines out of Zion, who "speaks and summons the earth from the rising of the sun to its setting" (vv. 1-2). The God who speaks does not come in silence or speak in even tones, but "before him is a devouring fire, and a mighty tempest all around him" (v. 3).

The fearsome imagery of God approaching in a storm leads to a courtroom scene similar to the prophetic motif of a covenant lawsuit such as those found in Isa. 1:18-20; 3:13-15; 41:1ff, 21ff; 43:9ff; Jer. 2:4-9; Hos. 2:4ff; and Mic. 6:1ff. Psalm 82 has a similar form.

Here, God "calls to the heavens above and to the earth, that he may judge his people" (v. 4). And who are the defendants in this case? That would be the entire people of Israel, who had entered into a covenant with God at Mount Sinai: "Gather to me my faithful ones, who made a covenant with me by sacrifice" (v. 5). [**Heaven and earth**]

The inaugural covenant ceremony had been accompanied by elaborate sacrifices and dashing of blood on the altar, with Moses also sprinkling blood on the people and saying

"See the blood of the covenant that the LORD has made with you in accordance with all these words" (Exod. 24:3-8).

With witnesses and defendants in place, God presides as judge over the case (v. 6). In practice, God also acts as the prosecuting attorney and chief witness, as we see in the following section.

When sacrifices are meaningless
(vv. 7-13, 16-22)

The poet/prophet speaks for God who addresses Israel as "my people" and testifies: "I am God, your God. Not for your sacrifices do I rebuke you; your burnt offerings are continually before me" (v. 7).

Sacrifices alone were not the issue. God had a complaint, but it wasn't for lack of animals being slaughtered at the temple. The problem was two-fold. First, the people may have had a misplaced concept of sacrifices as something God needed, perhaps accompanied by an idea that sending God smoke from burning meat was the extent of Israel's responsibility.

God rejected this idea: "I will not accept a bull from your house, or goats from your folds. For every wild animal of the forest is mine, the cattle on a thousand hills. I know all the birds of the air, and all that moves in the field is mine" (vv. 9-11).

Babylonians and Assyrians imagined that their gods depended on them for sustenance in addition to the cleaning and maintenance of their images. The Gilgamesh epic's version of the flood story depicts the gods as "swarming like flies" over sacrifices offered by Utnapishtim when he gained dry ground, because they hadn't been fed during the flood. [The care and feeding of the gods]

The Israelites imagined that God appreciated sacrifices and took note of the pleasing aroma, but had no instruction that God needed them for sustenance. Rather, "If I were hungry, I would not tell you," God insisted, "for the world and all that is in it is mine. Do I eat the flesh of bulls, or drink the blood of goats?" (vv. 12-13).

More important than misunderstanding, however, was misbehavior. Verses 16-22 charge the people with specific sins that render their sacrifices hypocritical. "But to the wicked God says: 'What right have you to recite my statutes, or take my covenant on your lips?'" (v. 16). Ritual worship is meaningless when offered as a payoff rather than as admiration and thanksgiving.

God charged the people with despising discipline and ignoring the law, saying "you cast my words behind you" (v. 17). They consorted with thieves and adulterers, spoke deceitfully, and slandered their own relatives (vv. 18-20).

Perhaps the people thought they were getting away with their misbehavior, or that God really was not so different from themselves, but God put that notion to rest: "These things you have done and I have been silent; you thought that I was one just like yourself. But now I rebuke you, and lay the charge before you" (v. 21).

Those who had abandoned God and followed their own desires could not do so without consequences: "Mark this, then, you who forget God, or I will tear you apart, and there will be no one to deliver" (v. 22).

"You who forget God." Those are chilling words. The verb is a participle: a literal translation would be "Consider this, (you) God-forgetters." The people might forget their covenant God, but God would not forget them – though they might wish otherwise.

But there was still an option to change their behavior, for the little word "lest" intervenes: "Consider this, you God-forgetters, *lest* I tear you apart ..." The conjunction *pen* can mean "lest," "otherwise," or "else."

How could Israel change their ways and avoid the ugly fate of God-forgetters?

What God wants
(vv. 14-15, 23)

What God wanted was for people to worship with their hearts in the right places and to understand that the sacrifice God desires most is not a bloody animal, but sincere thanksgiving and praise. Such persons could expect God to hear the prayers they offered.

"Offer to God a sacrifice of thanksgiving, and pay your vows to the Most High. Call on me in the day of trouble; I will deliver you, and you shall glorify me" (vv. 14-15).

"Pay your vows" is not just code for "keep the covenant," but refers to specific promises people may have made in conjunction with making special requests from God. It speaks of people who live in a trusting relationship with God and feel confident in offering prayers of both praise and petition.

The closing verse of the psalm makes it clear that more is involved. Worshipers should not only understand God's attitude toward sacrifice, but also pay attention to God's words and treat one another rightly if they are to come with clean hearts that are acceptable to God.

"Those who bring thanksgiving as their sacrifice honor me; to those who go the right way I will show the salvation of God" (v. 23).

What does it mean for modern believers to "go the right way"? We do not live under the same covenant described in this psalm. We do not bring animals for sacrifice when we come to worship, but we also are challenged to follow the right way.

Jesus spoke of choosing a narrow gate rather than following the wide and easy road that leads to destruction (Matt. 7:13). For Christians, to walk in the right way is to follow Jesus. Following Jesus involves denying our selfish desires (Matt. 16:24). To follow Jesus is to obey his command to love others as he loved us (John 13:34-35).

That is the sacrifice Jesus taught – one that might involve a sacrifice of time or money or even pride, but all in the name of love. It's easy for modern Christians, like the Israelites, to fall into the trap of doing what we think is "just enough" to get by and still be considered in good standing with God or the church.

Psalm 50 challenges us to consider whether we are God-forgetting people paying lip service, or true followers who "go the right way."

The Hardest Question
What is a "covenant lawsuit"?

German scholar Hermann Gunkel, a pioneer of form criticism, identified eight examples of what he called a "prophetic lawsuit" (*Gerichtsrede*): Isa. 1:18-20; 3:13-15; 41:1ff, 21ff; 43:9ff; Jer. 2:4-9; Hos. 2:4ff; and Mic. 6:1ff. He noted that Ps. 50:7-13 and Psalm 82 have similar forms.

Gunkel imagined the background of such lawsuits to be found at the city gate, though Ernst Würtwein argued that they were grounded in cult practice. Herbert Hoffman preferred the term "covenant lawsuit" and imagined the lawsuits taking place in the heavenly council, with the form of the suit being influenced by Hittite suzerainty treaties.

The prophetic lawsuit was based on a belief that Yahweh and Israel had entered into a covenant with mutual responsibilities. The prophets' understanding of covenant shifted somewhat between the eighth-century prophets, who saw Yahweh as one who instituted the covenant and guaranteed it with divine oaths, and the seventh-century prophets, who followed the Deuteronomistic understanding of the covenant as a binding agreement sealed by oaths of loyalty by both parties.

In either case, Israel was expected to live up to their part of the covenant, with the primary responsibility being faithfulness to Yahweh over any other gods, and obedience to God's commands.

Covenant lawsuits typically included several elements, such as an appeal for heaven, earth, and all people to hear what God has to say. The lawsuits attest that God has the right to bring charges, and typically spell out God's complaint against the people, who have no defense. The texts typically include reminders of God's past faithfulness along with a verdict that Israel is guilty. This may be followed by a declaration that God will bring destruction or punishment, or it may outline conditions necessary for Israel to be reconciled in relationship with God.

Psalm 50 contains both the threat of destruction, and instructions for worship that pleases God and restores relationship.

(For an in-depth look at covenant lawsuits, see Richard M. Davidson, "The Divine Covenant Lawsuit in Canonical Perspective," *Journal of the Adventist Theological Society*, 21/1-2 [2010]:45-84.)

Third Reading
Romans 4:1-25 (RCL 4:13-25)*

Law and Legacy

For the promise that he would inherit the world did not come to Abraham or to his descendants through the law but through the righteousness of faith. (Rom. 4:13)

Several popular television series have been set in Victorian England, often focusing on its obsession with royalty and nobility, in which everything depends on one's ancestry or lineage. Lords and ladies promenade in their finery and gossip about other families while uniting in their sense of superiority over commoners.

Modern society relies less on honorific titles, but we remain aware that some people are born to wealth or privilege, while others must work to survive and work even harder to prosper or get ahead.

We honor that work ethic, though, and admire people who achieve by the sweat of their brow or through building a business. We like the idea of earning what we get. When carried into the spiritual realm, though, that attitude can prove detrimental.

We *earn* it!
(vv. 1-4)

The notion that we have to earn our salvation or future place with God is an old one. Paul often dealt with it in his missionary work and his writings, as he does here. Many of Paul's contemporaries took pride in earning a righteous standing with God through observing the laws and rituals of Judaism. Paul, however, had come to believe that God's operating premise was one of grace.

In the previous chapter, Paul declared that Christ had revealed the depths of God's free grace toward humankind:

> **Abraham and grace:** Paul's insistence that Abraham did not achieve righteousness through his works is fully in line with the Old Testament story. Though we often refer to God's "covenant" with Abraham, it was clearly more of a promise than a conditional covenant. According to Gen. 12:1-3, God came to Abraham, who had probably been raised to worship the moon god Sîn, and promised to make of him a great nation. Abraham followed God's command that he travel to Canaan, where the scriptures say the promise was repeated several times (Genesis 13, 15, 17, 18, and 22). The only story in which Abraham was required to respond to any ritual requirement is in Gen. 17:1-14, the Priestly account that instituted circumcision as a perpetual way of marking his descendants as having a special relationship with God. Abraham did not always act in what we would consider righteous ways. Twice, for example, he passed his wife Sarah off as his sister and allowed foreign kings to take her into their harems so he could avoid a perceived threat to his own safety. Yet, God still counted his belief as "righteousness."

"… since all have sinned and fall short of the glory of God; they are now justified by his grace as a gift, through the redemption that is in Christ Jesus" (Rom. 3:23-24). Jesus himself had suggested that nothing brought more joy to God than the opportunity to grant grace to a repentant sinner (Luke 15:7).

Paul was concerned because some believers had professed trust in Jesus, but thought that they were still required to observe Jewish law. To counteract the inherent

---

This text is also read on the Second Sunday of Lent in Year B. Verses 1-5 and 13-17 are read for the Second Sunday of Lent in Year A.

legalism in their faith, Paul challenged them to look to the past and consider the foundation of their heritage. Even Abraham, the illustrious ancestor of the Hebrews, had been saved by faith and not works, he said.

Adopting a favorite style of rhetoric, Paul posed a question that his hearers might ask, and then answered it. "What about Abraham?" he asked (v. 1). Shouldn't "Father Abraham" be a prime example of one who was saved through works? After all, Gen. 26:5 claims that God had praised the patriarch, saying: "Abraham obeyed my voice and kept my charge, my commandments, my statutes, and my laws."

Even so, Paul insisted that Abraham's faithfulness was not motivated by a desire to earn God's love, but a belief that God had already shown grace to him. Paul recalled Gen. 15:6, where God renewed a promise to make of Abraham a great nation. In response, "Abraham believed God, and it was reckoned to him as righteousness." Thus, Paul argued, not even Abraham could boast of having earned his relationship with God (v. 2). [**Abraham and grace**]

In Paul's mind, Abraham's faithfulness in keeping the law, his good works toward others, and his unquestioning obedience to God's commands were all expressions of gratitude to God, not attempts to earn God's favor. If Abraham had worked for his reward, he would not have earned it (v. 4), but instead he trusted in God's promise and received God's blessing through grace.

He *saves* us!
(vv. 5-8)

Abraham experienced God's grace, but the scriptures portray him as being faithful from the beginning. What about those who are not so righteous as the iconic Abraham? Paul called upon another ancient example of faith and trust, but one whose reputation was less sterling.

David was remembered as Israel's greatest king and a man after God's own heart, but David also had a dark side. In his most glaring lapse, David had not only committed adultery with Bathsheba, but also tried to cover his crime by ordering that her faithful husband Uriah be sent to a certain death in battle (2 Samuel 11). Could God's grace also justify sinners (v. 5)?

Paul answered in the affirmative. David repented of his sin, cried out to God in repentance, and experienced God's cleansing grace (v. 6). To illustrate, Paul could have

---

> **David's prayer:** Paul apparently regarded the superscription to Psalm 32, "Of David," as an indication that the psalm was literally a prayer of repentance offered by David. More than two-thirds of the psalms have superscriptions, which are not original to the psalms, but were added by later editors. The expression *lᵉdawîd* can mean "of David," in the sense of "belonging to David," but could also mean "to David," or "for David," as in "dedicated to David."
>
> Psalm 51 has an even more specific superscription, claiming to be the actual prayer David prayed following Nathan's convicting confrontation in 2 Samuel 12.
>
> Whether David really wrote Psalm 32 is not central to Paul's argument. Whether it is a prayer of David or some other sinner, the psalm declares a belief that God is willing to forgive repentant sinners by grace.

described David's confession of sin from 2 Sam. 12:13, but instead he quoted from the opening verse of Psalm 32, which was commonly attributed to David.

The psalm expresses the joyful relief of one "whose iniquities are forgiven and whose sins are covered," the overwhelming release of "one against whom the Lord will not reckon sin" (vv. 7-8). The remainder of Psalm 32, like the more familiar Psalm 51, suggests that the psalmist experienced God's grace for one simple reason: he acknowledged his guilt and asked for forgiveness. [**David's prayer**]

Us means *all*
(vv. 9-25)

Some of Paul's readers may have brought up the issue that both Abraham and David were Jews: perhaps God's grace was more evident toward them than toward Gentiles. Shouldn't non-Jews have to do something to earn their right to relationship with God (v. 9)? Can the uncircumcised expect the same rights and privileges as those who bear the mark of God's covenant people?

Paul answered the question with another, returning to his initial appeal to Abraham: "Was God's grace shown to Abraham before or after he was circumcised?" The answer can only be *before* – that is, while he was still technically a Gentile (v. 10). Abraham had been born in Ur and lived much of his life in the northern Mesopotamian city of Haran. According to the stories in Genesis, Abraham was 75 when God called him, but was not circumcised until he had been in Canaan for 24 years. [**Counting years**]

> **Counting years:** According to the stories, Abraham was 75 when he left Haran for Canaan (Gen. 12:4), and he had been in the land 10 years when he conceived Ishmael by Hagar (Gen. 16:3). The command to circumcise in Gen. 17:1-14 took place when Abraham was 99 years old (Gen. 17:1), and Ishmael would have been about 13 years old.

God's grace toward Abraham clearly predated his circumcision, so Paul argued that circumcision was given to Abraham as a "seal" of the righteousness he had already experienced *by faith* – an outward mark of an inner relationship. Thus, Paul presented Abraham as the father of all believers, circumcised or uncircumcised, who put their trust in God (v. 11-12).

Circumcision is not required of Christians, but we may think of baptism as a similar "seal" on the relationship we have with God.

Paul's argument was not yet complete. He knew that someone might ask "But what about the law?" If circumcision was irrelevant to receiving grace, Paul argued, then the law was even more so. By Paul's reckoning, Abraham was "regarded as righteous" several years before his own circumcision and hundreds of years before Moses gave the law. Paul saw the law as a guideline for living as people whom God has already redeemed, not as the means of entering a relationship with God.

If the law had elevated obedience over faith, Paul argued, then the Abrahamic covenant of faith would become void and God's promises to Abraham's descendants would no longer apply (vv. 13-14). But, he claimed, the blessings of keeping the law were overshadowed by the curse of *not* keeping the law (the "wrath" of v. 15) – and no one can keep the law perfectly.

Thus, Paul contended that a right relationship with God is not based on the conditional covenant of the Mosaic law, but the prior Abrahamic relationship of faith and promise (v. 16a). Otherwise, he argued, we would be hopeless. But, if God still relates to humans through grace, all people still have the option of finding forgiveness: God's grace is "not only to the adherents of the law but also to those who share the faith of Abraham" (v. 16b). The promise to Abraham was not for the Jews only, Paul insisted, for God had said "I have made you the father of many nations" (v. 17a, citing Gen. 17:5).

Abraham's faith was such that he believed in a God "who gives life to the dead and calls into existence the things that do not exist" (v. 17b). God had promised to make Abraham the father of many nations, but he remained childless, even when he was very old, and his wife Sarah was long past menopause. Yet, Abraham believed that God could be trusted to fulfill the promise and bring life from their aged bodies, which were "as good as dead" (cf. vv. 18-21). When Abraham weighed all the reasons why he *could not* have children against the promise of God that he *could*, he chose to believe in God.

As a result, Abraham became not only the physical ancestor of the Jewish people, but "it was credited to him for righteousness" (v. 22, a quote from Gen. 15:6). That became a launch pad for Paul to insist that "it was credited to him" was written not just for Abraham, but "also for us, to whom God will credit righteousness – for us who believe in him who raised Jesus our Lord from the dead," because "He was delivered over to death for our sins and was raised to life for our justification" (vv. 23-25).

Modern believers who read this text may find Paul's theological argument to be hardly innovative, for Christianity has long accepted the principle of salvation by faith, and we don't need analogies based on Abraham to convince us. Even so, we can find in this text a powerful reminder of the influence one person can have. Nearly two millennia after Abraham's era and hundreds of years after the Abraham stories were written, Paul remembered his example and pointed to him as a model of faith.

What kind of legacy are we leaving for our descendants? Will they remember us as one who trusted in wealth and achievements apart from God, or as one who trusted a promise that goes as far back as Abraham and as far forward as our future hope?

The Hardest Question
How did the ancient Hebrews connect "salvation" with eternal rewards?

Paul's argument for salvation by grace makes logical sense, but we should realize that he was, in a sense, comparing apples and oranges. Ancient Hebrews such as Abraham did not think of salvation or righteousness as leading to an eternal reward. They believed that all who died had the same fate: a shadowy existence in an underground place known only as *Sheôl*. The Greeks held to a similar view, referring to the home of the dead as *hades*. We find a description of what one might expect in Job's painful complaint, when he wished that he were dead:

> Why did I not die at birth, come forth from the womb and expire? Why were there knees to receive me, or breasts for me to suck? Now I would be lying down and quiet; I would be asleep; then I would be at rest with kings and counselors of the earth who rebuild ruins for themselves, or with princes who have gold, who fill their houses with silver. Or why was I not buried like a stillborn child, like an infant that never sees the light? There the wicked cease from troubling, and there the weary are at rest. There the prisoners are at ease together; they do not hear the voice of the taskmaster. The small and the great are there, and the slaves are free from their masters. (Job 3:11-19)

Late in the Second Temple Period, during the centuries after some Jewish exiles had returned from Babylon to Jerusalem, various apocalyptic writings began to speak of a separation after death. Some apocryphal writings, including 1 Enoch 22 and 4 Ezra 7, imagined that a person's place in the afterlife would depend on how he or she had lived during their time on earth. Similar ideas developed in Greek thought, where influential writers such as Plato and Lucian taught that living justly would ensure a happier afterlife.

By the New Testament period, some Jews had come to believe in an afterlife featuring rewards and punishments, though it remained a matter of debate. This is reflected in gospel stories such as "the rich man and Lazarus" (Luke 16), but it remains a long way from the more detailed view of the afterlife developed by the early church.

Thus, Paul may speak of Abraham being counted as righteous and of David as being forgiven by grace, but neither Abraham nor David would have recognized God's favor as salvation to eternal life, as Paul did.

The prevailing theology of the Old Testament is based on both promise and covenant: God and Israel entered a covenant (Exod. 19:1-6, Exodus 24, later renewed several times in Deuteronomy and Joshua). The covenant promised temporal blessings if the people of Israel remained true to Yahweh (God's personal name, as revealed to Israel), but threatened trouble if they turned away.

Prior to the Second Temple Period, faithfulness to God was defined mainly as worshiping Yahweh alone and turning away from idols. Keeping the law and various ritual requirements became more prominent after the exile, especially as the early rabbis developed a "hedge about the law" consisting of hundreds of minor rules designed to keep people from breaking the more important laws. Jewish identity was established by birth and only occasionally by proselytism, and one did not have to keep the law to remain a Jew: the point of being faithful was the hope of earthly blessings for oneself and for Israel as a whole.

For most of Israel's history, "salvation" meant deliverance from trouble in the present world. Later notions of individual rewards after death were still developing during the New Testament period.

Paul's primary concern was that many new Christians were teaching that people must not only trust in Jesus, but also keep the Jewish law if they expected to be in right relationship with God and gain eternal life. Thus, while Paul's use of Abraham and David as analogies is useful in teaching the importance of faith over works, the comparisons can only go so far.

(For more on the development of views of the afterlife in Judaism, see Meghan Henning's article at http://www.bibleodyssey.org/en/people/related-articles/views-on-the-afterlife-in-the-time-of-jesus, sponsored by the Society of Biblical Literature.)

Fourth Reading
Matthew 9:9-13, 18-26

Life after Supper

Jesus turned and saw her. "Take heart, daughter," he said, "your faith has healed you."
And the woman was healed at that moment. (Matt. 9:22)

Do you have what it takes to follow Jesus? The lectionary's gospel readings for the next several Sundays focus on the theme of following Jesus. In these texts, Jesus treads some ground we might fear to travel, but also leads to places of high splendor. Along the way, he asks hard questions of opponents and friends alike. There are times when our task is to decide in which of those camps we belong.

Today's text combines two rather disparate stories: Matt. 9:9-13 narrates the memorable account of how Jesus called Matthew to be his disciple, and how the Jewish authorities reacted to it. Parallel accounts are found in Mark 2:13-17 and Luke 5:27-32.

The lection skips over a question about fasting in Matt. 9:14-17 and resumes with Matt. 9:18-26, which relates an intertwined story of a woman and a child who found healing in Jesus' touch. Parallel accounts appear in Mark 5:25-34 and Luke 8:43-48.

Follow me
(v. 9-11)

The time was early in Jesus' public ministry, and the place was apparently Capernaum (9:1), which Jesus had adopted as his home base while in Galilee: v. 1 names it as "his own town." Capernaum was also the home of Peter and Andrew, James and John. The town, whose name means "Village of Nahum," was located on the northwest shore of the Sea of Galilee. Modern visitors walk beneath a sign that proclaims Capernaum "the town of Jesus," and visit a Catholic church

Capernaum: Modern visitors to Capernaum can still sit in the remains of an elaborate limestone synagogue that was built in the fourth–fifth centuries, apparently over the basalt foundation of an earlier synagogue where Jesus taught.

that is built above the ruins of an ancient church thought to commemorate the site of Peter's house. **[Capernaum]**

One day, as Jesus walked past the tribute post operated by a turncoat Jew named Matthew, despised by most because he worked for the Romans, Jesus stopped and spoke briefly to the tax collector. All we have of the conversation is this: "Follow me." Amazingly, Matthew "got up and followed him" (v. 9).

We might wish that the late Paul Harvey had been relating the account so we would know "the rest of the story." It is likely Jesus had been developing a relationship with Matthew for some time, and this verse represents his challenge for Matthew to act on their friendship.

The more important issue is not the extent of their conversation, but the fact that Jesus called Matthew at all.

> **Working the road:** Matthew probably worked a booth on the main road: the *Via Maris* (or "Way of the Sea") passed by Capernaum on its way from Egypt and points south to Damascus and the east. Branches off the road led west to the coastal city of Acco (called Ptolemais in Jesus' time, later known as Acre). Matthew would have levied customs taxes on merchants who used the road to transport their goods, and he may also have had responsibility for collecting tribute from the merchants and fishermen of Capernaum.

Tax collectors of the first century were regarded as disreputable and unscrupulous persons who were prone to extorting more taxes or customs than they should. Men could bid for the position, promising to provide the Roman authorities with a certain amount of tribute in a given span. They were free to keep any amount over that total. **[Working the road]**

Since tax collectors dealt with both things and persons considered to be ritually unclean, they were also regarded as ritually impure. Additionally, Jews who collaborated with the Romans in collecting tax from other Jews were regarded as scurrilous traitors. None walked so close to the ground as a Jewish tax collector who stole from his own kindred. No one would have been a less likely candidate for apostleship than Matthew. Yet, Jesus reached far beyond the acceptable boundaries of Jewish society and called Matthew to be his follower and friend.

"Why?" we ask. "Why would Jesus choose such a scumbag to become his disciple?" The answer is simple: Jesus came to save everyone, including the lowest of the low. He wanted to reach out to the outcasts of society as well as the inner circle.

Matthew offered Jesus quick access to the rabble of Capernaum by throwing a party and inviting his friends. Matthew's cronies were likely to have been as disreputable as he was – prostitutes, maybe; card sharks and loan sharks; dealers in stolen goods. Other friends may not have been particularly felonious, but simply on the outs with the religious establishment.

Jesus refused to look down on any person at Matthew's party. He sat with them, ate with them, laughed with them, talked with them. In joining the party, Jesus built relationships of trust, laying the groundwork for others to find faith.

While befriending Capernaum's outcasts, Jesus ran afoul of Capernaum's elite. The leaders of the synagogue were already uneasy with Jesus, who had an unnerving habit of healing sick people and teaching with an attitude of authority. They were hard-pressed to explain Jesus' miraculous powers without assuming that he was indeed blessed by God, but they also expected different behavior from God's chosen messengers. Surely God's prophet would know how important it was to keep the law and avoid outcasts to maintain his personal purity.

Yet, Jesus was an enigma. He taught and healed as a prophet of God, but he ate and drank with partying pagans. The Pharisees approached Jesus' other disciples (who may have been staying outside, as good Jews should), and asked them to explain why Jesus was eating with tax collectors and sinners. The word "sinners" in this case does not describe particularly immoral or iniquitous persons. It was used by the Pharisees to describe the *'am ha'aretz* or "people of the land," the common people who did not follow all the laws of *kashrut* (keeping kosher) with the same single-minded zeal of the Pharisees.

When Jesus heard about the inquiry, he confronted the interrogators himself.

Learn from me
(vv. 12-13)

Jesus responded in what appears to be a straightforward way: "Those who are well have no need of a physician, but those who are sick. Go and learn what this means, 'I desire mercy, not sacrifice.' For I have come to call not the righteous, but sinners" (vv. 12-13). This could imply simply that Jesus was working among the sinners because they needed him most, rather than spending time with Pharisees who were spiritually healthy and didn't need him.

By challenging the Pharisees to learn from Hosea, Jesus appears to have implied that the men who questioned his motives were not righteous, but *self*-righteous. They were not *well*, but spiritually ill.

Whether he ministered to Pharisees or publicans, Jesus accepted them where they were. Physicians do not wait for their sick patients to get well before treating them, and Jesus did not wait for his "bad" friends to become good before reaching out to them.

According to Matthew (but not Mark and Luke), Jesus canceled all their arguments with the single brief quotation from Hosea, a prophet who was held in high esteem by the

Pharisees for his opposition to idolatry and impurity. Yet, they had missed Hosea's teaching about the kind of behavior that truly pleases God. Thus, Jesus responded: "Go and learn what this means, 'I desire mercy, not sacrifice.'"

"I desire mercy, not sacrifice." What pleases God is not the careful ritual of sacrifice and legalistic adherence to the law. What pleases God is the kind of compassion toward persons that is characterized as *mercy*. Jesus' critics would reject countless people in their efforts to remain pure, but God's love does not exclude anyone. To "learn what this means" is to understand that God's acceptance extends to all people. God would rather see us love people at the expense of ritual purity than to love purity at the expense of people. That desire did not change from Hosea's day until the time of Jesus. Neither can we presume that it has changed today.

Trust me
(vv. 18-26)

The second part of our text combines two stories, one of them contrasting a more open-minded synagogue leader with the Pharisees who had criticized Jesus. The main story concerns a man who asked Jesus for help when his daughter died, but it is interrupted by an ailing but trustful woman who met him on the way.

The first story begins with an important official making his way to Jesus. Matthew calls him only as a "ruler" (*archon*), though Mark 5:22 and Luke 8:41 add "of the synagogue." We are accustomed to stories in which such officials disparaged Jesus, but this one came in desperation that went beyond religious scruples. His daughter had died, leaving him nothing to hold onto beyond the slim hope that Jesus could restore her to life.

Jesus was sitting and teaching his disciples when the distinguished leader pushed his way through and knelt before Jesus, pleading "My daughter has just died; but come and lay your hand on her, and she will live" (v. 18). Luke identifies the leader as a man named Jairus, and suggests that the girl was not yet dead, but "was dying."

Jesus got up and followed the man, with his disciples tagging along (v. 19), when the procession was interrupted. A woman who had long suffered from persistent bleeding had slipped through the crowd and "touched the fringe of his cloak," hoping to be made well (vv. 20-21).

> **Flutes and funerals:** As if natural mourning were not enough, it was common in the first century for people to hire professional mourners to mark the occasion, including flute players and women skilled in wailing, probably a reference to high-pitched ululation. The Mishnaic tractate *Ketubot* concerns prenuptial agreements in addition to the responsibilities spouses bear to each other, including burial. According to *Ketubot* 46b, "Rabbi Yehuda says: Even the poorest man of the Jewish people may not provide fewer than two flutes and a lamenting woman, which it was customary to hire for a funeral, as these too are included in the duties of burial" (from *The William Davidson Talmud*, cited from Sefaria.org).
>
> The flutes were probably a form of reed or pan pipes that could produce mournful sounds.

Though Mark and Luke describe a more pointed confrontation, Matthew has Jesus pause just long enough to look at her and say "Take heart, daughter; your faith has made you well" (v. 22a). While Mark and Luke indicate that the woman was healed when touching Jesus, who sensed power going out of him, Matthew connects her healing with Jesus' comforting words: "And instantly the woman was made well" (v. 22b).

Matthew then turns back to the synagogue leader's daughter, whose death was being mourned by "flute players and the crowd making a commotion" (v. 23). [**Flutes and funerals**]

Jesus told the people to disperse, for the girl was "not dead but sleeping," generating laughter from the crowd (v. 24).

As with the previous story, Matthew has abbreviated longer accounts found in Mark and Luke, eliminating all conversation between Jesus, the girl's parents, and the disciples. After the noisy crowd had been put out of the house, Matthew says, Jesus "went in and took her by the hand, and the girl got up, and the report of this spread throughout the district" (vv. 25-26).

Matthew's accounts of the two healings are terse, focusing without elaboration on Jesus' power and growing popularity as more and more people came looking for Jesus.

Isn't that what we're doing when we get dressed on Sunday and make our way to church? In some way we are looking for Jesus, hoping to be healed, wanting to sense God's touch and feel that we are whole.

The church exists among people who believe we have already been touched, that we have already been healed. We come in worship to celebrate what God has already done for us, but we also come seeking continued wholeness, for we know that in this world we will yet be wounded and in need of healing, especially when the spiritual wounds are self-inflicted.

Many of us would confess that we often feel fragmented. We long for some power to put our pieces together so that life makes sense, our minds find peace, and our heart feels whole. We participate in a family of faith because there we find the encouragement to express our own faith, to reach out our hands, to touch the hem of Jesus' garment and feel his power flowing through us.

Sometimes, we are intensely aware of physical needs. Whether it is a new pain or an old one, it worries others. At other times, we are more in tune with emotional needs. We feel like we're on a mental roller coaster with more dips than climbs, one that sometimes ventures through dark tunnels. Our self-esteem may be in shambles, or our hearts broken, or our minds troubled with worry and care.

Medical doctors and therapists may help with our physical and emotional needs, but we have spiritual needs, too, and for those we need Jesus and the support of our worshiping community if we are to find wholeness.

Today's texts challenge us to learn from Jesus, to trust Jesus, and to follow Jesus. In doing so, we not only experience healing and wholeness for ourselves, but also do our part to bring healing to our world.

The Hardest Question
Can we take a closer look?

Amid the multiple stories involved in today's text, the "woman with the issue of blood" often gets short shrift. We may think of her as presumptuous, or be uncomfortable talking about her condition, probably a "female problem" such as endometriosis that involved a loss of blood through the vagina.

In a poor effort to understand the woman more clearly, I offer the following retelling of the story, which also draws on the longer account found in Mark 5:24-34 and Luke 8:42b-48.

You wouldn't have noticed her. If you had been there, in the crowd, in the pressing throngs of unwashed people who pushed and shoved and sought to get closer to Jesus, you wouldn't have seen her. In the ancient world, when you are a woman and you bleed all the time and you can't keep your clothes as clean as you like, you learn how not to be noticed. You walk a little faster, stoop a little lower, pull the headdress a little closer, stay closer to the edge of the road. This woman was a master of the art, and she should have been. She had been at it for 12 years.

Twelve years is how long she had been suffering from a problem with persistent bleeding. She had spent all that she had, Mark says, and endured much at the hands of those who passed for physicians in Capernaum. Even today, such problems are often hard to diagnose, despite sophisticated medical equipment. In our time and our culture, surgery can usually provide relief, but for this woman, that was not an option. In fact, she had run out of options. The only thing she had left was a handful of hope and a name she had heard.

Jesus: that was the name. People said he could heal the sick. Cripples walked. The blind saw. Lepers were cleansed. Nobody told her if bleeding women were cured, but she saw no reason why her disease should be treated any differently – no differently, except it was a lot harder to talk about. Trying to explain her problem to Jesus in front of a crowd would certainly be indelicate and embarrassing. But she couldn't miss the chance that Jesus might heal her! What could she do?

What *could* she do?

"I will touch him," she thought. "If he is a man of such power, if the healing grace of God flows through him, then all I really need to do is touch him – just to touch his garment – to touch the very *hem* of his garment. If the power of God is in him, I shouldn't have to say a word. I won't have to bother him or embarrass myself. I will find a way to touch him. Quietly. Quickly. I won't draw attention to myself. But I *will* touch him."

And so the woman set her mind, and she made her plans. Jesus was coming to Capernaum. It shouldn't be hard to touch him there. Capernaum was such a small place that you could never get lost in its few streets – but you could get lost in the crowd. That was the plan. Wait until Jesus came into town. Stand off to the side, then merge into the crowd. Slip over to within an arm's length of Jesus. Reach out and touch his garment. Ease back out at the next side street. Go home and check to see if it worked.

That was the plan, and it did work. She didn't have to go home and check. She felt within her body that she was healed. When the power of Christ flowed into her, she knew it. Her plan had worked to perfection.

It worked to perfection except for the part about remaining unnoticed. Just as she knew when she was healed, Jesus knew when she touched him. Others were touching him constantly, no doubt, but he knew when *she* touched him. There was something different. Her touch was light, but it was empowered by faith. Jesus was never content to deal with physical ills alone. He wanted to heal her whole person. So, he stopped the entire procession to pursue the quiet woman's greater healing.

"Who touched me?" Jesus asked. His disciples looked at their teacher as if he were a madman. They had seen scores of people touching Jesus, pressing against him. They had no way of knowing that one tiny tap among all the others was a touch of trust. Only two people knew that: Jesus, and the woman with the fingers of faith. Knowing that she had been healed, and knowing that she had been discovered, she stepped from the crowd, trembling with fear and trembling with joy and trembling with an inner presence she could not understand, and she fell to her knees before Jesus. Tearfully, she told him the whole story.

And Jesus told her a story about wholeness. He called her "daughter," though she was no doubt older than he, for she was a daughter of faith. "Daughter," he said, "take courage; your faith has made you well." Mark's version adds: "Go in peace, and be healed of your disease." Healing had already taken place, but Jesus' assuring words confirmed that she was not only healed, but also on the road to better health in every way.

Season after Pentecost: Proper 6

First Reading
Genesis 18:1-15, 21:1-7*

Not Dead Yet

"Is anything too wonderful for the LORD? At the set time I will return to you, in due season, and Sarah shall have a son." (Gen. 18:14)

Have you ever gotten news that seemed too good to be true – news so good that you could only laugh in disbelief? Maybe you won a big prize, or were selected for an honor, or got an unexpected promotion or raise. Maybe someone gave you an extravagant gift, or you learned that your first grandchild was on the way.

Today's lesson tells the story of a couple easily old enough to have great-great-grandchildren, but they were being told that they would soon conceive their *first* child. No wonder they laughed. I suspect we would have giggled, too.

An abandoned hope

Genesis 18 is part of the story of Abraham and Sarah that begins in the latter part of Gen. 11:26 and extends through Gen. 25:11. After spending much of his life in northern Mesopotamia, Abraham (then known as Abram) received a call from Yahweh, instructing him to leave his home behind and go "to a land that I will show you." The call was accompanied by an expansive promise that the LORD would bless Abraham and make of him a great nation, blessing others through him (12:1-3). Abraham was already 75 years old, but he pulled up stakes and moved on, though he did not yet know his destination.

God led Abraham to the land that would later become Israel, repeating or expanding the promises at several points along the way. In 13:14-18, God promised to make

Abraham's offspring as the dust of the earth, and to grant them "the length and breadth of the land" for them to live on. This made it clear that the promise involved both progeny and property.

Despite God's promise, years passed with no babies in sight, and Abraham so despaired of having children that he prepared to designate Eliezer, his steward, as his heir (15:1-3). Yahweh appeared again to assure Abraham that he would have a child of his own, then led him outside. "Look toward heaven and count the stars, if you are able to count them," Yahweh said. "So shall your descendants be" (15:4-5). Abraham responded with faith, the narrator said, "and the LORD reckoned it to him as righteousness" (15:6).

That promise was followed by a spooky night-time ritual of covenant making. God instructed Abraham to cut in half a three-year-old heifer and a three-year-old goat, placing the halves across from each other, along with a dove on one side and a pigeon on the other, with a path between them. As evening approached, Abraham fell asleep, "and a deep and terrifying darkness descended upon him." Yahweh again insisted that Abraham's descendants would inherit the land, and Abraham watched as "a smoking fire pot and a flaming torch" passed between the two rows of animal parts as a sign of God's commitment to following through. [**Covenant, or promise?**]

Genesis 18:1-10 is also read for Proper 11 in Year C.

Covenant, or promise? The eerie ceremony of Gen. 15:7-20 reflects an ancient tradition of "cutting a covenant," in which two parties making a covenant would apparently kill and divide an animal, then walk together between the pieces as a way of acknowledging they might be cut in half if they didn't keep their end of the bargain (Jer. 34:18). In this story, however, two symbols of God's presence passed between the carcass parts as Abraham watched. This indicates that the ceremony served more as a solemn promise from God to Abraham than a formal covenant between two parties. God alone guaranteed the promise.

Still another promise is found in 17:1-22, where God changed Abram's name to Abraham and Sarai's to Sarah (both are dialectical variants of the same names, which mean "Exalted Father" and "Princess"). Speaking to Abraham, God promised specifically that *Sarah* would have a child, after which Abraham could have texted "ROTFL" (text-speak for "Rolling On The Floor Laughing"). For modern texters, it rarely means more than a smile, but Abraham was literally on the floor: "Then Abraham fell on his face and laughed, and said to himself, 'Can a child be born to a man who is a hundred years old? Can Sarah, who is ninety years old, bear a child?'" (17:17).

While Abraham was laughing, God was serious. Something about this promise was different, for it contained a new stipulation that Abraham must obey: he was to begin the practice of circumcision and require his children to maintain the custom throughout all generations (17:9-14). [**Why so many stories?**]

Why so many stories? The several repetitions of God's promise to Abraham serve to emphasize the promise, but also reflect multiple streams of tradition that the author wanted to preserve. Stories of the promise in Genesis 12, 13, 15, and 18 derive from what critical scholars call the "Yahwist" source. Note that in each of them, God is referred to as "LORD," indicating the name "Yahweh." The promise account in ch. 17 comes from a different source known as the Priestly writer, who preferred to call God "Elohim" prior to the revelation of God's name as Yahweh in Exod. 6:2. In Genesis 17, then, the deity is called "God," the typical translation of Elohim. The Priestly writer was also especially concerned with ritual matters such as circumcision, which he alone claims that God commanded in conjunction with the promise (17:9-14).

A hospitable man
(18:1-8)

When we come to Gen. 18:1-15, God's promise of progeny is repeated, but this time in a more personal manner. Abraham had been in the land for more than 20 years. Some years before, at Sarah's urging, Abraham had fathered a son by Hagar, his wife's handmaid (16:1-16). He seemed satisfied enough for Ishmael to be his heir (17:18), but God had other plans.

The story has Abraham encamped at a favorite spot called "the oaks of Mamre," which was near Hebron, in a hilly area west of the Dead Sea. As he sat napping in the doorway of his tent in the heat of a dry afternoon, the old man looked up to find three men standing nearby. The trio must have been impressive in appearance, for Abraham ran to meet the visitors, bowed with his face to the ground, and begged them to rest in the shade and take refreshments before passing on, "since you have come to your servant" (vv. 1-5).

Hospitality was, and remains, an honored custom among Middle Eastern peoples. Even enemies could receive hospitality and protection if they sought it. We are not surprised, then, that Abraham received his visitors with warmth and generosity, but for these guests he put on a particularly extravagant display. Though pushing 100, Abraham *ran* to meet the visitors, *hurried* to ask Sarah to bake an abundance of bread, and again *ran* to the herd to select a choice calf to be slaughtered. He then organized a lavish and hefty meal with dishes of fresh bread, beef, milk, and curds (a form of yogurt). Treating the visitors as honored guests, he "stood by them under the tree while they ate" (v. 8). [**Setting the stage**]

Setting the stage: We don't know at what point Abraham recognized his guests as no one less than God and two angels, but his over-the-top show of hospitality began before he understood who the visitors were. In addition to the story's role in predicting Isaac's birth, the emphasis on Abraham's hospitality also serves to forcefully set the stage for contrasting the inhospitable behavior shown by the people of Sodom in the story that follows (18:16–19:29).

A wonderful promise
(18:9-15, 21:1-7)

At some point during or after the meal, the visitors asked "Where is your wife, Sarah?" (v. 9). Had Abraham told them his wife's name, or was their knowledge of her name the first indication of their supernatural identity? Abraham answered that Sarah had remained in the tent. This does not suggest that Sara was hiding or showing pique: it was customary for men to eat apart from the women, and for the women to remain out of sight.

One of the guests – presumably Yahweh – then declared: "I will surely return to you in due season, and your wife Sarah shall have a son" (v. 10). If Abraham had not yet guessed that his visitors were not ordinary people, that statement should have made it clear.

Sarah's tent was close enough for her to overhear the conversation. At 90 years old and long past menopause (v. 11), she had given up any hope of bearing children, but had not lost her sense of humor: "So Sarah laughed to herself, saying, 'After I have grown old, and my husband is old, shall I have pleasure?'" (v. 12). The thought of enjoying sex and getting pregnant by Abraham in their old age must have seemed ludicrous.

The notion was not at all absurd to Yahweh, however. "The LORD said to Abraham, 'Why did Sarah laugh, and say, "Shall I indeed bear a child, now that I am old?" Is anything too wonderful for the LORD? At the set time I will return to you, in due season, and Sarah shall have a son'" (vv. 13-14). [**At *what* time?**]

In the Hebrew, Yahweh's response comes across as incredulous, as if God couldn't believe that Sarah would doubt. A more literal translation would be: "Why, this? Sarah laughed, saying…" Yahweh's description of Sarah's statement is then more detailed and emphatic than previously reported. The narrator had mentioned only laughter at the thought of enjoying pleasure, but Yahweh quotes her as saying: "Indeed, *truly*, will I bear a child when I am old?"

Yahweh went on to ask, "Is anything too wonderful for the LORD?" The word translated as "wonderful" (NRSV) comes from a verb that can mean "to be extraordinary" or "to be amazing." Since wonderful things can be remarkably difficult to accomplish, it can also mean "to be difficult." Thus, NET has "Is anything impossible for the LORD?"

> **At *what* time?** God's promise in v. 10 is especially emphatic, using a special Hebrew construction that combines two forms of the verb. The literal rendering, "returning, I will return," would be understood as "I will surely return."
>
> But when would God return? The phrase could mean "according to the time of life" or "time of living," or perhaps "time of her life." Some take "living" in the sense of "reviving," as the land does in spring, and see it as an indication that Isaac would be born the next spring. If interpreted as "time of her life/living," it might be a reference to the completion of Sarah's pregnancy. The term is used only here in vv. 10 and 14, and in 2 Kgs. 4:16-17, all in the context of a predicted birth.

and NIV 11 has "Is anything too hard for the LORD?" This is probably the better sense in this context.

The answer to the question, of course, is "No." Nothing is too wonderful, too marvelous, too difficult for the LORD – even the gift of a child to a 90-year-old woman and her centenarian husband.

Fearing that God might be angered by her doubt, Sarah denied having laughed (v. 15), but she did indeed have pleasure *and* a son, according to the story in 21:1-7, where the text says that God remembered the promise, and that Sarah conceived and bore a son in her old age – at just the time Yahweh had predicted (21:1-3).

Abraham was 100 years old when he circumcised his new son (21:4-5), and laughter was again the order of the day. Previously, both Abraham and Sarah had laughed in the relative privacy of their tents, but when the boy was born, they happily named him "Isaac" (*Yitzhak*), which means "he laughed."

"God has brought laughter for me," Sarah said: "Everyone who hears will laugh with me" (21:6). According to the narrator, the proud new mother could not resist stating the obvious: "Who would ever have said to Abraham that Sarah would nurse children? Yet I have borne him a son in his old age" (21:7).

Who would ever have said it? God had said it, more than once, and what God says, God does.

Today we may still laugh at the prospect of God granting a baby to an aged woman, but Christian descendants of Abraham can rejoice even more in remembering how God, in due season, granted another baby – not to an old woman past the age of childbearing, but to a young woman who remained a virgin.

And that son brought joy to the world.

The Hardest Question
When did Abraham realize he was entertaining angels – and God?

The story is carefully told so that the reader will know who is visiting Abraham before Abraham does: "The LORD appeared to Abraham by the oaks of Mamre, as he sat at the entrance of his tent in the heat of the day" (v. 1). Some effort is given to describing Abraham's gradual realization that someone was there: the Hebrew says "he lifted his eyes and looked, and behold, three men were standing across from him" (v. 2). The preposition I've translated as "across" can mean "against," "on," or "over," but the guests clearly weren't looming over Abraham. The text suggests that the strangers were nearby, but they must have held back at a respectful distance, waiting to see how they would be received. After all, Abraham had to run to meet them.

Abraham's quick and extravagant response may lead one to think that Abraham immediately recognized them as supernatural, but it is more likely that he thought they were people of some nobility who were passing by. The previous stories suggest that God had spoken to Abraham several times before, but none suggested that Yahweh had appeared in human form.

One of the strangers must have been more impressive than the other two and was presumably the leader, for Abraham addressed only him: "My lord, if I find favor with you, do not pass by your servant" (v. 3). The title 'adônāy could be used for God, but also as an honorific for nobility or someone who had authority over another.

Abraham asked the trio to stop, rest, and take a meal, adding "after that you may pass on" (vv. 4-5). This suggests that Abraham still thought of them as travelers passing by his tent. He did not yet understand who they were or that they had come to bring him a message before going on to Sodom and Gomorrah.

Abraham remained respectful throughout the meal as he would have if the guests had been human nobility. There is no indication that he thought of them as supernatural: if so, he would probably have been scraping and bowing rather than standing beside them beneath the tree.

Although it is possible that they would have questioned Abraham about his family during the meal, the story suggests that the question "Where is your wife, Sarah?" came out of the blue (v. 9). The men's knowledge that Abraham's wife was still living – and named Sarah – may have been Abraham's first clear hint that his guests were more than human.

The lead speaker's confident insistence that he would return, and that Sarah would give birth to a child, was an added indicator that the stranger was a human-like manifestation of Yahweh. Further evidence of divine knowledge follows Sarah's response. The text says that when Sarah overheard Yahweh's promise, she "laughed to herself, saying …" (v. 12). Yet, though Sarah had laughed silently and spoken only within herself, Yahweh knew how she had responded: "What's this? Why did Sarah laugh and say …?" (v. 13).

If Abraham still had questions about his guest's identity, they would have been answered when Yahweh asked "Is anything too wonderful for the LORD?" (v. 14). Sarah, too, must have realized the speaker's identity, for she "denied, saying 'I did not laugh'; for she was afraid." Sarah feared, but Yahweh had the last word: "No, but you did laugh" (v. 15).

When the guests prepared to move on and Abraham walked with them, there was no longer any doubt that he was bargaining for Lot's life with no one less than Yahweh.

Season after Pentecost: Proper 6

Optional First Reading
Psalm 116 (RCL 116:1-2, 12-19)*

Paying Vows

This text is also read for the Third Sunday of Easter in Year A. A commentary on Psalm 116 appears for that Sunday in Year A, Volume 2 of this commentary.

Second Reading
Exodus 19:2-8

On Being Special

Now therefore, if you obey my voice and keep my covenant, you shall be my treasured possession out of all the peoples. Indeed, the whole earth is mine, but you shall be for me a priestly kingdom and a holy nation. (Exod. 19:5-6a)

Have you ever felt special to someone? We like to think that we are special to our parents, our spouses or friends, or our children. Honest teachers admit that some students are more special to them.

Fred Rogers endeared himself to generations of children by telling them that they were special, and that he liked them just the way they were.

Today's text is about a people who had the opportunity to become truly special to God.

A promise fulfilled
(vv. 2-3)

In the background of today's text is the account of Moses' introduction to Yahweh in a burning bush that was not consumed. The story in Exodus 3 is introduced by the Elohist, who locates it on "Horeb, the mountain of God." After charging Moses with the task of leading the Israelites from Egypt, Yahweh promised "I will be with you; and this shall be the sign for you that it is I who sent you: when you have brought the people out of Egypt, you shall worship God on this mountain" (Exod. 3:12).

According to Exodus 19, there came a day when Moses returned to the mountain. This time he was not leading a small flock of sheep, but a huge and noisy multitude of men and women. God had spoken to Moses the last time he stood on Horeb/Sinai's slopes, and Yahweh spoke to him again. After the people arrived, "Moses went up to God," and "the LORD called to him from the mountain" with

> **Another version:** Here's my translation of Exod. 19:4b-6: "Thus shall you say to the family of Jacob, and declare to the children of Israel: 'You yourselves have seen what I did to the Egyptians, and how I lifted you up on wings of eagles, and I brought you to myself. And now, if you will pay careful attention to my voice, and will keep my covenant, you will be to me a special treasure among all the peoples – for all the earth is mine – and you will be to me a kingdom of priests, and a holy nation.' These are the words which you will speak to the children of Israel."

instructions for what he was to declare to the Israelites (v. 3). [**Another version**]

This is one of the most powerful texts in all the Old Testament. It begins with a stirring call to remember God's work. It offers to us a framework for response to God's grace. And, it gives to believers a special role within God's kingdom. It is God's way of saying "You are special. Let's work together."

A call to remember
(v. 4)

"You have seen what I did to the Egyptians," Yahweh said, "and how I bore you on eagles' wings and brought you to myself" (v. 4).

We all need reminding, every now and then, of what God has done for us. With their own eyes, the Hebrews had seen the plagues strike Egypt. They had seen the waters roll back so they could cross the sea that led to freedom, and then watched the same waters close in and crush the pursuing Egyptians.

But God did not stop with deliverance. As the people marched through the wilderness, God hovered over them like a mother eagle. The people offered very little in the way of cooperation and much in the way of complaints, but God provided water, and food, and rest. God carried them when they could not carry themselves.

So it was that Moses reportedly used this same image years later when preaching by the banks of the Jordan. God had borne Israel, Moses said, "As an eagle stirs up its nest, and hovers over its young; as it spreads its wings, takes them up, and bears them aloft on its pinions" (Deut. 32:11-12).

God had brought the people to Sinai for a purpose. God wanted Israel to learn how to fly, and had brought them there to teach them.

A framework for response
(v. 5a)

God's offer of a covenant to Israel would require a response: "Now therefore, if you obey my voice and keep my covenant ..." (v. 5a).

Take note of the "if" ('im). The promise was conditional. When our English Bibles read "obey my voice," they are translating a special Hebrew construction that combines an infinitive absolute with the finite form of the same verb for emphasis. Literally, it means "if you will hearingly hear," or "if listening, you will listen." To truly hear God's voice is to obey God's command. This passage is the preface to the Ten Commandments. God was offering to Israel a covenant based on the offer of divine grace and relationship, but there was also a part for Israel to play. [**Did you *hear* me?**]

In our time, God continues to offer us the opportunity of a covenant relationship, not just through words carved in stone, not just through a Deuteronomistic tit-for-tat relationship of blessing and cursing, but through the Word made flesh, through Jesus Christ. As with Israel, though,

---

Did you *hear* me? Many readers can identify with the picture of a parent who tells a child to do something, but the child is slow to obey. The exasperated parent then says "Did you hear me?" Most of us heard that as children, or we may have spoken it to our own children. Hebrew has no special word for "obey," because "hear" suffices. To hear is to obey.

---

our participation in God's covenant family begins with acceptance and continues with obedience.

The obedience God looks for is best expressed through faith and loyalty. As Yahweh called upon Israel to live in obedience, so Jesus said to his followers "If you love me, keep my commandments" (John 14:15). In all three synoptic gospels, Jesus makes it clear that his commandments are to love God and to love others with the same kind of unselfish love he demonstrated toward us.

A special identity
(vv. 5b-6a)

If Israel would respond through faith and obedience, God offered them a special identity: "You shall be my treasured possession out of all the peoples. Indeed, the whole earth is mine, but you shall be for me a priestly kingdom and a holy nation" (vv. 5b-6a).

God promised to make of Israel a special treasure. The text utilizes a technical word, *s̆gullâ*. An ancient Near Eastern king could look out over his realm and say "all this land is mine, these people are mine, all the harvest is mine." There is a sense in which this would be true. But, if he took out a sword his father had given him, or a ring from his wife, or looked at the face of his newborn child, he could say "this is *really* mine, my special treasure."

Israel could become not only God's special treasure, but also a kingdom of priests and a holy nation. The Hebrews developed an elaborate system of priests and priestly functions, but the basic duty of a priest was – and is – to represent God to others, and to represent others to God.

Ordination is not required to serve God and become a channel of God's grace and love. Priests have a responsibility to serve as the mediator of God's message to the world. Through prayer and action, priests are to represent others before God, and to represent God to others.

When people take this relationship and responsibility seriously, they can become "a holy nation." In this sense, holiness does not refer to purity alone, but to distinctiveness. The Hebrew concept of being "holy" is to be "set apart" as a people called to worship God and to work in God's behalf.

This Old Testament promise was so memorable that the author of 1 Peter called upon it in his own charge to New Testament believers: "But you are a chosen race, a royal priesthood, a holy nation, God's own people, in order that you may proclaim the mighty acts of him who called you out of darkness into his marvelous light. Once you were not a people, but now you are God's people" (2:910a).

Followers of Jesus do not live under the same covenant stipulations as Israel, but there is much about this text that we, like the author of 1 Peter, can understand as applying to those who relate to God through the new covenant.

We, too, are called to be a special people. And we, too, are challenged to live up to our calling.

Fully trusting in God is a bit like stepping off a cliff and believing God will catch us. To truly follow Christ, we must step from the security of our cultural nest, believing that God has a better life in store for us.

How sad it is to think of an eagle that never leaves the nest and never achieves the joy of flight or the potential that God has placed within it. And how sad to think of a person who never leaves the security of the familiar to discover the abundant life that God has in store for those who will receive it.

It is equally grievous to imagine a church that won't leave its nest. It is the church that should serve as our flight training school. It is the community of faith that gives us opportunities to stretch our wings and soar to new spiritual heights. The people of God should challenge us if we start getting lazy and spend our time circling on the wind: we need our spiritual family to challenge us. It is the people of God who recognize our giftedness and encourage our participation in doing God's work.

The church is not just a hangar where we go to retreat – it is a flight deck that sends us on mission. To the extent we prove ourselves obedient and willing to follow God's way, we can fly. And even if we should run into sudden storms or microbursts or wind shear, God is still with us and will aid us.

We may remember the unforgettable words of Isaiah: "But those who wait for the Lord shall renew their strength, they shall mount up with wings like eagles, they shall run and not be weary, they shall walk and not faint" (40:31).

When my son Samuel was a toddler, the two of us were hanging out in the cul-de-sac beneath a full moon that was high over a neighbor's house, framed by several trees, huge and bright and fringed with faint clouds. I showed the moon to Samuel, and a big grin came over his face.

"Moon!" he said. Then, reaching up with his arms, he made as if to jump and said "Reach! Reach!" It was a special thing to see the wide-eyed innocence of a little child who thought he could reach the moon.

Do we ever feel just idealistic enough and childlike enough to think that we can shoot for the moon, and make it? When we put our trust in the Lord and follow his way, the moon is just the beginning of the places we can go.

The Hardest Question
Can you imagine?

As a way of introducing this text in a sermon, I once tried to imagine a scenario in which Moses would have observed an eagle catching a fledgling on its wings. Anecdotal evidence suggests that such behavior exists, though to my knowledge it has never been recorded. Whether such stories are truth or legend does not impact the power of the metaphor, the image of a mother eagle bearing its young on her wings. For effect, we'll call our story "Just Be-Claws."

High on a rugged spur of a desolate mountain, deep in the Sinai desert, there lived a young golden eagle with the heart of a chicken. His father bore the family name "Nesher," which is Hebrew for "Eagle," and his mother's name was "Canaphim," which means "Wings." I'm sure you understand that all the eagles in that part of the world speak Hebrew.

After the young eaglet was hatched in that high mountain aerie, he quickly developed his own personality, but that is not the kind of approach that gets you ahead in the society of eagles. The youngster was afraid of heights, and he tended to hold on so tightly to the woven brush making up his nest that he quickly picked up the nickname "Teffrey," which is short for "Tepherim," which we would translate as "Claws."

As young Claws began to grow toward maturity, his parents persistently pushed him toward the edge of the nest, because that is what good eagle parents do. Yet, every time Claws peered over the rim to look down at the valley floor several thousand feet below, he got the same quiver in his stomach that he felt the first time his mother brought him the chewed-up remains of a desert mouse for supper. He kept hoping that he would learn to like heights as much as he had grown to love mice, but it was a slow process.

Claws knew, of course, that one day he would have to leap from the nest and learn to fly and hunt for himself. His sister had moved out of the nest days ago. He intended, however, to put it off as long as he could.

Time passed and Claws showed no curiosity or desire to fly. Ultimately, however, his mother Canaphim decided to take matters into her own wings. She sensed an opportunity on a day when her sharp eyes picked out movement on the lower slopes of the mountain. It was a man bringing a flock of sheep to pasture on the tender grass that appeared for a brief time each year.

Claws had never seen a sheep, much less a man, so when his mother called, he momentarily dropped his defenses and crept up to look over the edge and test his own eagle eyes. He was just thinking of how those sheep looked remarkably like little white ants when he felt a gentle but forceful push from behind. Before he had time to clamp down with his viselike talons, the young eagle found himself falling over the edge of the nest and hurtling toward the valley floor.

Now, let's give him some credit. Claws *tried* to fly. He flapped his wings a few times, though not necessarily at the same time, and he could not gain any purchase on the air. Claws, of course, was horrified. Kicking his feet more than his wings, he soon resigned himself to a quick death on the rocks below.

As he hurtled downward, the features of the valley floor began to expand rapidly: trees, rocks, and even the sheep grew larger and larger. Falling closer and closer to the earth, Claws could even see the astonished look on that lonely shepherd's upturned face. But then suddenly, he felt an unexpected movement beneath his frantic feet. The mother eagle had circled overhead to watch her son's descent. When it became evident that he would not make it on his own, she

stooped and dove. With extraordinary speed and accuracy born of many years of hunting swift desert rodents, she swooped beneath the frightened eaglet and caught him on her powerful back.

As Claws dug in with all his might, she absorbed the shock with outstretched wings and went into a shallow glide right over the startled sheep. With practiced ease, she began to move her wings, beating the air in long, sweeping strokes, gradually gaining altitude in a slow, graceful, circling climb back toward the nest.

When Claws finally reopened his eyes, he looked from right to left and back again, watching his mother's wings at work in midair. "Oh," he thought, "so that's how you do it!" He tentatively spread his own wings again and felt the rush of air lift him slightly from his piggyback perch. Claws found his fear being transformed into exhilaration.

Sensing that Claws was ready for another try, his mother went into a gradual dive. The onrushing air swept Claws free and immediately his wings went into action, but slower and more steadily than before. One, two, three beats and he found himself gaining altitude, then gliding smoothly downward, then climbing again with long, powerful, heart-throbbing strokes.

Down below, the solitary shepherd stared in open-mouthed fascination. He was unable to let the moment pass in silence, so he let out a hoarse cheer for the young eagle. Then he began talking to himself, as shepherds are prone to do. "Well, Moses," he muttered, "there's something you never saw in Egypt."

And he thought perhaps it was the most marvelous thing he would ever see, until he looked back up at the mountainside – and beheld a burning bush.

Optional Second Reading
Psalm 100*

Good God!

Make a joyful noise to the LORD, all the earth. (Ps. 100:1)

Do you ever find joy hard to come by? Multiple factors have left many people in a numbing state of ennui. The COVID-19 pandemic seemed to turn the world upside down for more than two years. Millions of people changed jobs. Housing prices skyrocketed and inflation ramped up, leaving many without hope of owning a home. Racial inequality persisted and restrictive laws targeting women and sexual minorities revealed an ugly rancor from legislators who claimed to be righteous. Political polarization grew. Unnecessary wars led to thousands of needless deaths. Some days, it seems that chaos reigns.

Can we still be thankful?

Making the effort to turn from trouble to thanksgiving is a worthy exercise, and Psalm 100 is a perfect text for that. The poem makes deep and meaningful claims about who God is, who humans are, and how the two should relate. The song calls us to be thankful that God is, that God has created us, and that God has called us into relationship.

Whether global trials have left us relatively unscathed or deeply scarred, Psalm 100 can speak to us. It was written for people on both ends of the spectrum and in between. It was written for every person who believes, and even for those who do not believe. It is a joyful invitation for all people on earth to celebrate God, and to celebrate God's goodness.

The psalm is only five verses long, and it falls naturally into two parts, each containing a call to praise followed by a rationale for worship. The first three verses call us to celebrate the belief that the LORD is *God*. The last two verses call us to celebrate that the LORD is *good*. If we can remember no more than that, we understand the main point of the psalm.

Celebrate: the LORD is God!
(vv. 1-3)

The psalm begins with an imperative invitation that might have been spoken by a worship leader in the temple courts: "Make a joyful noise unto the Lord, all the earth!" (v. 1). No word meaning "joyful" is found in the text, but it is often inserted to reflect the worshipful context. The Hebrew literally reads: "Shout to Yahweh, all the earth!"

In the context of praise, one would expect such shouts to be joyful. The phrase "all the earth" implies that the call to worship Yahweh is universal.

What type of joyful noise might the poet have had in mind? The psalm as a whole is clearly a hymn of praise, and it appears to be associated with the worshipers' entrance into the temple courts. Thus, as liturgical churches may play or sing an introit while worship leaders enter the sanctuary (often to the musical shout of an organ), the psalm may have served as a brief call to worship, inviting pilgrims massed outside to come forward into the temple courts.

As a rule, Anglo Baptists in America rarely shout in church outside of an unhappy business meeting. Conversely, many ethnic congregations and churches with Pentecostal leanings anticipate joyful interjections from the congrega-

---

*Psalm 100 is also read for Proper 29 of Year A.

> **Calypso 100:** Here's my take on a modern paraphrase of Psalm 100, to be sung to a Caribbean beat.
>
> Verse 1 (vv. 1-2)
> Praise the Lord in the holy temple.
> Make a joyful noise and sing.
> We will worship our God with gladness.
> Praise the Lord for everything.
>
> Verse 2 (v. 3)
> Know ye that the Lord is God, now.
> God has made us and is our king.
> We're like the sheep within God's pasture.
> What a blessed joy to sing!
>
> Verse 3 (v. 4)
> Come on in with great thanksgiving.
> Come into God's courts with praise.
> Lift your hallelujahs up now,
> Bless God's precious holy name.
>
> Verse 4 (v. 5)
> For you know the Lord is good now,
> Showing love that will not end.
> God is faithful and eternal,
> Always here to be our friend.

tion. Here as in other areas, culture plays a large role in influencing our style of worship.

The psalmist calls us to shout with joy. Does that mean we should seek a hymn leader such as Otis Day from the 1978 movie *Animal House*, singing "Shout! A little bit louder now, Shout! A little bit louder now, Shout! Real loud now, Shout! Come on now…"?

Perhaps not. But what do we need?

When it comes to praising God in church, it's not the volume that counts, but the attitude. Shouting joyfully is just the first of three responses the psalmist calls for in gathering for worship. We are not only to make a joyful noise, but also to "worship the Lord with gladness" and "come into his presence with singing" (v. 2).

"Shout," "worship," and "come" are all imperative verbs. The psalmist has no role for wallflowers at the temple: all were called to worship and to sing.

It would be lovely to know what joyful tunes or harmonies the people of Israel might have sung, but we cannot.

But imagine: if a songwriter were to pen something akin to Psalm 100 today, what sort of tune would she use? I like the thought of setting Psalm 100 to a joyful, Caribbean beat with kettle drums – something that makes hearers want to join in, and maybe even to move. **[Calypso 100]**

Psalm 100 calls us to praise the Lord, and to do so with joy. Now the important question is "Why?" And the first answer is this: because the one we praise is *God*.

Verse 3 calls worshipers to "*know* that the LORD is God." In Hebrew, the word we translate as "know" implies personal, intimate knowledge that comes through experience. That is where worship begins.

There is a difference between knowing about someone and knowing them. The psalmist tells us that we can go beyond the simple knowledge that Yahweh is God: we can *know* God in a personal and intimate way, even as a shepherd and his sheep know each other.

We come to know other people through spending time together. Should learning to know God be any different? Can we expect to know God without spending time in prayer, meditation, or through the simple wonder of appreciating the glorious world we have been given?

Knowing God involves both talking and listening. We may speak in joy or in tears, with easy words of thanks or hard words of sorrow and complaint. Whatever we have to say, God is willing to hear. But are we equally willing to listen, attuning our spiritual ear to whatever manner God chooses to speak to us?

This is emphasized by the poet's use of God's personal name that was revealed to Moses. The name Yahweh may derive from a verb form meaning something akin to "the one who is" or "the one who causes to be." English translations typically render "Yahweh" as LORD, in all capital letters. **[The LORD is God]**

Why do we worship Yahweh? "Elementary," the psalmist might say: "because Yahweh is God!" There really is a God, he insists, and we know God's name, and we know that Yahweh cares for us in a special way.

There really is a God, to whom we owe our being. "It is he that hath made us," v. 3 declares, "and we are his" (NRSV). As God's people, we are like sheep in God's pasture, a common metaphor in Psalms (23:1, 28:9, 74:1, 77:21, 78:52-53, 80:1, 95:7). This claim tells us something about our basic identity in life. It tells us who we are, from

> **The LORD is God:** We can't be sure how YHWH, the Hebrew Bible's special name for God, should be pronounced. This is in part because ancient Hebrew was written without vowels, and before vowel notations were added, the Hebrew people came to believe that God's name was too sacred to pronounce. So, when the scribes later added vowel points to the text, they put the vowels for "Adonai" (a generic word meaning "Lord") with the consonants that we would render YHWH. In German, the same consonants would be rendered as JHVH. Early scholars translating the Bible into German didn't recognize that the Hebrew used the consonants for Yahweh and the vowels for Adonai. They read them together, giving rise to the name "Jehovah," a King James standby born as a Germanized version of two interlaced Hebrew names for God.

whence we came, and where we belong. We came from God, who created us, and we belong in God's fields, where the one who made us also cares for us.

Celebrate: the LORD is good!
(vv. 4-5)

Some interpreters see vv. 1-4 as an extended call to praise, with v. 5 furnishing the reason for praise. I prefer to see a two-part structure in which vv. 1-2 serve as an initial call to praise, with a reason for it given in v. 3. This is followed by a second call to praise in v. 4, with a second reason that worship is due in v. 5.

We can envision the worship leader, having opened the service with an initial burst of jubilation, now inviting the people to come forward to the temple's inner courtyard: "Enter his gates with thanksgiving, and his courts with praise! Give thanks to him, and bless his name!" (v. 4).

Here we have three more enthusiastic imperatives: "Enter!" "Give thanks!" "Bless!" The psalmist understood the human need to acknowledge the Creator and to respond with thanksgiving and praise.

Again, we ask: Why should we offer such praise? Because Yahweh is not only God (v. 3), but also *good* (v. 5): "For the LORD is good; his steadfast love endures forever, and his faithfulness to all generations."

God's goodness is shown in a steadfast or faithful love for God's people. The word translated "steadfast love" (*chesed*) comes from a verbal root meaning to be good or kind. It is commonly translated with words such as "kindness," "loving-kindness," or "mercy." As a divine attribute, it also carries the connotation of loyalty or commitment to covenant promises, leading to its frequent translation as "steadfast love." The word is used 120 times in the Psalms alone.

In choosing this term and combining it with "faithfulness," the psalmist insists that God's love is not volatile or shallow. It is a deep love, an abiding love, an eternal love. Believing this, those who trust in God need never feel alone: God's love is dependable and sure.

But what are some of the ways we see evidence of God's creative power and enduring love despite the troubles that surround us? Can we recognize it in giant bales of hay that dot the fields, in the smell of the crisp fall air, in the colors of leaves and the songs of birds?

Can we see glimpses of God's love in the devotion of a spouse, or a child – or parents whose love never stops? Are we fortunate enough to sense it in the support of friends who truly care about our well-being? [**Things, and thanks**]

Some people may feel more in tune with adversity than with accomplishment. We may have been too often disappointed by those whose love is unsteady and whose promises are empty. We may have borne the brunt of the painful COVID pandemic and its many-tentacled consequences of job losses, social isolation, and the upheaval of schools and workplaces.

For many, the poet's happy praise may ring hollow. Like Israel in exile, we may wonder how we can sing Yahweh's praise while in a strange land, yet the poet behind Psalm 137 found the faith and hope to persevere.

Psalm 100, indeed, may speak most clearly to those whose lives are hard, for in dark days the assurance of God's

> **Things, and thanks:** When she was a little girl, Barbara Ann Kipfer began to make a list of all the little things that made her happy. She started with an ordinary spiral-bound notebook, and soon she had filled it up. As she grew older, she continued making lists of things that gladdened her eye and brought wonder to the heart. She included items such as ancient alphabets, lighthouses, onions on a hot dog, honeysuckles, and tubs of ice cream.
>
> After 20 years of doing this, Kipfer persuaded Peter Workman to publish her list in a book called *14,000 Things To Be Happy About* (Workman Publishing, 1990).
>
> Consider starting your own list. What are some things, large or small, that make you happy and give you cause for thanking God?

loyal love is particularly welcome – and that makes it worthy of praise. When life seems fragile and friendships fickle, it is a comfort to be reminded that the Lord we worship is a God who wants to be known.

With the psalmist, we can declare that the Lord we worship is not just truly God, but also truly good.

The Hardest Question
Is it "We are his," or "Not we ourselves"?

How should we properly translate the second line of Ps. 100:3? The question has long provided an interpretive conundrum. Should it be something similar to "It is he that hath made us, and not we ourselves" (the familiar option followed by KJV and NAS95), or "It is he that has made us, and we are his/we belong to him" (NRSV, NET, HCSB, NIV)?

The problem is not so much one of translation as of choosing which textual option to translate. The received Hebrew text at the heart of scholarly editions was handed down through hundreds of years by special scribes known as the Masoretes, who took careful note of inconsistencies or apparent problems with the text.

The Masoretes would not change the text that had been passed on, but at places where they believed the text may have been incorrectly preserved, they added marginal notes containing what they perceived to be a better reading. Scholars refer to the main text as *ketiv* (what is written), and the alternate, preferred text as *qere* (to be read).

In Ps. 100:3, the *ketiv* and the *qere* reading are two different words that are spelled differently but pronounced identically, which explains the potential confusion. Both words (or word combinations) are pronounced as "low," which provides an English analogue: we pronounce the words "lo" and "low" the same, but they mean different things.

The *ketiv* reading uses the negative particle *lōʾ*, leading to the translation "not we ourselves," even though there's no word for "ourselves" in the text.

Scribes and scholars have tended to judge this as an inferior reading, in part because there's no indication that anyone was claiming that the Israelites had created themselves, so it appears to answer a question no one was asking.

The *qere* reading (*lô*) is a combination of the preposition *l-*, meaning "for" or "belonging to" and the third-person pronoun *ô*, meaning "him." The combination generally gives the sense of "belonging to him" or "his." This leads to translations such as "we are his," which fit the context better.

Ancient texts were all copied by hand, and substituting *lōʾ* for *lô* would be an easy mistake to make.

Some scholars favor a third translation option, noting that the *ketiv* reading *lōʾ* was also occasionally used as an interjection meaning "indeed" or "surely," resulting in "surely we are his people and the sheep of his pasture."

Whichever translation we choose, the end result is the same: God is creator, and we are God's creation; we relate to God as sheep in God's pasture who follow and depend on the shepherd.

Season after Pentecost: Proper 6

Third Reading
Romans 5:1-11 (RCL 5:1-8)*

Hopeful Peace

Fourth Reading
Matthew 9:35–10:23 (RCL 9:35–10:8 [9-23])

The World Needs Healing

When he saw the crowds, he had compassion for them, because they were harassed and helpless,
like sheep without a shepherd. (Matt. 9:36)

Do you like change? All of us go through times of transition in life. We experience movements between stages of life, changing relationships, jobs, and in other ways. Perhaps you have been involved in a church or a business that was growing so quickly that additional staff members were needed – or one that was declining to the point of having to combine jobs.

Transitions may come as the result of an intentional change in the focus or operational strategy of an organization or movement.

Whatever the cause, times of transition can be challenging. Today's text marks an intentional transition in Jesus' ministry as he empowered his closest disciples to go out and expand his work of preaching and healing.

That work is not finished: today's disciples still have work to do.

Focus on Jesus
(9:35-38)

Our text begins with a summary of Jesus' ministry that is almost a verbatim repetition of 4:23. "Then Jesus went about all the cities and villages, teaching in their synagogues, and proclaiming the good news of the kingdom, and curing every disease and every sickness" (9:35).

The writer of Matthew portrays Jesus as having an inclusive ministry to *all* the cities and villages. He did not avoid places with bad reputations or differing ethnic makeups, but reached out to all people through preaching, teaching, and healing.

This suggests that Jesus may lead us not only to places where we are comfortable, but also to those settings where we may be distinctly uncomfortable.

Jesus' ministry met educational needs as he taught in the synagogues throughout the area. He worked to help people understand how his life and work fit into God's plan through the ages.

Jesus met spiritual needs as he "proclaimed the good news of the kingdom" in the synagogues and elsewhere.

Jesus also ministered to the physical needs of those who surrounded him, "… curing every disease and every sickness." He had compassion not just for people's lost souls; he cared about their crippled feet, their troubled minds, and their bleeding sores.

That is why Christ-followers through the years have supported not only preaching and teaching, but also education, hospitals, and social ministries. All of these continue the work of Christ.

But why would Jesus give himself to such a mission to begin with? Because of love: "When he (Jesus) saw the crowds, he had compassion for them, because they were harassed and helpless, like sheep without a shepherd" (9:36).

When we look at the world with a Jesus-centered view, do we not also see many people who seem lost or troubled? Contemporary disciples can easily get caught up in "cocooning" and become blind to the needs of others. If we don't see their needs, then we are not motivated to feel compassion, and thus we don't feel responsible for helping them.

A harvest awaiting: I once served a church that included several tobacco farmers. Trying to understand them and their culture, I sometimes helped out with the field work. One morning around 6:00 a.m. I watched a farmer nervously pacing. The second leaves were ready to be primed and put into the barns, but several men he had hired for the harvest were sleeping off a hangover. He needed men in the field, but they remained in bed.

What is our excuse for failing to join Jesus in the fields of need?

When Jesus looked at the multitudes, he saw them distressed and downhearted. Jesus still calls his followers to see the needs of the elderly, who are often lonely and afraid. He calls on us to see the disillusioned people who have given up on church, to see the open eyes and tender hearts of youth who are so easily influenced and so in need of good examples and loving friends, to see the grimy hands and innocent hearts of children who are growing up in a world that is far from innocent.

Jesus emphasized both need and opportunity: "The harvest is plentiful, but the laborers are few; therefore ask the Lord of the harvest to send out laborers into his harvest" (9:37-38).

Surveys show a persistent rise in the number of people who claim no religious affiliation. A small minority of churches are thriving, but most are in decline, some with little hope of recovery. The age of "Christendom" has passed. Sunday is no longer considered sacred: it is a day for sports and shopping and taking it easy. We live in a new world, but the harvest is still plentiful. [A harvest awaiting]

Jesus told his disciples to pray that the Lord would send out laborers. As it turned out, they were about to become the answer to their own prayer. If we are convicted and compassionate enough to pray earnestly for missions, we will also be convicted and compassionate enough to share the love of Jesus in our own daily living.

Focus on disciples
(10:1-4)

The summary of Jesus' activities and his challenge to pray for laborers is followed by the disciples' own commission to head for the fields. "Then Jesus summoned his twelve disciples and gave them authority over unclean spirits, to cast them out, and to cure every disease and every sickness" (10:1).

It's hard for us to imagine being invested with such power, and despite scattered reports of miraculous healings, we don't see evidence of people with a consistent gift of healing today. Jesus' granting of healing power to the disciples was a special gift for a special time: even then it may have been a temporary sign of the gospel's truth and power. Seeing people cured of physical ills in Christ's name could encourage people to believe he could manage their spiritual ills, too.

Only here, deep into his gospel, does the writer of Matthew list the 12 disciples who were closest to Jesus. Mark and Luke name them much earlier (Mark 3:13-19, Luke 6:13-16). Listing the disciples' names in conjunction with their impending mission gave a more formal sense to the moment, similar to a commissioning ceremony in which candidates' full names are called.

The synoptic gospels and Acts all have lists of the 12 disciples who became known as "The Twelve," and as apostles. [Apostles] There are differences among the lists, generally explained by an assumption that some disciples may have gone by different names (see "The Hardest Question" below). Matthew lists them with a bit of commentary: "first, Simon, also known as Peter, and his brother Andrew; James son of Zebedee, and his brother John; Philip and Bartholomew; Thomas and Matthew the tax collector; James son of Alphaeus, and Thaddaeus; Simon the Cananaean; and Judas Iscariot, the one who betrayed him."

The names are listed in pairs, perhaps echoing Mark's observation that Jesus sent them out "two by two" (Mark 6:7). The writer has put the two sets of brothers together and identified Matthew as "the tax collector." The second Simon's appellative does not mean he was from Canaan: "Cananaean" derives from an Aramaic word sometimes

Apostles: Matthew 10:2 is the only time the word for "apostles" appears in Matthew. The Greek term apostolos means "one who is sent with a message." This is what made them apostles and not just disciples: they were sent out to proclaim the good news that in Jesus the kingdom of God had come near.

Over time, the term "apostle" came to have a more honorific sense, but its primary meaning is "one sent with a message." In that sense, all believers are called to be apostles.

translated as "zealot." He is called "Simon the Zealot (*zēlōtēs*) in Luke 6:15 and Acts 1:13.

Simon was apparently an enthusiastic supporter of Jewish independence from Rome, but it is unclear whether the activist opposition party known as Zealots had yet been organized.

The disciples' names are less important than their number. The selection of 12 disciples parallels the 12 foundational tribes of Israel and has obvious symbolic value: Jesus was laying the foundation of a new covenant.

Focus on ministry
(10:5-23)

The following verses begin a lengthy collection of teaching materials that Matthew has combined in the form of instructions to the disciples before they go out on mission (10:5-42). Instructions for the journey in Mark 6:8-11 and Luke 9:3-5 are much shorter. [**Discourses**] Matthew seems more interested in the collected teachings than the mission itself: unlike Mark (6:12, 30) and Luke (9:6, 10), he says nothing about the disciples' departure or return.

Matthew is also unique in beginning with a stern order that we may find confusing: "Go nowhere among the Gentiles, and enter no town of the Samaritans, but go rather to the lost sheep of the house of Israel" (10:5b-6).

We know that Jesus intended the gospel for all people, as texts such as Matt. 28:19-20 and Acts 1:8 make clear. The writer of Matthew believed, however, that Jesus intended for the gospel to be shared first among "the lost sheep of Israel" before being extended to the Gentiles. His purpose, it appears, was to express a belief that in God's plan of redemption, Jesus came as the ultimate fulfillment of God's plan for Israel. Once the gospel had been preached among the Jews, it could then be extended to all nations.

The disciples' mission, echoing 10:1, was to "proclaim the good news, 'The kingdom of heaven has come near.' Cure the sick, raise the dead, cleanse the lepers, cast out demons" (10:7-8a). In other words, the disciples were to do

> **Discourses:** Matthew 10:5-42, which the writer puts in the context of Jesus' instructions to the disciples, is the second of five lengthy discourses that Matthew attributes to Jesus. The others are 5:1–7:27, 13:1-52, 18:1-35, and 24:3–25:46.

> **Baggage:** According to Matthew, Jesus' disciples were not to profit from their newfound power, nor were they to take along any "emergency money" or even the normal small bag that would be packed for a typical journey (v. 9). Though filled with God's power, they were to live as those who were powerless. Purposeful poverty would give the disciples the freedom to accept help from others, and it would force them to depend on God for sustenance during the mission. In addition, the urgency of the mission demanded that the disciples travel lightly, unencumbered by excess baggage.

precisely what Jesus had been doing: preaching the gospel and healing the sick. They were not just to talk like Jesus, but to act like him: with compassion and self-sacrifice. We may not be empowered with gifts of miraculous healing, but are there ways in which we can live so that others see evidence of Jesus in us?

The core message Jesus instructed his disciples to proclaim was a simple quotation from his own preaching: "the kingdom of God has come near" (v. 7, cf. Matt. 4:17). Astute readers may wonder why Jesus did not instruct the disciples to call for repentance, as Jesus did. Perhaps Jesus simply wanted the offer of salvation to receive primary emphasis. Individuals who sought further information about the kingdom would have ample opportunity to learn more about repentance and salvation, but the central message was this: "the kingdom of God is near!"

A literal reading of Jesus' traveling instructions that follow seems to suggest that Jesus sent the disciples out penniless, barefoot, and without even a staff. His emphasis was not on asceticism, however, but on expediency: perhaps the point is that they didn't need extra luggage. The mission was apparently to be of short duration, and they were to depend on the hospitality of receptive hosts in each town. [**Baggage**]

The disciples were to expect both warm receptions and cold rejections, and to continue the work in either case. The fear of rejection has kept countless Christians from sharing their faith or even acts of caring with others. It's important to know that rejection does not indicate failure when we are being faithful.

Fields of need surround us. Where – and when – will we go?

The Hardest Question
Who were the 12 disciples?

Careful readers are aware that the three synoptic gospels and Acts all include lists of the 12 disciples, but the lists are not identical. How do we deal with the presence of different names?

The disciples' names are listed in Mark 3:16-19, Matt. 10:2-4, Luke 6:13-16, and Acts 1:13. In each list, Simon Peter is named first and Judas Iscariot is last (except in Acts, where he no longer appears). Peter, apparently, was consistently thought of as the primary leader among the disciples.

All four lists put the disciples into three groups of four. The two sets of brothers are always listed first: Simon Peter and Andrew, James and John (Mark lists them in the order Peter, James, John, and Andrew, perhaps emphasizing significance over fraternity).

The second set of four in each list includes Philip, Bartholomew, Thomas, and Matthew. Bartholomew is not a given name, but a reference to his father: the Greek *Bartholomaios* reflects the Aramaic phrase *Bar Talmai*, which means "son of Talmai." Many scholars think he is the same person who is called Nathanael in John 1:46.

The name Thomas is also a descriptor: it comes from an Aramaic word that means "twin." The Greek word *didymus* also means "twin," and the Fourth Gospel refers to him as "Thomas, also called the Twin (Didymus)," as in John 11:16, 20:24, and 21:2. We have no knowledge of who his twin was.

The Gospel of Matthew is the only one that identifies Matthew as "the tax collector," which seems to reflect Matt. 9:9, in which Jesus calls Matthew, who was "sitting at a tax booth." The parallel story in Mark identifies the tax collector as "Levi the son of Alphaeus" (Mark 2:14).

The third set of four includes James the son of Alphaeus (to distinguish him from James the son of Zebedee), and Simon the Cananaean/Zealot. Thaddeaus appears in Mark and Matthew (a textual variant calls him Lebbaeus), but in Luke and Acts he is called "Judas son of James." Some scholars have proposed that he changed his name from Judas to Thaddaeus after Jesus' betrayer gave the name "Judas" an infamous reputation. Thaddaeus could mean something akin to "warmhearted."

Matthew, Mark, and Luke understandably list Judas Iscariot last among the apostles. The meaning of "Iscariot" is unclear: some scholars think it means "Judas, man of Kerioth." Since Kerioth was in southern Judea, that would make him the only apostle who did not come from Galilee. Other possible meanings have been suggested, ranging from "assassin" to "hypocrite" to "redhead." Acts 1:15-23 explains how the remaining disciples chose Mathias to replace Judas so there would still be 12 apostles.

The number 12 was clearly intended to parallel the 12 foundational tribes of Israel, symbolizing that in some way Christ had come to establish a new foundational covenant, not just for Israel, but for all people.

We know very little about the disciples' activities after Jesus' resurrection. Though the others are named in Acts 1:13, only Peter, James, and John play any part in Luke's narrative. This is understandable, as the disciples were all Jewish and probably remained active in the Jerusalem church, working among other Jews. As the Book of Acts describes the shift of the gospel to the Gentile world, the focus moves to missionaries such as Paul and his colleagues.

Many traditions exist about later activities of the disciples. One tradition, for example, claims that John took Jesus' mother Mary to Ephesus and lived there. Another asserts that Peter went to Rome and was martyred there, insisting on being crucified upside down because he wasn't worthy to die in the same manner as Christ. How much confidence we can place in such traditions remains uncertain: tradition is a powerful thing, but not always historically accurate.

First Reading
Genesis 21:8-21

Not Long Alone

So Abraham rose early in the morning, and took bread and a skin of water, and gave it to Hagar, putting it on her shoulder, along with the child, and sent her away. And she departed, and wandered about in the wilderness of Beer-sheba. (Gen. 21:14)

Have you ever faced a major setback that led to a surprising leap forward? Sometimes we complain that our progress in life feels like "three steps forward and two steps back," or even worse, "two steps forward and three steps back."

Still, an apparent obstacle or reversal may turn into an unexpected advantage. Some of the most successful entrepreneurs crashed and burned in their early ventures, but they learned from failure to create a better product or a more effective business model. Any number of people have been rejected or discarded by someone they had expected to love for life, but kept going forward and found greater happiness, whether alone or with a new and better matched partner.

Today's text describes a mother and son who were cast from a comfortable camp into a desert wasteland. On the verge of losing all hope, they discovered that they were not alone, and had an impressive future ahead of them.

Trouble in the camp
(vv. 8-13)

The book of Genesis recounts multiple predictions that Abraham would become the father of a multitude, but he struggled to become the father of one. At one point his aged wife Sarah lost all hope of bearing a child of her own and decided to use her Egyptian handmaid as a surrogate birth mother. She encouraged Abraham to inseminate Hagar, the plan was successful, and Hagar became pregnant (16:1-3). Unfortunately, Hagar then "looked with contempt

---

> **Hearing and seeing:** Both hearing and seeing are important images in Gen. 16:7-14. First, God told Hagar to name the child "Ishmael," adding, "for the LORD has given heed to your affliction" (16:11). In Hebrew, Ishmael is *yishmā'ēl*, which means "God heard," or "God heeded."
>
> The image of sight comes from Hagar's response: she is the only person in scripture credited with giving God a new name. "You are El-roi," she said, which means "God of seeing" (16:13). Hagar was amazed that she had seen the angel of the LORD (an Elohistic euphemism for the appearance of God in human form) and lived, for it was commonly believed that no one could see God and live (Gen. 32:30, Exod. 33:20).

---

on her mistress" (16:4) and Sarah responded in kind, treating Hagar so harshly that the slave girl ran away (16:5-6).

Through a beautiful but often-overlooked encounter between Hagar and the "angel of the LORD," God not only provided for Hagar's needs in the wilderness, but also promised that her son Ishmael would grow into a "wild ass of a man" and become the progenitor of uncounted offspring, though he would live at odds with his kindred (16:7-12). [**Hearing and seeing**]

God intended for Sarah to have a child, however, and Gen. 18:1-15 recounts a personal encounter in which God visited Abraham's camp and told him that despite their old age, he and Sarah would soon have a natural-born son. They both laughed at such a preposterous idea, but in the face of all odds, Sarah gave birth to a boy. They named him Isaac, meaning "he laughed," and Sarah declared that "God has brought laughter for me" (Gen. 21:6).

Playing, or mocking? While we might prefer to think positively of Ishmael, the story is told from Sarah's perspective, and she clearly saw his behavior in a negative light. The only other times the same word is used in an absolute sense (without modifiers) are Exod. 32:6 and Judg. 16:25, both implying negative actions. In the first case, the rebellious Israelites made a golden calf and then started to "play," or "revel." In the second, the Philistines called for the blinded Samson to "play for" or entertain them. In two other instances, the verb is used with an adverbial phrase: Potiphar's wife wrongly accuses Joseph of mocking them by assaulting her (Gen. 39:14, 17). Another usage, which describes an adult Isaac as playing with or "fondling" his wife, is more neutral, though seen with disapproval by King Abimelech (Gen. 26:8).

Sarah's good humor did not last, however.

In their earlier encounter, God had instructed Hagar to return to Sarah with a more respectful attitude (16:9), and the text implies that she did. We read nothing more of their relationship for more than a decade, until the day when Abraham and Sarah held a feast to celebrate Isaac's weaning, which typically happened near a child's third birthday.

The happy celebration turned sour when Sarah found fault with something Ishmael, who would have been a teenager by then, was doing. A literal reading of v. 9 could be "Then Sarah saw the son of Hagar the Egyptian, which she had borne to Abraham, playing." The interpretive problem lies in our understanding of the last word, which is a participle formed from the same verb meaning "to laugh" that was the basis of Isaac's name.

The participle is formed from an intensive stem, which can give it nuances ranging from "he laughed" to "he played" to "he mocked" (laughing derisively). The NRSV assumes that Ishmael was innocent of ill will, translating the verse to say that Sarah saw Ishmael "playing with her son Isaac" (adding "with her son Isaac" after the early Greek version). The NET, on the other hand, casts Ishmael's behavior in a negative light, choosing the more critical shading of the verb: "Sarah noticed the son of Hagar the Egyptian – the son whom she had borne to Abraham – mocking" (see also NIV 11 and NAS 95). **[Playing, or mocking?]**

Whatever brought Ishmael to Sarah's attention, she apparently could not bear the thought of Hagar's son being on a par with Isaac. Forgoing their names, she insisted that Abraham "cast out this slave woman with her son, for the son of this slave woman shall not inherit along with my son Isaac" (v. 10). We are not surprised to read that "was very distressing for Abraham on account of his son" (v. 11), for he loved Ishmael and did not share Sarah's insecure jealousy.

Nevertheless, the narrator says God told Abraham to go along with Sarah and send them away, promising that Ishmael would become the father of a nation of his own, while the people to be known as Abraham's descendants would be descended from Isaac, the chosen son of Abraham and Sarah together (vv. 12-13).

Deliverance in the desert
(vv. 14-21)

Abraham acceded to Sarah's demand, sending Hagar and Ishmael into the wilderness with nothing more than a small supply of bread and water. They went miles to the south "and wandered about in the wilderness of Beer-sheba," apparently lost. It would not have taken many days for both food and water to run out, and soon Hagar despaired for their lives. The narrator does not record any speech from Ishmael, though he later says that "God heard the voice of the boy."

Ishmael would have been in his teens, according to the canonical chronology, but the story speaks as if he were much younger, using a term typically employed for a small child. **[How old was Ishmael?]** After their scant provisions were exhausted and thirst had taken its toll, Hagar "cast the child" under a bush and then went "about the distance of a bowshot" away, believing the boy would die soon and not wanting to watch (v. 15-16).

The NRSV's translation "she cast the child under one of the bushes" gives the impression that Hagar tossed a small child she had been carrying into the shrubs. The verb is used only in the causative stem, and usually means something like "throw" or "fling." It's the same word used to indicate that Joseph's brothers threw him into a pit (Gen. 37:20, 22, 24), that the Israelites threw down the king of Ai's body by the city gate (Josh. 8:29), and that angry priests threw Jeremiah into a cistern (Jer. 38:6, 9). In this sense, we might also use the word "dumped." Ishmael would have been too big for his mother to fling away from her, but we have the impression that the boy, having grown weak, may have been leaning on her for support, and she dropped him in the shadow of a bush.

How old was Ishmael? The account of Gen. 21:9-19 appears to portray Ishmael as a young boy, old enough to walk but still being held by the hand. The canonical chronology suggests that he could have been as old as 18, however. He was 13 when Abraham circumcised him, according to 17:25. Abraham had been 75 when he left Haran (12:4) and had been in the land for 10 years when Sarah suggested that he get Hagar pregnant (16:3), which would make him 86 when Ishmael was born (see 16:16). Abraham was 100 when Isaac was born, according to Gen. 21:5 – which would make Ishmael about 14 at the time. The feast Abraham threw to celebrate Isaac's weaning would have been about three years later, making Ishmael about 17, and quite old enough to carry the goatskin container of water that Abraham reportedly put on his mother's shoulder.

We can only put so much trust in biblical chronologies, however, as writers were typically not as concerned as we are about chronological accuracy. Some modern writers reconcile the difference in the way Ishmael is portrayed by pointing out that the various stories come from two different sources, or that some of the narrative is misplaced, but that makes for a forced and unsatisfying explanation. Perhaps it is best to imagine that the narrator, in focusing on the desperate circumstances of Hagar and her son, considered that the story would be more poignant if Ishmael was portrayed as a much younger child.

Hagar "lifted up her voice and wept," the text says (v. 16), and we assume Ishmael must have been crying, too, for comfort arrived when "God heard the voice of the boy" and "the angel of God called to Hagar from heaven, and said to her, 'What troubles you, Hagar? Do not be afraid, for God has heard the voice of the boy where he is'" (v. 17). Hagar had hidden Ishmael from her own sight, but he was not hidden from God.

The angel instructed Hagar to help the boy up and lead him by the hand, "for I will make a great nation of him" (v. 18). He then "opened her eyes" to a nearby well, from which she could refill the water skin and revive her son (v. 19).

Both God and Hagar looked after Ishmael as he grew, according to v. 20: "God was with the boy, and he grew up; he lived in the wilderness, and became an expert with the bow." While they lived in the wilderness of Paran, south of the Negev and close to Egypt, Hagar arranged a marriage for him with an Egyptian woman (v. 21) – and that's the last we hear of Hagar.

It is also the last we hear from Sarah. Surprised?

A tale of two mothers

We would not expect Sarah to appear in ch. 22, the story of how Abraham came close to offering Isaac as a burnt sacrifice. If she had known what Abraham was up to, it would surely have been the death of her. Indeed, the next chapter begins with Sarah's death in Hebron and the account of how Abraham purchased a burial cave for her – but much time had passed, for Isaac was then 40 years old.

The narrator portrays Sarah with ambivalence. He admires her beauty and her willingness to play along with Abraham's tricks, but he also sees Sarah as the first to give up on the promise by resorting to surrogate motherhood rather than trusting God to grant her a child. Given Sarah's age, we can understand why, but in the narrator's mind, she succumbs to a shadow that darkens as she turns against both Ishmael and her handmaid, who had obediently allowed Abraham to impregnate her.

The narrator also shows mixed feelings about Hagar. She obeys her mistress and accepts her role as a surrogate mother, but adopts a spiteful attitude toward Sarah after becoming pregnant. When treated harshly, she runs away, only to return and bear the child, then be forced to leave the camp with no more thanks than a loaf of bread and a skin of water. In the wilderness, she dumps Ishmael under a bush and retreats, leaving him to die alone rather than staying to comfort him in what she expected would be his last moments.

Despite Hagar's weak moments, she is granted two conversations with God. In the first encounter, God speaks to her, and she speaks to God. Indeed, she assigns to God a new name – *El Roi* – the only person in scripture said to have done so (16:13). In the second encounter, Hagar does not speak, but God provides water and again promises that her offspring – like Abraham's – will multiply beyond counting.

While biblical tradition asserts that the Israelites were descendants of Abraham through Isaac and then his son Jacob's 12 sons, it likewise assigns to Ishmael 12 sons who became progenitors of their own tribes. As Jews look to "Father Abraham," Muslims of Middle Eastern descent also consider Abraham to be their ancestor, but through his firstborn son, Ishmael.

Unfortunately, many Christians look at Muslim people with disdain similar to Sarah's attitude toward Ishmael. We would do well to remember that Ishmael was also blessed by God.

The Hardest Question
Why did Paul call Hagar the mother of Israel?

Although their stories are told in Genesis, both Sarah and Hagar reappear in the interpretive tradition of scripture, and in curious ways. Sarah is named in the company of Abraham in Isa. 51:2 as the mother of Israel's faith. Similarly, we assume that Isaiah had Sarah in mind when he spoke of the barren mother who would give birth to many (54:1-3).

Sarah and Hagar also appear in the New Testament, where Paul treats them in surprising fashion. In an argument for salvation by faith, Paul twists the Genesis traditions with a bold metaphor that aligns Hagar with Mount Sinai and the law, giving birth to children who are destined to slavery. In Paul's metaphor, which quotes from Isa. 54:1, he sees Jews who are enslaved to the law as descendants of Hagar, while Christian believers, like Isaac, are descendants of Sarah and the true "children of the promise" (Gal. 4:24-31).

This is doubly interesting, because in the Genesis tradition, Hagar serves as a counterpoint to the notion that God's care was limited to the chosen people of Israel. Hagar's only narrated conversations are with the same God whom Abraham served, and that same God made promises to Hagar not unlike those made to Abraham.

Walter Brueggemann has pointed out that Hagar "functions in the narrative to keep the horizon of Israel open to 'the other' who also has legitimate claims to make upon the promise of God" (*Introduction to the Old Testament: The Canon and Christian Imagination* [Westminster John Knox, 2003], 50).

So, while in Genesis Hagar is a reminder of God's persistent care for the "unchosen" and Sarah is the mother of the Israel, Paul chose to reverse the two: He portrayed the slave woman Hagar as the spiritual mother of Jews who were enslaved to the law, while depicting Sarah as the mother of Christians who trust God by faith and become "true children of the promise."

Optional First Reading
Psalm 86 (RCL 86:1-10, 16-17)*

The Up Side of Down Days

Turn to me and be gracious to me; give your strength to your servant; save the child of your serving girl. (Ps. 86:16)

Hard times come, and they come for everyone. Sorrow strikes. Health wanes. Debts mount. Relationships flounder. And what do we do?

Many of us – especially men – do our best to push on with stoic equanimity unbothered by trials, even the most challenging ones, even when we are at a loss and don't know what to do.

The psalmists knew something that we often overlook or undervalue: the benefits of lament, of expressing our confusion, giving vent to our grief, and admitting our feelings of helplessness and loss.

Individual and community laments make up nearly a third of the psalms, and today's text is one of them. It is the prayer of an individual who feels oppressed and cries out to God, and he (or possibly she) was not alone: similar laments are found scattered throughout the psalms. **[Whose prayer?]**

A prayer for help
(vv. 1-7)

The psalm begins with a profession of the poet's low standing as one who is poor and needy, but that does not prevent him from addressing God with a quadruple imperative: "Incline your ear, O LORD, and answer me, preserve my life, for I am devoted to you; save your servant who trusts in you" (vv. 1-2a).

Pleas for help are accompanied by professions of devotion that the psalmist hoped might motivate God to respond in a positive way. "For I am devoted to you" is

---

> **Whose prayer?** A superscription associates Psalm 86 with David, but not in the usual way. Instead of *lᵉdawîd*, which could mean "of," "by," or "for" David, this one is called *tᵉfillâ lᵉdawîd*, "a prayer of David."
>
> David may have faced a variety of circumstances where such a prayer would have been appropriate, but there is no other evidence that it came directly from his prayer life.

---

literally, "because godly (am) I," or "because I am loyal." The adjective *chāsîd* is used today to describe Ultraorthodox Jews who seek to follow rabbinic law to the letter.

The psalmist characterizes himself as God's servant, awkwardly interjecting "You are my God" between "save your servant" and "who trusts in you." The disjointed syntax may reflect the deep emotion of the petitioner, who can't call God's name often enough.

Perhaps you have heard people pray in a way that interjects "God," "Lord," or "Jesus" into every expression of petition or praise. Seven times in the psalm, the poet uses the pronoun for "you" (*'atâ*) with respect to God (vv. 2, 5, 10 [twice], 15, and 17). He refers to God as Yahweh four times (vv. 1, 6, 11, 17), and as *'adōnāy* ("lord") seven times (vv. 3, 4, 5, 8, 9, 12, 15).

Imperative verbs and motivational phrases continue in vv. 4 and 5: "Be gracious to me, O Lord, for to you do I cry all day long. Gladden the soul of your servant, for to you, O Lord, I lift up my soul." The word for "soul" is *nefesh*, which refers to one's inner being, the essence of what makes them who they are.

Psalm 86:11-17 is read in Year A on Proper 11. This study includes the entire psalm.

Verse 5 follows the common pattern of praising God's nature in hopes that God will continue to live up to the divine reputation: "For you, O Lord, are good and forgiving, abounding in steadfast love to all who call on you." He will return to this reflection on Exod. 34:6 in v. 15.

Two more imperative verbs intensify the appeal in v. 6, more strongly than the NRSV would suggest. "Give ear" is the causative form of a verb based on the noun for "ear." Shakespeare imagined Mark Antony saying "Friends, Romans, countrymen, lend me your ears" as he eulogized Julius Caesar. Even more forcefully, the psalmist calls on God to "give ear," or "listen up."

The word translated "listen" is also a causative form, which is by nature intense. It implies something sharper than "listen," and could best be translated as "pay attention." If Hebrew had used exclamation marks, one would surely have followed "Listen to my prayer, O Lord, pay attention to the sound of my plea!"

In v. 7 the psalmist expresses confidence that God will indeed hear and respond as he cries out in his "day of trouble."

He may have been a "poor and needy" servant, but he did not lack in *chutzpah*.

A God who can help
(vv. 8-13)

Having done all that he could to attract God's attention, the psalmist turned to flattery in a further attempt to gain a favorable response. This is not to suggest that his praise was not sincere, but it could be read as flattery, nonetheless. Thankful reminders of God's greatness in power and compassion toward the needy might inspire a desire to maintain the divine name:

"There is none like you among the gods, O Lord, nor are there any works like yours. All the nations you have

> **The depths:** The Hebrews thought that all who died went to Sheol, thought to be so deep beneath the surface of the earth that it was also called "the Pit" (Job 33:18, 22, 24, 28, 30; Ps. 7:15, 16:10, 28:1, 30:3, 69:15; and others). Writers often spoke of the "depths of Sheol" (Deut. 32:22, Prov. 9:18, Isa. 14:14). Surprisingly, as here in v. 13, writers expressed their distress as if they had already been in Sheol, and God had delivered them (see also Ps. 30:3, 88:6; Jonah 2:2).

> **Henotheism:** Early on, the Israelites could be described as henotheists, acknowledging the existence of many gods, but ideally worshiping only Yahweh, thought to be supreme among the gods. The first commandment appears to acknowledge this position: "You shall have no other gods before me." Over time, encouraged by the eighth-century prophets, Israel's religious leaders moved toward proper monotheism with the belief that Yahweh was the only true god.

made shall come and bow down before you, O Lord, and shall glorify your name. For you are great and do wondrous things; you alone are God" (vv. 8-10).

The eruption of praise begins with an image of Yahweh ruling over other gods in concert with God's rule over other nations, who worshiped different gods. "There is none like you among the gods" is a quotation from the "Song of Moses" in Exod. 15:11. He moves, however, from henotheism to monotheism with a profession that "You alone are God." [**Henotheism**]

Having professed himself to be wholly devoted and fully trusting in God (v. 2), the psalmist yearns to know even more of how God would have him live: "Teach me your way, O LORD, that I may walk in your truth; give me an undivided heart to revere your name" (v. 11).

Here the verbs remain imperatives, but the appeal is that the psalmist might grow ever closer to God. "Give me an undivided heart" could be rendered as "make my heart united." Wholehearted reverence was the goal, and awe-filled respect for God led to wholehearted and constant thanksgiving: "I give thanks to you, O Lord my God, with my whole heart, and I will glorify your name forever" (v. 12).

Verse 13 can be read as a testimony of past deliverance, but it should probably be understood as a declaration of hope for the psalmist's current situation, which seems dire. The first part has no verb. Literally, it reads "For your steadfast love (is) great over me." The verb in the second part is in the perfect tense, which is typically translated as past, as in the KJV, the NIV11, and the NRSV: "you have delivered my soul from the depths of Sheol." [**The depths**]

The perfect tense was sometimes used to express such certainty of a future event that it was described as past, however, a practice so common among the prophets that grammarians call it the "prophetic perfect." The NET renders it as "and will deliver my life from the depths of Sheol," regarding it as a future perfect: "for he will have delivered my life."

A plea for survival
(vv. 14-17)

The final verses of the psalm shift from praise and confidence to complaint and a renewal of the psalmist's plea. "O God, the insolent rise up against me; a band of ruffians seeks my life, and they do not set you before them" (v. 14).

The poet professes to be in grave danger, with a gang of violent men seeking his life – an apt time for prayer if ever there was one, though probably not one so carefully structured. Again, the psalmist finds his hope in the Hebrew Bible's central credo regarding the character of God as being "merciful and gracious, slow to anger and abounding in steadfast love and faithfulness" (v. 15.

References to this declaration of faith, reportedly announced by Yahweh's own self in Exod. 34:6, are scattered throughout the Old Testament, including several occurrences in the psalms (Exod. 34:6; Num. 14:18; Jer. 32:18; Joel 2:13; Jon. 4:2; Nah. 1:3; Ps. 103:8, 145:8).

If God was truly merciful and gracious and abounding in steadfast love, the psalmist reasoned, then God should deliver him from his distress: "Turn to me and be gracious to me; give your strength to your servant; save the child of your serving girl" (v. 16).

A cursory reading of the NRSV might lead one to say "Wait! Look! The author is a woman who is praying for the life of her child!" We might like the idea of a woman's voice in the psalms, but this one, it appears, was written by a man who wanted to express humility by describing himself as "the son of your female servant" (a literal translation), or more smoothly, "your handmaiden's son."

With the full-throated cry of a child, he concludes his petition with yet another imperative: "Show me a sign of your favor, so that those who hate me may see it and be put to shame, because you, LORD, have helped me and comforted me" (v. 17).

As in v. 13, the verbs are in the perfect tense, but probably to be read as future perfects designed to express confidence. His enemies will be shamed "because you, Yahweh, will help me and comfort me."

Psalm 86 may sound familiar to us, not just because it is so much like many other psalms of lament, but because it may bear more than a passing resemblance to our own prayers. When we find ourselves in times of strain and stress – and especially in distress – we may also pray with fervent imperatives, begging God to help, praising God for past faithfulness, expressing our devotion, appealing to God's grace and compassion.

We also may declare confidence that God will respond, and promise praise when deliverance comes. In the process, whether we get the answer we hoped for or not, we will have undergone the healthy exercise of expressing our pain, making known our hopes, and leaving it with God.

The Hardest Question
Was the author of Psalm 86 a copycat?

Psalm 86 is one of nearly 20 psalms that express the personal lament of a person who feels oppressed. Similar psalms include Psalms 3, 9, 10, 13, 35, 52, 55, 56, 57, 62, 69, 70, 109, 120, 139, 140, 141, and 143. Twelve psalms expressing similar sentiments come before this one.

The psalm seems so highly formulaic throughout that Robert Alter observed: "A reader who has been going through the Book of Psalms in sequence by this point will have encountered almost every line of this poem, with minor variations, elsewhere" (*The Book of Psalms: A Translation with Commentary* [W.W. Norton, 2007], 303).

Does the familiar ring of the psalm make it somehow inferior to others, or suggest that the psalmist was guilty of plagiarism? No, it does not. The psalms of lament naturally share similar themes of distress, whether they relate to sickness, the fear of death, or the oppression of enemies. As such, they also call on a similar vocabulary of stock phrases and familiar expressions. There are only so many ways to say "hear my payer" or "deliver me" from danger.

The profession of God's grace, mercy, steadfast love, and faithfulness was so comforting that it appears in full in two other psalms, and vocabulary taken from it is even more common.

We may find the same to be true in our own prayers. If we grow up in church and hear others praying on a regular basis, we are likely to pray in much the same way. How often have we heard others praise God's goodness in creation or use expressions such as "if it be your will" and "in Jesus' name."

I remember being taught that a prayer should be structured using the acronym PRAY – that our prayer should begin with *Praise* and move to *Repentance* before we *Ask* our requests and then *Yield* to God's will.

If we put a charismatic young minister in charge of a youth group, before long the youth are likely to begin expressing their prayers with similar vocabulary, expressions, and fervency as the leader they admire.

The similarity of Psalm 86 to other psalms of lament does not mean that the author lacked originality – only that he shared similar concerns and vocabulary with other psalmists in similar situations.

Second Reading
Jeremiah 20:7-13

Fire in the Bones

If I say, "I will not mention him, or speak any more in his name," then within me there is something like a burning fire shut up in my bones; I am weary with holding it in, and I cannot." (Jer. 20:9)

Have you ever been caught between two options, and not liking either of them? Sometimes we find ourselves in a bind, between the proverbial rock and a hard place, feeling damned if we don't and damned if we do.

Jeremiah knew that feeling, and that's precisely what today's text is about. **[Jeremiah's context]** Words of God can be painful, even to the one who speaks them.

Heated words and burning bones
(vv. 7-9)

Jeremiah speaks some hard words in this text, words of fierce complaint, and they are directed squarely at God. We can understand his bitterness best by looking to the previous chapter.

Jeremiah had a history of antagonistic encounters with Jerusalem's high priest, named Pashur, who appears to have been a toady of king Jehoiakim (609–598 BCE), the same preening monarch who sliced a copy of Jeremiah's prophecies into strips and tossed them into a firepot used for heating (Jer. 36:1-26).

According to Jer. 19:1-13, at God's instructions Jeremiah had called for senior leaders and priests to gather in the valley of Hinnom near the "Potsherd Gate," where Jerusalem's garbage was hauled away. There he preached a blistering sermon against Judah's kings and its people. He accused them of deserting Yahweh and participating in all manner of wickedness, from theft, murder, and lying to worshipping Baal and sacrificing children on a raised altar or "high place" they had built in the valley, called "Tophet."

The unusual word "Tophet" is often explained as a derogatory term consisting of the consonants for the Aramaic word for "stove" and the vowels for the Hebrew

---

Jeremiah's context: According to Jer. 1:1-3, Jeremiah's ministry stretched from about 627 to 586 BCE, beginning in the hopeful years of King Josiah's religious reforms, and extending through the rule of the foolish king Jehoiakim (609–598) who disdained and persecuted prophets.

Jeremiah was still active when the Babylonians conquered Judah in 597 and took captive Jehoiakim's son, Jehoiakin (598), replacing him with his uncle Mattaniah, whom they renamed Zedekiah (598–587). Jeremiah urged Zedekiah to submit to Babylon, but the king refused. Zedekiah joined Egypt in rebelling against the Babylonians, who returned and destroyed Jerusalem. Jeremiah survived and relocated to Egypt, where he continued to preach and to communicate through letters with exiles who lived in Babylon.

Much of Jeremiah's preaching echoes the retributive theology found in the Book of Deuteronomy: a belief that those who obeyed God's law would prosper, while the disobedient would be punished.

The book of Jeremiah contains several laments sometimes referred to as confessions. Our text (Jer. 20:7-13) is either the last or the next to last, depending on whether vv. 14-18 are regarded as part of the same lament. Earlier lamentations can be found at 11:18-12:6, 15:10-21, 17:14-18, and 18:18-23.

One can make a good argument for including Jer. 20:14-18 with vv. 7-13, but we will follow the lectionary and focus on the first part.

word "shame." In Jeremiah's eyes, the altar where children were sacrificed was a shameful place of burning.

Jerusalem's residents apparently believed the priest's smug assertions that Yahweh would protect the temple and never allow Jerusalem to be destroyed. Similar themes of judgment and false confidence are found in Jeremiah's memorable "temple sermon" (7:1-15), where Jeremiah lambasted the people, asking how they could worship other gods "and then come and stand before me in this house, which is called by my name, and say, 'We are safe!' – only to go on doing all these abominations?" (7:10).

Now Jeremiah stood amid the detritus in the Valley of Hinnom and symbolically shattered a pottery jar, declaring that God would break the city and its people so thoroughly that it could never be mended and that passersby would hiss at the horror of the city's destruction and the bloody slaughter of its people (19:10-13).

If that were not enough, Jeremiah returned to the city, entered the temple, and continued to preach, declaring Yahweh's word of disastrous judgment against a stiff-necked people (19:14-15).

To no one's surprise, the high priest took offense at Jeremiah's criticism. Pashur had Jeremiah beaten, locked in stocks, and subjected to public ridicule through the night. Upon his release, Jeremiah was even more enflamed. He nicknamed Pashur "Terror-all-around" and predicted that he and his family would join other people of Judah in being taken captive to Babylon (20:1-6).

This is the literary setting that precedes Jeremiah's sharp complaint against God in 20:7-9, accusations so fierce that similar grievances came to be known in English as "jeremiads."

Jeremiah accused God of "enticing" him, of deceiving and duping him into answering a call that would bring him only grief, making him a laughingstock (v. 7). God impelled him to speak, but would give him only words of doom and destruction. When his fierce proclamations weren't immediately fulfilled, Jeremiah became a subject of derision and scorn (v. 8), for the false prophets who claimed Jerusalem would never fall seemed more accurate than Jeremiah.

What should one do in a situation like that? Jeremiah was tempted to simply keep his mouth shut and not subject himself to ridicule, but when he tried to remain quiet, the message from God fought to get out, like a fire in his bones that cried for release (v. 9).

Wouldn't you have complained, too? God had put Jeremiah in a no-win situation. He could preach the divine word and suffer public ridicule, or stifle it and face inner torment.

What would *we* choose?

Fearful words and a fearsome God
(vv. 10-12)

Jeremiah sensed that he was the target of a whispering campaign by those who sought to discredit him. As if to mock him, their whispers echoed the nickname Jeremiah had given the false priest Pashur (v. 3): "Terror is all around!" [Terror all around]

Were the people taunting Jeremiah with sarcasm, quoting his own words against him?

Even the prophet's "friends" had turned against him, watching for him to stumble. The NRSV translates the idiom "men of my peace" (a typical description of those who care about one's well-being) as "my close friends," but it's likely that Jeremiah's language was ironic, and "my so-called friends" (NET) is probably a better translation.

Jeremiah's complaint in v. 10 repeats themes from v. 7. Jeremiah had accused God of "enticing" or "deceiving" him and prevailing against him. Now Jeremiah accuses his "friends" of plotting to do the same, hoping they could lure him into a bumble so they could engineer his downfall and prevail over him.

The prophet was not without hope, however. He was confident that Yahweh stood with him "like a dread warrior." As a result, it would be his opponents who would stumble, not him. It is they who would bear lasting shame, not him (v. 11).

As painful as it was to suffer ridicule for declaring a judgment that was slow in coming, Jeremiah was confident that the prophecy *would* be fulfilled. His faith might be

---

Terror all around: An optional translation is that Jeremiah was saying "Those who would cause me terror are everywhere" (NET). Similar expressions are found in Jer. 6:25 and Ps. 31:13.

tested along the way, but in the end, he believed that God would prevail and he would be vindicated (v. 12).

We may be less likely than Jeremiah to think that God has engineered hard times for the sole purpose of trying us, but we all experience difficult days, and they can be a trial. How do we respond to the trials of life? God sees "the heart and the mind," Jeremiah says. What does God see in us?

Happy words and hopeful praise
(v. 13)

Readers may be taken aback when the painful cries of vv. 7-12 suddenly give way to confident praise. How do we explain the sharp transition? Even a casual reader can see that v. 13 seems totally out of place. Between Jeremiah's bitter complaint (vv. 7-12) and a wretched wish that he had never been born (vv. 14-18) is a lilting call to praise: "Sing to the LORD; praise the LORD! For he has delivered the life of the needy from the hands of evildoers."

It's as if a heartbroken person who was pouring out his or her grief in counseling should pause between sobs to jump up and sing, "If you're happy and you know it, clap your hands!"

An obvious and possible explanation is to suggest that a later editor of Jeremiah's work couldn't bear to let the prophet's aggrieved indictment of God stand as the last word, and so he inserted the confident call to praise to indicate that the prophet fully expected God to deliver him. This is implied by an extra space separating v. 13 from vv. 12 and 14 in the NRSV, as if it doesn't fully belong to either.

If that were the case, however, why would the writer not have placed the joyful call at the end of v. 18, following Jeremiah's embittered complaint: "Why did I come forth from the womb to see toil and sorrow, and spend my days in shame?"

If an editor wanted to lighten the mood or ameliorate Jeremiah's charges against God, that would be the place to do it.

While the jarring shift in mood may seem strange to us, it is not an uncommon element in laments found in the book of Psalms, where joyful outbursts interrupt painful pleas with some regularity.

The book of Jeremiah, in its final form, was composed after the Babylonian king Nebuchadnezzar had defeated Judah, destroyed Jerusalem, and carried many leading Israelites into exile. It was written, then, with an exilic audience in mind. [**The book of Jeremiah**]

> **The book of Jeremiah:** While Jeremiah preached in and around Jerusalem during the late seventh and early sixth centuries, the written collection of his prophecies would have first been read by people living in exile, far from Jerusalem.
>
> For Israel-in-exile, whether held captive in Babylon or having escaped to Egypt, the prophet's words would be a reminder that the words of God he had proclaimed had been fulfilled. Judgment had come, but the prospect of hope remained. If they would turn back to following God, they might also sing praise once again.

If Jeremiah had seen or heard that Pashur and his other tormentors had been led away as he had predicted, it could have been cause for rejoicing, and the addition of a short chorus celebrating his exoneration would be fitting.

For most of his career, though, Jeremiah preached warnings that went unheeded and made predictions that went unfulfilled. He sought to serve God and faithfully live out his calling – indeed, the fire in his bones would not let him do otherwise – but it was a hard road to travel and rewards were few.

Jeremiah's complaint is the prayer of an honest man who is willing to shoot straight with God. God did not respond by blasting Jeremiah for impertinence or by assuaging his fears, but by simply giving him another hard word to proclaim (if the events of ch. 21 follow those of ch. 20). Such satisfaction as Jeremiah found would have to come in the knowledge that he was being obedient to the call.

Painful prayers such as this one remind us that God respects sincerity, and almost certainly prefers a plainspoken prayer to a pretty one. Whether we are called to speak hard words, to do hard things, or to love hard people, faithful service to God can be difficult. We may wonder if it's worth the effort. Our prayers may echo more complaints than confidence, but God can take it.

We should not be afraid to pray with both vigor and candor, for God understands our complaints and cherishes our hopes – and will send us right back to work.

The Hardest Question
How can a lament shift so quickly to praise?

Laments are common in the book of Psalms and in books such as Lamentations, Jeremiah, other prophetic works, and Job. In Psalms, we find both individual laments and community laments. In some cases, an individual may speak for the community. Laments are clearly prayers, written in the first person and addressed directly to God, speaking honestly about the individual's or community's pain and hopes for deliverance.

In the most basic sense, laments usually begin with a cry for help (entreaty), which is followed by a description of the petitioner's distress (complaint), generally followed by an expression of trust that God either will or has already responded to the prayer.

Complaints may speak of the petitioner's distress in specific or metaphorical terms. Sickness, death, mistreatment, and enemies are commonly cited. If enemies are involved, their taunts are often quoted.

Most psalms of lament include some expression of trust in God, that God will surely intervene. The expression of trust often includes elements designed to motivate God to respond to the prayer, motifs such as an appeal to God's justice, faithfulness, or trustworthiness. In doing so, the petitioner suggests that God must answer the prayer in order to be known as a just and faithful God who vindicates those who trust in him.

In some cases, laments include vows, conditional promises that the worshipper will repay God's favor through public praise.

Surprisingly, laments in the Psalms, with the exception of Psalms 39 and 88, typically conclude with a note of praise to God for having heard (and answered?) the prayer, expressing a note of surety that often seems quite surprising when contrasted with the deep distress that characterized the beginning of the prayer (see Psalm 13, for example).

How do we explain the sharp polarity between lament and praise?

In some cases, the shift to praise may indicate an expression of subjective faith that God will answer. For example,

the psalmist's fear of his enemies in Psalm 3 concludes with hopeful praise in vv. 3-6.

The words of praise in some psalms appear to have been added after the person praying had experienced the requested deliverance. In Ps. 41:4-10, a psalmist prays for release from those (including friends) who had turned against him. But then the tenor of the psalm changes: "By this I know that you are pleased with me; because my enemy has not triumphed over me. But you have upheld me because of my integrity, and set me in your presence forever. Blessed be the LORD, the God of Israel, from everlasting to everlasting. Amen and Amen" (41:11-13).

In yet other psalms, the shift to praise may indicate the aggrieved one's response to an "oracle of salvation" offered by a temple priest or prophet. Psalm 12, which includes an oracle of salvation in vv. 5-6, may be an example. (Consider also Eli's response to Hannah's prayer in 1 Samuel 1, and her resultant change of mood.)

Finally, it is possible that in some psalms of lament, the apparent confidence is really the promissory part of a vow to praise God if deliverance is forthcoming. In these cases, the conjunction often translated as "for" might better be translated in the equally legitimate sense of "when." Consider Psalm 54, which moves from entreaty (vv. 1-2) to complaint (v. 3) to trust (vv. 4-5), and then to the promise of an offering when God delivers him (vv. 6-7).

When we consider Jeremiah's lament in Jer. 20:7-13, the best option seems to be the second one: that Jeremiah had voiced his complaint to God, longing for deliverance from those who sought to subvert him (vv. 7-12). After being vindicated when his enemies were carried into exile, the change of affairs was acknowledged with the later addition of v. 13.

Optional Second Reading
Psalm 69:1-18 (RCL 69:7-10, [11-15], 16-18)

Beaten Down but Looking Up

Answer me, O LORD, for your steadfast love is good; according to your abundant mercy, turn to me. (Ps. 69:16)

The lectionary theme of lament for Proper 7 continues with a second psalm of lament (in addition to Psalm 86), an optional reading for Jeremiah's lamentation (Jer. 20:7-13). These are read in concert with Hagar's plaintive cry in the wilderness (Gen. 21:8-21) and New Testament readings that explore the trials of temptation (Rom. 6:1b-11) and the call to follow Jesus despite opposition (Matt. 10:24-39).

Can life never be easy, or at least a bit less fraught?

It certainly was not easy for the author of Psalm 69, whose abject sorrow inspired some New Testament writers to describe Jesus' passion in similar ways. [**Psalm 69 in the New Testament**]

A superscription names the tune of the song "According to 'The Lilies,'" and associates it with David, who had many enemies and was criticized at least once for his religious zeal (2 Sam. 6:16, 20-23). It is much more likely that the psalm arose during the exile or in the early post-exilic days, however, when Jerusalem and the cities of Judah were in need of rebuilding (vv. 35-36).

The psalm, which is written from the experience of an individual but could express sentiment of the community, is structured around pleas for help (vv. 1a, 6, 13-18, 22-25, 27-28, 29b) that alternate with expressions of complaint (vv. 1b-5, 7-12, 19-21, 26, 29a). A declaration of hope and praise concludes the psalm (vv. 30-36).

The lectionary reading excerpts scattered texts between vv. 7 and 18, but those selections require context. We'll give primary attention to vv. 1-18 with a brief look at the remaining verses, which repeat similar themes.

Don't let me drown!
(vv. 1-5)

The psalm begins with an image of drowning, a common metaphor for one who feels close to death. "Save me, O God," the psalmist prays, "for the waters have come up to my neck" (v. 1). [**Up to the neck?**]

The poet abounds with watery metaphors. He first speaks of sinking in "deep mire," like quicksand, "where there is no foothold," but then switches to the image of sinking in deep water as "the flood sweeps over me" (v. 2).

The metaphor of deep water recedes in v. 3, for the flood he has experienced is one of tears. "I am weary with my crying; my throat is parched. My eyes grow dim with waiting for my God."

Many of us know what it is like to weep until our eyes are swollen and our tears run dry, especially in situations

---

Psalm 69 in the New Testament: Early writings among the church fathers undoubtedly went too far in reading Psalm 69 as a prophecy of Jesus' zeal and passion, but elements of the psalm are reflected in the stories of Jesus. In v. 9, for example, the psalmist claims "It is zeal for your house that has consumed me." Following the Fourth Gospel's early account of Jesus cleansing the temple, it is said that "His disciples remembered that it was written, 'Zeal for your house will consume me'" (John 2:17)

Similarly, the psalmist's complaint that he was given poison for food and vinegar to drink (v. 21) may be reflected in John 19:28-29, where the soldiers responded to Jesus' thirst with sour wine.

> **Up to the neck:** Literally, the psalmist claims that waters have reached his *nefesh*, or very soul or life. The KJV has "unto my soul," which the NASB20 renders as "threatened my life." The NRSV, NIV11, and NET use a more visual image of "up to my neck" to indicate that his life was in danger.

where me may have felt betrayed or despised by people we thought should support us.

The psalmist envisioned his opponents as outnumbering the hairs of his head, people "who would destroy me, my enemies who accuse me falsely. What I did not steal, must I now restore?" (v. 4).

Had the psalmist been accused of literal theft, or does he speak in metaphor? Whatever the case, he feels wronged, like an innocent victim being pressed to confess to a crime he did not commit.

The poet did not pretend to be perfect: "O God, you know my folly; the wrongs I have done are not hidden from you" (v. 5). The psalmist admitted his failures to God, but still cried in anguish at being singled out and persecuted for things he had not done.

Don't let me be shamed!
(vv. 6-12)

The psalmist lamented that his reputation had been wrongfully besmirched, but his concern went beyond himself. He knew that others looked to him as an example, and he did not want the unfounded tarnish on his reputation to interfere with others' faith.

"Do not let those who hope in you be put to shame because of me, O Lord GOD of hosts; do not let those who seek you be dishonored because of me, O God of Israel" (v. 6).

The poet's situation reminds us of Jeremiah, who spoke God's true word in the face of a religious system that rejected him, had him arrested, and even put in stocks (Jer. 20:1-3). The priests controlled the narrative of what was and was not acceptable. It's more likely, however, that the psalmist had other enemies in mind.

We are reminded of how social media, negative advertising, and ideology-driven news outlets can be used to spread lies and distortions about unfavored political candidates or officials. It's unfair. It's despicable. And yet, it's effective.

The psalmist believed just such a negative campaign was being waged against him, one so effective that he lived in shame and had become alienated even from his own family (vv. 7-8).

How many families are divided today, even among Christians, where painful lines are drawn between believers who focus on justice and concerns for the poor, and family members who think Jesus would promote fewer taxes and more guns?

"It is zeal for your house that has consumed me," the psalmist said, a sentiment later cited to describe Jesus' cleansing of the temple (John 2:17). The poet's opponents do not appear to be temple officials, as in Jeremiah's case. They may have been secularists who had no use for the temple and who resented those who displayed religious fervor – or they could have been people who had no connection to Israel's faith.

"The insults of those who insult you have fallen on me," the psalmist said (v. 9b). Whether he wept or refrained from food or wore sackcloth to express mourning and pour out his heart to God, he was met with insults and gossip, even "the drunkards make songs about me" (vv. 10-12).

Perhaps the poet had a prophetic streak. Isaiah reportedly went about naked for three years as a prophetic sign (Isa. 20:2-3). Jeremiah wore a wooden yoke to symbolize Judah's coming defeat (Jeremiah 27–28). Ezekiel claimed to have lain in the streets of Babylon facing a model of besieged Jerusalem for more than a year as a sign of the length of exile (Ezek. 4:1-7).

No doubt, those prophets would have been subject to ridicule even though they believed they were acting in God's behalf. The psalmist, evidently, felt similarly bombarded with insults. What he saw as personal devotion, his community saw as religious fanaticism.

Don't hide from me!
(vv. 13-18)

The brief pleas of vv. 1a and 6 give way to a much longer request in vv. 13-18, where the poet prays for a time when God will show favor. Addressing God in the imperative mood, he joins other psalmists in appealing to God's reputation for faithfulness and compassion: "in the abundance of your steadfast love, answer me" (v. 13).

> **The Pit:** The Hebrews thought that all who died went to Sheol, a dark abode thought to be so deep beneath the surface of the earth that it was often called "the Pit" (Job 33:18, 22, 24, 28, 30; Ps. 7:15; 16:10; 28:1; 30:3; 69:15; 88:4, 6; 103:4; 143:7; Prov. 1:12; 28:18; Isa. 14:15, 19; 38:18; 51:14; Ezek. 26:20; 28:8; 31:14, 16; 32:18, 23, 24, 25, 29, 30; Jon. 2:6).

The NRSV takes the last words of v. 13, "with your faithful deliverance," as a segue into the next verse, which harks back to the complaint of vv. 1b-2: he wants to be saved from the quicksand, the deep waters, the floods that wash over him so that "the deep" threatens to swallow him and "the Pit" is ready to "close its mouth over me" (vv. 14-15). [**The pit**]

In v. 16 the psalmist again reinforces his appeal with vocabulary from Israel's credo that God is "merciful and gracious, slow to anger, and abounding in steadfast love and faithfulness" (Exod. 34:6). "Answer me, O LORD," he prayed, "for your steadfast love is good; according to your abundant mercy, turn to me."

Increasingly emboldened, he unleashes a string of further imperative and jussive verbs: "Do not hide your face from your servant, for I am in distress – make haste to answer me. Draw near to me, redeem me, set me free because of my enemies" (vv. 17-18).

The psalmist's daring prayer may seem presumptuous to our ears, but they are the words of a desperate man who clearly feels overwhelmed and put upon by critics who have made his life miserable.

He turns back to complaint in vv. 19-21, lamenting that his pitiless enemies have broken his heart with insults and sought to poison his food. He prays that their plans will backfire.

"Let their table be a trap to them" leads to a prayer that their eyes will be darkened and that their loins will tremble – perhaps he hopes that poison intended for him (whether real or metaphorical) will prove toxic to them as well, leaving their camp a desolation of empty tents (vv. 22-28).

A final appeal for divine salvation (v. 29) gives way to a testimony of confidence that God will respond favorably both to him and to the people of Israel, that they might once again inhabit Jerusalem and rebuild the towns of Judah.

Many of us face low spots in life and may at times feel wrongly accused. It is unlikely that religious zealotry is at the heart of our woes, but whatever the cause, the psalmist provides a model of an honest believer who lays his or her cards on the table, whether complaints or concerns, fears or hopes.

Then again, given that the psalmist's sense of rejection was related to his intense devotion to God, we might wonder if our lack of rejection by others could indicate that our convictions aren't meaningful or outward enough for anyone to notice.

Is our faith too easy? A few barbs from secular friends could be a sign of something good.

The Hardest Question
Can we know when Psalm 69 was written?

We cannot identify the setting of Psalm 69 with certainty, though it is unlikely to belong to David's reign in the 10th century, as the superscription claims.

Internal evidence suggests that it belongs to the exilic or early postexilic periods. For example, v. 26 seems to suggest an exilic setting: "For they persecute those whom you have struck down, and those whom you have wounded, they attack still more." Perhaps the psalmist has in mind the exile as the means by which God had "struck down" or disciplined the people, leaving them victims of enemies who make it even worse.

If this is the case, "they" could refer to captors who made fun of the psalmist's faith, or to fellow Hebrews who had lost confidence in God and scoffed at his persistent devotion. If the psalm was written later, after a fraction of the exiles had returned to find Jerusalem in ruins, the reference could be to neighboring peoples, who Ezra and Nehemiah describe as decidedly unfriendly.

Further evidence may be found in the hopeful prediction of the closing verses, which assume that both Jerusalem and other towns of Judah are in need of rebuilding and currently uninhabited by Hebrews: "For God will save Zion and rebuild the cities of Judah; and his servants shall live there and possess it; the children of his servants shall inherit it, and those who love his name shall live in it" (vv. 35-36).

Third Reading
Romans 6:1-11

The Power of Temptation

Therefore we have been buried with him by baptism into death, so that, just as Christ was raised from the dead by the glory of the Father, so we too might walk in newness of life. (Rom. 6:4)

We may as well admit it: We're sinners – every one of us. Even those of us who profess to be Christian – we are sinners, too. We don't like to acknowledge this, but the truth is there, and we can't hide it. We would rather focus on the positive, and build up our self-esteem, and hear how wonderful we are. And sometimes, we need a good shot of self-esteem, but most of us are far more self-centered than we need to be already. That's natural.

We like to sing about positive things, not negative ones. We don't especially like hymns that remind us of our sinful state. Those that remain in our hymnbooks tend to focus on forgiveness and grace for our sin: "Christ Receiveth Sinful Men" and "Grace, Greater Than Our Sin." We prefer more uplifting songs. That's natural, too.

But even so, we can't get around the simple truth that we are sinners, every one of us, and we may as well stand up on our seats and shout it to the world because everyone else knows it anyway.

Some years back, when a group of laymen called the "Promise Keepers" was going full force, newspapers reported that 60,000 men gathered in a stadium in Charlotte, N.C., for a rally and did cheers reminiscent of a football game. One side of the stands would shout "We love Jesus, yes we do! We love Jesus – how about you?" Then the other side would shout the same thing back, and it would go on for a while, each side measuring their love for Jesus in decibels and hoarse throats.

Maybe it would be appropriate for our congregations to periodically do a call-and-response cheer with the choir. We could shout: "We are sinners, one and all! We are sinners – how about y'all?" Could we get into that? Probably not.

It's not natural to celebrate sin in church, or even to acknowledge it, but it *is* very natural to *be* a sinner in church, to be subject to temptation. We know it – we just don't like to talk about it. We like to pretend that we're not so bad, or quietly compare ourselves with people who are worse, but deep inside we know that the dry rot of sin affects us all.

We may be inclined to think of our sins as surface manifestations similar to pimples that appear for a while but then dry up, but the infection of sin goes to the core of every one of us, and we know it is true. Or do we?

Out with the old …
(vv. 1-4)

Having noted the reality and pervasiveness of sin in ch. 3, Paul turned to the gift of grace made available in Christ (chs. 4–5). He concluded that "where sin increased, grace abounded all the more, so that, just as sin exercised dominion in death, so grace might also exercise dominion through justification leading to eternal life through Jesus Christ our Lord" (5:20b-21).

With ch. 6, Paul raises an interesting argument, one that he may have heard on the lips of others who found it hard to follow the straight and narrow. Or, it might have occurred to him that some might take his reference to sin increasing and grace abounding a little too literally.

We can't be sure if Paul was addressing a type of Christian hedonism or building a straw man, but he raised the question of whether it was permissible or even preferable for believers to continue in sin, since God delights in forgiving sinners. Would more sin and more opportunities to forgive increase the divine happiness? [**Another angle**]

Paul would have none of it: "What then are we to say? Should we continue in sin in order that grace may abound? By no means! How can we who died to sin go on living in it?" (vv. 1-2). Paul could not leave the question with no more explanation than a flat "No!" He goes on to explain the rationale behind his answer.

The notion of dying to sin was central to Paul's understanding of baptism as a life-changing event: "Do you not know that all of us who have been baptized into Christ Jesus were baptized into his death? Therefore we have been buried with him by baptism into death, so that, just as Christ was raised from the dead by the glory of the Father, so we too might walk in newness of life" (vv. 3-4).

Many people, sadly, think of baptism as little more than a possibly embarrassing public ceremony that is the

price you pay for a ticket to heaven. Others regard baptism as little more than a landmark event such as the first day of school or graduation.

Paul insisted that it was far more than that. It was not an initiation rite to be performed so one could join a club. Nor was it a magic trick like putting a flower into a hat and pulling out a rabbit. Paul saw it as a complete transformation through union with Christ.

Paul's understanding of baptism appears to have involved total immersion in water, the most obvious way to symbolize one's burial of the "old self." Thus, one emerges from the water as Christ was raised from the dead, now a new person with a new mission and a new walk and a new sense of union with Christ.

In Paul's teaching, baptism marks a transition as Christians become dead to sin and alive to Christ: suggesting that one should freely continue in sin was a non-starter. [**More than baptism**]

Surely Paul knew that overcoming sin would be hard, and he had much to say about that in the succeeding chapters. Our proclivity to sin does not go away, and habits formed over many years are unlikely to disappear overnight. Sin is not something we can quit cold turkey, baptized or not.

We sometimes read of people who become hoarders, refusing to throw anything away, even food scraps and things that are clearly trash. Their homes begin to reek with the festering garbage, but they don't notice because they have lived in it for so long, and they can't bear to give it up.

Persons like that typically suffer from a type of mental illness, but all of us suffer from a spiritual illness that is hard to shake. Paul believed that Christ could bring spiritual healing, and that baptism celebrated a transition from sin's deadly detritus to a clean, new life. That must have been more than some of his parishioners wanted to hear.

In with the new …
(vv. 5-11)

Leaving the old behind can be hard, but we are not alone in the struggle: we trust that Christ is with us to help us. "For if we have been united with him in a death like his, we will certainly be united with him in a resurrection like his" (v. 5). Read in isolation, Paul's words sound like an affirmation of a future resurrection with Christ, but he has more in mind than that.

We are called to resurrection living while in this life: "We know that our old self was crucified with him so that the body of sin might be destroyed, and we might no longer be enslaved to sin. For whoever has died is freed from sin. But if we have died with Christ, we believe that we will also live with him" (vv. 6-8).

Paul's argument may appear to be directed toward the future, but again Paul is speaking of life with Christ amid the daily challenges of life in this world, because we have become new people. "We know that Christ, being raised from the dead, will never die again; death no longer has dominion over him. The death he died, he died to sin, once for all; but the life he lives, he lives to God" (vv. 9-10).

As professed believers, we take on a new identity. To be successful, we must think of ourselves in new ways. Accepting and living into our new identity is essential for shaping the new lives we are called to live.

This is difficult for us, because we find it hard to be whole-hearted at anything. We compartmentalize our home life, our business life, our church life. An occasional Sunday morning may belong to Jesus, but the rest of our time is our own. Jesus may get a small contribution, but the rest of our money belongs to us. Paul saw it differently. Christ did not come to save our souls and leave the rest of us untouched, but to redeem our whole selves.

As Christ overcame death – once for all – so Paul believed Christ empowered Christians to overcome sin, period. As Christ "lives to God" in his resurrected state, "so you also must consider yourselves dead to sin and alive to God in Christ Jesus" (v. 11).

The result, he continued, is that believers should "not let sin exercise dominion in your mortal bodies, to make you obey their passions" (v. 12).

If only the living of it were as easy as Paul's argument for it! This is why we need the church to support us, encourage us, and hold us accountable. This is why we need friends who share our convictions. This is why we need to spend time in Bible study, reflection, and prayer.

A new title may be accorded us in a moment, as when a Ph.D. graduate can first be addressed as "Doctor." But it takes time, effort, and the support of others who also bear the name "Christian" if we are to open our lives fully to the union with Christ that Paul proclaimed.

The Hardest Question
How did Paul interpret baptism?

Charles Talbert offers a helpful summary of Paul's views on the theological significance of baptism:

"Paul's theology of baptism rules out any understanding of the rite as exclusively something the baptized individual does (e.g., 'promises the baptized person makes to God'). Baptism is not the time one promises to be good for the rest of one's life. This moralizing view of the rite is alien to Paul. It is rather a time when the church preaches Christ's death, burial, and resurrection in dramatic form. It is a time when the person being baptized is enabled by God to die to sin and rise to a new life. It is a time when the baptized is allowed to participate for the first time corporately in the church's proclamation of the gospel. If the church is constituted by the proclamation of the Word, entrance into the church is facilitated by one's participation in that proclamation.

"Paul's practice involved the baptized person in both individuation (= becoming an individual) and participation in community. Much church life today is polarized into two camps: one wants to emphasize community, and the other stresses individualism. The issue, in extreme form, becomes 'the herd' versus 'the autonomous individual.' Neither is a Pauline position." (*Romans*, Smyth & Helwys Bible Commentary [Smyth & Helwys, 2002], 179).

For Paul, then, baptism has both individual and collective dimensions. We are not baptized as "Lone Ranger" Christians, but as part of a community of "individuated" believers. The corporate aspect of our faith and practice strengthens our individual lives, while we as individuals build up the faith community.

Fourth Reading
Matthew 10:24-39

The World Needs Shaking

Those who find their life will lose it, and those who lose their life for my sake will find it. (Matt. 10:30)

All of us who read the Bible have our favorite passages. It's inevitable that we may love comforting texts such as Psalm 23 or John 14, or more challenging passages like Micah 6 and 1 Corinthians 13. The creation stories are poetically beautiful, the psalms can be inspiring, and heroes like Ruth, Daniel, and Esther make us smile.

Other texts are more troubling; for example, the psalmist's wish for someone to take his enemy's babies and dash them against a rock (Ps. 137:9). Reading genealogical lists (Genesis 5 and 1 Chronicles 1–9), cultic instructions (Exodus 25–31, 35–40), and tribal boundaries (Joshua 13–23) can be downright boring.

If you read today's text, chances are you won't like it for other reasons. Who looks forward to the prospect of persecution, family division, and self-sacrifice? Who cares for language that sounds like all or nothing?

And yet, there it is. It's part of scripture, the gospel of Matthew's version of several texts also found in Mark or Luke, along with a few words from traditions found in Matthew alone.

What shall we do with this troublesome text? Is there more to it than meets the eye?

Follow the leader
(vv. 24-25)

First, we consider the context. The Jewish author who wrote in Matthew's name probably penned his gospel about 50 years after Jesus' resurrection, so he was not only relying on traditions passed down in the early church, but also reflecting the realities of his own day.

Those realities apparently included aggressive resistance to the early church from both Jews and Gentiles. Thus, the author emphasized Jesus' challenge for his followers to be both fully committed to the gospel and fully prepared to expect opposition.

Today's text comes within what the author has constructed as a lengthy set of instructions to the Twelve as Jesus sent them out to preach and heal the sick in his name. Matthew's version (10:5-42) is considerably longer than the instructions given in Mark 6:8-11 and Luke 9:3-5, probably influenced by the difficult situation in which his readers lived in the late first century.

In vv. 16-23, Jesus told the disciples they were going out "like sheep into the midst of wolves," where they could expect to be flogged in the Jewish synagogues and dragged before Gentile authorities (vv. 17-20). Such conditions would not have been common during Jesus' ministry, but could have characterized the time of Matthew's writing when family members might betray one another and persecution had become common in some areas (vv. 21-23).

We must understand vv. 24-25 in the light of this. Jesus had not yet suffered, but his passion was well known by the time the gospel was written, and readers would understand that his reference to disciples not being greater than their teacher or servants than their masters was intended to say that if Jesus faced opposition, his followers could expect no less.

The mention of Beelzebul reflects an earlier reference to the "ruler of demons" in 9:34 and anticipates a more specific charge in 12:22-32. In both texts, certain Pharisees had accused Jesus of casting out demons by the power of "the prince of demons," who some called Beelzebul. Depending on the source, Beelzebul was thought of as one of the chief demons, or as an alternate name for Satan.

In a play on words, since Beelzebul in Aramaic means something akin to "lord of the manor" or "master of the house," the writer quotes Jesus as using a Greek word (*oikodespótēn*) to say "If they have called the master of the house Beelzebul, how much more will they malign those of his household!" (v. 25b).

The point, again, is that those who follow Jesus faithfully can expect the same kind of treatment that Jesus received, including painful opposition. Only the masochists among us look forward to tribulation, but have you ever considered the idea that a measure of persecution could be good for the church?

When all is going smoothly, it is easy for believers to become so comfortable in our faith that we don't take the challenge of following Jesus seriously, making it easier to focus on petty things that have little to do with true faith. Believers facing persecution, however, are more likely to realize what really matters, and to get serious or get out.

Know who to fear
(vv. 26-33)

The theme of standing strong in the face of trouble continues into the next section, where the author emphasizes the importance of being open about one's faith, even when

---

The Messianic Secret: Jesus' instructions that the disciples should keep certain truths to themselves led William Wrede, a Lutheran theologian from Germany, to propose in 1901 a theory he called "the Messianic Secret." He noted that Jesus not only ordered the disciples not to tell anyone he was the Messiah (Mark 8:29-30), but also warned persons who had been healed not to tell anyone, as in Mark 1:43-45. Wrede also included the idea that Jesus told the disciples he had revealed secrets of the Kingdom of God to them while speaking to the crowds in parables (Mark 4:11).

Wrede's explanation of the secretive commands has since fallen from favor, but it does appear that Jesus wanted certain things kept quiet until the time was right, not wanting to provoke a rebellion among the people or more opposition from the authorities before he was ready to bring his earthly ministry to a close.

The price of a sparrow: The author of Matthew said sparrows could be bought two for a penny. The Romans didn't use the word "penny" or "farthing" (KJV), of course. The word used was assarion, the name of a small copper coin valued at 1/16 of a denarius. Since a denarius was sometimes the measure of a day's pay for a common laborer, the two sparrows could be purchased for less than a half-hour's labor.

Luke's gospel portrays the sparrows as being even cheaper. Luke locates this group of sayings in a different context, where he has Jesus ask "Are not five sparrows sold for two pennies?" (Luke 12:6).

The reference to God's care for sparrows recalls the Sermon on the Mount, where Jesus pointed out that God provided for the birds of the air, who neither sowed nor reaped (Matt. 6:26).

Sparrows were likely among the cheapest items sold in the market: If God cared for them, shouldn't humans be considered of much greater value and thus even more worthy of divine attention?

---

threatened. Commitment to Jesus is not something to be kept secret, but publicly proclaimed. There had been times, early in his earthly ministry, when Jesus instructed his disciples to keep certain teachings to themselves. This is especially evident in Mark, as when Peter professed that Jesus was the Messiah, but Jesus "sternly ordered them not to tell anyone about him" (8:29-30). [**The Messianic Secret**]

But that was then. Things that had to remain under wraps during Jesus' earthly ministry were to be shouted from the housetops after the Resurrection. The author set Jesus' instructions as a word to the disciples before their preaching mission, but Matthew's audience was the post-Easter church: truths once held close were to be proclaimed openly and without fear (vv. 26-27).

Boldness could be dangerous. Still, Jesus insisted that one should not fear those who could harm the body, but instead the one who holds sway over eternity. Faithful followers can be fearless when they remember that our present life is but a brief glimpse of what lies beyond (v. 28).

Using a "how much more?" argument, Jesus noted that sparrows were so insignificant that two could be bought for a penny, and yet God took notice of them. How much more could God be trusted to care for human believers, whose every hair was subject to God's attention (vv. 29-31)? [**The price of a sparrow**]

> **Eating sparrows?** Crystal King, citing an ancient Roman cookbook written by Apicius, notes that songbirds were included in the Romans' diet: "little birds, such as figpeckers, sparrows, thrushes and ortolans were often defeathered, then cooked whole, to be eaten, bones and all" (from "Everything you ever wanted to know about: The Food of Ancient Rome," https://www.crystalking.com/thefoodofancientrome).

Some may wonder why anyone would want to buy or sell sparrows, whatever the price. Like other small birds and even dormice, sparrows were roasted and eaten as delicacies in Roman cuisine. Matthew's readers lived within a Roman culture and would have seen the bargain birds sold in the marketplace. [**Eating sparrows?**]

Expect division
(vv. 32-39)

Believers need not fear others when God is on their side, but who can be confident of God's favor? The writer believed a person's greatest fear should be what Jesus thinks of him or her. Only those who faithfully acknowledge Jesus on earth can expect Jesus to acknowledge them in heaven, according to vv. 32-33. The allusion to the judgment was a reminder that those who denied Christ in the face of persecution would themselves be denied by Christ.

The closing verses of this section are perhaps the most filled with angst. Though we think of Jesus as the "Prince of Peace" and the source of ultimate peace, being sold out to Jesus is no guarantee of familial peace. "I have not come to bring peace, but a sword," Jesus said (v. 34). Choosing to follow Christ when others did not could set parents against children or children against parents (vv. 35-36).

In so many words, Jesus was saying that if push comes to shove, faithful followers will choose the call of Christ over the desires of family. This does not mean such conflict is inevitable. When families are united in trusting Christ – or in rejecting him – faith may have little effect on domestic harmony. Even within Christian families, conflict can arise when one or more family members take Jesus more seriously than others, or if they choose to express their faith in different ways.

What happens when one member of a married couple feels called to full-time ministry or to devoting substantial time and money to volunteer ministries, while the other partner doesn't feel so inclined? Conflict can result.

Similarly, consider the widespread polarization we currently face in America. Untold family gatherings have been ruined by hot debates over political elections or Supreme Court decisions, and people on both sides of divisive issues may believe they are arguing from the position of a faithful Christian.

Christians are not immune to evil's pernicious ability to turn people against each other, not just between nations, but within nations, churches, and families. Choosing to follow Jesus' way can be painful and hard, even divisive. But those who give first place to their personal comfort and self-fulfillment will find that what they achieve in this life will not last. Those who give themselves fully to the service of Christ are the ones who find the true life that is not only abundant, but also eternal.

Whether we like thinking of such things or not, these purport to be the words of Jesus (v. 39), so we should best pay attention. Living with a Jesus-centered worldview may not be easy or make us popular, but it will make us whole.

The Hardest Question
Who was Beelzebul – or is it Beelzebub?

The character known as Beelzebul probably goes back to 2 Kings 1, in which Israel's king Ahaziah had been injured in a fall and sought the aid of Baal-zebub, the god of the Philistines who lived in Ekron. Baal-zebub means "Lord of the flies."

It is possible that the actual name was Baal-zebul, meaning "Lord of the house," and that the Hebrew narrator changed it to Baal-zebub as a derogatory nickname.

By the first century CE, a developing belief in demons in Judaism had come to speak of Beelzebub as a fallen angel turned prince of demons. In the Testament of Solomon, a pseudepigraphal work with roots in the first century, "Beelzeboul" appears as one of seven named demons.

In the New Testament, Beelzebul appears as the "prince of demons," basically equivalent to Satan (Mark 3:22; Matt. 10:25, 12:25, 27; Luke 11:15, 18-19). In each case, Jesus was accused of casting out demons by the power of Beelzebul. Jesus rejected the charge as ridiculous, as in Matt. 12:23-28:

All the crowds were amazed and said, "Can this be the Son of David?" But when the Pharisees heard it, they said, "It is only by Beelzebul, the ruler of the demons, that this fellow casts out the demons." He knew what they were thinking and said to them, "Every kingdom divided against itself is laid waste, and no city or house divided against itself will stand. If Satan casts out Satan, he is divided against himself; how then will his kingdom stand? If I cast out demons by Beelzebul, by whom do your own exorcists cast them out? Therefore they will be your judges. But if it is by the Spirit of God that I cast out demons, then the kingdom of God has come to you."

References to Beelzebul in popular demonology do not require that we share similar beliefs. Jesus spoke to the people of his day and in the language of his day, using the same references to Beelzebul, Satan, or hell that were common parlance among his hearers. Belief in Beelzebul died out in Jewish thought, but the idea of a demonic Beelzebub persisted in some Christian circles, as echoed in the highly imaginative writings of John Milton (*Paradise Lost*) and John Bunyan (*Pilgrim's Progress*).

First Reading
Genesis 22:1-19

The Closest Call

He said, "Do not lay your hand on the boy or do anything to him; for now I know that you fear God, since you have not withheld your son, your only son, from me." (Gen. 22:12)

Can you begin to imagine being asked to bind your only child, lay him on an altar, slice his throat, and light a fire beneath him? The very thought is horrifying beyond measure. Yet, the Bible insists that God asked Abraham to do that very thing – as a test – to determine if he was truly faithful and worthy of the blessing God had already promised several times before. [**The source of the story**]

As it has come down to us, the story is both warmly touching and deeply troubling. It speaks of confident faith on the part of Abraham and Isaac: Abraham trusts God, and Isaac trusts Abraham. Yet, such testing seems abusive. Would God command a father who had waited 100 years for a son to take that beloved child and return him to God as a burnt sacrifice?

In the late 1960s, British Baptist G. Henton Davies argued that God would not have put Abraham through such a terrorizing trial. In a commentary written for the Broadman

> **Context:** In Genesis 21, Abraham had lost his son Ishmael after giving in to Sarah's demand that he and his mother be sent away. God had promised to make a great nation out of Ishmael, even though he would not be the ancestor of the promised people. Would God also find a way to keep the promise alive if Abraham obeyed his command to sacrifice Isaac?
>
> Abraham's obedience to God's initial call (Gen. 12:1-9) cut him off from his past: if he obeyed the new command, it would cut him off from his future. Yet, the story portrays Abraham as apparently confident that the God who had previously worked miracles in his life could still fulfill the promises made time and again.

Bible Commentary, he offered a psychological argument that Abraham, aware that some of his pagan neighbors occasionally sacrificed their children, had convinced himself that God had called him to do the same thing.

Publication of the commentary stirred such controversy that it was recalled and assigned to a new writer, Clyde Francisco. Francisco allowed that Abraham may well have asked himself whether he loved his god as much as some of his pagan neighbors loved theirs, but insisted that "It was not a test that Abraham gave himself … a man so signally led and blessed by God would have had to hear from God himself the actual imperative to make the sacrifice" ("Genesis," in the *Broadman Bible Commentary*, vol. 1 [Baptist Sunday School Board, 1973], 187-188).

While modern readers can certainly debate whether they believe God would have asked such a thing, the bibli-

> **The source of the story:** Scholars often note that Genesis 22 is one of the most carefully crafted stories in the Old Testament. The story refers to God as Elohim (mostly, but not always) and has some other characteristics of the source generally known as the Elohist (E), so it is often labeled as an Elohistic story. The simple, bare-bones telling of the story, however, smacks of the Yahwist (J) source, which was probably earlier, and preferred to speak of God as Yahweh. The story uses Yahweh as a name for God in vv. 11, 14, 15, and 16. It is likely that the story was very old, perhaps first written by the Yahwist, then later edited by the Elohist.

cal writer had no doubt, and we must deal with the story from his perspective. **[Context]**

The writer masterfully evokes deep emotion without using a single word of feeling. He never speaks of fear, or pain, or heartache, or conflicting emotions – and yet the artful and often repetitive arrangement of actions and words grabs the reader's heart, and squeezes.

A terrifying test
(vv. 1-8)

The story begins with an excruciating demand. The narrator knows it is a test, and the reader knows (v. 1), but Abraham knows only that God has told him to "Take your son, your only son Isaac, whom you love, and go to the land of Moriah, and offer him there as a burnt offering on the mountain that I shall show you" (v. 2).

How could Abraham not protest? Why is there no questioning? Could anyone truly trust God so ardently that he or she would slaughter a child with no word of complaint?

The author presents Abraham as an icon of trustfulness, so any recriminations or self-doubts he might have entertained remain hovering in the background. This engages the reader more deeply: we must imagine what was going on in Abraham's mind and heart and belly as he got up early the next morning, chopped wood for the sacrificial pyre, bound it onto his donkey, and gathered his son and two servants to begin a long journey fraught with uncertainty (v. 3).

Sarah does not appear in this story, though she had a prominent role in the previous chapter: the future lies in Abraham's hands alone. Will he follow through? If he does, what happens to the promise? Will Sarah have yet another child somewhere past 110 years old?

The narrator relates the journey in dreamlike silence. No words were spoken until the third day, when Abraham saw the mountain ahead, and told the servants to stay with the donkey while "the boy and I will go over there; we will worship, and then we will come back to you" (v. 5). Is Abraham so trustful that he believes God will somehow let him escape the wrenching task ahead, or is he soft-peddling misdirection so the servants remain ignorant of his plans? Surely, they, like Isaac, would have known that everything needed was present except the sacrifice.

The author of Hebrews claimed that Abraham planned to sacrifice Isaac, but expected him to be resurrected (Heb. 11:17-19). In this way, he could explain Abraham's words to the servants as fully truthful.

But back to the story: narrative tension builds as the author tells how Abraham laid the large bundle of wood on his son's back – indicating that Isaac would have been a young man of some size – while Abraham himself carried a smoldering pot of coals and a sharp knife (v. 6). The implication is that a boy might hurt himself if entrusted with such dangerous items, but both the danger and the items rest with Abraham.

As they walked, Isaac spoke for the first and only time, voicing the long-unspoken question: "Father! ... The fire and the wood are here, but where is the lamb for a burnt offering?" (v. 7).

Again, we do not know if Abraham's reply reveals exorbitant trust or careful dissimulation: "God himself will provide the lamb for the burnt offering, my son" (v. 8). Abraham knew that Isaac was the intended victim, but God had also provided Isaac, so his response could be truthful without being specific.

For the second time, we are told that "the two of them walked on together" – a poignant picture that needs no further description.

A tension-filled climax
(vv. 9-14)

Once they had arrived at the mountain – traditionally identified as Mt. Zion, the future home of Jerusalem and the temple – the narrative moves quickly, as if the author wants to get the chilling tension over with. Abraham built an altar, no doubt with Isaac's help in gathering large stones and fitting them into a stable platform. He laid the wood in order to facilitate lighting it on fire at the appropriate time. "He bound his son Isaac" – with no reported resistance or protest from the boy, though it's hard to imagine such a thing could have been done in silence. He then took his beloved son and "laid him on the altar, on top of the wood" (v. 9).

The pivotal moment arrives with v. 10, as "Abraham reached out his hand and took the knife to kill his son." The word translated as "kill" normally means "slaughter," as in slaughtering an animal by slitting its throat. Can you

> **The angel of Yahweh:** Did an angel call out to Abraham, or was it God? The text speaks of "the angel of Yahweh," but in the Hebrew Bible the expression "angel of Yahweh" implies that God's own self is present through the angelic interme- diary. Note that the angel speaks "from heaven" (vv. 11, 14), and clearly speaks for Yahweh: "Now I know ..." (v. 12), "'By myself I have sworn,' says Yahweh ..."
>
> The narrator's use of the "angel of Yahweh" assures the reader that Yahweh is present, but provides just enough distance for the recipient of Yahweh's word to avoid having seen God personally – an event commonly thought to have fatal consequences.

imagine Isaac lying with throat bared and terror in his eyes? Can you stand with Abraham as he takes Isaac's hair in one hand and holds the knife poised in the other, trying to work up the nerve to begin the downward slice?

At what point did the angel of Yahweh step in to stop Abraham's hand? Did he wait until Abraham had commit- ted to the stroke, or call out as soon as he raised the knife? We don't know, but our stomachs twist at the thought. Finally, mercifully, God spoke: "Abraham, Abraham!" Feel the hope in Abraham's heart as he replied "Here I am!" (v. 12). [**The angel of Yahweh**]

And then there was relief: "Do not lay your hand on the boy or do anything to him; for now I know that you fear God, since you have not withheld your son, your only son, from me" (v. 12).

"Now I know." Did God really need to put Abraham through such a trial in order to know he was faithful? The author does not explain: his purpose is to magnify Abraham's trust rather than to question God's justice. As Abraham had "lifted his eyes and saw" the mountain earlier that day (v. 4), now he "lifted his eyes and saw" a ram in a thicket of brush, held fast by his entangled horns.

Abraham caught the ram and offered it as a sacrifice in place of his son, praising God by calling the place *"Yahweh Yireh,"* usually translated as "the LORD will provide" (v. 14), though the word *yireh* normally means "he sees." The story has been replete with images of seeing, as in the earlier story of God's provision for Hagar, who called God "El-roi," meaning "God who sees" (Gen. 16:13). The same root is used in both cases: *yireh* is the third-person singular imperfect form of the verb; *rōeh* is the masculine singular participle.

The narrator has succeeded in portraying Abraham's stalwart faith: what Isaac thought of the whole scenario remains unsaid.

A renewed blessing
(vv. 15-19)

With Abraham having passed the test, Yahweh uttered a surprising oath, repeating and expanding on previous promises to make Abraham's offspring as numerous as the stars of heaven and the sand of the seashore, so prosperous that other nations would share in the blessing. [**A self- directed oath**]

With no further fanfare or mention of Isaac, the text says Abraham returned to the servants he had left at the foot of the mountain, and they returned to Abraham's camp in Beersheba and life went on.

What might this story of testing – and the story of Jesus – say to modern believers who seek to please God? Hebrews 2:18, speaking of Jesus, reminds us that "Because he himself was tested by what he suffered, he is able to help those who are being tested." Paul, in writing to the Corin- thians, insisted that "God is faithful, and he will not let you be tested beyond your strength, but with the testing he will also provide the way out so that you may be able to endure it" (1 Cor. 10:13).

Abraham's dark story may seem troubling, but it is worth the stress it may cause us. It is a masterpiece of liter- ature, written with a simple economy of style that points us inexorably toward one single question: "Could you pass this test? Would you be willing to sacrifice your child for God?"

> **A self-directed oath:** Typically, biblical oath-takers swore by their god (or gods), or occasionally by the king – someone who had authority to punish them if they did not fulfill the oath. The standard form, usually much abbreviated in the text, was "May God do so and so to me, if I do not do such and such." The oath was an invitation for God to invoke a penalty if the person did not keep his oath.
>
> God's words were typically considered to have the force of an oath, for there was no higher or more authorita- tive being to which God could appeal. Thus, Gen. 22:16ff is especially forceful: "'By myself I have sworn,' says Yahweh: 'Because you have done this, and have not withheld your son, your only son, I will indeed bless you ...'"

Another version: Here is my translation of the story, intentionally rendered in a rather literal way in hopes of preserving some of the Hebrew flavor in the storyteller's art. Take note of what images stand out, either through repetition or by their simplicity.

And it happened, after these things, that God tested Abraham, and God said to him, "Abraham!" and he said, "Here I am." And (God) said, "Take now your son–your only son–the one you love–Isaac–and go–you–to the land of Moriah, and offer him up as a burnt offering on one of the mountains that I will tell you. And Abraham rose up early in the morning, and he saddled his donkey, and he took two lads with him–and Isaac, his son. And he cut wood for the burnt offering, And he started out for the place that God told him. On the third day, Abraham lifted his eyes and saw the place from a distance.

And Abraham said to the lads, "Stay here with the donkey, and I and the boy will go over there: we will worship, and we will return to you." And Abraham took the wood for the burnt offering and put it on Isaac, his son, and he took in his hand the fire and the knife, and they went on–the two of them–together. And Isaac spoke to Abraham, his father, and he said "My father!" And he said, "Here I am, my son." And he said, "Look, the fire and the wood, but where is the lamb for the burnt offering?" And Abraham said, "God will provide for himself the lamb for the burnt offering, my son." And they went on–the two of them–together.

And they came to the place that God told him, and there Abraham built an altar, and he laid out the wood, and he bound Isaac, his son, and he put him on the altar, on top of the wood, and Abraham stretched out his hand and took the knife to slaughter his son–but an angel of Yahweh called out to him from the heavens and said "Abraham! Abraham!" And he said, "Here I am!" And he said, "Do not stretch out your hand to the lad, and do not do anything to him, for now I know that you fear God, for you did not withhold your son, your only son, from me. And Abraham lifted his eyes and saw, and look!–a ram–one–was caught in a thicket by its horns. And Abraham went and he took the ram, and he offered it up as a burnt offering instead of his son. And Abraham called the name of that place "Yahweh Yireh," as it is said today, "On the mountain of Yahweh it will be provided."

And the angel of Yahweh called out to Abraham a second time from the heavens, "By myself I swear, says Yahweh, that because you have done this thing and did not withhold your son, your only son, that I will surely bless you and I will greatly multiply your descendants like the stars of the heavens or the grains of sand on the seashore, and your descendants will take over the stronghold of their enemies, and by your offspring they shall bless themselves–all the nations of the earth–because you heard my voice." So Abraham returned to his lads, and they started out together for Beersheba, and Abraham dwelt at Beersheba.

Before we respond with a blithe, "No, I could not," we must ask if the real question is to which god and on what altar will we sacrifice them. Will we ignore our children and sacrifice them to the god of success or business or personal achievement.? Will we fail to teach them the importance of love and ethical behavior, thus sacrificing them to the god of selfishness? Will we raise our children without teaching them about the living God of the universe, sacrificing them on the altar of our own faithlessness?

There is a risk involved in teaching our children about the power of God and the love of Jesus. They may take us seriously. They may determine to love other people even when it is difficult, to serve others even when it is danger-ous, or to give of themselves in manifold ways for the glory and the love of God. It's a risk we take when we carry them up the mountain of faith and introduce them to the wild and awesome God of Abraham.

No faith, no ethic, no religion is worth having if it does not ask for sacrifice. Christianity makes no claim to be a religion without cost, a cuddle-blanket designed only to meet the needs of its adherents. What are we willing to sacrifice for God? [**Another version**]

The Hardest Question
Where was Mount Moriah?

The question of Mount Moriah's location must also address whether the term indicated a place name, or if it means something else.

The story says that God told Abraham to sacrifice Isaac on "one of the mountains I will show you" somewhere "in the land of Moriah" (v. 2). Literally, it is "mountain that I will tell you." Verse 3 says Abraham headed toward the mountain God had shown him – actually "that God had told him about" – and v. 4 says Abraham saw the place, still far away. After God provided a ram as a substitute for Isaac, "Abraham called that place 'The LORD will provide'; as it is said to this day, 'On the mount of the LORD it shall be provided'" (v. 14). "The LORD will provide," in Hebrew, is "*yahweh yireh*," as preserved in some translations ("Jehovah-jireh" in the KJV).

Later Jewish traditions came to believe that a large stone on Temple Mount was the site of Abraham's sacrifice, further sanctifying the site as appropriate for the temple.

We read in 2 Chron. 3:1 that Solomon built the temple "on Mount Moriah," on the former threshing floor of "Ornan the Jebusite," which David had purchased and designated as the temple site.

The image of Moriah as an unsettled mountain but future home of Jerusalem is at odds with an earlier story in which Abraham is said to have paid tithes to Melchizedek, described as the "King of Salem," indicating that Jerusalem was already a walled city.

The Septuagint (an early Greek translation) preserves the name as "*Amoria*," suggesting "in the land of the Amorites." Earlier, Abraham had built an altar at a place called Moreh, near Shechem (Gen. 12:6). Thus, some scholars believe the place was on a hill near Shechem, which would jive with an early Samaritan belief that the sacrifice took place on Mt. Gerizim, which is in that area.

Muslims believe that Ishmael, rather than Isaac, was the intended victim, and identify the place as "Marwah," locating it near the Kaaba, in Mecca, Saudi Arabia.

But it is possible that "Moriah" was not intended as a place name. It is derived from the same verbal root (*rā'â*) found in references to when Abraham "lifted his eyes and saw," and when he named the place "Yahweh Yireh" (as noted above, *yireh* normally means "to see," but can have the sense of providing, as when we say "I'll see to it").

The Hebrew *mōrîyâ* can be interpreted as a *hif'il* (causative) participle, meaning "cause to be seen," or "show," which relates to the idea that Abraham would receive a revelation at the place of sacrifice. The Septuagint, an early Greek translation, rendered the phrase as "the land of heights," using a word (*hypsēlos*) that typically referred to a place above the earth and associated with divine beings. Catholic translations based on the Vulgate call it the "land of visions," rather than "land of Moriah." Possibly seeking to preserve a distinction from the term *mōrîyâ*, the Hebrew of vv. 2 and 3 do not use a word for "show," but for "tell."

Optional First Reading
Psalm 13

How Long, O LORD?

How long, O LORD? Will you forget me forever? How long will you hide your face from me? (Ps. 13:1)

Have you ever felt that God had forgotten you, or was ignoring you? Have you ever grown so frustrated or at wit's end that you were reduced to a few plaintive words such as "Oh God," or "Why me?"

Welcome to the psalmist's world – or at least to a part of it. In Psalm 13 we find a pointed psalm of lament without the meandering soliloquies and jumbled structure common to longer laments. This one is compact and classic, an ideal model for a lecture on biblical lamentations.

The little psalm moves from concentrated pain and earnest demand to effusive praise. It offers extravagant emotion and virtually no explanation, leaving a largely blank slate on which to post our own laments, whatever they may be. It is an invitation to both complaint and confidence.

A plaintive question
(vv. 1-2)

The psalm opens with a volley of five acerbic questions for God, four of them including the demanding accusation "How long?" We can imagine the heartfelt cry of someone who has come to the end of their rope and fears they can no longer hang on. [**How long?**]

"*How long,* O LORD? Will you forget me forever? *How long* will you hide your face from me? *How long* must I bear pain in my soul, and have sorrow in my heart all day long? *How long* shall my enemy be exalted over me?" (vv. 1-2, emphasis added).

> **How long?** The Hebrew expression translated "how long" is 'ad-'anah: "until when?"

The anguished petitioner feels abandoned by God, whose reputed compassion and steadfast love seem to have fallen by the wayside. The psalmist senses that God has not just forgotten him, but has intentionally hidden the divine face, a symbol of blessing. Job likewise complained that God's face had become hidden (Job 13:24). Other psalmists mourned that God had turned the divine countenance from them (Ps. 44:24, 88:14), or pleaded that God would not hide God's face from them (Ps. 27:9, 69:17, 102:2, 143:7).

Why might God hide the divine countenance? Not surprisingly, the writer of Deuteronomy and the prophets attributed God's turning away to the people's persistent sin (Deut. 31:17-18, 32:20; Isa. 1:15, 59:2, 64:7; Jer. 33:5; Mic. 3:4).

Given that common biblical motif, some interpreters argue that the author must have been guilty of a major sin and had experienced hardships he attributed to divine punishment. Prayers of contrition may not have changed the situation, leaving the psalmist to feel that God had turned away – similar to a friend giving the cold shoulder. How long would God turn away? Hadn't the lesson been learned already?

That's one option, but not the only one. The writer speaks of bearing "pain in my soul" and "sorrow in my heart all day long." The NRSV rendering "bear pain in my soul" may be misleading: the Hebrew asks "How long must I take counsel in my soul," which is more indicative of worry than pain, a sorrowful state that holds through the day as well as the night.

What is it that torments the psalmist with such anxiety? It could be personal failure, or misfortune in life – or it could be an enemy. The sufferer asks: "How long shall my enemy be exalted over me?"

The prayer is so bare in detail that we can't tell if the "enemy" is a personal rival who is making life miserable, or a debilitating disease, or a metaphor for the inner turmoil that plagues the writer with a sense of frustrated defeat.

Sometimes we may find ourselves in a similar situation, feeling bombarded with cares on every side and unable to pinpoint any one source of pain that plagues us. We feel at a loss, stuck in a dark tunnel with no light at the end, and we wonder: How long?

A forceful plea
(vv. 3-4)

With vv. 3-4 the plaintiff stops questioning and starts demanding: "Consider and answer me, O LORD my God! Give light to my eyes, or I will sleep the sleep of death, and my enemy will say, 'I have prevailed;' my foes will rejoice because I am shaken."

Now we learn that the psalmist fears death. The implication is that of a physical demise, to "sleep the sleep of death," though the death may yet be metaphorical for defeat or utter loss. If his enemies had hoped for death, they would celebrate that, rather than rejoicing simply "because I am shaken."

The pained petitioner speaks boldly. The word translated as "consider" more commonly means "look," and it is both intensive and imperative: the NET has "Look at me! Answer me!"

This more apt rendering helps us see the connection to v. 1, where the psalmist charged God with looking away and hiding the divine face. The stricken worshiper demands to be seen, heard, and answered.

Few of us would consider such a bold prayer to be appropriate, but the psalmist's boldness is testimony to a relationship once enjoyed, but now in question. The frank brazenness of the plea is testimony to a belief that God welcomes all prayers, even the angry and accusing ones. It suggests that God may respect an honest prayer with all its attendant ugliness far more than a pretty petition that hides true emotion behind floral language.

The psalmist walks in the dark valley of the shadow of death, but has not lost hope of seeing the light, and will not leave God unaware of the fact.

A surprising song
(vv. 5-6)

Did the psalmist leave this anguished poem aside and come back to it on a better day? Did a priest offer a promise of divine intervention? Did the very act of crying out for a hearing prove cathartic and hopeful?

Any of these are possible explanations for the unexpected turn in vv. 5-6, for now the petitioner breaks into a testimony of joyful praise.

Really?

Not so fast.

The NRSV appears to assume the prayer has been answered: "But I trusted in your steadfast love; my heart shall rejoice in your salvation. I will sing to the LORD, because he has dealt bountifully with me."

A closer look at the verb forms reveals another and more likely reading that exhibits a more hopeful tone, but still wishful. Verse 5 begins with a forceful addition of the first-person pronoun to a verb in the perfect tense: "*And I, I have trusted in your steadfast love.*" The afflicted one expresses confidence of having done everything possible, putting their trust in God.

The next verb can and probably should be read as a jussive wish rather than a certain statement of the future (the jussive and imperfect forms are the same): "*may my heart rejoice* in your salvation." The psalmist's prayerful stance has brought hope, but not yet certainty. Similarly, the next verb should be translated as cohortative: "*let me sing to Yahweh* when he has vindicated me."

The particle *ki*, which precedes the last phrase, is usually translated as "for" or "because," but in conditional circumstances it can also be rendered as "when." Like other psalm writers who prayed in similar circumstances, this one concludes with a promise to praise God when the prayer has been answered. Neither vindication nor abject praise have yet arrived, but the darkness has given way to hope that better days are on the horizon. **[Vows in the psalms]**

The wretched but hopeful author of Psalm 13 offers a helpful strategy for dealing with overwhelming trials. Feeling lost and even abandoned by God, the psalmist cried

> **Vows in the psalms:** Though often unrecognized, many psalms of lament that appear to conclude with praise are actually making promises in hopes of future deliverance, though the poetic nature sometimes obscures the conditional nature (Ps. 22:21-22, 61:7-8, 69:29-30, 109:29-30). The conjunction normally translated as "and," often left untranslated, can have the sense of "when." And, the preposition *kî*, usually translated as "for" or "because," can also have the sense of "when."
>
> Many psalms speak of paying vows (Ps. 22:25; 50:14; 61:8; 66:13; 116:14, 18) – all of them promises spoken by an individual: "I will pay my vows to the LORD."
>
> (For more on vows in the psalms, see my book, *Vows in the Hebrew Bible and the Ancient Near East* [Sheffield Academic Press, 1992], 150-161; or an earlier article, "Conditional Vows in the Psalms of Lament: A New Approach to an Old Problem," in *The Listening Heart: Essays in Psalms and Wisdom in Honor of Roland E. Murphy, O. Carm.*, ed. Ken Hoglund, et. al. [JSOT Press, 1987], 77-94.)

out with brutal honesty, laying his or her dire situation before God – and leaving it there.

Many of us are familiar with a hymn called "Leave It There." It was written by Charles Albert Tindley, who was born in Maryland in 1851. His father was a slave, but his mother was free. His mother died when he was young and an aunt took him in so he could remain free, but he was often hired out to help support the family.

Self-taught until he could take correspondence courses, Tindley became a Methodist minister whose sermons were so captivating that membership at the "Tindley Temple" in Philadelphia approached 10,000.

Tindley wrote many hymns and would often break into song during his sermons. One of his best remembered was "Leave It There," which recalled the struggles of his youth and echoed the approach of the psalmist. The chorus urges believers to "Take your burden to the Lord and leave it there" (https://hymnary.org/person/Tindley_CA).

The poet would, no doubt, continue to deal with daily struggles as best he could, but with renewed confidence that God was aware, and with trustful hope that God continued to care.

The Hardest Question
What's with the superscription?

A superscription to Psalm 13 reads "To the music director: a psalm of David." That seems a strange notation: we would expect an address to the choirmaster to include a tune or other instruction, like "with stringed instruments" (Psalms 4, 10, 55, 61, 67, 76), "for the flutes" (Psalm 5), or with the cryptic name of a tune or musical style such as "According to the Sheminith (Psalms 6, 12, mentioned in 1 Chron. 15:21), or "According to the Gittith" (Psalms 8, 81, 84).

Four psalms include "According to Lilies" (Psalms 45, 60, 69, 80). One of those is additionally labeled "A love song" (Psalm 45), and two of them connect "lilies" with "covenant" (Psalms 60, 80). Three psalms are to be sung "according to Jeduthun," known to be a temple singer and musician (Psalms 39, 62, 77, mentioned in 1 Chron. 16:41-42; 25:1, 3, 6, 12). Another tune was called "The Deer of the Dawn" (Psalm 22), and four were apparently sung to the surprising title *'al-tashchēt*, "Do Not Destroy" (Psalms 57, 58, 59, 75).

A few of the superscriptions imaginatively attempt to connect the psalm to a particular event in David's life: when David escaped from Saul (Psalm 18), when Nathan confronted David about Bathsheba (Psalm 51), when the priests of Nob were betrayed by Doeg (Psalm 52), when David was betrayed by the Ziphites (Psalm 54), when David ran into trouble in Gath (Psalm 56), when David fled from Saul to a cave (Psalm 57), when Saul sought to kill David (Psalm 59), and after a battle in Syria (Psalm 60).

Psalm 13 is one of 14 psalms that associate them with David and perhaps add "a song," but nothing in the way of a tune or other instruction (Psalms 11, 13, 19, 20, 21, 31, 40, 41, 64, 65, 68, 109, 139, 140).

The preposition *l*, typically translated "of" as in "A psalm of David," can also mean "by," "for," or even "in the manner of." Perhaps there was a traditional style of music or chanting associated with David, so that no additional tune or instruction was required. In the end, however, the precise purpose of addressing the choirmaster with nothing more than "A David psalm" remains as mysterious as the specific troubles facing the author of Psalm 13.

Second Reading
Jeremiah 27–28 (RCL 28:5-9)

The War of the Words

As for the prophet who prophesies peace, when the word of that prophet comes true,
then it will be known that the LORD has truly sent the prophet. (Jer. 28:9)

Our society features many "experts" and commentators who offer such differing opinions that it's hard to know whom to believe. One politician predicts national disaster if a certain bill is passed, while another sees only ruin if it fails.

Radio talk show hosts speak as if they know with certainty what is best for the country, while others dismiss their diatribes as political spin or a play for ratings. Division reigns and compromises are few.

Our text derives from a similarly contentious period in Judah's history, when national policies were up for debate and prophets stood on opposing sides, each claiming to have a word from God. Perhaps a look at Jeremiah's experience can offer insight for our own time.

A yoke in the background
(27:1-22)

Here is the setting: around 597 BCE, the stout armies of Babylon swept through Judah, encamped about the gates of Jerusalem, and demanded that the city surrender. After a long siege, the victorious invaders looted the city's treasures, including vessels of gold and silver from the temple and palace (2 Kgs. 24:13). King Nebuchadnezzar forced many of the city's leading citizens into exile, including its young king, Jehoiachin (also called Jeconiah, 2 Kgs. 24:6-15).

Nebuchadnezzar replaced Jehoiachin with his uncle Mattaniah, changed the new king's name to Zedekiah, and required him to pay an annual tribute to Babylon in return for allowing the city to remain intact. **[A name change]**

> **A name change:** Why Nebuchadnezzar changed Mattaniah's name to Zedekiah is not clear: both are good Hebrew names. Mattaniah means "gift of Yahweh," and Zedekiah means "righteousness of Yahweh." Perhaps Nebuchadnezzar changed Mattaniah's name as a sign of his authority over the new king, but allowed him to keep a Hebrew name since he remained in Jerusalem.
>
> In contrast, the book of Daniel speaks of Hebrew captives who were given Babylonian names (Dan. 1:6-7).

During the early years of Zedekiah's reign, there was much inner turmoil among the leaders who remained in Jerusalem. Should they resign themselves to Babylonian domination, or rebel and refuse to pay the demanded tribute?

At one point, envoys from Moab, Edom, Ammon, Tyre, and Sidon met with Zedekiah in Jerusalem to consider an alliance that could break free of the Babylonian yoke, perhaps with Egypt's assistance. Nationalistic prophets predicted that Babylon would fall, but Jeremiah argued that God had given the nations into Babylon's hand, and that they should take their punishment and submit rather than rebel. Whether Jeremiah's preaching made a difference we do not know, but nothing came of the proposed alliance.

Jeremiah, who often used visual aids to get his point across, fashioned a yoke of wooden bars and leather straps, then wore it on his neck as a symbol of Babylon's sway over Israel and its neighbors (27:3-7). **[Symbolic acts]**

Attributing Judah's defeat to God rather than to Babylon, Jeremiah claimed that God considered the

Symbolic acts: The yoke of chs. 27–28 is not the only attention-getting prophetic symbol that Jeremiah used, often expressly at God's command.

Jeremiah once wore a linen loincloth for some time without washing it, then buried it among the rocks by a river. When he later dug it up, it was rotted and useless. He displayed it as a symbol of Judah's faithlessness before God (13:1-14).

He proclaimed that God had told him not to take a wife or have children, lest they suffer and die as would the families who would go into exile (16:1-13).

In a familiar story, Jeremiah spoke of a visit to a potter's house, where he saw the potter crush and rework a pot that had become spoiled in his hand, as God would destroy the nation in hopes of rebuilding it anew (18:1-12). Later, Jeremiah took a finished pot and shattered it before priests and officials of Israel to indicate the nation's coming destruction (19:1-15).

He used two baskets of figs – one good, one bad – to distinguish between the earliest wave of exiles (the good figs) and those who remained behind with King Zedekiah (24:1-10).

Babylonian king Nebuchadnezzar to be his *servant* (27:6). The idea was so offensive that the word was dropped from the Greek translation, not only here, but also in 25:9 and 43:10. Nebuchadnezzar would not have considered himself to be a servant of Yahweh, but the prophet believed that Nebuchadnezzar's imperialism served the purposes of God. In that sense, the Babylonian king was not so much a servant, but a tool.

Jeremiah insisted that those who refused to accept Babylonian hegemony would lose everything, while those who submitted could retain their holdings. Jeremiah cautioned the people to ignore "your prophets, your diviners, your dreamers, your soothsayers, or your sorcerers, who are saying to you, 'You shall not serve the king of Babylon,'" for their prophesy was a lie (27:7-11).

Temple "vessels": The furnishings not plundered in 597 BCE were too large for easy transport, or made of less valuable material than the silver and gold dishes and implements that were initially taken. The temple was still equipped with impressive bronze pillars, the large "bronze sea" used for ceremonial cleansing, and various other incense stands and ritual vessels made of iron or bronze. Jeremiah's reference to "temple vessels" likely referred to all items of value that were considered sacred, not just those used to hold grain, wine, or oil.

"Diviners," "dreamers," "soothsayers," and "sorcerers" were all practitioners of magical or occult arts that were commonly found in the ancient Near East, but who were forbidden from practicing their trade in Israel (Lev. 19:26, 31; 20:6, 27; Deut. 18:9-14). It is not surprising that such persons' advice would be diametrically opposed to Yahweh's counsel. To be successful, fortune-tellers need to say what people want to hear. Jeremiah flatly accused them of lying (27:10), and predicted that further disasters would come, including the loss of all remaining implements used for worship in the temple (27:12-22). [**Temple vessels**]

Jeremiah found no joy in Babylonian rule, but he believed Judah's defeat was a justified punishment for the nation's desertion of Yahweh. Resisting Babylon would be tantamount to rebelling against the God who had given them into Nebuchadnezzar's hand. Willing submission to Babylon was not ideal, but still better than a deeper disaster.

A prophetic conflict
(28:1-11)

Today's text, from Jeremiah 28, is tightly connected to ch. 27. Both begin with "In the same year," both are concerned with a conflict between prophets over how Judah should respond to Babylon, and both involve the symbolism of a yoke. The lectionary reading encompasses only 28:5-9, but those verses mean little if not read and studied within their larger context. For this reason, we will consider all of ch. 28.

In 28:1, we meet one of the prophets with whom Jeremiah had been sparring. Hananiah, surprisingly, is not identified as a false prophet. Rather, his credentials appear to be good: the narrator refers to both Jeremiah and Hananiah as prophets. Both use the proper form for prophetic oracles ("Thus says the LORD of hosts ..."), and both speak for God using the word "I." Rather than prejudice the text with pejorative labels, the narrator allows the reader to judge which prophet is true.

A day came when Jeremiah and Hananiah faced each other in the temple courts, as if meeting for a debate, with a crowd of both people and priests looking on (v. 1).

Hananiah spoke first, expanding an earlier message. "Thus says the LORD of hosts, the God of Israel: I have broken the yoke of the king of Babylon ..." (v. 2). Hananiah went on to predict that the temple's sacred items would be

> **The prophetic perfect:** In Hebrew, the perfect tense is used largely for past or completed action. Prophets sometimes used the perfect tense to emphasize the certainty of their predictions, even though they had not yet happened.
>
> Some translators prefer to translate Hananiah's oracle in v. 2 literally ("I have broken the yoke," NRSV, KJV, HCSB, NAS95), while others acknowledge that the act is not yet fulfilled and translate it as future ("I will break the yoke," NET, NIV).

returned within two years, along with king Jeconiah and the rest of the exiles (vv. 3-4). [**The prophetic perfect**]

Did Hananiah believe his own forecast? It is unlikely that he should be seen only as a court prophet pushing King Zedekiah's agenda, for his prediction of Jehoiachin's return would not be welcome news to the man who had replaced him.

Is it possible that Hananiah wanted so badly to see the vessels and people returned that he convinced himself it would happen? If so, he would not have been the first or last to practice self-deception.

When we want something to be true, we have a way of convincing ourselves that it is true or acceptable. For example, we may want to think that God is fine with it if we choose to live extravagantly while ignoring the poor, to enhance our comfort by excluding those who are different, or to get blissfully high while endangering others. If we want something to be true, we can often talk ourselves into believing it – but that doesn't make it so.

Jeremiah wished Hananiah's prediction could be true. Thus, he responded with a hearty "Amen," or "So let it be!" A limited sentence in bondage to Babylon would certainly be welcome news (vv. 5-6).

Jeremiah didn't believe Hananiah, but he knew that Yahweh sometimes changed course despite earlier declarations (Exod. 32:11-14, for example). In the absence of a clear word of the Lord, Jeremiah simply reminded Hananiah and the other listeners that Israel's greatest prophets were known mainly for their prophesies of judgment (vv. 7-8). Prophecies of peace were rare, and no one who predicted peace should be regarded as a prophet until his or her words came true (v. 9).

Hananiah responded by taking the yoke Jeremiah had been wearing from his neck and breaking it. Turning Jeremiah's object lesson to his own purposes, he declared that God would break the yoke of Babylon and bring restoration within two years (vv. 10-11a).

It seems surprising that Jeremiah meekly submitted to Hananiah's actions, despite his disbelief that the competing prophet was correct. Apparently, Jeremiah thought the matter was worth additional consideration and prayer. He refrained from further comment and "went on his way" (v. 11b), at least until he had something clear to say.

Jeremiah's response suggests that everyone – and especially those who claim to speak for God – could benefit from taking time to reflect and seek divine direction before speaking potentially divisive words.

How often have we popped off in the heat of the moment and made claims that were either hurtful or simply wrong? What can we learn from Jeremiah's decision, when he had no clear word from God, to hold his tongue?

A certain word
(28:12-17)

The prophet waited, and "sometime after," things became clear, as "the word of the LORD came to Jeremiah" (v. 12). Yahweh instructed him to tell Hananiah that the wooden yoke he had broken would be replaced by one of iron. Nebuchadnezzar and his descendants would rule with an even harsher hand until their own time of judgment came due (vv. 13-14, cf. 27:6-7). The reference to his authority extending even to wild animals, as in 27:6, was a means of underscoring the extent of Nebuchadnezzar's ruling power.

Jeremiah did not think of Babylon as a more righteous nation, but as a people whom God used to fulfill the divine purpose of punishing the rebellious people of Judah. Jeremiah believed that God had given the nations and even the wild animals into Nebuchadnezzar's hand for three generations, but not permanently. Elsewhere Jeremiah predicted that Babylon's time for judgment would come, and its people would become slaves to others (27:1-7).

The chapter closes with a harsh warning to those who mislead God's people by misrepresenting God's word: Jeremiah predicted that Hananiah would die within the year (vv. 15-17), and the narrative says that the prediction was fulfilled.

In our own world, it seems that every few years, especially as significant dates approach, contemporary "prophets" arise to predict the end of the world or the return of Christ. When natural disasters or terrorists strike, we can be sure that one or more self-styled or high-profile prognosticators will label the calamity as divine punishment against nations or cities that tolerate what the so-called prophet perceives as sin.

Jeremiah's words remind us that prophecy is serious business. Those who take it upon themselves to speak for God face an awesome responsibility, and those who misrepresent the divine word must answer to a fearsome God.

The responsibility doesn't end with the speakers, though. Those who listen have a duty to judge carefully and prayerfully whether they believe a message accurately reflects the teachings of scripture and the love of Christ.

God gave us good minds and receptive hearts for a reason. Let's use them.

The Hardest Question
How do you identify a real prophet?

Our airwaves, print media, and digital devices are flooded with the claims of would-be prophets of both secular and religious leanings. How do we know whom to believe, if anyone?

The Bible does not deal with secular prophets who make forecasts relative to the economy, the stock market, sporting events, or the weather. Nor does it speak of politicos who warn of national decline if certain persons are elected or if contested legislation is passed. When judging such prognostications, it's best to check the speaker's or writer's reliability against his or her past record.

It turns out, that's also one of two biblical criteria used to judge those who would speak for God. The book of Deuteronomy attributes to Moses – whose prophetic credentials were unquestioned – a speech in which he reportedly told the Israelites to look out for others who would come after him, claiming to speak for God. He warned them that they shouldn't believe just everyone:

But any prophet who speaks in the name of other gods, or who presumes to speak in my name a word that I have not commanded the prophet to speak – that prophet shall die." You may say to yourself, "How can we recognize a word that the LORD has not spoken?" If a prophet speaks in the name of the LORD but the thing does not take place or prove true, it is a word that the LORD has not spoken. The prophet has spoken it presumptuously; do not be frightened by it. (Deut. 18:20-22)

Don't listen to anyone who claims to speak in the name of other gods, Moses told them – and don't believe prophets, and don't trust in anyone who predicts things that don't happen. And, by the way, prophets who speak for false gods or who falsify Yahweh's words are subject to death. Yikes!

Jeremiah appears to have had this passage in mind when he challenged Hananiah, saying that those who prophesy peace can't be proven true until peace arrives – a scenario he would welcome but did not expect (Jer. 28:7-9). And, when he was confident that Hananiah had proclaimed a false message, Jeremiah successfully predicted that the false prophet would die within a year (Jer. 28:15-17), thus boosting his own prophetic record.

Such criteria seem well and good, but there's an inherent problem: The only sure way to prove that someone is a prophet is to wait and see if his or her predictions come true. If the predictions go beyond the prophet's lifetime, he can only be recognized as legitimate in retrospect, after the people who needed to heed the message are also dead.

Micah felt the sting of that dilemma. He preached during the latter half of the eighth century. He prophesied doom for the wicked leaders of Israel, and the northern kingdom fell to Assyria in 722 BCE. So far, so good, but Micah also called on Judah and Jerusalem to repent and renew their commitment to God, predicting that Jerusalem would be laid waste and turned into a heap of ruins if they didn't (Mic. 1:3-12).

Jerusalem was indeed destroyed, but it was the Babylonians who did it, and not until a century after Micah was dead. He appears to have been discredited during his lifetime, spending much of it in silence.

How, then, can one judge the validity of a prophet's message while there's still time to respond to it?

Jeremiah pointed to tradition as one sign of caution. Prophets prior to him were mainly known for forecasting war and ruin rather than peace. So, he suggested, anyone who prophesied peace was automatically suspect. But there were prophets both before and after Jeremiah who proclaimed apocalyptic hopes of a coming day when God will set all things right. We wouldn't set aside Isa. 2:2-4, Mic. 4:1-4, or Jeremiah's own "book of consolation" (Jeremiah 30–33) on those grounds.

How can Christians today judge whether to believe what they hear from TV evangelists, radio preachers, or even from their own pulpits? How can they know if the speaker is speaking for God or simply voicing his or her own culturally shaped beliefs?

In the New Testament, where various people were reported to be prophets but not all of them real, Paul considered the "discernment of spirits" to be a spiritual gift (1 Cor. 12:4-11).

Short of feeling gifted with spiritual discernment, believers can employ other strategies. First of all, one should ask if the speaker's words resonate with the scripture. Saying "the Bible says so" does not provide a sufficient reason for one to believe the message, even if the speaker can quote one verse after another. One must also judge if the speaker or writer has considered the cultural context of passages, how they fit into the larger context of the Bible, and how the Bible's developing understanding of God might impact the scripture's interpretation.

Additionally, we should consider if the speaker has taken into account positive developments in human society. We no longer consider slavery to be appropriate, for example, even though it was accepted within the ancient cultures reflected in the Bible. We should no longer believe a "prophet" who advocates for slavery, or for segregation, or for unequal treatment of fellow humans – even if such things happened in the Bible. We have advanced in other ways, too. We have a much better understanding of how the universe functions and of how long the earth has been around. We know much more about medical and psychological matters. We should be skeptical of prophets who argue that everything in Genesis 1 should be read literally.

Biblical prophets were marked by their perceptivity to the world around them as well as their receptivity to the leading of God within. One who would speak for God today should do the same.

Most of all, it's important that we consider whether a would-be prophet's words reflect the teaching and example of Jesus, who brought a new way of understanding law and grace and the love of God. If we can't imagine Jesus agreeing with the message being preached, perhaps we shouldn't follow it, either.

Optional Second Reading
Psalm 89 (RCL 89:1-4, 15-18)

Steadfast and Forever?

I will sing of your steadfast love, O LORD, forever; with my mouth
I will proclaim your faithfulness to all generations. (Ps. 89:1)

This Sunday offers two optional readings for the Old Testament, both of them psalms, and both psalms of lament. They are quite different, however.

Psalm 13, only six verses long, begins with a hollow cry of longing, but moves to hopeful trust. Psalm 89 covers 52 verses in which the first 37 offer full-throated praise before turning to an accusation of divine betrayal. Both center around the issue of God's perceived hiddenness and the question of how long it will last.

Either psalm offers a helpful reminder that we are not the first to feel disappointed in God, that God has let us down or failed to keep certain promises, whether God made those promises or not.

No matter how sophisticated our theology, in the backs of our minds, many of us hold to an idea that God has promised to always protect us and provide for us. When something happens, when trouble comes, it is quite natural for us to feel let down, to think that God has been sleeping on the job.

Psalm 89 offers a case study for asking two important questions. First, *can* we realistically expect God to protect us from trouble? And, if God *doesn't* keep a shield about us, what can we expect when trouble comes? [**The text**]

The text: The lectionary reading comprises only vv. 1-4 and 15-18, which may be very well for an out-of-context liturgical reading, but are hardly adequate if one hopes to grasp the message of the psalm as a whole. While an in-depth verse-by-verse study would be impractical, we will give some attention to the entire psalm.

Ethan's opinion?
(vv. 1-37)

Masoretic tradition holds that Psalm 89 was written by Ethan the Ezrahite, who was legendary for his wisdom. When the author of 1 Kgs. 4:31 wanted to impress his readers with the extent of Solomon's great wisdom, he said that Solomon was wiser even than Ethan the Ezrahite, who was presumably one of David's wisest counselors. That, unfortunately, is all we know about Ethan.

If indeed Ethan was a contemporary of David, and if he really wrote this psalm, it must have been late in David's reign, perhaps when some military defeat seemed imminent. It is much more likely that the psalm was written many years later – at least in its final form – during the exilic or postexilic period, and attributed to Ethan in hopes that his wise reputation would add stature to the psalm. [**A long history?**]

It is a long song, a strange sort of song that begins with powerful praise to the God who was faithful to David (vv. 1-4), the One who created the heavens and the earth (vv. 5-12), and who rules over all with righteousness, justice, and loving kindness (vv. 13-18).

With v. 19, the psalmist reprises an oracle from 2 Samuel 7, in which God had made certain promises to David. When David offered to build a house for Yahweh to dwell in, God turned the tables and insisted that no earthly house was necessary. Instead, God would build for David a dynastic house. The promise appears to be unconditional and unending, an assertion that David's descendants would

A long history? Psalm 89 can be understood as a unity, but it probably had a long history of composition, with the earlier sections focused on praising God written first (vv. 1-18), perhaps in parts that were later combined. At some point the oracle concerning David and its elaboration (vv. 19-37) could have been added to form a royal psalm that could have been used on coronation days or other public events honoring the king. After the kingdom fell and the dynasty of David had come to an end, the painful lament questioning God's continued presence and love (vv. 38-51) may have rounded out the psalm. A brief benediction in v. 52 marks the end of Book III of the psalms (Psalms 73–89).

Marvin Tate offers a detailed review of suggestions in *Psalms 51–100*, vol. 20 of Word Biblical Commentary (Word Books, 1990), 413-19.

rule upon the throne of Israel for all time. That would not exempt future kings from punishment if they turned away from God, for the promise was understood as an eternal commitment to Davidic rule.

In Ps. 89:19-37 the psalmist remembers that promise, and elaborates on it. Indeed, a reference to David in vv. 1-4 makes it clear that the entire psalm is built around that promise and its implications. As he celebrates God's blessing on David in vv. 19-37, he adds promises not included in 2 Samuel 7, and elevates David to near the level of divinity. David was Yahweh's "firstborn, the highest of the kings of all the earth," he claimed (v. 27). More than once, he recalls the promise that God's covenant with David would last *forever*.

In vv. 31-32, the psalmist even remembers the proviso that rebellion would be punished, but he glosses over it with a reminder that God would never break his covenant (vv. 33-34), and then launches into quoting a supposed divine promise in which God swore that David's line "shall continue forever, and his throne endure before me like the sun. It shall be established forever like the moon, an enduring witness in the skies" (vv. 35-37).

Scripture contains no other record of God making such a promise, but it reflected a popular belief. Late in the seventh century BCE, when the Babylonians threatened and prophets such as Jeremiah called on the people to repent or be destroyed, many scoffed at the thought that anything bad could happen to Jerusalem. That's where David's descendant lived! That's where God had promised

to make David's descendants rule forever, as sure as the sun and moon (see Mic. 3:9-12, Jer. 7:1-15).

Whining Time
(vv. 38-51)

But the kingdom was lost to the Babylonians, and the person who wrote this psalm in Ethan the Ezrahite's name was devastated over its demise. He accused God of breaking promises that the Judahites had thought were inviolable. God had "spurned and rejected" David's line, "renounced the covenant," and "defiled his crown in the dust" (vv. 38-39).

The walls of Jerusalem were broken and the capital city in ruins, plundered by passersby and scorned by neighbors as enemies exulted over the broken scepter and fallen throne (vv. 40-45).

The psalmist had turned from praising God's creation to celebrating God's promise to crying over God's perceived betrayal. Two celebratory movements gave way to a mournful requiem as it turns into a sad song.

Any of us are subject to whining if we believe God has disappointed us. Some people, like the psalmist, let it all hang out. When they get frustrated or angry, God hears about it.

Others may express their disappointment by trying to gloss over it. They think it's inappropriate to get mad at God, so they pretend they are not. They still attribute trials to God, but try to explain them away as lessons designed to teach them something.

Many people, however, respond to disappointment in God by simply giving up. If God isn't going to take any better care of them, they think, what's the use of being faithful? If God hasn't solved my financial woes or taken care of a loved one's drinking problem, why keep praying? If God wouldn't cure my mother's cancer or keep my marriage together, why should I bother going to church?

There is no shortage of people who tried to live a faithful Christian life for a while, but when God didn't live up to their expectations, they gave up.

The problem is not with God's promises, but with our expectations. The psalmist believed that God had promised to keep David's son and David's city and David's country on top of the world, no matter what.

He was wrong, even if his song is in scripture. He ignored his own words, for he quoted God's reminder that sinful behavior would lead to troublesome consequences (vv. 30-32) – and the scriptures are very careful to say that is why Jerusalem ultimately fell – but he gave it no more attention. All he could see was the image of Jerusalem in ruins and no son of David on the throne and the promises of God laying broken all over the ground.

Bigger Pictures

The psalmist's limited perspective could not see that God was not through with Israel. In keeping with 2 Sam. 7:14-15, God was not breaking a promise, but acting on the condition that David's descendants who turned away from God would face consequences "punished with the rods of men," but not be abandoned.

"Ethan the Ezrahite" had no way of knowing that God's promise ultimately would transcend the concept of a physical king on a throne in Jerusalem, and that it would reveal a spiritual king on a heavenly throne.

In time, the prophets began to foresee a day when God would raise up a "shoot out of the stump of Jesse," a descendant of David, who would usher in a new age of deliverance.

New Testament writers saw those prophetic hopes fulfilled when Jesus came into the world as a scion of David who was destined to become all that David was not, as one who would reign forever on an eternal throne within a whole new concept of what "kingdom" means.

This is why we can be patient with the frustrated author of Psalm 89. He couldn't back up far enough to see the big picture, and a lot of the picture had yet to be painted.

Today we can look back and see what he could not see, the part of the picture that includes the coming of Christ as the true and eternal son of David. We can see how God's promise did in fact prove to be true, even though the psalmist thought he had been forsaken.

But what about the parts of the picture that *we* can't see because they haven't been painted yet? What about the ways in which we think God has let us down?

God has promised many things. The scriptures speak of divine promises to grant forgiveness and live both abundant and eternal to those who trust in Christ (Rom. 6:23; John 3:16, 10:10). God has promised to be present in the Spirit through all our trials (John 16:13).

But God never promised us all flowers and fun. Indeed, God could not offer us perfect protection and human freedom at the same time – and I suspect that most of us would still choose freedom if the choice were ours.

The Hardest Question
What *can* we expect?

Questions arising from Psalm 89 might lead us to wonder that if God has not promised to provide perfect care for me and my family, what *can* I expect? An illustration from football may suggest an analogy. Our temptation is to imagine that we are the quarterback, we've got the ball, and God is like a huge offensive lineman who runs interference for us and knocks down anyone who tries to tackle us.

In truth, it's best to picture ourselves as one of the players who *doesn't* have the ball, but is doing his or her best to help the team. In this scheme, God is not out in front blocking for us but on the sidelines, coaching us. God encourages us to do our best, and helps us to understand when we make mistakes. While the game is being played, God is always present, but we are the ones who play the game. We face the big defensive tackles and the trap plays and the personal fouls of life. When we are injured, God is there with us, even as the coach always runs onto the field when one of his players is hurt.

God helps us up, helps us to heal, and helps us to learn from the experience and to be a better player because of it. It may take some time, and not all of us will be stars, but we can all contribute, and we can all get better at what we do, because we know that we have a coach who is always looking for ways to help us reach our potential.

When I think about this question, I always come back to a verse of scripture that I printed on green tape with a label maker and stuck to the bottom of my desk lamp when I was still in high school: "And we know that all things work together for good to them that love God, to them who are the called according to his purpose" (Rom. 8:28, KJV). Nothing in that verse says that all things are good, or that God will only allow good things to happen. But everything about it says that God is good, and that God is able and willing to work with us *through* anything, and bring something good out of it.

If I didn't believe that, I would likely have dropped out a long time ago. When we have realistic expectations of God, we learn to accept and learn from what God *has* promised, rather than spending our time being mad about what God *has not* promised.

Sometimes, we just can't help but to sing a sad song – but we don't have to make it into a gold record.

Third Reading
Romans 6:12-23

Law and Grace

For the wages of sin is death, but the free gift of God is eternal life in Christ Jesus our Lord. (Rom. 6:23)

Few texts generate as much resistance as Paul's insistence that we do not belong to ourselves. We live in a culture that values personal freedom and self-determination above all else. *I* decide how I will live. *I* make choices about what I perceive to be acceptable and unacceptable. *I* am in control of my destiny. *I* am entitled to life, liberty, and the pursuit of happiness. These are my inalienable rights.

Paul would argue that our penchant for self-sufficient mastery of our own ship is a boatload of malarkey. We can't serve ourselves: we're either slaves to sin, or slaves to God. There is no in-between.

That's bad news for people who like to think of faith as just one of several aspects involved in a life that they control – and doesn't that describe most of us?

Leave the old master
(vv. 12-14)

The lectionary draws no less than 15 readings from Romans during the Season after Pentecost in Year A, with six of them coming from chs. 6–8. While readers may grow tired of Paul's fervent and persistent advocacy for the gospel as he understood it, there is much to be learned, and most of us probably need the lessons.

Commentators often suggest that Romans 6 promotes a progression from justification (vv. 1-11) to sanctification (vv. 12-23), as if we are first saved and then go on the road toward holiness, but it is not that simple.

Justification and sanctification are two sides of the same coin: when we are put right with God through Christ, we are called to live and love in the right way. Verses 1-11 do

Not everyone: The history and ramifications of slavery continue to haunt our society, but many people don't want to admit it. Legislators in some states have passed laws prohibiting schools from teaching the obvious truth that racism is deeply embedded in the culture as part of the legacy of slavery. The fear, apparently, is that white children may get their feelings hurt if they learn how cruel past generations have been to Black people – or how our present generation remains complicit in the persistent oppression of minority peoples, especially people of African and Latin descent.

As one who grew up in a racist community of the South, I wish someone had pricked my conscience at a much earlier age, rather than allowing attitudes of superiority and privilege to harden: they take continuous effort to deconstruct.

focus more on the theme of justification, but also encourage believers to "walk in newness of life" (v. 4) and to live free of sin (vv. 5-8). Verses 12-23 highlight the ideal of sanctification, but also speak of moving from law to grace (v. 14). The two are intertwined.

That is not to say there is not a shift between the two parts. In vv. 1-11, Paul speaks primarily in the indicative, stating his views and elaborating on them. In vv. 12-23, he shifts to the imperative or cohortative mode and the second person plural, urging his readers to put his teachings into action.

As distasteful as it is to our modern ears, Paul's central metaphor in vv. 12-23 is one of slavery. We think of slavery as a 300-year dark blot on the history of our country, and as an undeserved curse on a people who still suffer from its repercussions. [**Not everyone**]

Paul, however, lived in a world that embraced slavery as a fact of life. Upwards of a quarter of the population in ancient Rome consisted of slaves. Unlike America's history of chattel slavery consisting almost entirely of African people, slaves in Rome could be from any ethnic background. They could be captured in war, bought for a price, born to a slave, or acquired in other ways. People sometimes sold themselves to pay their debts. They worked on every level of society, from grunt labor to educators and public servants. Some were highly respected, but whatever their station, they were beholden to a master – under the dominion of another.

Paul believed that all people were naturally slaves to sin unless they had been redeemed by Christ. Following his baptism analogy from vv. 1-11, he insisted: "Therefore, do not let sin exercise dominion in your mortal bodies, to make you obey their passions" (v. 12). For Paul, "mortal body" refers to more than one's physical nature: it incorporates one's needs and wants, hungers and desires.

"No longer present your members to sin as instruments of wickedness," Paul said, "but present yourselves to God as those who have been brought from death to life, and present your members to God as instruments of righteousness" (v. 13).

Paul adopts something of a martial tone here: the word for "instruments" is *hopla*, which was commonly used for a soldier's equipment, whether weapons or armor. Our bodies and actions can be used as weapons of wickedness to promote and strengthen sin, or as the armor of righteousness to defend against it. We recall Paul's encouragement to the Ephesians to "put on the whole armor of God" (Eph. 6:10-17).

We all choose sides and fight as slaves to one side or the other, Paul said. For Christians, the issue of masters was settled: "For sin will have no dominion over you, since you are not under law but under grace" (v. 14).

Living into that new identity, however, could be quite *un*settling.

Serve the new master
(vv. 15-19)

In v. 15, Paul returns to the question he had asked in v.1: "What then? Should we sin because we are not under law but under grace?" Some might still lean toward the idea that

---

> **Not quite through:** Paul might have resonated with a church that had a message board by the highway where the pastor would post clever slogans. One week the message said, "If you're done with sin, come on in!" Below it, however, someone had taped a placard that read, "But if you're not quite through, call 567-8432."

---

an abundance of grace could easily overshadow a modicum of sin. Can't we focus on what we want and still be forgiven?

The Hebrews did not draw a sharp distinction between body and soul, but the Greeks did, and Paul was writing to believers in Rome, most of whom would have been steeped in Greco-Roman culture. Some thought that the soul was inherently good and the body inherently evil, but since the two were separate, it didn't matter what one did with the body. Antinomianism comes in many shades.

Paul, who had asked the question to make a rhetorical point, would not quibble: "By no means! Do you not know that if you present yourselves to anyone as obedient slaves, you are slaves of the one whom you obey, either of sin, which leads to death, or of obedience, which leads to righteousness?" (vv. 15b-16).

The slave metaphor returns with a vengeance: you can tell which master you belong to by which master you obey, Paul said, and you can't belong to both sin and Christ. The word "obey" is in the present tense, suggesting continuous action. Serving sin leads to death, while obedience to Christ leads to righteousness.

We struggle to make that choice, though, don't we? We prefer a stance somewhere between, one that allows us to feather our own nests and follow our own desires but still remain in good standing with God. [**Not quite through**]

We may not want to choose, but Paul insisted that people who have trusted Christ have already chosen and must live out their choice: "But thanks be to God that you, having once been slaves of sin, have become obedient from the heart to the form of teaching to which you were entrusted, and that you, having been set free from sin, have become slaves of righteousness" (vv. 17-18).

Still, we know that none of us are perfectly righteous or completely immune to sin. Commentators often suggest that to be freed *from* sin comes from being freed *to* Christ. When we are prayerfully attentive to following Christ and open to the Spirit, we are free from the tyranny of sin to overwhelm us with unhelpful desires or purely selfish motives. We are free to experience the abundant life and to anticipate the eternal life that Jesus promised.

Scholars debate what Paul meant by "to the form of teaching, to which you have been entrusted." We might think it more logical to say that teachings had been entrusted to believers rather than the other way around, but Paul was still using the slave metaphor. By speaking of the "form" (*typos*) of teaching he probably had in mind the teachings of Jesus that believers were called to follow, and indeed to Jesus himself. Jesus and his teachings don't belong to believers: they belong to Jesus.

Paul's reference to his readers' wholehearted obedience was probably overstating the case. If his readers had truly become "obedient from the heart" to Christ, he wouldn't have had to work so hard to promote choosing righteousness over sin.

Paul understood that truly walking the walk was difficult, so he almost apologized for repeatedly breaking it down: "I am speaking in human terms because of your natural limitations. For just as you once presented your members as slaves to impurity and to greater and greater iniquity, so now present your members as slaves to righteousness for sanctification" (v. 19).

One way or another, Paul sought to help his readers live into their new identity. He was like a drill sergeant with a band of new recruits, reminding them every day that they are no longer civilians but soldiers, and that soldiers serve best when they obey orders and look out for one another.

Modern motivational speakers sometimes encourage people to "fake it 'til you make it," to do what a successful person does until the behavior becomes natural. Paul wanted believers to fully adopt their identity as followers of Christ who had been saved by grace and called to righteous living.

Find eternal life
(vv. 20-23)

People who serve sin have no obligation to be righteous, Paul said, but they ultimately gain nothing from it: "The end of those things is death" (vv. 20-21). Believers, on the other hand, have no obligation to continue in sin, but to live in ways that lead to a holy life: "But now that you have

been freed from sin and enslaved to God, the advantage you get is sanctification. The end is eternal life" (v. 22).

The word for sanctification, *hagiasmós*, could also be translated as "holiness." It builds on the Hebrew idea of being set apart for God, being different from the world. Israel's traditions remembered that God's initial challenge at Sinai was to obey God's teaching and keep the covenant, with the result that "you shall be my treasured possession out of all the peoples … you shall be for me a priestly kingdom and a holy nation" (Exod. 19:5-6).

New Testament teachings went beyond the appeal of being God's special people to the promise of joining God throughout the ages, for "The end is eternal life."

Condensing and repeating his thought, Paul concluded with a sentence that countless Sunday School pupils have been taught to memorize: "For the wages of sin is death, but the free gift of God is eternal life in Christ Jesus our Lord" (v. 23).

The word used for "wages" was typically used for a Roman soldier's salary. It was something he earned to keep him going, mainly subsistence wages. A life of sin also pays wages, Paul said. It may keep us going and reward us with pleasure, but at the end of the road, there's only the end of the road. The wages of sin is death.

A gift is something different than wages. It is something we do not earn, but are freely given. The gift is not forced on us, however. We choose to accept God's grace, and once we accept it, we belong to Christ, no longer to sin. As slaves to Christ, we live to God, and at the end of the road we find that the road never ends, but life goes on and on with God.

The Hardest Question
What does Paul mean by saying believers "have become obedient from the heart to the form of teaching to which you were entrusted"?

Most of us are familiar with nature documentaries that point out how some animals, especially birds such as ducks and geese, are genetically programmed to imprint on their mother and follow her. Arranging for them to hatch in the presence of a human can cause them to imprint on that person. Chinese rice farmers have long used the process to lead ducks to the fields to eat destructive snails. In 1996, a Canadian man named Bill Lishman gained notoriety by raising a flock of geese from hatchlings and teaching them to migrate by following his ultralight plane.

Humans can also be imprinted by the influence of others or by habitual actions. The words translated as "form" in "form of teaching" (v. 17, NRSV) was the word *typos*, the root of our word "type," as in "typewriter." In Greek writing of the period, *typos* was used in the sense of "stamping" or "imprinting" – the mark made by the stroke of a pen, the imprint of a seal, or by one thing striking another.

Charles Talbert cited the Jewish philosopher Philo as writing that Moses, in teaching others to follow God, "stamped upon their minds, as with a seal, deep imprints (*typoi*) of holiness, so that no … smoothing in the course of years should ever blur their distinctiveness" (*Special Laws* 1.5+30).

In another section of the same work, he spoke of a student who took lessons from a teacher and learned them so well that by recalling the memory, "he stamps a firm impression of them on his soul" (*Special Laws* 4.18+107).

Paul's comment that the "form of teaching" (*typon didachēs*) to which believers had been entrusted suggests a strong imprinting of identity and ownership. As Talbert observed, "This may very well be yet another way of saying that in the new covenant the law is written on their hearts (Jer. 31:31-34)" (see *Romans*, Smyth & Helwys Bible Commentary [Smyth & Helwys, 2002], 169).

Fourth Reading
Matthew 10:40-42

The World Needs Kindness

Whoever welcomes you welcomes me, and whoever welcomes me welcomes the one who sent me. (Matt. 10:40)

In the summer of 1971, as a 19-year-old college student who had rarely left the state of Georgia, I trusted God and set out to spend the summer in Indonesia.

Never before or since have I experienced as many examples of the type of hospitality that today's scripture talks about. When I learned that my airline ticket could become an around-the-world flight for an additional $200, my home church pastor raised an impromptu offering, and he started it with a $20 bill from his own pocket (more than $140 in 2022 dollars).

I wrote letters to missionaries from Georgia serving in Tokyo, Hong Kong, and Singapore, asking if I could visit with them on my way to Indonesia. All of them welcomed me warmly, offering lodging and food and an introduction to their work.

To this day, when I recall how Griff and Ducky Henderson picked me up from a sweltering airport in Hong Kong and offered me ice-cold lemonade, I think of Jesus' encouragement to offer a cup of cold water to "one of these little ones." I certainly felt very small against the backdrop of new lands and new cultures.

Two different families hosted me during my summer in Semarang, on the island of Java. The Indonesian people were uniformly kind and welcoming, introducing me to their city and their culture and their churches.

While traveling home, my first visit to Israel came courtesy of a missionary family there.

As a young man finding joy in serving and growing and learning all I could about God's work in the world,

my experience was enriched immeasurably by people who understood the meaning of Matt. 10:40-42.

Welcoming Jesus
(v. 40)

Our brief text for the day concludes what the writer of Matthew has designed as a lengthy discourse on mission (vv. 5-42). The discourse begins (10:5-14) in a similar fashion to mission-sending stories in Mark 6:7-13 and Luke 10:1-16, then shifts to various comments on the trials faithful Christians might expect in an unfriendly world (10:15-39) – texts that would have spoken directly to believers in the author's circle of influence many years later.

With v. 40 the conversation turns to what sort of hospitality the disciples-on-mission should expect from people they encountered in their travels. As representatives of Jesus, they should be received with the same kindness that would be offered to their teacher: "Whoever welcomes you welcomes me," Jesus said, "and whoever welcomes me welcomes the one who sent me."

The teaching recalls a Jewish concept known as *shaliach*, from the Hebrew verb meaning "sent." The principle is that when someone sends a messenger, the messenger

---

Welcoming the messenger: The Jewish concept of *shaliach* is mentioned in the Mishnah, where the tractate *Berakot* says "[This is on the principle that] a man's agent is like [the man] himself" (Berakot 5:5, translation by Jacob Neusner, *Mishnah: A New Translation* [Yale University Press, 1988]).

should be accorded the same courtesies that would have been offered to the sender. [**Welcoming the messenger**]

In the context of this passage, the 12 disciples were being sent out to proclaim the kingdom of God and to heal the sick through the power of Christ. Some people would welcome them, but some would not. If they should encounter wholesale rejection in a town, Jesus said, they were to leave and ceremonially shake the dust from their feet on the way out (v. 14).

During Jesus' public ministry, and also when Matthew was written more than a generation later, many people refused to accept either Jesus or his message. Those who follow Jesus on mission can expect a welcome from some, but a cold shoulder from others.

Welcoming the faithful
(v. 41)

In vv. 40-42, the discourse is spoken to the disciples, but pertains more directly to those who had the option of showing hospitality to Jesus' representatives. The ideal choice would be to show kindness rather than coldness. According to Matthew, Jesus promised significant rewards to persons who welcomed those sent in his behalf.

Those who showed hospitality to a prophet would receive the reward of a prophet, he said, while those who welcomed a righteous person would receive the reward of the righteous person. That did not mean that prophets and righteous people were in the habit of handing out rewards for good service. Rather, it looked forward to eternal rewards, when those who had shown hospitality to prophets or righteous people would receive the same rewards as those they had welcomed.

But who are the prophets and righteous people? It is likely that Jesus used both terms with reference to the disciples he was sending out. We need not quibble over distinctions, however.

The point is not that we should look for prophets or saints so we can host them and receive the reward (presumably greater than our own) that is due to them. The point is that we are called to show warm hospitality to others because it is the right thing to do, without regard to their reputation or title. The author is thinking of eternal rewards: it's hard to imagine a better reward than a heavenly home, and we can't really expect that anyone will have more "stars in their

Degrees of reward? Some Christians argue that there will be varying degrees of rewards in heaven, believing that while all Christians inherit eternal life, certain ones will have gained more treasures in heaven than others. Texts such as Matt. 5:11-12, 6:1-20, and 19:28-39 are cited to suggest that God will reward some more than others. Other Christians may find such arguments helpful as an incentive to more faithful living, but not everyone finds that position to be convincing.

The book of Revelation speaks of elders and martyrs having designated places in heaven, but the entire book belongs to the apocalyptic genre, rich in symbolism and not intended to be taken literally. In any case, does having a special place to stand or a special song to sing make one's reward greater than another?

Our goal is not to serve Christ in hopes of greater heavenly rewards – or earthly ones, for advocates of the prosperity gospel. None of us can say for sure what lies beyond this life, or what our "reward" will be like. Our calling is to serve others because that is what Christians do, because that is what Christ did, and we are called to be like Christ.

An old hymn written by Eliza Edmunds Hewitt in 1897 that remains popular among bluegrass gospel fans is "Will There Be Any Stars in My Crown?" The second verse goes like this, followed by the chorus:

> In the strength of the Lord let me labor and pray,
> Let me watch as a winner of souls;
> That bright stars may be mine in the glorious day,
> When His praise like the sea-billow rolls.
>
> Will there be any stars, any stars in my crown
> When at evening the sun goeth down?
> When I wake with the blest in the mansions of rest,
> Will there be any stars in my crown?

The tune is catchy, but many will find the theology to be sketchy (hear Allison Kraus sing it here: https://www.youtube.com/watch?v=9qOkoE-723g).

crown" than others. [**Degrees of reward?**] Showing hospitality to others – and not just to itinerant evangelists, but to all who need it – is what faithful believers are called to do.

Welcoming the little ones
(v. 42)

The closing verse continues in the same vein, this time promising rewards to "whoever gives even a cup of cold water to one of these little ones in the name of a disciple."

Little disciples? We would not normally think of the disciples, all of whom were grown men, as "little ones" (*mikrōn* in Matt. 10:42), but Jesus sometimes used diminutive terms to speak of the disciples affectionately or to indicate that they were still young, inexperienced, and growing in the faith. Mark 10:24 has Jesus address the disciples as "children" (*tékna*), and the gospel of John has Jesus speak to them as both "little children" (*teknía*, 13:33) and "children" (*paidía*, 21:5).

Later, Paul was fond of similar terms. In addition to many references to all believers as "children of God," Paul spoke of Timothy as his "child in the Lord" (*téknon*, 1 Cor. 4:17). He spoke to the Corinthians "as children" (*téknois*, 2 Cor. 6:13), and he addressed the Galatians as "my little children" (*tékna*, Gal. 4:19).

It would not be that unusual for Jesus to call his disciples "little ones."

Some commentators argue that this should be regarded as a reference to the disciples who were being sent out on mission, suggesting that Jesus also had the disciples in mind when he spoke of "little ones" in Matt. 18:6, 10, and 14. Verse 40 spoke of one who welcomed "a prophet in the name of a prophet" and "a righteous person in the name of a righteous person," using the same word at the beginning and end. Here, it is "one of these little ones in the name of a disciple," so it's possible that "little ones" and "disciple" are parallel terms. [**Little disciples?**]

In Matthew's context, vv. 40-42 speak to the believer's responsibility to show hospitality to various traveling emissaries of Jesus – but how might this text speak to us? In our world, traveling evangelists who walk from place to place, carry no money or luggage, and depend entirely on local hosts to house and feed them are virtually non-existent.

On rare occasions, a church family may be called on to take a visiting preacher to lunch. If a guest speaker spends multiple days leading a revival or teaching a Bible study, the church nearly always provides a nice hotel room. How can *we* offer the kind of hospitality Jesus called for?

It may be helpful to note that the people needing hospitality in Matt. 10:40-42 were representatives of Christ. Later in the same gospel, Jesus said those who would inherit the kingdom would be those who had shown hospitality to him – who gave him food and water when hungry; who welcomed him as a stranger; who clothed him when naked, cared for him when sick, and visited him in prison.

People in the crowd who had never hosted Jesus asked him how that could be. When had they fed him when hungry, clothed him when naked, or visited him when sick or in prison? When had they welcomed him as a stranger?

We are familiar with Jesus' response: "Truly I tell you, just as you did it to one of the least of these who are members of my family, you did it to me" (25:40). That was not so different from his statement in 10:40: "Whoever welcomes you welcomes me, and whoever welcomes me welcomes the one who sent me."

Welcoming "these little ones" and caring for "the least of these" sound very similar, do they not?

Jesus' Jewish heritage was replete with commands for faithful Hebrews to welcome strangers and show kindness to marginalized people (Lev. 19:33-34, Deut. 15:10-11, Prov. 19:17, among others). Early in his own ministry, Jesus announced that he had come to "to bring good news to the poor . . . to proclaim release to the captives and recovery of sight to the blind, to let the oppressed go free, to proclaim the year of the Lord's favor" (Luke 4:18b-19).

As he went about during the years of his ministry, Jesus was constantly healing those who were sick and afflicted, without regard for their religion or social status. When thousands gathered to hear him teach, he fed them.

We recall an admonition from the writer of Hebrews: "Do not neglect to show hospitality to strangers, for by doing that some have entertained angels without knowing it" (Heb. 13:2).

We have only the rarest call to entertain an itinerant minister, but we do not lack in opportunities to welcome strangers and show hospitality to those who live on the fringes of society. In doing so, do we not also show warmth and care to the "little ones" or "least of these" that Jesus equated with ministry to himself?

When we look at the world through a Jesus-centered lens, there is no question that we will find opportunities for showing kindness and hospitality on every hand. The question is how we will respond to what we see.

The Hardest Question
Who were the "prophets" and "righteous people" of whom Jesus spoke?

When Jesus said, "Whoever welcomes a prophet in the name of a prophet will receive a prophet's reward; and whoever welcomes a righteous person in the name of a righteous person will receive the reward of the righteous" (Matt. 10:41), who was he talking about?

Given that these verses conclude a section framed as a discourse between Jesus and his disciples, some scholars believe that both "prophets" and "righteous people," along with "little ones" in the next verse, are all references to the disciples who were being sent out. There was a sense in which the disciples were being sent as prophets, proclaiming the advent of the kingdom of God. As people who trusted Jesus and sought to follow his way, they could have been considered "righteous ones." But, as people who were still inexperienced and still unsure of Jesus' mission, they could be described as "little ones" in terms of their faith journey.

Other scholars believe the author of Matthew designed his gospel mainly as a message to people who would have been active in his own time and sphere of influence, probably 80–90 CE, somewhere in the Roman world.

During that period in the early church's development, it was not unusual for itinerant evangelists or teachers to travel from place to place, trusting people in the local churches to provide food, lodging, and perhaps needed clothing along the way. Such travelers could have included prophets, for some believers were considered to have the gift of prophecy (Rom. 12:6; 1 Cor. 12:10; 14:10, 22; 1 Tim. 4:14).

Some scholars think "righteous ones" in Matthew's mind might refer to notable teachers or leaders, though there is little evidence to support the distinction. Jesus seems to have used "prophets," "righteous ones," and "little ones" in this text as alternate terms for those whom he had sent into the world as his representatives.

In the late first century, itinerant preachers and teachers were still quite active among the churches as well as taking the gospel to new frontiers. Though they had not met Jesus personally, they felt no less called or sent by him, and those to whom they ministered had the same opportunity to welcome them as they would have welcomed Jesus.

In an earlier lesson, we pointed out that Matthew's gospel, unlike the gospels of Mark and Luke, contains no account of the disciples departing or returning from the mission to which Jesus had appointed them. The author of Matthew may have intentionally omitted such references as a way of emphasizing a belief that Jesus' call for disciples to go forth preaching and healing was still underway in his own time.

First Reading
Genesis 24:34-67 (RCL 24:34-38, 42-49, 58-67)

The Backstory

And they blessed Rebekah and said to her, "May you, our sister, become thousands of myriads;
may your offspring gain possession of the gates of their foes." (Gen. 24:60)

Have you ever read a novel or watched a movie that began in the middle and left you confused? Skillful writers will find ways, as the story moves along, to fill in the backstory – aspects of the story that readers or viewers need in order to understand the actions, motives, or personalities of the characters.

For example, the movie version of *Forrest Gump* opens with a feather gently riding the soft currents of a warm Savannah breeze, then landing on the foot of a young man who sits at attention while waiting on a bench at a bus stop. We don't know who he is, why he is on the bench, or why he speaks so oddly. But we learn through a series of flashbacks that tell the story of Forrest's life to that point.

Biblical stories also have backstories that are important if we are to understand the characters involved. Today's text provides the background to a series of lessons on the memorable life of the patriarch Jacob, one of the Bible's most colorful characters.

A servant's mission
(vv. 34-41)

Today's lectionary text needs a backstory of its own, for it plops the reader down right in the middle of an elongated narrative. A servant of Abraham is making a speech before dinner in the home of one of Abraham's relatives, in the far-off city of Haran. What brought him to that place?

The story began with Abraham, whom God had called to become the father of a great nation at a time when Abraham and his wife Sarah were childless, old, and unlikely to become parents (Gen. 12:1-9). After many years and several misadventures, however, they had a son, and they named him Isaac (21:1-7).

In today's story, Isaac is 40 years old, and his mother Sarah has died. Abraham decides it is time for Isaac to marry, so he sends a trusted servant to find a wife for him while Isaac remains behind, grieving for his mother. **[Poor Isaac]**

Determined that Isaac should not marry one of the local Canaanite women, Abraham sent his emissary on a

---

Poor Isaac: Careful readers can't help but note that Isaac, for all the hope placed in him before his birth, is rarely given space in the narrative to exercise his own personality. When Isaac appears in the narrative, he most often appears as Abraham's son or Jacob's father, not as his own man. And, in most stories, Isaac is passive and we wonder if he might suffer from developmental challenges. He was born to aged parents.

As a boy of indeterminate age, he is strong enough to carry wood but says nothing as Abraham comes close to slitting his throat (Genesis 22). In a time when people typically married quite young, Isaac was still unmarried and apparently living in his mother's tent at the age of 40. Did he need special care?

Abraham does not seek a wife for Isaac until Sarah dies, and Isaac is not allowed to travel to Haran or choose his own bride. Still, Isaac does not complain when his father arranges his marriage without consulting him (Genesis 24). Years later, as an old man, Isaac submits meekly as Rebekah and their son Jacob pull the wool over his eyes and manipulate him (Genesis 27). Even the stories in which Isaac appears to show initiative (Genesis 26) are virtual repeats of stories attributed to Abraham, as if Isaac had no independent adventures.

A serious oath: Abraham's instruction for his servant to "put your hand under my thigh" while swearing an oath of fidelity is attested in other ancient cultures, and is similar to a later oath in which Jacob (then called "Israel") called upon Joseph to swear that he would not bury him in Egypt (Gen. 47:29).

The implication is that the servant either held or put his hand beside Abraham's genitals, perhaps in recognition of the genitals as the "vehicle of life" (Terrence Fretheim, "Genesis" in *The New Interpreter's Dictionary of the Bible* [Abingdon Press, 1994], 510). The genitals also suggest, in this situation, the importance of fertility and the propagation of the family through Isaac's descendants. (For an extended discussion of this, see D.R. Freedman, "Put Your Hand Under My Thigh — the Patriarchal Oath," *Biblical Archaeology Review* 2 [1976]: 2-4, 42.)

long journey north to Haran, where his extended family had settled (Gen. 11:31). The servant is not named, but may have been his trusted steward Eliezer, who would have been Abraham's heir if no children had been born (15:2).

We enter the story after Abraham has assigned his servant the task, swearing him to fidelity through an oath that apparently involved touching his genitals (24:1-9). With 10 loaded camels, the servant completed the long journey to Haran and stopped by a well to pray for God to identify the right maiden (24:10-14), who quickly revealed herself by drawing water for the servant and his camels (24:15-21) – no easy task. [A serious oath]

The servant rewarded the young woman with a gold nose ring and two heavy gold bracelets before learning that she was Rebekah, the granddaughter of Abraham's brother Nahor, and thus a perfect match for Isaac (12:22-24). When Rebekah invited the servant to lodge at the family compound, he offered a heartfelt prayer of thanksgiving (24:25-28). Once there, he met the woman's brother,

Laban, who pointedly took notice of Rebekah's new jewelry before taking charge of the camels and inviting the servant to dinner (24:29-33).

Today's text picks up here, as dinner is served, but the servant refuses to be seated or to eat before announcing his mission. In short order, he describes how Abraham had amassed great wealth, how Isaac had been born, and how he had been bound by an oath to procure a wife for Abraham's heir. The servant notes that Abraham insisted that a wife be chosen from his extended family, but tactfully omits the patriarch's instruction that Isaac himself should under no circumstance travel to Haran (24:6).

An answered prayer
(vv. 42-53)

With the backstory in place, the servant met with Rebekah's father Bethuel and her brother Laban to discuss a potential marriage. Such decisions were generally made by male authority figures, not by the prospective bride.

As a man on a mission, the servant explained how he had prayed for God to reveal the chosen woman by means of her willingness to water the camels, how Rebekah had met every requirement, and how he had thanked God for answered prayer. [Wells and weddings]

The servant then put the wedding ball in his hosts' court: Would they agree to a marriage between Rebekah and Isaac?

Bethuel and brother Laban politely protested that there was little for them to say, since Yahweh's will had apparently been made known (vv. 50-51). Pleasantries aside, Rebekah's family could expect the payment of a generous dowry and other gifts of hospitality (remember the 10 camels). The servant did not disappoint them, distributing rich gifts to Rebekah and other family members (v. 53).

Wells and weddings: The story about Isaac and Rebekah's union is a variation on a familiar "betrothal type scene" in the Bible, in which a man and a woman meet at a well and a marriage ensues (for example, Jacob and Rachel in Gen. 29:1-14 and Moses and Zipporah in Exod. 2:15-22). When Jesus met the Samaritan woman at the well, the story also has overtones of marriage, though they related to the woman's multiple previous marriages (John 4:1-26).

In Old Testament betrothal scenes, the man typically has traveled to a far country when he stops for water at a community well, one of the few places where one could conveniently meet marriageable maidens. In the accounts involving Jacob and Moses, the men draw water in a show of chivalry, but in Genesis 24 it is the maiden who draws water for the servant, as an answer to his prayer for a sign.

As Robert Alter notes, "There is surely some intimation in all this of the subsequent course of the marriage of Isaac and Rebekah – he in most respects the most passive of the patriarchs, she forceful and enterprising" (*Genesis: Translation and Commentary* [W.W. Norton, 1996], 115).

A marriage made in Haran
(vv. 54-67)

Rebekah's family sought to delay her departure for 10 days of farewells, but when the steward insisted on leaving immediately, Rebekah was finally given a voice in the matter: "they called Rebekah, and said to her, 'Will you go with this man?' She said, 'I will'" (v. 58). Rebekah's unexpectedly willing attitude to travel far from home and marry a man she had never met is reminiscent of Abraham's readiness to leave his family behind as he followed God's leadership "to a land that I will show you" (Gen. 12:1).

Fittingly, Rebekah's family blessed her as she left – a literary pointer to the father's blessing that Rebekah would later help her son Jacob steal from his brother Esau. The blessing itself – a wish for many offspring who would prosper and "gain possession of the gates of their foes" – foreshadows Israel's efforts to take possession of the "Promised Land" many years later, after the exodus from Egypt. [**Foreshadowing**]

The long journey south to the Negeb (a near-desert area in southern Israel) is passed over quickly, but the initial meeting between the two lovers-to-be plays out in cinematic style. From atop her camel, Rebekah saw Isaac at a distance, wandering in the field. Lest he see her in an unladylike position aboard the camel, she slid to the ground and covered her face with a veil, as was the custom before a wedding.

The narrator passes over any mention of a marriage ceremony, and there may not have been one. He says only that Isaac "brought her into his mother Sarah's tent" where "he took Rebekah, and she became his wife; and he loved her" (24:67).

There is much to unpack in these few frames of action. The significance of Isaac taking Rebekah to his mother Sarah's tent is that she becomes the new matriarch of the family. Abraham remarried after Sarah's death (25:1), but

his new wife Keturah did not get Sarah's tent: that belonged to Rebekah and Isaac, through whom the promised line would continue.

Although the new union was an arranged marriage, we are told that "Isaac loved her," and was comforted after the loss of his mother. The text says nothing about whether Rebekah loved Isaac, but her earlier eagerness to get on with the journey suggests that she was a willing partner in the marriage.

The story of Isaac and Rebekah's marriage seems far removed from courtship as known in Western culture, though arranged marriage is still the custom in some Eastern cultures.

What might Christians in a modern Western context learn from this account of a strange practice in a strange land?

We first consider how the story fits into the larger context. Genesis 12–50, often called the "Patriarchal History" or "Stories of the Ancestors," focuses on themes of divine guidance and human obedience in the lives of the patriarchs, in addition to God's covenant promise to Abraham that he would become "a great nation" (Gen. 12:2). Each generation of patriarchs faced tests of faith and had to overcome obstacles before seeing the birth of children: Isaac himself is most famous for having been born, after all hope had failed, to a 100-year-old father and a 90-year-old mother.

For the line to continue and the "nation" to grow, Isaac would also have to marry and have children. The servant's experience of answered prayer is replete with the theme of divine guidance, reminders that God desires to be at work in the lives of those who seek to follow God's way.

By the end of the story, there is no doubt in the reader's mind that Isaac has found the right woman, but a question yet remains: Will she have children? This will be the subject of next week's Old Testament reading.

The Hardest Question
What can we learn from this story?

Isaac appears as more of a bridge character between Abraham and Jacob than as an individual in his own right. Yet, bridges are important. God used Isaac and Rebekah as links in the generational chain that led to the formation of

---

Foreshadowing: In another instance of foreshadowing, the narrator's observation that Laban took notice of the gold ring and bracelets given to Rebekah before he personally unloaded the camels (to examine what else he had brought?) is an early suggestion that he has a greedy and sneaky streak, one that will come full flower in his later interactions with Jacob, who accused him of constantly changing his wages.

Israel. We may sometimes feel as insignificant or incompetent as Isaac was portrayed to be, but do we believe God can do important work through us, too?

The servant's fervent prayer for divine leadership is an impressive reminder that we also can – and should – seek God's guidance, especially when facing major decisions. We may not have an experience quite like that of Abraham's servant, but prayer – and listening for God's response – may help to clarify our thinking and give us a sense of divine leadership. For people who pray "Thy will be done," it is important to discern what God's will might be.

Before sending his servant to find a wife for Isaac, Abraham required him to swear that he would make every effort to fulfill his responsibility. Yet, knowing that success was not guaranteed, Abraham agreed that if the servant failed to find an appropriate wife, so long as he did his best, he would be absolved of his oath. This may offer some comfort for times when we strive to be faithful or build up the church, but see little in the way of results. Abraham's response may suggest that God is also more concerned with the measure of our obedience than the extent of our success.

First Optional First Reading
Psalm 45 (RCL 45:10-17)

A Royal Wedding

The princess is decked in her chamber with gold-woven robes; in many-colored robes she is led to the king; behind her the virgins, her companions, follow. (Ps. 45:13b-14)

Psalm 45 can be a difficult one to read in our culture. It sings obsequious praise to a king at a time when we want nothing to do with kings. It paints the king's bride as little more than arm candy, a flashy but submissive ornament who should be glad for the opportunity to serve her "lord." It longs for everlasting dominion through the king's begetting of sons who will become "princes in all the earth."

Do we *really* want to study this psalm? Can it be worth our time and effort, even for the occasionally needed exercise of interpreting *against* the text?

Let's find out. The psalm includes several issues and at least one very curious verse to ponder, provided we appropriately consider the entire psalm rather than the lectionary limit to the latter half.

Praise for the king
(vv. 1-9)

Psalm 45 is clearly a royal psalm designed to celebrate a king's wedding. A superscription identifies the psalm as "a love song," but any love expressed grows from the psalmist's sycophantic devotion to the king. It includes no hint of romance between the king and the young bride about to join his trophy collection. **[A love song]**

The psalmist could have written for a newspaper's society column, or could have reported for a celebrity magazine. This is the only psalm in which the poet applauds his own literary skill: "My heart overflows with a goodly theme," he gushes. "I address my verses to the king; my

> **A love song:** A superscription to the psalm informs the choir director that the psalm should be sung to a tune or beat known as "Lilies" (*shōshanîm*), and attributes it to the Korahites, a known family of temple singers. It is furthermore identified as a "Maskil," which may suggest a "skilled" construction, but may also be a further instruction related to the psalm's performance, or an indicator that it belongs to a certain class of psalms. Thirteen psalms are labeled as Maskils (Psalms 32, 42, 44, 45, 52, 53, 54, 55, 74, 78, 88, 89, 142). An additional note describes Psalm 45 as "a love song."

tongue is like the pen of a ready scribe" (v. 1). The word translated "ready" normally means "quick" or "rapid." A scribe who could write rapidly, similar to a skilled secretary taking dictation, would be a valued member of the court.

The poet is clearly enamored with the king: "You are the most handsome of men; grace is poured upon your lips; therefore God has blessed you forever." The flowery word behind "you are most handsome" (*yāfyāfîtā*) is an irregular intensive form of the verb *yāfâ*, "to be beautiful," and is used only here.

The king is also skilled in oratory or conversation, per the poet, who uses "lips" as a metonymy for speech: "grace is poured upon your lips." To all appearances, then, the king is divinely blessed, a reputation the psalmist expects to last forever.

Quickly the poet switches from beauty to warfare: the king is not only handsome and well-spoken, but also powerful, with a "mighty sword" that contributes to his "glory and majesty" (v. 3). The psalmist cheers for the king to mount his war chariot and "ride on victoriously for the cause of truth and to defend the right" (v. 4a). He imagines the king's right hand – a symbol of his power – accomplishing things so great that they demonstrate his fearsome deeds (v. 4b).

Like Egyptian artists who flattered their pharaoh by portraying him as larger than life, skewering enemies with arrows and crushing them with his chariot, the poet attributes victories to the king's military prowess: "Your arrows are sharp in the heart of the king's enemies' the peoples fall under you" (v. 5). [**The mighty king**]

If the entire psalm is an interpretive conundrum, v. 6 brings an internal puzzle. Consider the NRSV: "Your throne, O God, endures forever and ever" (v. 6a). Has the poet's abject admiration elevated the king to the level of divinity?

It was not unusual for Egyptian or Mesopotamian kings to claim that the gods had granted them divine status, and the coronation hymn of Psalm 2 contains a hint of divine sonship even in Israel. There, the newly crowned king speaks: "I will tell of the decree of the LORD: he said to me, 'You are my son; today I have begotten you'" (Ps. 2:7).

The author of Psalm 45 appears to have gone one step further, as a literal reading of the text says "Your throne, God, (is) forever and ever." The word translated "God" is *'elohîm*. Psalm 45 falls within the "Elohistic Psalter" (Psalms 42–72) in which the divine name *yhwh* has been largely replaced by *'elohîm*.

In either case, the poet appears to be employing a royal hyperbole, speaking of the king as God's representative on earth, so closely identified that he could be addressed – at least in the context of his divinely endorsed throne – in terms of divinity.

The psalmist briefly attests that the king's reign, symbolized by the royal scepter and anointed by God "with the oil of gladness" beyond all companions, is one of equity and righteousness, opposed to all wickedness (v. 6b-7).

Quickly, however, he becomes lost in praise for the physical manifestations of the regent's glory. He wears aromatic robes "fragrant with myrrh and aloes and cassia," and dwells in "ivory palaces" featuring the glad music of stringed instruments (v. 8).

The king has many possessions, among them his wives, many of them marriages of political expediency. Stories of David, Solomon, and Ahab speak to the common practice of kings marrying the daughters of neighboring monarchs as a means of cementing political alliances. Absalom's mother, for example, was the daughter of the king of Geshur (2 Sam. 3:3).

The poet enthuses that "Daughters of kings are among your ladies of honor" (v. 9a). Though translators and commentators rarely point it out, "ladies of honor" must be a euphemism for other wives. There would be no point in a king having princesses from other countries hanging about as "ladies of honor," like Victorian nobility visiting their cousins for extended periods.

Knowing that the king had multiple wives, it is not unreasonable to suppose the current wives would have been expected to attend future weddings and welcome (to the extent possible) the new member of the harem to which they all belonged.

Whether "the queen in gold of Ophir" at the king's right hand is his current "Number One" wife or the new bride is unclear (v. 9b). Most translators and commentators take it as a reference to the new bride, though she is not "led to the king" until v. 14, though the chronology doesn't necessarily follow the verse order. [**Gold of Ophir**]

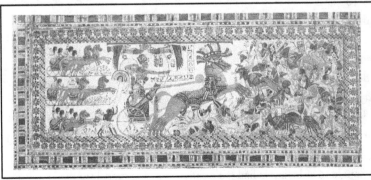

The mighty king: The painted wood panel in this image depicts the Egyptian king Tutankhamun defeating his enemies in a manner not unlike the description of the king in Ps. 45:5. (The photograph, by Yann Forget in *Le Musée absolu* [Phaidon, 2017], 10-2012, is in the public domain [https://commons.wikimedia.org/wiki/File:The_Pharaoh_Tutankhamun_destroying_his_enemies.jpg]).

> **Gold of Ophir:** Ophir refers to an unknown location, often thought to be in southern Arabia, though other locations have been suggested. The region was famous for producing fine gold. "Gold of Ophir" is also mentioned in Isa. 13:12 and Job 28:16.

Interpretation is complicated because the word "queen" (NRSV, NAS20) is a rare word, probably a loan word from Akkadian. It appears to refer to a royal consort in Neh. 2:6, and an Aramaic cognate is used of royal wives in Dan. 5:23. NIV11 and NET have "bride," while Craigie translates it as "consort."

It is likely that the psalmist refers to the bride, since he finally turns his attention to her in the next verse – or at least to her appearance and her perceived responsibilities.

Advice for the bride
(vv. 10-15)

The poet presumes to instruct the princess bride on how she should approach the coming marriage, but he does so solely in regard to what benefits the king, not her: "Hear, O daughter, consider and incline your ear; forget your people and your father's house, and the king will desire your beauty. Since he is your lord, bow to him …" (vv. 10-11).

Some readers compare the charge favorably with God's call for Abraham to leave his country and kindred (Gen. 12:1-3), but Abraham was not called to *forget* his home or family. Indeed, when it was time to find a wife for Isaac (Genesis 24, a companion text for this Sunday), he remembered them and sent his steward back to his homeland to procure a wife from among his kindred. Isaac's son Jacob likewise returned to their ancestral country and kin.

Insisting that the new bride forget her family and homeland seems cruel, but the psalmist seems to have thought it would be the only way for her to fit into the royal court, showing loyalty not to her family or home country, but to the king alone: "Since he is your lord, bow to him."

Depending on when the psalm was written, the psalmist's concern may have been that the princess would bring her home country's god and a competing cult into the kingdom. Solomon was praised for having many wives, but was also condemned for worshiping their gods (1 Kgs. 11:1-8). Ahab's wife Jezebel, daughter of the king of Tyre, famously sought to stamp out Yahweh worship in Israel and replace it with the cult of Baal (1 Kgs. 16:31-33; 18:3-4, 17-19).

To honor the new bride's place in the Israelite king's court, the psalmist said, rich people of Tyre would honor her with gifts, "with all kinds of wealth" (vv. 12-13). This may indicate that the woman's father was the king of Tyre, with whom both David and Solomon had good relations, and who would have likely remained an ally of sorts at different periods.

It also suggests that the promise of a rich dowry and good relations with Tyre may have been a motivating factor in the wedding.

Verses 14-15 describe the bride's elaborate costume. The vocabulary is difficult and a specific image is elusive, but her robes seem to have been either embroidered or multi-colored and embellished with gold. She is accompanied by ladies in waiting, whom the psalmist describes as delighted to be part of the bridal procession.

Blessings for the king
(vv. 16-17)

The psalm closes with a prediction or blessing that the king would beget sons, some of them no doubt by his new wife, that he would establish as "princes in all the earth" (v. 15). How we read this depends on whether we interpret the word $h\bar{a}$ $\bar{a}rets$ as "the earth" (NRSV, NAS20), or as "the land" (NIV11, NET). The word can be used for either one, but with decidedly different connotations.

Is the poet envisioning an empire of divinely sponsored world dominion to be ruled with the assistance of the king's sons, or does he imagine that future sons will be given positions of responsibility within the land of Israel or Judah?

While that is unclear, the psalmist's hope for the king's reputation is clear: he intends to praise the king with such celebration that his sterling reputation would be remembered from generation to generation, "forever and ever."

Puzzles for interpreters

What are we to do with a psalm like this? The Bible contains no more blatant example of patriarchy, male domination, and female submission than this. While some conservative believers hail male superiority as a model for life in any age, most of us recognize the inequity and injustice inherent in such a view.

Years ago, when Marabel Morgan's *The Total Woman* was popular within certain sectors, I recall hearing a beautiful young pastor's wife gush that "If my husband is the king, that means I get to be the queen!"

I thought it meant that she had been brainwashed.

Surely, we should not teach/preach this psalm as a paean for patriarchy.

Should we, then, teach/preach it as an anti-text, pointing to its culturally conditioned flaws in favor of our more enlightened view? That practice is hedged with limitations.

Many interpreters through the years have chosen to read the text as an allegory of Christ and the church. Allegorical interpretation is fraught with danger, and this is no exception. As Patricia Tull has noted, "If we try to allegorize this bride as the church and the king as God, we are left with a deity whose interest in us is superficial and political, who will love us, conditionally, if we forsake all our prior relationships" (*Feasting on the Word, Year A*, vol. 3 of Accordance electronic ed. [Westminster John Knox Press, 2011], par. 15526).

While studying the psalm has value, if only to recognize how off-target we believe the psalmist may have been, it can be difficult to redeem in a sermon. Some may be up for the challenge, but with six other RCL text options for Proper 9, most preachers are likely to find easier pickings among them.

The Hardest Question
How do we deal with a text that, by all appearances, refers to a Hebrew king as a god?

Verse 6, embedded in an address to the king on his wedding day, literally reads "Your throne, God, (is) forever and ever." Most major translations preserve the reading "Your throne, O God" (NRSV, NIV11, NAS20).

Some interpreters resolve the discomfort grammatically by taking 'elohîm in an adjectival sense, reading it to mean "Your divine throne endures forever and ever." This suggests no more than that kingship in Israel/Judah was established by God. Robert Alter translates it as "Your throne of God is forevermore" (*The Book of Psalms: A Translation with Commentary* [W.W. Norton, 2007], 159). An adjectival or attributive use of the divine name would be unusual, however.

Mitchell Dahood takes another approach, reading the noun meaning "throne" as a verb with the sense of "to enthrone," thus, "The eternal and everlasting God has enthroned you" (*Psalms I*, Anchor Bible [Yale University Press, 1966], 273, followed by Peter S. Craigie, *Psalms 1–50*, vol. 19 of Word Biblical Commentary [Word Books, 1983]).

Some interpreters may sidestep the issue by assuming that the text does not pertain to the king at all, but the poet has chosen to interrupt his address to the king with a burst of praise to God, whose throne endures forever, and who loves righteousness and hates wickedness. The following verses assume that v. 6 refers to the king, however.

The author of Hebrews resolved the issue – if he ever saw it as a problem – by reading Psalm 45 as a straightforward prophecy of Christ being enthroned as the divine king. In Heb. 1:5-9, while praising Christ as superior to angels, the writer cited several Old Testament texts as direct prophesies of Christ, with Ps. 45:6-7 playing the starring role:

- For to which of the angels did God ever say, "You are my Son; today I have begotten you"? (Ps. 2:7)
- Or again, "I will be his Father, and he will be my Son"? (2 Sam. 7:14)
- And again, when he brings the firstborn into the world, he says, "Let all God's angels worship him." (Deut. 32:43, Ps. 97:7)
- Of the angels he says, "He makes his angels winds, and his servants flames of fire." (Ps. 104:4)
- But of the Son he says, "Your throne, O God, is forever and ever, and the righteous scepter is the scepter of your kingdom. You have loved righteousness and hated wickedness; therefore God, your God, has anointed you with the oil of gladness beyond your companions." (Ps. 45:6-7)

Another popular option, as mentioned above, is to read the psalm as an allegory in which the king represents Christ and his new bride represents the church.

None of these readings are entirely satisfactory. Perhaps our best option is to take the text as it is and sit with the discomfort of contemplating a psalmist so smitten with a king who was so blessed by God that he has difficulty seeing the difference.

Second Optional First Reading
Song of Songs 2:1-17 (RCL 2:8-13)*

A Time for Love

My beloved speaks and says to me: "Arise, my love, my fair one, and come away..." (Song 2:10)

Bible studies from the Song of Songs may be even scarcer than sermons from its beautiful but mysterious poetry, but the ancients were inspired enough to preserve it as a part of the scriptures. This may seem strange, because the Song never mentions God or Israel, has no religious themes, and is frankly, exotically, erotically focused on human intimacy and sex with no real mention of marriage – or of sin.

During the first century, as the rabbis were trying to tie down the loose ends and establish the limits of the Hebrew Bible, many thought the Song of Songs should not be included. The influential Rabbi Akiva insisted, however, saying "Heaven forbid that there should be division in Israel about the holiness of the Song of Songs, for there is not one day in the whole of eternity that equals the one in which the Song of Songs was given to Israel. For all the Writings are holy, but the Song of Songs is the holiest" (*Mishna Yadayim* 3:5).

So, what wisdom might we find in this surprising book?

The Song of Songs is one of five short books that the Hebrew Bible refers to as the Megillot, each of which is associated with one of the annual feasts. The Song of Songs is typically read among Ashkenazic Jews (of Eastern European ancestry) on the Sabbath before the Feast of the Passover. Among some Sephardic Jews (of Spanish or Mediterranean ancestry), it is read on the eve of every Sabbath.

Why Passover? Some of the rabbis interpreted the Song as an allegory for the love relationship between God and

---

Why not Solomon? The Song of Songs, largely a collection of love poems, probably came to be associated with Solomon because two of the poems speak of the male lover as a king (1:4, 12), and several verses mention Solomon–though always in the third person, as someone else talking about him (3:6-11, 8:11-12). Solomon's accomplishments were both celebrated and exaggerated: the author of 1 Kings claimed that Solomon wrote 1,005 songs (1 Kgs. 4:32), and that he had an unlikely harem of 700 wives and 300 concubines (1 Kgs. 11:3). This would have given him quite the reputation of a paramour, though certainly not in the passionate or committed nature of the lovers who must struggle to see each other in the Song of Songs.

Solomon was also known as a patron of the arts, and associating the book with him would have heightened its reputation. Even so, most modern scholars doubt seriously that Solomon had anything to do with its composition. Not only is Solomon described in the third person; much of the vocabulary reflects a period hundreds of years after Solomon ruled. Its final composition almost certainly belongs in the postexilic period, long after Solomon's reign, and perhaps as late as the third century.

Israel. The Passover marked the beginning of the Exodus and Wilderness period, which prophets later idealized as a type of "honeymoon" between Yahweh and Israel.

The book is sometimes called the Song of Solomon, from its first verse, a superscription calling it "The song of songs, which is to/of/by/for Solomon." Solomon is an unlikely author, though a later editor associated the poems with him, perhaps as a dedication. [**Why not Solomon?**]

---

*This text is also read for Proper 17 in Year B.

The alternate name, "Song of Songs," is a Hebrew expression meaning "the greatest song." Bibles favored by Catholics call it "Canticles," after the title in the Latin Vulgate.

The short book's 117 verses comprise anywhere from five to 50 different poems, depending on how one counts them. Poetry is notoriously difficult to translate, and the Song has more *hapax legomena* (words used only once in the Bible) than any other book in either Testament, making an accurate translation even more difficult. About 11 percent of the words in the Song do not appear elsewhere in the Bible, leaving translators to rely on cognates from other Semitic languages and make educated guesses.

Some scholars have labored to identify a cohesive plot and identify speaking parts, but the book resists a clear structural analysis. The Song is a rather loose collection of love poems that may refer to more than one couple.

Just how the Song functioned in Israel's life and worship is unclear. Perhaps it is best to simply regard it as a collection of ancient love songs that celebrate young love, the discovery of love, sexual awakening, and the hopes of the lovers.

One possible reason for the popularity of these songs and their eventual collection could be that they often speak of forbidden love, of love that cannot be expressed in the public square or that might not be approved of by the public officials. Several of the poems speak of lovers who seem mismatched by their culture's standards, but who sought to overcome the obstacles and be with their true chosen partner.

Forbidden love has remained a common theme in literature or popular music through the years: we can easily think of *Romeo and Juliet*, *West Side Story*, or the movie version of *Titanic*, among others. In the postexilic period, the theme might have had special resonance for the many people who were caught in Ezra or Nehemiah's campaign to prevent intermarriage between "pure" Israelites and any of their ethnically mixed neighbors, or to force divorces when such marriages had already occurred (Ezra 10:1-44, Neh. 13:23-31).

Unlike the wholly patriarchal character of Psalm 45, the other optional reading for Genesis 24, the female lover in the Song is not a passive ornament for the man's amusement, but she plays a positive and powerful role. She appears just as bold as he in describing what she admires, what she wants, and how she plans to find time with her lover. She is assertive and sexual and clearly appreciates the joy of intimacy apart from its role in procreation or patri-archal family systems. She often speaks of her mother's house and her mother's bedchamber, both of which speak of female power and autonomy.

The frequency with which the woman speaks suggests the distinct possibility that a woman could have written all or part of the Song of Songs.

Love desired
(vv. 1-9)

Our text describes an encounter involving a young woman who could have been named "Flower," for she describes herself as "a rose of Sharon, a lily of the valleys" (v. 1), and her beloved describes her as "a lily among brambles" (v. 2). She describes her beau in lavish terms as a rare find, "like an apple tree among the trees of the wood" (v. 3). Remembering a previous rendezvous, she recalls "I sat in his shadow, and his fruit was sweet to my taste." The image of shade suggests both protection from the blazing sun and the delight of a secretive location, a figurative description of their happy and obviously sexual encounter. [Apples]

The notion of taste continues in v. 4, where she speaks of "the banqueting house" (literally, "house of wine"), a metaphor for the feast of love they share. She recalls asking for raisin cakes and apples for sustenance in her love-sick state (v. 5), but the cure she most desires is to be in her beloved's arms: "O that his left hand were under my head and that his right hand embraced me" (v. 6).

The first part of v. 6 has no verb: "his left hand under my head" could thus be rendered in different ways. "His left hand [is] under my head," and "[O that] his left hand [were] under my head" are two options. Whether she is wishing for his embrace or describing it depends on the translator's understanding of the surrounding context.

The healing power of a lover's embrace is reflected in Egyptian love poetry, as in these lines: "My salvation is her

---

Apples: Apple trees were not native to Palestine. Then, as now, the kind of apple trees that produce good fruit must be carefully cultivated, and to find such a tree "in the wood" would be an unexpected boon.

Apples, though uncommon, were known throughout the ancient Near East, and often associated with themes of romantic love and sexual fertility. References to apples or apple trees occur several times in the Song: 2:3, 5, 7, 9; 8:5.

coming in from outside; when I see her, I will be healthy. When she opens her eye, my body is young; when she speaks, I will be strong. When I embrace her, she exorcises evil from me" (from the Chester Beatty Papyri, C 5:1-2, cited in notes to Song 2:6 in the New English Translation).

Enamored with thoughts of love, the maiden calls on her companions, the "daughters of Jerusalem," to swear that they will not "awaken or arouse love" until "it delights" (literally), sometimes translated "until it is ready" (v. 7, NRSV). Here, as in many other places in the Song, "love" is not abstract, but descriptive of physical passion. The meaning seems to be that one should be cautious, and not arouse one's ardor before the time is right.

Anticipating a new encounter, the maiden exults in the sound of her beloved's voice and the sight of his approach (v. 8). She describes him as being like a gazelle or a young stag (v. 9), "leaping upon the mountains, bounding over the hills." Both stags and gazelles, sure-footed residents of the area's mountain crags and open plains, were associated with male virility.

The maiden anxiously watches for his arrival, and happily spots him standing behind the wall, peeking through the lattice – a suggestion that their tryst is both secret and exciting.

Love invited
(vv. 10-15)

With v. 10, the beloved arrives, and his voice – quoted by the woman – is heard in the next several verses. The man is just as eager to see the woman as she is to be reunited with him.

With the passing of winter rains (v. 11) – when planting was done – springtime offered a window of opportunity for other pursuits. Kings led their armies forth to war in the spring because the troops weren't needed in the fields until harvest (2 Sam. 11:1).

The same freedom brought the man to his beloved, declaring that spring had arrived, and it was time for romance. He speaks of flowers, birdsong, fig trees, and fragrant vineyards, all possible background settings for secretive expressions of their passion (vv. 12-13).

Despite her earlier enthusiasm, the woman appears to have become fearful. The male lover speaks of her as a dove hiding in a cliffside cavity (v. 14). He calls her to come out of hiding so he can see her face and hear her voice, "for your voice is sweet, and your face is lovely." [Chiasm]

> **Chiasm:** The latter part of v. 14 offers a nice example of a chiastic parallelism, in which elements appear in reverse order: face-voice-voice-face.
>
> Let me see your face,
>   let me hear your voice;
>   for your voice is sweet,
> and your face is lovely.

With v. 15, the woman speaks again, apparently giving voice to her fears. Whether she is speaking to her lover or to a wider audience is unclear, but she appeals for someone to "catch the foxes, the little foxes that ruin the vineyards, for our vineyards are in blossom."

Foxes are mentioned several times in the Hebrew Bible, always in a negative sense (Judg. 15:4, Neh. 4:3, Ps. 63:10, Lam. 5:18, Ezek. 13:4). With a taste for sweet grapes, they could cause significant damage to a vineyard. Thus, well-tended vineyards were surrounded by sturdy fences or hedges and included a watchtower so someone could keep an eye out for intruders (see, e.g., Isa. 5:1-2).

Earlier, the man had spoken of vineyards in blossom, and now the woman returns to the image as a metaphor for their love, which appears to be threatened. Several of the poems in the Song speak of lovers who don't match up with social conventions and are thus discouraged from meeting, leading them to meet at night or in clandestine outdoor settings.

Who were the foxes that threatened the couple's blossoming love? The poem does not say, but evidence in other parts of the Song point to possible ethnic or class differences. In 1:5 she speaks of being "black but beautiful," which probably relates more to social class than to race, for she attributes her dark skin to being forced to work outdoors as a vine-keeper.

In ch. 5, when the woman goes out in search of her lover, she is caught and beaten by night watchmen, though the cause of her offense is not clear. Someone doesn't want them to be together.

Love enjoyed
(vv. 16-17)

Whatever obstacles they had to overcome, the lovers achieve their rendezvous, and the woman describes their mutual commitment: "My beloved is mine and I am his," she says. Then, with a description of sex barely veiled in metaphor, she adds: "he pastures his flock among the lilies" (NRSV, or

'Anî l^edôdî: A variation of the expression "I am my beloved's, and my beloved is mine" appears at 2:16, 6:3, and 7:10. The first line of 6:3, *'anî l^edôdî, v^edôdî lî* (literally, "I belong to my beloved, and my beloved belongs to me"), has become a popular phrase for incorporation into jewelry such as necklaces, bracelets, and rings.

In the photo, a ring bears the unpointed Hebrew script (right to left) for *'ani ledodi, vedodi li.*

NET: "he grazes among the lilies," v. 16). The woman hopes their encounter will last through the night ("until the day breathes and the shadows flee"), urging her beloved to "be like a gazelle or a young stag on the cleft of the mountains" (v. 17). [*'Anî l^edôdî*]

What do we do with such a frank and erotic description of love? Interpreters have employed a variety of approaches in trying to make sense of the text, or to make it palatable to prudish readers. Many have resorted to allegory, reading the Song as a love story between God and Israel, or between Christ and the church.

Allegory may have been the most popular approach, but it is exegetically the least satisfying, for it imposes an interpretation that the text does not invite.

In the end, we may regard this and other texts from the Song of Songs as a welcome biblical endorsement of the wonder and beauty of love, passion, and sexual expression as being among God's most beautiful and praiseworthy gifts.

Both the man and the woman consider each other to be rare and cherished finds. Surely that kind of joyful, devoted relationship has something sacred about it, something worthy of poetry and song, and even of scripture.

The Hardest Question
How do we interpret the message of the Song of Songs?

The Song of Songs, with its frequent and graphic references to sex – and its complete absence of any reference to God – has left both Jewish and Christian interpreters uncomfort-

able. How do we understand this elegant but racy collection of love poems?

Through the years, expositors have developed a variety of interpretational approaches. Perhaps the most popular tactic is to treat the Song as an allegory about God's love relationship with Israel or the church. That approach works better in a generic fashion than a specific one, however: it's one thing to speak of the church as the bride of Christ, but quite another to describe the relationship in a graphic, physical, sexual way.

It appears clear that the poets or writers who contributed to the Song of Songs had other things in mind when composing the alluring and erotic poetry that makes up the book. They certainly made no effort to spell out any sort of connection or allusion to the man and woman as God and Israel.

It is quite possible to recognize the book as a frank celebration of sexual love as God's good gift to humankind. The lack of specific references to God or marriage, along with the abundance of creation images, suggest that the book's main purpose may be simply to extol God's good gift of human sexuality and its expression in loving relationships – even in situations outside of typical societal bounds.

Perhaps it is best to recognize that the poetry of the Song can be read on more than one level. On the surface, the poetry speaks openly about love and sex, eroticism and intimacy, the excitement of longing for the touch of a loved one.

On a different level, the song could be read as a commentary on the theme of barriers such as race and class or religion and family that can interfere with love. Like *West Side Story* or *Romeo and Juliet*, it can be seen as a plea for understanding of and acceptance for relationships between people from different backgrounds. This would have been especially apropos during the postexilic period, when religious leaders were demanding that Hebrew men and women should avoid intermarriage with non-Jews.

On a more abstract level, one could possibly read the song as an allegory of longing and love, pursuit and courtship between God and people. But one should be aware that such an interpretation is imposed from without by later tradition or current readers, and almost certainly was not the author's (or authors') intent.

Second Reading
Zechariah 9:9-12

Prisoners of Hope

Return to your stronghold, O prisoners of hope; today I declare that I will restore to you double. (Zech. 9:12)

Hard times are a fact of life for all of us. Sooner or later, less or more, we will encounter rough patches or bleak days that may leave us struggling to put one foot in front of the other.

The hedgerow that seems so impenetrable may be a pile of bills that a job loss has rendered us unable to pay, or an unexpected illness that has put us on the sidelines for an indefinite period. It may have its roots in a strained relationship, a broken heart, or a colossal mistake that we regret but can't change.

How do we move forward when prospects seem dismal? We go with hope.

Hope will not always guarantee success or grant quick relief from trial, but it keeps us on our feet and moving.

Today's text speaks of a promising future for a downtrodden people who live in exile but have not given up, because they are prisoners of hope.

A little-known prophet

The encouraging words are found in the book of Zechariah, which comes next to last in both the "Book of the Twelve" (or "Minor Prophets") and the Old Testament.

The book consists of two main parts. The first eight chapters contain a series of visions precisely dated between 520 and 518 BCE, less than 20 years after the first group of exiles from Judah had returned to Jerusalem in hopes of rebuilding the city.

When the pioneering exiles returned to Jerusalem, beginning about 538 BCE, they found the city in ruins. New homes had to be built and farms planted, but a

---

A two-part book: The latter section of Zechariah can be further divided into two sections (chs. 9–11 and chs. 12–14), each of which begin with the words "Oracle of the Lord," an unusual expression that also begins the following book of Malachi.

The oracles found in chs. 9–14 defy precise dating. Some scholars find clues to suggest they originated with a different prophet in an earlier period, but most modern scholars believe they derive from a period as much as 200 years after Zechariah's time, as the Persian Empire was beginning to fade and the Greeks were ascendant, with Jerusalem caught in the middle.

As early as 1638, Joseph Mede suggested that the latter part of Zechariah was written much earlier, and by Jeremiah, because when the author of Matthew quoted Zech. 11:12-13 regarding Judas' payment of 30 pieces of silver, he attributed it to Jeremiah (Matt. 27:9-10). Mede suggested that the Holy Spirit was using Matthew to correct a misattribution of the texts to Zechariah as the prophetic books were being shaped by early editors.

Some early scholars followed Mede's suggestion. Others have dated the oracles in Zechariah 9–14 to periods ranging from the eighth century onward, but a late postexilic date is most likely. Though we cannot ascribe authorship with certainty, we will refer to the writer as Zechariah.

---

drought hampered their efforts. Officials from neighboring sub-provinces conspired to slow reconstruction efforts.

Efforts to rebuild the temple languished for more than a decade, but with the arrival of Zerubbabel as governor in 520 BCE, the prophets Haggai and Zechariah saw him as a potential messiah: despite his Babylonian name ("Seed/offspring of Babylon), Zerubbabel was a descendant of

David. Though he was not a king, his position as governor inspired hope for a brighter future. With encouragement and support from the two prophets, Zerubbabel led an effort to rebuild the temple, dedicating it in 515 BCE.

The hard but hopeful prophecies of Zechariah 1–8 are carefully dated to this period. In contrast, chs. 9–14 adopt a different style and take on an apocalyptic cast, looking beyond the immediate future to a day of ultimate restoration. Many scholars believe they may have been added at a later time, perhaps by a different prophet. [A two-part book]

Zechariah, whose name means "Yahweh remembers," was known as the head of a priestly family (Neh. 12:6). He is described as the son of Berechiah and the grandson of Iddo in 1:1, though Ezra 5:1 and 6:14 call him the son of Iddo. The term *ben* normally means "son," but can also refer to a more distant but direct descendant. Like Ezekiel, Zechariah would have been both priest and prophet.

In chs. 1–8, Zechariah sought to assure the struggling settlers that God was concerned about their welfare, and he spoke of a glorious kingdom to come. In chs. 9–14, he pronounced judgment on foreign lands and on Judah's leaders, but promised that God would restore the scattered people of both Israel (10:1-12) and Judah (chs. 12–13). The nations of the earth would come against Jerusalem but be defeated, so that God would rule over all the earth and be worshiped by all nations (ch. 14).

A peace-loving king
(vv. 9-10)

Today's text contains one of the most familiar and beloved prophecies to be quoted in the New Testament: the prediction of a powerful but humble king who would ride into Jerusalem on a donkey and establish a reign of peace.

The verses preceding the text (9:1-8) set the stage for the king's entrance by declaring that Yahweh would clear out Israel's closest enemies, beginning with Syria to the northeast, moving to Phoenicia on the northwest, and then south to drive out Philistines to the west and southwest before returning to Jerusalem to "encamp at my house as a guard." [Safe in Jerusalem?]

In a separate oracle, the next two verses anticipate that a human king would come to join Yahweh in the newly

---

Safe in Jerusalem? The claim found in Zech. 9:8 is reminiscent of the false prophets of Jeremiah's day who claimed that Jerusalem's residents were safe, no matter how they behaved, because Yahweh would not allow the temple to be destroyed (cf. Jer. 7:1-15). That was manifestly not true, for the temple was leveled by the Babylonians just a few years later.

The promise in Zech. 9:8 looks to a future day when Yahweh would make Jerusalem as invulnerable as the earlier false prophets had claimed it would be: "Then I will encamp at my house as a guard, so that no one shall march to and fro; no oppressor shall again overrun them, for now I have seen with my own eyes."

Such a time still awaits the arrival of the "New Jerusalem" spoken of in New Testament apocalyptic: the second temple, built in Zechariah's day and magnificently expanded by King Herod, was utterly destroyed by the Romans in 70 CE, following a Jewish rebellion. The former temple mount is now home to two historic mosques, the Dome of the Rock (Mosque of Omar) and the Al-Aqsa Mosque, both of which were built shortly before or after 700 CE and have stood for 1300 years, far longer than the tenure of Solomon's temple and the Second Temple combined.

---

liberated city, riding into Jerusalem amid shouts of jubilation from "daughter Zion" and "daughter Jerusalem."

"Zion," though just part of the city, was often used in parallel with Jerusalem as a whole. Here, as in other texts, the city is personified as a woman (2 Kgs. 19:21; Isa. 37:22; Lam. 2:13, 15; Mic. 4:8; Zeph. 3:14). Zechariah envisioned a future population of Jerusalem gathering to "rejoice greatly" and "shout aloud" as they welcomed the coming king.

What can we know about this mysterious man who rides a donkey to his coronation? God would have already eliminated potential enemies, so he would not arrive as a conqueror. [No enemies?] Even so, the coming king would be called "triumphant" and "victorious" as well as "humble" (NRSV).

The NRSV's use of "triumphant" is puzzling: the word (*tsadiq*) would be better translated in the normal sense of "righteous" (NIV, HCSB). A righteous or just (KJV) king is one who upholds Israel's covenant with Yahweh and rules wisely with justice for all persons.

The word "victorious" literally means "saved," or "delivered," as in the KJV's awkward but accurate "having salvation." The term does not carry the New Testament sense

No enemies? The text of Zech. 9:9 implies that the coming king could claim the throne without conflict because Yahweh had swept Israel's borders clean of would-be enemies such as Syria, Phoenicia, and Philistia (9:1-8). He is then said to do away with war and establish dominion "from sea to sea and from the river to the ends of the earth" (v. 10).

There is a problem with this, however: the text says nothing about Persia, which defeated Babylonia in 538 BCE and rose to become the sole superpower of its day. As Zechariah watched the efforts to rebuild the ruined temple of Yahweh and prophesied of Jerusalem's future glory, the area surrounding the city was merely a sub-province of Persia, called "Jehud" (pronounced "yeh-HOOD," a Persian version of "Judah"). Jehud was led by a governor who was appointed by the Persians, paid tribute to their overlords, and were subject to Persian authority.

The Persian Empire (also called the Achaemenid Empire) was largely unchallenged for domination of the known world for 200 years, with territories stretching from the Indus Valley in the east to the border of Greece and as far south as Egypt. Internal dissension and a series of victories by the Greek Alexander the Great culminating in the Battle of Gaugamela in 331 BCE led to the dissolution of the empire.

Whether Zechariah 9 dates to the late sixth or late fourth centuries, as variously speculated, the absence of the Persians from 9:1-8 is puzzling. Greeks are mentioned in v. 13, with an indication that Judah and Ephraim (the former northern and southern kingdoms) together would defeat them.

One way to understand the order of events is to recognize that vv. 1-8, vv. 9-10, and vv. 11-13 probably originated as separate oracles, explaining the lack of consistency between them.

of "being saved from sin," but suggests that Yahweh had delivered the coming king from all enemies and dangers. God had won the victory for him.

Perhaps this helps to explain the king's modesty. He would not be proud and haughty as Absalom was, or as some other kings of Israel had been. Rather, he would be marked by the humility needed to rule with compassion and justice.

The word translated as "humble" normally means "poor" or "afflicted," but can also carry the sense of meekness or gentleness (KJV). Moses was said to be "meek" (Num. 12:3), and a form of the word is used for the "suffering servant" of Isa. 53:4.

As a mark of his modesty, the king would not arrive in a chariot or astride a warhorse, but on the back of a donkey.

Poetic repetition emphasizes the king's humility, using three different words for "donkey" or "ass." Literally, he would be "riding on a donkey (*hamôr*); on a male donkey (*'ayîr*), the son (*ben*) of a female donkey (*'âtôn* – though surprisingly, the MT has the plural form *'atônôt*)."

A misunderstanding of this poetic repetition led the translators of the Greek Septuagint to imagine two animals, a stance followed by the KJV, which says he was "riding upon an ass, and upon a colt the foal of an ass" – an image that would have the king straddling two animals, or perhaps standing with a foot upon each, like a circus performer.

Zechariah declared that the coming king's rule would be so peaceful that weapons of war could be eliminated: "I will cut off the chariot from Ephraim and the horse from Jerusalem. The bow of war will be removed, and he will proclaim peace to the nations" (v. 10a).

This poetic promise imagines not only peace, but also the reunification of the northern tribes (called "Ephraim") who had been scattered by the Assyrians in 722 BCE, and the people of Judah (Jerusalem), who had been exiled by the Babylonians in several waves beginning in 597 and increasing in 587 BCE.

Afterward, the king's dominion would stretch "from sea to sea," and "from the Euphrates River to the ends of the earth" (v. 10b: "the river" typically refers to the Euphrates).

Zechariah would have had a far more limited vision of the earth's extent than that of modern readers, but he declared that the king's peaceful rule would extend throughout the world that was known to him, and beyond.

A God-blessed people
(vv. 11-12)

The new king's rule would not be the only good news: God would bring new waves of returning exiles to Jerusalem. The promise of deliverance in vv. 11-13 may have originated separately, but it is bound to the previous verses in such a way that the prophet continues to address daughter Jerusalem: the "you" in "As for you …" is feminine.

The oracle is unusual because it speaks of God having a "covenant of blood" with Jerusalem (v. 11a). Similar expressions are found only in Exod. 24:8, a reference to blood sprinkled on the altar during the covenant ceremony at Sinai, and in Jesus' words of institution at the Lord's Supper (Mark 14:24).

Javan? The Hebrew word used for "Greece" is "Javan" (pronounced *Yāvān*), a Hebrew spelling of "Ionian." The area known as Ionia was in western Turkey, but populated by a tribe of Greeks known as Ionians. As sea-traders, they were known to the Hebrews and other peoples who lived along the periphery of the Mediterranean Sea. The term also appears in Gen. 10:2, 4; Ezek. 27:13; Isa. 66:9; Joel 3:6; Dan. 8:21, and 11:2.

In this context, the "covenant of blood" may refer to God's promise to David in 2 Samuel 7 that one of his descendants (that is, of his bloodline) would always sit on the throne (2 Samuel 7, 23:5; Ps. 89:4, 29; 132:11). Thus, later prophets foresaw a time when God would fulfill the "forever promise" and return a Davidic king to the throne.

The oracle looks to a time when all of Israel's exiles would be released from the "waterless pit" of their imprisonment (v. 11b), possibly a reference to Joseph's release from a pit into which his brothers had thrown him (Gen. 37:18-28).

As "prisoners of hope" who had not given up on God during their exile, Zechariah said, they would "return to the stronghold" (Jerusalem) and find new prosperity (v. 12). That the exiles would include persons from both Israel and Judah becomes clear in v. 13: with a striking metaphor, the prophet declares that Yahweh would bend Judah as a bow, and "fill" it with Ephraim as an arrow to be released against the people of Greece, who followed the Persians as empire builders. [Javan?]

The military imagery of v. 13 may seem at odds with the peaceful king who enters the city in v. 10, but the prophet used both pictures to capture his readers with the hope of a new and better future.

Christian worshipers recall how Jesus modeled his ministry and teaching on the image of a peaceful king who would bring spiritual deliverance through humility and service. All four gospels recount the story of how Jesus entered Jerusalem on Palm Sunday in just the manner described by Zech. 9:9, riding on a young donkey. Both Matt. 21:5 and John 12:15 cite portions of Zech. 9:9, while the shouts of "Hosanna! Blessed is he who comes in the name of the Lord," found in all four gospels, derive from Ps. 118:25-26.

Zechariah, like Jesus, spoke to a discouraged and downtrodden people who were desperately in need of hope

lest they give up on God altogether. Their messages served – and continue to serve – to capture our hearts with a sense of expectancy. Though we may sometimes feel shackled to the daily grind or bound by moments of crisis, we can find inspiration to keep pushing forward, for in Christ we are prisoners of hope.

The Hardest Question
Does God break a bow or use it?

One who reads today's text closely cannot help but be puzzled by what appear to be two diametrically opposite statements.

In v. 10, the prophet imagines a peaceful king who enjoys a peaceful rule of world dominion established by God, who "will cut off the chariot from Ephraim and the war horse from Judah; and the battle bow shall be cut off, and he shall command peace to the nations."

But in v. 13, the martial metaphor remains active: "For I have bent Judah as my bow; I have made Ephraim its arrow. I will arouse your sons, O Zion, against your sons, O Greece, and wield you like a warrior's sword."

How can the prophet speak of an end to war in one verse while imagining a military Israel being unleashed against Greece just three verses later? How can the battle bow be "cut off" in v. 10, but bent and loaded for war in v. 13?

The most likely explanation is to recognize not only that vv. 9-10 and vv. 11-13 originated as separate oracles, but also that prophetic predictions were quite varied, not necessarily in chronological order, and cannot always be reconciled. Some oracles imagine a warrior king who will lead Israel to victory over its enemies and re-establish the nation as a world power, while others speak of an age of peace in which all peoples will worship God, with Jerusalem as the focus of the world.

In today's text, a vision of world harmony led by a peace-loving king in Jerusalem is followed by a separate oracle that predicts a successful military campaign. That thought continues through v. 17, which some scholars see as the proper end of the oracle beginning in v. 11.

The variety of prophesies led emerging Judaism to hold in tension the twin hopes of a messiah who would come to lead a military victory, and a messianic age led by a king of peace.

Jesus' ministry emerged in the midst of this tension. The Zealots (including some of his own disciples) pressured Jesus to use his power to defeat Rome, and were disappointed when he identified with the humble servant king who would rule in peace.

Optional Second Reading
Psalm 145 (RCL 145:8-14)*

How Great Is God?

Great is the LORD, and greatly to be praised; his greatness is unsearchable. (Ps. 145:3)

The Jerusalem temple had a well-organized music program, with singers, musicians, choirmasters, and perhaps even resident psalmists. If the temple had offered a "contemporary worship" option with a praise team leading the music, there's no doubt that Psalm 145 would have been their bread and butter.

It's rather long, for one thing, and somewhat repetitive. Most of all, it's about praising the greatness and goodness of God, revealed in marvelous ways. It is a happy, joyful song, a song that could inspire worshipers to lift their hands, dance, and smile.

It is the last of the psalms with a superscription associating it with David, or with anyone else, and the only one to be labeled, simply, "Praise" (*t'hillâ*). It introduces a string of psalms that close the Psalter with expressions of rapturous admiration for God: Psalms 146–150 all begin with "Praise the LORD" (or in Hebrew, *hallelû-yâ*).

Psalm 145 appears more often than any other in the Jewish prayer book, and rabbinic discussion in the Jewish Talmud holds that anyone who recites Psalm 145 three times a day will be assured a place in the world to come because it is not only a memorable acrostic, but also praises God's sustenance to all creation (*Berakhot* 4b:16-20).

Hymnary.org cites several pages of hymns with some connection to Psalm 145. The Revised Common Lectionary uses selections from Psalm 145 for Sunday readings no less than five times.

To get the full effect of this memorable encomium, we will address the entire psalm rather than the selected verses for any particular Sunday.

God is great
(vv. 1-7)

As noted above, the psalm is an acrostic, with each verse beginning with a consecutive letter of the Hebrew alphabet. Similar patterns are found in Psalms 24, 34, 37, 111, 112, and 119. The acrostic pattern served as an aid to memorization, but also emphasized the theme of total praise to God, "from A to Z," or in this case, from *alef* to *tav*.

The first seven verses leave no question that the psalmist's purpose is to offer lavish adoration to God. "I will extol you, my God and King, and bless your name forever and ever" (v. 1). The reference to God as king links the psalm to the theme of divinely ordained kingship in Psalms 2, 45, and others. [Extol]

The psalmist's praise is both intense and lasting. It is "forever and ever," a thought repeated in v. 2, which promises not just eternal, but daily adoration. Overflowing with gratitude and worship, he sings: "Great is the LORD,

> **Extol:** The word for "extol" is an intensive, passive, cohortative form of a verb that means "to be high," meaning something akin to "may you be lifted up by me"–"I will extol you" or "I will exalt you" offers a smoother reading.

---

*Psalm 145:1-8 is read for Proper 20 in Year A; 145:1-5, 18-21 is read for Proper 27 in Year C; 145:8-9, 15-21 is read for Proper 13A; and 145:10-19 is read for Proper 12 in Year B. This commentary will incorporate the full chapter, vv. 1-21.

and greatly to be praised; his greatness is unsearchable" (v. 3), a sentiment that has inspired several modern praise choruses.

The poet is not alone in singing praise, however, for he attests: "One generation shall laud your works to another, and shall declare your mighty acts" (v. 4). Hebrews often drew on traditional memories of God's mighty acts in delivering Israel from Egypt, parting the sea, and aiding in victories over their enemies.

Though distant in time, celebrations such as Passover continue to encourage people of Hebrew descent to relive those events as if they were present in the loins of their ancestors.

The theme continues as the psalmist promises to meditate on "the glorious splendor of your majesty and on your wondrous works" (v. 5). He will proclaim "the might of your awesome deeds" and "declare your greatness" (v. 6), celebrating "the fame of your abundant goodness" and singing aloud of God's righteousness (v. 7).

God is gracious
(vv. 8-13)

The extravagant piling up of descriptors for God's striking deeds leads the poet to explore laudable aspects of the divine character, beginning with a near quotation from Exod. 34:6, rephrased so that it begins with the word for gracious (*channûn*), the appropriate letter to begin the next verse. "The LORD is gracious and merciful, slow to anger and abounding in steadfast love" (v. 8). That sentiment, reportedly God's self-revelation to Moses, served as a credo so memorable that it is quoted in Num. 14:18, Jer. 32:18, Joel 2:13, Jon 4:2, Nah. 1:3, and Ps. 103:8 and 145:8.

God's goodness and compassion extend "over all that he has made" (v. 9), so it is appropriate that "all your works shall give thanks to you, O LORD" (v. 10a).

Glorious splendor: The psalmist stretches language to the breaking point, but Hebrew has only so many words to describe majesty or glory, so a repetition of vocabulary is not surprising. For example, in v. 5, he meditates on "the glorious splendor" (*hadar k^evôd*) of God's majesty, while v. 12 praises "the glorious splendor (*k^evôd hadar*) of your kingdom," reversing the words but to the same end.

One might expect the poet to rhapsodize on all the elements of nature and all peoples offering praise to God, as in Psalm 148, but he keeps the focus on God, as the faithful ones offer blessings to God (v. 10b), speak of God's glory and power (v. 11), tell of God's mighty deeds (v. 12a), and make known "the glorious splendor of your kingdom" (v. 12b). [**Glorious splendor**]

God's kingdom and sovereignty are both glorious and everlasting, "and your dominion endures throughout all generations" (v. 13a).

God is faithful
(vv. 14-21)

The final section begins with a verse that may or may not have been found in the original text. The acrostic nature of the psalm leads us to expect a verse beginning with *nun*, but that verse is missing from the Masoretic Text (see "The Hardest Question" below for more). Most modern translations accept a reading found in the Dead Sea Scrolls and the Septuagint that supplies the missing verse with a statement that segues nicely from one section to the next: "The LORD is faithful in all his words, and gracious in all his deeds" (v. 13b).

The following verses explore the compassionate nature of God in responding to human needs, especially those expressed in prayer. "The LORD upholds all who are falling, and raises up all who are bowed down," he says (v. 14). Those who believe this promise naturally turn to God in trust for daily needs: "The eyes of all look to you, and you give them their food in due season. You open your hand, satisfying the desire of every living thing" (vv. 15-16).

The poet speaks idealistically. Surely among those hearing these words in Israel's worship, reading them later, or reciting them frequently would be people who had experienced droughts or hard times. God did not and does not always "satisfy the desire of every living thing" – or at least, not every desire.

Still, the poet declared God to be trustworthy, attentive, and doing what is right: "The LORD is just in all his ways, and kind in all his doings" (v. 17). Even when times are hard, "The LORD is near to all who call on him, to all who call on him in truth" (v. 18). [**All**]

> **All:** The fullness of God's sovereignty over all things is emphasized by the word "all" (*kol*), which appears no less than 17 times in Psalm 145.

People need more than daily sustenance. Sometimes they find themselves facing illness, poverty, danger, or other trials. They yearn to be delivered from their state of exigency, and the psalmist insists that "He fulfills the desire of all who fear him; he also hears their cry, and saves them" (v. 19).

Moreover, God is constantly on guard to protect the righteous, the thankful worshiper declares: "The LORD watches over all who love him, but all the wicked he will destroy" (v. 20).

The closing verse echoes the opening gush of praise, both for himself and for coming generations: "My mouth will speak the praise of the LORD, and all flesh will bless his holy name forever and ever" (v. 21).

What might have been the original setting of such a praise-filled psalm? One might think it reflects a time of prosperity when ebullient thanksgiving would come naturally. Many scholars, however, think it may have arisen during the postexilic period as a celebration of the exiles' opportunity to return home, even though reclaiming the ruined city of Jerusalem was fraught with difficulty.

Praise is appropriate, even when it does not come easy. The expression of joyful trust can remind the suffering that God has not forgotten them, even if they feel more like singing one of the many psalms of lament. "The LORD upholds the fallen, and raises up all who are bowed down."

Many in the Black church understand this. Despite centuries of suffering and continuing oppression through a society that has long privileged whiteness over people of color, worship in many predominantly Black churches remains joyful and hopeful. A Black minister of my acquaintance once explained the apparent dichotomy in part by saying "We are not rejoicing in what is, but in what will be."

Times will come when lament is appropriate, but even those times can invite praise to a God who is both sovereign and compassionate, a God who offers hope for all our days.

The Hardest Question
What about the missing *nun*?

Observant readers may note that, although Psalm 145 is designed as an acrostic, with each verse beginning with a consecutive letter, the psalm contains only 21 verses, while the Hebrew alphabet (or *alefbet*) contains 22 letters.

This is because a verse beginning with the letter *nun* is missing. How do we explain that? One might assume that the original text had a verse beginning with *nun*, but it was accidentally omitted during copying at some point, and subsequent copies of the dominant tradition also lacked the verse.

Some manuscripts, however, include a verse beginning with *nun*: "faithful is Yahweh in all his words, and gracious in all his deeds," with the first word being *ne'amān*, "faithful."

This reading does not appear in the most common Hebrew manuscripts, but it does appear in 11QPs^a from Qumran, the Greek Septuagint, and one of the Syriac targums. Though other acrostic psalms associated with David are also missing a letter (Psalms 25, 34, 37), Leslie Allen has argued "structural considerations affirm its genuineness" (*Psalms 101–150*, vol. 21 of Word Biblical Commentary [Word Books, 2002], 367).

The verse is accepted and appears in most modern translations, including the NRSV, as v. 13b: "The LORD is faithful in all his words, and gracious in all his deeds."

The rabbis, however, depended on the Masoretic text, which did not have the verse, and sought to explain the missing *nun* in a different way. In a very circular Talmudic argument, Rabbi Yohanan argued that the missing line referred to the downfall of the enemies of Israel, which he said was a euphemism for Israel itself. The missing line, he said, was supplied by Amos 5:2: "Fallen, no more to rise, is maiden Israel; forsaken on her land, with no one to raise her up." That verse begins with a *nun*, as the word for "fallen" is *nāflâ*.

Believing that David wrote the psalm, Rav Nahman bar Yitzhak added that David had been divinely inspired to omit the verse, foreseeing that Amos would later write the needed verse, also through divine inspiration. Since the next verse begins with a *samekh* and declares that "The Lord upholds the fallen," he argued, it shows that David was inspired to offer hope and encouragement to Israel that, despite Amos' later prediction of a fall, God would uphold the fallen and raise up all who are bowed down (*Berakhot* 4b:21-22; for an easily accessible text, see *The William Davis Talmud* at sefaria.org).

Christian readers may be less likely than Talmud scholars to accept the rabbis' reasoning, but one must admire their creativity. For our purposes, we'll simply acknowledge that the question of the missing *nun* remains open.

Third Reading
Romans 7:15-25a

What I Want, and What I Do

For I know that nothing good dwells within me, that is, in my flesh.
I can will what is right, but I cannot do it. (Rom. 7:18)

The lectionary does not tire of Paul's elaboration on the problem of sin. In Romans 5–6 he urges Christian readers to consider themselves dead to sin through baptism and alive to Christ. He insists that believers are no longer in bondage to the strong pull of wickedness, but free to choose a life of right choices and service to Christ.

He knows, however, that such choices are not easy, and in ch. 7 he continues the discussion, arguing that sin had power to subvert even the law because prohibitions against various sins could inspire wrongdoing that might not have been considered otherwise. "Yet, if it were not for the law, I would not have known sin," Paul contended. "I would not have known what it is to covet if the law had not said, 'You shall not covet'" (v. 7).

We may assume that Paul was speaking for himself: most of us did not need to be told it was wrong before wishing we owned certain things that were not in our possession.

Moving on, Paul turned to the inner conflict one experiences in temptation, and dared to confess that he also struggled to do the right thing.

A refreshing confession
(vv. 15-20)

Many of us may find it encouraging to know that the fiery apostle had faced a fierce opponent in temptation, too. Paul was a star among missionaries, a tower of strength among Christians, a font of wisdom and a bastion of maturity. If anyone should have it together, it would be Paul. It's almost liberating to hear his confession – and his strange way of dealing with it:

"I do not understand my own actions. For I do not do what I want, but I do the very thing I hate. Now if I do what I do not want, I agree that the law is good. But in fact it is no longer I that do it, but sin that dwells within me. For I know that nothing good dwells within me, that is, in my flesh. I can will what is right, but I cannot do it. For I do not do the good I want, but the evil I do not want is what I do. Now if I do what I do not want, it is no longer I that do it, but sin that dwells within me" (vv. 15-20).

On the surface it seems almost as if Paul is evading personal responsibility by saying "it is no longer I that do it, but sin that dwells within me." In fact, he says it twice, in vv. 17 and 20.

What was Paul getting at?

The passage under consideration has provoked much debate. On the surface, it appears that Paul, the stalwart Christian extraordinaire, is a miserable and wretched man who can't control his passions and lives in a state of frustration because sin continues to have its way with him.

But how does that match up with Phil. 3:4-6, where he claims "If anyone else has reason to be confident in the flesh, I have more: circumcised on the eighth day, a member of the people of Israel, of the tribe of Benjamin, a Hebrew born of Hebrews; as to the law, a Pharisee; as to zeal, a persecutor of the church; as to righteousness under the law, blameless"?

Prosopopoeia: This Greek term, from the world of rhetoric, describes the practice of speaking through an imaginary person to make a point. "Suppose that I'm in the following situation ..." Such presentations were often somewhat theatrical, and Paul's use of "I" no less than eight times suggests that possibility.

Even the most devout: The outspoken reformer Martin Luther, as bold and outspoken as anyone, declared: "Though I lived as a monk without reproach, I felt I was a sinner before God" (*Martin Luther as a Monk*, 1521).

Could this be the same man speaking?

The central questions seem to be (1) Who is Paul talking about when he says "I"? Is he speaking autobiographically, or rhetorically? And (2) If Paul is speaking autobiographically, is he discussing his current Christian experience, or his former pre-Christian life?

Given that Paul's other writings do not hint at the same kind of deep struggle he describes in Romans 7, many recent scholars presume he is using a rhetorical device to speak hypothetically, as in: "Let's say that I don't understand my own actions ..." In this case, he used the pronoun "I" but was assuming the identity of someone else for the sake of the argument. [*Prosopopoeia*]

If this is the case, then the argument effectively begins in 7:13 with the question "Did what is good, then, bring death to me? By no means! It was sin, working death in me through what is good, in order that sin might be shown to be sin, and through the commandment might become sinful beyond measure."

His argument in vv. 14-25, then, would be understood as an answer to the question in v. 13, building a case that the law is good, even though sin can distort it for evil purposes. In that sense, it could refer to the life of anyone who depends on the law for righteousness, but who finds himself or herself unable to overcome sin, for sin had co-opted the law to inspire new fields of wrongdoing. The law itself was good, but sin used it for bad ends, and the person who sought righteousness through the law was forced to admit defeat. [**The surest way**]

Paul's hypothetical "I" – if that's what it was – could have included either Jews or God-fearing Gentiles who had been taught that keeping the law was necessary for a proper relationship with God.

This brings us to the second question: If the hypothetical "I" Paul speaks of could include himself prior to his conversion, perhaps his argument is both rhetorical and autobiographical, but speaking of his former self. Some interpreters read the text in this way, though they continue to struggle with Paul's claim in Philippians to have been "blameless" with respect to the law.

One possible solution is to note that the contexts of Romans 6–8 and Philippians are quite different: In Philippians the discussion of the nature of sin or Paul's relation to it was not the subject at hand. There, as in Gal. 1:14, he could speak proudly of his accomplishments in Judaism while also acknowledging that they had not brought him to experience the grace he had come to know in Christ.

It remains possible that Paul was speaking of himself in the present; that despite his Damascus Road conversion and full-throated commitment to Christ, he continued to struggle with sin, unable to live as virtuously as he wished.

Most of us, I suspect, read the text this way because it speaks to our own experience. We also have trusted in Christ and consider ourselves to be Christian, but we continue to struggle with temptations on every hand.

O, wretched readers that we are! If only Paul had prefaced his argument with something akin to "This is how it was before I became a Christian," or "Suppose I found myself in this situation," or "I still contend with sin every day." But he did not, and he speaks in the present tense, not as if in his former life.

Our own experience, along with autobiographical confessions of people as devoted as Pope John XXIII and Mother Theresa, make it clear that we all continue to struggle with sin – but that's not the end of the story. [**Even the most devout**]

The surest way: Many parents have discovered that telling a child not to do something often has the effect of increasing the child's desire to do that very thing. Adults can have the same experience. A friend once allowed me to spend a night in his home while he and his wife were away. His only request was: "Don't go into our bedroom." I wouldn't have thought of it otherwise, but he left me really curious to see what was in there.

A promised solution
(vv. 21-25a)

"So I find it to be a law that when I want to do what is good, evil lies close at hand. For I delight in the law of God in my inmost self, but I see in my members another law at war with the law of my mind, making me captive to the law of sin that dwells in my members" (vv. 21-23).

Paul continues to discuss the relationship between the law, which is good, and evil, which can pervert even the most positive guide for life.

Whether evil derives from a demonic force, as some imagine, or from one's own natural bent toward self-gratification, as others see it, it is still a force to be reckoned with. Sin is like an inborn addiction that we never fully get over but continue to deal with every day.

Gaining freedom from sin requires more than willpower: we all know people who have differing degrees of self-restraint, but none who are accomplished enough to eliminate every less-than-righteous thought or action.

The good news is that God does not require moral perfection. That's where grace comes in. "Wretched man that I am! Who will rescue me from this body of death? Thanks be to God through Jesus Christ our Lord!" (vv. 24-25a).

Christ does not free us from the temptation to sin, but does set us free from the ultimate penalty of sin. Christ sets us free to say no, even when we don't always exercise that freedom properly.

Paul would not have us continue to sin that grace may abound. No, he has argued effectively against that position in previous chapters. But neither would he have us live in a state of defeat, thinking ourselves to be hopelessly trapped in a quagmire of sin.

Paul understood that the road to recovery begins with acknowledgement of our true condition as slaves to sin, but who can choose to seek redemption through the grace Christ offers.

The key to our salvation, then, is grace. "All have sinned and fall short of the glory of God," Paul tells us, but we can be "justified by his grace as a gift, through the redemption that is in Christ Jesus" (Rom. 3:23-24).

In other words, as others have pointed out in various ways, we might agree that "I'm not okay and you're not okay and God knows we're not okay, but when we come to him in repentance and confession, he looks at us with grace born of love and says 'It's okay – I love you anyway. I forgive you.'"

Maybe we have been touched by that kind of grace. Maybe our spouse has forgiven us and loved us even when we didn't deserve it. Maybe our parents or children have been willing to overlook our faults and love us anyway. Maybe we have a friend who really knows how rotten we are, but he or she still accepts us. Such wonderful gifts are but a taste of the grace of our God, who sees behind our masks and knows our deepest heart and loves us still. Paul knew the depth of his human weakness, but he also knew the ascending wonder of God's grace, who could look upon his wretched condition and say "there is therefore now no condemnation for those who are in Christ Jesus."

In Christ, we are guilty, but not condemned. We are weak, but given the strength of God's Spirit to hold us up and see us through. We are human, but touched by divinity. That's why a perennially favorite hymn begins with the words "Amazing grace – how sweet the sound, that saved a wretch like me." … Amazing, indeed.

The Hardest Question

Can AA offer insight?

When commentators discuss Paul's apparent struggle with sin that he can't overcome in Romans 7, the subject of 12-Step programs often comes up. Members of groups such as Alcoholics Anonymous and Narcotics Anonymous struggle with powerful addictions that they also have difficulty controlling.

Persons in similar programs must begin with an honest acknowledgement of their addiction and inability to overcome it alone. The second step turns to hope for recovery, despite setbacks, through acknowledging a higher power and then surrendering to the higher power (Step 3) to move forward.

They also know the fourth step: the necessity of taking a deep dive into one's past, having the courage to name past mistakes, even the painful ones. The next step involves confession: having the integrity to admit those failings to oneself, to God, and to another trustworthy person.

The next steps involve expressing the willingness to have God forgive those shortcomings and the humility to let the past remain in the past. They involve seeking to make amends to anyone they may have harmed, and taking responsibility for one's own actions.

The final steps involve the discipline to continue admitting mistakes and dealing with them one at the time, the awareness needed to stay in touch with God, and acts of service that focus on others rather than personal desires, often by investing in others who are new to the program. The community aspect of 12-Step programs – the mutual support that members receive from each other – is a powerful element in promoting recovery.

These programs certainly resonate in many ways with the dilemma Paul describes in Rom. 7:15-25. Where many people fall, whether they are in a recovery program or not, is at the point of discipline and continuing acceptance of responsibility for actions. The first few steps are crucial, but the principles behind them must remain present and acted upon.

Scripture and psychology agree that we are all needy, driven, troubled people, in need of some sort of salvation that is not just a once-for-all ticket to heaven, but a key to better living every day. "Wretched man that I am!" Paul said. "Who will deliver me?"

I like the way Will Willimon once put it: "The key to our salvation is not positive thinking or self-induced self-esteem, but God's grace which frees us from having to define ourselves solely on terms of our good achievements" (*Pulpit Resource* [July-September 1996], 5).

Principles from recovery programs remind us that, while Paul's emphasis on grace is an essential starting place, we also need to receive from and contribute to a supportive community.

Fourth Reading
Matthew 11:16-30 (RCL 11:16-19, 25-30)

The World Needs Rest

Come to me, all you that are weary and are carrying heavy burdens, and I will give you rest. (Matt. 11:28)

"Red rover, red rover, send Mary right over!" So we sang in one of my favorite playground games as a young boy. Two lines of children, facing each other and holding hands, would call for someone in the other line to run over and try to break through their line. If the runner failed, they would join that line. If they succeeded, they would take a "captive" and return to their home line. It was one of the few games boys and girls played together.

In the opening verses of today's text, Jesus references children's games as an illustration of how people responded both to him and to John the Baptist: it seemed that most people didn't want to play.

To those who won't play
(vv. 16-19)

Today's text is part of a narrative section following the second of five major discourses that Matthew uses to organize his gospel. Jesus had warned his disciples that they would experience rejection as he commissioned them to go out and preach (9:35–11:1), and the theme of rejection carries over into the following narrative.

The Revised Common Lectionary text skips from Matt. 11:16-19 to 11:25-30, bypassing the oracles of woe in 11:20-24. Since they are an integral part of the text, however, we will include a brief look at them in our study.
[The source]

The text is preceded by a discussion of John the baptizer. Even he had apparently begun to wonder about Jesus, so he sent some of his disciples to ask if Jesus truly

> **The source:** Scholars regard most of Matt. 11:16-30 as deriving from a written source document that Luke also used. It's commonly called "Q," an abbreviation for the German word *Quelle*, which means "source." Matthew and Luke use elements from Q in different contexts, however. Matthew 11:16-19 has a parallel in Luke 7:31-35, while the oracles in Matt. 11:20-24 appear in Luke 10:12-15, and the prayer of Matt. 11:25-27 is found in Luke 10:21-22. Matthew 11:28-30, sometimes called "The Great Invitation," comes from material reflected only in Matthew.

was the Messiah, "the one who is to come" (vv. 2-3). Jesus told them to tell John what miraculous things they saw him doing (vv. 4-6). Then he turned to the crowds, describing John as the prophesied messenger sent to prepare the way for the messiah, like a new Elijah (vv. 7-15).

Religious leaders, however, had rejected both John and Jesus. "But to what will I compare this generation?" he asked. "It is like children sitting in the marketplaces and calling to one another, 'We played the flute for you, and you did not dance; we wailed, and you did not mourn'" (vv. 16-17).

Perhaps Jesus imagined a group of girls who wanted to play "wedding," but the boys would not do the circle dance typically done by men. Maybe the boys wanted to play "funeral," but they couldn't get the girls to imitate the professional mourners who typically keened loud laments.

John was a hard-edged, locust-eating ascetic who wore uncomfortable clothes, lived in the desert, and called for repentance. Many people regarded him as too intense. They

Deeds, or children? While Matthew has "Wisdom is vindicated by her deeds" (*ergon*, 11:18b), the parallel passage in Luke has "Wisdom is vindicated by all her children" (*téknōn*, Luke 7:35).

Both Matthew and Luke knew the phrase from the same source: whether they had two different versions of Q, or whether one of them changed the expression for greater clarity, is unknown. Many Greek manuscripts follow a tradition that replaced the word "deeds" with "children" so Matthew's wording would match with Luke, but the oldest and best manuscripts have "deeds."

accused him of having a demon and would not sing his mournful song of repentance (v. 18).

Jesus, in contrast, enjoyed parties with good food and drink, and wasn't above tapping into divine power to keep the wine flowing after a wedding. He befriended tax collectors and sinners and called others to join the circle of gospel liberation, but many would not dance (v. 18a).

Chorazin: The village of Chorazin, located a few miles north of Capernaum, was constructed mainly of local basalt. The third-century synagogue whose remains are pictured here was in the center of the village.

John was too strict for them, and Jesus was too loose. They didn't want to mourn with John or to dance with Jesus. They could not recognize the new reality before them. But Jesus said, "Wisdom is vindicated by her deeds" (v. 18b). **[Deeds, or children?]**

His own generation might reject Jesus, but he would ultimately be vindicated by his works.

To those who won't repent
(vv. 20-24)

Matthew continues the theme of rejection in the following verses. Jesus "began to reproach the cities in which most of his deeds of power had been done," the author says, "because they did not repent" (v. 20). Other texts tell us that Jesus spent most of his active ministry in Galilee and even made his home in Capernaum, by the sea of Galilee (Matt. 4:13).

Chorazin was a few miles northwest of Capernaum, and Bethsaida was a few miles to the east, along the shore. Jesus was well known in those towns and did many "deeds of power" there. Still, the people as a whole did not repent and turn to him. **[Chorazin]**

If the same miracles had been done in the pagan cities of Tyre and Sidon, Jesus said, the people would have been moved to repent in sackcloth and ashes (v. 21).

This teaching suggests that those who have been most exposed to the gospel are more accountable than those who have not heard about Jesus. At the judgment, Jesus said, the people of Tyre and Sidon – even the people of Sodom – would fare better than residents of the towns who knew Jesus best (vv. 22-24).

To those who want rest
(vv. 25-30)

The harshness of vv. 20-24 softens as Matthew pictures Jesus pausing to offer a prayer: "At that time Jesus said, 'I thank you, Father, Lord of heaven and earth, because you have hidden these things from the wise and the intelligent and have revealed them to infants; yes, Father, for such was your gracious will" (vv. 25-26).

If Jesus spoke Aramaic, as we think, he probably would have used the term *Abba* for "father," an intimate term not unlike "Daddy" or "Papa." A surface reading of the prayer seems to absolve those who rejected Jesus of responsibility, implying that it was God's will to hide the truth from "the wise and intelligent" and reveal it to "infants."

In the lead-up to this prayer, however, Jesus was holding people accountable for choosing to reject him. It is unlikely that he would contradict himself by asserting that their rejection was predestined.

Instead, Jesus was probably using sarcasm. His reference to "the wise and intelligent" clearly points to the highly trained scribes and Pharisees, the experts in interpreting the Jewish law. He portrays them as being stubbornly proud of their knowledge and unwilling to accept the possibility that they could be wrong. Thus, they failed to perceive that Jesus had come to inaugurate the inbreaking of the kingdom of God in a fashion wholly different from what they expected.

In contrast, those who were like "infants" – a word that can also mean "simple" – were not so devoted to authoritative preconceptions. They were more open to accepting the revelation of Christ, even if it did set the traditional interpretation of the Law on its head. Later Jesus would emphasize this more clearly by calling a child to him and saying "Truly I tell you, unless you change and become like children, you will never enter the kingdom of heaven. Whoever becomes humble like this child is the greatest in the kingdom of heaven" (Matt. 18:3-4).

It is God's gracious will that *anyone* who comes to Christ in childlike faith is welcomed into the kingdom – but Jesus knew that some would refuse to budge from their set beliefs and ways.

Verse 27 sounds surprisingly like ideas more characteristic of the Fourth Gospel, as Jesus turned from his prayer and announced: "All things have been handed over to me by my Father; and no one knows the Son except the Father, and no one knows the Father except the Son and anyone to whom the Son chooses to reveal him."

Jesus' primary critics considered themselves experts on all matters of the law and of understanding God. They prayed to God as "Father" just as Jesus did, but Jesus made it clear that they did not know God as he did. Using an intensive form of the verb for "to know," he insisted that no one truly knew the Father but the Son, and those to whom he chose to reveal such knowledge: knowing the Father involved far more than comprehension of the Torah.

Jesus cannot be understood in terms of preconceived human notions, but only as God knows him and has revealed him to be.

The next three verses, found only in Matthew, are among the most beautiful and comforting words in scripture: "Come to me, all you that are weary and are carrying heavy burdens, and I will give you rest. Take my yoke upon you and learn from me; for I am gentle and humble in heart, and you will find rest for your souls. For my yoke is easy, and my burden is light" (vv. 28-30).

We often misinterpret these words, reading them as an invitation for overworked people to lay down their burdens and follow Jesus on an easy path. Not so. The "burden" Jesus has in mind is the Jewish law, especially as taught in the oral tradition of the rabbis, who developed no less than 613 commandments to "build a fence around the law" by adding hundreds of specific prohibitions designed to prevent anyone from getting close to breaking the written commandments.

In the gospels, the word "burden" is always used in reference to burdens of the oral law. Elsewhere Jesus criticized the religious leaders who "Tie up heavy burdens, hard to bear, and lay them on the shoulders of others; but they themselves are unwilling to lift a finger to move them" (23:4).

The law was sometimes referred to as a "yoke," the wooden harness used to attach oxen plows or heavy carts. Jesus also had a yoke, but his understanding of the law was not harsh and burdensome. Rather, it was "easy" (better translated as "kind") and "light." Following the metaphor, his yoke had no sharp edges or splinters to cut when pulling, but was smooth and well fitting, "kind" to the one who wore it. While the rabbis rained down 613 esoteric laws, Jesus said the law could be boiled down to loving God with our whole being and loving our neighbors as ourselves (22:37-40). Living in this way, believers could bypass petty rules and focus on "the weightier matters of the law: justice and mercy and faithfulness" (23:23).

Jesus did not say "obey the law" or even "come to God," but "Come to *me*." When we come to Jesus, following his example and learning from him, we learn to obey the true spirit of the law. In doing so, we find rest for our souls.
[Rest for the soul]

> **Rest for the soul:** Some scholars believe this passage may be influenced by wisdom sayings in ch. 51 of the apocryphal book Sirach (also known as Ecclesiasticus). Others note a similarity with Jer. 6:16: "Thus says the LORD: Stand at the crossroads, and look, and ask for the ancient paths, where the good way lies; and walk in it, and find rest for your souls. But they said, 'We will not walk in it.'"
>
> When we stand at the crossroads of life, we can trust Jesus to show us "where the good way lies," that we may "walk in it" and find rest for our souls.

When we find such rest, we become a living example to others who are burdened with fruitless attempts to find meaning in life, and can become channels of blessing as we point them to the good way, the way of Jesus.

The Hardest Question
Why is "wisdom" important to Matthew?

The author of Matthew shapes much of Jesus' teaching in the form of wisdom traditions from the Hebrew Bible, even to the extent of using the kind of synonymous parallelism common to the book of Proverbs. The books of Proverbs, Job, and Ecclesiastes were considered part of the "Wisdom literature," and several psalms, such as Psalm 1, also echoed clear wisdom themes.

Wisdom was not just a noun suggesting knowledge and what to do with it. In some cases, as in Proverbs 8, Wisdom was personified as a woman who had been present with God from the very beginning, aiding in creation.

There Wisdom says: "I have good advice and sound wisdom; I have insight, I have strength. By me kings reign, and rulers decree what is just; by me rulers rule, and nobles, all who govern rightly. I love those who love me, and those who seek me diligently find me" (vv. 14-17).

She goes on to say: "Ages ago I was set up, at the first, before the beginning of the earth. When there were no depths I was brought forth, when there were no springs abounding with water. Before the mountains had been shaped, before the hills, I was brought forth— when he had not yet made earth and fields, or the world's first bits of soil. When he established the heavens, I was there, when he drew a circle on the face of the deep, when he made firm the skies above, when he established the fountains of the deep, when he assigned to the sea its limit, so that the waters might not transgress his command, when he marked out the foundations of the earth, then I was beside him, like a master worker; and I was daily his delight, rejoicing before him always, rejoicing in his inhabited world and delighting in the human race" (vv. 23-31).

Several wisdom-oriented Jewish works such as Sirach (also called "Ecclesiasticus") and Wisdom (also called "The Wisdom of Solomon") are included in the Apocrypha. They echo similar themes, especially Wisdom 7–8.

The Greek word for "wisdom" is *Sophia*, so in some traditions Wisdom was regarded as a feminine aspect of Yahweh, or even as God's wife or consort. Identifying Jesus with Wisdom was an important theme in the developing Christology of the early church. Matthew appears to have regarded Jesus as Wisdom incarnate. Paul's writing was less obvious, though he once referred to Christ as "the power of God and the wisdom of God" (1 Cor. 1:24).

First Reading
Genesis 25:19-34

Birth Rights and Wrongs

And the LORD said to her, "Two nations are in your womb, and two peoples born of you shall be divided; the one shall be stronger than the other, the elder shall serve the younger." (Gen. 25:23)

Have you ever seen a rough-looking biker or other person wearing a T-shirt with the slogan "Born to Lose," or heard one of several songs by the same name? Apparently, the fatalistic notion that one might come into the world with the fates stacked against him or her is a common thought.

The book of Genesis contains the story of a man who seemed born to lose, a red-haired outdoorsman named Esau. His brother Jacob, however, could have sewn a patch on his shepherd's robe declaring that he was "Born to Win." **[Framed by losers]**

Do either of those life scripts resonate with you? How we think of ourselves in relation to the world – as winners or losers, as competent or hopeless – can have a great impact on whether we find success in life, or whether we surrender to our own script of failure. A look at Jacob and Esau might offer helpful insights as we imagine what yet lies ahead for us.

Esau was technically the older brother, but his twin brother Jacob was given the name "Israel" and became not only the father of the famous 12 tribes of Israel, but also a mirror or memory in which Israel could see itself facing difficult obstacles (some self-inflicted), but yet surviving.

Jacob and Esau were twin sons of Abraham's son Isaac and his wife Rebekah. Like Abraham and Sarah, the couple appears to have had difficulty getting pregnant. This fits neatly into the common motif of patriarchal wives having difficulty bearing children in Genesis 12–50.

God had promised countless progeny to Abraham, but he and Sarah remained childless for many years. So, we are not surprised to learn that Isaac's beloved wife Rebekah

Framed by losers: The stories of Abraham close with the genealogy of Ishmael (25:12-18), the son who had been born to Abraham by the Egyptian maid Hagar. This genealogy serves as a literary bracket to close one story and mark the beginning of another. The stories of Abraham's son Isaac – which some would see as a subset of a larger Jacob cycle (25:19–36:43) – begin with what appears to be a genealogy of Isaac's descendants ("These are the descendants of Isaac …," Gen. 25:19), but it is really an account of the birth of Jacob and Esau, his only children of which we have any record.

There is good reason to see the larger picture as a Jacob cycle in which the chosen one's story is bracketed by the genealogy of Ishmael (25:12-18) and the genealogy of Esau (36:1-43). Both Ishmael and Esau were the eldest sons of a "chosen" patriarch, but passed over as leader of the next generation. Terrence Fretheim has noted "This bracketing of the chosen by the non-chosen may be a way in which these groups of people are held together, not least in the service of God's mission of blessing all 'families' (28:14)" ("Genesis," in *The New Interpreter's Dictionary of the Bible* [Abingdon Press, 1994], 518-19).

bore no children during the first 20 years of their marriage (v. 21). Isaac is said to have been 40 years old when he married Rebekah (v. 20), but he was 60 years old when Jacob and Esau were born (v. 26). Many things had happened in the intervening years – probably including most of what reportedly takes place in the following chapter, where children are not mentioned. Ancient Hebrew writers cared far less about putting things in chronological order than modern writers. Since the most important thing for us to know about Isaac is that he was Jacob's father, this story is told first.

Two prayers and an oracle
(vv. 19-23)

None of the Abraham stories say that he prayed for Sarah to conceive, though we can presume that he did. Stories about Isaac are limited, but at some point he is said to have prayed for Rebekah to have a child, "and the LORD granted his prayer, and Rebekah conceived" (v. 21). Not only did Rebekah conceive; she conceived twins.

The story tells us that Rebekah also prayed, not to get pregnant, but because she was pregnant, and it proved to be exceedingly difficult. The twins reportedly "struggled together" in her womb (literally, "they crushed each other," a sign of things to come), making Rebekah so miserable that she prayed and wondered why it had to be that way (v. 22). **[A miserable pregnancy]**

The text says that "Rebekah went to inquire of the LORD," using the same sort of language typically employed to describe a visit to a sanctuary or a conversation with a priest, in which one would seek a divine oracle.

In Rebekah's day, however, there was no sanctuary or priesthood for the God of Abraham, unless we are to presume something established by Melchizedek, who is called "priest of the God Most High" in Gen. 14:18, and to whom Abraham paid tithes (Gen. 14:20). Melchizedek is not mentioned in the patriarchal narratives after that episode, however, so we have no way of knowing where Rebekah traveled, how she went about "inquiring of the LORD," or how she received the oracle in v. 23.

By whatever means it came about, the tradition holds that Rebekah received an oracle from God explaining that her difficult pregnancy involved twins, along with a prophecy of how the brothers' lives would play out. The oracle is couched in poetry, as shown below in this rather literal translation, with suggested clarifications in parentheses:

Two nations are in your womb,
And two peoples will be separated from your belly,
And (one) people will be stronger than the (other) people,
And (the) great (older?) will serve the small (younger?).

The firstborn son, it seems, was born to lose.

> **A miserable pregnancy:** Rebekah may have done more than complain about the difficulty of her pregnancy. Translators of the NRSV, relying on the witness of an early Syriac version, have her saying, "If it is to be this way, why should I live?" The preserved Hebrew text literally says "If it is thus, why am I this (way)?" Whether Rebekah considered her situation a matter of life or death is uncertain.

Two births and a struggle
(vv. 24-26)

The narrator delights in wordplay while describing the twins' births. Esau is described as "red" (*'admônî*), using the same word translated as "Edomite." The land inhabited by the Edomites is characterized by reddish sandstone mountains, scrub, and deserts. Esau is also depicted as "hairy," using a word that sounds akin to "Seir," an alternate name for the Edomites' homeland. The name "Esau" also draws on some of the same sounds.

Jacob is said to have been born holding on to Esau's heel (*'aqēv*); thus he is called "*Ya'aqōv*," which could mean something such as "heel-grabber," "supplanter," "grasper," or "over-reacher."

We note that the narrator describes Esau entirely in physical terms, such as what he looked like (red and hairy), but not what he does. In contrast, the narrator describes Jacob only in terms of action – we don't know what he looked like, but are told that he was grabbing at Esau's heel, as if he were trying to pull his twin brother back and beat him out of the womb. Jacob's competitive nature is clear from the beginning: he was born with a determination to win.

Two boys and a bad deal
(vv. 27-34)

The story of the boys' disparate proclivities and their parents' dysfunctional partiality is familiar to us. Isaac is partial to Esau because he loves to eat wild game, and Esau's nature is the ancient equivalent of a man who wears camouflage and drives a pickup with a gun rack in the back. Jacob, on the other hand, is a homebody who likes to cook, which pleases his mother.

As Isaac and Rebekah's years of childlessness are telescoped into a single verse, so are the adolescence and growth to manhood of Esau and Jacob. In vv. 25-26, they

> **More on wordplay:** Curious about the words? In the first bit of wordplay, the term for "cook" (*zîd*) sounds like the word used earlier for both "hunter" and "game" (*tsayîd*). This may subtly suggest a relationship between the cook and the hunter.
>
> The second instance comes into play with what Esau says when he asks for some of Jacob's cooking. Literally, he says, "Please cause me to swallow the red stuff, this red stuff, for I am famished." The word I've translated as "red stuff" is *hā'ādōm*, which literally means "the red." Without the article, it is identical to the word for Edom. Thus, the narrator adds, "he was called Edom." Esau will later be known as the ancestor of the Edomites.

are born. In v. 27, they "grew up" and became men – men who lived out the prediction of the oracle that preceded their birth.

Wordplay is also important in the story of how Jacob persuaded Esau to sell his birthright for a bowl of stew. The story does not identify what Jacob was cooking when Esau came in from the field, only that he "was famished." Later we learn that it was a stew made with lentils.

The words for "cook," "hunter," and "game" in Hebrew have similar sounds, suggesting perhaps that the hunter may fall victim to the cook.

A second instance of wordplay is Esau's request for the "red stuff" (a literal translation) that Jacob is cooking. Literally, he says "Please feed me the red (stuff), this red (stuff), for I am faint." The word for "red stuff" is the same as the word for Edom. Later in the narrative, Esau will be called the ancestor of the Edomites. [**More on wordplay**]

Note again how differently the characters are portrayed. Jacob is conniving, clever, and looking toward the future, while Esau appears to be so shortsighted and impulsive that he thinks less of his birthright than a bowl of thick lentil soup, thinking he will die if he doesn't eat and the birthright will be no use to him. Thus, the text says, "he despised his birthright."

The text leaves us wondering what things we may have "despised" in serving ourselves over God. Are there ways in which we, like Esau, have "despised" our birthrights as children of God, called to live and love in ways that honor God and better the world? Have we let physical desires or appetites eclipse our inclinations to obey God and serve others?

Although Esau is the one who seemed to care little for his birthright, the narrator shows no empathy for the conniving way in which Jacob obtained it. Are we ever inclined to use shady means to get ahead or take advantage of other people? If our success comes at the cost of cheating another, is it worth it?

The reader may wonder whether either Jacob or Esau knew about the oracle Rebekah had reportedly received. Since the prophecy predicted that the older son would serve the younger, would Rebekah have kept that news from her favorite son, or have used it to encourage him? Given these thoughts, we likewise wonder if Jacob's actions were necessarily an indication of his personality, or if they were shaped by what his mother believed to be his destiny.

What shapes us?

The Hardest Question
Why would God choose Jacob over Esau?

One of the conundrums of biblical interpretation — especially in Genesis — is why God would choose a seamy character like Jacob to become the "Father of Israel," the progenitor of the 12 sons who would give rise to the 12 tribes, at least according to one biblical tradition. Some tribal lists don't match up with the classic 12, such as Deuteronomy 33 (which omits Simeon); Judges 1 (which includes Caleb and Kenites but omits Reuben, Levi, Issachar, and Gad); and Judg. 5:2-31, which mentions Ephraim, Benjamin, Zebulun, Issachar, Reuben, Dan, Asher, and Naphtali, along with Machir, but lacks five of the traditional tribes.

Sticking with the tradition, why should only one of Isaac's two sons be chosen to carry on the promise to Abraham and beget the "children of Israel," and why would it be Jacob rather than the officially older brother, Esau? Jacob's character is present in his name, which means something akin to "heel-grabber," as if he was holding Esau's heel in utero, trying to hold him back so he could be the firstborn. Jacob's determination to supersede Esau is evident in the finagling way he obtained Esau's birthright under duress by requiring it as payment for a bowl of soup, and in the way he disguised himself as Esau to deceive his blind father and receive the blessing destined for the firstborn.

Jacob's shady ways continue through much of his life, including his relationship with his father-in-law Laban, who matched Jacob in the art of hoodwinking. The story of their relationship is one of cheating and deceiving each other.

So why choose Jacob? The narrator goes out of his way to paint Esau as unworthy. He first depicts him as a physical freak who came out of the womb covered with red hair, "like a hairy mantle" (v. 25). The image of Esau as a hunter portrays him as a rustic who was less civilized than Jacob, and his willingness to trade his birthright for a bowl of lentil stew, thinking he would otherwise die of starvation, sketches him in as an obtuse bumbler.

While Jacob traveled to Haran to obtain a "proper bride" from the family, Isaac held him up as an example and told Esau not to marry Canaanite women (Gen. 28:6). A previous text suggested that he had been consorting with Hittite women, for Gen. 27:46 has Rebekah complaining to Isaac, "I am weary of my life because of the Hittite women. If Jacob marries one of the Hittite women such as these, one of the women of the land, what good will my life be to me?" Since Canaanites were off base, Esau married a cousin, a daughter of Abraham's son Ishmael, in addition to other wives he already had (Gen. 28:9). Gen. 33:2-3, however, assumes the other wives were Canannites, for the genealogy of Esau claims "Esau took his wives from the Canaanites: Adah daughter of Elon the Hittite, Oholibamah daugh-

ter of Anah son of Zibeon the Hivite, and Basemath, Ishmael's daughter, sister of Nebaioth."

So, though Jacob was sneaky, Esau was regarded as worse, living without regard for either God or his parents. Jacob, despite his duplicitous nature, is depicted as having a personal encounter with God in which he made a vow and promised to worship God (if God fulfilled the vow, Genesis 28). He later wrestled with God at the Jabbock (Genesis 32), where God changed his name from Jacob ("Heelgrabber") to Israel ("He struggled with God"), saying "for you have striven with God and with humans, and have prevailed" (Gen. 32: 28).

The biblical writers, for the most part, were aware that all people are flawed, even those who are primary leaders. Abraham acted deceitfully in claiming that Sarah was his wife rather than his sister (Genesis 12, 20). Moses was denied entrance to the Promised Land for striking a rock rather than just speaking to it (as God had instructed him) to bring out water (Num. 20:7-13). David committed both adultery and murder (2 Samuel 11).

It was important for the biblical writers to demonstrate God's ability to do good and important things through imperfect people, including Jacob. While Jacob fell short in multiple ways, Esau was depicted as worse. Though he also reportedly became the ancestor of a nation, it was the nation of Edom: Israel's perpetual enemy

Optional First Reading
Psalm 119:105-112

A Lamp and a Light

Your word is a lamp to my feet and a light to my path. (Ps. 119:105)

Are you a person who likes rules, or someone who prefers to freewheel it through life? While some people relish the thought of life without restrictions, such an approach can lead to personal or societal chaos. Others recognize the value of holding to certain standards of behavior in individual or corporate life. They take comfort in knowing basic and acceptable guidelines for living, and in seeking to follow them.

The poet behind Psalm 119 was a big fan of God's rules, which he speaks of with a variety of near synonyms in referring to God's Torah, God's word, God's way, and God's laws, statues, decrees, commands, precepts, ordinances, and so forth. The psalm could be described as a wisdom psalm or as a Torah psalm: those who are wise know the value of studying and following the written law. The psalmist was so enamored with following God's guidelines for life that he devoted no less than 176 verses to the subject, divided into 22 sections, one for each letter of the Hebrew alphabet. **[A party for the law]**

A lengthy poem on the delights of God's law is bound to include considerable repetition. For this reason, a close look at one section can give us an overview of the entire psalm.

> **A party for the law:** Commentator Leslie C. Allen waxed poetic himself in describing Psalm 119: "This elaborate acrostic is a literary festival of prayer and praise held in honor of Yahweh's self-revelation to Israel" (*Word Biblical Commentary*, vol. 21 [Thomas Nelson, 1983], 184).

> **Thy word:** Many people who memorized Ps. 119:105 did so from the KJV, and are more familiar with the phrasing: "Thy word is a lamp unto my feet, and a light unto my path." Others recognize these words from a popular praise song, "Thy Word," by Michael W. Smith and Amy Grant. (A YouTube version can be found at https://www.youtube.com/watch?v=oRBc188biCs.)

Light on the path
(vv. 105-106)

Our text begins with one of the most familiar verses, not only in Psalm 119, but also in the entire psalter. Many people can recite it from memory: "Your word is a lamp to my feet, and a light to my path."

The psalm comes from a period when the Torah, the first five books of the Bible, had become accepted as the standard guideline for Israel's living. "A lamp to my feet is your word, and a light to my path" (a literal translation of v. 105). Here, "your word" is a reference to the Torah, to God's guidelines for living. **[Thy word]**

How do we navigate the twists and turns of life? How do we make decisions about personal behavior, about the use of our resources, about our treatment of others? Is it all a matter of how we feel at any given moment? If making our way through life is unstructured or lawless, we find ourselves in a constant state of uncertainty and unrest.

That is why the psalmist celebrated the structure and guidelines for life offered by the law. We don't have to walk in darkness or uncertainty when it comes to how we should relate to God and to others. At the heart of the law are the

Ten Commandments. The first four deal with the most basic question: how we relate to God. We worship God alone. We don't bow down before idols or make images of God. We don't treat God's name lightly or swear falsely by it. We honor God on a special day each week, resting and focusing on the worship of God (Exod. 20:1-11).

The remaining commandments guide our relationships with others. We show respect to our parents, a reminder that the home is a training ground for the world. We don't kill people, or violate our spouse's trust through adultery. We don't steal, or tell lies about others, or lust after what other people have (Exod. 20:12-17).

The books of Exodus, Leviticus, and Numbers contain many other laws specific to Israel: rules for eating, rules for worship, rules regarding ritual purity, rules about hygiene, rules about making cloth and sowing seed. These regulations were designed mainly to set the Israelites apart as a distinct people: They circumcised males and the men didn't ever trim their sideburns. They ate *kosher* food and covered their heads when praying, They didn't crossbreed cattle or weave wool and cotton in the same garment. To one who took great pride in his or her ethnic heritage, the rules offered a clear path to living as a faithful Jew.

Christian believers don't concern themselves with the distinguishing tenets of being Jewish, and many modern Jews happily shave their sideburns and wear blended fabrics. That doesn't mean, however, that we aren't to be distinctive in our behavior, or that we have no guidelines for living. Jesus affirmed a common rabbinic teaching that the two laws of first importance were to love God with all our hearts, and to love our neighbors as ourselves.

How can we stand apart as Christian believers? Jesus put it succinctly in "a new commandment, that you love one another. Just as I have loved you, you also should love one another. By this everyone will know that you are my disciples, if you have love for one another" (John 13:34-35).

Whether we have in mind the Old Testament law or the teachings of Jesus, we can be grateful that God has not left us without direction. The psalmist declared that he had sworn an oath to observe God's righteous ways (v. 106). Jesus suggested that we avoid oaths, but called for a full commitment no less.

Obstacles on the way
(vv. 107-110)

While praising God for the gift of guidelines, the psalmist acknowledged that having a map did not mean a path without obstacles. He spoke of being so "severely afflicted" that he feared for his life (v. 107), though he did not name the affliction. Whether it was illness or enemies, we do not know, though he claimed to have been willing to risk his life for God's way: "I hold my life in my hand continually, but I do not forget your law" (v. 109). [**A handful of life**]

If v. 110 further expounds on his affliction, the psalmist's afflictions may have come from opponents he believed to have evil intent: "The wicked have laid a snare for me, but I do not stray from your precepts."

While the poet's recitation of his troubles suggests a connection with the happy praise of the previous verses, it was precisely because he sometimes traveled a dark road that he needed God's teachings as a lamp to his feet and a light to his path. We wouldn't dare drive down a dark highway without headlights, and we trust that other vehicles will be using their lights, too.

Have you ever faced a troubled or perilous time of life when the way forward seemed clouded and obscure? Many believers testify of finding their way through such trials on the strength of trusting God and seeking to follow God's way without regard to the outcome.

Despite his trials, the psalmist found time and reason to praise God. Following the lead of other psalmists, he regarded his words of praise as an offering to God: the phrase translated as "offerings of praise" literally means "free will offerings of my mouth" (v. 108). The term for "free

---

A handful of life: The psalmist's claim that "I hold my life in my hand continually" (v. 109) appears to be a metaphor for the willingness to risk one's life for a cause. A similar metaphor appears in Judg. 12:3, a story about Jephthah, one of Israel's less successful judges. Jephthah argued with certain leaders of Ephraim who had come to confront him. They should have been his allies but had not aided him in fighting off a threat from the Ammonites. "When I saw that you would not deliver me," Jephthah said, "*I took my life in my hand,* and crossed over against the Ammonites, and the LORD gave them into my hand. Why then have you come up to me this day, to fight against me?"

will offerings" typically referred to material gifts such as those offered for the construction of the tabernacle (Exod. 35:29, 36:3), for the first temple (2 Chron. 31:14), or for the second temple, built after the return of the exiles (Ezra 1:4, 8:28).

It may have been during the exile – when there was no temple and no practical way to bring a physical offering to God – that Hebrews began to think of verbal praise to God as being equivalent to material gifts.

A heart to follow
(vv. 111-112)

The psalmist did not think of God's teachings as something to be called upon in an emergency, like candles and flashlights that modern folk break out when a storm comes and the power goes out. Rather, he trusted God's law as a lifelong guide for a lifelong journey, a source of comfort and joy as well as direction: "Your decrees are my heritage forever," he wrote: "they are the joy of my heart" (v. 111). The poet was in it for the long haul: "I incline my heart to perform your statutes forever, to the end" (v. 112).

Are there scripture verses that you rely on to help you through the day? Christians are less likely than the Hebrews to think of the Bible as a law book, but we will be more fervent and faithful followers if we rely on its teachings as a guide for daily life.

In Scripture we find much in the way of direction, though we must be careful to allow for context as we interpret it: many of the legalisms found in the Pentateuch were specific to Hebrew people living within a particular culture in a long-ago world. Even so, the values expressed in the Ten Commandments remain valid guidelines for both relating to God and for civilized living. Teachings about the importance of loving our neighbors, caring for widows and orphans, showing hospitality to others, and making room for aliens or strangers (read "immigrants") in our land are fully in line with Jesus' call to love one another as he loved us.

If we, like the psalmist, believe that other people bear harmful intent toward us, we can remember Jesus' challenge to turn the other cheek and go the extra mile, showing kindness even to our enemies (Matt. 5:38-48).

When we face unexpected tragedy, hardship, or illness, we can recall the promise that those who love God can trust

---

Lawful hymns: A search for Ps. 119:105 on hymnary.org turns up no less than 155 related hymns. One of the most familiar is "Wonderful Words of Life," written by Philip P. Bliss and published in 1874. Note how the first verse echoes themes from the text:

Sing them over again to me,
Wonderful words of life,
Let me more of their beauty see,
Wonderful words of life.
Words of life and beauty,
Teach me faith and duty,

Beautiful words, wonderful words,
Wonderful words of life,
Beautiful words, wonderful words,
Wonderful words of life.

God to bring something good from even the darkest of days and the deepest of falls (Rom. 8:28).

Loving Jesus is a wonderful thing, but those who love Jesus also bear a responsibility to learn about Jesus, including the biblical testimony of God's work among humans before Jesus' time on earth. The psalmist loved God, but also loved and appreciated God's law. Those who love Jesus best also love Jesus' teachings, and they seek to follow them – always. [**Lawful hymns**]

The Hardest Question
How does the acrostic structure of Psalm 119 work?

Psalm 119 is not only the longest chapter in the Bible, but it is also the most carefully structured. The psalm is a lengthy and elaborate acrostic poem, consisting of 176 verses divided into 22 sections consisting of eight verses each. Within each section, each verse begins with the corresponding Hebrew letter. Thus, the first section contains eight verses, all beginning with the letter *alef*. Every verse of the second section (vv. 9-16) begins with *bet*, and so forth.

Our text for the day comes from the 10th section (vv. 105-112), in which each verse begins with the letter *nun*, equivalent to the English "n." Making each verse work as an acrostic can require the use of unusual word forms or convoluted sentence structures.

Verse 105 begins with the word *nĕr*, meaning "lamp." Literally, it reads "(A) lamp to my feet (is) your word, and (a) light to my path."

Verse 106 begins with the *nifal* form of a verb that means "to swear." The verb is *shāvʿā*, but in the *nifal* stem – used to make verbs passive – it begins with a *nun* (*nishbaʿti*), so it reads "I have sworn an oath and confirmed it, to keep your righteous ordinances."

Verse 107 also begins with a passive verb, so that *ʿănâ* ("to afflict") begins with a *nun*: "I am afflicted mightily: Yahweh, give my life according to your word."

Verse 108 begins with the plural form of the word for freewill offerings, *nidbôt*. "Freewill offerings of my mouth, please accept, Yahweh; and your ordinances, teach me."

The familiar word *nefesh* begins v. 109. The word means something akin to "essence of life." It is often translated "soul," but should not be understood in the dualistic Greek notion of the soul being separate from the body. It is what makes one alive. "My life (is) in my palm continually, but your law (Torah) I do not forget."

Verse 110 begins with a rather unusual use of the verb *nātan*, which normally means "give" or "set." Here it is used to mean "prepared" or "laid": "They have laid, the wicked, a snare for me; but from your precepts I do not stray."

A word that can mean "my heritage" (*nāchalti*) begins v. 111: "My heritage (are) your decrees forever; for the joy of my heart they are."

Finally, v. 112 begins with a verb (*nāiti*) that can mean "to stretch out" or "to incline": "I incline my heart to perform your statues forever, always."

Knowing the Hebrew words may not mean much to most readers, but perhaps it can help us to appreciate the author's artistry and the efforts that went into this psalm – especially considering that there are 21 other sections of eight verses, each to begin with a corresponding letter of the Hebrew *alefbet*. The subject may be straightforward and somewhat repetitive, but the care that went into the poem's construction was far from simple.

Second Reading
Isaiah 55 (RCL 55:10-13)*

The Fertile Word

For you shall go out in joy, and be led back in peace; the mountains and the hills before you shall burst into song, and all the trees of the field shall clap their hands. (Isa. 55:12)

We know what it's like to suffer through a brutal winter that seems interminable. We long for the warmth and the green and the blossoms of spring as daffodils do battle with lingering snow and overnight freezes to lift their yellow faces sunward.

In time, the Bradford pears burst into clouds of bloom, the redbuds blossom, the cherry trees explode, the dogwoods unfurl their crosses, and all seems right with the world.

Today's text imagines a day when God will spark a spring to end all springs, a day when mountains will shout and trees applaud the homecoming of God's people.

Isaiah 55 is such a hopeful text that parts of it appear multiple times over the lectionary's three-year cycle. Given that the chapter contains only 13 verses, and all of them are connected, our approach is to consider one study of the entire chapter: ministers or teachers can tailor the study to particular times of the year.

The text is an enthusiastic invitation for Israel – and for all who will – to get on board with God, to accept God's gift of covenant promises, and to follow God on a journey of justice that leads to the Promised Land. The spiritual and metaphorical appeal of Isaiah 55 is universal, and it remains one of the Bible's most beautiful invitations to relationship with God. [**More context**]

More context: Isaiah 55 concludes the second of three major sections in the book of Isaiah.

Chapters 1–39 belong mainly to the pre-exilic period of the late eighth and early seventh centuries BCE, calling Israel's people to repent and trust God lest they be carried into exile.

Chapters 40–55 belong to a later period, and are addressed to the sixth-century exiles, living in Babylon, paying the price of a previous generation's rebellion.

The final section, chapters 56–66, appears designed to encourage those exiles who returned to Jerusalem and surrounding areas after Babylon was defeated and the Persian king Cyrus allowed the captives to return home.

Today's text may belong to the period immediately following Cyrus' edict of 538 BCE, which gave the exiles permission to return home and rebuild Jerusalem. The text may best be understood as a call for Israelites to leave their homes in Babylon and undertake the arduous journey back to Jerusalem.

There were many who wondered why they should do so: the Babylonians had allowed the Israelites a considerable amount of freedom to carry on their business and even to accumulate property. Few remained who remembered Jerusalem, and apparently there was no great rush of people anxious to leave what they had worked for in Babylon and return to an uncertain, hostile existence in a new Persian province consisting of Jerusalem and its immediate environs.

Isaiah 55 appears multiple times in lectionary readings: vv. 1-5 are read for Proper 13 in Year A, vv. 1-9 for the third Sunday in Lent of Year C, and vv. 10-13 for Proper 10 in Year A, the eighth Sunday of Epiphany in Year C, and Proper 3 in Year C. A study is more fruitful if it includes vv. 1-13.

God's promises: God's offer in v. 3 promises nothing less than life, continuing a long string of imperative verbs: "Incline your ear, and come to me; listen, so that you may live" (v 3a). In Hebrew thought, the concepts of "listening" and "obeying" were closely linked: to truly hear was to obey. Here, the repetition of "incline your ear" and "listen" implies that the hearers must not only hear the prophet's words, but also obey his teaching, if they are to experience the life he promises.

The latter part of v. 3 is difficult to translate. Literally, the text says "I will cut for you (plural) a covenant everlasting, my steadfast love (to) David confirmed." The word behind "confirmed" is a reflexive participle from the verb *'āman* (English "amen"), meaning "to confirm" or make sure. Thus, it could be translated as an adjective such as "sure." The NRSV renders it "I will make with you an everlasting covenant, my steadfast, sure love for David."

The awkwardness comes from the lack of any preposition or comparative associated with the name of David, which stands alone. Most scholars believe the intended sense is that the promised covenant is to be "like" God's sure promises to David. In essence, then, Isaiah promises that God's everlasting covenant with David has been transferred to the people, who are now free to return to Jerusalem in hopes of building a new and lasting kingdom.

A thirsty people
(vv. 1-5)

The oracle in Isaiah 55 may have been preached in a public marketplace, for it sounds like a sales pitch from someone hawking wares in the crowded streets of Babylon. Vendors selling potable water, bread, wine, milk, and other comestibles would have been commonplace in any ancient urban setting, just as they are today.

Isaiah offered food and water that are beyond price, but freely offered. It may have been a hard sell, however, for there was no visible food or drink in his hands.

The prophet's offer appears to work on two levels. On the surface, he may have been promising the availability of good water and abundant provisions in the Promised Land for those who would return. On another level, Isaiah spoke of priceless spiritual food that can be found only – but freely – in relationship with God.

In either case, Isaiah charged that the "bread" his hearers were buying in Babylon was not real bread, and that their efforts to build fortunes in exile could not fully satisfy.

The prophet offered "rich food" to those who would "listen carefully" and choose rightly.

Isaiah's free offer of food and drink is not unlike Jesus' parable of the great supper, in which God invites all people to come and eat at the heavenly table (Luke 14:15-24, John 7:37-38, Rev. 22:17). Both are freely offered, yet many are hesitant to accept.

In addition, the prophet promised that the eternal covenant God had made with David – that his descendants would always lead Israel (2 Sam. 7:8-16, 23:5; 1 Kgs. 8:23-26; Psalm 89) – would be transferred or extended to all Israel (vv. 3-5). **[God's promises]**

"I will make with you an everlasting covenant," Isaiah said, echoing language from God's promise to make for David an everlasting house. The promise, however, carried with it a responsibility. Because of God's blessings, David became "a witness to the peoples, a leader and commander for the peoples" (v. 4).

Israel was also called to be a witness, no longer in the sense of political leadership, but as spiritual guides. In particular, they were to live as a testimony before nations that do not know God: "you shall call nations that you do not know, and nations that you do not know shall run to you ..." (v. 5a).

While David in his promised "house" was a witness to the people he ruled, Israel is also promised an everlasting future in which she is to be a witness to people who do not know God.

The prophet believed that if the exiles would trust God and return to build up Jerusalem as a people fully committed to God's way, they would become such an inspiration that other nations would "run" to them in search of the secret to success and life that they have discovered in "the LORD your God, the Holy One of Israel, for he has glorified you" (v. 5b).

An awesome God
(vv. 6-9)

How does one enter this promised relationship? How does one "Seek the LORD while he may be found, call upon him while he is near" (v. 6)? In cultic-oriented contexts such as Deut. 12:5 and Ps. 105:4, "to seek the LORD" is to come and worship in the temple. For the prophets, however, seeking the Lord involved more than temple worship: it called for a commitment to following God's way.

Notice the piling up of imperative verbs in this text. Isaiah calls on the people to "come" (twice), "buy" (twice), and "eat" (v. 1); to "listen carefully," "eat," and "delight yourselves" (v. 2); to "incline your ear," "come to me," and "listen" (v. 3); to "see" (vv. 4-5); to "seek the LORD" and "call upon him" (v. 6). The use of imperative verbs emphasizes a call for human response in God's offer of redemption.

Isaiah and his fellow exiles in Babylon could not "seek God" by going to the temple, but God's presence was not dependent on a temple. For Isaiah, seeking God began with repentance (v. 7). Thus, he called on the wicked to forsake their wicked ways, and the unrighteous their unworthy thoughts. The prophet, writing at the end of the exile, may also have been encouraging people to accept Cyrus' offer to return home and rebuild the temple while the opportunity was available. [**Seeking God by seeking justice**]

To "return to the LORD" (v. 7) means to repent. Indeed, the Hebrew word for "turn" or "return" is the same word used for "repent." To repent is to turn about; to turn away from a self-oriented life to a God-directed life, from a sinful life to a righteous life.

The prophet's call to repentance led to a promise of pardon. If the people would seek the Lord, they would find mercy. Isaiah believed that the exiles' time in Babylon had paid the penalty for the sins of the ancestors. They were now free to "get out of jail" and return home to rebuild Jerusalem.

For some hearers, accustomed to Babylonian ways and settled in their Babylonian homes, Isaiah's words may have sounded like foolishness. From a human point of view, the call to pull up stakes and return to an uncertain future made little sense. But God knew things the people did not know, Isaiah said. "For my thoughts are not your thoughts, nor are your ways my ways, says the LORD" (v. 8).

Human minds are limited, but God's knowledge knows no boundaries: "For as the heavens are higher than the earth, so are my ways higher than your ways and my thoughts than your thoughts" (v. 9). As much as we may like the idea of understanding everything, we have to acknowledge that God remains far beyond our full comprehension, always shrouded in mystery. God's ways are higher than our ways, but how can we know when a prophetic message truly reflects God's ways?

A fruitful word
(vv. 10-13)

Isaiah returned to the image of the heavens as higher than the earth and built on it to assure the people he was an authentic channel of God's powerful and effective word. The metaphor takes on more depth when we understand that in Hebrew, the notions of "word" and "deed" are connoted by the same term. God's words and God's deeds go together. Just as rain and snow come from the heavens to water the earth and make it fruitful, so God's spoken word would accomplish its purpose (vv. 10-11).

And what was that purpose?

In this context, it was the return of Israel to the land of promise. Isaiah painted the kind of glorious image we'd only expect to see in a happy-ending movie. He envisioned a joyful journey of gleeful people enjoying a new era of peace, with nearby mountains happily serenading and roadside trees applauding the people as they marched past like heroes on parade (v. 12). We can almost hear Julie Andrews singing, "The hills are alive with the sound of music …"

The rough thorn bushes and briers in the ruins of Jerusalem would give way to fragrant cypress and myrtle trees, Isaiah said, which would stand as a living reminder of God's deliverance for Israel. The true memorial of God's

Memorial trees: The Haas Promenade, a memorial park overlooking Jerusalem, features trees reminiscent of Isaiah's promise.

work, however, could not be seen in tall trees, but in a faithful and fruitful people. [**Memorial trees**]

Unfortunately, those who did return to Jerusalem did not experience a happy homecoming. The city was a ruin, the neighbors were rude, and the land was facing a drought. How do we square the prophet's pretty picture with the ugly scene the returnees encountered?

Isaiah's over-the-top metaphor may have been sparked by the overwhelming joy of realizing that the exiles could finally return home. Though his hyperbolic description of their return did not match the desolate scene they would find in Jerusalem, the prophet looked beyond the ruined land to a spiritual spring when God and people would live together in a joyful setting not unlike Israel's tradition of Eden.

Sometimes, things must get worse before they get better. How often have we anticipated a delightful vacation, only to be sidetracked by cranky children, long lines, or bad weather? Despite the difficulties, we manage to make good memories and remember the trip fondly, carsickness and all.

I can remember imagining how much enjoyment a small, shaded patio might add to my backyard. But before the first relaxing glass of lemonade, there were weeks of backbreaking labor to dig out the spot, build a retaining wall, level the ground, fill in the substrate, fit the pavers, and landscape the surroundings. I can lie in a hammock and read to the music of birds and wind chimes now, but it

didn't spring from the earth like flowers leaping up to greet one of Disney's cartoon heroines.

There is a future for us, and it is bigger and more beautiful, happier and more peaceful than the Jerusalem we know will ever be. Despite the best prophetic efforts, from Ezekiel's visions to John's apocalypse, we cannot know exactly what that future will be like.

The one thing we can hang our hopes on is that we serve a God who wants to be known, and who wants to bless us. As we "seek the LORD while he may be found," we embark upon a journey through valleys and hills that may be more stressful than musical, but we do not travel alone – and when we can be confident that the end of the road brings us closer to God, every step will be worth the effort.

The Hardest Question
How can "word" and "deed" be the same thing?

In Hebrew, the same term can be used to mean "word" or "deed." It can, for that matter, also mean "thing," though generally in the sense of a thing that is done. The word is *dābar*, and it can be used for words and deeds of humans or of God.

Isaiah 55:10-11 makes maximum use of this dual meaning: God's promised word and God's actions are interconnected. As Claus Westermann has put it, "God's word is a word that does things" (*Isaiah 40–66*, Old Testament Library [Westminster Press, 1977], 289).

This thought dominates prophecy in both the Old and the New Testaments. Hebrews 4:12 declares "Indeed, the word of God is living and active, sharper than any two-edged sword …" John's gospel likens not only Christ's work, but also Christ himself, to the word of God: "In the beginning was the Word, and the Word was with God, and the Word was God. … All things came into being through him …" (John 1:1, 3a).

The prophets' declaration of God's word was risky, because it was not grounded in tradition or in the temple: it had nothing to stand on but the word itself, and its fulfillment. The very nature of this risk, however, made its pronouncement a bold and meaningful act.

The authentic declaration of God's word, by its nature, will be fulfilled. It may not always be fulfilled in the way we expect: Isaiah's promise of a rose-garden reception for the returning exiles did not happen, but the point of the prophecy was that Israel would be delivered from their bondage in Babylon, and that promise was fulfilled.

As Westermann notes (p. 290), we must be careful not to assume that God's word is on some sort of autopilot, to be fulfilled without our cooperation. Isaiah proclaimed a word of deliverance and restoration to Israel, but they had the responsibility of hearing and acting upon it: God would not set them on a magic carpet and whisk them off to Jerusalem without their cooperation and consent.

Nor would God's fulfillment of the word necessarily follow the precise pattern envisioned by the prophets, who often spoke in metaphorical language. We have no record of mountains singing or trees cheering as the exiles made their way home, but they got there.

"The only thing that is absolutely certain is that prophecy inevitably results in fulfillment," Westermann writes. "The word never returns void."

"But," he reminds us, "the God who fulfills his promises is always one whose thoughts and ways are immeasurably greater than those of men" (p. 291).

God's words and deeds are inextricably bound together, and our response is a third strand in the rope. As we work together, God's word is accomplished and sure. As the author of Ecclesiastes said, "A three-ply cord is not easily broken" (Eccl. 4:12).

Optional Second Reading
Psalm 65 (RCL 65:[1-8], 9-13)

Showers of Blessings

By awesome deeds you answer us with deliverance, O God of our salvation;
you are the hope of all the ends of the earth and of the farthest seas. (Ps. 65:5)

Perhaps you can recall attending an annual convention or other meeting that might include denominational dignitaries along with lay people. A pastor or priest who is tasked with the opening prayer comes to the microphone with a carefully scripted prayer of thanksgiving that displays the speaker's polished elocution but seems a bit short on heart.

Psalm 65 strikes me as just that kind of prayer: it is beautifully written and laden with impressive imagery, but told from a third person perspective and often in the passive voice. It is as if the psalmist observes a world of reasons for gratitude to God, but without much personal participation.

The accomplished but subdued approach is likely due to the communal nature of the psalm. It would have been used, no doubt, in Israel's formal liturgy, with the priest offering praise on behalf of the people rather than as a personal expression of faith. **[Head notes]**

Satisfied people
(vv. 1-4)

The solemnity of the psalm does not detract from its significance. It falls naturally into three sections, each including "God" in the lead verse, and each focusing on a different aspect of God's creative and sustaining work.

The first section reflects a human response to God's offer of relationship. "Praise is due to you" translates an unusual phrase that would read literally as "For you, silence, praise, O God in Zion." Translators often slightly emend

Head notes: A superscription to Psalm 65 informs the choirmaster that it is "of David," and "a song." How this information would prove instructive is unclear, unless "of David" indicates both a tune and a collection, and "a song" suggests it is to be sung rather than read. Occurring within the "Elohistic Psalter" (Psalms 42–72), the psalm addresses God as *'elohîm* rather than Yahweh.

the noun for "silence" into a verbal form and give it the sense of "wait." Thus, "Praise awaits you."

Both subject and verb are singular in the next line: "a vow will be paid." Most modern translations render them as plural, which seems to be called for, though the NASB20 follows the KJV in retaining the singular form.

The passive construction of v. 1 suggests the more formal approach of a prayer in behalf of the larger community, but v. 2 turns to a more active mode, addressing God as the one who hears prayers. The NRSV and NIV11 translate the participle *shōmē'a* optimistically. It normally means "hear" and can also mean "obey." Hebrew has a verb that means "to answer," and the poet uses it in v. 5. It's a stretch to think of God obeying our requests, but in the context of seeking forgiveness, one might be confident of a response.

The psalmist wrote from a clear Hebrew perspective, but believed all people had access to God: "To you all flesh shall come. When deeds of iniquity overwhelm us, you forgive our transgressions" (vv. 2b-3).

A cherished credo held that God was consistently compassionate, merciful, and willing to forgive sins (Exod.

34:6), and it was often reflected in the psalms, sometimes quoted in full (Ps. 86:5, 15; 103:8; 145:8).

As a Hebrew, the psalmist saw the locus of God's presence and the seat of grace as found in the Jerusalem temple: "Happy are those whom you choose and bring near to live in your courts. We shall be satisfied with the goodness of your house, your holy temple" (v. 4).

Joyful days
(vv. 5-8)

God was thought to be particularly present and accessible in the sanctuary, but not limited to it. "By awesome deeds you answer us with deliverance, O God of our salvation; you are the hope of all the ends of the earth and of the farthest seas" (v. 5).

The verse includes an interesting combination of attestations: it begins with typical nationalistic vocabulary for God's having delivered Israel through mighty deeds, but shifts to the idea that God is "the hope of all the ends of the earth and of the farthest seas."

This remarkably universalistic outlook is consonant, however, with the following affirmations of God's role in creating all things and all peoples. Only God had the strength to establish the mountains (v. 6) and "silence the roaring of the seas, the roaring of their waves, the tumult of the peoples" (v. 7).

Israel's creation tradition spelled out in Genesis 1 and reflected elsewhere presumed a primordial state of chaotic waters before God stepped in to create a dome-like "firmament" in their midst and solidified a surface beneath to make way for a bubble of air that could support life. Earthly seas continued to recall the wild waters above and below, stormy waves that only God could tame and control.

[Waters upon waters]

> **Waters upon waters:** The ancient Hebrew cosmogony did not conceive of an infinite void beyond the earth, populated by star-filled galaxies separated by inconceivable distances. They imagined that the earth stood on pillars with waters beneath, and that the heavenly firmament held back waters above. They understood that ordinary rains came from clouds, but feared the possibility that God might wreak havoc by opening "the windows of heaven" with destructive force (Gen. 7:11, 8:2; Isa. 24:18). They also believed that God could bless the earth with abundance in the same way (Mal. 3:10).

Keeping the reference to humans as part of God's creation in mind, the psalmist declared God's ability to quiet the tempestuous actions and turbulent relations of "the peoples" as well as the waters. Given humanity's persistent penchant for conflict, one wonders which is the more difficult task.

People from one end of the earth to the other are so awed by the wonder of God's creation, it causes them to shout for joy. Translations differ for the final phrase. Some see signs of morning and evening praising God as if personified. NRSV has the poetic "you make the gateways of the morning and the evening shout for joy" and NASB20 has "You make the sunrise and the sunset shout for joy," while in NIV11 the subject offering praise is more abstract: "where morning dawns, where evening fades, you call for songs of joy."

Another approach, one that may honor the parallel structure more clearly, keeps the people from the remotest parts of the earth in mind. A literal reading could be, "from the going out of the morning to the evening you cause it/him/humankind to sing for joy." The obvious reference to east and west led to the NET translation: "you cause those living in the east and west to praise you."

Creation itself, along with the people who enjoy it, is called to praise the author of its existence.

Happy valleys
(vv. 9-13)

In the last section, the psalmist turns from God's role in creation to one of magnanimity and sustenance. God not only created the earth, but also looks after it, most notably by providing water. In vv. 9-11, God is the actor: God visits the earth, waters it, and enriches it, thus providing the people with grain (v. 9). God waters the furrows of the fields with rain, settling the freshly plowed earth and softening its crusty ridges (v. 10). In the harvest, God "crowns the year" with good, so much so that even wagon tracks have sprouted a rich bounty (v. 11).

This happens because "the river of God is full of water" (v. 9). In God there is no lack of resources to be poured upon the earth. The combination of v. 4's reference to God's presence in the temple and v. 9's praise for God's limitless supply of water recalls Ezekiel's vision of a crystal river flowing from God's temple and going forth to water the trees that line its banks. The water was so fresh and abundant, Ezekiel said, that it would turn the Dead Sea into a living lake with abundant fish (Ezek. 47:1-2).

The subject shifts from God to creation in the closing verses. With inspiring bucolic imagery, the psalmist portrays a grateful earth: "The pastures of the wilderness overflow, the hills gird themselves with joy, the meadows clothe themselves with flocks, the valleys deck themselves with grain, they shout and sing together for joy" (vv. 12-13).

The psalmist's stately prayer seems perfect: a generous God has created a perfect earth and sustains it with abundant water so that the fields are lush with grain. Planet and people alike praise God for all good things. But we know that all things are not good, not always. The psalmist tacitly acknowledges this with the opening affirmation that God forgives human iniquities and has the power to calm "the tumults of the peoples."

Praise for earthly abundance would not be so impressive if not for the awareness that some years are less than prosperous. In the American West, 25 years of drought have contributed to massive forest fires and historically low water levels in Lake Powell and in Lake Mead, on which up to 25 million people depend. Droughts in Africa, India, and other places that don't have the infrastructure of giant lakes for backup lead to periodic famines and many deaths. Overpopulation in some areas, and economic disparity even where resources are rich, remind us that all is not right with the world.

We celebrate years of plentiful rain and fertile fields, because we know it's not always that way. An Amish farmer who had experienced two years of bumper crops once confided to me that he was worried that trouble was coming: he knew that some years are not as prosperous.

The psalm, then, is not a naïve painting of a perfect world that can't be spoiled, but a salute to the God whose abundant might and generosity has created a world of fecundity and promise, but also one in which humankind has a role to play.

In both Gen. 1:1–2:4a and 2:4b-25, God creates the world, but then assigns humans the responsibility of caring for it. The river of God may be full of water, but people play a role in ensuring that everyone has access to it.

The Hardest Question
Does v. 1 speak of single or multiple vows?

In Hebrew life, as in the wider ancient Near Eastern neighbors, it was customary to appeal to the deity for a boon in times of exigency, and to promise some kind of offering in return if the prayer received a positive response.

In Hebrew, this was called a *neder*, consistently translated as "vow." Readers should keep in mind that vows in this context are not unconditional, as we consider wedding vows or monastic vows to be, but highly conditional. If a request is made and God comes through, the promised vow must be paid in conjunction with ceremonial actions and offerings made at the temple (Leviticus 22, Numbers 30).

The psalms contain examples of vows being made, though the poetic nature sometimes obscures the conditional nature (Ps. 22:21-22, 61:7-8, 69:29-30, 109:29-30). The conjunction normally translated as "and," often left untranslated, can have the sense of "when." And, the preposition *ki*, usually translated as "for" or "because," can also have the sense of "when."

Many psalms speak of paying vows (Ps. 22:25; 50:14; 61:8; 66:13; 116:14, 18) – all of them promises spoken by an individual: "I will pay my vows to the LORD."

Though individual vows were understandably most common, national or community vows were possible. Numbers 21:1-3 relates a story from Israel's time in the wilderness, when an enemy threatened. "… Then Israel made a vow to the LORD and said, 'If you will indeed give this people into our hands, then we will utterly destroy their towns. The LORD listened to the voice of Israel, and handed over the Canaanites; and they utterly destroyed them and their towns; so the place was called Hormah.'"

One might guess that a similar vow was made before the putative defeat of Jericho, because a lone individual named Achan determined to keep some of the plunder for himself, leading to a disastrous result in the next battle, and even more so for Achan and his family (Joshua 7).

The singular nature of v. 1b, "a vow shall be paid," suggests the possibility that the psalm accompanied the payment of a vow on behalf of the community, or in the community's presence. Vows in the psalms typically offer the promise of public praise or testimony.

The remainder of the psalm makes no reference to the payment of a vow, however, so it is more likely that v. 1 speaks generically of both praise and payment being due to God. (For more, see my book, *Vows in the Hebrew Bible and the Ancient Near East* [Sheffield Academic Press, 1992], 150-161, or an earlier article, "Conditional Vows in the Psalms of Lament: A New Approach to an Old Problem," in *The Listening Heart: Essays in Psalms and Wisdom in Honor of Roland E. Murphy, O. Carm.*, ed. Ken Hoglund, et. al. [JSOT Press, 1987], 77-94.)

Season after Pentecost: Proper 10

Third Reading
Romans 8:1-11

Mindful Spirituality

To set the mind on the flesh is death, but to set the mind on the Spirit is life and peace. (Rom. 8:6)

Spirituality is a crucial dimension of human life. Seminaries and divinity schools develop programs of spiritual formation. Both ministers and laypersons seek trained spiritual directors to serve as life coaches of a higher order. Ministers, rabbis, yogis, and other disciples of the inner life promote quiet retreats or daily meditation to nurture one's spiritual life.

Corporality is less talked about, perhaps because we're all familiar with the hard pull of hunger for physical gratification through food and drink, sex and play, chilling out and being entertained. We don't need special training to help us focus on desire, idolize our bodies, or obsess over financial security.

The Apostle Paul knew what it was like to be torn between the spirit and the flesh. He devoted considerable discussion in Rom. 7:14–8:5 to the inherent tension between spirit and body, good and evil, aspirations to godliness and the reality of failure.

Where does one find the power to overcome temptation and move beyond? Paul celebrated a belief that "the law of the Spirit of life has set us free from the law of sin and death" (Rom. 6:2).

Still, Paul knew that spiritual liberation is not a one-time experience: we live in our bodies every day of our lives, and are constantly subject to temptation.

As we go forward, we should note that when Paul speaks of "the flesh," he does not mean the physical body alone, but includes the mind that directs it. The dichotomy

---

The malleable mind: We are often reminded of how pliable the mind is. News stories abound of how terrorists have kidnapped children and used various methods to brainwash them, filling them with hatred and then sending them out as suicide bombers. Others become radicalized through exposure to Internet sites or the influence of a person skilled in mental manipulation. On the other hand, positive influences may also shape our thinking.

In most cases, though we remain subject to peer pressure, political propaganda, and subliminal influences, we retain the ability to choose our own way. Paul's concern is whether we choose the self-directed way of "the flesh," or the Christ-directed way of "the Spirit."

---

in this text is not just body versus spirit, but the human mind/spirit versus the indwelling Spirit of Christ.

The question to ask is: Who, or what, is in control of our minds? What influence has the most power over our decision-making: our human desires, or "the mind of Christ" (Phil. 2:5-8)? [**The malleable mind**]

Spirit and flesh
(v. 1-6)

Paul began Romans 8 by celebrating the redeeming work of Christ, which has "set you free from the law of in and of death" (vv. 1-2). He believed that Christians find true life in voluntarily submitting their will to the Spirit of Christ, rather than leaving their thoughts to be blown about by worldly whims.

---

* Romans 8:6-11 is also read on the Fifth Sunday in Lent in Year A.

Selfish works and spiritual fruit: When Paul talks about the works of the flesh versus the fruits of the spirit in Gal. 5:19-23, the "works of the flesh" constitute a catalogue of negative traits: "fornication, impurity, licentiousness, idolatry, sorcery, enmities, strife, jealousy, anger, quarrels, dissensions, factions, envy, drunkenness, carousing, and things like these" (Gal. 5:19-21). In his mind, the self-focused life is bound for trouble.

In contrast, the term "Spirit" (*pneuma*) speaks of the total person in relation to God. The fruits of the Spirit listed in Gal. 5:22-23 – "love, joy, peace, patience, kindness, generosity, faithfulness, gentleness, and self-control" – reflect the presence and the activity of God in the daily life of the believer.

The default mode for humans is to think as the culture thinks. Paul often used the Greek word for "flesh" *(sarx)* to describe the nature of a human without Christ. In this he sets "flesh" and "spirit" against each other as two poles of human experience, not as a separate body and soul. While "of the flesh" can refer in a literal sense to the physical body, Paul more commonly uses it in the sense of a person's determination to trust in self rather than God.

Paul saw humans as living in bondage to their human failings, redeemable only by the work of Christ, who came in the form of a human to deal with the problem of sin and set us free to focus our minds on the Spirit (vv. 3-5).

In Paul's mind, trusting in self can lead only to death. Thus, he wrote "To set the mind on the flesh is death, but to set the mind on the Spirit is life and peace" (v. 6). Some translations avoid the uncomfortable word "flesh" and speak of those who are "carnally minded" (KJV) or have "the mind of sinful man" (NIV). Maintaining the word "flesh" reminds the reader that our minds are firmly interconnected with our bodies and in touch with our physical desires.

Paul's phrase, "to set the mind" (NRSV) translates the noun form of a verb that means "to think," or "to set one's mind or heart on something." Thus, "it denotes the whole action of the affections and will as well as of the reason" (Fritz Rienecker, *A Linguistic Key to the Greek New Testament: Romans–Revelation*, trans. Cleon L. Rogers Jr. [Zondervan, 1980], 19). A more literal translation is: "for the mindset of the flesh (is) death, and the mindset of the Spirit (is) life and peace."

For Paul, the results of following the way of the flesh or the way of the Spirit are self-evident and the proper choice between them is obvious. It involves choosing between hurtful behaviors that lead to disquiet and death, or helpful actions that promote peace and life. The character and quality of our daily experience, as well as our eternal destiny, is determined by the direction in which we set our minds. [**Selfish works and spiritual fruit**]

A mortal mind
(vv. 7-8)

The power of the mind is an awesome thing. We are familiar with the significant effects of positive thinking or negative thinking. We may have read articles or heard testimonies of people who credit their health or success to positive mental attitudes. Doctors agree that hopeful and positive attitudes are important aids to healing.

We may also have observed persons who enter a downward spiral because of negative thinking. We may have experienced it ourselves. Unhealthy thinking habits can ultimately affect our emotional and physical health. These ways of thinking can become "hard-wired" into our brains, and they are difficult to overcome.

Behavioral coaches sometimes teach the art of "reframing," of literally training our minds to see things differently and think in more positive ways. Paul understood the need for believers to reframe their thinking by setting their minds on the Spirit rather than on the flesh. This, he believed, was essential for both life and peace.

Having established the basic "flesh vs. spirit" dichotomy in v. 6, Paul elaborates in vv. 7-11. The mind that is "set on the flesh" is hostile to God, Paul said: "it does not submit to God's law – indeed it cannot" (v. 7). A "fleshly" mind cannot submit to God because it has already submitted to self. As Jesus reminded us, no one can serve two masters (Matt. 6:24).

Paul saw nothing but danger in being sold out to the worldly idea that a person can be self-sufficient, that one does not need God. The acclaimed southern writer Flannery O'Conner gave voice to that idea through a self-absorbed character named Hazel Motes. At some point in the short story titled "Wise Blood," someone mentioned the subject of redemption. In response, Hazel sneered, "Any man who owns a good car don't need redemption." [**Redemption**]

> **Redemption:** Preacher, professor, prolific writer, and Methodist bishop Will Willimon once pointed out that Flannery O'Conner's Hazel Motes speaks for many modern Americans: "If you have a good Chevrolet with a working transmission, a good heart rate, suitably low blood pressure, a pension plan, you don't need redemption. We have, through our earnest good efforts, redeemed ourselves" (*Pulpit Resource* [October–December, 1995], 56).

As long as we think our own efforts can achieve all the security that matters, our mind cannot submit to God or please God (v. 8), because God is not even in the picture. The "mind of the flesh," by definition, is opposed to and closed to the mind of God.

A spiritual mind
(vv. 9-11)

Having pointed squarely to the mindset that leads to death, Paul challenges his readers to steer clear of that rocky shoal and anchor their minds firmly in the safe harbor of the Spirit: "But you are not in the flesh; you are in the Spirit, since the Spirit of God dwells in you" (v. 9a). Those who belong to Christ also possess the Spirit of Christ, and the Spirit of Christ possesses them (v. 9b). Thus, having the Spirit is not a "second blessing" for super-surrendered Christians, but an essential aspect of what it means to live in relationship with Christ.

Paul speaks of the indwelling of the Spirit as both present and future. He indicates that the believer's new position in the realm of the Spirit came about at the moment he or she trusted Christ, and that the Spirit of God continues to indwell the believer: "But if Christ is in you, though the body is dead because of sin, the Spirit is life because of righteousness" (v. 10).

Note that Paul makes little distinction between the "Spirit of God," the "Spirit of Christ," and "Christ in you." These are equivalent expressions, all referring to the same reality, and suggesting that something approaching a Trinitarian view was present in Paul's thought.

Scholars have spilled much ink over the meaning of Paul's assertion that, while "the body is dead because of sin, the Spirit is life because of righteousness." He seems to be saying that, even for believers, our physical nature is still destined for a physical death, even as those who live in the flesh are destined for an eternal death.

Though our bodies are mortal, where the Spirit is, there is life and true righteousness. Believers who trust God's Spirit experience a new kind of life (Rom. 6:4), a fruitful life (Gal. 5:22-23), the abundant life that Christ has promised (John 10:10).

Paul believed that life in the Spirit also has a future component. The Spirit who dwells in us is the same Spirit responsible for raising Jesus from dead. Thus, he said, the Spirit will also raise us, even our mortal bodies, from the dead (v. 11). The Christian belief in resurrection retains a hint of the ancient Jewish belief that the body is somehow connected to the spirit even after death. In some way beyond our understanding, our resurrection with Christ will have both a physical and spiritual component. As we often remind ourselves in funeral eulogies, "this mortal shall put on immortality" (1 Cor. 15:53).

To the Corinthians, Paul described Christ's resurrection as the "firstfruits," assuring Christ-followers that they would participate in a full and final harvest of life (1 Cor. 15:23). Thus, the Spirit now present in us will bear fruit in our future resurrection and full participation in the kingdom of God. This assertion brings us back to where we began in v. 6: a mind set on the flesh leads to death, but a mind set on the Spirit leads to life.

Paul effectively uses this promise to remind readers that their thinking should include a future component. While it is wise to avoid the dilemma of being "so heavenly minded that we are no earthly good," Christians know there is more to the equation than what feels good at any given moment.

Our human side wants to enjoy luxury, leisure, and financial security. We want to be happy, to have fun, and enjoy pleasure. Paul would not suggest that we be fiscally irresponsible or deny every delight, but he clearly called upon believers to revamp their priorities. While more money in the bank and a vacation home to call our own might be nice, generosity to the poor and personal involvement in assisting others might be better.

Salvation involves more than the promise of "pie in the sky," but God's promise is nothing to be sneered at. Paul believed we have been promised an eternal home with Jesus, an everlasting experience of joy and peace.

To sacrifice our future hope on the altar of present pleasure is a bad deal – a deal Paul hopes his readers will be wise enough to reject.

The Hardest Question
I believe, but still struggle with temptation. Is something wrong with me?

A surface reading of the text might lead to the idea that once we trust in Christ and receive the Spirit, everything is hunky-dory and we no longer have to worry about temptation – but we all know it doesn't work that way.

Paul understood this. Though we may speak of "dying to sin" and "being raised with Christ," and though we may have prayed to receive the Spirit of Christ within us, our humanity does not cease. Temptations do not go away. As long as we live in our mortal bodies and possess a mortal mind, we face daily choices about whether we will orient our behavior toward selfish or godly goals.

James D.G. Dunn explains it this way: In speaking to the Romans, "Paul means neither that they have left the flesh wholly behind, nor that they are in a constant state of inspiration or permanent ecstasy. The phrases 'in flesh' and 'in Spirit' are much looser than that, as Paul's usage elsewhere confirms (cf., e.g., 14:17 and Gal. 2:20). What Paul assumes is not that the process of salvation is complete but that it has begun, not that their total being has been completely transferred to another realm but that a decisive transfer of allegiance and lordship has already taken place, not that moral effort has been rendered unnecessary but that the inner compulsion of God's Spirit has become the most important factor at the level of primary motivation and enabling" (*Romans 1–8*, vol. 38A of Word Biblical Commentary [Zondervan, 1988], 443-444).

Are there practical ways in which we can set our minds toward a life governed more by the Spirit than the flesh? Charles Talbert suggests a prayer-centered, three-step approach that involves a progressive "emptying" of self-orientation to make more room for the Spirit's influence.

First, he says, make a list of everyone you can think of who has offended you that you haven't forgiven – from childhood onward. Then, "Pray through that list until everyone has been released to Jesus," he says, even if God is also on the list because we have harbored anger toward heaven. This is necessary, Talbert says, "… because anger and grudges take up space in the self that only God needs to fill."

Second, Talbert writes, make a list of everything you can remember for which you need to be forgiven, then "Pray through that list until Jesus takes every one," emptying clutter from the mind.

Third, Talbert advises, "make a list of all the areas of your life over which Jesus does not have absolute control. Pray through that list until every one is open to him and subject to redecorating rights by him." In this way, we release our hold on the idols that take up space in our lives that ought to belong to God.

Only then, Talbert says, are we ready to ask God to come in and fill the empty space so that we may truly be led by the Spirit (*Romans*, Smyth & Helwys Bible Commentary [Smyth & Helwys, 2002], 210).

As long as we live in a mortal body, we are subject to the struggles that all humans face. Paul expressed hope that one day, even our mortal bodies will be perfected and given new life through the Spirit. In the meantime, we must consciously remember to take out the trash of our unworthy thoughts to make adequate room for the Spirit.

Fourth Reading
Matthew 13:1-23 (RCL 13:1-9, 18-23)

The World Needs the Word

But as for what was sown on good soil, this is the one who hears the word and understands it, who indeed bears fruit and yields, in one case a hundredfold, in another sixty, and in another thirty. (Matt. 13:23)

When I was in college at the University of Georgia, a former president of the Baptist Student Union who had gone off to seminary came back to speak in a chapel service. Using the parable before us today, he titled his message "A Species Analysis of Dirt."

As a science major learning to identify the species of everything from bacteria to broccoli to bears, I was all in with the title. It was also helpful, because we often call this text "the parable of the sower" after v. 13, but it's not just about the sower or the seeds: it's about the soils. **[Structure]**

The Revised Common Lectionary skips over vv. 10-17, in which Jesus was asked to explain why he taught in parables, focusing on the parable and its interpretation alone. Nevertheless, we will give some attention to those verses, as they help us to understand Jesus' purpose and strategy in utilizing parables for teaching.

A dirty story
(vv. 1-9)

Why did Jesus perch himself on a boat and tell this particular story, and why was it so memorable that all three synoptic gospels include it (cp. Mark 4:1-9 and Luke 8:4-8)? Several accounts leading up to ch. 13 reflect the theme of rejection: The religious leaders of the day opposed Jesus outright, and while curious crowds came out to hear the new teacher, few chose to follow him on the path of discipleship.

When the gospel of Matthew was written many years later, rejection was still a problem. Faithful followers had been spreading the gospel for 50 years or more, but the response was disappointing. Converts were few, and the movement faced resistance.

Jesus – and the author of Matthew – used the parable in part to reassure faithful followers that their work was not in vain as they sowed the seed of the gospel. They would not always get a hoped-for response.

The story is grounded in ancient farming techniques that would have been commonly known. Carefully

---

Structure: Matthew 13:1-52 comprises the third of five major teaching discourses apparent in the structure of Matthew. Though Jesus had used analogies before, this is the first time the author uses the word "parable" to describe Jesus' teaching, and the chapter is a collection of parables having to do with the kingdom, or dominion, of God.

Scholars are divided over whether the chapter contains seven or eight parables, depending on whether v. 52 is counted as a parable. Here is a representative outline of the structure:

1. The Parable of the Soils (13:1-9) and Commentary (13:10-23)
2. The Parable of the Wheat and the Weeds (13:24-30)
3. The Parable of the Mustard Seed (13:31-32)
4. The Parable of the Leavened Loaves (13:33) and Commentary (13:34-43)
5. The Parable of the Hidden Treasure (13:44)
6. The Parable of the Pearl (13:45-46)
7. The Parable of the Dragnet (13:47-50)
8. The (Parable of the?) Scribe Trained for the Kingdom (13:51-52)

marked and cultivated fields or garden plots as we know them were not the rule. Simple boundary stones typically marked property limits, and small landowners often used as much of their land as possible. When planting time came, some farmers would broadcast seed across whatever area might be promising. Plowing often took place *after* sowing, turning the seeds under the soil along with whatever vegetation remained from the previous year. [**Sow first, plow later**]

Jesus pointed to realities of life that anyone who had walked through rural areas would have observed. Seed that fell on or near hardened paths were likely to be gobbled up by birds and never have a chance to sprout.

Seed that fell on a thin layer of soil above a limestone shelf – commonly found in Palestine – would sprout quickly with sufficient rain but wither before reaching maturity because the ground would dry out quickly, with no room for a healthy root system.

Wheat or barley tossed into scrubby areas might also get a good start, but even though the surface weeds and thorns might have been plowed under, they would come back and grow strong, choking out the once-promising grain.

Finally, seed spread in good, deep soil with few weeds could be trusted to grow unhindered and produce the expected harvest.

And that's the story Jesus told in vv. 3-8. The only real surprise was in the remarkable harvest from the good soil: "some a hundredfold, some sixty, some thirty." Farming in antiquity typically resulted in multiples of 7–10 times the amount of grain planted: a harvest of 30–100 times more would have been rare and memorable.

Jesus told the story with no further explanation other than a warning: "Let anyone with ears listen!" (v. 9).

A curious question
(vv. 10-17)

Despite the presence of crowds so thick that Jesus had to teach from a boat (vv. 1-2), v. 10 presumes a different setting, one in which the disciples could come separately to Jesus and ask "Why do you speak to them (i.e., the crowds) in parables?"

The word "parable" (*parabolē*) literally means "cast alongside," as in two things that are set side by side for comparison. New Testament parables grew from similarly figurative Old Testament teachings. The Hebrew *mashal* was not just an explanation, but also carried the sense of a teaching that was enigmatic, as a riddle designed to provoke curiosity and further thought.

Jesus told the disciples: "To you it has been given to know the secrets of the kingdom of heaven, but to them it has not been given" (v. 11). Those who had proven receptive to God's offer of grace could grow in understanding and assurance of a place in the kingdom, but those who rejected Jesus would lose the opportunity they once had (v. 12).

Parables weren't just illustrations designed to clarify a point: sometimes they did the opposite. Jesus spoke of himself as carrying on in the tradition of Isaiah, who God instructed to be faithful in preaching to the people of Jerusalem despite their stubborn refusal to hear the message or see their need for repentance (vv. 13-15, citing Isa. 6:9-10).

Parables weren't designed to make people stubborn or to prevent them from entering the kingdom, but they could not be understood by those whose intentional stubbornness left them as outsiders. [**The secret life of parables**]

In contrast, Jesus said, those who chose to follow him were more blessed than prophets and saints of the past who would have longed to hear what Jesus was teaching them (vv. 16-17).

A secret explanation
(vv. 18-23)

Verse 18 brings us back to the parable in question and Jesus' explanation of it.

We should note that scholars through the years have proposed many ideas about how we should interpret parables. Early church fathers and their followers tended to read many parables as allegories, with each part of the parable representing something. After the advent of critical scholarship of the Bible, it became common to argue that Jesus' parables originally had only one central point, but that the gospel writers, reflecting early Christian traditions, added allegorical elements to them. In recent years, it has become more common to acknowledge that parables can have different levels of meaning, and that readers naturally bring their own contexts to the text and interpret through different lenses.

As Jesus explained it, the sower and the seed remain constant: what is different in each case is the type of soil on which the seed falls. Three types of soil yield little or no fruit, while one type of soil produces three levels of abundant fruit.

The hard ground by the path describes those who are so resistant to the gospel that they don't even try to understand it. Whatever interest might be sparked by a Christian friend or a moment of crisis is quickly swept away (v. 19).

Some people are like shallow soil over a rocky shelf. They respond to the gospel quickly, but their faith is shallow, and withers when challenged by opposition or hard times. Persecution was more common in Matthew's day than ours, but believers may still face ridicule from others. Or, they may have unrealistic expectations that God will protect them from harm, and fall away when the hard edges of life intrude through illness, divorce, or financial struggles (vv. 20-21).

When high-pressure evangelists sell the gospel like fire insurance, drawing people down the aisle to escape the prospect of hell, it's like seeding shallow ground. Meaningful faith must have roots that go deeper than a desire for a free ticket to heaven. It doesn't last.

Jesus knew that some believers would hear the gospel and respond with all good intentions, but later be led astray by emerging temptations that choke out their faith. Children, for example, may trust Jesus in all sincerity, but they face growing temptations with every passing year. Promising faith may give way when "the cares of the world and the lure of wealth choke the word, and it yields nothing" (v. 22).

When the seeds of selfishness and materialism are allowed to grow unhindered, they grow deep. Overcoming human selfishness without deep spiritual roots is like trying to eradicate a stand of kudzu with a garden hoe. It's a lost cause.

But there is good soil that makes room for strong roots to ground the faith. The good soil, Jesus said, would bring a harvest of 30, 60, or even 100 times more than was planted. In ancient times, those multiples would range from impressive to miraculous.

Jesus knew, and the author of Matthew knew, that rejection is a reality of life. We can't count on every seed we plant to sprout or grow, to reach maturity or to produce fruit. And yet, we are called to sow with the promise of an ultimate harvest that is hard to imagine.

The parable challenges us to look inward and work the soil of our own hearts so that we are not too hard to receive the word, not too shallow to give it root, not too encumbered with worldly cares to grow in faith and discipleship.

As we look to our own makeup, we also look outward. We are not to give up on others whose hearts are hard, for they may yet be softened by the rains of repentance. We cannot ignore those who quickly fall away, but must help them to transplant their lives and find room for deep roots. We dare not turn away from persons whose lives are overgrown with temporal concerns, but continue reminding them of eternal matters.

Discouragement comes easy, but Jesus holds before us the promise of an abundant harvest. As Christ himself continued to serve faithfully despite disappointment, so he calls us to sow good seed in a world of need.

The Hardest Question
Could the seeds reflect the *Shema*?

Swedish New Testament scholar Birger Gerhardsson has argued that the parable of the sower and the soils intentionally reflects the *Sh^ema*, the Old Testament commandment found in Deut. 6:4-9 ("The Parable of the Sower and Its Interpretation," *New Testament Studies* 14:2 [1967-68], 165-193).

The *Sh^ema* begins: "Hear, O Israel: The LORD is our God, the LORD alone. You shall love the LORD your God with all your heart, and with all your soul, and with all your might. Keep these words that I am commanding you today in your heart" (Deut. 6:4-5).

Faithful Jews of Jesus' day repeated the *Sh^ema* twice each day in keeping with the command to recite them "when you lie down and when you rise" (Deut. 6:6-7), and many Jewish people maintain the practice today.

Gerhardsson suggested that the *Sh^ema* was so well known that Jesus may have intentionally alluded to it in the parable. First, the rejection of the seed by the hard ground contradicted the command to love God with all of one's heart. Similarly, the shallow ground that did not sustain growth in times of persecution or trouble could indicate an unwillingness to love God with all the soul. Finally, the weed-filled soil that choked out the good seed with worldly cares and selfish attitudes pointed to a failure to love God with all of one's might.

The *Sh^ema* was popularly recited as the greatest of all commandments in the first century, as reflected in Jesus' conversation with the "rich young ruler." That, along with the gospels' interest in portraying Jesus as the fulfillment of the Old Testament, strengthens the proposed connection. By Jesus' day, however, Jews had become so Hellenized that it was popular to add the word "mind" to the sequence of heart, soul, and might (Mark 12:30, Luke 10:27), or to substitute it for "might" (Matt. 22:37). This makes the possible comparison less neat.

Reading the parable as a reflection on following the *Sh^ema* could be seen simply as a different way to allegorize it, but there still may be value in helping believers think through their level of love and loyalty to God through Christ.

First Reading
Genesis 28:10-22 (RCL 28:10-19a)

Climbing Jacob's Ladder

"And he was afraid, and said, "How awesome is this place!
This is none other than the house of God, and this is the gate of heaven." (Gen. 28:17)

Have you ever wished you could meet God personally – while still on this side of the border between life and death? Have you ever imagined what it would be like to hear God speak a blessing directly to you?

If such a thing should happen, how do you think you would respond? With shock and awe? With humble gratitude? Is there any chance you would pull out a contract and ask God to sign on the dotted line to confirm that the promised blessings would be fulfilled?

That is very close to what Jacob did when God unexpectedly appeared to him in a dream near a place called Bethel. Although the lectionary text stops at Gen. 28:19a, the story is woefully incomplete if we do not continue through v. 22.

Two stories
(vv. 10-15)

This familiar story follows the even more memorable account – not included in the lectionary – of how Jacob disguised himself as Esau and swindled his brother out of the blessing his blind and aged father Isaac had intended to bestow on the oldest son (27:1-40). Esau was rightfully angry and plotted to kill his conniving twin, but Rebekah sent Jacob away before his brother could act. While traveling toward Haran, where he would seek refuge with his uncle Laban, Jacob had an unexpected encounter with the divine.

The account appears to contain two stories in one, a well-edited composite of the two oldest source documents behind the Pentateuch, usually called "J" and "E." The J source is so named because the narrator typically refers to God as "Yahweh," the special name by which God was called. It is called "J" rather than "Y" because German scholars who first identified the source spelled the divine name *yhwh* as *jhvh* (which explains the derivative spelling "Jehovah"). The E source is denoted in part by its characteristic use of "Elohim," a plural form of the generic Semitic term for "god," as the preferred divine name.

While the older J source tends to speak of Yahweh as appearing physically in the form of a man, the E source imagines God as being more distant, appearing in dreams or through the medium of an angel. In this story, the larger frame of the story appears to be E, which speaks of a dream where Jacob glimpses a stairway to heaven. Though we commonly think of "Jacob's ladder," the word is more suggestive of a broad staircase: angels are both ascending and descending upon it – an unlikely image for a ladder.

In the middle of E's dream sequence, however, we find a theophany from the J source, in which Yahweh appears and speaks directly to Jacob.

The editor/narrator manages this transition seamlessly by inserting Yahweh's appearance at v. 13 and by using a double-duty combination of a preposition that can mean "upon," "by," or "beside," with an attached pronoun that can mean either "he" or "it." Thus, the resulting word can be translated to indicate either that God stood "upon it" (that is, upon the stairway, from the perspective of E's dream sequence) or "by him" (beside Jacob, from the perspective of J's theophany).

Yahweh audibly addresses Jacob, self-identifying as the God of his grandfather Abraham and his father Isaac. Yahweh repeats to Jacob the basic promise of land and offspring that was previously made to Abraham and Isaac, but then expands it with a promise to be with him everywhere he goes, to watch over him, and to return him safely back to his homeland. Yahweh concludes with the ringing affirmation "I will not leave you until I have done what I have promised you."

Two responses
(vv. 16-22)

When Jacob awakes from the dream, he is convinced that he has stumbled upon the very gateway to heaven. At first, he is overcome with awe and immediately marks the spot by taking the stone he had used to bolster his head and standing it on end, then anointing it with oil to sanctify the place as a holy site. Appropriately, he calls the place "Bethel," a Hebrew term meaning "house (*beth*) of God (*el*)." [**From pillow to pillar**]

In v. 20, however, Jacob appears less worshipful and more distrustful. Although Yahweh had made a solemn and unconditional promise to bless Jacob, he responded with a very conditional vow designed to withhold his worship until God has fulfilled all the promises.

In the ancient Near East, vows were not simply formal promises, as we think of them, but conditional bargains in which a person, usually in a state of exigency, asked a favor from God and promised something in return, but only if God granted the request.

From pillow to pillar: Jacob's act of setting up a stone pillar to mark a sacred spot follows a familiar pattern in the Old Testament. Laban would later set up a pillar as a witness to his final parting from Jacob (Gen. 31:51-52). Samuel set up a stone called "Ebenezer" (stone of help) to commemorate God's aid in a victory over the Philistines (1 Sam. 7:12). Later, Absalom set up a pillar as a memorial to himself (2 Sam. 18:18).

Pillars were commonly associated with the worship of Baal or other foreign gods, however (2 Kgs. 3:2, 10:26-27), so in time the process came to be frowned upon: Deut. 16:22 forbids it.

Earlier, when Jacob persuaded his brother Esau to trade his birthright for a bowl of stew (25:29-34), Jacob had sealed the deal by requiring him to swear an oath. Now, before he fully accepts God's offer, Jacob initiates a conditional vow designed to bind God to the previous promises: he wants to see the promises fulfilled before he agrees to join his forbears in acknowledging and worshiping God.

We can't help but note that Jacob's vow (vv. 20a-22) does not mention the central pledge of land or progeny. Instead, Jacob focuses on God's promises of personal patronage and divine protection. This seems to underscore Jacob's self-centered nature. Not only does he focus on personal aspects of the promises, but he also intensifies them. Not satisfied with God's general promise to "watch over" him, Jacob asks specifically for food and clothing. Not satisfied to know that God will bring him back to the land, Jacob asks that he be brought back "in peace."

Though raised in a family of Yahweh worshipers, Jacob holds out even his acceptance of Yahweh as God until he sees the promises fulfilled. In this way, the vow also serves as a framing device for much of the narrative that follows. The vow will be mentioned again in 31:13, when God reminds Jacob of it and tells him to return home, and it is not completed until 35:1-7, when Jacob finally returns to Bethel, builds an altar and offers sacrifices after a peaceful reception by his brother Esau.

Two questions

Chances are that none of us have had an experience such as Jacob's. We haven't slept in the wilderness with our head on a rock or awakened to a vision of God standing beside our bedroll, promising to make us the progenitor of a nation.

So, why do we bother to study this text? What can we learn from it?

Reading this story suggests that we never know where we might meet God, or at least, feel an overpowering sense of the divine. There is nothing we can do to reach God, but the Bible insists that God can reach us, that heaven may come down to meet us in the midst of our need and our fear and our running away. [**Awakening to the presence of God**]

Jacob learned that he could run from his brother, but he could not run from God. God came to Jacob in the

> **Awakening to the presence of God:** Consider Elizabeth Achtemeier's comment on Jacob's surprise visit from God:
>
> "Jacob wakes with a shudder, and in shivering awe he comes to the realization that this is none other than the place where heaven and earth meet. This is the gate of heaven. The Lord has invaded my world, he realizes. I am not alone on this journey.
>
> "Somewhere on our journey through life, we all have had a similar experience –that heaven has invaded our ordinary realm, that we are not alone in our world, but that we are accompanied on our pilgrimage by a mysterious presence, whose name is Jesus Christ. Surely if ever heaven descended to this earth, it did so in that man of Nazareth, and now he walks the road with us, as we go on our common journeys" (*Preaching from the Old Testament* [Westminster/John Knox, 1989], 65).

middle of nowhere, bringing surprising words of grace and promise and a future. Even when Jacob responded with a guarded vow that showed his own lack of trust, God did not give up on him, and neither does God give up on us.

As we walk our common journeys, as we run from our fears, as we pursue our dreams, God comes to us. Sometimes, when we least expect it, God comes to us in the form of a person or a dream or a sudden conviction or even a sermon that touches the heart. When God comes, we may not respond with great maturity or faith – we may try to work the same kind of distrustful deal with God that Jacob did – but God accepts what trust we have, and continues to work with us and lead us to other times when we may meet God again and grow in our devotion.

A second thing to observe is that the text virtually shouts of blessing. Jacob had done nothing to deserve God's beneficence. Indeed, one would think that his conniving ways would have earned him some sort of divine retribution. But, the story suggests that it was in God's mind to bless Jacob as the chosen one to become the head of a new nation. Although Jacob had to leave home and would gain wealth through his wits and work rather than an inheritance from Isaac, he was blessed in many ways.

We should note that Esau was also blessed. Although he did not receive his father's official blessing to the first-born, with Jacob's departure he inherited everything. This gave to Esau even more property than he would have had if the estate had been divided the normal way, with the older son getting twice the share of the younger.

Esau's behavior was no more commendable than Jacob's: he is roundly criticized for marrying two Hittite women and making life bitter for Isaac and Rebekah (26:34-35). Yet, he is also blessed.

Can you think of ways in which God has blessed you, even though you can also think of ways in which you have fallen short of God's purposes for you?

The Hardest Question
What about the angels on the ladder?

The story of Jacob's dream says that "he dreamed that there was a ladder set up on the earth, the top of it reaching to heaven; and the angels of God were ascending and descending on it" (v. 12). What is the significance of this?

As noted above, the word translated as "ladder" (*sullām*) could probably mean either "ladder" or "stairway." The word is a *hapax legomena* – this is the only time it appears in the Old Testament. To translate, we rely on both context and any cognates we can find.

The context indicates some type of structure that reaches from earth to heaven, broad enough for angels to pass each other while going up and coming down. This clearly implies a staircase. Ladders are typically narrow and designed for one person.

The angels, or "messengers of God" (*mal'akê 'elohîm*), do not appear to have wings in this account, necessitating a visionary structure for conveyance. The image of angels climbing a ladder is comical enough: the picture of them working around each other while ascending and descending – all the way from heaven to earth and back – seems even more ludicrous.

The Hebrew word *m'sillâ*, apparently from the same root, is commonly used to mean a "raised way" or "highway." The Akkadian cognate *simmiltu* is a specialized word that means "stairway" or "ramp." Thus, it seems clear that the dream does not depict angels stumbling over each other on a ladder – unless it was a truly magnificent ladder that was easily traversed – but making their way up and down a broad staircase or ramp.

But what are these "messengers of God" doing in the story? On the one hand, they reflect the belief that God sometimes either sent an angel or appeared in the form of an angel when communicating with humans or carrying out divine business. An angel appeared to Hagar in the desert (Genesis 16 and 21). No less than three angels (one of them God) appeared to Abraham (Genesis 18), then two of them went on to rescue Lot and wreak havoc against Sodom and Gomorrah (Genesis 19). An angel appeared in the nick of time to stay Abraham's hand as he was about to sacrifice Isaac at God's command (Genesis 22).

All of these stories are derived from the Yahwist or Elohist sources, with J describing an "angel of Yahweh" and E depicting an "angel of God." Both sources give the impression that such encounters were a theophany in which the deity appeared in the form of an angel, and that seems to be the case in Genesis 28, where Jacob sees angels traveling between heaven and earth before realizing that Yahweh is standing beside him (or possibly, upon the ladder/staircase).

In relating Jacob's dream imagery, the story implies a belief that there is constant contact between heaven and earth, and the gap is easily crossed by divine messengers. Jacob appears to have interpreted the vision in a localized sense, thinking he had happened upon the very gateway to heaven and the house of God on earth, albeit an invisible one (v. 17), leading him to name the place *bêth-el*, or "House of God."

Jacob's vow implied that if God followed through on the promises, he would return to Bethel and establish the pillar he had erected as the heart of a sanctuary where he would pay tithes (v. 22).

The vow was not fulfilled until many years later, as related in Gen. 35:1-8, following a story of how Jacob's sons, led by Simeon and Levi, had connived to murder the men of Shechem despite previously peaceful relations. Afterward, the account says that God instructed Jacob to go on to Bethel and dwell there. After collecting and burying all foreign gods and related jewelry from the people with him, he was to build an altar in Bethel and worship God there. He did so, the text says, building an altar and naming the place "El Bethel" or "God of Bethel."

A following story from the Priestly source offers an alternate account of Jacob's encounter with God at Bethel. In it, God appeared to Jacob "when he came from Paddan-aram" and blessed him, renewing the promise of both progeny and property, and changing Jacob's name to "Israel." Afterward, Jacob reportedly set up a pillar of stone and consecrated it with oil and a drink offering as he named the place "Bethel" (Gen. 35:9-15). That story mentions no angels, saying only that "God appeared to Jacob" and later "God went up from him at the place where he had spoken with him" (Gen. 35:9, 13).

Optional First Reading
Psalm 139 (RCL 139:1-12, 23-24)*

A Life Exposed

Where can I go from your spirit? Or where can I flee from your presence? (Ps. 139:7)

How many people do you think know you very well – or do you think *anyone* really knows you? Even the most introverted among us want to be known by someone. Few things hurt worse than thinking no one understands us, and few things are more frustrating than feeling that we don't understand ourselves.

We can spend a lot of time and money in therapy, trying to gain insight from someone who is skilled at helping us to see things more clearly, and sometimes that's exactly what we need to do. Still, we would also like to feel known without resorting to professional help.

The poet who wrote today's text may have believed other people misunderstood him, but he was convinced that God knew him through and through. **[Why the gap?]**

Psalm 139's superscription reads "To/for the director, a psalm to/for/by David." The psalmist appears to stand accused by others but pleads with God for vindication. Imagining that David faced similar situations, the author connected it with Israel's most beloved king.

A close analysis of the psalm, however, reveals multiple words and constructions that are more common to late Hebrew than early, suggesting that the psalm may not have been composed until the postexilic period, when the influence of Aramaic on the Hebrew language was becoming more evident.

The form of the psalm is hard to pin down. The first 18 verses are hymnic and include elements of praise, while vv. 19-24 are more like a lament. Scattered throughout are elements of Israel's wisdom literature, including images common to the book of Job. Overall, the psalm should be read as the personal prayer of someone who appears to have been accused of wrongdoing, but who feels innocent of the charges. We can imagine him coming into the sanctuary and offering this prayer, asserting that the God who knows him from stem to stern, both inside and out, should also affirm his innocence.

A knowing God
(vv. 1-6)

There are times when we wish God did not know us so well: it's hard to plead innocence when we know we are guilty, or to claim faithfulness when we know how often we fall – and we assume that God knows us even better than we know ourselves.

Why the gap? The lectionary text for this lesson, "Proper 11A," is Ps. 139:1-12, 23-24. But why leave out the beautiful soliloquy of vv. 13-18, where the psalmist rhapsodizes on how God knew him from the womb, and how he was "fearfully and wonderfully made"? The lectionary includes that text as an option on three other Sundays –Epiphany 2B, Proper 4B, and Proper 18C – but avoids the troublesome theme of vv. 19-22 altogether.

Psalm 139 appears here because of its reference to God's presence both in heaven and on earth, reflecting the story of Jacob's dream in the first reading for the day.

Rather than chop up the psalm, we'll consider it as a unit for each of those Sundays.

---

*Psalm 139:1-5, 12-17 is also read for the Second Sunday of Epiphany and Proper 4 in Year B, and for Proper 18 in Year C. This commentary includes the entire chapter.

When we feel wrongly accused, however, we long for others to understand our position, especially God. It is probably in that setting that we are to imagine the psalmist coming before God and praying "O LORD, you have searched me and known me" (v. 1).

The psalmist waxes eloquent on the extent to which he believes God's knowledge extends. He imagines that God is in the heavens, far away from earth, and yet God knows not only whether he sits or stands, but also every thought in his head (v. 2). No matter where he travels, where he sleeps, or what he does, God knows about it (v. 3) before the psalmist does: "Even before a word is on my tongue, O LORD, you know it completely" (v. 4).

Verse 5 suggests that the psalmist may have been ambivalent about God's pervasive knowledge: the terms used for "you hem me in" often describe a restrictive situation, and the notion of God's hand being laid on someone can have negative connotations. The petitioner appears to think of God's fencing him in as more protective than oppressive, however. He speaks of God's knowledge as being "too wonderful for me," and "so high that I cannot attain it" (v. 6).

A present God
(vv. 7-12)

God is not only aware of the psalmist's every thought and action, the poet writes, but also present with him. He imagines what it would be like to try running away from God, or to hide from God's spirit (v. 7). He thinks first on a vertical axis: if he could ascend as high as the heavens, or to the depths of Sheol, he would find God there (v. 8). The ancients did not think of Sheol as a place of blessedness in the presence of God, but as a shadowy place for the dead, where there were neither rewards nor punishments. Even so, the psalmist believes that Sheol exists under God's sovereignty, and not apart from God's presence.

With v. 9, the poet thinks horizontally: if he should "take the wings of the morning" (a reference to the East) or venture to the farthest limits of the sea (the West), he would not be beyond God's presence or care: "even there your hand shall lead me, and your right hand shall hold me fast" (v. 10). [**East and West**]

If distance is no obstacle to God, what about darkness? Could the psalmist hide from God under the cover of night? (v. 11). No, for "even the darkness is not dark to you; the night is as bright as the day, for darkness is as light to you" (v. 12). God's presence and perception knows no bounds. Distance means nothing, and darkness means less: no one can hide from God.

Do you find such thoughts to be comforting, or intrusive? Do you delight in believing that God knows your every move, or does the idea seem suffocating? The psalmist takes a mainly positive approach: he does not think of God as a nosy neighbor or an invasive voyeur, but as one who knows his heart and who cares about his well-being.

A creating God
(vv. 13-18)

The prayerful person behind Psalm 139 believed that God not only knew him thoroughly, but also had known him from the very beginning – and was in fact involved in his creation: "for it was you who formed my inward parts; you knit me together in my mother's womb" (v. 12). This verse is often cited by people who oppose abortion in any circumstance to affirm a belief that every fertilized egg should be regarded as a fully human being. That goes well beyond the intent of the psalmist, who was not arguing the extent to which personhood begins at conception, or that God inspires every conception. His purpose was to revel in the thought that God had known him and had been involved in his life from the womb.

The following verse, though much beloved, is notoriously difficult to translate. The NRSV, following close to the KJV, reads this way: "I praise you, for I am fearfully and wonderfully made. Wonderful are your works: that I know very well" (v. 14; NIV 11 and HCSB are similar).

East and West: When reading the Old Testament, we should remember that the biblical authors wrote from the perspective of their geographical location – including an assumption that the earth was huge but flat and limited in size, covered by a dome-like firmament.

Whether in Palestine or Babylon, Hebrew writers would observe the sun rising in the East, thus "the wings of the morning" would suggest a location as far east as one could go. Likewise, from either Palestine or Babylon, the Mediterranean Sea was to the West. To "settle at the farthest limits of the sea" would be to go as far west as one could go. From one end to the other, the psalmist believed, God was present.

An alternate translation attributes the fearsome wonder to God rather than the psalmist's frame: "I will give you thanks because your deeds are awesome and amazing. You knew me thoroughly" (NET).

The first words of v. 14, "I will praise you, because …" are clear. What comes after that is a puzzle. There is no word corresponding to "made," which translators sometimes supply to make sense of the verse. The first word after "because" or "for" is a reflexive (*nifal*) participle from a verb that means "to fear." In this form, it can mean "to be fearful" or "to be filled with dread." The next word is the *nifal* form of a verb that usually means "to be wonderful," "to be difficult," or "to be distinct." As the text stands, it is a finite verb in the first person, so it could mean "I am awesome" or "I am distinct." The next word appears to be a participle formed from the same verb, meaning "one being amazing."

A literal reading of the whole phrase could be "because fearsomely, I am awesome! Amazing are your works!" Some early translators, whether following a different text or believing the verb should be read as applying to God rather than the psalmist, emended the verb to second person so it could be translated: "because fearsomely, you are awesome!"

However we read the verse, the point is clear: God's work is frighteningly impressive and extends even into the womb. As a result, the poet believed that nothing about him could be hidden from God, whose vision can penetrate not only the womb, but also the "depths of the earth" (v. 15), where he claims, poetically, to have been shaped.

The psalmist believed that God could see his future as well as his past. From the time "Your eyes beheld my unformed substance," he said, "In your book were written

---

Waking, or at the end? The latter part of v. 18 has proven itself a puzzle to translators. Poetry often uses awkward syntax, and can be difficult under the best of circumstances. The first part, though missing some elements common to prose, seems clear: "I count them, they are greater than sand" must indicate something akin to "If I should count them (God's thoughts), they would outnumber the (grains of) sand."

The conundrum comes in the last phrase. A literal reading of the received text would be "I awaken, and I (am) still with you." Some scholars believe this makes little sense, and emend the verb to a proposed form of a different word meaning "to end." Thus, the NRSV has "I come to the end – I am still with you."

The NIV11 has a footnote regarding the alternate view, but stays with the received text: "When I awake, I am still with you." There is good reason for this. As it is, the text could make sense if we imagine the task the psalmist was up against. Some people count sheep to put themselves to sleep. If the psalmist had tried to count divine thoughts that outnumbered the sands of earth and sea, he would surely fall asleep long before he was done – and when he awoke, he and God would still be together.

---

all the days that were formed for me, when none of them as yet existed" (v. 16). [**Is our death predetermined?**]

How much of our future God knows may make for an interesting debate, but it doesn't matter in the end: the important thing is the confidence that God truly knows us, and God is with us through all the up-and-down days of our lives. Such thoughts are vast and weighty indeed (v. 17), far more than we can comprehend. Fortunately, we don't have to understand a host of divine thoughts that would outnumber every grain of sand on earth: in the end, we can believe that God is with us, and we are with God (v. 18). [**Waking, or at the end?**]

A searching God
(vv. 19-24)

Verses 19-22 seem out of joint and out of place. Having spent the major portion of the psalm praising God's perceptive omnipresence and creative power, the psalmist suddenly turns to an imprecatory tirade against wicked people, especially against "bloodthirsty" people who appear to be threatening him (v. 19), and those who speak maliciously against God (v. 20).

Is our death predetermined? Verse 16 seems to imply that God has set the course and extent of our lives, even before we are born. This seems overly deterministic. Whether God has a heavenly calendar with a death date for each of us already circled, we cannot know. Some people, like the psalmist, emphasize divine sovereignty and take comfort in the thought that God already knows how our life will turn out, and how long it will last. Others lean more to a belief that God grants each of us the freedom to make our own decisions – choices that can clearly impact the length of our lives. If someone's life is shortened by preventable diseases because he or she insisted on chain-smoking, eating with abandon, and avoiding exercise, should we blame God for that?

As noted above, the psalmist appears to have come before God in hopes of being vindicated against some sort of charges that had been brought against him. He began the psalm by saying, in so many words, "You know me, O God. You have always known me. I can't even comprehend how well you know me and everyone else."

Now we learn that "bloodthirsty" and "malicious" people not only seek his harm, but also speak against God. The psalmist wants it known that he is on God's side, and God knows that he is innocent. He hates those whom he believes God hates, and he counts them as enemies (vv. 21-22).

Though some of his earlier musings cast God's oversight as borderline oppressive, now he welcomes it, for he believes God will find him righteous and save him from his enemies. "Search me, O God, and know my heart; test me and know my thoughts. See if there is any wicked way in me, and lead me in the way everlasting" (vv. 23-24).

The word translated as "wicked" in v. 24 comes from a verbal root that means "to hurt" or "to cause pain." The word rendered "everlasting" often means "eternity," but can indicate both antiquity and the days to come.

The psalmist intentionally contrasts the "hurtful way" with the "everlasting (or ancient) way." Perhaps his enemies had accused him of causing pain or grief to others, but he challenges even God to find a hurtful bone in his body. The psalmist insists that is not the way he rolls: he prefers to walk in the way of God, the ancient way that leads throughout eternity.

Do you share the psalmist's confidence? Is your life so upright that your prayer could challenge God to search your heart and life for any harmful thought or motive? If so, congratulations! If not, what kind of prayer might be more appropriate?

The Hardest Question
Why does the psalmist say he was made "in the depths of the earth"?

The psalmist knows he was "knit together" in his mother's womb (v. 13), but also speaks of "being made in secret, intricately woven in the depths of the earth" (v. 15). Both expressions are metaphors, and while we are taught not to mix metaphors in writing, the Hebrews had no such concerns. The latter metaphor could reflect early beliefs about humans being made from the dust/clay of the earth, even though ancient people knew that babies grow inside of women.

Consider Job 10:8-11, which credits God with fashioning Job from dust: "Your hands fashioned and made me; and now you turn and destroy me. Remember that you fashioned me like clay; and will you turn me to dust again? Did you not pour me out like milk and curdle me like cheese? You clothed me with skin and flesh, and knit me together with bones and sinews."

In Job 1:26, Job declares his faithfulness despite the loss of his children and his wealth: "Naked I came from my mother's womb, and naked I shall return there. The LORD gave, and the LORD has taken away; blessed be the name of the LORD."

As it reads, Job's statement gives the impression that he believed he would die and return to his mother's womb, but this is manifestly not the case. He knows he will return to the earth, dust to dust. As we often speak of "mother earth," the ancients knew that we all in some way emerge from the earth and return to it. Human mothers are a crucial link in the cycle of life, which metaphorically begins in the earth and through burial returns to the earth. Earthly elements and women's wombs do not act alone in creating life, however: the psalmist believed that God was intimately involved throughout the process.

Season after Pentecost: Proper 11

Second Reading
Isaiah 44:6-20 (RCL 44:6-8)

The Real Thing

Thus says the LORD, the King of Israel, and his Redeemer, the LORD of hosts:
I am the first and I am the last; besides me there is no god. (Isa. 44:6)

Idolatry: It's not a word that often comes to mind, not one we would typically apply to our lives. But it's the subject of this Sunday's second reading. Why should we care? Why should we not? Perhaps we're not as guiltless as we think. Read on.

The first and only God
(vv. 6-8)

When one lives in a land that worships many gods, how to choose between them? Isaiah 44 falls in a section that was probably written in the last years of the Babylonian exile, and it contains several confrontational speeches in which the prophet speaks for the God of Israel, insisting that Yahweh is the only true god, and that all others are pretenders (41:1-5, 41:21-28, 43:8-15). The oracle in 44:6-8 takes up the same theme, along with elements of salvation or encouragement for Israel. [**Second Isaiah – and others?**]

The speech begins with God's self-identification as "Yahweh of hosts," both the king and redeemer of Israel (v. 6). The use of "redeemer" would remind the exiles that God had stepped in as a loyal kinsman and delivered Israel before. The same Yahweh who had brought the Israelites from captivity in Egypt could bring them home from Babylon. The same God who had defeated Philistines and Ammonites and Syrians in Israel's behalf could deliver them again.

The naming of God as "king" was a reminder that God's rule was unchanged. Israel was in bondage because of God's discipline, not because of God's weakness. Israel owed Yahweh both loyalty and service.

> **Second Isaiah – and others?** Today's text comes from the second major section of the Book of Isaiah (chs. 40–55), often referred to as "Second Isaiah" or "Deutero-Isaiah."
>
> Both textual and thematic clues make it evident that these chapters belong to the late exilic period, shortly before Cyrus conquered the Babylonians and allowed the Israelites to return home. Some elements of the text may have been added even later.
>
> A close reading suggests that Isa. 44:1-22 contains multiple oracles and other bits that have been stitched together as the document grew. Some scholars regard vv. 1-8 as a single unit, while others believe vv. 1-5 form a discrete unit, and that v. 6, introduced by the typical oracle formula "Thus says the LORD," begins a new oracle extending through v. 8.
>
> It's obvious to a careful reader that vv. 9-20 have a different style. While the prior verses are clearly poetic, vv. 9-20 read as prose. There are some poetic elements, namely occasional bits of repetition characteristic of Hebrew poetry, but the meter is uneven and clearly unlike that of the verses on either side.
>
> Some scholars believe vv. 21-22 belong with vv. 6-8 as the concluding part of a salvation oracle, having been separated when the satirical essay against idolatry (vv. 9-20) was inserted.
>
> The lectionary chooses vv. 6-8 as a stand-alone oracle, but the following send-off of idolatry is too juicy for us to ignore, so we'll include it in our study for today.

The introduction to the oracle, then, calls for faithfulness even as it offers hope in the one true God: "I am the first and I am the last; besides me there is no god" (v. 6b). The expression "the first and the last" is a merism, a figure of speech in which two very different things are named (like "good and evil" or "heaven and earth"), but we are to large effigies ensconced on platforms in the innermost sanctums. The images were commonly made from a wooden core covered with thin plates of iron, bronze, silver, or gold. [**Images**]

Verse 7 is a direct challenge to such gods, as Yahweh asks the demanding question: "Who is like me? Let them proclaim it, let them declare it and set it forth before me."

The first evidence of the other gods' impotence is their inability to speak or to answer Yahweh's challenge.

In contrast, the God of Israel not only speaks, but also announces in advance what will happen. In other settings, the proof of a true prophet is that when he speaks for God, his words come true (Deut. 18:22, 1 Sam. 3:19, Isa. 48:3-5, Jer. 28:9, Ezek. 33:33). Here, it is the test of a true god: Can other deities declare what is yet to come? Yahweh issues a dare: "Let them tell us what is yet to be."

With v. 8, the prophet addresses the exiles, but on the same theme. Still speaking for God, he tells them not to fear, but to remember: "Have I not told you from before and declared it? You are my witnesses!"

Prophets who spoke for Yahweh had long predicted that Israel's faithlessness would lead them to national ruin and to exile. The deportees to whom the prophet spoke were witnesses that the forecast of national judgment had come to pass.

If God could send the people into exile, however, God's power could surely bring them out. Returning to the thought of v. 7, Yahweh asks "Is there any God besides me? There is no other rock; I know not one."

The image of God as a steadfast rock was common to Hebrew thought, especially in the Psalms, including Ps. 18:31, which echoes Isaiah: "For who is God except the LORD? And who is a rock besides our God?" [**God as a rock**]

The prophet's challenge remains as pertinent today as it did to those who lived and mourned by the waters of Babylon more than 2,500 years ago. Exile can take many shapes, not all of them related to physical captivity. Broken relationships leave us feeling exiled from others. Depression can be as isolating as solitary confinement. Poverty brings its own kind of exile.

In bleak times of relational, emotional, economic, or spiritual exile, where do we turn? Can we also trust in the

Images: Images of the gods from temples would typically have been covered with precious metal and carried away as trophies of war or melted down. Few of those, and only very small ones, have survived. Stone images of the gods or their representations are more common.

As one example, the *Queen of the Night*, also known as *the Burney Relief*, is often thought to be a representation of Ishtar, or possibly, Eresh-kigal. (Image courtesy of the British Museum, Creative Commons license.)

understand that the reality includes everything in between. There was no god before Yahweh, and there will be none after: it stands to reason that there are likewise no other gods between those times. Similar expressions are found in Isa. 41:4, 43:12, 48:12 and in Rev. 1:8, 1:17, 22:13.

While v. 6 is addressed to Israel, v. 7 is directed toward any would-be gods the people might be tempted to worship. The Babylonians recognized many gods, from leading deities such as Marduk and Ishtar to minor ones like Ninkasi and Ninkilim, the goddess of beer and the god of rats.

Individuals kept small statuettes of personal gods in their homes, but massive temples to deities like Shamash (the sun god) and Ishtar (goddess of love and war) featured

---

God as a rock: The prophetic oracles of Isa. 44:1-8 echo themes from Deuteronomy 32, which portrays a sermon in which Moses drew heavily on the metaphor of God as a rock, beginning with v. 4: "The Rock, his work is perfect, and all his ways are just ..."

Moses charged that Jacob's descendants had abandoned God and "scoffed at the Rock of his salvation" (Deut. 32:15). They were "unmindful of the Rock that bore you" (Deut. 32:18), and fell before their enemies only when "their Rock had sold them, and Yahweh had given them up" (Deut. 32:30).

As Israel faced enemies, Moses reportedly said "Their rock is not like our Rock," (Deut. 32:31 – the upper and lower case letters for "rock/Rock" are provided by translators). God would disperse Israel's enemies, Moses said, and afterward would ask "Where are their gods, the rock in which they took refuge ...?" (Deut. 32:37).

The similarity between Isaiah's oracle and Moses' speech extends to a rare term for the people of Israel, "Jeshurun." The moniker appears only four times in scripture: at Deut. 32:15 and 33:5, and Isa. 44:2. In both Deut. 32:15 and Isa. 44:2, Jeshurun is used in parallel with Jacob.

The meaning of the name "Jeshurun" is probably "upright ones," derived from the Hebrew verb *yāshar*, "to be upright." A note in the NET describes it as a "term of affection," citing M. Mulder, who wrote that it speaks of Israel "in an ideal situation, with its 'uprightness' due more to God's help than his own efforts" (*Theological Dictionary of the Old Testament*, vol. 6 [Eerdmans, 1974], 475).

God of Israel as the eternal one who will never forsake us, a rock on which we can stake our hope and build our future?

Is there any other god in whom we can trust?

The trouble, we know, is that we all have tried other gods. We have sought to find peace and fulfillment and happiness in other people, in financial security, in pleasure, or in enlightenment.

We have tried these things, and found them little more capable than the gods who inhabited Babylonian temples, to which we now turn.

The fake and phony gods
(vv. 9-20)

The style of the text shifts sharply with v. 9. While vv. 6-8 are written in the poetic form of an oracle, vv. 9-20 read like a satirical essay on the foolishness of idolatry. The text is so different in approach that most critical scholars consider it a later addition, and its sarcasm is so biting that one doubts it would have been added while the author was still living among the people he was mocking.

Those who make idols are "nothing," the writer says, "and the things they delight in do not profit." The word translated as "nothing" is the same term (*tōhû*) that describes the empty formlessness existing before creation (Gen. 1:1). The expression "does not profit" was a favorite of Israel's wisdom teachers: something that does no good is useless.

While the people of Israel were witnesses of Yahweh's mighty acts of deliverance (v. 8), the writer insists that idol worshippers have nothing to talk about. Their "witnesses neither see nor know" because their gods do nothing to be seen or experienced, offering their worshipers nothing but shame.

In the preceding oracle, Yahweh asked, "Who is like me?" Now the writer asks "Who would fashion a god or cast an image that can do no good?" (v. 10). Why would a human artisan make something that can do nothing and call it a god? (v. 11).

In the process of critiquing those who worship idols, the writer provides an interesting description of the craftsmen's work in fashioning them. The blacksmith works over a forge, shaping an image or hammering plate metal, so intent on his work that he neglects to eat or drink and grows weak (v. 12).

The unspoken question is, "How can a mortal man with failing strength make a god with divine powers?"

The woodworker takes a large block of wood and marks the parts to cut away, then shapes it into an image to be set up in a temple (v. 13). To illustrate the foolishness of the enterprise, the writer takes the image backward in time to when it was a tree in the forest, then a seedling to be planted and nourished by the rain (v. 14).

We can almost hear the writer laughing as he sets up the inanity of someone who starts with a tree trunk, chips and carves away to fashion an idol, then builds a fire to warm himself and roast his dinner from the scraps he had chipped away. Part of the wood he burns, and part of it he makes into an idol to which he bows and prays "Save me, for you are my god!" (vv. 15-17).

The silliness of the project seems mind-boggling to the writer, who cannot comprehend how anyone could fail to understand its foolhardy nature (vv. 18-19). "He feeds on ashes," the author concludes. "A deluded mind has led him

<table>
<tr><td>

Where does God live? When you were a child, were you ever admonished not to run or speak loudly in church, because "This is God's house"? Have you passed on similar thoughts to children in your own life? Perhaps we should give more thought to statements that are well meaning, but could also be heard to imply that God lives only in certain holy places, rather than in the nitty-gritty of our daily lives.

</td></tr>
</table>

astray, and he cannot save himself or say, 'Is not this thing in my right hand a fraud?'" (v. 20).

The satire is overdone. None of the ancients who employed idols in their worship were foolish enough to think that the idol and the god were the same thing. The images used in worship were physical representations of what they believed to be a spiritual reality.

But the author has a point to make. The Hebrews were to be different. As far back as the second commandment, they were forbidden from making images to depict God. Still, humans have always wanted something to see or hold, and the Israelites were prone not only to acknowledging the idols of their neighbors, but of making images for the worship of Yahweh, also.

Christians also must be careful to remember that devotional objects are, in themselves, not sacred. Crosses, icons, and statues of saints may remind us of God – as do country chapels and soaring cathedrals – but they are neither God nor God's abode. **[Where does God live?]**

The true God is known through faithful acts of power and deliverance, Isaiah insisted, acts that were witnessed by ancestors and saints that have come before us. But the Israelites delivered from Egypt and the believers present at Pentecost are not the only witnesses. We also may know the joy of God's saving grace, the peace of God's presence, and the assurance of God's steadfast love.

Steeples and stained glass may be inspiring, but the God we seek is known through Spirit and power that changes hearts and lives: we are witnesses.

The Hardest Question
Were the Israelites guilty of idolatry?

The book of Deuteronomy retrospectively warns the Israelites against the worship of gods "made by human hands, objects of wood and stone that neither see, nor hear, nor

eat, nor smell" (Deut. 4:28). Consequences for following such gods would be serious: "If you do forget the LORD your God and follow other gods to serve and worship them, I solemnly warn you today that you shall surely perish" (Deut. 8:19, among many others). Those who enticed family members, friends, or neighbors to worship other gods should be executed on the spot, according to Deut. 13:6-9.

Idolatry was serious business, but incredibly tempting, because the Old Testament charges Israel with constantly going after other gods. Judges 2:12, for example, says "they abandoned the LORD, the God of their ancestors, who had brought them out of the land of Egypt; they followed other gods, from among the gods of the peoples who were all around them, and bowed down to them; and they provoked the LORD to anger." Similar charges can be found in narratives such as Judg. 2:17-19, 10:13; 1 Sam. 8:8; 1 Kgs. 9:9, 14:9; and 2 Kgs. 22:17 – to name a few.

The prophets often accused the Hebrews of abandoning Yahweh for other gods, which inevitably involved images of some sort. Jeremiah became livid at the thought of Israelites making offerings to other gods: "The children gather wood, the fathers kindle fire, and the women knead dough, to make cakes for the queen of heaven; and they pour out drink offerings to other gods, to provoke me to anger" (Jer. 7:18, one among many references to the worship of other gods in Jeremiah).

Other gods were named, including Baal (Hos. 11:2, Zeph. 1:4) and Astarte (Judg. 2:13, 10:6; 1 Sam. 7:3-4), and Asherah (2 Kgs. 23:4-7). Citing every text that criticizes idolatry in Israel would make for long and boring reading.

Perhaps it is more pertinent to consider the ways in which Hebrews of the Old Testament period sometimes employed images in their worship of Yahweh. Although the second commandment made it clear that the Hebrews were not to make images of God, the people struggled to obey, as we can see in a string of Old Testament stories.

Narrative accounts describe an inherent inclination toward idolatry: while Moses was still on Mount Sinai receiving the law, according to Exodus 32, the Israelites persuaded Aaron to fashion a golden calf to represent the god who had delivered them from Egypt. Although their intentions may have been good, the radical nature of Moses' violent response (32:25-29) was designed to reveal the seriousness of the matter.

While still in the wilderness, after God sent a plague of serpents in response to Israel's persistent complaints, Moses prayed for God to remove the serpents. Instead, God told Moses to fashion a bronze serpent and put it on a pole as a promise of healing for those who looked upon it (Num. 21:4-9). In time, however, the people began to worship the image, calling it "Nehushtan." Later, during a time of religious reform, Hezekiah ordered it to be destroyed (2 Kgs. 18:4).

In the book of Judges, after Gideon led Israel to victory over their oppressors, he refused their offer to become king but foolishly took gold booty from the victims and fashioned an "ephod" from it. Gideon set up the image in his hometown, "and all Israel prostituted themselves to it there, and it became a snare to Gideon and his family" (Judg. 8:26-27). Gideon, who had once destroyed an altar to Baal and an Asherah pole belonging to his father, apparently made the image in honor of Yahweh, who had given him the victory, but "it became a snare" to the people.

When internal division led to a separation between the northern and southern tribes, Jeroboam became the first king of the northern kingdom, which came to be known as Israel, while the southern kingdom was called Judah. Not wanting his subjects to travel to Jerusalem (in Judah) to worship, Jeroboam had temples built for their use in Bethel and Dan, each containing a golden calf (1 Kgs. 12:25-33). The calves were almost certainly intended to be representative of Yahweh, but it was still regarded as a great sin. The authors of 1–2 Kings judged all later kings of Israel on the basis of whether they turned aside "from the sins of Jeroboam son of Nebat, which he caused Israel to commit – the gold calves that were in Bethel and in Dan" (2 Kgs. 10:29, among others).

Even things made with Yahweh's consent and direction were subject to misuse, as with the bronze serpent mentioned above. The Ark of the Covenant was thought of as the "footstool" (1 Chron. 28:2) or "mercy seat" above which God could be met (Exodus 25–26). When threatened by the Philistines, the elders persuaded Eli's sons to carry it into battle as a symbol of God's presence, thinking that God would not allow the sacred Ark to be captured. The strategy seemed promising, as the Philistine opponents grew afraid and shouted, "Gods have come into the camp!" To show displeasure, however, Yahweh allowed the Philistines to defeat the Israelites and capture the Ark.

Israel's struggles with idolatry, as noted in the lesson, are not unique. We all struggle with the temptation to assign sacred significance to things, whether crosses or churches or even (especially) the Bible. Things may remind us of God or teach us about God, but they should never be confused with God.

Season after Pentecost: Proper 11

Optional Second Reading
Psalm 86 (RCL 86:11-17)*

The Up Side of Down Days

*Psalm 86:1-10, 16-17 is read on Proper 7 of Year A.
A commentary on Psalm 86 is included in this volume under that Sunday.*

Third Reading
Romans 8:12-25*

In the Flesh, of the Spirit

... for if you live according to the flesh, you will die; but if by the Spirit you put to death the deeds of the body, you will live. (Rom. 8:13)

Children often bear a physical likeness to their parents: "She looks just like her mother," we say, or "He gets his height from his grandfather." We know that genetics play a role in physical similarities among family members, but adopted children may also take on noticeable characteristics of their parents. We can often see the similarity in their politeness (or lack of it), and sometimes in their general approach to life in general, whether positive or negative.

None of that is surprising, but we also know that children may choose to rebel and try to be everything that their parents are not: they may look like their parents, but not act like them. A well-behaved model child and a full-throated rebel can emerge from the same set of siblings.

Today's text happens to include references to God as Father, to Christ, and to the Spirit, so it is often read on Trinity Sunday. The purpose of the text, however, is not to explain the Trinity, but to talk about what it means to be children of God.

Children of flesh
(vv. 12-13)

Paul's language may seem strange to us: How often do we use the word "flesh"? The word Paul used is *sarx*. In the most basic sense, it was the graphic Greek term to describe bodily flesh, though it could be used of the body in general.

Paul gave the term a metaphorical sense by applying it to human nature, especially in its negative aspects.

In essence, Paul's argument is straightforward. He was calling on believers to live a righteous and holy life for the simple reason that they belonged to God, and not to the flesh, or to the world.

It's easy for us to excuse all kinds of behavior by saying "it's just human nature," or "I can't help myself." Paul insisted that we are not obligated to follow the weaker or more salacious aspects of human nature: we are not "debtors" to our human condition, "to live according to the flesh" (v. 12). While we are by nature *in* the flesh, we are not obligated to be *of* the flesh by surrendering to every bodily temptation.

Instead, we have an option, and a much better one that we would be wise to choose: "for if you live according to the flesh, you will die; but if by the Spirit you put to death the deeds of the body, you will live" (v. 13).

Note that Paul spoke to his readers as "brothers," in a sense that clearly indicated both brothers and sisters (as in NRSV, NIV 11, NET). Paul recognized that he was in the same boat as other believers, using the pronoun "we" to include himself in the conversation.

Paul knew, as we do, that all of us who live in human skin are destined to die, but he clearly had in mind more than the physical death of the body. We may all succumb in a physical sense, but if we put our trust in God's Spirit

---

Romans 8:12-17 is read on Trinity Sunday in Year B.

A similar thought: Moses, according to the Deuteronomist, also admonished the Israelites to choose between life and death:

"See, I set before you today life and prosperity, death and destruction. For I command you today to love the LORD your God, to walk in obedience to him, and to keep his commands, decrees and laws; then you will live and increase, and the LORD your God will bless you in the land you are entering to possess.

"But if your heart turns away and you are not obedient, and if you are drawn away to bow down to other gods and worship them, I declare to you this day that you will certainly be destroyed. You will not live long in the land you are crossing the Jordan to enter and possess.

"This day I call the heavens and the earth as witnesses against you that I have set before you life and death, blessings and curses. Now choose life, so that you and your children may live and that you may love the LORD your God, listen to his voice, and hold fast to him. For the LORD is your life, and he will give you many years in the land he swore to give to your fathers, Abraham, Isaac and Jacob" (Deut. 30:15-20, NIV 11).

rather than human inclinations, we may live in other ways, including eternally.

In a similar message to the Galatians, Paul had written: "If you sow to your own flesh, you will reap corruption from the flesh; but if you sow to the Spirit you will reap eternal life from the Spirit" (Gal. 6:8).

One could argue that the abundant life we can know in Christ is also qualitatively different than life that is limited to what the world has to offer, but Paul is probably looking toward eternity.

As a former rabbi, Paul may have intentionally called upon the rhetoric of Deuteronomy, where a sermon attributed to Moses includes a similar challenge for the Israelites to choose life and prosperity over death and destruction by loving God and obeying the commandments (Deut. 30:15-20). **[A similar thought]**

The admonitions of both Paul and Moses move from a righteous life to the promise of an inheritance, but while Israel was promised (through obedience) a land to call their home, Christ-followers are promised (through the Spirit) that they will become "heirs of God and joint heirs with Christ" (v. 18).

But what are these "deeds of the body" that Christians must overcome by the Spirit? The word *praxis* simply means

"actions" – things that we do. Here Paul uses the word *sōma* for "body" rather than *sarx*, possibly for variety, since *sōma* doesn't usually carry a negative connotation.

Eating, drinking, sleeping, and working could all qualify as "deeds of the body," but what Paul has in mind are those actions that feed human desires without thought for whether they are right or cause harm to others.

Only with the Spirit's help can we "put to death" selfish inclinations that threaten our very lives. We cannot fail to note that Paul was not directing these words as threats to unbelievers: he was writing to the church in Rome. Paul did not subscribe to the all-too-common notion that one could "accept Christ" as a fire insurance policy and then continue to behave as he or she wished. Following Jesus is serious business, and overcoming sin is a task that endures as long as we inhabit our bodies.

Children of God
(vv. 14-17)

While those who follow only human desires are doomed to experience only human life, Christ has made possible a better option: "For all who are led by the Spirit of God are children of God," Paul said (v. 14).

It's hard to comprehend that name, "children of God." Paul's readers would have been familiar with the concept. Greek royals and even renowned philosophers sometimes described themselves as favored sons of a patron god. Paul also used the masculine "sons," but it is clear that he had in mind all people.

Reflecting a belief in God's creative activity in the world, sometimes we speak of all people as "children of God," and there is a sense in which that is true – especially for those who are still children. But Paul had a deeper relationship in mind, not determined by our generic humanity, but by our specific choice to follow God's way, trusting in Jesus and being led by the Spirit.

Some ancients posited that the gods had created humans to be their servants, but Paul believed we have a higher calling: "For you did not receive a spirit of slavery to fall back into fear, but you have received a spirit of adoption. When we cry, 'Abba! Father!' it is that very Spirit bearing witness with our spirit that we are children of God ..." (vv. 15-16).

> **Cry "Abba! ... Father!"** The word translated as "cry" in v. 15 derives from *krazō*, which could mean "call out," "shout," or even "croak." It carries a sense of urgency, as when two blind men pursued Jesus "and shouted 'Have mercy on us'" (Matt. 9:27), or even when the disciples saw Jesus walking on the water through the storm, and "screamed" (Mark 6:49).
>
> Note also that "Father!" is not just a translation of "Abba!" but represents an emphatic cry in both Aramaic and Greek: "*Abba! Ho patēr!*" Sometimes, in our own sense of urgency or fear, we may cry "Jesus! Lord," or "Oh God–Jesus!"
>
> Paul wasn't suggesting that all prayer must derive from urgency, but wanted readers to know that God is like a caring parent who is always attentive to the children's cries.

Slaves are motivated by fear: the fear of punishment or starvation, the fear of being sold or separated from family, even the fear of death. Christian believers do not relate to God as slaves to their master, but as children to a loving parent.

The Jews of Paul's day did not call God "Father," even in prayer, considering such a term far too familiar. In fact, they avoided using God's name altogether, preferring circumlocutions such as "the Holy One, blessed be he," or even "the Name."

It may be hard for us to imagine how radical-sounding it was for Paul to suggest that we can call God not only "Father," but also "Abba" – an Aramaic term equivalent to "Daddy." Paul wanted to emphasize how close a relationship we can have with God when we choose to be Spirit-led rather than self-led. **[Cry "Abba! ... Father!"]**

If we are children of God, Paul went on to say, then we are also "heirs, heirs of God and joint heirs with Christ" (v. 17a). What does that even mean? In one sense, it could mean that we experience the glory of God that was lost through sin. Christ knew and experienced God's glory. In

> **Who is crying?** When writing to the Galatians, Paul used similar language, with an interesting twist: "And because you are children, God has sent the Spirit of his Son into our hearts, crying, 'Abba! Father!' So you are no longer a slave but a child, and if a child then also an heir, through God" (Gal. 4:6-7).
>
> Note that in this text it is "the Spirit of his Son" who has "come into our hearts, crying, 'Abba! Father!'" While this sounds contradictory, it is not. Paul's message to the Romans emphasized that only when we are led by the Spirit can we cry to God in such a personal way.

his farewell prayer with and for the disciples, Jesus prayed for the Father to restore to him the glory he had known before (John 17:1, 5).

Elsewhere, Paul often connected our "inheritance" with participation in the kingdom of God, as in 1 Cor. 15:50, where he insisted that "flesh and blood cannot inherit the kingdom of God" (see also 1 Cor. 6:9-11, Gal. 5:21, Eph. 5:5).

Sharing in Christ's glory sounds amazing, but if we are to share Christ's glory, we are also to share in his suffering. We are joint heirs, Paul said, "if, in fact, we suffer with him so that we may also be glorified with him" (v. 17b). **[Who is crying?]**

What? *Suffer?* If we are to live in Christ, we take the difficult along with the delightful. Suffering was and is an inevitable part of God's purpose for Christ and the church. Paul told the Philippians, "I want to know Christ and the power of his resurrection and the sharing of his sufferings by becoming like him in his death" (Phil. 3:10).

Suffering, then, does not indicate defeat, but takes on a positive theological meaning. Here, Paul may have in mind more than the persecutions he and others would suffer. He has urged his readers to "put to death" their human desires. Giving up a life dedicated to pleasure may seem like suffering to some, but if one is not willing to resist temptation, how will he or she respond to real trouble?

Children of the future
(vv. 18-25)

Paul's call to a family relationship with God looks toward what he anticipates as a glorious future in vv. 18-25. Present sufferings could not compare with "the glory about to be revealed in us," he said (v. 18), probably reflecting a common belief that Jesus would return soon and bring in a new age.

Even creation itself "waits with eager longing for the revealing of the children of God," Paul said (v. 19), connecting a renewal of creation with "the freedom of the glory of the children of God" (v. 20-21).

In this, Paul connected the potential suffering of believers with an unusual reference to the suffering of creation, which he metaphorically described as "groaning in labor pains until now" (v. 22). As creation has groaned in anticipation of God's future, so Christians "groan inwardly" while waiting for the ultimate fulfillment of what it means to be adopted by God, "the redemption of our bodies" (v. 23).

Some might give up on a such a blessed future, Paul knew, and he could offer no hard evidence that his future vision was sure, so he emphasized the importance of hope. "It was in hope that we were saved," he said, not in certainty. "Now hope that is seen is not hope," he added, "For who hopes for what is seen?" (v. 24). If the future was now and we were bathed in the joy of heaven, there would be no need to hope for it, but that day has not arrived.

The glorious future Paul had discussed was not a proven certainty with a defined date of arrival, but a hope that could not be seen or proven. Still, it was worth suffering for and waiting for with patience, he said (v. 25).

People of an earlier age might have had some difficulty with Paul's metaphor of creation groaning, but those who now live in the "Anthropocene Age" – the one in which humans have begun to appreciably shape and change the earth – know the cost of pollution, depletion of resources, and runaway climate change. We see the weather changing and sea levels rising, and sense the earth groaning.

We may be less likely than Paul to anticipate Christ's return in our lifetime, but we can be confident that whatever future God has in store for us, it will be worth all our hopes.

The Hardest Question
Did Paul espouse a Trinity?

Romans 8:12-25 is shot through with references to God, to the Father, to Christ, and to the Spirit, and to "the Spirit of God." Even so, we cannot assume that Paul had a concept of the Trinity that matches the doctrines worked out in church councils hundreds of years later.

Paul did not try to explain the relationship between God, Christ, and the Spirit, but spoke of them all as aspects of divinity that relate to humankind. Nor can any of us fully explain how God the Father, Son, and Holy Spirit relate. God's nature remains a mystery beyond human comprehension.

One early attempt is associated with Sabellius, a third-century priest and theologian, who taught a doctrine that is sometimes called "modalism" or "modalistic Monarchianism." His idea was that God was perceived by believers as one of three ways of seeing one God. This is largely considered to be non-Trinitarian, because he did not argue for three distinct persons within the Godhead, but three different modes of perception for one God. This is not unlike the inadequate attempt to relate the Trinity to a man who can be a Father, a Son, and a husband – one person but perceived in three different ways.

Others, both ancient and modern, have suggested what some call a "Social Trinity," which posits that the three persons of the Godhead exist as three separate divine beings who live in a loving and cooperative relationship. The problem with this is that seems to give us three gods, not one.

Perhaps the most popular way of understanding the Trinity is a model that may be called the "Immanent" or "Ontological Trinity." This was the classical view of Augustine, later amplified by Karl Barth and others. It says that God should be thought of as three "persons" who share one "essence." That is, God is one, but is known to us through three "modes of being." Some commentators will find that satisfactory; to others it sounds like philosophical word games.

If it is hard for us to understand how one God could be manifest in three different ways, we must remember that we can hardly expect to understand all divine mysteries.

Perhaps the most profitable thing for us is not to worry too much about just how the Trinity works, but to ask ourselves, instead, why God chose to become known as Father, Son, and Holy Spirit.

I wonder if it is because God is willing to do whatever it takes to communicate with us and to lead us into relationship. The Old Testament testifies that God self-identified as one God, whose name is Yahweh. Thus, the *shema*, the core creed of Judaism, begins with "Hear O Israel, Yahweh is God, Yahweh is one!" Yet, God appeared in various ways: in a burning bush, in the form of a visiting messenger, from the midst of a whirlwind, in the form of an angel, in a still, small voice. One God was revealed in various ways.

In Jesus Christ, God was revealed in the form of a human person. People who have trouble relating to God as an invisible, heavenly creator may be able to connect much better when they see God's love through the eyes and the words of Jesus. We speak of Jesus' birth as the "Incarnation," which means that God became human in Jesus

Christ so that Jesus was both God and human at the same time – another concept that boggles our mind.

As Jesus prepared to leave the earth, he promised his followers that he would continue to relate to them through the Holy Spirit. In later scriptures, the Spirit is sometimes called the Spirit of God, and at other times the Spirit of Christ. To know the Holy Spirit's presence is to know Christ's presence, and to know God the Father's presence. The Spirit is the way in which God relates to us in this world, in this age. We speak of Father, Son, and Holy Spirit, but all are one in purpose, will, and love.

Fourth Reading
Matthew 13:24-30, 36-43

The World Needs Patience

Then the righteous will shine like the sun in the kingdom of their Father. Let anyone with ears listen! (Matt. 13:43)

D arn that Darnel – he goes out drinking every Saturday night and then shows up for church just in time to sing in the choir. Should such a weedy character be rooted out?

And what about Dannie? Everything can be going okay and then she pops up like a dandelion in a fescue lawn and starts some gossipy conversation that just ruins everything.

And don't get me started on Charlie. He kind of looks at everybody in a creepy sort of way that makes people uncomfortable. Wouldn't worship be better without him around?

Do such thoughts ever occur to you? We dig weeds out of our gardens and flower beds. Should we do the same in our churches? That's not a new question.

A practical question
(vv. 24-30)

The "parable of the wheat and the tares" is the second in a series of parables found in Matthew 13, and it appears only there among the biblical gospels. A shorter version of it appears in the apocryphal Gospel of Thomas, which adapted it from Matthew. **[Ins and outs]**

Matthew portrays parables as containing coded knowledge that would not be accessible to everyone. Thus, Jesus tells the story in public but explains it only in private conversation with his disciples.

The story is straightforward. Like the parables of the sower before it and the mustard seed that follows, it grows from the common experience of Galilean farmers.

A certain farmer planted a field of wheat, using good seed, but a subversive enemy came behind and sowed weeds

Ins and outs: The Gospel of Thomas reflects an early heresy known as "Gnosticism." The Gnostics claimed to have secret mystical knowledge that could enable the initiated to ascend through various spiritual "spheres" on their way to heaven. Gnostics made a clear division between those who were "in" and "out," those who had the secret knowledge and those on the outside. Thus, the Gospel of Thomas adapts the "wheat and weeds" parable from Matthew as a way of illustrating their idea of a separation between those with and without the Gnostic community. The parable appears in logion 57:

> Jesus said, "What the kingdom of the father resembles is a man who had a [good] (kind of) seed. His enemy came at night and scattered grass seed in with the good seed. The man did not let them pluck out the grass, saying to them, 'Do not, lest you (plural) go to pluck out the grass and then pluck out the wheat along with it. For, on the day of the harvest the grass will be obvious, and it will be plucked out and burned.'" (From Bentley Layton, *The Gnostic Scriptures: Ancient Wisdom for the New Age* [Doubleday, 1987], accessed at http://www.earlychristian writings.com/thomas/gospelthomas57.html.)

in the same field. As the plants neared maturity, the farmer's servants recognized weeds among the wheat and asked what should be done. The farmer understood that removing the weeds would damage the wheat, so he decided to let both grow until harvest time, when the two could be separated and used for different purposes.

A bit of background may help us understand this agrarian tale more clearly. Farmers in the ancient Middle East generally broadcast seed rather than planting in rows, and then plowed to turn the seed under.

The weed in question, called "tares" in the KJV, is designated by the Greek term *zizania*. It could refer to noxious weeds in general, but typically described a plant known as "darnel," a plague of ancient farmers. The grassy weed, also known as "bearded darnel" or "false wheat," is virtually indistinguishable from regular wheat when the plants are young. Only when heads of grain begin to form do their differences become apparent.

As they grow, the tough roots of the hardy darnel plant intertwine with the wheat. By the time the plants become distinguishable, the roots are so enmeshed that it's impossible to pull up one without the other.

The two have to be separated, though, because darnel seeds are poisonous. Ingesting them can cause dizziness, nausea, hallucinations, and in sufficient quantities even death.

So, despite the added labor, darnel had to be identified and separated from wheat as it was being harvested. Then it could be bundled up and used to fuel cooking fires or pottery kilns.

A cautionary answer
(vv. 36-43)

Everything makes good sense so far, though we might wonder what kind of enemy would be motivated to raise or find enough darnel seeds to sabotage someone's fields with harmful weeds.

The disciples wondered, too. The author has them wait while Jesus added the parable of the mustard seed and the parable of the leaven (vv. 31-33, readings for next week).

In vv. 34-35, Matthew returns to the idea that Jesus told parables – intentionally obscure in meaning – that were in keeping with divine instructions to Old Testament prophets that they should prophesy even though many would not understand them or accept their words (vv. 11-15).

Jesus' teaching fulfilled "what had been spoken through the prophet," the author wrote, citing: "I will open my mouth to speak in parables; I will proclaim what has been hidden from the foundation of the world."

The citation does not come from a prophetic book, but is adapted from Ps. 78:2: "I will open my mouth in a parable; I will utter dark sayings from of old." The psalm was attributed to Asaph, who "prophesied under the direction of the king" (David), according to 1 Chron. 25:2.

Jesus was regarded as a descendant of David, and Psalm 78 was largely a recital of God's saving acts in history, so early believers came to consider Jesus as the one who fulfilled God's ultimate work of salvation. Some also saw Ps. 78:1-2 as a prophecy of Jesus' teaching in parables, revealing hidden mysteries of God's work among humans.

After Jesus retreated from the crowds and entered a house – unidentified, but often thought of as Peter's home in Capernaum – the disciples asked him to explain "the parable of the weeds of the field."

What follows in Matthew is a strongly allegorical interpretation. Scholars are divided as to whether the interpretation goes back to Jesus, or to the author of Matthew's special source, or if it was the author's own interpretation of Jesus' words for his setting.

The allegory goes like this: The one who sowed the good seed is "the Son of Man" (Jesus), while the enemy who sowed weeds is the devil (*diabolos*). The field is the world, the good seed are "the children of the kingdom," and the weeds are "the children of the evil one."

The time of harvest represents the final judgment at the end of the age, when angels would separate the children of the kingdom from the children of the evil one. The latter would be thrown "into the furnace of fire, where there will be weeping and gnashing of teeth," while the righteous would "shine like the sun in the kingdom of their Father" (vv. 37-43).

Some readers may find it odd that angels would be involved in separating people for judgment, but they also appear in Matt. 24:30-31 as being dispatched to gather the elect in the eschaton. Angels are also described as having a role in judgment in Matt. 16:27 and 25:31-33.

Matthew was especially concerned about those who caused others to stumble (see 18:6-7), and in our text the angels gather "all causes of sin and all evil doers." The word behind "causes of sin" is *skándala*, from which we get the English words "scandal" and "scandalize." The translation "evildoers" is literally "those who do lawlessness." The word "lawlessness" comes from *anomía*, which is composed of the word for law (*nomos*) with the negative prefix *a*. They live without recognition or respect for the law – in this sense, biblical teachings of right and wrong.

The allegory makes use of stock phrases and images common to apocalyptic writings in the first century, includ-

Fire and sun: The image of the angelic reapers throwing the wicked into the fire (vv. 41 and 50) is taken from Dan. 3:6, where those who refused to worship the king's image would be thrown into a "fiery furnace." The developing concept of hell was drawn from the image of the valley of Hinnom (gê hinnōm in Hebrew and transcribed as Gehenna in Greek). Located on the southwest side of Jerusalem, the narrow valley was used for many years as the city's trash dump, where refuse was piled, dead animals or bodies were sometimes abandoned, and fires were perpetual. Jeremiah accused certain kings of Judah of having offered sacrifices to Baal and even sacrificing their children to Molech at a place called "Topheth" (which means "burning") in the Valley of Hinnom. Jeremiah cursed the valley, saying it would become a scene of slaughter and punishment (Jer. 7:30-34, 19:1-9). Not surprisingly, it came to symbolize a place of judgment.

The author of Matthew was particularly fond of the phrase "gnashing of teeth." He used it six times (8:12; 13:42, 50; 22:13; 24:51; 25:30), but it appears elsewhere only in Luke 13:28.

While judgment will bring punishment for the wicked, according to the text, the righteous will be rewarded, and will "shine like the sun in the kingdom of their Father" (v. 43). The verb for "shine" is the same one used of Jesus in Matthew's version of the Transfiguration story (17:2), and recalls a phrase from Dan. 12:3: "Those who are wise will shine like the brightness of the sky, and those who lead many to righteousness, like the stars forever and ever."

ing the concept of a supernatural evil power who opposed God and a burning hell for his followers. While some readers remain comfortable with such eschatological imagery, we may also recognize the metaphorical nature of some ancient concepts. We don't have to believe in a personal devil or that the loving God we worship will consign non-believers to eternal torment in order to understand the parable. **[Fire and sun]**

The primary point of the parable is not that there will be a judgment and an ultimate separation between good and evil: that was assumed. The intent of the parable is to answer the question of why such judgment was delayed, and to remind believers that judgment is God's business, not ours.

"The field is the world," Jesus is reported to have said. The most casual observance makes it clear that the world includes positive and productive people on the one hand, along with "bad seed" who muck things up on the other hand.

Sadly, the same is true of the church, which is within the world. As some have observed, the church is not "solely holy." Some members take Jesus seriously. They seek to live by his teachings, centering their worldviews and their lives around loving God and loving others as Jesus instructed us to do. They are generous with their time and their talents and their resources. They build community, keep the wheels turning, and point the church in the direction of ministry.

We also know, as harsh as it sounds, that the church includes people who are more like weeds than wheat. Some may draw on the church's resources without giving anything in return. Others may hinder the church's mission by clinging tightly to narrow or racist attitudes that would cut off the church from its wider community. Others may bring embarrassment or harm to the church through their public behavior.

Sometimes, when we look inside our own minds and motivations, we may recognize elements of both weeds and wheat. Which will win out?

What do we do with weeds among the wheat? Should we practice the kind of church discipline that publicly rebukes wayward members or revokes their standing on the church roll? If so, where should we draw the lines? There may come a time for a certain measure of discernment: a later story in Matthew suggests that when someone persists in harmful or toxic behavior and resists all efforts at reconciliation, they should be treated "as a Gentile or a tax collector" (18:15-17). **[A holy ambiguity]**

But Jesus' parable suggests that we can never know about weeds, and sometimes we can't even be sure about wheat. Wheat and darnel were so similar that some ancient people thought the darnel weeds were just good wheat gone bad. Could bad weeds become good wheat?

Let them both grow, Jesus said. Take care of them both while they grow, wait until the harvest, and let the reapers sort things out. Judgment is God's business, not ours – and aren't we glad? It's so easy for us to judge prematurely, or wrongly, or incompletely. We rarely know the whole story. We don't know others' hearts.

We may recognize members of the Christian community who seem to be on a different track and maybe even holding the church back, but our calling is to be patient with them and to love them no less.

As Jesus said, we who have ears to hear had better listen. We can never tell about weeds.

A holy ambiguity: Consider these thoughts from Theodore J. Wardlaw, as he ponders the instruction to let weeds and wheat grow together:

> There is a strategy in these words of restraint that pushes away from premature clarity regarding such matters of discernment and makes room instead for a holy and purposeful ambiguity. This is not a vague and ungrounded "whatever" kind of ambiguity, but an ambiguity that is both wise and intentional. In our impatience with others, we often want to bring matters to a head and so determine whether others are in or out; but the God who is glimpsed in this parable models for us an infinite patience that frees us to get on with the crucial business of loving, or at least living with, each other. . . .
>
> On such a journey as this, it is not our job to determine who is within and who is beyond this God's attention. It is rather our job to imagine everyone as belonging to this God, and there-fore, with all that we can muster, to endeavor to embrace, through Jesus Christ our Lord, God's holy and purposeful ambiguity. (From *Feasting on the Word,* Year A, vol. 3 of Accordance electronic ed. [Westminster John Knox Press, 2011], para. 16588.)

The Hardest Question
What is this weed?

Wheat and darnel are virtually indistinguishable until they mature enough for the heads of grain to form. At that point, wheat forms heads of grain in neat rows, while the heads of darnel are more gangly. Mature wheat turns brown, while the seeds of darnel are black.

Grains of the darnel plant not only dilute the wheat, but they are also poisonous enough to kill if eaten in suffi-cient quantities. Darnel seeds cause dizziness and nausea and have such hallucinogenic properties that the plant's scientific name is *Lolium temulentum:* the Latin word *temulentus* means "drunk."

Through the years, some people have taken advantage of the weed's hallucinogenic properties. Reportedly, follow-ers of Persephone and Demeter in ancient Greece used it to induce a frenzied state. In Europe, it was sometimes used as an anesthetic, but also baked into "dazed bread" or brewed into beer as a means of intentionally getting high. The plant

is mentioned in a variety of literary illusions including Shakespeare, who portrayed King Lear has having darnel in his crown. (Source: Howard Thomas, Jayne Elisabeth Arther, and Richard Marggraf Turley, "Remembering Darnel, a Forgotten Plant of Literary, Religious, and Social Significance," *Journal of Ethnobiology* 36:1 [March 2016], 29-44, cited by Sarah Laskow at *Atlas Obscura,* https://www.atlasobscura.com/articles/wheats-evil-twin-has-been-intoxicating-humans-for-centuries.)

In the illustration, darnel is the plant on the left, and wheat is on the right (from Otto Wilhelm Thomé *Flora von Deutschland, Österreich und der Schweiz* 1885, Gera, Germany: Public Domain).

Modern agricultural methods have eliminated darnel as a threat, though it can still be a problem for subsistence farmers in underdeveloped countries.

First Reading
Genesis 29:1-30 (RCL 29:15-28)

Jacob Meets His Match(es)

So Jacob served seven years for Rachel, and they seemed to him but a few days because of the love he had for her. (Gen. 29:20)

Have you ever unwrapped a gift, hoping it was something you wanted? Perhaps the size and weight were right for that blue sweater you'd been hinting about, or a new cordless screwdriver. With keen anticipation, you worked through the wrapping paper, only to discover that the blue sweater was a pink housecoat, or that the cordless screwdriver was a book.

It can be hard to hide our disappointment when reality turns out to be quite different from our expectations, and life surprises us. Try to imagine, though, the astonishment on Jacob's face when he awoke on the morning after his wedding night to discover that his new bride – veiled the night before – was not the woman he expected.

The text in context
(vv. 1-14)

The backstory of today's text, which the lectionary unfortunately limits to vv. 15-28, is Jacob's arrival in Haran after fleeing from his brother Esau and encountering God while camping along the way.

The narrator reports that, as Jacob approached the outskirts of the city, he came upon a well (vv. 1-3). The reader imagines it to be the same community water source at which his mother Rebekah had impressed Abraham's servant years before (Genesis 24). As in that story, Jacob's appearance at the well fits into the familiar betrothal type scene, but with several twists befitting Jacob's unique personality.

First, he encountered other shepherds, inquired if they knew Laban, and in short order learned that Laban's daugh-

> **More on context:** This text is part of a larger literary unit usually assigned to the Yahwist source, or to an edited composite of material from the Yahwist (J) and the Elohist (E). The unit, stretching from Genesis 29–31, is bound together by at least three running themes.
>
> The first theme is an ongoing battle of wits between Jacob and Laban, his mother's brother. Jacob has slickly managed to manipulate his way through life until he gets to Haran, but there he meets his match in chicanery by having to deal with his deceptive and conniving uncle Laban. Although Jacob will ultimately gain the upper hand, he endures many trials along the way.
>
> The second theme has to do with Jacob becoming the father of 11 sons and a daughter through a variety of circumstances involving four different women. Again, Jacob the mastermind finds the sandal on the other foot as he becomes a pawn of his two wives.
>
> The third theme is seen in an ongoing testimony that God was involved in all the previous encounters, blessing Jacob in his dealings with Laban and "opening the womb" of Leah or Rachel at certain times.

ter Rachel was then approaching the well. The shepherds explained the custom of waiting for all to arrive before removing the stone cover on the well, but Jacob impetuously removed it himself to prepare for Rachel's arrival (vv. 4-8). Jacob's action suggests not only that he was strikingly strong, but also that he had no qualms about violating custom in the service of his own interests. [**More on context**]

Secondly, while Abraham's servant had stood by while Rebekah drew water for his caravan of camels, Jacob eagerly drew water for the flock of animals Rachel had brought to the well (vv. 9-12). Was he simply being gallant, or trying to impress the beautiful Rachel? Knowing Jacob, we are inclined to believe the latter.

After his long and lonely sojourn in the wilderness, Jacob was overcome with emotion to learn that the captivating young woman was his cousin. Following her home, he received a warm and happy welcome from Rachel's father Laban – but the initial warmth was in sharp contrast to the cold duplicity that would follow (vv. 11-12).

Two women, one love
(vv. 15-20)

Hospitality can only last for so long without some sort of official arrangement. So, after Jacob had stayed for a month with Laban's family, a time in which he apparently pitched in and did chores with the rest of them, Laban sought to engage the industrious young man in a binding contract. His query, "Why do you serve me for nothing?" (v. 15) was an opening bid in negotiating the wages he would have to pay for Jacob's continued labor.

Perhaps the narrator intentionally built irony into Laban's question about why Jacob would "serve" him for nothing. The reader knows by now that Jacob serves no one, including God, for any purpose that does not serve himself – but he is willing to do what is necessary to get what he wants: Rachel, Laban's daughter. But he knew that Laban would demand a steep price for her hand.

Fleeing Esau, Jacob had apparently left home with little in the way of money or other resources. His family's wealth was in livestock, which he could not transport while on the run. With no money to pay as a bride price, Jacob offered to indenture himself to Laban for seven years as payment for the woman he loved. This suggests something about the depth of Jacob's desire for Rachel. How many of us would pay seven years' wages for the privilege of marrying our spouse?

As he negotiated, Jacob was aware that Laban had another unmarried daughter who was older, so he carefully specified that his labor would be in exchange "for your younger daughter, Rachel" (v. 18).

We have learned from vv. 16-17 that Rachel's older sister was named Leah, and that she was apparently less attractive than Rachel. The text mentions only her eyes, which are ambiguously described as "tender" or "soft," possibly in the sense of "weak."

Whatever the case, she was no match for Rachel, who is portrayed as both shapely in form and beautiful in appearance. The NRSV muddles the translation, describing her as "graceful and beautiful," though the text clearly comments on both her figure (literally, "beautiful of form/outline") and her overall comeliness ("beautiful of appearance").

While Rachel's physical appeal is the only characteristic given by the text, we have no way of knowing what other intangibles may have attracted Jacob to her. The narrator leaves no doubt, however, that Jacob was deeply smitten with Rachel, and Laban agreed to the arrangement. The seven years of labor seemed like a few days, we are told, "because of his love for her" (vv. 19-20).

A honeymoon surprise
(vv. 21-24)

What happened next is a familiar story. The seven years passed, and Jacob insisted that Laban give him Rachel, whom he identified as his wife: since betrothals were binding, the term was not inappropriate.

The manner of Jacob's request seems rather crude. "Give me my wife," he said, "my time is up and I want to go in to her" (v. 21). The Hebrew expression translated "go in" (or "go into") was not a euphemism, but a common way of saying "have sex with her."

The crassness of Jacob's request may be the narrator's way of emphasizing Jacob's eagerness to consummate the marriage, perhaps without looking closely at his bride. After a day of wedding festivities in which men and women were largely separate, and after an evening banquet that probably involved some heavy drinking, Laban brought a veiled Leah into Jacob's dark tent instead of Rachel, "and he went into her" (vv. 22-24).

The narrator says nothing about Rachel's whereabouts, only that Jacob slept that night with Leah, not realizing until morning's light that his bedmate was the older, unwanted sister. The author indicates that Jacob finally got his comeuppance. Although he was younger, he had tricked his way into receiving the birthright and blessing that rightfully belonged to the older brother. Now, though he had bargained for the younger sister, he was tricked into wedding the older one. As Jacob deceived his blind father who depended on touch, he in turn was flummoxed by darkness and an over-reliance on feel. Perhaps Leah had spoken as if she were Rachel, even as Jacob had claimed to be Esau.

One bride, or two?
(vv. 26-30)

When Jacob realized that he had been deceived, he complained to Laban, who calmly insisted that local custom dictated that the older sister must marry first. He added that he was not averse to having his hard-working son-in-law marry Rachel, too – something custom did allow – but it would cost Jacob an additional seven years of labor (vv. 26-27). [**Seven more years?**]

With little choice in the matter, Jacob accepted the offer. After a week with Leah, he was allowed to marry Rachel, with seven years of labor yet to go. "So Jacob went in to Rachel also, and he loved Rachel more than Leah" (vv. 28-30).

We notice that neither woman is given a voice in the story. Today, we would judge that both women were mistreated by having the course of their lives determined for them. For Leah it appears worse, because she is clearly less favored: the narrator emphatically tells us that Jacob loves Rachel. On the other hand, if Leah's "weak eyes" might have prevented other men from ever wanting to marry her, the arrangement might ultimately have served her well.

Still, we are left to wonder what the women thought about the arrangement. Was Rachel as in love with Jacob as he was with her? Was she aware of Laban's plans before the wedding? Did she cooperate willingly? How did Leah feel about this arrangement? Did she want to marry Jacob? Did she worry that her marriage to Jacob was cloaked in deception?

We don't know the answer to these questions, but they lead us to examine our own motives in our relationships with others. In our marriages and other relationships, do we seek others' good, or focus on our own needs? Do we

---

Parenthetical notes: You will note the parenthetical indications, with each wife, that Laban gave possession of their respective handmaids to them: Zilpah to Leah and Bilhah to Rachel. This information will become important later, as both Rachel and Leah insist that Jacob have sex with their handmaids in an effort to sire children they can call their own – actions that recall childless Sarah's insistence that Abraham beget a child by her handmaid Hagar (Gen. 16:1-4).

---

relate to others with honesty, or harbor hidden agendas? [**Parenthetical notes**]

A final thought: the story of Jacob and Laban, Leah and Rachel is not a pretty one. It is hard for us to find redeeming qualities in the multiple layers of deceit and the ways in which people were manipulated like pawns. Yet, before all was said and done, something good emerged: Jacob and his wives would produce children who would become known as the fathers of the 12 tribes of Israel.

Despite our failures and foibles, our manipulations and machinations, God still manages to work through us: imagine the thought.

The Hardest Question
What was it with Leah's eyes?

Translations differ in their description of Leah, who is said to have had distinctive eyes. But what made them distinctive?

The Hebrew word used to describe Leah's eyes in v. 17 is *rakôt*, an adjective that means "tender," "soft," or "delicate." The word could possibly indicate that Leah's vision was poor, or that her eyes were particularly sensitive to light, so that she squinted, but the narrator's intent is unclear.

Some translators take the term to be a derogatory description. Thus, the NIV and NAS95 translations say that Leah had "weak" eyes, and the HCSB says they were "ordinary." The KJV and NET are more ambiguous, describing Leah as having "tender" eyes, while the NRSV stretches the translation to say her eyes were "lovely."

Some commentators suggest that a reference to Leah's "tender eyes" might have been a backhanded compliment, implying that Leah's eyes were her only attractive feature.

Whatever allure there may or may not have been in Leah's eyes, for the narrator she paled in comparison to Rachel, who had both an attractive figure and a pretty face.

Seven more years? It is unlikely that Jacob had to wait seven more years before marrying Rachel: Laban asked only that he "finish this daughter's bridal week" ("complete the period of seven for this one"), at which time he could marry Rachel, even though she came with an obligation to work for Laban an additional seven years. Jacob ended up getting two wives instead of one, but not two for the price of one.

Optional First Reading
Psalm 105 (RCL 105:1-11, 45b)*

Don't Forget

O give thanks to the LORD, call on his name, make known his deeds among the peoples. (Ps. 105:1)

All of us took history courses in high school: world history, American history, the history of the state in which we lived. Learning about history is good, but learning *from* history is better. Ideally, lessons from the past should inform our present living with an outlook toward a better future.

American history has many bright spots: a pioneering spirit, a constitution that values equality and justice, a commitment to preserving and defending freedom.

We also have blots on our history, however, and many people prefer to keep those aspects of history under wraps, or revised in a way that makes them more palatable. The story of how American settlers took over the land that Native Americans had inhabited for thousands of years is often told as if it happened with no conflict, as if "peace" treaties were voluntary, as if the "Trail of Tears" never happened, as if assigning Native peoples to reservations was for their benefit.

Even more egregious is the way many history courses – at the direction of some state legislatures – whitewash America's dark history of slavery and the endemic racism that still pervades the country and privileges white people in ways that continue to oppress people of color.

We need to remember the good and the bad, and that is what we find in Psalms 105 and 106. Both are historical psalms that are intentionally paired in the psalter, both begin and end with a call to praise the LORD, and both

> **Historical psalms:** Psalms 105–106 are not the only historical psalms. Psalm 136 reprises God's mighty works for Israel in 26 verses, each of which concludes with "for his steadfast love endures forever." Psalm 78 is reminiscent of Psalms 105–106 together. It is a lengthy recitation of God's blessings, Israel's failures, divine anger and punishment, and Judah's ultimate vindication.

provide a brief review of Israel's history. Their approach is quite different, however: Psalm 105 reprises the good and powerful deeds God had done in support of God's covenant with Israel. Psalm 106 relates how the people had failed to appreciate God's blessings to the point of frittering them away through flaunting their covenant responsibilities. [Historical psalms]

The lectionary draws on piecemeal readings from Psalm 105 four times in Year A (Proper Sundays 12, 14, 17, and 20), in addition to a selection from Psalm 106 on Proper 23. Our approach to the readings from Psalm 105 would be the same in each case, so we will offer one study that covers the entire chapter.

A call to remember
(vv. 1-6)

Psalm 105 begins and ends with elements of praise, but its primary purpose is to inspire hope and confidence in God among a downtrodden people. By reciting positive events

---

In addition to this reading, Ps. 105:1-6, 16-22, 45b is read for Proper 14 in Year A; Ps. 105:1-6, 23-26, 45b is read for Proper 17 in Year A; and Ps. 105:1-6, 37-45 is read for Proper 20 in Year A. This commentary will include the entire chapter, vv. 1-45.

from Israel's history – events that recall God's promise to Abraham and the displays of power involved in fulfilling the promise – the psalmist encourages worshipers to trust that God still has power to bless Abraham's descendants, no matter their situation.

That is why he can challenge worshipers to "give thanks to the LORD, call on his name," and proclaim God's deeds as they sing praises and tell of God's wonderful work. Whatever their circumstances, they can "glory in his holy name" (vv. 1-3).

"Seek the LORD and his strength," the psalmist charges: "seek his presence continually" (v. 4). Two different verbs are used (*dārash* and *bāqash*), both in the imperative plural form. The verbs could be used in the context of pilgrimage, but also in everyday usage. The significant thing is that the people were challenged to seek God as a source of strength, and to do so continually. Remembering God's "wonderful works" on Israel's behalf could be a helpful way to bolster strength when people felt in need of another miracle (v. 5).

In v. 6 we find the first indication that the psalmist finds more strength in Genesis than in Deuteronomy, more comfort in remembering Abraham than David. While we might expect the psalmist to identify his audience at the beginning, the poet has waited until now: his appeal is to "offspring of his servant Abraham, children of Jacob, his chosen ones."

A covenant with Abraham
(vv. 7-11)

The next section brings further clarity to the psalmist's favored theological perspective. He begins with an emphatic pronoun for "he" (*hu*) that isn't grammatically necessary, but adds punch to the affirmation that "*He* is the LORD our God," a God whose "judgments are in all the earth" – perhaps a reminder that God's rule extends to lands of exile (v. 7). God is likewise one who does not forget promises, but "is mindful of his covenant forever, of the word that he commanded, for a thousand generations" (v. 8).

The covenant the psalmist had in mind was not the conditional covenant made at Sinai and elaborated in Deuteronomy. That covenant hadn't worked out well because it called for severe punishment if the people failed to keep it, and they had fallen far short. The exile was the natural outworking of that covenant, based on faithfulness to the law, and it seemed hopeless to think the people would ever do better.

For this reason, many took comfort in an older covenant – more of an outright promise than a covenant with stipulations – the promise they believed God had made to Abraham, the promise that assured him of countless descendants and a land in which they could live.

Thus, the covenant the psalmist recalls in v. 8, the covenant he says God never forgets, is "the covenant that he made with Abraham, his sworn promise to Isaac, which he confirmed to Jacob as a statute, to Israel as an everlasting covenant, saying, 'To you I will give the land of Canaan as your portion for an inheritance'" (vv. 9-11).

A history of faithfulness
(vv. 12-44)

Having stated his premise, the psalmist reflects on elements of Israel's history in which God had been faithful to the promise. While Abraham and his family remained small, he said, wandering about as strangers in the land, God "allowed no one to oppress them; he rebuked kings on their account" (vv. 12-14).

The poet apparently had in mind stories such as Abraham's reported encounters with the kings of both Egypt and Gerar (Gen. 12:10-20, 20:1-18). In both stories, Abraham pretended that Sarah was his sister and she was taken into the local king's harem, only to have God rebuke them. Isaac, according to Gen. 26:1-11, had a similar experience in Gerar.

The emphatic claim that God rebuked the kings by saying "Do not touch my anointed ones, do my prophets no harm" (v. 15) does not derive from the biblical accounts, but apparently from the poet's imagination.

The next mighty work was one of provision, as the psalmist recounts a famine that led Jacob's family to find refuge in Egypt, possible only because God "had sent a man ahead of them, Joseph, who was sold as a slave" (vv. 16-17). Again, the psalmist's creative license comes to the fore as he describes Joseph wearing fetters on his feet and a collar of iron as he faced test after test until the king released him from prison and "made him lord of his house, ruler of all his possessions" (vv. 18-22).

Land of Ham? We might expect v. 23 to speak of Jacob's family living in the "land of Goshen," as described in Gen. 45:10 and 46:28-29, a fertile area in the Nile delta. Instead, he surprisingly describes it as the "land of Ham." This reference goes back to the "Table of the Nations" in Genesis 10, which imaginatively describes the population of the known world by the three sons of Noah and their descendants. The descendants of Shem reportedly settled mainly in the Middle East and became ancestors of the Semites. The descendants of Japheth were said to have gone north and west, thus becoming the ancestors of the Greeks, Romans, and Europeans.

The descendants of Ham are said to have settled in a variety of places. One of Ham's sons was named Mizraim, the Hebrew name for Egypt, and another was named Cush, the Hebrew word for what is now Ethiopia and Somalia.

The connection of Ham with the continent of Africa led to a harmfully twisted interpretation of scripture used to endorse African slavery. A story in Gen. 9:20-27 says that Noah invented wine and passed out naked in his tent from over-imbibing. Ham saw him there, and apparently made light of the situation to his brothers. This offended Noah, who placed a curse—not on Ham, but on Ham's son Canaan—saying he would become the slave of Japheth, who would dwell in the tents of Shem.

Whether Canaan was the original target of the curse, or whether it was adapted later, the Hebrews used the story as a theological justification for the Israelites (descendants of Shem) to conquer and enslave the people of Canaan.

Proponents of African slavery later claimed that the so-called "curse of Ham" turned him black and sent him to Africa, where his descendants were destined to become slaves of the descendants of Japheth.

That paved the way for his father Jacob and his brothers to come and live as aliens in Egypt, where "the LORD made his people very fruitful, and made them stronger than their foes," who then turned against them (vv. 23-25). **[Land of Ham?]**

Verses 26-36 relate a colorful account of how God sent Moses and Aaron to deliver the people through calling on God to strike the Egyptians with one dread plague after another until they were weakened so that, "Then he brought Israel out with silver and gold and there was no one among their tribes who stumbled," leaving the Egyptians glad to be rid of them (vv. 37-38). God guided the people through cloud and fire, and provided for them both food and water because "he remembered his holy promise, and Abraham, his servant" (vv. 39-42).

Painting a rosy picture of Israel's occupation of Canaan, the psalmist sings, "So he brought his people out with joy, his chosen ones with singing. He gave them lands of the nations, and they took possession of the wealth of the peoples" (vv. 43-44).

Only in the last verse is there a hint that Israel also has a responsibility in this covenant, "that they might keep his statutes and observe his laws" (v. 45). Even there, we recall that the psalmist had defined the covenant with Abraham and promise to Isaac as something "he confirmed to Jacob as a statute, to Israel as an everlasting covenant, saying 'To you I will give the land of Canaan as your portion for an inheritance'" (vv. 10-11).

In the psalmist's mind, then, keeping the statutes (*chōq* in both vv. 10 and 45) and laws (*torah*, v. 45) consisted mainly of living in the promised land of Canaan – a much easier prospect than avoiding adherence to other tempting gods and treating one another with justice.

A question of approach

How should modern readers approach this psalm, which celebrates a divine promise remembered as unconditional and unbreakable, while ignoring the conditional covenant that had governed most of Israel's history, at least as far as its theologians were concerned?

While the psalm is long on memory, it is short on responsibility. It focuses on a belief that God had picked out Abraham and his descendants to be God's chosen people ("chosen" appears in vv. 6 and 43), no matter what. The psalm recounts happy memories of God's deliverance and provision without recalling days of complaining and unfaithfulness. There is no mention of the covenant at Sinai, but much emphasis on the "covenant" promises to Abraham, Isaac, and Jacob (vv. 8, 9, 10).

It seems that the psalmist has given up on Israel fulfilling the covenants spelled out in Exodus and Deuteronomy, and has put all his hope in the Genesis accounts of God's promise to Abraham, which he describes as "an everlasting covenant" good "for a thousand generations" (vv. 7-11).

Should we also adopt this belief that God has promised Israel the land of Canaan as an everlasting inheritance, no matter what? Under the conditions of the Sinai/Deuteron-omistic covenant, the Hebrews could not uphold their end of the bargain, and they lost the land that had been given. Should the older promise to Abraham then override the people's failure and guarantee the land anyway? There are many who use this argument to insist that the modern state of Israel should still have rights to all the land of Canaan, including what is occupied by Palestinians.

Imagine how a Palestinian Christian feels when reading this psalm. Or, for that matter, consider the entire notion of Canaan as Israel's divine inheritance from the perspective of the Canaanites, who were minding their own business before the Israelites showed up.

Texts such as this one have a way of stirring up more questions than answers, and none of the answers are easy. What we *can* take from the psalm, at the very least, is a reminder of the importance of remembrance. We who claim the name of Christ would do well to recall what God has done for us: a mighty deed in the work of Christ that made grace available to all people, a deed that overshadows any story of martial conquest or miraculous provision for physical needs.

Our promised land is not of this earth.

The Hardest Question
When was Psalm 105 composed?

Psalm 105, probably written within the priestly circle, offers no specific information about its composition, but various clues suggest that it was written from an exilic or postexilic perspective. First, as noted in the lesson, it is carefully paired with Psalm 106, which includes an account of Israel's defeat and prays "Save us, O LORD our God, and gather us from among the nations" (Ps. 106:47), an obvious indication of exile.

Second, the psalm has much to say about God's covenant promise to Abraham up to Israel's entry to Canaan, but says nothing about the conditional covenant at Sinai that was expounded in Deuteronomy and constantly violated through the years. This was characteristic of the postexilic period, when Israel's theologians found little comfort in rehashing a covenant the nation had never been able to keep, and focused more on the earlier promises to Abraham, which were said to be perpetual. See, for example, references from Second and Third Isaiah, all of which reference Abraham (Isa. 41:8, 51:1-2, 63:16). Nehemiah, likewise, late into the postexilic period, praised Yahweh as "the one who chose Abram and brought him out of Ur of the Chaldeans and gave him the name Abraham" (Neh. 9:7).

Third, the psalm appears at the end of Book IV of the Psalms (Psalms 90–106), most of which appear to reflect concerns from the exilic and postexilic periods.

Finally, Psalm 105 was evidently known and popular during the postexilic era, because the book of 1 Chronicles, one of the last Old Testament books to be written, quotes directly from Ps. 105:1-15 with just a few variations. The Chronicler, who clearly wrote as a promoter of the priest-hood, typically expanded stories from 1–2 Samuel and 1–2 Kings to enlarge the roles of David and Solomon and to associate them more closely with the development of worship and priestly matters. In constructing an account of David bringing the Ark of the Covenant into Jerusalem, the Chronicler inserted Ps. 105:1-15 as a song of praise that David reportedly sang (1 Chron. 16:8-22). The same account attributes to David citations from Ps. 96:1-13a (1 Chron. 16:23-25) and 106:47-48 (1 Chron. 16:35-36). Surprisingly, none of those psalms bear superscriptions associating them with David: the Chronicler alone makes that connection.

Second Optional First Reading
Psalm 128

A Blessed Man

Happy is everyone who fears the LORD, who walks in his ways. (Ps. 128:1)

Are you happy? Many Americans are obsessed with the subject. Surveys asking what people want most often find happiness at the top of the list. The Declaration of Independence declares that all people have inalienable rights to life, liberty, and the pursuit of happiness. Who doesn't want to be happy?

Yet, chances are that the more effort people put into pursuing happiness, the less likely they are to find it. A quote from social worker Richard Lessor appeared on motivational posters in the 1970s, contending that "Happiness is like a butterfly: the more you chase it, the more it will elude you; but if you turn your attention to other things, it will come and sit softly on your shoulder" (the quote is often erroneously attributed to Henry David Thoreau).

Metaphors aside, happiness is more likely to emerge as a byproduct of other activities than when pursued as an end goal. Researchers consistently find that people are happiest when they focus more on others than themselves.

The author of today's text testified to the same truth more than two millennia ago: for him, the primary "other" we should be concerned with is God.

A happy walk
(vv. 1-4)

Psalm 128 is labeled as a "Song of Ascents," which makes it one of 15 "pilgrim songs" collected in the psalter (Psalms 120–134). The psalm also contains clear elements of wisdom such as that expressed in the book of Proverbs, making it one of several psalms that portray clear wisdom

---

> **Psalms of Ascent:** Psalms 120–134 are known as the "Psalms of Ascent," for each begins with the superscription *shir ha-ma'alôt*, which means "a song of going up." As Robert Alter has noted, "The verb 'ascend' or 'go up' is the technical term used for pilgrimage" in Hebrew (*The Book of Psalms: A Translation and Commentary* [W.W. Norton, 2007], 435).
>
> The Psalms of Ascent are typically thought of as pilgrim songs that would have been sung by Jews who were climbing into Jerusalem to worship in the holy city at one of the three annual festivals that drew pilgrims from near and far.
>
> Some scholars, on the other hand, argue that the psalms were sung by Levite temple singers as they climbed the 15 steps leading into the temple. The psalms share a common theme of praising Zion and hoping for a good future. It is likely that they date from the Second Temple period: at least one (Psalm 126) speaks specifically of the exiles' hoped-for return to Jerusalem.
>
> A few writers take a different approach, suggesting that the term is a musical notation, and that "psalm of ascent" could have described "an ascent in pitch or a crescendo in the song" (Alter, 435), but most scholars find the concept of pilgrim songs to be most satisfying.

themes (see also Psalms 1, 36, 37, 49, 73, 112, 127, 128, and 133). [**Psalms of Ascent**]

Despite being just six verses long, the psalm displays no clear structure. We have chosen to approach it in two parts, seeing the first four verses as a didactic hymn drawn from the wisdom tradition, and the last two verses as a blessing. The psalm, in essence, says "this is the recipe for happiness" (vv. 1-4), and "let's hope it works!" (vv. 5-6).

All of us are familiar with articles or Internet posts by lifestyle gurus or even preachers who promise "Three steps to a happy life" or "Seven keys to prosperity." The psalmist believed that only one thing was required: "Fear the LORD."

In this setting, the word "fear" does not imply horror or panic, but a deep sense of reverence before God that plays out in one's daily life. Israel's wisdom teachers, thought to be professional sages employed to teach young men from well-to-do families or to serve as royal advisers, firmly believed that success in life was a contractual matter: those who showed true respect to God by carefully following the law should enjoy prosperity, while those who thought little of God and chose self-directed ways were on a road to misery.

Israel's community of the wise may have been responsible for the final compilation of the psalter, for it begins with a classical wisdom teaching. Psalm 1 insists that those who reject sinful ways and follow God's teaching will prosper like fruitful trees that never wither because they are planted by streams of water. The wicked, in contrast, are like chaff driven by the wind, for "the way of the wicked will perish."

The author of Psalm 128 focuses on the positive side of the equation: "Happy is everyone who fears the LORD, who walks in his ways" (v. 1). A beautiful aspect of this psalm is the poet's identification of joy in simple and solid things: meaningful work, a committed partner, and children. [**Simple things**]

While some people would describe these things as "what matters most in life," the text does not intend to suggest that those who are single or childless are incapable of happiness. Israel's sages uniformly addressed their instructions to men, and in Israelite culture every man hoped to marry and father children, especially sons ("children" in v. 3 is literally "sons").

On the other hand, women in the ancient world also assumed that happiness was found in marriage and children: unmarried or childless women were considered unfortunate at best, or cursed at worst.

Simple things: John Durham has observed that "One of the gifts of the true poet is an uncanny sensitivity to the profound truths of life at its most uncomplicated. And a second gift is the ability to set forth these truths with eloquent simplicity" ("Psalms," in *The Broadman Bible Commentary*, vol. 4 [Broadman Press, 1971], 430).

Blessings and cursings: The psalmist knew the teachings of Deuteronomy, a covenant of blessings and cursings between God and Israel. Deuteronomy 28 is a notable text that describes the happy blessings that would result from obedience, while depicting in gory detail the curses that might follow if the Israelites went after other gods: potential curses outnumber the blessings three to one. The thought of working hard to till the earth and raise crops—only to see them taken over and eaten by an enemy—was a particularly memorable curse (Deut. 28:30-34).

Modern readers can recognize that the psalmist was celebrating his culture's ideals without limiting our own concept of a happy life to matrimony and progeny.

Every person needs meaningful work or tasks, whether paying or not, to have a sense of purpose in life. If all we do is eat and sleep, existing in the world without contributing to it, where is the joy in that?

The ability to "eat the fruit of the labor of your hands" (v. 2) was a sign of blessing and happiness during a time of peace when neither enemies nor poverty threatened. We find great satisfaction in earning our own living, or in eating food from our garden or kitchen. Even those who aren't in the workforce can find purpose and satisfaction in supporting others through cultivating meaningful relationships. Persons who have no close relatives or children of their own can still relate actively to others and feel part of the family.

For many people, including the psalmist, family is at the heart of happiness. Addressing men, he connects contentment and prosperity with a wife who is "like a fruitful vine" within the house, bearing children who would grow "like olive shoots" around the table (v. 3).

The agricultural metaphors were not accidental. Grape vines were common symbols of fertility, on the one hand, and the source of wine, on the other – both signs and sources of joy for one who has them. Sprouts near the base of olive trees can be transplanted to produce more trees and more olives. In the ancient Near East, olive trees were – and continue to be – highly valued as a source of both food and olive oil, an all-purpose product that could be used for cooking, cosmetics, medicinal purposes, lighting the home, or trade. [**Blessings and cursings**]

The metaphors are simple but profound. Happiness is not found in fame or wealth or even good health, but in meaningful work, in close relationships, and in the legacy we leave behind. Verse 4 concludes the hymnic lesson by returning to the initial thought, switching from "happy" to a near synonym, "blessed": "Thus shall the man be blessed who fears the LORD."

The psalmist addressed men in his original context, but we may be confident that the hymn applies to women, too.

A happy wish
(vv. 5-6)

Israel's sages held to the traditional belief that obedience and prosperity went hand in hand, but they knew that life was not so simple. After all, the books of Job and Ecclesiastes also came from Israel's wisdom community, calling into question the whole notion of a guaranteed *quid pro quo* theology. They knew that God was more than the manager of a heavenly storehouse who dispensed blessings in return for behavior-based coin.

Perhaps that is why the psalm closes with a hopeful blessing, a God-directed wish that the promised ideal might become reality. When we consider how this psalm would have functioned in Israel's worship, we can imagine a choir singing the first four verses, promising happiness to those who fear God and follow God's teachings. Afterward, a priest may have stepped forward to pronounce the benediction found in vv. 5-6: "The LORD bless you from Zion! May you see the prosperity of Jerusalem all the days of your life. May you see your children's children. Peace be upon Israel!"

Do you see all the blessings tied up in those few lines? The prominence of Zion/Jerusalem connects with the poem's function as a "Psalm of Ascent," probably associated with pilgrims coming to Jerusalem for worship. The Israelites did not think Yahweh was limited to the holy city. Even so, they believed that God's presence was powerfully associated with the temple in Jerusalem. Thus, Yahweh's blessings would come "from Zion."

Furthermore, the prosperity of individuals was directly tied to the prosperity of Jerusalem: neither the people nor the city could flourish unless there was peace in the land and the people were free to raise their crops and families, pursue economic advancement, and worship without hindrance.

The poet's benediction wishes not only prosperity, but also longevity for both Jerusalem and the worshiper. He prays for the city to remain prosperous "all the days of your life," and for worshipers to grow old enough to see their grandchildren.

Knowing one's grandchildren was a triple blessing. Aside from the inherent delight of seeing one's children bear children, the presence of both children and grandchildren implied that the happy God-fearer would not be poor or alone in old age, but would be secure in having offspring to provide for and look after him or her.

Furthermore, ancient Israelite religion did not include the concept of life after death, other than a shadowy existence in Sheol for both the righteous and the wicked. For those who wrote and sang this song in Jerusalem, one's posterity was tied to one's descendants. Without a belief in life that continued beyond one's time on earth, one's best hope was to live on through future generations who would keep his or her memory alive.

The psalmist's hope was connected to a belief that the nation and its individual members would demonstrate their reverence for God by following God's ways. "Peace be upon Israel" is a wish that nation and people alike would – in words echoed by *Star Trek*'s Dr. Spock – live long and prosper.

Do you consider yourself to be a happy or blessed person? What makes you feel that way? Have you noticed that when you trust God, work hard, and invest in others, happiness finds *you*?

The Hardest Question
How should we understand the structure of Psalm 128?

For a short text of only six verses, the intended structure of Psalm 128 has proven to be a surprising puzzle, perhaps because the poet skillfully worked several repetitive themes into its lines.

Some scholars believe the psalm falls neatly into two parts, with the first four verses functioning as a wisdom psalm in which the first part is a chiasm, and the latter two verses are a blessing, possibly spoken by a priest in response to the psalm.

"Chiasm" is a literary term describing a series of statements that move through stages from one subject to another and back again. Chiasms can be as short as this one, with only two stages, or long and complex. Notice the integrated structure as the psalmist moves from a third-person principle to a second person promise and back again (Option 1 in the box below).

The end of the chiasm provides a natural break, leading to the blessing, which repeats the themes of blessing (v. 5) and fruit/children (v. 6).

While this structure may seem obvious, other scholars see a more natural division between vv. 3 and 4, with the return to blessing in v. 4 beginning a new section rather than serving as a bookend for the first section. They see the same pattern of a shift from third to first person, and note that the progression of fearing God (v. 1), prosperity (v. 2), and children (v. 3) is repeated in vv. 4, 5, and 6 (Option 2 in the box below).

While a case could be made for either view, the second option takes little account of the benedictory nature of vv. 5-6, which is different in character (if not in content) from the preceding verses. Thus, we have chosen the first option for this study.

Option 1

(third person) Happy are those who *fear the LORD* (v. 1)
    (second person) You will eat the *fruit* produced by your labor (v. 2)
    (second person) Your wife will be a *fruitful*, your children like sprouts (v. 3)
(third person) Blessed are those who *fear the LORD* (v. 4)

Option 2

(third person) Happy are those *who fear God* (v. 1)
    (second person) You will *prosper by enjoying the fruit* of your labor (v. 2)
        (second person) Your wife will *bear children* like olive shoots (v. 3)
(third person) Blessed are those *who fear God* (v. 4)
    (second person) May the LORD *bless you with prosperity* (v. 5)
    (second person) May you see *your children's children* (v. 6)

Second Reading
1 Kings 3:1-15 (RCL 3:5-12)

A Listening Heart

Give your servant therefore an understanding mind to govern your people,
able to discern between good and evil; for who can govern this your great people? (1 Kgs. 3:9)

"Did you hear me?" Most of us heard those words at some point as we were growing up: perhaps one of our parents told us to mow the lawn or wash the dishes, and we were slow to comply. *"Did you hear me?"* – usually conveyed with impatience – sent a clear message that life would be much better if we would listen to our parents and do what they say.

We may as well confess that those of us who have children of our own, or who have taught school, have probably used the same words. We want to get across the lesson that successful people listen to those who are wiser, and learn to follow their lead.

Solomon understood this, or so we surmise from today's familiar text, but there's more to the story than meets the eye (or ear).

The lectionary reading is 1 Kgs. 3:5-15, but to appreciate the full picture, we will include all of vv. 1-15.

Pharaoh's son-in-law
(vv. 1-2)

When we come to 1 Kings 3, Solomon has recently succeeded his father David as king of Israel, and over a short period of time he reportedly revamped the royal court and consolidated his rule.

What we often overlook is that Solomon is presented as a living conundrum. His name (*shlōmōh*) is derived from the word *shālôm*, which relates to peace or wholeness, but Solomon began his reign by executing three persons who could threaten his rule (the military chief Joab, his brother

Adonijah, and a critic named Shimei), while banishing another who had promoted the cause of his brother (Abiathar the priest). He solidified his "peace" by dint of the sword. [**Three deaths and a banishment**]

A second disconnect is that Solomon would become known as a man of unmatched wisdom, but the wisdom he is first known for was rooted in brute force. David had instructed Solomon to keep close to God and follow the law (2 Kgs. 2:1-4), but then charged him to see that neither Joab nor Shimei should die in peace (2 Kgs. 2:5-9). In both cases, David told Solomon to use his *wisdom* in determining how and when to do the bloody deed (vv. 6, 9).

A third surprise is that, while Solomon emerged as the chosen son of David, he also chose to marry an Egyptian princess and thus become pharaoh's son-in-law (3:1). The narrator carefully avoids naming the Egyptian king, probably because he wants the reader to keep in mind the story of the cruel pharaoh who had oppressed the Israelites long before, and to be wary of Solomon's penchant for marriage alliances.

With these narrative touches and more to come, the editor of 1 Kings manages to praise King Solomon as a monarch of unparalleled wisdom and prosperity, but with a shadow over him.

He wants to praise Solomon, but the praise is not unqualified. For example, in telling us that Solomon brought his new wife into Jerusalem, there is a reminder that he had not yet finished "building his own house and the house of the LORD and the wall around Jerusalem." The implication that Solomon was completing his own

Three deaths and a banishment: Before David's death, he instructed Solomon to engineer the deaths of both Joab and Shimei (1 Kgs. 2:5-9). Joab had long served as the chief of David's army, but had also crossed David by murdering two rival military leaders, Abner (2 Sam. 3:20-30) and Amasa (2 Sam. 20:1-12), even though David had been cultivating good relationships with them. On top of that, he had supported David's oldest son, Adonijah, for the throne instead of Solomon. Shimei, from Saul's extended family, had cursed David and thrown stones at him as David fled Jerusalem during Absalom's *coup d'etat* (2 Sam. 16:5-14).

When Solomon's brother Adonijah, who had also sought the throne, asked permission to marry Abishag, the concubine who had been brought to David in his old age, Solomon saw his request as a ploy for power. He ordered Benaiah, the captain of the guard, to execute Adonijah, so "He struck him down, and he died" (1 Kgs. 2:13-25).

Solomon then sent for Abiathar, who had long served David as priest – but who had also supported Adonijah's claim for the throne. He did not kill Abiathar – probably because he was an anointed priest – but banished him to the village of Anathoth (2 Kgs. 2:26-27).

When Joab learned that Solomon was purging potential enemies, he fled to the tent that housed the Ark of the Covenant and grasped the horns of the altar before it. This was a traditional place of sanctuary, but Solomon ordered Benaiah to kill him even there. "Then Benaiah son of Jehoiada went up and struck him down and killed him …" (2 Kgs. 2:28-34).

Having eliminated these rivals, Solomon elevated Benaiah to commander of the army, and appointed Zadok – a priest who had supported him over Adonijah – as high priest.

There was one rival to go: Solomon took Shimei, who had cursed his father and who had the potential of causing unrest among the northern tribes, and put him under house arrest. Solomon ordered Shimei not to leave the city, under penalty of death, but three years later, Shimei went to reclaim two slaves who had run away to the city of Gath. Solomon called him to account, and ordered Benaiah to kill him: "and he went out and struck him down, and he died" (2 Kgs. 2:36-46a).

Solomon's name indicated that he was a man of peace, but when "the kingdom was established in the hand of Solomon" (2 Kgs. 2:46b), it was a hand that wielded a sword.

palace before building the temple or fortifying the city suggests that his priorities may have been misplaced.

Furthermore, we read that those who wanted to worship Yahweh were still sacrificing on outdoor shrines or "high places," a practice that would later be expressly forbidden, but that remained popular precisely because Solomon had not yet built the temple, where sacrifices could rightly be offered.

David's son and successor
(vv. 3-9)

The theme continues in v. 3, where we are told that Solomon "loved the LORD" and "followed in the statutes of his father David," but with a qualifier: "*only*, he sacrificed and offered incense at the high places." **[High places]**

Two things deserve comment. First, while Solomon is said to have "loved Yahweh," the text does not say he followed the teachings of Yahweh, but that he "walked in the statutes of his father David." David was known for his piety, righteousness, and desire to follow God's will for most of his life. But David went off the rails after falling in lust with Bathsheba and having her husband Uriah killed (2 Samuel 11). David's life went downhill after that, and the

writer of 1 Kings portrays his last days as those of a weak and bitter old man who was more interested in vengeance than in peace: he urged Solomon to be faithful to Yahweh (2:1-4), then instructed him to kill Joab and Shimei while rewarding Barzillai of Gilead (2:5-9).

While the concept of "walking in the statutes" of Yahweh is uniformly positive, to walk in the statutes of another human is less so. Ezekiel spoke of how God had warned Israel in the wilderness not to follow the statutes of their parents (Ezek. 20:18), but of God alone.

Thus, while the narrator offers a basically positive assessment of Solomon as "walking in the statutes of his father David," we know that his model is flawed.

Second, the author expresses displeasure that Solomon offered sacrifices on the high places. Indeed, he reports that Solomon did so on a massive scale: v. 4 says that he went to the principal high place in Gibeon (about 7 miles northwest of Jerusalem), and offered a thousand burnt offerings.

Even allowing for exaggeration, why would anyone offer such extravagant sacrifices? The words used speak of whole burnt offerings, rather than the more typical "peace offerings" that were ritually sacrificed but mostly eaten by worshipers. The verb forms suggest that this was Solomon's

High places: People of the ancient Near East commonly offered sacrifices in outdoor settings, and often on hills or mountains that had an impressive view or seemed closer to the gods.

For the author of 1 Kings – called the "Deuteronomist" because of his interest in illustrating theological themes from the book of Deuteronomy – worship on the high places was too tinged with pagan practices to be acceptable, and after the temple was built, it became anathema (2 Kgs. 14:4; 15:4, 35).

For every king of Judah who followed Solomon, the writer's judgment was based largely on whether he tore down the high places (good king), tolerated worship on the high places (mediocre king), or participated in worship on the high places (evil king).

In 1 Kgs. 3:2-4, both the people and Solomon are said to have worshiped and offered sacrifices on the high places, but only because there was not another option: Solomon had not yet built the temple. Thus, while the note that Solomon offered massive sacrifices on the main high place at Gibeon appears to be a positive thing, there is a shadow over it.

The round altar pictured, at Megiddo, was used by Canaanite worshippers as far back as the third millennium BCE. Note its position on a high place, overlooking the Jezreel Valley.

hopes that God would speak to them in a dream. Whatever Solomon's motive, he evidently had a royal pavilion set up during these sacrificial outings so he could stay overnight. On one occasion, whether Solomon had sought the encounter or not, God reportedly spoke to him in a dream (v. 5). **[Divination by dreams]**

God, according to the story, appeared to Solomon and offered to bless him, asking the new king to name what he most desired. Solomon replied with a show of humility, praising God for the loyalty shown to his father David, and recognizing that his place on the throne was a continued sign of God's "great and steadfast love" (v. 6).

Even though he was already a father, had eliminated his rivals, had established a core of supporters, and had entered at least one political marriage alliance, Solomon spoke of himself as "only a little child" who did not know how to go out or come in. The obvious exaggeration was designed to indicate Solomon's awareness that he still had much to learn if he was to govern Israel well (vv. 7-8).

Perhaps Solomon was already smart enough to know that if he had the discernment to do the right things, success in other areas would follow. In either case, he chose wisdom as his wish: "Give to your servant therefore an understanding mind to govern your people, able to discern between good and evil …" (v. 9).

The NRSV's "an understanding mind" is an apt translation, but it is helpful to recognize that Solomon's literal request was for "a listening heart." The Hebrews considered the heart to be the place where options were considered and decisions were made. They also connected the act of listening with obedience: to truly listen is to obey.

Solomon's desire to "discern between good and evil" employs a figure of speech called a merism, which states two very different things while meaning to include everything in between. It wasn't just an ability to label things as "good" or "evil" that Solomon needed, but an ability to judge rightly and make good decisions, to lead wisely and to establish justice for all people. Solomon recognized the enormity of the multiple tasks of good governance and leadership as he asked, "for who can govern your great people?"

Asking for a "listening heart" showed that Solomon sought to understand God's desire, and to follow it. He was still new to the "game of thrones," but knew enough to recognize that he would need God's help in order to rule

custom, rather than a one-time event. Was the burning of such valuable food resources the new king's way of seeking legitimacy by demonstrating loyalty to Yahweh in public fashion, or did he wish to stress by example the importance of serving Yahweh? Nothing in scripture calls for such extravagant sacrifices.

From another angle, is it possible that Solomon was actively seeking to receive a word from God? The ancients sometimes offered sacrifices and then slept in holy places in

Divination by dreams: The Old Testament contains many stories of people receiving a message from God in a dream. These dreams do not seem to be sought, and the recipients do not have to be Hebrews. Abraham, Jacob, Joseph, Gideon, and Daniel are but a few famous Hebrew dreamers, but Egypt's pharaoh and Babylon's Nebuchadnezzar also received messages in dreams.

The book of Deuteronomy speaks of prophets who claim to be able to seek messages from God through dreams (Deuteronomy 13; cp. Jeremiah 23). It does not discount the practice, but warns against false prophets who claim to have received a word from God in a dream when they have not.

At a low point in his life, King Saul actively sought a word from God, including the use of dreams, but was unsuccessful: "When Saul inquired of the LORD, the LORD did not answer him, not by dreams or by Urim, or by prophets" (1 Sam. 28:6).

Documents preserved from Israel's neighbors speak of how persons would sometimes sleep in a temple or other sacred place in hopes of receiving a message from the gods, and scholars speculate that the Hebrews also knew the practice.

Whether Solomon was hoping to receive a divinely inspired dream by sleeping on the high place is uncertain, but possible.

What do you need? When considering Solomon's options in asking something of Yahweh, one might note that Solomon was already capable of getting as rich as he wanted to be through taxing his subjects, and he later became very successful at setting up a productive system of royal finance.

Likewise, Solomon had already demonstrated a willingness to take the lives of his rivals: he knew how to do that. The one thing totally out of his hands was long life.

---

effectively over a people who had demonstrated their willful ways many times over.

It's hard to imagine what it would be like to have a conversation in which God offered to grant anything we wished. Solomon asked for a heart that was open and obedient to following God's way. What would be on *our* wish list?

God's chosen leader
(vv. 10-15)

Solomon's request was pleasing to God, according to v. 10, who was impressed that the king had asked for "understanding to discern what is right" rather than for long life, riches, or the lives of his enemies (v. 11). [**What do you need?**]

To reward Solomon's astutely humble request, God agreed to grant him "a wise and discerning mind" unmatched in either history or prospect (v. 12). God also promised to grant Solomon what he had not asked for: "riches and honor" beyond that of any other king for all of his life (literally, "days," v. 13).

We note that God's promise replaces the potential request for triumph over enemies with "honor," a word that

could also mean "glory." Solomon could enjoy those blessings for as long as he lived. But how long would that be?

Verse 14 includes a conditional element: Solomon could have long life, but only "if you will walk in my ways, keeping my statutes and my commandments, as your father David walked – then I will lengthen your life."

Awaking from his dream, Solomon realized the importance of the vision. The first fruit of his "listening heart," apparently, was the realization that sacrifices to Yahweh should be offered in Jerusalem, on the altar before the tent housing the Ark of the Covenant.

Solomon then returned to Jerusalem, where he offered both whole burnt offerings and "sacrifices of well-being" and "provided a feast for all his servants" (v. 15).

That was a good start, but would Solomon live up to the ideal of a listening heart that heard and obeyed God's lead? Would God live up to the divine promises?

We might be curious about Solomon, but more importantly, to whom are *our* hearts listening? God has not pledged to us the worldly riches, power, or legendary wisdom of Solomon, but through Christ we have the offer of forgiving grace, steadfast love, and the abiding hope of God's present Spirit – all of which call us to faithful service.

Are our hearts open to God's promises and God's leading? Are we listening?

The Hardest Question
Did Solomon live a long life?

The answer to this question is not that hard, so far as the biblical record is concerned, but requires a bit of digging. God promised to Solomon a long life, but only if he would "walk in my ways, keeping my statutes and my commandments, as your father David walked" (1 Kgs. 3:14).

How did that work out? We know that Solomon did become famous for his wisdom, for his riches, and for his power. God had promised those without condition. But what about the conditional promise that an obedient Solomon could live a long life?

We don't know how old Solomon was at his death, being told only that he died after ruling Israel for 40 years (1 Kgs. 11:41-43, 2 Chron. 9:29-31). Solomon could hardly have been older than 30 when he came to the throne, for he was born several years after David had established himself as king in Jerusalem, where he ruled for 33 years (1 Kgs. 2:10-12). This would give Solomon a lifespan of 70 years at most, possibly equivalent to the biblical threescore and 10 (Ps. 90:10) but hardly an example of a lengthy life.

Was this due to God's failure to follow up on a promise, or Solomon's failure to meet the conditions? Sadly, Solomon did follow something of the pattern of his father, who rose to power as a faithful follower but got off track later in life. He turned away from Yahweh, and apparently God kept the promise to make the length of his life conditional on the extent of his obedience, though the narrator makes no editorial comments about it.

The first part of Solomon's reign is described in mostly glowing terms, as he oversaw the building of the temple, the expansion of Jerusalem, and growing international power.

Along the way, however, Solomon was also marrying a variety of foreign women, including some from nations with whom intermarriage was expressly forbidden. The marriages were probably designed to cement alliances with neighboring kings, but the narrator insists that "Solomon clung to these in love." Altogether Solomon had 700 princesses and 300 concubines, according to 1 Kgs. 11:1-3. The number is clearly exaggerated to make an impression in a world that measured royal power by the size of the king's harem and his ability to father numerous children. His "princess" wives would have represented marriage alliances with neighboring kings.

Solomon's wives, who would have brought their own gods with them, "turned away his heart after other gods," the text says, so that his heart was no longer true to Yahweh, as his father David had been. David had his faults, but remained a steadfast Yahwist, and was never accused of worshiping other gods.

Solomon not only built temples for his wives' gods, but also worshiped in them, the narrator says, following Astarte of the Sidonians, Milcom of the Ammonites, and going so far as to build high places for the "abominations" Chemosh of the Moabites and Molech of the Ammonites (1 Kgs. 11:4-8, both said to have accepted child sacrifice). The result, as the remainder of 1 Kings 11 relates, was that Yahweh was no longer pleased but grew angry at Solomon, raised up enemies against him, and declared that the kingdom would be torn apart, leaving his son with only a single tribe. Apparently, the offer of "length of days" was another casualty: Solomon lived a full life, but not an overly long one. Even the credit of a 40-year rule sounds more formulaic than actual.

We can't help but note that, while Solomon's one request was for a "listening heart" that could discern God's will, his later downfall resulted when his wives "turned away his heart after other gods," so that it was listening to Yahweh no more.

Optional Second Reading
Psalm 119:129-136

Steady as She Goes

Keep my steps steady according to your promise, and never let iniquity have dominion over me. (Ps. 119:133)

Psalm 119 gets considerable airplay during the season after Pentecost in Year A, as the Revised Common Lectionary features selections from it for Proper Sundays 1, 2, 10, and 12. This is not surprising, given that Psalm 119 contains 176 verses divided into 22 sections, each of which could have been a separate psalm.

What binds the sections together is an acrostic structure and a thoroughgoing celebration of the importance of keeping God's law, depicted with a variety of synonyms, at least six of which occur in each section. [**Law language**]

The structure is as carefully detailed as the theme: each of the 22 sections features a consecutive letter of the Hebrew alphabet (or *alefbet*), and each contains eight verses beginning with that same letter. Today's reading features the letter *pe*, roughly equivalent to the English letter "p," though more versatile in pronunciation. Depending on its position relative to other letters, it could be pronounced as a "p" as in *peh*, for "mouth, or as an "f" as in *nefesh*, often translated as "soul" or "inner being."

Appreciation for the law
(vv. 129-130)

A structure based on a sequence of letters is bound to have some artificiality to it, so some verses may appear random. In this section, however, the psalmist has managed to incorporate some discernable movement.

The section begins with words of admiration for the law and a profession of allegiance to it. "Your decrees are wonderful," the poet declared in an attitude of prayer, "therefore my soul keeps them" (v. 129).

Law language: The psalmist populated Psalm 119 with eight thematic terms describing God's teaching, repeating them again and again: most of them appear in each of the 22 sections. These eight terms are generally translated as "law" (*tōrâ*, used 25 times), "decrees/covenant terms" (*'edût*, 23 times), "statutes/laws" (*chōq*, 22 times), "commandments/commands" (*mizwâ* 21 times), "ordinances" (*mishpat*, 22 times), "word" (*dābar*, 24 times), "precepts/charges" (*piqûd*, 20 times), and "promise/saying" (*'imrâ*, 20 times). Occasionally the psalmist uses terms such as God's "paths" or "ways" to get across the same ideas.

James Luther Mays described the effect of the acrostic structure and repetitive lexicon of stock words in this way: "So he used the alphabet to signal completeness and the whole vocabulary to represent comprehensiveness ... Within the control of the formal structure, the same thing is said in 167 different ways, in a progression that moves through the alphabet without ever moving from its single subject" (*Psalms*, Interpretation: A Bible Commentary for Teaching and Preaching [Westminster John Knox Press, 2011], 381-382]).

Many of us tend to think of laws and legal decrees as necessary and obligatory, but rarely as something "wonderful." A closer look at the word may help us to appreciate it. The verse begins with a noun, *p^elā'ōt*, which is related to a verb that means "to be difficult," in the sense of being beyond one's abilities. The psalmist saw God's ability to design the law as beyond human capability and thus wonderful in its scope and worthy of following.

Modern readers may liken the beginning of v. 130 to the unfolding of a map to reveal its secrets, but the translation is an interpretation. The verse begins with *pētach*, or "doorway," from a verb that means "to open." A literal reading would be "A doorway, your words, shines understanding (on the) naïve."

God's instructions, the poet believed, were like light shining into the life of an immature person, bringing understanding and showing them the way to go. Today we may talk about education as the doorway to opportunity, equipping people for a better life. While we focus on teaching skills for daily competence or financial success, the psalmist saw an understanding of God's all-encompassing law as the highest goal.

A plea for strength to follow
(vv. 131-135)

Knowing what is right and having the discipline to do it are two different things, and the second can be more difficult than the first. The psalmist understood this, and shifted from appreciation to a string of requests for divine aid in adhering to the divine way.

Needing a word beginning with *pe*, the poet chose *peh*, the word for mouth: "With open mouth I pant, because I long for your commandments" (v. 131). Like an exhausted runner panting for air or a thirsty traveler panting for water, he pictured himself open-mouthed, panting for the refreshing air of the commandments, the water of God's teaching.

He knew, however, that following God's way was more strenuous than knowing it. To follow God's way, he would need God's help: "Turn to me and be gracious to me, as is your custom toward those who love your name. Keep my steps steady according to your promise, and never let iniquity have dominion over me" (vv. 132-133).

The poet was not putting the ball entirely in God's court: he fully intended to follow the narrow way, but longed for God to hold his hand along the steepest and most trying parts, the places where temptation was strongest and other forces sought to lead him astray.

Like all of us, the psalmist lived in community, and his or her interactions with other people could be either a distraction or a downright detriment to remaining true to the path. The words behind "human oppression" indicate something stronger than simple temptation to do wrong. When someone else treats us badly, we are most in danger of leaning on a human instinct to return the hurt rather than returning good for evil. Perhaps that is why Jesus stressed the importance of turning the other cheek and going the extra mile (Matt. 5:38-42).

"Make your face shine upon your servant," the devout poet prayed, "and teach me your statutes" (v. 135). The expression recalls the Aaronic blessing of Num. 6:24-26: "The LORD bless you and keep you; the LORD make his face to shine upon you, and be gracious to you; the LORD lift up his countenance upon you, and give you peace."

The psalmist believed God's very nature could be revealed in one's study of God's laws, statutes, ordinances, decrees, and any other guide to positive relationships with God and others. Even so, the poet knew that human study and human effort are not enough: God's benevolent assistance would be required.

Sorrow for times of failure
(v. 136)

The section closes with a woeful observation of human nature: "My eyes shed streams of tears because your law is not kept" (v. 136). The psalmist may have had in mind those times when he or she had failed to keep the law, but is more likely to have been weeping for the state of the community. How many neighbors followed God's teaching? How faithfully did local authorities or higher levels of government adhere to the law that was designed to define the proper course of life with God and with others?

The psalmist lived in the context of an ethnic people who were called to uniformly follow the same God and the same laws. Today, we lie in a pluralistic society in which people follow both different faiths, and no faith. Despite the claims of some, America was not founded with the purpose of being a "Christian nation." Although Judeo-Christian ethics clearly influenced the Constitution and our national values, the intent was not to impose Christian beliefs on all residents.

Today, Christian nationalism – often a thin disguise for white supremacy – is one of the greatest threats to the health of the nation. Many devoted believers weep at the way biblical teachings have been twisted and used to oppress other people, often in the name of Christ.

We do not celebrate the strict codes of conduct and worship known to the psalmist, but we also hold to the belief that Christ demonstrated and taught the importance of love for God and love for others, a core tenet that is easier to understand, but no less difficult to follow than the commands so praised by the psalmist.

Despite its ancient and provincial nature, this text offers a clear and present challenge to those who would see the world as Jesus sees it, relate to the world as Jesus taught, and weep for those who twist biblical teaching to serve their own ends.

The Hardest Question
How does the acrostic work in vv. 129-136?

The psalmist has arranged it so that each verse in today's text begins with the Hebrew letter *pe*. The section begins with *pᵉlā'ôt*, meaning "wonderful," as a description of God's law.

Verse 130 begins with *pētach*, meaning "doorway," the image of an opening through which the light of God's teaching shines to educate the untrained.

A double use of the letter opens v. 131: *pî-pā'artî* combines the word for "mouth" with the verb for "to open" to describe the poet's open-mouthed panting for God's teaching.

The next verse begins with an appeal: *pᵉnē-'ēlay* pleads for God to "turn to me" with grace and help for the way.

Verse 133 employs a word for "my steps," *pᵉ'āmay* in a prayer that God will direct them rightly, while the next verse begins with *pᵉdēnî*, a request for God to "deliver me" from those who would oppress or lead the psalmist astray.

The expression "your face" (*pāneka*) opens v. 135 with a request that God would shine the divine countenance toward the psalmist to strengthen and guide.

Finally, v. 136 begins with a compound expression for "streams of water" (*palgê-mayîm*) to describe torrents of tears flowing from the psalmist's eyes as she mourned to see that so many did not follow God's way.

Third Reading
Romans 8:26-39

Life in the Spirit

Likewise the Spirit helps us in our weakness; for we do not know how to pray as we ought,
but that very Spirit intercedes with sighs too deep words. (Rom. 8:26)

Have you ever known someone who could be described as "spirited"? That suggests an effusive personality that always seems to be "on." In today's text, Paul has much to say about what it means to be a person with spirit, but he has much more in mind than one's personality. He's talking about living in, with, and empowered by the Spirit of Christ.

In the Spirit, we have an intercessor
(vv. 26-27)

The Spirit, Paul says, acts as an advocate and supporter to believers. If it comforts us to know that other people are praying for us, how much more should it mean to know that the Spirit intercedes for us? "The Spirit helps us in our weaknesses," Paul said, acknowledging that none of us have sufficient strength to face every challenge alone. We may or may not know the extent of our weaknesses, or what to do about them. Paul added "for we do not know how to pray as we ought, but that very Spirit intercedes with sighs too deep for words" (v. 26). **[Groaning]**

Groaning: Paul's discussion of suffering in the world and the life of the believer is punctuated by three words based on the verbal root *stenázō*, "to groan," with different subjects. In v. 22 he says "the whole creation has been groaning in labor pains until now," and in v. 23 he says that he and his fellow believers "groan inwardly while we wait for adoption, the redemption of our bodies." In v. 26 he affirms that the Spirit cares for us and "intercedes with sighs (groans) too deep for words."

On days when it seems that no one understands us and we may not understand ourselves, it is a comfort to know that the Spirit not only understands us, but also voices our needs in ways beyond our understanding. The thought itself is almost beyond comprehension, beyond our words.

Verse 27 may come across as almost dualistic, with a functional separation of God from the Spirit, but Paul's intent is to assure his readers that God understands their needs because the Spirit understands them and brings them to God, because God "knows what is the mind of the Spirit." As the Spirit intercedes for the "saints," so their needs come before God.

Here, as elsewhere, we note that Paul was writing to a deeply flawed group of believers, and yet they were believers, so he called them "saints," people who were set apart for God's service.

In the Spirit, we have a present helper
(v. 28)

Few New Testament verses, especially among Paul's writings, are more beloved or memorized more often than v. 28: "We know that all things work together for good for those who love God, who are called according to his purpose."

Paul wrote these words with an assumption that everyone is subject to troubles. If only good things happened, it would not be necessary to tell us that God can work to bring something good from all things.

Knowing that trouble is to be expected takes some of the fear out of it. If we give up the idea that life is going to be perfect, we don't have to be paranoid about what might happen to mess up our dreams. Instead, we can trust that even when unexpected trouble comes, we are not alone – and that God can actually work with us to bring good things from hard times.

I was academically successful in high school, but not particularly popular. And, though I tried hard, I was never more than an average athlete. To deal with my lack of success in those areas, I adopted a philosophy I'd heard attributed to Confucius: "He who expecteth nothing is never disappointed." When you don't expect much, then every good thing that happens tastes especially sweet.

Romans 8:28 moves beyond that pessimistic philosophy, but also retains a helpful level of realism. In premarital counseling, good pastors and counselors try to help a couple develop a set of realistic expectations about their marriage. Otherwise, they may enter marriage with "pie in the sky" dreams that get shattered the first time they find a pair of dirty socks on the floor.

None of us are immune to misfortune: we can expect to face bad days, but not to face them alone. We must be careful not to go beyond what Paul says: he does not say that all things are good, or that all things are from God. The verse does not suggest that God is behind all our hard times.

The point of the verse is that God can work together with us in ways that bring good even from those things that are not good in themselves, and that is an amazing truth. Losing a job we love is not a good thing in itself, but it may lead to a better job, or to a re-evaluation of what we want from life. Experiencing a disease or an accident with lasting consequences cannot be called a good thing, but greater maturity may come from it, or an ability to comfort and counsel others facing similar circumstances.

The good that comes may not feel equal to the difficulty endured, but there remains some comfort in knowing that we are not alone: God is not only with us, but at work in us, and if we pay attention, we will see ways in which

---

Good from bad: As an exercise, consider looking back at some of the major setbacks you have faced, and identifying areas of growth or new experiences that emerged from them as God worked with you to bring something good out of the trial.

---

even the most arduous situations may give rise to something positive. [**Good from bad**]

In the Spirit, there is no condemnation (vv. 29-39)

Although some commentators read vv. 29-30 in support of a double-edged view of predestination, the focus is not on God predetermining that certain people would be saved and certain people lost. Rather, it is about God's desire to live in relationship with humans. Paul believed this was God's intent, even before creation, and that God knew some people would respond in a positive way. Knowing this, God "predestined" them "to be conformed to the image of his Son, in order that he might be the firstborn within a large family" (v. 29).

In stairstep fashion, Paul argued that those who were "predestined" were "called," and the called were "justified," and the justified would be in turn "glorified" with God in eternity (v. 30).

Following the declaration of God's salvific intent, vv. 31-39 are built around three rhetorical questions: "If God is for us, who can be against us?" (v. 31b); "Who will bring any charge against God's chosen ones?" (v. 33a); and "Who is the one who condemns?" (v. 34a). The implied answers are that no one can ultimately stand against us, bring charges against us, or condemn us.

Many people may stand or work against us while this world lasts, but no one can condemn us ultimately. Paul, of course, is using the language of the courtroom. God is both judge and the one who justifies. Christ, who died for us, also intercedes for us. In that setting, no force of evil can prevail.

This thought leads Paul to write some of the most beautiful, powerful, and comforting words to be found in scripture: "Who will separate us from the love of Christ? Will hardship, or distress, or persecution, or famine, or nakedness, or peril, or sword?" (v. 35).

Note the seven threats Paul lists as common to his world: hardship, distress, persecution, famine, nakedness, peril, the sword. If Paul were writing today, he might use words such as racism, rejection, hunger, homelessness, poverty, terrorism, or bombs. Those things do exist, as Paul acknowledged in a rather awkward citation from Ps. 44:22 (v. 36), and

> **Placating the spirits:** Years ago I visited a missionary family who worked with a small tribe in northern Thailand. The people were very poor, in part because they spent much of their small income on placating the spirits. When villagers learned that the missionaries were expecting a new baby, they were shocked that the father did not drown a pig in the river to ensure a safe birth.

they can affect our lives, but they cannot separate us from the love of God nor keep us from overcoming.

"No, in all these things we are more than conquerors through him who loved us," Paul insisted. "For I am convinced that neither death, nor life, nor angels, nor rulers, nor things present, nor things to come, nor powers, nor height, nor depth, nor anything else in all creation, will be able to separate us from the love of God in Christ Jesus our Lord" (vv. 37-39).

Again, Paul lists potential threats, 10 of them this time, all of which probably connote some dimension beyond earthly life alone: death, life, angels, rulers, things present, things to come, powers, height, depth, or anything else in all creation.

In Paul's day, many people believed that the world was ruled by a hierarchy of invisible spirits. Paul's reference to angels, rulers, powers, height, and depth may have been technical terms referring to particular classes of supernatural beings. He doesn't indicate whether he also believed in oppressive spiritual beings, but uses language and concepts known to his audience.

Many people today still fear evil spirits. In some Oriental cultures, buildings are traditionally constructed with upturned points on the corners of the roof to keep evil spirits from roosting there. In Thailand, "spirit houses" – like big, fancy bird-houses – can be found in many yards. Homeowners provide the "spirit house" and put food in it daily in hopes of keeping the spirits from invading the house where they live. [**Placating the spirits**]

> **Naming the demons:** As an exercise, consider what attitudes, actions, or worldviews could be considered demonic, to the extent that their existence stands in opposition to the will and the work of God. Sometimes, when we name the demons for what they are, we can fear them less, and oppose them more.

While that may sound silly to many western Christians, many people still believe there is a constant battle between evil powers and the spirits of God, between bad angels and good angels. The Bible sometimes hints at such things, perhaps because ancient peoples believed so firmly in this system of supernatural beings. Imaginative novelists have popularized the belief that we are surrounded by an invisible war between the forces of good and evil, between archangels and archdemons striving to dominate the world.

We shouldn't lose any sleep in worrying about wars between angels and demons fighting for control of the world, but there are demon-like evils that should concern us. Alcoholism and drug addiction are akin to demons, as they destroy both lives and families. Racism is demonic in the way it privileges one group of people while oppressing others. Any brand of religion that terrorizes or kills in the name of God could be called demonic. Twisting scripture for political gain and corrupting power is demonic. Whether those evil things have any relation to supernatural beings is immaterial. [**Naming the demons**]

The point is not to worry about whether we believe in a world full of supernatural spirits; the point is that we don't have to be afraid of them. Christ has overcome all that can separate us from God. Nothing can come between us and God's grace. That was Paul's point.

Many things in this world can separate us from our money, our homes, our family, but there is nothing that can separate us from the love of God. Whatever comes, God can help us deal with it and bring something good from it.

The Book of Revelation describes heaven as a place where there are no more tears. While in this world, we still have tears, but because of Christ, we can have no more fears.

The Hardest Question
Why so many questions?

Paul's argument in Rom. 8:31-39 contains no less than a dozen questions, asked in rapid-fire order, and not always followed by answers. Paul was skilled in the art of rhetoric, and one could speak of these as a string of rhetorical questions, chosen and emphasized in service to a final answer that should put the questions to rest.

"What then are we to say about these things?" (v. 31a) sets the tone for the questions and answers to come.

"If God is for us, who is against us?" (v. 31b) is followed by an answer that morphs into another question: "He who did not withhold his own Son, but gave him up for all of us, will he not with him also give us everything else?" (v. 32). Here is the key to the argument and the basis on which it turns: the self-giving work of Christ has overcome the power of evil in all its manifestations.

With Christ having redeemed us, "Who will bring any charge against God's elect?" The unstated answer is "No one," because "It is God who justifies" (v. 33).

If God has justified believers, then "Who is to condemn?" Again, Paul turns to the work of Christ to refute the possibility. "It is Christ Jesus who died, yes, who was raised, who was at the right hand of God, who indeed intercedes for us" (v. 34).

Since God in Christ has gone to this extreme to demonstrate divine love and call humankind to redemption, "Who will separate us from the love of Christ?" Various possibilities come in the form of yet another question that's really seven queries in one: "Will hardship, or distress, or persecution, or famine, or nakedness, or peril, or sword?" (v. 35).

The answer comes in the powerful affirmation that is such a mainstay in funeral services: "No, in all these things we are more than conquerors through him who loved us. For I am convinced that neither death, nor life, nor angels, nor rulers, nor things present, nor things to come, nor powers, nor height, nor depth, nor anything else in all creation, will be able to separate us from the love of God in Christ Jesus our Lord" (vv. 37-39).

Can there be any doubt about the effectiveness of well-placed questions?

Fourth Reading
Matthew 13:31-33, 44-52

The World Needs Wisdom

The kingdom of heaven is like yeast that a woman took and mixed in with three measures of flour until all of it was leavened. (Matt. 13:33)

Some things are just too difficult to describe in technical terms alone. How does one explain love, or pride, or an adrenaline rush?

When vocabulary and logic fail, stories come to the rescue. When Jesus tried to explain such difficult concepts as the Kingdom of God, he told stories that had the power to enlighten those who had the ears of faith and discernment to listen, while leaving hard-hearted or hard-headed people in the dark.

Today's text finds us again in Matthew 13, where the author has strung together a series of parables about the kingdom of heaven. Part of Jesus' task was to help his followers to unlearn some of their misguided ideas and to comprehend the true meaning of God's reign.

Many first-century Jews imagined the kingdom as arriving with a divinely assisted victory over Rome, led by a messianic warrior who would then rule as a mighty king – someone like David, only better.

But when Jesus thought of the kingdom of God, he had in mind the rule of God in the minds and hearts and lives of those who followed him. It was not an external empire encompassing the earth's population, but an internal relationship between God and those who follow God's way. The kingdom had begun in Jesus and was growing through the disciples and others who followed Jesus, but it was not yet all that it would be. Thus, the kingdom was both a present reality and a promised fulfillment.

Parables of mustard seed and leaven
(vv. 31-33)

The third parable in Matthew 13 is the first that is not given an interpretation. It appears in slightly different forms in Mark 4:30-32 and Luke 13:18-19. "The kingdom of heaven is like a mustard seed that someone took and sowed in his field," Jesus said. "It is the smallest of all the seeds, but when it has grown it is the greatest of shrubs and becomes a tree, so that the birds of the air come and make nests in its branches."

The story is not a botany lesson: mustard seeds are not in fact the smallest seeds (orchid seeds are smaller), but they were likely the smallest known in first-century Palestine. **[Mustard seeds]**

Jesus' hearers were familiar with a plant known as black mustard (*Brassica Nigra*). When left alone, it could reach 8–10 feet tall. It was spindly and not technically a tree, but large enough to attract birds that might perch on its branches and eat the seeds.

The primary point seems to be a straightforward analogy. As the mustard plant began as a tiny seed but grew into a large bush, so the kingdom of God had a small begin-

---

Mustard seeds: Modern readers might be familiar with mustard greens, but the ancients sometimes cultivated mustard for its seeds. As such a large plant, one wouldn't typically plant mustard in a small garden, but a few in a field could come in handy. Mustard seeds could be used as spices, for medicinal purposes, or even for the extraction of oil.

ning in Jesus and those who followed him, but it would come to an amazing fruition.

While the focus is on contrast and not allegory, many readers see in the birds an image of how the kingdom would grow to encompass people from every nation. The image calls to mind Old Testament texts that speak of trees in which birds come to nest in their branches (Dan. 4:10-12; Ezek. 17:22-24, 31:6). In Jewish thought, birds were sometimes used as symbols of the Gentiles.

Matthew paired the mustard seed with another story of mysterious and surprising growth: "The kingdom of heaven is like yeast that a woman took and mixed in with three measures of flour until all of it was leavened" (v. 33; cp. Luke 13:20-21).

While the NRSV and other translations say the woman "mixed" the leaven into the dough, the word used is *enkryptō*, which means "to hide." It's built from the root *kryptō*, which is far more common: *enkryptō* is used only here in the New Testament. English words such as cryptology and encryption, referring to secret codes, are derived from it.

Some interpreters try to find meaning in the idea that leaven was sometimes described in negative terms as a corrupting influence, as something Jews had to remove from their homes before Passover. But there are positive images to balance those. Jews ate leavened bread every other week of the year. Like leaven affecting bread, we can influence others, whether for good or bad.

"Yeast" is better translated as "leaven," something similar to sourdough starter. Every day, when a woman finished kneading the dough and prepared to bake bread, she would put a small piece of dough aside in a covered bowl: the yeast in it would continue fermenting and serve as leaven for the next day's bread.

The point of the story is again seen in the power of the leaven to spark amazing growth. Like a seed that grows underground and out of sight, the woman "hides" the leaven in the doughy mixture of flour and water. And what a mixture it is: the three measures of flour in the story would have been about 40–60 pounds. That would make enough bread for a party of 100 people or more.

God's kingdom, still hidden in the lives of Jesus and his disciples, would grow beyond measure and instill a spirit of celebration to boot.

Parables of a treasure and a pearl
(vv. 44-46)

After an interlude in which Jesus explained the purpose of parables (vv. 34-35) and the meaning of the parable of the wheat and the weeds (vv. 36-43), Matthew portrays Jesus as relating several other parables to the disciples alone.

Two parables are again paired. Both are found only in Matthew, and both emphasize not the surprising growth and size of the kingdom (as in the parables of the mustard seed and the leaven), but the kingdom's surpassing value – something so desirable that it calls for total discipleship.

The first story concerns a treasure hidden in a field, "which someone found and hid; then in his joy he goes and sells all that he has and buys that field" (v. 44). [**Finders keepers?**]

The point of the story is not to raise ethical questions about buying a field without disclosing its hidden treasure, but to portray participation in God's realm as so valuable that one should be willing to give up all else in order to find it. We do not possess the kingdom as we would a treasure. Rather, we are possessed by such a desire for relationship with God that we are willing to put God first in our lives.

The second story is similar: a certain merchant in search of fine pearls came across a single pearl so magnificent that he was determined to have it, so "on finding one pearl of great value, he went and sold all that he had and bought it" (vv. 45-46).

Merchants were generally considered to be shady characters in scripture, but it was not unusual for Jesus to appreciate people that others did not. We should observe that, once the man sold all that he had to buy the wonder-

---

Finders keepers? The parable of the hidden treasure in a field does not say anything about why the treasure-finder was poking around in someone else's field, nor does it speak to the ethics of buying someone's land without disclosing the presence of a massive treasure. Was he looking for treasure, like someone crisscrossing the beach or a historic battlefield with a metal detector? We typically imagine that the man was a hired hand sent out to plow, but the story does not say so. Nor does the story identify the treasure or say how long it had been there – things we would like to know. Presumably, if the owner of the field had known about the treasure, he would not have sold it, so perhaps the lucky finder/buyer felt justified in keeping it for himself.

> **Pearly drinks:** Readers might be interested to know that the Greek word for pearl is *margarita*. The alcoholic drink known as a margarita probably gets its name from the Spanish word for "daisy." It is similar to a brandy cocktail known as a "daisy" that was popular during Prohibition.
>
> Some ancient stories associate pearls and drinking, though alcohol was not involved. Pliny noted that pearls were considered of utmost value in the Roman empire – more valuable than gold or rubies. He and several other Latin writers recount a story in which Cleopatra reportedly bet Mark Antony that she could finish off 10,000,000 sesterces' worth of food and drink in a single meal. When it was time for the dessert course, a small dish of vinegar was brought to her. Cleopatra, according to the story, was wearing earrings made from the two largest pearls ever found, gifts of visiting kings. She removed one of her impressive pearls and put it in the vinegar, where it dissolved. She then drank it and won the wager by slurping up a highly valuable pearl.
>
> (While I found this story in Amy Jill Levine's *Short Stories of Jesus* [Harper Collins, 2014], 146-147, the source is Pliny, *Natural History* 9.119-21. It is also discussed in B. Ullman, "Cleopatra's Pearls," *Classical Journal* 52.5 [1957], http://penelope.uchicago.edu/Thayer/E/journals/CJ/52/5/Cleopatras_Pearls*.html.)

ful pearl, he was effectively no longer a merchant. There is no indication that he planned to sell it for a profit: he had become just a man with a very valuable pearl.

We presume the man who bought the field would make use of the treasure to buy what he needed, but how could the former merchant eat and where would he sleep if he had sold everything to buy a pearl? **[Pearly drinks]**

Practicality is not the point, which is that being a part of God's kingdom is so valuable and so important that it calls for complete surrender. But Jesus also recognized that we have human needs. We may recall his advice in Matt. 6:33, which encouraged people not to worry about material possessions: "But strive first for the kingdom of God and his righteousness, and all these things will be given to you as well."

A parable about good fish and bad fish
(vv. 47-50)

The seventh parable in Matthew's kingdom collection returns to the judgment theme of the parable of the weeds among the wheat. Here Jesus speaks of a net thrown into the sea that catches fish of every kind. The fishermen bring all the fish to shore, where they keep the good fish and

throw out the bad – presumably inedible or non-kosher fish (vv. 47-48).

Using vocabulary and phrases similar to v. 42, Jesus (or Matthew) explained it as a parable of judgment in which angels would "separate the evil from the righteous and throw them into the furnace of fire, where there will be weeping and gnashing of teeth" (vv. 48-49).

The point is that a time of separation will come, and only the righteous will remain within God's kingdom realm. For more on the symbolic language of judgment, see last week's gospel lesson.

A word about the wise
(vv. 51-52)

Having drawn his kingdom teachings to a close, Jesus asked the disciples if they understood. Probably overstating the case, they claimed that they did (v. 51).

Jesus then reminded them of their ongoing responsibility as teachers: having such understanding, they would need to explain the gospel and its kingdom implications to others. Using an analogy that some commentators consider to be an eighth parable, Jesus said "Therefore every scribe who has been trained for the kingdom of heaven is like the master of a household who brings out of his treasure what is new and what is old" (v. 52).

"Scribes" were the teachers of the law, rabbis who had been trained in understanding the written Torah as well as the oral law. They were the teachers of Israel. Jesus now speaks to the disciples as Christian scribes who could comprehend both the great treasures of the Old Testament scriptures and the teachings of Jesus – and could relate the two. With the emphasis on the latter, they could bring out "what is new and what is old." Matthew, no doubt, also had in mind Christian pastors and teachers of future generations. **[A self-portrait?]**

> **A self-portrait?** Commentators have often imagined that v. 52 is like the author's self-portrait: he thinks of himself as a Christian scribe who understands the new teachings of Jesus and is able to relate them to ancient teachings preserved in the Hebrew scriptures. Matthew constantly quotes from the Old Testament, seeing ways in which Jesus fulfilled or related to Israel's religious heritage.

As the church experienced kingdom growth, it would need trained teachers to help believers understand how the love of God stretched from creation to eternity in an ongoing tension of judgment and grace, and with a desire to encompass all people.

We teach by both word and example. Who can you bless by bringing out treasures, both new and old?

The Hardest Question
What's missing?

While Matthew has brought together several parables of the kingdom from a variety of sources, attentive readers might note that he omitted a related kingdom parable that he clearly had at his disposal. The author of Matthew often follows the gospel of Mark, who pairs the parable of the mustard seed with another short parable often referred to as "the seed growing secretly" (Mark 4:26-29).

Jesus said: "This is what the kingdom of God is like. A man scatters seed on the ground. Night and day, whether he sleeps or gets up, the seed sprouts and grows, though he does not know how. All by itself (*automatos*) the soil produces grain – first the stalk, then the head, then the full kernel in the head. As soon as the grain is ripe, he puts the sickle to it, because the harvest has come."

The main point seems to be that the kingdom was founded by God's initiative, and God could be trusted to bring it to fruition. The verse about the harvest is a rough quotation of Joel 3:13, an Old Testament prophecy regarding the surety of a coming judgment. The main point, then, is that the seed grows by itself. We can neither "bring in the kingdom" nor predict the time of its ultimate revelation.

We can't fully understand how the kingdom grows, but we can trust God that it will. Our tendency is to try and explain everything. I remember how delighted I was in biology class to learn something about how plants grow – how the apical meristem of a shoot undergoes continual mitosis, rapidly producing cells which then differentiate into xylem or phloem or cambium or epithelium – but none of that knowledge enabled me to actually make a seed grow. The seed grows by itself.

This is not to say that we have no place in the story. The first farmer was Jesus, sowing the seeds of the kingdom in the hearts and minds of his followers. But one of the secrets of kingdom growth is that Jesus' followers are called to continue sowing the seed of Christ's kingdom love. In other places, Jesus taught us not only to be faithful in sowing the seed by proclaiming the kingdom, but also to recognize that there is already a harvest in the field that needs to be brought in (Luke 10:2).

The growth of the kingdom is a cooperative venture. It is God who makes it grow, but we have a part in the sowing and the reaping as we work to bring others to Christ and as faithful subjects of the kingdom.

Why did Matthew not include this parable? Perhaps he wanted to pair the parable of the mustard seed with the parable of the leaven, and thought those were sufficient illustrations of how the kingdom grows mysteriously as the work of God. The other parables in the sequence emphasize the need for human response to the claims of the gospel.

First Reading
Genesis 32:22-31*

Wrestling with God

Then the man said, "You shall no longer be called Jacob, but Israel, for you have striven with God and with humans, and have prevailed." (Gen. 32:28)

I have never understood why people enjoy professional "rasslin'," as we called it when I was a boy and the Saturday afternoon matches on TV that we watched featured characters such as the mountainous Haystacks Calhoun, the masked "Mr. Wrestling," and a bad-guy tag team known as "the Assassins."

Does watching beefed-up men in tights being thrown around, choked, and stomped give viewers an adrenaline or testosterone rush? Do the theatrically staged violence and "hero vs. villain" aspects provide a vicarious way for people to give vent to their anger or frustrations? I don't know, but there's a market for it.

When most of us wrestle, it's likely to be a mental effort to overcome an unhealthy habit or to wrangle our finances into shape. Sometimes, though, we may find ourselves feeling as if we were wrestling with God over some personal struggle. We may plead, argue, or bargain with God, but few of us can claim to have engaged the divine in hand-to-hand combat.

There is one man who could. His name was Jacob.

Jacob's long and winding road: Jacob is the main character from Genesis 25–36 and takes the spotlight again near the end of the book, when he gathers his sons to his deathbed and blesses some of them, but not all (Genesis 49).

The name "Jacob" means "heel-grabber," an ancient version of "Sneaky Pete" or "Slimy Sam," and he lived up to it. At birth, Jacob tried to yank his twin Esau back into the womb. As an adult, he swindled Esau out of his birthright and tricked his father Isaac into giving him Esau's blessing. When his furious brother threatened murder, Jacob had to flee their base camp in Hebron. His mother Rebekah sent him far away, to the northern Mesopotamian city of Haran, to hole up with her brother Laban.

Along the way, Yahweh appeared to Jacob in a dream and promised to continue Abraham's blessing through him, though Jacob was skeptical and made a vow designed to hold God to the promise.

In Haran, Laban turned out to be as tricky as Jacob. He duped his nephew into marrying both of his daughters, Leah and Rachel, though Jacob wanted only Rachel. Jacob paid for his wives with 14 years of labor before earning a share of each year's newborn sheep and goats as a salary. Although Laban often changed the terms, Jacob connived to practice breeding methods that gained him a larger share of the livestock.

While outwitting Laban, Jacob found himself being traded back and forth between his two wives and their handmaids, Bilhah and Zilpah. In the process, he fathered 11 sons and at least one daughter (he would later see a 12th son born, but lose his beloved Rachel in the process).

A day came when Jacob – reportedly at God's instruction – decided to gather his wives, flocks, and other possessions for a return trip to his homeland (31:1-13). After a contentious parting from Laban (31:14-55), Jacob and his party traveled south along the eastern side of the Jordan River, stopping to camp near the fords of the Jabbok River, a tributary of the Jordan about 20 miles north of the Dead Sea.

---

*This text is also read for Proper 24 in Year C.

A long road

Jacob had traveled a long and winding road before we meet him in today's text. He was the son of Isaac and grandson of Abraham, with a much-deserved reputation as a rascal. Jacob cheated his brother Esau so badly that he had to flee for his life while still a young man. After spending 20 years or more in the northwest Mesopotamian city of Haran with his conniving uncle Laban, he prepared to return to his homeland as a prosperous man with a large family. [Jacob's long and winding road]

Traveling south along the eastern bank of the Jordan river, "the angels of God met him," the narrator says, leading Jacob to believe he had stumbled upon "God's camp" (32:1-2). This apparently encouraged him enough to send messengers to his estranged brother, alerting him that he was moving back toward home (32:3-8).

Still nervous about their reunion, in his message Jacob referred to his brother as "my lord Esau" and described himself as "your servant Jacob."

Jacob got no comfort from a following report that Esau had set out to meet him with a small army of 400 men. Attempting defensive measures, Jacob divided his family and property into two camps in hopes that one could escape if the other was attacked. He then prayed for deliverance, according to Gen. 32:9-12. Hoping to placate his

brother, Jacob sent a large gift of valuable livestock ahead of him (32:13-21), spaced out in several groups for maximum effect. [Praying for deliverance]

A midnight surprise
(vv. 22-25)

Jacob then took his wives, children, and all his possessions across a ford in the river to the south side of the Jabbok (now called Zarqa). Surprisingly, he then returned to the north bank to remain alone through the night.

Was Jacob being cowardly? Did he need some "alone time"? Did he want to pray for deliverance in private? The text doesn't say, nor does it tell as much as we'd like to know about what happened next.

A man appeared, we are told, and "wrestled with him until daybreak" (v. 24). The Hebrew word for "wrestle" comes from the same root that means "dust." Literally, it means "to get dusty," which is bound to happen when one wrestles in the dirt.

Because we have read the whole story, we know that the "man" (*'ish*) was either God or a supernatural stand-in in human form, but apparently with some self-imposed limitations. God had "stood by" Jacob and blessed him as he prepared to leave Canaan. God met him again as he prepared to re-enter the land – but this time, blessing was preceded by wrestling.

We don't know how or when Jacob concluded that he was dealing with a divine opponent. Commentators have proposed that he may have thought his assailant was Esau, or a river demon. The writer said the grueling match lasted through the night, but offers no details. [Jacob's opponent]

That Jacob should prove to be a strong opponent is not surprising. He was known for having moved a heavy stone well cover by himself (Gen. 29:1-10), and tenacity was his trademark. As daybreak drew near, Jacob's opponent saw that he "did not prevail" against Jacob through pure wrestling, so he struck him a blow that dislocated his hip (v. 25).

The word translated as "strike" can also mean "touch," and some read this to mean that God exercised supernatural power by just touching Jacob's hip and putting it out of joint. But, since the opponent is clearly portrayed as self-limited and unable to prevail, the probable intent is that the divine adversary maneuvered Jacob into a vulnera-

---

Praying for deliverance: Jacob's prayer in 32:9-12 is very similar in form to some of the psalms of lament. The prayer is couched in humility, but still contains manipulative elements, as Jacob uses God's own words in hopes of gaining protection, addressing his prayer to the god "who said to me, 'Go back to your country and your relatives, and I will make you prosper'" (32:9b).

In his prayer, however, Jacob did finally acknowledge his heritage and his place in the divine scheme to make Abraham's descendants like the sand of the sea. This is in contrast to Gen. 28:20-22, where he had ignored those promises to focus on personal interests for provision and safekeeping.

The only aspect of God's promise in Genesis 28 not yet fulfilled was a safe return to his homeland, and for that Jacob prayed, reminding God of the divine promise that his descendants would be like the sand of the sea, a promise that Jacob presumed would require God to protect the mothers and children in his family.

> **Jacob's opponent:** It has often been suggested that the story of Jacob at the Jabbok has its roots in an old story about a river demon who would threaten travelers attempting to cross the ford, much like the trolls who guard the bridge in the fairy tale "Three Billy Goats Gruff." One might also imagine that the narrow ford might be a place where thieves would lurk at night, so Jacob might have imagined his attacker was a bandit. Some readers also suspect Jacob might have thought his attacker was a stealthy Esau. In any case, Jacob had apparently crossed the ford multiple times without incident – but that was in daylight.
>
> Are we to read the account as a physical event? Interpreters often suggest that the entire story is an extended metaphor – that Jacob was really wrestling with himself and his mixed motives and his uncertain relationship with God. While we may find profit in thinking of the story this way, the text itself does not suggest it.

> **Strength from wounds:** Jacob was wounded in his wrestling with God, but in transformative ways. Sometimes, our greatest blessings come through our deepest wounds. We should not argue that God causes all our wounds, as in Jacob's story, but when we are alone in the night, when we are wounded by life, we are more likely to focus on the most important priorities. When we are hurting, we are more prone to seek solace in God. When we realize how badly we need help, we are more inclined to seek the presence of the One who is our ultimate help.

ble position and then struck his hip in such a way as to put it out of joint.

A sunrise blessing
(vv. 26-31)

Though the dislocation would have been extremely painful, Jacob held tight when his opponent said "Let me go," even though God reminded him that dawn was breaking. It was widely believed that anyone who saw God's face would die, so the request was for Jacob's benefit.

Still, Jacob was determined to wrangle a blessing from his adversary and was willing to risk his life in the effort.

The encounter switched from physical to verbal. God asked Jacob's name, which he readily supplied. God then gave him a new name: "You shall no longer be called Jacob, but Israel, for you have striven with God and with humans, and have prevailed" (v. 28). "Israel" can mean "God fights," but it could also be read to mean "he struggled (with) God." Given the context, the latter seems more likely.

We can't appreciate it in English, but for Hebrew readers the story contains several instances of wordplay: Jacob (*ya*◻*akōv*), Jabbok (*yabbōq*), and wrestle (◻*āvāq*) all share multiple consonants.

Unlike the stories of Jacob's grandfather, which consistently call him Abraham after his name was changed from Abram, the narrators continue to call Jacob by his birth name. When he is called "Israel" in a few later texts, it is generally in recognition of his role as father of the 12 sons who gave rise to the 12 putative tribes of Israel.

Jacob was not satisfied to receive a new name of his own, however: he wanted to know the name of his combatant. Was he still uncertain with whom he was wrestling, or did he hope that God would reveal a more personal name that might grant Jacob some advantage? We cannot be sure: God's only reply was "Why do you ask?" (v. 29).

Jacob did not learn the name of his opponent, but he did win a blessing. God refused to give Jacob what he wanted, but blessed him with what he needed, and that's all we know.

But Jacob also felt blessed in another way. He must have caught at least a shadowy glimpse of his opponent, for he named the place "Peniel" (more commonly spelled "Penuel"), which means "face of God." Proud of having survived the encounter, Jacob said "I have seen God face to face, and my life has been preserved" (v. 30).

One of the most vivid images in all of scripture is the next one, told with bare-bones simplicity: "And the sun broke out on him as he crossed over Penuel, limping on his hip" (v. 31). Jacob may have seen God and survived, but he did not emerge unmarked. [**Strength from wounds**]

Lessons to remember

Can such an arcane story speak to others who also struggle with God? Consider that Jacob's encounter with God was preceded by a prayer for deliverance (32:9-12), followed by the employment of a defensive strategy designed to protect his family. Jacob believed in praying for divine help, but also in doing what he could for himself. We can learn from that.

The nocturnal wrestling match with God, in some ways, combines both prayer and action: Jacob physically struggled with God, while also engaging in a conversation designed to elicit a blessing from God. Do our prayers come too easy, or do they reflect a serious spiritual struggle to become what God wants us to be?

Few of us could claim to have grappled with God in a physical sense, but Jacob's encounter at the Jabbok reminds us that God still comes to meet us on our own level, in our own imperfections, where we are, and offers blessing. We don't need to wrestle with or wheedle blessings from God: they are freely granted. [**Wrestling with God**]

Jacob's exchange with God reminds us that names are important – both the name we are given and the name we make for ourselves. God knows our names and needs. God didn't have to ask Jacob's name, but apparently wanted the cunning patriarch to confess his nature as one who overreaches. The new name God gave honored Jacob's continued willingness to reach beyond what was expected: as he had struggled with men, so he had struggled with God – and for the good.

Jacob's encounter reminds us that God can break into our lives at any time and lead us in new directions. Jacob apparently had few thoughts beyond protecting himself and his family when he encountered the unexpected visitor in the night. He was still walking when he emerged from the encounter, but his limp was a clear reminder that his life had been changed forever.

Jacob's story might also remind us of another time when God came to earth in human form for the purpose of blessing. Jesus became incarnate, intentionally self-limited during his life on earth. He struggled with temptation and weariness and frustration, just as we do. He engaged in match after match with opponents and critics. He wrestled in the garden with his own very natural desire to escape the cost of Calvary, but he held on to the end, taking our wounds upon himself. Because of that, we can also catch a glimpse of what God is like. We can be changed, and take on a new name, and set out on a new road to live out the meaning of "Christian."

The Hardest Question
Is there a connection between Genesis 28 and 32?

The very brief account of Jacob meeting "the angels of God" on his return to Canaan is reminiscent of an earlier meeting as he was leaving. Genesis 28 tells the story of how Jacob stopped for the night while journeying north, fleeing his brother and aiming for Haran.

At "a certain place," he went to sleep with his head on a large rock as his pillow. During the night, he had a vision of "the angels of God" ascending and descending a ladder (or more likely, a staircase) between heaven and earth" (28:10-12). Yahweh ("the LORD") then "stood beside him" and pledged that the promises given to Abraham would pass on to him (28:13-14).

Jacob responded by exclaiming "How awesome is the place! This is none other than the house of God, and this is the gate of heaven!" (28:16-17). The next morning Jacob turned his pillow upright to make a standing stone (*masseb*â) and reportedly named the place Bethel, which means "house of God" (28:18-19).

Jacob then did something surprising. Instead of gratefully accepting God's appearance and impressive blessing at face value, he sought to maneuver God into a ritually binding arrangement. Jacob made a vow to serve God. In the Hebrew Bible, a vow is always a conditional promise. So, Jacob vowed to return to Bethel and serve God – *if* God fulfilled all the promises *and* provided him with food, clothing, and a safe return home (28:20-22).

On Jacob's return, we find that he was once again met by angels. No details are given as in the meeting on his departure, but the angels were in sufficient number that Jacob once again believed he had come across a junction of sorts between heaven and earth, and he gave the place a name: "This is God's camp," he said, "So he called that place Mahanaim" (32:1). The word *mahᵃnā'im* is a dual form, meaning "two camps," perhaps in reference to Jacob's own camp and the angel's camp.

The narrative of Jacob's return contains no record of a conversation between him and the angels, but afterward Jacob prayed for deliverance (32:9-12), reminding God of the promises made in their first encounter. Soon thereafter, God again visited Jacob in the night. This time, God did not stand by and bless the crafty patriarch, but engaged Jacob in a wrestling match, dislocating his hip and blessing him after Jacob had struggled through the night. As he limped away, Jacob again pronounced a place name, calling the spot Peniel, which means "face of God," because he believed he had survived a face-to-face encounter with God.

Thus, a careful reader will note that Jacob was met by angels and had a direct encounter with God both on his exit and his return to Canaan. In both instances, he reportedly gave the places commemorative names. And, in both cases Jacob tried to verbally manipulate God, acting as a shrewd and determined operator trying to gain an advantage. After the second encounter, Jacob apparently recognized how fortunate he was just to have survived his encounter with God, and the narrator portrays him as a different person from that time forward. Jacob was not perfect – he still showed unfortunate favoritism to the sons of Rachel – but his relationship with God through the remainder of Genesis revealed much deeper humility, gratitude, and trust.

Optional First Reading
Psalm 17 (RCL 17:1-7, 15)

An Imperative Prayer

Wondrously show your steadfast love, O savior of those who seek refuge from their adversaries at your right hand. (Ps. 17:7)

"I deserve better than this," she said, before storming out of the house. "I was a model employee who worked hard every day," he claimed, "but I still got laid off." Maybe she did deserve better, and maybe he was the ideal hire, but bad things can happen to good people.

There are times when we may think we deserve better than we get, times when we're convinced that others are mistreating us even though we're in the right. It may be life that's doing us wrong, with a hint of suspicion that God may be behind the blows. That's how the author of today's text was feeling, and she made sure God heard about it.

A case for vindication
(vv. 1-5)

The first line of this poem tells us where the prayer is going. "Hear a just cause, O LORD" sets the stage for someone who thinks they are being unfairly treated to ask God to set things straight.

The petitioner presents himself or herself as someone who is just in every way, who never speaks deceitfully and is in the right (vv. 1-2), who harbors no wickedness and voices no verbal transgressions (v. 3), who avoids the ways of the violent but holds fast to God's paths (vv. 4-5).

How many of us could make such bold claims? We may think we don't deserve whatever unfairness is going on in our lives, but few of us would claim to be as faultless as the psalmist claimed to be.

The NRSV's version of v. 3 is misleading: it takes the verse as a conditional sentence that challenges God to come and test the petitioner: "If you try my heart, if you visit me by night, if you test me, you will find no wickedness in me;

my mouth does not transgress." The NIV11 offers a similar hypothetical action: "Though you probe my heart …"

The first three verbs, however, are simple perfects that indicate past action, as in the NET: "You have scrutinized my inner motives; you have examined me during the night. You have carefully evaluated me, but you find no sin."

Whether in prospect or retrospect, the outcome is the same: the psalmist is confident that God has found and will find him innocent on all counts, and plans to keep it that way: "I am determined I will say nothing sinful."

An unusual construction in v. 4 could be read as a simple reference to the psalmist's desire to follow God's way: "As for what others do, by the word of your lips I have avoided the ways of the violent." An alternate reading, however, sees the awkward "word of your lips" as something like an oath or interjection. Robert Alter translates it this way: "As for human acts – by the word of your lips! I have kept from the tracks of the brute" (*The Book of Psalms: A Translation with Commentary* [W.W. Norton, 2007], 49).

Following God's teaching and avoiding the ways of violent men, the poet could claim "My steps have held fast to your paths; my feet have not slipped" (v. 5).

Do you know anyone whose feet have never slipped, who have never wavered from the path of righteousness? The psalmist doesn't sound like anyone we know.

An appeal for help
(vv. 6-14)

The psalmist is so sure of his innocence and God's favor that he demands a hearing and a response: "I call upon you, for

At, or by God's hand? The NRSV translation is legitimate but confusing, as it is not clear whether it is those who seek refuge or the adversaries who are "at your right hand," which suggests a place of divine favor (Ps. 45:9, 80:17). The word order suggests it could be the adversaries, but that doesn't follow. Thus, one must read the awkward sentence carefully to understand that the psalmist, as one who seeks refuge in God, imagines herself to be positioned at God's right hand.

An alternate translation avoids the difficulty by taking the idiom of God's right hand as an image of power rather than a place of favor. The preposition b- (which appears before "your right hand") can have the locative sense of "in" or "at," but can also bear the instrumental sense of "by" or "with." Thus, one could read the sentence, as NIV11 and NET do, as a prayer that deliverance would come "by your right hand," a common idiom for divine power in the Hebrew Bible, and one made explicit in vv. 13-14a (see Exod. 15:6, 12; Job 40:14; Ps. 48:10, 60:5, 91:7, 108:6, 138:7, et. al.).

you will answer me, O God; incline your ear to me, hear my words. Wondrously show your steadfast love, O savior of those who seek refuge from their adversaries at your right hand" (vv. 6-7). **[At, or by God's hand?]**

The psalmist is so devout that he thinks of himself as the apple of God's eye, and prays that God would protectively enfold him "in the shadow of your wings" (v. 8). If the poet is thinking metaphorically, as with Moses' description of God carrying Israel on eagle's wings (Exod. 19:4, 32:11), the image would be like that of a mother bird sheltering her chicks. Psalm 91:4 promises that "he will cover you with his pinions, and under his wings you will find refuge," and Jesus used a similar metaphor to describe his care for Jerusalem (Matt. 23:37, Luke 13:34).

It is just as likely, however, that the poet was thinking of the wings of the cherubim above the Ark of the Covenant, where God's presence was thought to be especially powerful. Similar images of taking shelter beneath God's wings are found in Ruth 2:12 and Ps. 36:7, 57:1, 61:4, and 63:7.

The psalmist turns to say more about his enemies. They are wicked and deadly (v. 9), with hearts too fat with pride to have pity and prone to arrogant speech (v. 10). They are persistent, tracking the psalmist down and surrounding him "like a lion eager to tear, like a young lion lurking in ambush" (vv. 11-12).

Were the adversaries really out to murder the psalmist, or was the extravagant language a metaphor for their attempts to bring him down? If the author really was David, the reference could be literal: there were often times when people tried to kill him, most notably when Saul and thousands of men reportedly pursued him in the wilderness and tried to surround him. Other people in similar settings may have had enemies with lethal intent.

Verse 9 speaks of those "who despoil me." The word can mean "attack," "destroy," or "devastate." Clearly the psalmist thought someone was out to ruin him. Perhaps they had brought false charges against him in court. Whether they sought to ruin his reputation or his finances or his position in society, it was still a serious matter. The psalmist saw no way other than to petition for God's protective shelter.

Verse 13 implies that the enemies were truly after blood, for the psalmist prayed for God to "... confront them! Overthrow them! By your sword deliver my life from the wicked, from mortals – by your hand, O LORD – from mortals whose portion in life is in this world" (vv. 13-14a).

A close reader, especially of the Hebrew text, will note that the poet has switched back and forth between singular and plural when describing the opposition. The enemies are multiple in vv. 9-11, but in v. 12 the "lion eager to tear" is singular, "a young lion lurking in ambush."

Singular use continues into v. 13. Although the NRSV uses the plural, the psalmist prays for God to "confront him," "overthrow him," and wield the sword against the "wicked," a word that is singular but could be understood collectively. In v. 14 the poet reverts to the plural, speaking of "mortals whose portion in life is in this world."

At this point the translation gets tricky again. The remainder of v. 14 can be read as a lament that God has blessed such mortals with such prosperity that their bellies are full and they have abundance to leave to their children. NASB20, for example, has "And whose belly you fill with treasure; they are satisfied with children, and leave their abundance to their babies." NET follows a similar course.

Robert Alter (*The Book of Psalms*, 50) reads the verse as a prayer that God will bless the psalmist with prosperity. The word others translate as "riches" derives from a root that means "hidden," so he regards God's hidden or treasured ones as the referent: "And your protected ones – fill their bellies, let their sons be sated, and let them leave what is left to their young."

Another option is taken by NRSV and NIV11, which interpret the imperfect verbs in a jussive or precative sense, so that the enemies' bellies are stuffed with divine retribution: "May their bellies be filled with what you have stored up for then; may their children have more than enough; may they leave something over to their little ones" (NRSV).

This reading gives v. 14b an imprecatory sense, that God would render such harsh judgment on the psalmist's enemies that they would feel it for generations to come.

A confident hope
(v. 15)

One could make a case for any one of the three approaches, but the first seems to fit best when compared with the final verse. While mortals who find their reward in this world may have sufficient goods to satisfy their needs for generations, the psalmist has a different goal in mind. "As for me, I shall behold your face in righteousness; when I awake I shall be satisfied, beholding your likeness."

The psalmist's bold desire to see God's face runs against the traditional belief that death would be the result and anticipates that he would see God's face. Moses was told that he could not see God's face and live (Exod. 33:20), but he is also said to have spoken with God "face to face" (Exod. 33:11, Num. 12:8). Jacob claimed to have seen God's face after a night of wrestling with God (Gen. 32:30). [**Night vision**]

The psalmists sometimes spoke of worship so real that God's face might be revealed in it: seeking God through righteous living and fervent worship could bring God and the pious worshiper close fellowship. The psalmist's just (or

---

Night vision: The option of reading from Psalm 17 is in conjunction with the Old Testament reading from the account of Jacob's wrestling with God in Genesis 32. While Jacob wrestled with God through the night (Gen. 32:24-28), the psalmist wrote of God visiting in the night to test him (Ps. 17:3). Jacob received God's blessing and "called the place Peniel, saying 'For I have seen God face to face, and yet my life is preserved'" (Gen. 32:30). Psalm 17 closes with a desire to behold God's face in righteousness, and to awake satisfied, beholding God's likeness.

"righteous") cause in v. 1 neatly frames his wish in v. 15 to "behold your face in righteousness." While self-sufficient mortals may be satisfied with filled bellies, the psalmist's fulfillment is found in fellowship with God: "when I awake I shall be satisfied, beholding your likeness."

Some commentators have suggested that "when I awake" may indicate that the psalmist had embarked on an all-night prayer vigil at the temple, and others see it as a hope of resurrection beyond death, but neither is necessarily implied. Like the poet behind Psalm 27, this psalmist believes that righteous living and passionate worship would be rewarded with a special closeness to God: "'Come,' my heart says, 'seek his face!' Your face, LORD, do I seek" (Ps. 27:8).

The sharp dichotomy inherent in this psalm may leave us feeling uncomfortable. We would not think of ourselves as arrogant folk out to hurt the innocent, but do we have more in common with the mortals who seek satisfaction in this life than with the psalmist, whose dead aim was directed toward staying on the path that leads to satisfaction in God? What are our priorities?

The Hardest Question
What is the purpose of all the body language?

The psalmist must have been a fully embodied person, much in touch with the physical world. Take note of all the body language: God is to "give *ear*" to "*lips* free from deceit" (v. 1), to look with divine *eyes* upon the psalmist's right cause (v. 2), and to test their *heart* and see that their *mouth* does not transgress (v. 3).

The psalmist follows the word of God's *lips* so that their *feet* have not slipped from God's path (vv. 4-5). Verse 6 finds another appeal to God's *ear*, while v. 7 prays for deliverance by God's *right hand*, and v. 8 asks God to guard the psalmist as the apple (*pupil*) of the divine *eye* and hide her in the shadow of God's *wings* (v. 8).

Meanwhile, the wicked close their *hearts* (literally, with *fat*) to pity, speak arrogantly with their *mouths*, and set their *eyes* to knock the poet down (vv. 10-11).

In v. 14 the psalmist speaks of the oppressor's *bellies*, either observing that their bellies are filled and their abundance passed on to children, or praying that their bellies would be filled with the retribution God has in store for them, with grief enough to spill over onto their children – the intent is not clear.

Finally, filled with confidence, the poet longs to behold God's *face* and look upon the divine *likeness* (v. 15).

Why does the poet depend so heavily on bodily metaphors? Perhaps it was simply a style choice, but it is also likely that the intense bodily images throughout the psalm help to express the psalmist's deep longing for a hearing with God, and for justice to be done. By giving attention to the physicality of the vocabulary, the reader not only sees or hears the psalmist's pain, but also feels it.

Season after Pentecost: Proper 13

Second Reading
Isaiah 55:1-13 (RCL 55:1-5)*

A Stunning Invitation

Isaiah 55 appears multiple times in lectionary reading: vv. 1-5 are read for Proper 13 in Year A; vv. 1-9 for the third Sunday in Lent of Year C; and vv. 10-13 for Proper 10 in Year A, the Eighth Sunday of Epiphany in Year C, and Proper 3 in Year C. A study of vv. 1-13 is found under Proper 10 of Year A in this volume.

Optional Second Reading
Psalm 145 (RCL 145:8-9, 14-21)*

How Great Is God

*Psalm 145:1-8 is read for Proper 20 in Year A; 145:1-5, 18-22 for Proper 27 in Year C; 145:8-14 for Proper 9 in Year A; and 145:10-19 for Proper 12 in Year B. A commentary on the full chapter is found in this volume under the second optional first reading for Proper 9.

Third Reading
Romans 9:1-5

Hard Thoughts

For I could wish that I myself were accursed and cut off from Christ for the sake of my own people,
my kindred according to the flesh. (Rom. 1:3)

Would you be willing to give up your hope of eternity so someone else could enjoy it? We might forgo a dessert so a child could have a second helping, or give a few dollars to feed a homeless person, but most of us probably have limits to our self-denial.

Paul was so devoted to the idea of winning over Jewish people to Christ that he claimed a willingness to give up as much as any person could. His wish was rhetorical, but no doubt sincere.

Following Paul's inspiring crescendo of confidence in the faithful love of Christ in Rom. 8:31-39, chs. 9–11 come as a rather unwelcome shift as Paul transitions from exuberant praise to doleful despondency, and from trust in a Christ who will never leave his followers to distress for a people who have never made the connection.

The lectionary text serves as an introduction to the next three chapters.

Paul's great anguish
(vv. 1-3)

Happiness and grief can be thought of as two sides of the same coin. We wouldn't appreciate joy if we had not also known sorrow. Excitement for a child who wins a competition must share heart space with sadness for the children who did not. Grief for a lost loved one echoes the joy of their presence.

Paul's eloquent and ebullient paean to Christ's faithfulness in 8:31-39 appears to have reminded him of so many others who did not share the confidence of his relationship with God through Christ.

Paul was a fanatical follower of Jesus, but he could not forget the years he had spent as an equally zealous follower of God through the faith and practice of his Hebrew heritage. Only an experience as dramatic as his encounter with Christ on the road to Damascus (Acts 9) could have derailed his allegiance to Judaism.

That initial visionary encounter and following meetings and prayer sessions with other Christ followers left Paul overwhelmed with the exciting belief that all his hopes and dreams as a Jew longing for the Messiah had been fulfilled in Jesus, and it broke his heart that so many of his lifelong family of faith did not follow him in accepting Christ.

"I speak the truth in Christ," he wrote. "I am not lying, my conscience confirms it in the Holy Spirit – I have great sorrow and unceasing anguish in my heart" (vv. 1-2).

Speaking in doublets, Paul could hardly be more emphatic: "I speak the truth, I am not lying." He even calls on the Holy Spirit to confirm how deeply he felt it: the word translated as "conscience" comes from a compound that literally means "joint knowledge." [**Doublespeak**]

How deep was his concern? "For I could wish that I myself were cursed and cut off from Christ for the sake of my brothers, those of my own race, the people of Israel" (v. 3). Paul used the word "accursed" (*'anathema*) in other places (1 Cor. 16:22; Gal. 1:8, 9), but never with potential reference to himself. The word describes something

> **Doublespeak:** Paul's lament for his Hebrew kindred gains depth from the way he doubles up five successive attestations in emphasizing the reality and depth of his concern. His pattern of repetition is reminiscent of the parallelism common to Hebrew poetry, such as we find in the psalms of lament:
>
> I speak the truth in Christ
>   I am not lying.
> My conscience confirms it
>   by the Holy Spirit.
> I have great sorrow
>   and unceasing anguish in my heart.
> For I could wish that I myself were accursed
>   and cut off from Christ
> for the sake of my own people
>   my kindred according to the flesh.

set apart or dedicated to God, but not always in a positive sense. Luke 21:5 speaks of beautiful stones and gifts that were dedicated (using a verbal form of the word) to God in the temple compound. In the Septuagint, however, *'anathema* was used to translate the Hebrew word *cherem*, which describes something that was dedicated to God, but for destruction (Lev. 27:28; Deut. 7:26, 13:17).

One might notice that in the heat of the moment, Paul's talk of becoming accursed seems to overlook his own previous argument that nothing could possibly separate anyone "from the love of God in Christ Jesus our Lord" (8:39). However deeply he felt it, however, his language was rhetorical, not something he considered to be possible. He was arguing from passion, not from logic.

Why was Paul's grief so deep? Did he believe that all Jews who did not accept Jesus were "accursed," so that he was willing to exchange places with them? Paul's words have often been used to express just this belief: that the "old covenant" became void when the "new covenant" in Christ arrived, ending God's special relationship with Israel, a view typically known as "supercessionism." This, in addition, has contributed to antisemitic sentiment among some Christians who look askance at Jews who remain faithful to their tradition and don't turn to Jesus.

Seeking to understand Paul, then, requires a careful attention to nuance and context in addition to taking Paul's deep passion for evangelism into account.

It is not clear whether Paul's stated willingness to become *'anathema* for the salvation of the Jews means that he considered Jews who didn't follow Christ to be in a state of *'anathema*, destined to destruction. The first part of his more rational argument that follows may seem to suggest that, but he reaches a much more hopeful position that all Israel will be saved (11:25-32).

Israel's great blessings
(v. 4)

Paul was convinced that the Jewish people had a heritage of divine favor. "Theirs is the adoption as sons; theirs the divine glory, the covenants, the receiving of the law, the temple worship and the promises," he said (v. 4). [**Adoption**]

Some writers read this as two parallel triplets, linking adoption with receiving the law, divine glory with temple worship, and covenants with promises. When read aloud in Greek, the sequence has a poetic, almost rhyming quality that suggests careful composition.

Rather than using the term "Jews," Paul speaks of "the Israelites," recalling the long heritage of the Hebrews that became the foundation of what can rightly be called Judaism, which developed in the late postexilic period.

Paul had no trouble reciting advantages afforded to the Israelites. At God's initiative, they had entered a covenant that amounted to adoption as God's special people. They had been given guidelines for life within that covenant, and a system of worship to inspire them. Beyond (or before) this were "the promises," not only the promises to Abraham of descendants and land, but also the promises to David that one of his descendants would rule. Both were thought to be eternal promises.

Did Paul think the covenants and promises had been revoked, that Israelites who didn't follow Jesus had lost their connection with God? Was he more concerned that they

> **Adoption:** The expression "adoption as sons" translates a single word, *huiothesía*, which combines the word for "son" (*huíos*) and "adoption" (*thesis*). The word was a legal term used to mean "adoption as a son with full rights of inheritance." Paul keyed in on the "full rights of inheritance" aspect but was not arguing that God "adopts" only males, so it is appropriate to translate as "adoption as children." The same expression is used in Rom. 8:15, Gal. 4:5, and Eph. 1:5.

were missing out on a relationship that was even better? Or, did he have something else in mind?

The world's great messiah
(v. 5)

Paul understood the close connection between Jesus and his Hebrew heritage. "Theirs are the patriarchs, and from them is traced the human ancestry of Christ, who is God over all, forever praised! Amen" (v. 5).

While Paul affirms that the patriarchs "belong" to Israel, Christ does not. In a human sense, Jesus was descended from Israel, but as the Christ he was much more than a Davidic descendant. Paul appears to claim that Christ is, indeed, God. In that sense, Israel belongs to Christ, not the other way around.

The precise translation of the last part of the verse depends on how one punctuates it (the Greek has no punctuation other than a period at the end), and whether one translates *Christos* as "Christ" or as "Messiah," both legitimate. The NIV11 has "the Messiah, who is God over all, forever praised," while the NET renders it as "Christ, who is God over all, blessed forever." The NRSV reads "the Messiah, who is over all, God blessed forever."

All three versions have footnotes pointing to the alternate translations. How do we decide which is the best? One clue could be the literary context: the section begins with a deep expression of grief. Is it likely that Paul would shift to a doxology in just five verses? If not, then a straightforward affirmation of "Christ, who is God over all, blessed forever," might seem more likely. In that context, "blessed" is an attribute of Christ rather than a doxology to God, and the equation of Christ with God serves to reinforce Paul's sorrow by indicating a belief that in rejecting Christ, the Jewish community as a whole had also rejected Christ.

On the other hand, some observers question whether Paul would have equated Jesus with God so plainly: while he often speaks of God, Christ, and the Holy Spirit in ways that point to a relationship, he does not say "Christ is God." Unless we assume this is one time when he diverged from the pattern, it could be best to think of Paul speaking of Christ as the Messiah over all, and connect "God" with a doxology: "God (be) blessed forever."

Paul's sorrow – and hope – on behalf of his own people challenges modern believers to ask who it is that we grieve for, if anyone. Do our children or other family members have a relationship with Christ? Do our neighbors have a faith that gives them hope? We may not burn with the evangelistic fervor of someone who believes all people who don't trust Christ are destined for eternal punishment, but if our faith is meaningful enough to make a positive difference in our lives, wouldn't we want others to share a hopeful and joyful relationship with God?

If our faith doesn't make enough of a difference in our lives to be something we want to share, that's another subject entirely. But if our faith does mean so much that we want others to know it, not everyone will follow our lead, even among those we love the most. Then we, like Paul, must continue to pray and express our concern in loving (not pestering) ways, but ultimately leave them in the hands of God.

The Hardest Question
Why did Paul speak of both covenants and promises?

In v. 4, Paul speaks of Israel's advantages including both covenants (*diathēkai*) and promises (*'epangeliai*). Hebrew theology was not uniform, and shifted in emphasis over time. At times it focused on the idea of relationship as one of promise that challenged the people to be faithful out of gratitude, and at other times the emphasis was on a conditional covenant in which obedience was required if the relationship was to be beneficial.

Most stories in Genesis speak of God's outright promises to Abraham, Isaac, and Jacob that they would be blessed with progeny and property: their descendants would multiply extravagantly and live in the land of Canaan.

Stories from Exodus onward, after the promise of many descendants had been fulfilled, major on the idea of a conditional covenant relationship offered by God and voluntarily entered by the people as a whole (Exod. 19:1-6, followed by the Ten Commandments; Exod. 24:3-8, which included a pledge to obey the "book of the covenant"). The book of Deuteronomy later spelled out requirements of the covenant, replete with promises for obedience, along with curses for disobedience listed in excruciating detail. Covenant renewal ceremonies are described as taking place on the plain east of the Jordan (Deuteronomy 29), at Mount Gerizim and Mount Ebal (Josh. 8:30-35), and at Shechem (Joshua 24).

During the exilic and postexilic periods, Israel's prophets and theologians appear to have concluded that the people would never live up to the conditional covenant they believed God had offered at Sinai, and that the pre-exilic Deuteronomistic writers had developed so thoroughly. The defeat of Israel in 722 BCE and the devastation of Jerusalem in 587 BCE, followed by the exile, were seen as punishment for Israel's inability to be true to their end of the covenant.

As a result, later thought focused on the foundational promises to Abraham. Isaiah of the exile recalled God's promises to Abraham as a harbinger of hope (Isa. 41:8, 51:1-2), as did the postexilic prophet who wrote in Isaiah's name (Isa. 63.16). Nehemiah, likewise, late into the postexilic period, praised Yahweh as "the one who chose Abram and brought him out of Ur of the Chaldeans and gave him the name Abraham" (Neh. 9:7).

The promise to Abraham narrated in Genesis 17, the product of a priestly writer and also likely written after the exile, emphasized a belief that the promise to Abraham was everlasting: "I will establish my covenant between me and you, and your offspring after you throughout their generations, for an everlasting covenant, to be God to you and to your offspring after you" (Gen. 17:7; see also 17:19-22). The Priestly writer used the word "covenant" (b'rit) in an emphatic way, probably to stress a belief in God's commit-ment to it, but the relationship was more promise than covenant. Other accounts of God's promise to Abraham (Gen. 12:1-3, 15:12-21, 18:9-15), Isaac (Gen. 26:2-5), and Jacob (Gen. 28:13-15) – all from the Yahwistic source – are simple promises, open to the future but without covenant stipulations or assurance that possession of the land would be "everlasting."

The promise to David, in an account written in the late pre-exilic period, also had the character of a promise, not a covenant, though it was said to be an eternal one. When David sought to build a "house" for God, the prophet Nathan told him that God had promised to build a "house" (dynasty) for David, to establish his line on the throne forever: "When your days are fulfilled and you lie down with your ancestors, I will raise up your offspring after you, who shall come forth from your body, and I will establish his kingdom. He shall build a house for my name, and I will establish the throne of his kingdom forever" (2 Sam. 7:12-13).

That promise included a conditional element – that disobedience would be punished "with the rods of men" – but also the assurance that "I will not take my steadfast love from him" (2 Sam. 7:14-15).

Israel, then, had a history of both promises and covenants. Paul saw both as a sign of favor from God, so it was natural for him to include them both.

Fourth Reading
Matthew 14:13-21

A Picnic to Remember

Jesus said to them, "They need not go away; you give them something to eat." (Matt. 14:16)

Can you think of something you have done that everyone who knows you remembers? Hopefully it wasn't a public *faux pas* that became your most embarrassing moment. We would all like to be remembered, I suspect, not for our mistakes, but for the good things we have done, the love we have shown, the people we have touched.

In a setting where stories get told, you may notice that people often remember the same event in different ways, and some may insist they remember it correctly, even when shown evidence to the contrary.

We can be grateful for memories, and especially thankful that those who followed Jesus passed on their memories of his impressive miracles and inspirational teachings. Like us, those followers whose memories gave rise to the four gospels didn't all remember the same things, or recall the details in the same way.

Surprisingly, only one of Jesus' "mighty works" (not counting the resurrection) is recorded in all four gospels, and its story included a healthy dose of embarrassment for the disciples. We usually call it the "Feeding of the Five Thousand," and it's found in Matt. 14:13-21, Mark 6:30-44, Luke 9:10-17, and John 6:1-14.

The story's appearance in all four gospels tells us how significant the disciples considered this event to be. Broken bread and fish not only fed thousands of people, but also provided important lessons for those who would follow Jesus.

When needs become pressing
(vv. 13-16)

Many charitable organizations and denominational groups have become very good at meeting physical needs on a large scale. Through disaster relief units that are trained and ready to serve, dedicated volunteers have prepared and served literally millions of meals in the wake of disasters caused by earthquakes and hurricanes, tornadoes and terrorists, famines and wars.

When people are hungry, trained volunteers know what to do. They have trucks, equipment, and food supplies at the ready. Tell them that you need 5,000 meals by suppertime, and they won't blink an eye.

Tell a dozen bearded disciples who have neither training nor resources, and you'll get a different response.

As Matthew tells the story, Jesus and his disciples were already tired and in need of rest when this story begins. They had faced rejection in Nazareth (13:54-58) and had learned that Jesus' cousin John had been arrested and beheaded (14:1-12). Physically and emotionally drained, Jesus set out across the Sea of Galilee in search of a quiet place along the shore, but the word soon got out. By the time Jesus landed, he was greeted by a mass of people with a multitude of needs. **[A deserted place]**

Jesus didn't have to look hard to see physical needs, emotional needs, and spiritual needs. He "was moved with compassion" for the people, Matthew said (v. 14). Matthew typically abbreviates the stories taken from Mark, often by about one-third. Here, Matthew noted that Jesus was "moved with compassion" by the crowd (v. 14), but did not

A deserted place: The traditional site of Jesus' multiplication of the loaves and fish is at Tabgha, on the northwest shore of the Sea of Galilee, not far from the village of Capernaum. In the photo, the Church of St. Peter's Primacy is the gray stone building at right. The roof of the Church of the Multiplication of Loaves and Fishes is seen at left.

include Mark's comment that "they were like sheep without a shepherd" (Mark 6:34). Perhaps Matthew omitted that line here because he had already used a similar expression in Matt. 9:36.

For Jesus, compassion was not just something one feels, but something one does, even when tired. Jesus patiently waded into the crowd, taking the time to cure many who were sick.

As the day grew long, with no refreshment stands or food trucks around, the people began to grow hungry – as anyone would have. The disciples asked Jesus to call it a day and send everyone home for supper, but Jesus had other ideas. Maybe he wanted to show that the gospel has social as well as spiritual dimensions, or maybe he wanted a lot of people to witness an amazing act that they'd never forget.

Or maybe he just wanted to teach the disciples a lesson. "You give them something to eat," he said.

Imagine the look on the disciples' faces! Imagine how any of us would look if someone put us in charge of feeding 5,000 hungry men – not counting women and children – and to do so quickly, even though we had neither food to give them nor money to call a caterer.

If we didn't already know this story, how could we imagine it ever being done?

When disciples become prepared
(vv. 17-19)

Matthew has a tendency to tone down the implicit criticism of the disciples that is often found in Mark. Perhaps that is why he does not include their dumbfounded response (Mark 6:37) that even 200 denarii wouldn't be enough to buy sufficient bread. In John's version, it was Phillip who did the math (John 6:7) and said that six months of wages would hardly get them a mouthful apiece.

But Jesus had given the job to the disciples. How could they feed such a crowd? If we had only Matthew's gospel, we'd assume the disciples themselves had some provisions, but not much: "We have nothing here but five loaves and two fish" (v. 17).

Neither Matthew, Mark, nor Luke says anything about the small boy we know from the text in John, the boy Andrew found who was willing to share his meager fare.

Five loaves and two fish really aren't very much when the "loaves" are probably small circles of flatbread, and the fish are salt-dried sardines. **[Fish]**

Sometimes we might feel about as ill-equipped for other demands that come to hand, and we wonder how we can do what needs to be done. Jesus wanted the disciples to look beyond the normal human resources that came to mind. He wanted them to consider what could be done, not just on their own, but with God's help.

The story reminds us that serving Christ faithfully involves the willingness to obediently share what we have in assets or abilities, and to trust Jesus to make that enough.

Even so, Jesus' disciples must have been muttering to themselves as Jesus instructed the crowd to find a seat on the green grass – a reminder that though they had sought "a deserted place," it wasn't a desert. Matthew omits Mark's observation that Jesus told the disciples to

Fish: The most common commercial fish in the Sea of Galilee were a type of tilapia known locally as "St. Peter's Fish." These were typically hand-size, or larger. Sardines were also commonly caught. Their smaller size made them easy to preserve by drying and salting.

arrange the thousands of people in groups of fifties and hundreds (Mark 6:39-40), saying only that Jesus ordered the crowd to sit on the grass (Matt. 14:19a). Perhaps the author's purpose is to leave out extraneous material and sharpen the focus on Jesus.

All three synoptic gospels note that Jesus took the food in his hands and "looked up to heaven" before blessing and breaking the loaves (John says only that he gave thanks, John 6:11). This seems intended to remind both readers and those present that Jesus was never wholly apart from the Father, and drew his power from the fullness of the Godhead.

After saying that Jesus took the bread and fish in his hands, Matthew loses interest in the fish, saying only that Jesus "broke the loaves and gave them to the disciples, and the disciples gave them to the crowds" (v. 19b). The other gospels continue to include the fish, though almost as an afterthought.

If we can imagine the disciples' surprise when Jesus first told them it was their job to feed the multitude, let's consider how flabbergasted they must have been to discover that, no matter how many times they passed the baskets among the people, they always returned full.

The gospels are silent on the manner of the miracle. When Jesus broke the paltry provisions into fragments and put some in each disciple's basket, they probably expected nothing more than to offer an appetizer to two or three people each, but the food was replenished as quickly as it was removed, and everyone ate their fill.

Writers often note similarities between the feeding of the 5,000 and the Last Supper. The fish play a very minor role in the story, for example, while bread – especially Jesus' breaking of the bread – is front and center. Furthermore, the sequence of verbs used – "he took," "he blessed," "he broke," "he gave" – is precisely the same as in the Last Supper (Matt. 26:26-27).

Even with the absence of wine, the similarity in the way Jesus is said to have taken, blessed, broken, and shared the bread is a striking preview of the last meal he would share prior to the crucifixion.

How long did the disciples' initial excitement over the miraculous multiplication last before their task turned into mere labor? If the 12 alone were expected to serve the crowds, as the story implies, each would

---

The manner of the miracle: None of the gospels explain how the miracle took place, only that Jesus broke the bread and fish before giving it to the disciples, who distributed it to the people, and that there were 12 baskets of leftovers.

Some writers have speculated that the miracle was not really one of multiplication, but of sharing. In their view, the people in the crowd had food with them, but had kept quiet when the disciples asked for potential supplies. After hearing Jesus pray and seeing him set the example, however, they furtively brought out and shared the bread and fish they had brought, so that there was enough, and more than enough.

Such an explanation robs the story of its power, however. The whole point of the story is that Jesus is the Messiah who provides bread in the wilderness, even as God had provided manna for the Israelites. The 12 baskets of leftovers are more than an indication that each disciple returned with a full basket: they can be seen as symbolic of the 12 tribes of Israel.

Donald A. Hagner argues that the feeding of the 5,000 is designed to show that Christ came first to the Jews, as the fulfillment of their messianic hopes, while the feeding of the 4,000 in Matt. 15:32-38 demonstrates the extension of Jesus' provision to the Gentiles. In that story, the word for "basket" is a word typically used by Greeks, and the leftovers fill seven baskets, symbolizing Christ's provision for all nations (*Matthew 14–28*, Word Biblical Commentary, vol. 33b [Word Books, 1995], 419, 452).

---

have been responsible for carrying food to 500 or more people. And they thought they were tired before!

The job wasn't over when it was over, though. Whether by innate frugality or direct instruction, they returned to collect the leftovers and finished the day with 12 baskets of bread and fish – one for each disciple, if we assume that only the Twelve were involved. Their weariness must have known no bounds, but witnessing such an act of grace and power must have been energizing, too.

We can't overlook an important aspect of discipleship here: the work was done when Jesus looked to heaven, broke the food, and then gave it to the disciples for distribution to the hungry crowd. [**The manner of the miracle**]

To this day, that's the way it works when we seek to live out the kingdom of God on earth. We receive the blessings of God that come through Christ, then share them with others. Whether God gives us material goods or spiritual wisdom, a love for children or joyful enthusiasm, we are called to share with a world that is hungry for more than bread and fish.

When needs become opportunities
(vv. 20-21)

Jesus' miraculous multiplication of the bread and fish was a mighty witness to the multitude, but perhaps even more significant for the disciples. They learned from Jesus that deep compassion gives us energy to keep going, even when we're feeling drained.

They also learned by experience that the most overwhelming situations are not without hope. As Christ's followers trust in Jesus, offer to him their abilities, and obey his commands to love, marvelous things can be done – even in the face of obstacles that may seem insurmountable to us.

When all was done and the people finally went home, the presence of a full basket for each disciple suggests that Jesus' power not only makes our service effective in helping others, but also provides for our own needs.

The purpose of Christ's miraculous lesson was not just inspirational, but motivational. What physical and spiritual needs do we see in the world around us? What gifts can we offer toward meeting those needs? And what are we doing with that basket in our hands?

The Hardest Question
Why are the gospels so different?

With this study, as in other studies of the gospels, we take note of ways in which Matthew, Mark, Luke, and John tell the story of Jesus in ways that are both similar and different.

Even a surface reading shows that Matthew, Mark, and Luke are quite similar at many points, and they are called the "synoptic gospels" because of this ("synoptic" comes from Greek, meaning "seen together").

A few scholars have argued that Matthew was written first, and that Mark and Luke abbreviated what was found there. Most scholars, however, agree that Mark, the shortest of the gospels, was written first. Part of the evidence for this is that when Matthew and Luke include stories that follow the same order, it is in those sections that they have in common with Mark.

It is commonly thought that the gospel of Mark reflects the memories of the Apostle Peter, with whom Mark worked. The author of Matthew may have been the apostle, or someone writing in his name. We know Luke as the author of both Luke and Acts. He was a Gentile physician who had come to know Christ and sought to gain as much information as he could before writing his books, which were addressed to "Theophilus" (meaning "lover of God").

It seems evident that the authors of both Matthew and Luke had access to Mark's gospel, and included much of its material in their books, often in a slightly abbreviated form or shaped to emphasize their personal interests. Some interpreters believe Matthew was writing mainly to a Jewish audience, while Luke wrote for other Gentiles. Luke's gospel also gives extra attention to the role of women and to those who are sick or poor.

Matthew and Luke also share a number of Jesus' teachings in common that are not in Mark. This material is often attributed to an otherwise unknown collection of Jesus' "sayings" that scholars call "Q" (from "Quelle," a German word meaning "source").

In addition, both Matthew and Luke incorporate unique materials not included elsewhere, notably their separate narratives about the birth and infancy of Jesus: Matthew has more to say about Joseph's place in the story, while Luke focuses more on Mary. Both Matthew and Luke sometimes mix and match their various materials in different ways.

Thus, Matthew is thought to consist mainly of material from Mark, Q, and Matthew's distinctive source, while Luke consists of material from Mark, Q, and Luke's separate source.

John's gospel, which reflects a more philosophical approach and a more developed Christology than the synoptics, shows relatively little dependence on them. It was probably written toward the end of the first century, somewhat later than the snyoptics, which are often dated to around 60–90 CE.

The many differences between John and the synoptics make it all the more remarkable that the story of Jesus feeding the 5,000 appears in it, too: it is the only Galilean miracle of Jesus that occurs in all four gospels.

First Reading
Genesis 37 (RCL 37:1-4, 12-28)

Selling Joseph

Now Israel loved Joseph more than any other of his children, because he was the son of his old age;
and he had made him a long robe with sleeves. (Gen. 37:3)

If you have ever seen Andrew Lloyd Webber's musical *Joseph and the Amazing Technicolor Dreamcoat*, you've noted how he and lyricist Tim Rice wove the disparate stories of Jacob's son Joseph and his brothers into a cohesive story. The musical takes significant liberties with the account, as one might expect, but its playful mix of music genres could remind the reader of the various strands of tradition that go into the Joseph narrative – and what a narrative it is.

While we normally think of Genesis 37–50 as the story of Joseph, the latest editor called it the story of Jacob's family: "This is the story of the family of Jacob" (37:2). And, while Joseph has the starring role, Joseph's brothers play a significant part in the story. Father Jacob looms in the background throughout the story until he resurfaces near the end, insists on adopting Joseph's offspring as his own (47:29–48:22), and blesses (or condemns) his sons while predicting the future of their families (49:1-28). After Jacob's death, his sons carry his body (according to his instructions) back to Canaan for burial in the family tomb at Macpelah (49:29–50:13), but they return to Egypt.

Don't ignore the dreams: The lectionary text for the day is Gen. 37:1-4, 12-28, which begins with an explanation of why Joseph's brothers hated him (he was their father's favorite), then skips to the story of how they sold Joseph into slavery, omitting the account of Joseph's dreams in vv. 5-11. Since the dreams contributed much to the brother's antipathy toward Joseph, it is important that we include a brief discussion of them.

Though Jacob haunts the background, the lead character in our text for today is Joseph – and Joseph is in trouble. **[Don't ignore the dreams]**

A favorite son
(vv. 1-4)

The story begins with Jacob and his family having settled in the land of Canaan, where they lived as sojourners among the land's native peoples, probably near the southern town of Hebron (v. 1, cf. 35:27).

Years must have passed, because Joseph is said to be 17 years old when he ran afoul of his brothers. All of them appear to have worked as shepherds, with Joseph in a sort of apprentice role: a literal reading is "and he was a lad with the sons of Bilhah and Zilpah, his father's wives." His function included shuttling messages and probably provisions back and forth between Jacob's home base and the brothers' temporary field quarters.

Whether Jacob had intended for Joseph to report on his brothers is unclear, but the text says that on one occasion Joseph brought a "bad report" of them to his father (v. 2). Nothing more is said about it, but we may assume the older brothers would have considered him a tattletale, and they would not have been pleased. **[Jacob's brothers]**

Joseph's snitching, however, was not as troublesome as his obvious position as the favored son. Jacob must have known the perils of partiality – his brother Esau had been his father Isaac's favorite, while his mother Rebekah had

> **Jacob's brothers:** Jacob was assigned to work "with the sons of Bilhah and Zilpah, his father's wives." Bilhah and Zilpah were secondary wives: Jacob had wanted to marry Rachel, but his father-in-law Laban tricked him into marrying her older sister Leah first. After Leah had given birth to four sons (Reuben, Simeon, Levi, and Judah) while Rachel remained childless, Rachel persuaded Jacob to impregnate her handmaid Bilhah so she could claim the children. Bilhah bore Dan and Naphtali, after which Leah stopped getting pregnant and insisted that Jacob also take her handmaid, Zilpah – who bore Gad and Asher. Leah then gave birth to Issachar and Zebulon, along with a daughter, Dinah. Finally, Rachel was able to conceive, and bore Joseph, who immediately became Jacob's favorite as the first son of his favorite wife. Rachel later died giving birth to Benjamin somewhere near Bethlehem during the journey from Haran to Hebron.
>
> The older brothers with whom Joseph served in the field, then, were Dan, Naphtali, Gad, and Asher.

doted on him – but he carried the dysfunction into the next generation, openly indulging Joseph over his other children.

Jacob's preferential treatment of Joseph included the gift of a special cloak (v. 3). It was probably not "many-colored" (a tradition that began with the early Greek translation), but long-sleeved or possibly "embroidered." The same expression is used to describe the robe worn by Tamar, David's daughter, when she was raped by her brother Amnon (2 Samuel 13).

Whatever fashion statement the garment made, the point is that Joseph's robe was notably more special than the ordinary clothes worn by his brothers. Jacob's overt favoritism did not play well with Joseph's siblings, "who hated him, and could not speak peaceably to him" (v. 4).

A hated brother
(vv. 5-11)

The brothers' antipathy grew even deeper when Joseph told the family about his grandiose dreams (v. 5). The first was a vision of a freshly harvested grain field, where Joseph's sheaf of grain suddenly stood up and the brothers' sheaves came and bowed down to it (vv. 6-7). Predictably incensed by the notion that Joseph would rule over them, the brothers "hated him even more because of his dreams and his words" (v. 8).

A second dream was even more imposing: Joseph claimed to have dreamed that the sun, moon, and 11 stars all bowed down to him (v. 9). The sun and moon clearly represent his parents, though Joseph's mother Rachel had died giving birth to Benjamin, and the 11 stars his brothers. Understandably, the brothers' jealousy toward Joseph grew, and even Jacob offered a verbal rebuke, though he took no action, and "kept the matter in mind," no doubt wondering what the dream might mean (vv. 10-11).

A future slave
(vv. 12-28)

With fraternal enmity fully established, the narrator fast-forwards to another day and perhaps another season, when Joseph's brothers were said to be pasturing the flocks near Shechem, a city beneath Mount Gerizim. From Jacob's camp near Hebron, Shechem would have been more than 50 miles to the north, a journey of at least two or three days by foot. The brothers could have kept the flocks there for weeks or perhaps months at a time, so Jacob would have cause to seek a periodic report on their welfare, and that of the flocks. He dispatched Joseph to check on his brothers and bring back news (vv. 12-14).

Joseph made his way to Shechem, but could not find his brothers. When a local man found him wandering around the area and asked what he was up to, Joseph indicated that he was looking for his brothers. In typical story-telling style, the man said he had been near the brothers when they decided to move the flocks to Dothan, another 15 miles to the north and slightly west (vv. 15-17).

Another day's journey and Joseph saw his brothers in the distance – but they also saw him coming. Some of brothers proposed that they kill the troublesome dreamer and throw him into a pit, telling their father that a wild animal had killed the boy. Then "we shall see what will become of his dreams," they said (vv. 18-19). Reuben, the oldest brother, reportedly demurred, suggesting only that they throw him into a pit without hurting him. He must have implied that they would leave him in the pit, though the narrator says Reuben secretly planned to rescue Joseph and take him home (vv. 20-22).

Reuben's plan prevailed, though some still had blood on their minds. When Joseph arrived, they stripped off his special coat and threw him into a pit originally dug as a well or cistern but that was currently dry (vv. 23-24).

Who bought and sold Joseph? If the narrative of vv. 25-28 sounds confusing, there's good reason for it. Was Joseph bought and sold by Ishmaelites or Midianites?

The Ishmaelites' ancestry was traced to Abraham's first son, Ishmael, and the Midianites to a son of Abraham's second wife, Keturah, but they both became known as largely nomadic people who made their living as traders. Through the years, the distinction seems to have diminished, and the terms sometimes appear interchangeable as a catch-all label for wandering merchants. Genesis is not the only place that happens: Judg. 24:8 identifies the raiders who Gideon defeated as both Midianites and Ishmaelites.

Two traditions may have been combined here: it has been suggested that Reuben's defense and the Midianite traders derived from the Elohist source (37:18, 21-22, 24-25a, 28a, 29-30), while Judah's intervention and Ishmaelite merchants came from an older story by the Yahwist (37:19-20, 23, 25b-27, 28b, 31-32).

Aside from the different names, we note that the Ishmaelites and Midianites seem to make separate appearances. Even so, the discrepancies apparently didn't trouble the editor/narrator. He says the brothers sold Joseph to "the Ishmaelites," who carried him down to Egypt, but later indicates that "the Midianites" sold him to a man named Potiphar, in Egypt (v. 36).

In either case, there is an unexpected connection: Joseph, the chosen son of Jacob, the chosen son of Isaac, the chosen son of Abraham, becomes captive to the unchosen descendants of his great-grandfather.

As the brothers left Joseph in the pit and sat down to eat (apparently, they didn't want to kill Joseph on empty stomachs), a caravan of Ishmaelite traders happened to pass by on their way from Gilead (east of the Sea of Galilee) to Egypt, loaded down with various goods. It's likely that two different traditions have been combined in the story, for now it is Judah who speaks up to save Joseph's life, suggesting that they sell him to the Ishmaelites. In doing so they could avoid bloodguilt and make some money while still getting rid of Joseph.

The brothers agreed – apparently while Reuben was absent – so when some Midianite traders came by, they pulled Joseph from the pit and sold him for 20 pieces of silver (vv. 25-28) [**Who bought and sold Joseph?**]

In the meantime, Reuben returned to find Joseph gone and his plans for rescue thwarted. To cover their crime, the brothers slaughtered a goat and dipped Joseph's tunic in it,

later showing it to Jacob as evidence that a wild beast had devoured his favorite son. Jacob became distraught, as one might expect, and would not be comforted (vv. 29-35).

A modern lesson

The selling of Joseph is a familiar and entertaining story, but what might modern believers gain from it?

We should first look to the narrator's purpose in telling the story: he wants us to see how God can take a bad thing (the selling of Joseph) and turn it into something good (the deliverance of Jacob's family from famine). That does not make hurtful actions commendable, but it illustrates a belief that God can orchestrate human events for divine purposes, even when their intentions were not admirable. Later, when Joseph had ascended to power in Egypt, Jacob had died, and his brothers feared that Joseph might take vengeance on them, he offered forgiveness and claimed: "Even though you intended to do harm to me, God intended it for good, in order to preserve a numerous people, as he is doing today" (50:20). [**God in the background**]

God in the background: Scholars often note that, though God is often mentioned in Genesis 37–50, the deity plays a less active role than in the earlier patriarchal stories. While the narratives insist that God spoke directly to Abraham, Isaac, and Jacob, God never appears directly to Joseph. The reader may assume it is God who sends messages to Joseph via dreams, and the narrator leaves no doubt that God is with Joseph and blesses him, but God's overt involvement in announcing or fulfilling the promises shifts to the background.

For his part, Joseph builds no altars to Yahweh as his forbears did, and establishes no sanctuaries, yet manages to serve God within a land of other gods. He does not hear the Abrahamic promise of progeny from God, but from Jacob, and then not until 48:3-4, 21-22. Thus, Terrence Fretheim has argued, "The human community now becomes responsible for the transmission of the word of God" ("Genesis," in *The New Interpreter's Bible*, vol. 1 [Abingdon, 1994], 594).

The narrator's belief that providence was at work in Joseph's coming to Egypt is also apparent in 45:7-8, where Joseph told his brothers: "God sent me before you to preserve for you a remnant on earth, and to keep alive for you many survivors. So it was not you who sent me here, but God; he has made me a father to Pharaoh, and lord of all his house and ruler over all the land of Egypt."

If we live long enough, bad things will happen to us. Friends or family may treat us shabbily; colleagues in the workplace may undermine our advancement. We cannot always attribute poor treatment to God, as Joseph did, but we can trust that God has the ability to work in us, teach us, strengthen us, and ultimately bring something good from the situations we face.

Though it was not the author's primary intent, the story also reminds us of the dangers of family favoritism. When parents play favorites with their children – at any age – they sow seeds of jealousy, discord, and emotional issues that may play out over many years and repeat themselves in generations to come. Jacob apparently learned nothing from the pain of knowing that his father loved Esau more than him, and he passed that hurt on to his children by openly favoring Joseph over his brothers. Can we learn to do better?

The Hardest Question
How does the Joseph novella fit into the larger book of Genesis?

Genesis consists of two primary divisions: the "Primeval History" (chs. 1–11) and the "Patriarchal History," or "Stories of the Ancestors" (chs. 12–50). Abraham is first introduced in a genealogy (11:27-32), but his story begins in earnest with ch. 12. Abraham's story continues until his death (25:7-11), interlaced with stories about Isaac. Isaac takes center stage only briefly (25:19–28:9), and then mostly as a background character, for the narrator's primary interest is that he is Abraham's son and Jacob's father. Jacob comes to the fore at 28:10, continuing through ch. 35, though he doesn't die until the final chapter.

Family genealogies in Genesis often serve as framing devices to end one story and begin another, relating in meaningful ways with both. In this case, the genealogy of Esau in ch. 36 is an appropriate introduction to chs. 37–50, because both Esau's genealogy and the following "generations of Jacob" narrative emphasize the transition from an individual to a people.

According to ch. 36, Esau became the progenitor of the Edomites, a people living southeast of the Dead Sea and frequently at odds with Israel (twice the genealogy says "Esau, he is Edom"). Now Jacob – enabled by the timely and God-enhanced efforts of his son Joseph – also grows to become a people. After Jacob's wrestling match with God at the Jabbok, God had given him the alternate name "Israel" (Gen. 32:28): now Israel becomes the Israelites. By the time we reach the end of the section, Jacob's 12 sons have multiplied to at least the fourth generation, which could have comprised a considerable multitude of people.

In this way, the Joseph story provides an appropriate end to the book of Genesis, which is primarily concerned with God's promise of progeny – but it also serves as an effective lead-in to the book of Exodus, where the people of Israel have multiplied in Egypt, and the focus shifts to their consolidation as a nation and their quest to possess the Promised Land.

The final section of Genesis has long been recognized as a structured unit that includes material from disparate sources, but holds together well enough to be given titles such as "short story" or "novella." While the earlier narratives are often separate episodes bracketed by genealogies and stitched together by travel notes, chs. 37–50 appear to be a larger, more unified work. It might be helpful to consider a rough outline of the "novella":

I. 37:1-36 – Joseph the dreamer predicts prominence but falls from favor with his brothers, who sell him as a slave bound for Egypt.

II. 38:1-30 – As Joseph toils in Egypt, life goes on in Canaan, where older brother Judah fails to honor his daughter-in-law Tamar and then falls for her ploy to have a child, securing Judah's heritage.

III. 39:1–41:57 – Joseph rides a roller coaster to power in Egypt.
A. 39:1-23 – Joseph rises from bottom to top in Potiphar's house, then to prison.
B. 40:1-23 – Joseph rises from bottom to top in prison, then to Pharaoh's palace.
C. 41:1-57 – Joseph rises from dream interpreter to ruler in Pharaoh's palace.

IV. 42:1–45:28 – A reunion with his brothers fulfills Joseph's dreams.
A. 42:1-38 – Joseph's brothers beg to buy food but don't recognize Joseph, who speaks harshly but weeps privately, and tests his brothers' loyalty.
B. 43:1-43 – Joseph's brothers beg again, and are frightened when Joseph brings them to his house for lunch, seating them according to age.
C. 44:1-34 – Joseph tests his brothers' fraternal fidelity toward Benjamin, and they pass the test.
D. 45:1-28 – Joseph tearfully reunites with his brothers and invites the whole clan to live in his care.

V. 46:1–47:26 – Israel comes to Egypt.
A. A. 46:1-27 – Jacob sacrifices, receives a vision, and journeys with his family to Egypt.
B. B. 46:28–47:12 – Joseph settles Jacob's family in the land of Goshen.
C. C. 47:13-26 – Joseph uses stored grain to buy all of Egypt for Pharaoh.

VI. 47:27–50:26 – An incipient nation emerges.
A. 47:27–48:22 – Jacob adopts Joseph's sons (told in two versions).
B. 49:1-33 – Jacob's last words, of blessing and curse, look to the future.
C. 50:1-14 – Jacob dies in Egypt but is buried in Canaan.
D. 50:15-21 – Jacob's sons are truly reconciled.
E. 50:22-26 – Joseph dies in Egypt, but his burial in Canaan is delayed.

Season after Pentecost: Proper 14

Optional First Reading
Psalm 105 (RCL 105:1-6, 16-22, 45b)*

Don't Forget

In addition to this reading, Ps. 105:1-11, 45b is read for Proper 12 in Year A; Ps. 105:1-6, 23-26, 45b for Proper 17 in Year A; and Ps. 105:1-6, 37-45 for Proper 20 in Year A. A commentary on the entire chapter appears in this volume under Proper 12.

Second Reading
1 Kings 19:1-18

The World Needs Faith

Then there came a voice to him that said, "What are you doing here, Elijah?" (1 Kgs. 19:13b)

In *Canoeing the Mountains* (IVP Books, 2015), Tod Bolsinger writes about working as a consultant for a denominational organization that wanted to prepare for the future. Countless meetings and interviews and brain-storming sessions were conducted. Progress reports were composed and distributed. Many participants expressed excitement about the potential new direction. All seemed positive, but when the final proposal was presented, an underlying fear of change prevailed. After two years of intense work, the proposal was voted down.

Have you ever worked on a project for a long period of time, only to see it canceled? Or perhaps you have labored faithfully at a job for many years, but no one seems to notice or care? Experiences such as these can lead one to feel downhearted, or downright depressed. Sometimes things pile up until we reach the proverbial straw that broke the camel's back, and we find ourselves in danger of cracking. We think about giving up and wonder "What's the use?" If that happens, we may find ourselves walking beside the prophet Elijah.

The Revised Common Lectionary text for the day is 1 Kgs. 19:1-4 (5-7), 8-15a, but we won't be skipping any verses, stopping only at the point where Yahweh sends Elijah on a mission.

A downhearted prophet
(vv. 1-9a)

Perhaps we should not be surprised that Elijah's emotional crash came soon after the high point in his career. On Mt. Carmel, he had challenged 450 prophets of Baal to a game

> **Curses:** Jezebel's warning came in the form of a Hebrew oath, which consisted of a curse followed by a promise. Literally, it would read: "Thus may the gods do to me, and thus add more if by this time tomorrow I do not make your life like the life of one of them." The self-imprecation of calling upon the gods to punish her if she didn't keep the promise added serious emphasis to the threat: Jezebel meant business. A paraphrase could be "May the gods do whatever they want to me, and even more, if I do not make you as dead as one of the prophets of Baal by this time tomorrow."

of dueling gods. The prophets of Baal failed to bring fire from heaven, but Elijah's prayer to Yahweh resulted in a conflagration that consumed both sacrifice and altar (1 Kgs. 18:20-40). Soon Elijah had seen to it that the prophets of Baal were dead, many Israelites had turned back to Yahweh, and Elijah was on top of the heap.

Perhaps Elijah had not considered the political ramifications of such a big and bloody encounter. He already had a contentious relationship with King Ahab and his Phoenician wife Jezebel, the primary proponent of Baalism. When Jezebel learned what havoc Elijah had wreaked on her pagan prophets, the angry queen quickly sent him a warning in the form of an oath: "So may the gods do to me, and more also, if I do not make your life like the life of one of them (the dead priests of Baal) by this time tomorrow" (v. 2). [**Curses**]

The same Elijah who had bravely confronted 450 priests of Baal now quailed in fear before one angry queen and he fled for his life, running all the way from the northern kingdom of Israel to the town of Beersheba, near the

> **Seeking solitude?** Jerome Walsh notes that Elijah's actions reflect "a series of abandonments" as Elijah leaves his homeland for Judah, leaves settled land for the wilderness, and finally leaves all human companionship behind to venture on to Mt. Horeb alone (*1 Kings*, in Berit Olam: Studies in Hebrew Narrative and Poetry [The Liturgical Press, 1996], 266).

southern border of Judah. Beersheba was so far south that it was commonly cited alongside Dan, the northernmost city, to indicate the whole of Israel (Judg. 20:1; 1 Sam. 3:20; 2 Sam. 3:10; 17:11; 24:2, 15).

Elijah must have been quite a runner. Near the end of the previous chapter, we are told that he had outrun King Ahab from Mt. Carmel to the city of Jezreel, about 20 miles away, even though Ahab was in a horse-drawn chariot. Now we are told that – presumably leaving on the same day – he "fled for his life" to Beersheba, another 95 miles south as the crow flies, and undoubtedly longer by road and path – a true ultra-marathon.

Even that was not far enough: Elijah left his servant in Beersheba and traveled yet another day's journey south into the desert, losing himself in the lonely wilderness of the Negeb (v. 3). **[Seeking solitude?]**

Lost and alone, Elijah collapsed under a lonesome tree and prayed to die: "It is enough; now, O LORD, take away my life, for I am no better than my ancestors" (4b).

> **Touched by an angel?** The Hebrew does not specifically identify the visitor who brought Elijah food as an angel: the word used is *malak*, which means "messenger" (for example, the prophet Malachi's name means "My messenger"). The word could be used of human messengers, but it was also used of angelic messengers. The NRSV, based on the context, translates the word as "angel," for the appearance of a provision-bearing messenger in the middle of nowhere seems to suggest divine providence, and the second mention describes him as a "messenger of Yahweh."
>
> In either case, the Hebrew grammar indicates a level of surprise, for the messenger's touch apparently woke Elijah, who may not have expected to awaken at all. The NRSV has "All at once an angel touched him …," while NET has "All of a sudden an angelic messenger touched him …" A closer translation would be: "And look here … a messenger is touching him!"

The tree in question, called a "broom tree" in Spanish, is a variety of juniper, more of a large shrub than an actual tree. It can tolerate dry conditions, and it continues to grow in many parts of Palestine.

Note that the shrub is described as "one tree," or "a lone tree." Elijah's own loneliness is emphasized by his attempt to find shade beneath a solitary shrub that probably offered little comfort.

If Elijah had really wanted to die, he could have remained in Israel, where Jezebel would have been glad to assist him. But, for a while, he may have felt like it.

Elijah had been running without food or rest for several days. When he finally fell asleep under that isolated bush, it was because he had no other choice. He was completely worn out.

God knew what Elijah needed, so when the prophet woke up, it was to the unexpected touch of an angel. "Get up and eat," the visitor said, "or else the journey will be too great for you." Elijah saw a steaming cake of bread and a jug of water nearby. He ate and drank, lay down again, then ate and drank some more (vv. 5-7). **[Touched by an angel?]**

The Hebrew contains an interesting wordplay. When Elijah collapsed beneath the broom tree and asked God to take his life, he began by saying "I've had enough!" (v. 4). When the angel provided food for Elijah the second time, he told him to get up and eat, "for the journey is more than enough for you" (v. 7), using the same word (*rab*, which means "a great many," or "enough"). The NRSV has "too much for you," which gets the idiom but misses the repetition of "enough."

The angel's repetition of Elijah's own word provides God's answer: God is not through with Elijah; it's not yet enough.

Elijah did not eat again for 40 days as he journeyed on to the most sacred mountain in Israel's memory. Some called it Mt. Horeb, while others called it Sinai.

Using the last of his strength, Elijah climbed the hallowed hill until he came to a cave, perhaps the same cleft that had once sheltered Moses – the Hebrew text has "*the* cave," as if the reader should know the cave of which it speaks. There Elijah spent the night, not knowing what would be next (vv. 8-9a).

> **Silence:** Mother Teresa of Calcutta once spoke of our need for silence this way: "We need to find God, and God cannot be found in noise and restlessness. God is the friend of silence. See how nature – trees, flowers, grass – grows in silence; see the stars, the moon, the sun, how they move in silence … The more we receive in silent prayer, the more we can give in our active life. We need silence to be able to touch souls. The essential thing is not what we say, but what God says to us and through us. All our words will be useless unless they come from within – words which do not give the light of Christ increase the darkness" (Quoted in James Roose-Evans, *The Inner Stage* [Cowley Publications, 1990], 130).

An uplifting God
(vv. 9b-18)

What came next was a question: "Then the word of the LORD came to him, saying, 'What are you doing here, Elijah?'" (v. 9b).

Elijah responded with a litany of complaints that his faithful efforts had been for nothing, the people of Israel had deserted Yahweh, that he was the only prophet left, and now Jezebel was after him (v. 10). Elijah's protest revealed a self-pitying distortion of the situation. He ignored the faithful Obadiah and the 100 prophets God had kept safe (18:13), as well as the many who had repented following the miracle on Mt. Carmel (18:39-40). He couldn't see beyond his own grief.

God gave Elijah a chance to vent, then offered him a picture of something bigger than his frustrated self, calling Elijah to come out of his cave and stand on the mountain before Yahweh, "for the LORD is about to pass by" (v. 11) – reminiscent of the story of Moses standing in a cleft as Yahweh's glory passed by (Exod. 33:17-23).

Elijah did not come out, but remained in the cave as a howling wind blew past, "so strong that it was splitting mountains and breaking rocks in pieces before the LORD," but surprisingly, "the LORD was not in the wind."

After the wind came the frightful shaking of an earthquake, "but the LORD was not in the earthquake." On the heels of the temblor, Elijah felt the heat and heard the roar of a wildfire racing across the mountainside, but "the LORD was not in the fire," either (vv. 11-12).

When all the commotion ceased, an eerie silence settled over the land, so tangible that Elijah could *hear* it. Transla-

tors struggle to describe what Elijah experienced. The KJV says there was a "still, small voice," while the NIV has "a gentle whisper." Literally, the text says that Elijah heard a *qôl demāmâ daqqâ*: "a sound of a thin silence."

And that's where Elijah found the voice of God: in the silence. The rejection he had felt and the uncertainty of his future and the fierceness of his opposition may have seemed as fearsome as a storm wind, as tumultuous as an earthquake, as ravaging as a forest fire. But God was not behind that. God was not the author of Elijah's discontent.

Perhaps God wanted Elijah to learn that, in the midst of the storms of life that make it hard to get ahead, the upheavals that turn our lives upside down, and the burning heat of anger and disappointment and loss, God is still with us. In times like that, we may wish for God to speak up and make everything clear, but God does not work that way. More often, God is present in the sound of silence. **[Silence]**

The astute reader will note several parallels between Elijah's experience and that of Moses. Both met God on Mt. Sinai/Horeb. Moses fasted alone on the mountain for 40 days, while Elijah ate nothing for 40 days during his journey to Horeb. Both Moses and Elijah complained to God that they were left alone to carry the burden of Israel's recalcitrant people, and both were granted a theophany in which Yahweh appeared to them by "passing by."

When Elijah recognized the closeness of God, he covered his face with his mantle – proving that he didn't really want to die, for he was certain that God was present and the Hebrews believed that one who saw God would die.

Carefully, then, Elijah finally ventured to the mouth of the cave – still short of standing "on the mountain" as God had commanded – and again God asked: "What are you doing here, Elijah?" (v. 13).

It was the same question as before, because Elijah still had yet to answer it. And despite all he had learned, Elijah remained stuck in his despondency. He gave the same answer as before, complaining that Jezebel had been killing the prophets, that he was the only one left in Israel, and that he was next in line (v. 14).

It's easy to be hard on Elijah, but if we'd been standing in his place, chased into the desert by a wicked queen's death threat, we'd probably be rather self-absorbed, too.

> **A prayer for the silence:** Here's a suggested prayer to use in conjunction with teaching or preaching from this text, perhaps asking members to spend some moments in silence, as each one seeks to hear the gentle whisper of God's voice to us: "God, grant that we may be silent before you, that we may hear you … let us be open to you, that you may enter … empty before you, that you may fill us … let us be at rest in you, that you may be at work in us … let us be still, and know that you are our God … (silence) … Amen" (Adapted from Sir Paul Reeves, as quoted in *Homiletics* 4 [April–June, 1992], 49.)

Elijah's depressing response suggests that, if nothing else, he needed assurance that his lonesome life and his dangerous work had some meaning.

So it was that God did not offer Elijah a theological self-defense of divine actions or a neat analysis of Elijah's psyche. God answered by giving the prophet a new mission and the assurance that other faithful people remained (vv. 15-18).

Elijah had made the common mistake of thinking it was all about him.

Let's give another thought to God's insistence that Elijah listen to (or through) the silence. Our culture seems addicted to noise. Even people out for a solitary walk tend to wear earbuds to crank out music or podcasts. As the daily clamor of life assaults our ears, our minds crackle with inner static as we try to remember all the errands that need doing and the work that hasn't been done.

One potential blessing of the COVID-19 pandemic of 2020–2022 and the resulting social isolation was that we had more opportunities for silence and for listening to God. While some have called it "the Great Interruption," others thought of it as "the Great Pause." The noise continued, of course. We had the option of binge-watching the news or Netflix, but that could only satisfy for so long. With less time in traffic or in meetings or in watching sports, we had more opportunity to shed the insulating layers of noise and let our hearts and minds lie bare before God. [**A prayer for the silence**]

It doesn't matter how low we may feel, how battered and bruised, how fierce are the storms that surround us: God is there, speaking in the silence, if we are willing to become quiet enough, open enough, vulnerable enough to hear. There is meaning in this life. There is hope. There is

work for us, worthwhile work that will make a difference for Christ and for our world. Will we listen for it this week?

The Hardest Question
What *was* Elijah doing there?

Elijah's long journey south had to have a greater purpose than simply escaping Jezebel's murderous threats: the frazzled prophet traveled a day's journey south of Israel's southernmost city, then 40 days more into the desolate Sinai Peninsula.

It is unlikely that Elijah had traveled all the way to Mt. Horeb (an alternate name for Mt. Sinai) unless he had a purpose in mind. Some optimistic interpreters have suggested that Elijah made a pilgrimage to the root place of God's covenant with Israel so he could renew and revitalize his commitment to Yahweh, and to service as God's prophet. If that is the case, he didn't act like it.

Others have suggested, perhaps more accurately, that Elijah traveled to the mountain so associated with Moses in order to renounce his calling and throw in the towel. On the journey south, he asked God to put him out of his misery (19:4), which is one way of being released from his obligations. "I am no better than my ancestors" (19:4b) carries the sense of "I've been no more successful than the prophets before me" at persuading Israel to follow God faithfully.

When Elijah reached the mountain, he was full of complaints, suggesting that his efforts had been fruitless (19:10, 14). It is as if he were saying, "I give up." Jerome T. Walsh suggests that "The pilgrimage is an act of defiance, not devotion; the prophet does not seek renewal, he demands release; and the deity seems indifferent to Elijah's ultimatum" (*1 Kings*, Berit Olam: Studies in Hebrew Narrative and Poetry [The Liturgical Press, 1996], 281).

It's also possible that Elijah didn't have any particular agenda, that he was simply lost and searching for hope in the midst of a stormy career that had left him feeling like a failure.

In any case, God's question, twice offered, was most appropriate: "What are you doing here, Elijah?" (19:9, 13). The Hebrew construction puts emphasis on the word "here," as if God expected Elijah to be somewhere else and is asking "What are you doing *here*?" Some scholars have noted that, when God sent provisions to Elijah under the broom tree, the angel said he would need it for his "way" (*derek*), perhaps to fortify Elijah on the way back to his work in Israel. This would suggest that Yahweh was frustrated by Elijah's insistence on diverting from "his way" and continuing southward to Sinai. Thus the question: "What are you doing here?"

Elijah gave every appearance of wanting to give up and resign his office, but Yahweh refused to accept the resignation, instructing him to return to his "way" (using *derek* again). As a compromise, perhaps, God instructed Elijah to anoint Elisha the son of Shaphat to serve as his successor, showing the prophet that there was light at the end of the tunnel. (For more on this, see Walsh, 271-278).

In our prayers, it might be worthwhile to imagine that God is asking us what we are doing here – in this place, in this job, in this stage of life – and if there are situations in which we might be avoiding the way God has in mind for us.

Optional Second Reading
Psalm 85 (RCL 85:8-13)

Celebrate Salvation

Steadfast love and faithfulness will meet; righteousness and peace will kiss each other. (Ps. 85:10)

Brandon's parents had given him all the standard lectures about driving carefully and observing the speed limit when he first got his license. Like many parents, they continued to admonish him to drive safely, so when he was running late for school and got a speeding ticket, he was afraid they'd never forgive him.

They were disappointed, but responded with surprising calm. Brandon used some Christmas money he had saved to pay the fine. Though his parents continued to preach safe driving, it felt good to be back in their good graces.

A few weeks later, however, Brandon was texting one of his buddies on the way to school and failed to notice that the minivan in front of him had slowed to a stop. He didn't hit it *that* hard, but it was hard enough to cause some damage and shake up the children inside.

Would his parents ever forgive him *now*, or had his luck run out?

Forgiveness granted
(vv. 1-3)

Psalm 85 recounts a similar story, though on a larger level. The RCL includes sections from the psalm for the second Sunday of Advent in Year B (vv. 1-2, 8-13), while vv. 8-13 are on Proper 14 of Year A and Proper 10 of Year B. Verses 4-7 are omitted in all of the readings, perhaps because they appear to be contradictory to the rest of the psalm. It is better, however, that we deal with the tricky parts than to skip them, so we will consider the entire psalm in our study. **[Sons of Korah]**

> **Sons of Korah:** Psalm 85 is attributed to the "sons of Korah," or the "Korahites." They were a long-lived family of Levitical priests that David reportedly put in charge of various functions in the temple, such as gatekeeping (1 Chron. 26:19) and baking the ceremonial bread (1 Chron. 9:19). They must have also been active among the temple singers, as 11 psalms (42, 44–49, 84–85, 87–88) are attributed to them.

The first three verses proclaim a happy hymn of praise, recalling God's past acts of forgiveness and restoration. "LORD, you were favorable to your land," sang the psalmist: "you restored the fortunes of Jacob" (v. 1). This is probably not a reference to Israel's deliverance from Egypt, but to the Hebrews' return after the exile. They had lost their land to the Assyrians and Babylonians, but Cyrus the Persian had conquered Babylon in 539 BCE and allowed the Hebrews to return.

Verse 2 offers further evidence that the psalmist was thinking of the return from exile. Israel's Egyptian captivity was not traditionally associated with sin or rebellion among the Hebrews, but the exile was: prophets such as Isaiah, Micah, Amos, and Jeremiah drew a straight line between a sinful people and a defeated nation.

The psalmist's expression of gratitude seems to presuppose that a time of punishment or exile had come to an end. Israel's restoration had begun with divine pardon: "You forgave the iniquity of your people; you pardoned all their sin" (v. 2), leading God to turn away from anger and wrath (v. 3). **[Selah?]**

Selah: Verse 2 concludes with the word "Selah," a Hebrew term that is transliterated into English letters, but not translated into English words. The reason for this is straightforward: we don't know what it means.

The word – which was probably pronounced "seh-la" – appears 71 times in Psalms (scattered among 39 different psalms) and another three times in Habakkuk 3, which is a psalm. It may appear at the end of a stanza or section (as in 32:4, 5, 7), at the end of a psalm, or even at the end of a quotation (Ps. 44:9).

The most likely suggestion is that Selah has some musical significance. The term appears most commonly in psalms that have titles, and most of those identify the psalm with David or one of the known temple singers such as Asaph. Three quarters of the hymns with titles in which "Selah" appears have the indication "to the choirmaster" or "the leader." Psalm 85 follows this pattern.

Some think *selâ* might mark the spot for an instrumental interlude, a pause for reflection, or even a clash of cymbals. Sigmund Mowinkel proposed that it might indicate a point at which worshipers were expected to lie prostrate before God.

One possible interpretation is that *selâ* could be derived from the root *sll*, which means "to raise" or "lift up" – which could imply raising the voice, singing louder, or raising the volume of any instrumental accompaniment. This, however, is not certain.

The bottom line, as Robert Alter notes, is "Though there is general agreement that this is a choral or musical notation, there is no way of determining the meaning or the etymology" (*The Book of Psalms: A Translation with Commentary* [W.W. Norton & Co., 2007], 8).

Unless we were born without a conscience, we all know how it feels to be weighed down by a heavy burden of guilt, knowing that we have done wrong, have hurt someone, or have failed to live up to our calling. It's not a good feeling. Guilt can be poisonous if we wallow in it, but it can be invaluable if it motivates us to seek forgiveness from God, from others, or even from ourselves.

Have you ever sought such forgiveness, and felt the amazing sense of relief that comes with the knowledge that your sins have been pardoned and set aside?

If you're like most people, it's likely that your sense of freedom did not last long, because we all have a propensity to venture back into the realms of wrongdoing. If so, you have a headstart on understanding what the psalmist does next.

Forgiveness needed
(vv. 4-7)

With the happy praise for forgiveness still in the air, the psalm takes a shocking turn to a fervent lamentation that God has *not* forgiven the people (vv. 4-7). The psalmist pleads for God to "Restore us, O God our deliverer!" (v. 4, NET: the word "again" in the NRSV is interpretive, not in the text). Psalm 85 is not the only one to make such a sharp shift: a similar swing from happy joy to lament is echoed in Psalm 126.

"Will you be angry with us forever?" the psalmist asks (v. 5). "Will you not revive us again, so that your people may rejoice in you?" (v. 6).

The disjunctive shift from praise to lament is so sharp that the lectionary omits vv. 4-7 from the liturgical reading as if it's inappropriate, but the interlacing of praise and lament is common in the psalms. Guilty people may praise God for past forgiveness to set the stage for a renewed plea that God will forgive them once again.

As noted above, the postexilic period offers a likely context for Psalm 85. Verses 1-3 may recall the heady days of Israel's return from captivity, when prophets such as Isaiah of the Exile (Isaiah 40–55) declared that their time of punishment was over, that God had forgiven the sins that had brought them down. No doubt, many rejoiced at the news that they could return to Jerusalem.

When the Hebrews returned to Jerusalem, however, they still lived as subjects of the Persian Empire, occupying one small sub-province of the territory west of the Jordan. They found the beloved city in ruins and the neighbors unwelcoming. As the people scrambled to rebuild their homes and restore their farmlands, the enmity of surrounding peoples and an extended period of drought made life hard, and joy faded.

The return from exile began in 538 BCE, but not all at once. Waves of exiles returned at different times. The prophet Haggai, who returned with a group of exiles in 520 BCE, was heartbroken to see that the temple had not been rebuilt, and declared that God had plagued them with drought and hard times precisely because the people had not given priority to rebuilding the temple.

"You have looked for much, and, lo, it came to little," he proclaimed, "and when you brought it home, I blew it away. Why? says the LORD of hosts. Because my house lies in ruins, while all of you hurry off to your own houses.

Therefore the heavens above you have withheld the dew, and the earth has withheld its produce. And I have called for a drought on the land and the hills, on the grain, the new wine, the oil, on what the soil produces, on human beings and animals, and on all their labors" (Hag. 1:9-11; see also Hag. 1:6 and 2:15-17).

The prophet Zechariah, active about the same time, likewise charged the people with having followed the evil ways of their ancestors, and called for them to repent if they hoped for better days (Zech. 1:1-6).

Perhaps it was in a setting such as this that Psalm 85 originated as a prayer for forgiveness and restoration as the people thanked God for past forgiveness and asked for renewed favor as they returned to the task of building the temple, pleading "Show us your steadfast love, O LORD, and grant us your salvation" (v. 7).

The word translated "steadfast love" is *chesed*, a word so rich that it defies an exact translation. It suggests ideas of persistent compassion, kindness, and mercy that grow from a deep love that won't give up. Exod. 34:6 declares God's characteristic promise of steadfast love to Israel. God's promise to establish David's line on the throne insists "I will not take my steadfast love from him" (2 Sam. 7:14-15).

The promise was so memorable and appealing that in the psalms alone, God's "steadfast love" is either praised or requested 120 times. The psalmist knew that any hope for Israel's deliverance or salvation from its failures and its times of trial had to lie in the belief that God's *chesed* would not let them go.

Salvation coming
(vv. 8-13)

While vv. 1-7 are addressed to God, in vv. 8-13 the psalmist speaks to his audience – worshipers, hearers, or later readers – concerning his beliefs about God. Perhaps the speaker was recognized as a temple prophet, for he claimed the ability to hear and proclaim a message from God: "Let me hear what God the LORD will speak," he said (v. 8a, NRSV), or perhaps "I will listen to what God the LORD says" (NET). Both are legitimate translations.

But what is it that God will speak? "For he will speak peace to his people, to his faithful." The word translated "peace" is *shalom*. Like *chesed*, the concept of *shālôm* cannot be summed up in one word. It conveys the primary idea

> **Hearts, or folly?** The NRSV translates the last line of v. 8 as "to those who turn to him in their hearts," but the NET has "Yet they must not return to their foolish ways," similar to the rendering of KJV and NIV 11: "but let them not turn to folly."
>
> The latter readings are closer to a literal rendering of the text as it is: the NRSV follows an emendation of the text that changes some of the vowels so that it reads "to those who return to him in confidence." The NRSV reading has the advantage of being in parallel with the two previous lines, but the other translations have stronger textual support, and make good sense: God's word of peace to the people is appropriately accompanied by a call to remain on the right path and not return to foolish ways.

of wholeness or well-being that produces an inner peace that goes far beyond the absence of conflict. *Shālôm* is the outgrowth of God's salvation or deliverance, which the psalmist believed would be soon coming (v. 9). [**Hearts, or folly?**]

In v. 10 we find one of scripture's most charming images: "Steadfast love and faithfulness will meet; righteousness and peace will kiss each other." Here the psalmist imagines four of God's divine attributes as living agents who unite to bring salvation to the land through renewed prosperity. In personified form, "faithfulness will spring up from the ground and righteousness will look down from the sky" (or "heavens," v. 11), a reminder that fertile soil and appropriate rains are both gifts of God, for "The LORD will give what is good, and our land will yield its increase" (v. 12).

The psalmist believed that divine forgiveness and earthly fertility were intimately connected: when God's rich attributes of loving faithfulness and righteous peace were unleashed, both land and people would respond with fruitful growth reflecting God's presence among God's people. That, in the psalmist's mind, was of prime importance. When facing famine, the people naturally longed for abundant rain and prolific harvests, but the psalmist understood that their greatest need was for God to be with them: "Righteousness will go before him, and will make a path for his steps" (v. 13).

Americans are less closely connected to the land than our ancient counterparts. Despite the great swatches of farmland one may admire from an airplane window, less than two percent of families in America are actively involved in farming. Even so, we can appreciate the powerful metaphors connecting God's faithful love with redeeming grace that brings peace and wholeness to God's people, even as God's righteous acts call forth right living on our part.

Like the psalmist, we are often in need of hope for both now and the future. But unlike the psalmist, we know the ground of a hope that goes beyond abundant harvests. God in Christ came to bring the *shālôm* of abundant life, the fullest expression of salvation, and available to all.

The Hardest Question
How do we translate v. 6?

The rendering of v. 6 (v. 7 in Hebrew) varies little in English translations, but it is not as simple as it seems, and a surface reading might leave us thinking that the psalmist was mainly praying for a spiritual "revival" as understood in the revivalist tradition. A closer reading will give us a clearer view of the psalmist's intent. Here are representative translations:

- NRSV and HCSB: "Will you not revive us again, so that your people may rejoice in you?"
- NIV11: "Will you not revive us again, that your people may rejoice in you?"
- NET: "Will you not revive us once more? Then your people will rejoice in you!"

Let's take a closer look: the verse begins with a three-letter combination of the interrogative particle *heh* and the negative particle *lō*, which together can mean "Will not?" This is followed by the second person pronoun, which is not grammatically needed because person is already included in the meaning of the verbs that follow, "you will return," and "you will make alive." The addition of the pronoun

adds emphasis. Ordinarily, two consecutive finite verbs are joined by a conjunction such as "and" or "but," but here they appear side by side. A literal reading, then, is "Will you not, *you*, return, make us alive?"

Most English translations smooth out the reading by rendering the verb "return" in an adverbial sense as "again" or "once more," and by giving "make us alive" or "give us life" the nuanced meaning of "revive us." Thus, we get "Will you not revive us again?"

Those who have been given the second chance of a new life will naturally respond with praise. NRSV, NIV11, and HCSB read this as a resultant clause, "(so) that your people will rejoice in you." The Hebrew conjunction is the versatile *vav*, which commonly means "and," but can also be translated as "but," "so," or "then" in certain contexts. Here the NET keeps the same resultant sense but gives the petition the sense of a promise or vow by making the following clause a separate sentence: "Then your people will rejoice in you!"

Other translations have been proposed. The Septuagint rendered the opening expression as "O God," suggesting that the translators' copy of the Hebrew text began with the combination *h'al* or *'alh* instead of *hl'a*, or that the translators mentally reversed the letters of the Hebrew word, which would have contained no vowels.

One might think the old-time hymn "Revive Us Again" by W.P. Mackey may have derived from this verse, but all three verses of the hymn are concerned with Jesus as savior. The last line of the chorus, "Revive us again!" has no obvious connection with Psalm 85.

Third Reading
Romans 10:5-15*

No Distinction

*For there is no distinction between Jew and Greek; the same Lord is Lord of all
and is generous to all who call on him. (Rom. 10:12)*

Some texts are harder than others: that's the way it is with Bible study. Today's reading falls within a series of tricky texts from Romans chosen as epistle readings during the season after Pentecost.

The context is a lengthy discourse in which Paul argues at length about God's past, current, and future relationship to the Jews. In that context, Paul considers the subject of salvation, or being in a right relationship with God. Who is eligible for it, and how might one obtain it? For those of us who know the feeling of being lost and apart from God, that sounds like important stuff.

But what does Paul mean when he talks about "being saved," or "having salvation" (*sōtēria*)? It's far more than just getting our ticket punched for the heaven-bound glory train. Paul's message centers on having a right relationship with God that affects our daily lives as well as the potential for eternal life.

The righteousness of the law
(v. 5)

To understand Paul's argument in vv. 5-13, we need to look back at vv. 1-4, where he repeats an argument from the previous chapter relative to the place of the Jews in God's ongoing plan. That was a major issue for Paul, and it pervades his letter from chs. 9–11.

Paul had been born and raised as a Jew, then trained as an expert in the law and thus a leader among Jews.

He knew first-century Judaism from the inside out, and he was once such a stalwart defender of the faith – as understood by the Pharisee party – that he considered Jews who followed Jesus to be dangerous heretics, and therefore persecuted them.

But meeting Christ on the road to Damascus had changed Paul's life, and it changed his perspective on the law. He came to believe that God had given the law, not as a means for obtaining salvation, but as a life-guide for those who had already been granted the gift of a covenantal relationship with God.

Most Jews, in Paul's mind, had failed to understand this. Unwilling to accept God's gift of relationship to be guided by the law, he argued, they believed that one must first obey the law in order to have a right relationship with God.

Rather than seeing the law as a means for engendering faith and trust in the God who had already chosen them, they saw it as a means for earning God's favor through religious activity. As Paul Achtemeier puts it, "They were so religious that they did not want to settle for something God could give them. They wanted to be religious enough so that they could become partners with God in the matter of their salvation" (*Romans*, Interpretation [John Knox, 1985], 167).

Paul had come to believe that Christ was the "end" or "goal" of the law. The word *telos* can carry the sense of

---

Romans 10:8b-13 is also read on the First Sunday of Lent in Year C.

> **Tell us about *telos*:** In 10:4, Paul says that "Christ is the end of the law so that there might be righteousness for everyone who believes." Scholars debate whether the word *telos* should be translated as "end" (the more common meaning) or "goal," an alternate meaning. The problem is complicated by our own fuzzy approach to "end" and "goal" in English. While some draw a clear distinction between the two, in common usage the two words can be used in similar ways.
>
> The issue is whether Christ is "the end of the law" in the sense of abolishing the law as a means of relating to God, or whether Christ is the goal or fulfillment of the law in its purpose of encouraging trust in God.

either finality or fulfillment – or both. To help his readers understand the difference, Paul contrasts the righteousness that comes through the law (v. 5) and righteousness that comes through faith (vv. 6-13). [**Tell us about *telos***]

Quoting Moses, Paul illustrates "righteousness that comes through the law" with a quotation from Lev. 18:5: "the person who does these things will live by them." In other words, he implies, those who put their trust in the law must then live by the law.

Trusting in the law creates at least two problems. First, the very effort to keep the law becomes a type of idolatry. Paul believed that the idea of earning one's way into a right relationship with God was in effect a rejection of God's grace.

The second problem is that no one can perfectly keep the law, and "The whole problem with the law is that if one depends on fulfilling the law as the basis for one's relationship with God, that is the only basis that relationship will have" (Achtemeier, 168).

Christians may also find it hard to trust that God's grace is sufficient. Our traditions, our churches, our parents, or our peers may lead us to believe that we must follow a list of do's and don'ts if we're to be fully accepted by God. If we're trusting in our own behavior, however, we're not fully trusting in Christ.

The righteousness of faith
(vv. 6-13)

To explain the concept of faith over law, Paul creates a literary character named Righteousness-by-Faith, and gives her the power of speech throughout vv. 6-13: "But the righteousness that comes by faith says …" [**Righteousness-by-Faith**]

Speaking as "Righteousness-by-Faith," Paul cites phrases from Deut. 9:4 ("Do not say in your heart") and 30:12b ("Who will ascend into heaven?"), replacing the question "Who will cross over the sea?" from Deut. 30:13 with an allusion from Ps. 107:26, which says "they ascend into the heavens and descend into the abyss."

In the Deuteronomic context, Moses was arguing that the Israelites did not have to go in search of the law. It was neither in heaven nor across the sea, but as near to them as their own hearts. Thus, they did not need to send anyone on a quest to ascend to heaven or traverse the sea: the law was already in their midst.

Paul's substitution of "descending to the abyss" (from Ps. 107:26) for "crossing the sea" (from the main text Deut. 30:13) poses a vertical, rather than horizontal dimension. The word translated as "abyss" was commonly used to describe the depths of the sea, but it also provided an allusion to Sheol, the abode of the dead.

Paul mixed and matched the texts to contrast the vertical distance between the highest heaven and the deepest depths, in part because he has adapted the questions to refer to Christ rather than the law. We can see this in the interpretive comments he adds, characteristic of a Jewish midrash, denoted by parentheses in the text:

"Who will ascend into heaven? (that is, to bring Christ down), or Who will descend into the abyss? (that is, to bring Christ up from the dead)" (vv. 6b-7). Paul continues adding commentary with v. 8, taken from Deut. 30:14, where Moses insisted that "the word is very near to you, it is in your mouth and in your heart" – and Paul adds a parenthetical "that is, the word of faith that we proclaim."

> **Righteousness-by-Faith:** The personification of Righteousness by Faith as a character who speaks and instructs follows the Old Testament pattern of sometimes personifying wisdom as a woman (Prov. 1:20-33, 8:1–9:18). Paul is setting out to loosely cite a variety of Old Testament scriptures in support of his view that one should relate to God through trusting in God's grace. Using this literary approach enhances his argument "because it is not Paul's voice that reinterprets the OT passages but rather the scriptural personage called Righteousness by Faith" (Robert Jewett, *Romans*, Hermeneia [Fortress Press, 2007], 625.

By this method, Paul takes an Old Testament text about the nearness of the law, and reinterprets it with reference to the nearness of Christ, whose presence needs not be sought in heaven or in Sheol, but acknowledged as present and available to those who put their trust in God.

We don't have to go looking for Jesus in heaven, as if we could get there, or in the world of the dead, as if we could go there and come back. The righteousness that reconciles us to God is as near as the life and teaching and death and resurrection and spiritual presence of Jesus Christ.

As Moses had spoken of God's word being "in your mouth and in your heart," Righteousness-by-Faith declares that "one believes with the heart and so is justified, and one confesses with the mouth and so is saved" (v. 10). Paul goes on to adapt the promise of Isa. 28:16 to insist that "anyone who trusts in him will never be put to shame" (v. 11). Isaiah's prophecy spoke of a tested and precious cornerstone that God would lay in Zion, which Paul interpreted as a prophecy of Christ.

The reference to both heart and mouth leads Paul to declare that a saving relationship with God is available to all people, Jews and Gentiles alike, for "Everyone who calls on the name of the Lord shall be saved" (v. 13) – yet another Old Testament quotation, this time from Joel 2:32.

Paul's reference to "believing in your heart" and "confessing with your mouth" is not really a two-step process, as it is sometimes presented, but two sides of the same coin. Those who truly trust Christ inwardly will want to express their faith outwardly. In our postmodern, post-denominational, even post-Christendom society, it is common for people to think of faith as a purely personal thing that is no one else's business. We often hear the phrase "I'm spiritual, but not religious." In contrast, Paul expected those who believe inwardly to express their faith outwardly and identify with the believing community. [**Secret Service**]

The sharing life
(vv. 14-15)

Paul wanted his readers to remember that the world is filled with people – Jews and Gentiles alike – who need to hear the good news of salvation through faith. In vv. 14-15 he presents an effective string of rhetorical questions that could look back to Jews who have rejected Jesus, or forward to those who have yet to hear.

How can anyone call on someone they don't believe in? How can they believe if they haven't heard about them? How can they hear if no one brings them the message? How can someone preach the good news unless they are sent?

Still speaking as "Righteousness-by-Faith," Paul concludes with quotes from Isa. 57:2 and Nah. 1:15, both celebrating the idea that few things are more beautiful than the feet of people who run to bring good news.

No matter how attractive the preacher's feet, however, faith is not automatic. As those who proclaim need to be responsible witnesses, those who hear must be responsible listeners. "Faith comes from what is heard," Paul said, "and what is heard comes through the word of Christ" (v. 17). It is possible to hear with the ears but not listen with the heart. When our hearts are dulled by a spirit of self-sufficiency, whether it's a belief that we can be reconciled to God through obeying the law or just being a "good person," we can become spiritually hard of hearing.

While Paul's primary concern is the response of those who hear, his words also remind believers of our need to be good witnesses, proclaiming the good news through both word and deed. The question still lingers: "How can they believe in one of whom they have not heard?"

The Hardest Question
What is the significance of saying "Jesus is Lord"?

Romans 10:9, a part of today's text, probably reflects an early Christian confession that predates Paul. Here Paul says "if you confess with your lips that Jesus is Lord and believe in your heart that God raised him from the dead, you will

---

Secret service? An old story speaks of a woman who felt insecure and wanted to obtain a guard dog. She responded to an ad for a retired police dog, imagining that she would get an impressive German Shepherd to keep watch and intimidate intruders. She was disappointed when a policeman delivered a scrawny, pitiful looking animal. When she complained, the officer said "Now, Ma'am, don't let this dog's looks deceive you. He was in the Secret Service."

Following Jesus is not a secret service. We are not called to be "Lone Ranger" Christians or secret agents in the Lord's service. Trusting Christ is not just a private thing, but a public thing, so much so that Paul speaks of public confession as integrally linked to inner faith.

be saved." The English word "that" has been supplied to make the verse read more smoothly: a more straightforward translation would be "if you confess with your lips, 'Jesus is Lord,' and believe …"

The confession also appears in 1 Cor. 12:3, where Paul says "Therefore I want you to understand that no one speaking by the Spirit of God ever says 'Let Jesus be cursed!' and no one can say 'Jesus is Lord' except by the Holy Spirit."

Similar confessions appear in other texts. The hymnic text of Phil. 2:5-11, which Paul may have borrowed from the early church, concludes with "every tongue should confess that Jesus Christ is Lord, to the glory of God the Father."

In a sermon on the day of Pentecost, Peter concluded "Therefore let the entire house of Israel know with certainty that God has made him both Lord and Messiah, this Jesus whom you crucified" (Acts 2:36).

The confession is also implicit in the title "Lord Jesus Christ," which appears more than 60 times in the New Testament, from Acts through Jude.

But what does it mean to say "Jesus is Lord"? It is more than an individual confession of faith. We live in such an individualistic society that we tend to think of it as a personal confession that "Jesus is *my* Lord," but it is more than that. To say "Jesus is my Lord" could be taken to imply that other lords exist, and I have chosen Jesus from among the available options.

Thus, we do not confess that "Jesus is *my* Lord," but "Jesus is *Lord*." In doing so we affirm that Jesus is one with God, who is Lord over all. New Testament Christians did not give up on the monotheism taught by the Old Testament prophets. Jesus, though revealed on earth as the Son of God, is not a separate being, but the same Lord known in the Old Testament scriptures.

To confess "Jesus is Lord" is to assert that there is no other Lord. Early Christians living in the Roman Empire understood that many people considered the emperor to be a god, and that some emperors commanded their subjects to offer sacrifices and confess "Caesar is Lord." To declare that Jesus is Lord, by definition, affirms that Caesar is not.

Our society is no less pluralistic than the one in which Paul lived: there are many gods on the market, and multiple religions. While we may acknowledge positive aspects of other faiths, those who confess "Jesus as Lord" express their belief that the best aspects of other religions must ultimately point to Christ.

To confess "Jesus is Lord" is not to testify of a personal religious experience, but to acknowledge what we accept as the fundamental reality of Christian faith. Jesus is not one Lord among many from whom we can choose, but *the* one Lord through whom the world can be redeemed. Jesus is not just Lord of our lives, or Lord of the church, but Lord of all.

Fourth Reading
Matthew 14:22-33

Skiing Without a Boat

Jesus immediately reached out his hand and caught him, saying to him, "You of little faith, why did you doubt?" (Matt. 14:31)

The gospel of Matthew often deals with various aspects of the question, "Who is Jesus?" (See, for example, Matthew 7:28-29, 11:3, 13:54-56, 14:2). We all have some notion of who we think Jesus is. Perhaps a closer study of further lectionary readings texts from Matthew can help us gain a fresher notion of how the first disciples came to the gradual understanding that Jesus was more than an ordinary man.

Have you ever felt emotionally lost at sea on a stormy night, tossed by waves and frightened by darkness? The metaphor comes easily to mind. We all know what it is like to endure the tempests of life. Those who follow Jesus also know how to find hope even in the darkest night and the fiercest storm.

The biblical account of Jesus' famous water walk is found in Matt. 14:22-33, Mark 6:45-51, and John 6:15-21.

The parallels are marked by significant differences, most notably Matthew's solo inclusion of the episode with Peter. That story would have had special significance to the early church, which faced hard times and would have preserved this account as a reminder that Jesus offers hope and calm amid any storm. [**A misplaced story?**]

A quiet prayer
(vv. 22-23)

All accounts agree that the water-walking episode followed the exciting and tumultuous event in which Jesus fed thousands of people with a single boy's lunch of bread and fish. The natural uproar caused by the long day of teaching and miracle-working left Jesus exhausted and in need of quiet. So, Jesus sent the crowds away – and his disciples, too – while he stole into the hills to pray.

A misplaced story? Ancient authors typically cared far less about chronology than modern ones do, often arranging stories to suit a thematic purpose or theological agenda. That may be the case with this story.

Scholars often note that the story has similarities to the resurrection narrative, and suggest that its original context may have been a post-resurrection appearance: Jesus appears unexpectedly and the disciples think he is a ghost, but he calms their fears and brings them peace. The special attention paid to Peter is reminiscent of other stories surrounding the passion and resurrection. For example, in the garden Peter claimed that he could stand strong, but he sank into denial three times before the night was over. A story in John also describes a post-resurrection account in which Jesus met Peter and the Twelve by the seaside: Peter jumped into the water to go to Jesus, then Jesus offered him words of comfort and challenge.

As for the possibility that this story may originally have referred to a post-resurrection appearance, we note that Matthew also provides a different ending from Mark's account, portraying the disciples as falling in utter worship before Jesus and proclaiming him the Son of God, which seems more like a post-Easter phenomenon. Thus, some writers speculate that the church took the memory of a post-resurrection appearance and transposed it to an earlier time in Jesus' ministry. While this theory provides interesting speculation, we must recognize that the author of Matthew's gospel has placed it in its present context for a purpose, and it succeeds quite well in making the intended point.

In Matthew and Mark, Jesus seems to be motivated primarily by the need for quiet reflection. Jesus' popularity had skyrocketed, and people were clamoring for him to become king. John, in fact, says the crowds intended to seize Jesus and make him king by force (John 6:15). John also says that the miracle took place during Passover, which celebrated Israel's deliverance from Egypt and often gave rise to messianic fever.

Jesus' meteoric rise in fame must have tempted him to choose the route of popular political power. He needed a time of reflection and prayer to reaffirm his commitment to the servant role he had come to fulfill.

Jesus' actions offer a helpful lesson for modern disciples – especially those who experience some success in either personal or professional ministry. When we are lauded for our speaking, teaching, or unselfish service, we may be tempted to attempt greater things in hopes of greater praise. Jesus saw the danger of trusting in public acclaim. As the potential for greater and greater things drew near, Jesus pulled back to center himself on his true mission.

A noisy sea
(vv. 24-27)

While Jesus prayed on the quiet mountain, the disciples found themselves caught in one of the severe and sudden squalls that can sweep across the Sea of Galilee, which is well below sea level and surrounded by steep hills that can contribute to swirling winds. At about eight miles long and five miles wide, the Sea of Galilee is large enough to become extremely dangerous in a storm.

Jesus came to meet the disciples "early in the morning," according to the NRSV, less specific than the Greek text's "in the fourth watch of the night." The Greeks divided the night into four watches, the last of which extended from 3:00 to 6:00 a.m. Jesus had prayed far into the night, giving the disciples time to venture far from shore. [**How far out?**]

As the 12 tired men battled the battering wind, they must have been astonished to see Jesus coming toward them, striding confidently across the waves with the wind whipping his robe and hair. Is it any wonder they were terrified? Seeing such a thing in the dead of night, they assumed that the advancing apparition must be a ghost, perhaps of some fisherman who had drowned.

The disciples may have screamed as loudly as men allow themselves to do, but Jesus quickly quieted their fears, if not their curiosity. When he was close enough so they could hear him over the wind and waves, he said "Take heart, it is I; do not be afraid." Scholars have often noted that the Greek words "it is I" (*ego eimi*) are equivalent to the self-revelation of Yahweh to Moses as "I am" (*'ehyeh 'asher 'ehyeh*, Exod. 3:14). The Hebrew *'ehyeh* was translated as *ego eimi* in the Septuagint.

Matthew's gospel was likely written for a primarily Jewish audience, so his readers would have immediately seen the connection. God had self-identified as "I am" to Moses from a burning bush, and now Jesus uses the same words from a roiling sea. Neither Moses nor the disciples expected to meet God in such circumstances, but both were confronted by the great "I am."

A stammering disciple
(vv. 28-33)

As mentioned above, only Matthew includes the story about Peter's attempt to join Jesus on the water. Emboldened by the moment, but not entirely convinced that it was Jesus, Peter devised a thrill-seeking test: "Lord, *if* it is you, command me to come to you on the water" (v. 28). Note that Peter was not ready to jump in of his own accord, but he was ready to attempt anything at Christ's command.

Jesus' answer was simple: "Come." And, according to Matthew, Peter stepped onto the water and began to walk firmly toward Jesus. But then — as countless preachers and teachers have pointed out through the years — "when he noticed the strong wind, he became frightened." Peter, "the Rock," began to sink like a stone. Preachers often insist that

---

How far out? How far from shore were the disciples when Jesus came to them? The Sea of Galilee is about five miles wide at its widest point, and eight miles long. Mark's version of the story, on which Matthew probably depends, says only that they were "in the middle of the sea" (Mark 6:47). Matthew says that the boat was "many *stadia*" from shore (Matt. 14:24). One *stade* was equal to about 200 yards. John adds more specificity to the account, saying the disciples were "25 or 30 stadia" from shore (John 6:19). That distance, about three miles, would suggest they were close to the middle, about as far from land as one can get.

Peter began to sink "when he took his eyes off Jesus," but the story itself is concerned with Peter's faith as well as his focus.

There was a problem with Peter's faith (v. 31). As Malcolm Tolbert suggested, Peter had enough faith to begin, but not enough to finish (*Good News from Matthew* [Broadman Press, 1975], 133). Yet, when Peter began to sink and he realized that Jesus was his only hope for salvation, true faith was born. "This, then, is true faith: not the sublime achievement of an especially religious individual, but 'single minded' devotion to the Lord, to his biding and to his help" (Eduard Schweizer, *The Good News According to Matthew*, David E. Green, trans. [John Knox Press, 1975], 323).

Despite his impulsive nature and human weakness, Peter alone got out of the boat to go to Jesus. All of the disciples began this episode with abject fear, but moved to faith and worship (v. 33). Peter's role as a catalyst in the transformation recalls his crucial place in leading the early church in the stormy days after Pentecost.

When Jesus entered the boat, the storm ceased and the disciples began to worship him as the Son of God. Note the progression from unchecked fear to unequivocal faith: from Jesus' "I am" to Peter's "if it is you" to the disciples' "truly you are the Son of God!" If they remembered their synagogue lessons, they would know that only God could walk on water (Job 9:8, Ps. 77:19).

Wind for our sails: Here are some questions that may be helpful in guiding our thinking about this passage:

(1) On the temptation of trusting popularity (vv. 22-23): Imagine that the Bible study class you teach has outgrown the room you meet in, as people flock to hear your erudite delivery. Soon your class has to move into the sanctuary. The Adult Department Director suggests that your class could continue as a "superclass," or give birth to several new units that would be small enough to allow individual participation. How would you respond?

(2) Thinking of the disciples' surprise at meeting Jesus in the midst of a stormy sea (vv. 24-27), we are reminded that sometimes, when we least expect it, God's presence may come to us and inspire us. Have you ever experienced God in an unexpected place?

(3) Thinking of Peter's single-minded trust in Jesus as he began to sink (vv. 28-33), I'm reminded that I once heard someone say "You can't really say that Jesus is all you need until Jesus is all you have." Do you think this statement is true? Does it relate to Peter's experience?

Matthew's ending attributes far more faith to the disciples than Mark's story, in which they remain confused. Mark concludes with the observation that "they were utterly astounded, for they did not understand about the loaves, but their hearts were hardened" (Mark 6:51-52).

Who is Jesus? The disciples' growing belief is stated clearly: "truly you are the Son of God." **[Wind for our sails]**

The disciples' experience of growing in their developing faith and understanding of Jesus offers comfort to contemporary followers who also find their faith faltering and their assurance in need of assistance. All the disciples were uncertain about Jesus' identity. Even the great Simon Peter had doubts and fears, stumbling in the face of turbulent weather. But, as Peter extended his hand to Jesus as the only source of hope and salvation, Jesus was able to take Peter's "little faith" and nourish it so that Peter grew – through further fits and starts – to become the prime pillar of the early church.

Ben Witherington III puts it nicely: "Peter then has become the poster child of both faith and too little faith, of faith giving way to doubt and fear but also of faith overcoming one's initial fears" (*Matthew*, Smyth & Helwys Bible Commentary [Smyth & Helwys, 2006], 293).

God does not expect our faith to emerge full-blown. We must grow in faith even as our bodies grow, even as we grow intellectually and grow in maturity. We also face severe trials and howling storms, but Jesus is always there, looking upon our fear and doubt with grace unmeasured, ready to lift us up unto life.

The Hardest Question
What did the disciples mean when they called Jesus "the Son of God"?

The disciples' affirmation of faith that Jesus was the "Son of God" seems premature. Were they acknowledging Jesus as being one with God?

Exactly what the disciples would have meant in this situation is uncertain, but it is probably not a full-blown belief in Jesus as a divine incarnation. Keep in mind that, in Mark's version, their response is limited to astonishment and befuddlement.

Donald Hagner suggests that "Here, 'Son of God' is probably understood by the disciples as the unique messenger of God, God's messianic agent, and not, as the later church will make explicit, the actual incarnation of God" (*Matthew 14–28*, Word Biblical Commentary [Word Books, 1995], 424).

Ben Witherington III, in contrast, implies greater understanding: "Only God's divine offspring could do what the disciples had just witnessed" (*Matthew*, Smyth & Helwys Bible Commentary [Smyth & Helwys, 2006], 294). Witherington notes that the disciples' response in this story goes well beyond the ending of a similar account in Matt. 8:23-27, where the bewildered men say only "What sort of man is this, that even the winds and the sea obey him?"

Asking what the idea of Jesus as the Son of God meant to the disciples is a matter of curiosity. Asking what Jesus as the Son of God means to us is the more important question.

Index of Lectionary Texts
Year A, Volume 3

CPSIA information can be obtained
at www.ICGtesting.com
Printed in the USA
JSHW070907240223
38152JS00001B/12